صحيح مسلم

Ṣaḥīḥ Muslim

With the Full Commentary by

Imam al-Nawawī

Translated and Edited by

Adil Salahi

VOLUME

•FIVE•

THE ISLAMIC FOUNDATION &
ICMG AUSTRALIA

Ṣaḥīḥ Muslim: With Full Commentary by Imam al-Nawawī, volume 5

First published in England by

THE ISLAMIC FOUNDATION,

Markfield Conference Centre,
Ratby Lane, Markfield,
Leicestershire, LE67 9SY,
United Kingdom
Website: www.Islamic-foundation.com
Email: Publications@islamic-foundation.com

Quran House, PO Box 30611, Nairobi, Kenya

P.M.B 3193, Kano, Nigeria

Distributed by
Kube Publishing Ltd
Tel: +44 (0) 1530 249230
Fax: +44 (0) 1530 249656
Website: www.kubepublishing.com

With special thank you for the immense contribution of ICMG Youth Australia.

Cataloguing-in-Publication Data is available from the British Library

ISBN: 978-0-86037-719-1 *casebound*
ISBN: 978-0-86037-714-6 *paperback*
ISBN: 978-0-86037-724-5 *ebook*

Cover Design by: Jannah Haque
Typesetting by: nqaddoura@hotmail.com
Printed by: Elma Printing, Turkey

بسم الله الرحمن الرحيم

CONTENTS

BOOK OF TRAVELLERS' PRAYERS

BOOK OF FRIDAY PRAYER

BOOK OF EID PRAYER

BOOK OF PRAYER FOR RAIN

BOOK OF PRAYER AT A SOLAR ECLIPSE

BOOK OF FUNERAL PRAYER

TRANSLITERATION TABLE

Arabic Consonants

Initial, unexpressed medial and final: ء ’

ا	a	د	d	ض	ḍ	ك	k
ب	b	ذ	dh	ط	ṭ	ل	l
ت	t	ر	r	ظ	ẓ	م	m
ث	th	ز	z	ع	‘	ن	n
ج	j	س	s	غ	gh	هـ	h
ح	ḥ	ش	sh	ف	f	و	w
خ	kh	ص	ṣ	ق	q	ي	y

With a *shaddah*, both medial and final consonants are doubled.

Vowels, diphthongs, etc.

Short:	ـَـ	a	ـِـ	i	ـُـ	u
Long:	ـَا	ā	ـِي	ī	ـُو	ū
Diphthongs:			ـَوْ	aw		
			ـَيْ	ay		

In the name of God, the Most Compassionate, the Ever Merciful

PREFACE

We live in a time when people can spread their views around the globe at the touch of a button. Yet such views may come from people of little knowledge who can confuse and even misguide others. This is a concern that has become particularly acute with the widespread misrepresentation of Islam, both by those hostile towards it, and, unfortunately, even those who claim to profess it. Through their evil but eloquent schemes, such people can misrepresent the sacred teachings of this religion, and direct the ignorant and the ill-fated to perpetrate heinous crimes against both an innocent public and an innocent religion. Such deception and misinterpretation has sadly become all too common in our day, and among its causes is, undoubtedly, the relative inaccessibility of sound Islamic scholarship and literature in the English language. An additional cause is the suggestion that there is no difference between experts and non-experts. It is as though God never declared in His Book: *'How can those who know be equal to those who do not know?'* (39: 9)

A plethora of problems can arise when non-experts begin to consider themselves experts on a subject matter. One can vividly illustrate with the example of a person who requires medical attention. A sensible individual would choose to be treated by a medical professional—an expert in the field—rather than risk their health by consenting to a medical procedure from someone who fancies themselves a doctor simply because they have read a medical textbook in their spare time. Indeed, there are serious legal consequences for those who claim to practice medicine without a recognized licence—one which is granted because they have been through rigorous training and examination. Such legal repercussions are entirely appropriate of course, for such frauds place people's worldly lives at risk. Yet why is it that when it comes to our health we seek an expert opinion, but when it comes to our everlasting Hereafter so many of us prefer to follow someone who considers himself an expert after reading just a couple of books? Simply put: why do we risk our eternity by following those who are not qualified? Why do we not seek out recognized experts? As God the

Almighty says: *'ask the people of knowledge if you do not know.'* (16: 43) It is precisely to address this gap between scholarly works and non-scholarly opinions that we have endeavoured to produce this invaluable resource.

After reading the entirety of *al-Minhāj* in Turkish, the Director of Organisational Management at Islamic Community Milli Gorus (ICMG) Youth Australia, Adem Temel, conducted a meeting with our small team in which we studied the book and recognized how blessed we were to have access to such a stupendous work. It was evident that the renowned scholar and author of *al-Minhāj*, Imam al-Nawawī, may God have mercy on him, had wisdom and knowledge many today are in desperate need of. Indeed, *al-Minhāj* is one of the greatest and most respected commentaries on *Ṣaḥīḥ* Muslim. While an English translation of a hadith can struggle to convey its apparent meaning, let alone the appropriate context and other subtleties, commentaries by experts like Imam al-Nawawī can shed light on hadiths more comprehensively and thus give us greater access to the intended meaning while guarding us against misunderstanding. During a subsequent meeting, our team compared the Turkish translation of *Fī Ẓilāl al-Qur'an* with the English translation by Dr Adil Salahi and were impressed by the remarkable consistency between the two translations. Immediately thereafter, the team made the decision to contact Dr Salahi with a view to proposing that he translate Imam al-Nawawī's *al-Minhāj* into English. We were overjoyed to hear his positive response.

A number of people and organizations have contributed to this project. Firstly, this work would not have been possible without Adil Salahi's mastery of both the Arabic and English languages. His love of Prophet Muhammad, peace and blessings be upon him, and his dedication to making knowledge accessible has led to the translation of significant works from the Islamic literary heritage. Second, the ICMG Youth Australia and Kube Publishing (UK) teams worked closely to meet all project timelines. Third, many individuals and groups volunteered to support this project both physically and financially. Lastly, and most importantly, God, the Almighty, guided us, brought ease, and opened closed doors to make everything possible.

'... and my success can only come from God. In Him I put my trust, and to Him I will return.' (11: 88)

Halim Erbasi
ICMG Youth Australia
Director of Education

BEFORE YOU READ

There are some important points that the reader, particularly a student of Hadith, needs to bear in mind when using this book. Although these have been explained in the Introduction to the first volume, it is considered worthwhile to remind readers of the editorial method followed in this work.

1. Numbering and references

It is surprising, but there has never been a full and serial numbering of hadiths in *Ṣaḥīḥ* Muslim, and hence references to hadiths vary. A hadith is often referenced by book and chapter: 'Related by Muslim, Book of Faith, Chapter so-and-so', and so forth. This is a difficult method of referencing, particularly because the headings of some chapters run into two or three lines, or even longer. The fullest numbering of the hadiths in *Ṣaḥīḥ* Muslim is that given in *al-Muʿjam al-Mufahras li-Alfāẓ al-Ḥadīth*, but many hadiths are left without numbers. These are versions of the previous hadith, differing only in their chains of transmission, and it was probably felt that they should count with the earlier and often more complete version.

Al-Muʿjam al-Mufahras is a concordance of the words of the Prophet's hadiths listed in the most important nine anthologies: al-Bukhārī, Muslim, Abū Dāwūd, al-Tirmidhī, al-Nasā'ī, Ibn Mājah, as well as Mālik's *al-Muwaṭṭa'*, Ahmad's *al-Musnad* and al-Dārimī's *Sunan*. It was prepared by a group of forty Western researchers of Islamic studies under the supervision of Arent Jan Wensinck (1882–1939) and edited by the Egyptian scholar Muhammad Fu'ād ʿAbd al-Bāqī (1882–1967).[i]

---

i. Shaykh Muhammad Rashīd Riḍā gave an English copy of *A Manual of the Early Muhammadan Traditions* by Arent Jan Wensinck, Professor of Arabic and Islam at the University of Leiden in Holland, to one of his regular students, Muhammad

However, *al-Muʿjam al-Mufahras* gives a serial number to each 'book' in Muslim's *Ṣaḥīḥ*. Thus, it lists the numbers of the hadiths in the Book of Faith from 1 to 380, and then begins the numbering in the Book of Cleansing from 1. As such, it does not give a complete serial numbering to the entire anthology. I have therefore decided to provide serial numbering, giving every hadith its own numbered identification. In doing so, I follow the method adopted by the late hadith scholar Mūsā Shāhīn Lāshīn (1920–2009) in his 10-volume commentary, *Fatḥ al-Munʿim fī Sharḥ Ṣaḥīḥ Muslim*. This method does not assign a number for a hadith that differs from the one before it only in its chain of transmission, but that has exactly the same text.

Muslim's *Ṣaḥīḥ* has been translated into English by Abd al-Hamid Siddiqui. The translation is well circulated and its better known edition, published by Dār al-Salām, is available online. After looking carefully at this translation, I have decided to provide my own. However, the translation gives a full serial numbering of the hadiths listed by Muslim, bringing the total to 7,190 hadiths. This is different from Lāshīn's method of numbering, which brings the total to 6,571 hadiths. To make it easier for readers who wish to refer to Dār al-Salām's translation, I give the number in that translation in brackets before the chain of transmission.

Fu'ād ʿAbd al-Bāqī, and asked him to translate it into Arabic. ʿAbd al-Bāqī, who was working as a translator at the Agricultural Bank in Cairo at the time, complied and translated the book, but first he wrote to Wensinck for his permission. Wensinck expressed delight at the idea and also sent ʿAbd al-Bāqī a copy of the first part of a concordance of the Prophet's hadiths that he and other researchers were working on. ʿAbd al-Bāqī reviewed the work and found many mistakes. He made a list of these and sent it to Wensinck, who was delighted with the input and recruited ʿAbd al-Bāqī as editor of the entire *al-Muʿjam al-Mufahras* concordance.

Al-Muʿjam al-Mufahras is published in Arabic in eight volumes and is indispensable for any researcher in Islamic Studies. Words are listed alphabetically, and a short sentence or phrase in which the word occurs is given. Then the hadith which includes the sentence or phrase is referenced to any of the nine anthologies. ʿAbd al-Bāqī's role is acknowledged by Wensinck in the Introduction, and working on this concordance enabled Muhammad Fu'ād ʿAbd al-Bāqī to subsequently undertake his own highly acclaimed concordance of the Qur'an.

Thus, three sets of numbers are included before the chain of transmission of each hadith. The first is a complete serial number following Lāshīn's method. The second is that of *al-Muʿjam al-Mufahras* and the third is that of Dār al-Salām's translation given in brackets. Where Lāshīn or *al-Muʿjam al-Mufahras* does not give a hadith a number, because it is the same as the hadith before it, I follow the convention of giving it the mark '000'. Thus, either of the first two numbers may be replaced by 000. Where Dār al-Salām's translation omits a hadith or does not give it a number, I give it the mark '0'. The pattern of numbering is simplified, as follows:

Lāshīn – *Al-Muʿjam* – (Dār al-Salām)

This applies to all the hadiths that are entered in the anthology itself, beginning with the Book of Faith. Imam Muslim wrote a long introduction to his work, explaining his method. In it, he includes ninety-two hadiths and statements by the early scholars of Hadith. These are given separate numbers, from 1 to 92. Only a few of these are entered in *al-Muʿjam al-Mufahras*, because the majority are attributed to scholars of Hadith. Whichever is entered in *al-Muʿjam al-Mufahras* its number is stated. Dār al-Salām's translation does not include this introduction.

When a hadith is entered in any of the other five anthologies considered to be the most authentic, I mention these in a footnote. Where no such information is given, it means that the hadith is entered only in Muslim's anthology. The Arabic original of each hadith is given immediately after the English translation, but this applies to the main body of the anthology, not to Muslim's introduction.

Imam Muslim divided his anthology into books, each covering an important area of the Islamic faith, such as the Book of Faith, the Book of Prayer, etc. He did not make further classification. It was left to Imam al-Nawawī to divide each book into chapters, and give headings to these. These chapters were later given numbers in *al-Muʿjam al-Mufahras*. The headings and their numbers are given in this translation. However, as many headings tend to be long, I have tried to reduce them while retaining the elements highlighted in the headings. It should be pointed out, however, that some of these chapters are not given numbers. Where no number is given to a chapter in *al-Muʿjam al-Mufahras*, it appears without a number in this translation.

There are a few instances where the same number is given to two consecutive hadiths. In order to indicate that this is not an error, but merely following the Arabic original, the repetition is indicated by the symbol [R].

2. The chain of transmission

Hadith scholars were very specific in their terminology. Therefore, when they used synonymous words, they imparted clear distinction to them. Thus, the words *ḥaddathanā*, *akhbaranā*, *anba'anā*, and *ʿan*, have different meanings, although linguistically speaking they are very similar and denote receiving information from a named person. However, *ḥaddathanā* is used to refer to a process whereby the teacher reads out the hadith to his students, whether he is narrating from memory or reading out loud directly. *Akhbaranā* and *anba'anā* are practically identical in meaning. However, the first refers to a process whereby a student is reading aloud from his teacher's books in the presence of the teacher. *Anba'anā* does not specify this process, but means that the information was passed on by the teacher or in his presence. *ʿAn*, on the other hand, does not specify any process, nor does it specify that the reporter actually heard the teacher's narration or his student's reading out in his presence. Indeed, it could, thus, mean that the reporter heard the hadith from a colleague who was in the teacher's circle at the time.

In order to reflect these differences, 'narrated' is the term used here for *ḥaddathanā*, 'reported' for *akhbaranā*, 'mentioned' for *anba'anā*, and 'from' for *ʿan*. However, any of the first three ways could involve a one-to-one situation in which the reporter is the only one present with his teacher. In Arabic, this is marked by changing the last letter in the three Arabic words, using 'ī' instead of 'ā'. Thus the words become *ḥaddathanī, akhbaranī,* and *anba'anī*. To reflect the difference in the English translation the words 'to me' have been used after 'narrated', 'reported' and 'mentioned' to indicate the one-to-one situation, while the three words on their own indicate the presence of others when the narration took place.

Readers will also note that in some hadiths the chain of transmission includes the mark [H]. This is indicated in Arabic by the use of the letter [Ḥ], and it may occur once, twice, or even more in the chain of transmission of the same hadith. What this signifies is that the hadith is narrated by two or more chains of transmission, but these join up at some stage. Rather than give them separately, repeating the names of reporters from where they join up to the Prophet's companion, Hadith scholars use this way to indicate that the different chains are joined at this point.

Another symbol used in the chain of transmission is [R], but this is much less frequent. It simply indicates that the number given to a particular hadith is repeated, which means that the number has been given to more than one hadith instead of giving each of them a separate number.

Sometimes Muslim narrates a hadith from three of his teachers and uses the word 'narrated', but their methods of learning from their teacher whom they quote differ. Muslim is too careful and meticulous to overlook this fact. He makes this clear by immediately adding something like: 'The first said "narrated" and the other two said "reported".'

3. Word usage

The usage of some Arabic words need to be explained. The word 'imam' is often used in reference to some scholars quoted in this work. It is also used in reference to both Muslim and al-Nawawī. There is, however, a very clear difference in the use of this word by Sunni Muslims and the Shia.

Linguistically speaking, *imām* means 'leader' and is often used, particularly in books of Islamic Jurisprudence, or *fiqh*, to refer to the ruler or the head of state, whether he has the title of caliph or some other title. It is also commonly used to refer to the person who leads congregational prayer. In this second usage, there is no difference between the one who leads the prayer and anyone in the congregation, except that the imam leads and the congregation follow.

A far more common usage of the word is as a title of respect added before the name of a scholar who is recognized for his high achievement and scholarship. This is how it is mostly used in this work. It may, however, also be used here in the sense of the 'leader of congregational prayer' when this topic is discussed, but as such will be clearly identified at that juncture. A scholar who is considered an imam has no special distinction, apart from what his scholarship gives him; he does not enjoy any special status. It will be noted in this work that the views of some such scholars are outlined, and discussed or rejected. This is clearly a matter of scholarly difference that does not detract from the high standing of the scholar or the one who differs with him.

The Shia have a totally different concept of 'imam'. They give this status to twelve people starting with ʿAlī ibn Abī Ṭālib, the Prophet's cousin, followed by eleven of his descendants through Fāṭimah, his wife and the Prophet's daughter. To the Shia, those imams were infallible and enjoy a rank that is almost equal to that of the Prophet. Indeed, the way some Shia speak of the third Imam, al-Ḥusayn, the Prophet's grandson, gives at times the impression that they rank him above the Prophet himself. Moreover, the Shia believe that the twelfth Imam was taken away and did not die: he will return at some point when he will bring justice to the world. This Shia concept is absolutely unacceptable to Sunni Muslims who do not recognize any such status as belonging to anyone.

We speak of a hadith having a chain of transmission and we mention 'transmitters'. We also use the words 'reporter' and 'narrator'. These three words are used interchangeably and they refer to the people named in the chain of transmission. These have the same status with regard to how the Prophet's statement or action is taught and learnt. When we use the verb 'narrate' we are referring to the action of stating the hadith, whether by reading it out loud or otherwise. However, the word 'narrate' is often used in Islamic literature in reference to the works of the leading scholars of Hadith and what they include in their anthologies. Thus, we often see phrases like 'al-Tirmidhī narrated ...', 'al-Bukhārī narrated ...'. It is felt that it is better to distinguish the mere quoting of a hadith and its entry in an anthology. Therefore we use the word 'narrate' to indicate quoting a hadith and the word 'relate' to mean the 'entry in a Hadith anthology'. Thus, we say: 'al-Bukhārī relates in his *Ṣaḥīḥ*', or 'al-Bayhaqī relates in *Shuʿab al-Īmān*', or 'al-Nasāʾī relates in *al-Sunan al-Kubrā*'.

The words Abū and Abī are often used in the names of hadith reporters and scholars. These two are the same word, but the endings are case markers according to their position in the sentence. Invariably, Abū is used at the beginning of the sentence and when not preceded by a name, while Abī is used when preceded by the word 'ibn'. There are other situations that indicate which of the two should be used. Both words mean 'father of' and their use indicates an appellation of respect.

The word *mawlā* is used to describe some reporters and other persons mentioned in the commentary. This word is one of the few Arabic words that denote opposite meanings. Linguistically, it means both 'master' and 'slave', and it is used in the Qur'an to refer to God as the *mawlā* of the believers. When someone is referred to as the *mawlā* of another or of a tribe, it most frequently refers to a slave who was set free. He then allied himself with his former master or with his tribe, as this was a recognized practice in Arabia both under Islam and prior to it.

It will be noted that the phrase 'but God knows best' is used very frequently in al-Nawawī's commentary and by the scholars he quotes: this is a mark of humility. They express their views but shy away from presenting these as the true and correct view, to the exclusion of anything different. It is akin to saying that 'this is what I know, but ultimate knowledge rests with God'.

The word hadith is used with a capital or small 'h' and this usage indicates a difference. When it is used with the lower case first letter it refers to a single statement by the Prophet. Hence, the reference to one or more statements by the Prophet is always with the lower case. When it is used with a capital first letter, it refers to the Hadith discipline, which is a specialized branch of study, concerned with the Prophet's statements, actions and approvals.

4. Arrangement

Imam al-Nawawī discusses three areas in relation to every hadith included in Muslim's anthology: 1) The general meaning of the hadith and its message. He also outlines the important points it includes and highlights any rulings that it stipulates or may be based on it. 2) The chain of transmission: he identifies the different reporters, giving some information about them and their full names if they are mentioned by first name or by appellation. He also highlights any useful point that the chain provides, and explains any subtle point that reflects Muslim's careful and meticulous scholarship. 3) He explains the language of the hadith, stating the meanings of individual words, particularly those that may be unfamiliar to readers or became rarely used. Where a word, phrase or sentence may have more than one meaning, he discusses these and shows which, if any, is unacceptable. However, he does not follow a single pattern in the arrangement of his commentary. Sometimes, he begins by discussing the chain of transmission, but often he discusses the general meaning first. He may also start by explaining the language and the meaning of individual words.

In this English version, liberty has been taken to follow a consistent pattern. The meaning of the hadith is given first and then its explanation, under the subheading 'text explanation', is provided. This is followed with any discussion al-Nawawī gives concerning the chain of transmission, using the subheading 'transmission'. The information al-Nawawī provides about the meaning of individual words and the pronunciation of unfamiliar words and names has been ignored, because these are already reflected in the translation. However, when he discusses alternative meanings, what is considered useful to English readers is included. If it is a matter of pronunciation or a grammatical aspect that does not affect the meaning or the message of the hadith, this has been disregarded.

5. Quotations and references

In his monumental work, al-Nawawī cites numerous quotations from various scholars. At times, he mentions the work from which the quotation is made, but in most cases this is not done. Although his work has been checked and verified several times, and published many times in different countries, none of these undertook the task of checking the original works in order to provide detailed references. There are several reasons for this omission. Many of the original works have not been published, but remain in manuscript form held in different libraries in various countries. Moreover, many of these works are voluminous. For example, al-Nawawī often quotes from Imam al-Ḥaramayn, who wrote a large number of books. As mentioned in the biographical note on Imam al-Ḥaramayn, one of his books is published in twenty-one volumes. Although a discerning scholar may have a good guess as to the book from which a particular quote is taken, finding it may require several hours, if not days of hard work. Imam al-Nawawī died 750 years ago and we cannot blame him for not citing his references according to modern methods of citation. It should be remembered that all the books he read were written in long hand and manuscripts of the same book differed in size, number of pages and style of writing. Readers and students must simply trust to his scholarship and piety with all that he quotes from other scholars. May God bless them all for their meticulous and faithful scholarship.

6. Notes and editorial liberty

In certain cases, it is felt that a note should be added within the text to explain certain points or add a particular perspective. This is not surprising considering that the book was written nearly eight centuries ago. In order to make the addition very clear, it is preceded by the word 'Note' and given an independent paragraph.

In a few cases, a sentence is started by mentioning the author's name before mentioning what he says, such as 'al-Nawawī considers these hadiths self-explanatory, adding only …', and in a very few cases, a short comment by the author is not included in the translation, because time has made it irrelevant and including it would be either confusing or require a long explanatory footnote. Since it is unlikely to concern the reader, it is felt that omission is better. Such liberty is taken only in cases where it is felt that had the author lived in our time, he would have approved of such omission.

Adil Salahi
London
February 2019

BOOK OF TRAVELLERS' PRAYERS

CHAPTER 1

PRAYER WHEN TRAVELLING AND SHORTENING IT

[1327–1]. (Dar al-Salam 1458) Yaḥyā ibn Yaḥyā narrated:[i] he said: I read out to Mālik; from Ṣāliḥ ibn Kaysān; from ʿUrwah ibn al-Zubayr; from ʿĀʾishah, the Prophet's wife; that she said: **'When prayer was made a duty, it was two *rakʿahs* each, when at home and when travelling. Later, prayer on a journey remained the same but it was increased when at home'.**

حَدَّثَنَا يَحْيَى بْنُ يَحْيَى، قَالَ قَرَأْتُ عَلَى مَالِكٍ عَنْ صَالِحِ بْنِ كَيْسَانَ، عَنْ عُرْوَةَ بْنِ الزُّبَيْرِ، عَنْ عَائِشَةَ، زَوْجِ النَّبِيِّ صَلَّى اللهُ عَلَيْهِ وَسَلَّمَ، أَنَّهَا قَالَتْ فُرِضَتِ الصَّلَاةُ رَكْعَتَيْنِ رَكْعَتَيْنِ فِي الْحَضَرِ وَالسَّفَرِ، فَأُقِرَّتْ صَلَاةُ السَّفَرِ وَزِيدَ فِي صَلَاةِ الْحَضَرِ.

[1328–2]. (Dar al-Salam 1459) Abu al-Ṭāhir and Ḥarmalah ibn Yaḥyā narrated to me: both said: Ibn Wahb narrated; from Yūnus; from Ibn Shihāb. He said: ʿUrwah ibn al-Zubayr narrated to me that ʿĀʾishah, the Prophet's wife, said: **'When God commanded [Muslims] to pray, He ordered it to be two *rakʿahs*. He later made it complete when at home, while prayer during a journey remained as it was in the first instance'.**

وَحَدَّثَنِي أَبُو الطَّاهِرِ وَحَرْمَلَةُ بْنُ يَحْيَى، قَالَا: حَدَّثَنَا ابْنُ وَهْبٍ، عَنْ يُونُسَ، عَنِ ابْنِ شِهَابٍ قَالَ: حَدَّثَنِي عُرْوَةُ بْنُ الزُّبَيْرِ، أَنَّ عَائِشَةَ، زَوْجَ النَّبِيِّ صَلَّى اللهُ عَلَيْهِ وَسَلَّمَ

i. Related by al-Bukhari, 350; Abu Dāwūd, 1198; al-Nasāʾī, 454.

قَالَتْ: فَرَضَ اللهُ الصَّلاَةَ حِينَ فَرَضَهَا رَكْعَتَيْنِ، ثُمَّ أَتَمَّهَا فِي الْحَضَرِ. فَأُقِرَّتْ صَلاَةُ السَّفَرِ عَلَى الْفَرِيضَةِ الأُولَى.

[1329–3]. (Dar al-Salam 1460) ʿAlī ibn Khashram narrated to me:[i] Ibn ʿUyaynah reported; from al-Zuhrī; from ʿUrwah; from ʿĀ'ishah that **'When prayer was first made a duty, it was in two *rakʿahs*. Prayer during travel remained the same, but prayer at home was made more complete'.**

Al-Zuhrī said: **'I said to ʿUrwah: "How is it, then, that ʿĀ'ishah offers the prayer complete when she is travelling?" He said: "She justified it as ʿUthmān did".'**

وَحَدَّثَنِي عَلِيُّ بْنُ خَشْرَمٍ، أَخْبَرَنَا ابْنُ عُيَيْنَةَ، عَنِ الزُّهْرِيِّ، عَنْ عُرْوَةَ، عَنْ عَائِشَةَ أَنَّ الصَّلاَةَ أَوَّلَ مَا فُرِضَتْ رَكْعَتَيْنِ. فَأُقِرَّتْ صَلاَةُ السَّفَرِ وَأُتِمَّتْ صَلاَةُ الْحَضَرِ.

قَالَ الزُّهْرِيُّ فَقُلْتُ لِعُرْوَةَ مَا بَالُ عَائِشَةَ تُتِمُّ فِي السَّفَرِ؟ قَالَ: إِنَّهَا تَأَوَّلَتْ كَمَا تَأَوَّلَ عُثْمَانُ.

[1330–4]. (Dar al-Salam 1461) Abu Bakr ibn Abi Shaybah, Abu Kurayb, Zuhayr ibn Ḥarb and Isḥāq ibn Ibrāhīm narrated:[ii] ʿAbdullāh ibn Idrīs (Isḥāq said: 'reported' and the others said: 'narrated'); from Ibn Jurayj; from Ibn Abi ʿAmmār; from ʿAbdullāh ibn Bābayh; from Yaʿlā ibn Umayyah. He said: **'I said to ʿUmar ibn al-Khaṭṭāb: [God says:] "You will incur no sin by shortening your prayers, if you have reason to fear that the unbelievers may cause you affliction". (4: 101) People now live in security'. He said: "I wondered the same as you wonder, and I asked God's Messenger (peace be upon him)**

i. Related by al-Bukhari, 1090; al-Nasā'ī, 452.
ii. Related by Abu Dāwūd, 1199 and in a similar text, 1200; al-Tirmidhī, 3034; al-Nasā'ī, 1432; Ibn Mājah, 1065.

about it. He said: 'This is a charity God has given you. You should accept His charity'."'

وَحدَّثَنَا أَبُو بَكْرِ بْنُ أَبِي شَيْبَةَ وَأَبُو كُرَيْبٍ وَزُهَيْرُ بْنُ حَرْبٍ وَإِسْحَاقُ بْنُ إِبْرَاهِيمَ، قَالَ إِسْحَاقُ أَخْبَرَنَا وَقَالَ الآخَرُونَ حَدَّثَنَا عَبْدُ اللهِ بْنُ إِدْرِيسَ، عَنِ ابْنِ جُرَيْجٍ، عَنِ ابْنِ أَبِي عَمَّارٍ، عَنْ عَبْدِ اللهِ بْنِ بَابَيْهِ، عَنْ يَعْلَى بْنِ أُمَيَّةَ، قَالَ: قُلْتُ لِعُمَرَ بْنِ الْخَطَّابِ: "لَيْسَ عَلَيْكُمْ جُنَاحٌ أَنْ تَقْصُرُوا، مِنَ الصَّلاَةِ إِنْ خِفْتُمْ أَنْ يَفْتِنَكُمُ الَّذِينَ كَفَرُوا"، فَقَدْ أَمِنَ النَّاسُ. فَقَالَ: عَجِبْتُ مِمَّا عَجِبْتَ مِنْهُ، فَسَأَلْتُ رَسُولَ اللهِ صَلَّى اللهُ عَلَيْهِ وَسَلَّمَ عَنْ ذَلِكَ، فَقَالَ: "صَدَقَةٌ تَصَدَّقَ اللهُ بِهَا عَلَيْكُمْ، فَاقْبَلُوا صَدَقَتَهُ".

[000–000]. (Dar al-Salam 1462) Muhammad ibn Abu Bakr al-Muqaddamī narrated: Yaḥyā narrated; from Ibn Jurayj. He said: ʿAbd al-Raḥmān ibn ʿAbdullāh ibn Abi ʿAmmār; from ʿAbdullāh ibn Bābayh; from Yaʿlā ibn Umayyah: **'I said to ʿUmar ibn al-Khaṭṭāb…' the same as Ibn Idrīs' narration.**

وَحدَّثَنَا مُحَمَّدُ بْنُ أَبِي بَكْرٍ الْمُقَدَّمِيُّ، حَدَّثَنَا يَحْيَى، عَنِ ابْنِ جُرَيْجٍ قَالَ: حَدَّثَنِي عَبْدُ الرَّحْمَنِ بْنُ عَبْدِ اللهِ بْنِ أَبِي عَمَّارٍ، عَنْ عَبْدِ اللهِ بْنِ بَابَيْهِ، عَنْ يَعْلَى بْنِ أُمَيَّةَ قَالَ: قُلْتُ لِعُمَرَ بْنِ الْخَطَّابِ. بِمِثْلِ حَدِيثِ ابْنِ إِدْرِيسَ.

[1331–5]. (Dar al-Salam 1463) Yaḥyā ibn Yaḥyā, Saʿīd ibn Manṣūr, Abu al-Rabīʿ and Qutaybah ibn Saʿīd narrated:[i] Abu ʿAwānah (Yaḥyā said: 'reported' and the others said: 'narrated'); from Bukayr ibn al-Akhnas; from Mujāhid; from Ibn ʿAbbās. He said: **'God has made prayer obligatory through your Prophet (peace be upon him): at home four *rakʿahs*, on a journey two *rakʿahs* and only one *rakʿah* in situations of fear'.**

---

i. Related by Abu Dawud, 1247; al-Nasa'i, 455, 1440, 1441 and 1531; Ibn Majah in a shorter version, 1068.

حَدَّثَنَا يَحْيَى بْنُ يَحْيَى وَسَعِيدُ بْنُ مَنْصُورٍ وَأَبُو الرَّبِيعِ وَقُتَيْبَةُ بْنُ سَعِيدٍ، قَالَ يَحْيَى أَخْبَرَنَا وَقَالَ الآخَرُونَ حَدَّثَنَا أَبُو عَوَانَةَ، عَنْ بُكَيْرِ بْنِ الأَخْنَسِ، عَنْ مُجَاهِدٍ، عَنِ ابْنِ عَبَّاسٍ قَالَ: فَرَضَ اللهُ الصَّلَاةَ عَلَى لِسَانِ نَبِيِّكُمْ صَلَّى اللهُ عَلَيْهِ وَسَلَّمَ: فِي الْحَضَرِ أَرْبَعًا، وَفِي السَّفَرِ رَكْعَتَيْنِ، وَفِي الْخَوْفِ رَكْعَةً.

[1332–6]. (Dar al-Salam 1464) Abu Bakr ibn Abi Shaybah and ʿAmr al-Nāqid narrated: both from al-Qāsim ibn Mālik. ʿAmr said: Qāsim ibn Mālik al-Muzanī narrated; Ayyūb ibn ʿĀ'idh al-Ṭā'ī narrated; from Bukayr ibn al-Akhnas; from Mujāhid; from Ibn ʿAbbās. He said: **'God has made prayer obligatory through your Prophet (peace be upon him): two *rakʿahs* for a person on a journey, four *rakʿahs* for a person at home and one *rakʿah* in situations of fear'.**

وَحَدَّثَنَا أَبُو بَكْرِ بْنُ أَبِي شَيْبَةَ وَعَمْرٌو النَّاقِدُ، جَمِيعًا عَنِ الْقَاسِمِ بْنِ مَالِكٍ، قَالَ عَمْرٌو: حَدَّثَنَا قَاسِمُ بْنُ مَالِكٍ الْمُزَنِيُّ، حَدَّثَنَا أَيُّوبُ بْنُ عَائِذٍ الطَّائِيُّ، عَنْ بُكَيْرِ بْنِ الأَخْنَسِ، عَنْ مُجَاهِدٍ، عَنِ ابْنِ عَبَّاسٍ قَالَ: إِنَّ اللهَ فَرَضَ الصَّلَاةَ عَلَى لِسَانِ نَبِيِّكُمْ صَلَّى اللهُ عَلَيْهِ وَسَلَّمَ: عَلَى الْمُسَافِرِ رَكْعَتَيْنِ، وَعَلَى الْمُقِيمِ أَرْبَعًا، وَفِي الْخَوْفِ رَكْعَةً.

[1333–7]. (Dar al-Salam 1465–1466) Muhammad ibn al-Muthannā and Ibn Bashshār narrated:[i] both said: Muhammad ibn Jaʿfar narrated; Shuʿbah narrated; he said: I heard Qatādah narrating from Mūsā ibn Salamah al-Hudhalī. He said: **'I asked Ibn ʿAbbās: "How should I pray if I am in Makkah and I do not pray with the imam?" He said: "Two *rakʿahs*. Such is Abu al-Qāsim's sunnah".'**

---

i. Related by al-Nasā'ī, 1442 and 1443.

حَدَّثَنَا مُحَمَّدُ بْنُ الْـمُثَنَّى وَابْنُ بَشَّارٍ، قَالا: حَدَّثَنَا مُحَمَّدُ بْنُ جَعْفَرٍ، حَدَّثَنَا شُعْبَةُ قَالَ: سَمِعْتُ قَتَادَةَ يُحَدِّثُ عَنْ مُوسَى بْنِ سَلَمَةَ الْهُذَلِيِّ، قَالَ: سَأَلْتُ ابْنَ عَبَّاسٍ كَيْفَ أُصَلِّي إِذَا كُنْتُ بِمَكَّةَ إِذَا لَمْ أُصَلِّ مَعَ الإِمَامِ؟ فَقَالَ: رَكْعَتَيْنِ سُنَّةَ أَبِي الْقَاسِمِ صَلَّى اللهُ عَلَيْهِ وَسَلَّمَ.

Muhammad ibn Minhāl al-Ḍarīr narrated: Yazīd ibn Zurayʿ narrated; Saʿīd ibn Abī ʿArūbah narrated [H]. Muhammad ibn al-Muthannā narrated; Muʿādh ibn Hishām narrated; my father narrated; both from Qatādah, with the same chain of transmission: **a similar text.**

وَحَدَّثَنَاهُ مُحَمَّدُ بْنُ مِنْهَالٍ الضَّرِيرُ، حَدَّثَنَا يَزِيدُ بْنُ زُرَيْعٍ، حَدَّثَنَا سَعِيدُ بْنُ أَبِي عَرُوبَةَ، ح. وَحَدَّثَنَا مُحَمَّدُ بْنُ الْـمُثَنَّى، حَدَّثَنَا مُعَاذُ بْنُ هِشَامٍ، حَدَّثَنَا أَبِي جَمِيعًا، عَنْ قَتَادَةَ، بِهَذَا الإِسْنَادِ نَحْوَهُ.

[1334–8]. (Dar al-Salam 1467) ʿAbdullāh ibn Maslamah ibn Qaʿnab narrated:[i] ʿĪsā ibn Ḥafṣ ibn ʿĀṣim ibn ʿUmar ibn al-Khaṭṭāb; from his father. He said: **'I was in Ibn ʿUmar's company [travelling] on the way to Makkah. He led us in Ẓuhr Prayer, offering it in two *rakʿahs*. He then moved forward and we moved with him until he reached his camel where he sat, and we sat with him. He then happened to turn his face towards the place where he prayed and saw some people standing [in prayer]. He asked: "What are these people doing?" I said: "They are praying the sunnah". He said: "Were I to pray the sunnah, I would rather have completed my [obligatory] prayer. My nephew, I accompanied God's Messenger (peace be upon him) on travel and he never offered more than two**

i. Related by al-Bukhari in a shorter version, 1102; Abu Dāwūd, 1223; al-Nasāʾī in a shorter version, 1457; Ibn Mājah, 1071.

rak'ahs until God gathered his soul. I accompanied Abu Bakr and he never offered more than two *rak'ahs* until God gathered his soul. I also accompanied 'Umar and he never offered more than two *rak'ahs* until God gathered his soul. Then I accompanied 'Uthmān and he never offered more than two *rak'ahs* until God gathered his soul. God says: 'In God's Messenger you have a good model [to follow]' (33: 21)".'

وَحَدَّثَنَا عَبْدُ اللهِ بْنُ مَسْلَمَةَ بْنِ قَعْنَبٍ، حَدَّثَنَا عِيسَى بْنُ حَفْصِ بْنِ عَاصِمِ بْنِ عُمَرَ بْنِ الْخَطَّابِ، عَنْ أَبِيهِ قَالَ: صَحِبْتُ ابْنَ عُمَرَ فِي طَرِيقِ مَكَّةَ. قَالَ: فَصَلَّى لَنَا الظُّهْرَ رَكْعَتَيْنِ، ثُمَّ أَقْبَلَ وَأَقْبَلْنَا مَعَهُ حَتَّى جَاءَ رَحْلَهُ وَجَلَسَ وَجَلَسْنَا مَعَهُ. فَحَانَتْ مِنْهُ الْتِفَاتَةٌ نَحْوَ حَيْثُ صَلَّى، فَرَأَى نَاسًا قِيَامًا، فَقَالَ: مَا يَصْنَعُ هَؤُلَاءِ؟ قُلْتُ: يُسَبِّحُونَ. قَالَ: لَوْ كُنْتُ مُسَبِّحًا لَأَتْمَمْتُ صَلَاتِي. يَا ابْنَ أَخِي، إِنِّي صَحِبْتُ رَسُولَ اللهِ صَلَّى اللهُ عَلَيْهِ وَسَلَّمَ فِي السَّفَرِ، فَلَمْ يَزِدْ عَلَى رَكْعَتَيْنِ حَتَّى قَبَضَهُ اللهُ. وَصَحِبْتُ أَبَا بَكْرٍ، فَلَمْ يَزِدْ عَلَى رَكْعَتَيْنِ حَتَّى قَبَضَهُ اللهُ. وَصَحِبْتُ عُمَرَ، فَلَمْ يَزِدْ عَلَى رَكْعَتَيْنِ حَتَّى قَبَضَهُ اللهُ. ثُمَّ صَحِبْتُ عُثْمَانَ، فَلَمْ يَزِدْ عَلَى رَكْعَتَيْنِ حَتَّى قَبَضَهُ اللهُ. وَقَدْ قَالَ اللهُ "لَقَدْ كَانَ لَكُمْ فِي رَسُولِ اللهِ أُسْوَةٌ حَسَنَةٌ".

[1335–9]. (Dar al-Salam 1468) Qutaybah ibn Sa'īd narrated: Yazīd (meaning Ibn Zuray') narrated; from 'Umar ibn Muhammad; from Ḥafṣ ibn 'Āṣim. He said: **'I was ill, and Ibn 'Umar came to visit me. I asked him about praying the sunnah during travel. He said: "I travelled with God's Messenger (peace be upon him) and did not see him offering sunnah prayer. Were I to pray sunnah, I would have completed [the obligatory prayer]. God says: 'In God's Messenger you have a good model [to follow]'."'**

حَدَّثَنَا قُتَيْبَةُ بْنُ سَعِيدٍ، حَدَّثَنَا يَزِيدُ (يَعْنِي ابْنَ زُرَيْعٍ) عَنْ عُمَرَ بْنِ مُحَمَّدٍ، عَنْ حَفْصِ بْنِ عَاصِمٍ قَالَ: مَرِضْتُ مَرَضًا، فَجَاءَ ابْنُ عُمَرَ يَعُودُنِي. قَالَ: وَسَأَلْتُهُ عَنِ السُّبْحَةِ فِي

السَّفَرِ. فَقَالَ: صَحِبْتُ رَسُولَ اللهِ صَلَّى اللهُ عَلَيْهِ وَسَلَّمَ فِي السَّفَرِ، فَمَا رَأَيْتُهُ يُسَبِّحُ. وَلَوْ كُنْتُ مُسَبِّحًا لأَتْمَمْتُ. وَقَدْ قَالَ اللهُ تَعَالَى: ''لَقَدْ كَانَ لَكُمْ فِي رَسُولِ اللهِ أُسْوَةٌ حَسَنَةٌ''.

[1336–10]. (Dar al-Salam 1469) Khalaf ibn Hishām, Abu al-Rabīʿ al-Zahrānī and Qutaybah ibn Saʿīd narrated:[i] they said: Ḥammād (who is Ibn Zayd) narrated [H]. Zuhayr ibn Ḥarb and Yaʿqūb ibn Ibrāhīm narrated to me; both said: Ismāʿīl narrated; both from Ayyūb; from Abu Qilābah; from Anas that **'God's Messenger prayed Ẓuhr in four *rakʿahs* in Madinah and prayed Asr in two *rakʿahs* at Dhul-Hulayfah'.**

حَدَّثَنَا خَلَفُ بْنُ هِشَامٍ وَأَبُو الرَّبِيعِ الزَّهْرَانِيُّ وَقُتَيْبَةُ بْنُ سَعِيدٍ، قَالُوا: حَدَّثَنَا حَمَّادٌ (وَهُوَ ابْنُ زَيْدٍ) ح. وَحَدَّثَنِي زُهَيْرُ بْنُ حَرْبٍ وَيَعْقُوبُ بْنُ إِبْرَاهِيمَ، قَالَا: حَدَّثَنَا إِسْمَاعِيلُ، كِلَاهُمَا عَنْ أَيُّوبَ، عَنْ أَبِي قِلَابَةَ، عَنْ أَنَسٍ أَنَّ رَسُولَ اللهِ صَلَّى اللهُ عَلَيْهِ وَسَلَّمَ صَلَّى الظُّهْرَ بِالْمَدِينَةِ أَرْبَعًا، وَصَلَّى الْعَصْرَ بِذِي الْحُلَيْفَةِ رَكْعَتَيْنِ.

[1337–11]. (Dar al-Salam 1470) Saʿīd ibn Manṣūr narrated:[ii] Sufyān narrated; Muhammad ibn al-Munkadir and Ibrāhīm ibn Maysarah narrated; they heard Anas ibn Mālik say: **'I offered Ẓuhr Prayer with God's Messenger in Madinah in four *rakʿahs* and I offered ʿAṣr Prayer with him at Dhul-Hulayfah in two *rakʿahs*'.**

حَدَّثَنَا سَعِيدُ بْنُ مَنْصُورٍ، حَدَّثَنَا سُفْيَانُ، حَدَّثَنَا مُحَمَّدُ بْنُ الْمُنْكَدِرِ وَإِبْرَاهِيمُ بْنُ مَيْسَرَةَ، سَمِعَا أَنَسَ بْنَ مَالِكٍ يَقُولُ: صَلَّيْتُ مَعَ رَسُولِ اللهِ صَلَّى اللهُ عَلَيْهِ وَسَلَّمَ الظُّهْرَ بِالْمَدِينَةِ أَرْبَعًا، وَصَلَّيْتُ مَعَهُ الْعَصْرَ بِذِي الْحُلَيْفَةِ رَكْعَتَيْنِ.

---

i. Related by al-Bukhari in longer versions, 1547, 1548, 1551 1712; 1714, 1715, 2951 and 2986; Abu Dāwūd, 1796 and 2793; al-Nasā'ī, 476.

ii. Related by al-Bukhari, 1089 and in a longer version, 1546; Abu Dāwūd, 1202 and in a longer version, 1773; al-Tirmidhī, 546; al-Nasā'ī, 468.

[1338–12]. (Dar al-Salam 1471) Abu Bakr ibn Abi Shaybah and Muhammad ibn Bashshār narrated:[i] both from Ghundar; Abu Bakr said: Muhammad ibn Jaʿfar Ghundar narrated; from Shuʿbah; from Yaḥyā ibn Yazīd al-Hunāʾī. **He said: 'I asked Anas ibn Mālik about shortening prayers. He said: "God's Messenger (peace be upon him) offered his prayers in two *rakʿahs* when he had travelled three miles or three *farsakhs*[ii] (the doubt is by Shuʿbah)".'**

وَحَدَّثَنَاهُ أَبُو بَكْرِ بْنُ أَبِي شَيْبَةَ وَمُحَمَّدُ بْنُ بَشَّارٍ، كِلَاهُمَا عَنْ غُنْدَرٍ، قَالَ أَبُو بَكْرٍ: حَدَّثَنَا مُحَمَّدُ بْنُ جَعْفَرٍ، غُنْدَر، عَنْ شُعْبَةَ، عَنْ يَحْيَى بْنِ يَزِيدَ الْهُنَائِيِّ قَالَ: سَأَلْتُ أَنَسَ بْنَ مَالِكٍ عَنْ قَصْرِ الصَّلَاةِ فَقَالَ: كَانَ رَسُولُ اللهِ صَلَّى اللهُ عَلَيْهِ وَسَلَّمَ إِذَا خَرَجَ مَسِيرَةَ ثَلَاثَةِ أَمْيَالٍ، أَوْ ثَلَاثَةِ فَرَاسِخَ، (شُعْبَةُ الشَّاكُّ) صَلَّى رَكْعَتَيْنِ.

[1339–13]. (Dar al-Salam 1472) Zuhayr ibn Ḥarb and Muhammad ibn Bashshār narrated:[iii] both from Ibn Mahdī; Zuhayr said: ʿAbd al-Raḥmān ibn Mahdī narrated; Shuʿbah narrated; from Yazīd ibn Khumayr; from Ḥabīb ibn ʿUbayd; from Jubayr ibn Nufayr. He said: **'I went with Shuraḥbīl ibn al-Simṭ to a village which was seventeen or eighteen miles away. He offered his prayer in two *rakʿahs*. I spoke to him and he said: "I saw ʿUmar praying in two *rakʿahs* at Dhul-Hulayfah. I questioned him and he said: 'I am doing as I saw God's Messenger (peace be upon him) do'."'**

حَدَّثَنَا زُهَيْرُ بْنُ حَرْبٍ وَمُحَمَّدُ بْنُ بَشَّارٍ، جَمِيعًا عَنِ ابْنِ مَهْدِيٍّ، قَالَ زُهَيْرٌ: حَدَّثَنَا عَبْدُ الرَّحْمَنِ بْنُ مَهْدِيٍّ، حَدَّثَنَا شُعْبَةُ، عَنْ يَزِيدَ بْنِ خُمَيْرٍ، عَنْ حَبِيبِ بْنِ عُبَيْدٍ، عَنْ جُبَيْرِ بْنِ

i. Related by Abu Dāwūd, 1201.

ii. *Farsakh* is equal to three Arabian miles, and a mile is estimated to be equal to 1848 meters. Thus, a *farsakh* is equal to 5,544 metres.

iii. Related by al-Nasāʾī, 1436.

نُفَيْرٍ قَالَ: خَرَجْتُ مَعَ شُرَحْبِيلَ بْنِ السِّمْطِ إِلَى قَرْيَةٍ عَلَى رَأْسِ سَبْعَةَ عَشَرَ أَوْ ثَمَانِيَةَ عَشَرَ مِيلاً، فَصَلَّى رَكْعَتَيْنِ. فَقُلْتُ لَهُ، فَقَالَ: رَأَيْتُ عُمَرَ صَلَّى بِذِي الْحُلَيْفَةِ رَكْعَتَيْنِ، فَقُلْتُ لَهُ، فَقَالَ: إِنَّمَا أَفْعَلُ كَمَا رَأَيْتُ رَسُولَ اللهِ صَلَّى اللهُ عَلَيْهِ وَسَلَّمَ يَفْعَلُ.

[1340–14]. (Dar al-Salam[i]) Muhammad ibn al-Muthannā narrated the same to me: Muhammad ibn Ja'far narrated; Shu'bah narrated; with the same chain of transmission but he said Ibn al-Simṭ without naming Shuraḥbīl. He said: **'He went to an area called Dūmīn near Ḥumṣ, at a distance of eighteen miles'.**

وَحَدَّثَنِيهِ مُحَمَّدُ بْنُ الْـمُثَنَّى، حَدَّثَنَا مُحَمَّدُ بْنُ جَعْفَرٍ، حَدَّثَنَا شُعْبَةُ، بِهَذَا الإِسْنَادِ. وَقَالَ عَنِ ابْنِ السِّمْطِ، وَلَمْ يُسَمِّ شُرَحْبِيلَ، وَقَالَ: إِنَّهُ أَتَى أَرْضًا يُقَالُ لَهَا دُومِينُ مِنْ حِمْصَ عَلَى رَأْسِ ثَمَانِيَةَ عَشَرَ مِيلاً.

[1341–15]. (Dar al-Salam 1473–1474) Yaḥyā ibn Yaḥyā al-Tamīmī narrated:[ii] Hushaym reported; from Yaḥyā ibn Abi Isḥāq; from Anas ibn Mālik. He said: **'We travelled with God's Messenger (peace be upon him) from Madinah to Makkah and he offered prayers in two *rak'ahs* each until he went back'. I asked: 'How long did he stay in Makkah?' He said: 'Ten days'.**

حَدَّثَنَا يَحْيَى بْنُ يَحْيَى التَّمِيمِيُّ، أَخْبَرَنَا هُشَيْمٌ، عَنْ يَحْيَى بْنِ أَبِي إِسْحَاقَ، عَنْ أَنَسِ بْنِ مَالِكٍ قَالَ: خَرَجْنَا مَعَ رَسُولِ اللهِ صَلَّى اللهُ عَلَيْهِ وَسَلَّمَ مِنَ الْـمَدِينَةِ إِلَى مَكَّةَ، فَصَلَّى رَكْعَتَيْنِ رَكْعَتَيْنِ حَتَّى رَجَعَ. قُلْتُ: كَمْ أَقَامَ بِمَكَّةَ؟ قَالَ: عَشْرًا.

---

i. In the Dar al-Salam edition, this hadith is entered as a part of the hadith before it and given no number.

ii. Related by al-Bukhari, 1081 and in a shorter version, 4297; Abu Dāwūd, 1233; al-Tirmidhī, 548; al-Nasā'ī, 1437; Ibn Mājah, 1077.

Qutaybah narrated: Abu ʿAwānah narrated [H]. Abu Kurayb narrated; Ibn ʿUlayyah narrated; both from Yaḥyā ibn Abi Isḥāq; from Anas; from the Prophet (peace be upon him): **the same text as Hushaym's narration.**

وَحَدَّثَنَاهُ قُتَيْبَةُ، حَدَّثَنَا أَبُو عَوَانَةَ، ح. وَحَدَّثَنَاهُ أَبُو كُرَيْبٍ، حَدَّثَنَا ابْنُ عُلَيَّةَ، جَمِيعًا عَنْ يَحْيَى بْنِ أَبِي إِسْحَاقَ، عَنْ أَنَسٍ، عَنِ النَّبِيِّ صَلَّى اللهُ عَلَيْهِ وَسَلَّمَ، بِمِثْلِ حَدِيثِ هُشَيْمٍ.

[1342–000]. (Dar al-Salam 1475) ʿUbaydullāh ibn Muʿādh narrated: my father narrated; Shuʿbah narrated; Yaḥyā ibn Abi Isḥāq narrated to me. He said: I heard Anas ibn Mālik say: **'We set out from Madinah for the pilgrimage...'. He added the same text.**

وَحَدَّثَنَا عُبَيْدُ اللهِ بْنُ مُعَاذٍ، حَدَّثَنَا أَبِي، حَدَّثَنَا شُعْبَةُ قَالَ: حَدَّثَنِي يَحْيَى بْنُ أَبِي إِسْحَاقَ، قَالَ سَمِعْتُ أَنَسَ بْنَ مَالِكٍ يَقُولُ: خَرَجْنَا مِنَ الْـمَدِينَةِ إِلَى الْحَجِّ. ثُمَّ ذَكَرَ مِثْلَهُ.

[1343–000]. (Dar al-Salam 1476) Ibn Numayr narrated: my father narrated [H]. Abu Kurayb narrated; Abu Usāmah narrated; both from al-Thawrī; from Yaḥyā ibn Abi Isḥāq; from Anas; from the Prophet (peace be upon him): **the same text but he did not mention the pilgrimage.**

وَحَدَّثَنَا ابْنُ نُمَيْرٍ، حَدَّثَنَا أَبِي ح. وَحَدَّثَنَا أَبُو كُرَيْبٍ، حَدَّثَنَا أَبُو أُسَامَةَ، جَمِيعًا عَنِ الثَّوْرِيِّ، عَنْ يَحْيَى بْنِ أَبِي إِسْحَاقَ، عَنْ أَنَسٍ، عَنِ النَّبِيِّ صَلَّى اللهُ عَلَيْهِ وَسَلَّمَ: بِمِثْلِهِ، وَلَمْ يَذْكُرِ الْحَجَّ.

Text Explanation

In the first hadith, No. 1327, ʿĀ'ishah says: 'When prayer was made a duty, it was two *rakʿahs* each, when at home and when travelling.

Later, prayer on a journey remained the same but it was increased when at home'.

Scholars express different views regarding the shortening of prayers when a person is on a journey. Al-Shāfiʿī, Mālik ibn Anas and the majority of scholars say that both shortening the prayers and praying them in full are permissible, but shortening prayers is better. My own view is that offering the prayer complete is better, but also, I look at it differently and say that both completing and shortening the prayer are equally valid. The correct and well-known view is that shortening prayer when travelling is better. Abu Ḥanīfah and many scholars say that shortening prayers on a journey is a duty and praying them in full is wrong, citing this hadith in support and saying that on most occasions the Prophet and his Companions shortened their prayers. Al-Shāfiʿī and scholars who agree with him cite in support of their view a number of well-known hadiths related by Muslim and others, stating that the Prophet's Companions travelled with God's Messenger (peace be upon him), and some of them shortened their prayers and some prayed complete. Some of them fasted [if they travelled during Ramadan] and some did not. None of them criticised the others. They also said that ʿUthmān prayed in full, as did ʿĀ'ishah. This is the apparent meaning of the Qur'anic verse: 'When you go forth on earth, you will incur no sin by shortening your prayers.' (4: 101) This means permissibility and incurring no sin. The hadith that says: 'prayer was made obligatory in two *rakʿahs*', means that two *rakʿahs* were obligatory to those who wish to limit themselves to that. Two more *rakʿahs* were added as obligatory for anyone in residence, while the shorter prayer remained permissible and valid if one wished to stick to it. Given the permissibility of offering the prayer in full is confirmed by good evidence, it must be upheld.[i]

In hadith No. 1329, al-Zuhrī asks ʿUrwah: 'How is it, then, that ʿĀ'ishah offers the prayer complete when she is travelling?' He said:

---

i. This is the argument al-Nawawi provides in support of his view preferring completing prayers when travelling.

'She justified it as 'Uthmān did'. Scholars differ in their explanations of such justification. The correct view endorsed by leading scholars is that they considered both shortening prayers and offering them in full to be permissible, and they chose one of the two permissible options, which was to pray in full. Some scholars suggested that 'Uthmān was the leader of the believers and 'Ā'ishah was their mother, which meant that wherever they were, they were in their own homes. This argument is rejected by leading scholars on the basis that the Prophet was more entitled to this than either 'Uthmān or 'Ā'ishah, as were Abu Bakr and 'Umar.

Other arguments are provided and rejected by leading scholars, such as that 'Uthmān married in Makkah, but this is rejected on the basis that the Prophet travelled with his wives and shortened the prayers. Another argument suggests that 'Uthmān did so because of the Bedouins who travelled with him. He wanted to make sure that they would not think that prayers were always in two *rak'ahs*, both at home and when on a journey. This is countered by the fact that this applied during the Prophet's lifetime and he shortened the prayer. Moreover, by 'Uthmān's time, prayer and its rulings were far better known. A further argument is that 'Uthmān intended to stay in Makkah after his pilgrimage, but this is countered by the fact that any stay in Makkah for more than three days was forbidden to the Muhājirīn, and 'Uthmān was one of them. Yet another argument says that 'Uthmān owned some land in Mina, but this is countered by the fact that this does not require him to pray in full and stay there. The correct view is the first [which makes clear that it is permissible to shorten prayers and to offer them complete when on a journey].

The view of al-Shāfi'ī, Mālik, Abu Ḥanīfah, Ahmad and the majority of scholars is that shortening prayers is permissible during every legitimate travel. Some early scholars make it a condition that it should be travel accompanied by fear, while others say that it must be travel to perform the pilgrimage, or the umrah, or to face an enemy, and others still said that it must be travel for some legitimate purpose. Al-Shāfi'ī, Mālik, Ahmad and the majority of scholars say that it is not permissible if the travel involves doing something in disobedience of God, but Abu Ḥanīfah and al-Thawrī say that it is permissible even then.

Al-Shāfiʿī, Mālik and their disciples, as well as al-Layth, al-Awzāʿī, those that are well versed in Fiqh among Hadith scholars and others maintain that shortening prayers is only permissible during travel that covers at least two stages, equal to forty-eight Hashimite miles.[i] Abu Ḥanīfah and other Kūfī scholars say that for shortening prayer, the travel must be of a distance equal to three stages or more. This is also attributed to ʿUthmān, Ibn Masʿūd and Ḥudhayfah. Dāwūd and scholars of the Ẓāhirī School say that prayer is shortened in long and short travel, even in a journey of three miles [i.e. less than six kilometres].

In hadith No. 1330, the narrator Yaʿlā ibn Umayyah asks ʿUmar ibn al-Khaṭṭāb about the Qur'anic verse and ʿUmar says: 'I wondered the same as you wonder, and I asked God's Messenger (peace be upon him) about it. He said: "This is a charity God has given you. You should accept His charity".' This confirms that it is permissible to say that God has been charitable to us, or has given us a charity, or to pray to Him to give us a charity. Some early scholars say that it is discouraged, but this is clearly wrong. I clarified this in my book *al-Adhkār*. The hadith makes clear that it is permissible to shorten prayers in situations other than that of being in fear. It also shows that when someone sees a better versed person doing something he finds problematic, he should ask him about it.

Hadith No. 1331 quotes Ibn ʿAbbās: 'God has made prayer obligatory through your Prophet (peace be upon him): at home four *rakʿahs*, on a journey two *rakʿahs* and only one *rakʿah* in situations of fear'. A number of early scholars, such as al-Ḥasan, al-Ḍaḥḥāk and Isḥāq ibn Rāhawayh, implemented this hadith according to its

i. A Hashimite or Arabian mile is a little longer than a British mile, and this distance is considered to be equal to about 84 kilometres. Al-Nawawi provides here estimates of this distance according to what was known at the time: 'A mile is 6,000 arm lengths, and an arm length is equal to the width of 24 average fingers, and a finger is equal to the width of six hairs'. It appears that a hair was a known measure and does not equate to normal human hair.

apparent meaning. Al-Shāfiʿī, Mālik and the majority of scholars say that prayer in a situation of fear consists of the same number of *rakʿahs* as offered in a situation of security, which means that at home it is offered in four *rakʿahs* and in two *rakʿahs* only if on a journey. It is not permissible to offer it in one *rakʿah* in any situation. They understand this hadith by Ibn ʿAbbās as meaning one *rakʿah* with the imam and one alone, as clearly stated in authentic hadiths reporting how the Prophet and his Companions prayed when they were in fear of being attacked. This understanding is necessary to reconcile all the relevant evidence, but God knows best.

In hadith No. 1334, Ibn ʿUmar is told that some people were praying sunnah as they were with him on a journey. He said: 'Were I to pray the sunnah, I would rather have completed my [obligatory] prayer'. What he meant is that he did not agree with either praying the sunnah or completing the obligatory prayer in four *rakʿahs*. The recommended practice is to shorten the obligatory prayer and not to offer the sunnah. This applies to the regular sunnah with each of the obligatory prayers. As for other voluntary prayers, Ibn ʿUmar used to offer these when he was on a journey. It is reported that the Prophet did these, as authentically reported. Scholars are agreed that offering general voluntary prayers during travel is desirable, but they differ with regard to the regular sunnah prayer. Ibn ʿUmar and other scholars discourage these, while al-Shāfiʿī, scholars of his school and the majority consider these desirable also. The evidence they cite is in the hadiths speaking of the desirability of offering sunnah prayers generally, the hadith stating that 'God's Messenger prayed the mid-morning (Ḍuḥā) sunnah in Makkah on the day when Makkah fell to Islam' and the two *rakʿahs* of the Fajr sunnah when they slept until after sunrise, as well as other hadiths mentioned in the *Sunan* anthologies. Moreover, they take this on the basis of analogy with the general voluntary prayers. It may be that the Prophet used to pray the sunnah prayers where he encamped and Ibn ʿUmar did not see him because praying the sunnah at home is better than praying it at the mosque. Or perhaps the Prophet did not pray the sunnah at times in order to make clear to his Companions that it is permissible to leave it out. Some scholars say that the sunnah prayers should be left out during travel because completing the obligatory prayers is more important. In answer, we say that the sunnah prayer is left to us; everyone may choose to perform it or not. Therefore, it is a kindness to make it available and everyone chooses to do it or not in order to earn its reward or to leave it out, incurring no sin.

In the same hadith, the narrator says: 'I then accompanied ʿUthmān and he never offered more than two *rakʿahs* until God gathered his soul'. Muslim mentions later in a hadith narrated on Ibn ʿUmar's authority: 'And with ʿUthmān for a part of his reign as caliph, and he subsequently offered his prayers complete'. In one version, for eight years or six years. It is well known that ʿUthmān offered his prayers in the complete version after six years of his reign. Scholars understand this report as meaning that ʿUthmān never prayed more than two *rakʿahs* on a journey, other than at Mina, until he passed away. The well-known reports that ʿUthmān prayed the full number of *rakʿahs* are understood to refer to how he prayed at Mina in particular. In his narration, ʿImrān ibn al-Ḥuṣayn explains that ʿUthmān's offering of the prayers complete was in Mina. The narrations stated later in Muslim's *Ṣaḥīḥ* have the same meaning.

Shortening the prayers at Arafat, Muzdalifah and Mina is permissible for pilgrims other than those who live in Makkah and its surrounding area. It is not permissible to the people of Makkah and those living at a distance less than that which permits shortening prayers. This is the view of al-Shāfiʿī, Abu Ḥanīfah and the majority of scholars. Mālik, however, says that the people of Makkah, Mina, Muzdalifah and Arafat also shorten their prayers. He considers undertaking the pilgrimage as the reason for shortening the prayers, while the majority of scholars consider that the reason is being in travel, but God knows best.

Hadith No. 1336 mentions that the Prophet offered Ẓuhr Prayer in four *rakʿahs* in Madinah, then offered ʿAṣr in two *rakʿahs* only at Dhul-Hulayfah. The distance between Madinah and Dhul-Hulayfah is six or seven miles. This is part of the evidence cited by the Ẓāhirī scholars to support the opinion that shortening prayers applies in all travel, whether of a long or short distance. The majority of scholars say that shortening prayers does not apply for journeys of a distance less than two stages, while Abu Ḥanīfah and others say it must be at least three stages. They rely on reports by some of the Prophet's Companions. The present hadith does not provide evidence in support of the view of the Ẓāhirī scholars. The hadith speaks of the Prophet's travel to Makkah on his Farewell Pilgrimage. It was then that he prayed four *rakʿahs* in Madinah and then travelled. The 'Aṣr Prayer became due when he was at Dhul-Hulayfah, and he prayed it there in two *rakʿahs*. Dhul-Hulayfah was not his destination. Hence, the hadith gives no evidence in support of this view.

The traveller may start to shorten his prayers from the moment he departs his town or village, or he leaves his people's camp, if that is where they live. This is the sum of the relevant rulings, but their details are well explained in books of Fiqh. This is our view and the view of all scholars, with the exception of a poor (*i.e. ḍaʿīf*) report attributed to Mālik saying that it begins after having travelled three miles. It is also reported that 'Aṭā' and a number of Ibn Masʿūd's disciples suggest that a person intending to travel may shorten his prayers before starting his journey. A different view attributed to Mujāhid is that a traveller does not shorten his prayer on the day he starts his journey until nightfall. All these reports are contrary to the sunnah and the unanimity of scholars of earlier and recent generations.

In hadith No. 1338, the Prophet used to shorten his prayers to two *rakʿahs* at a distance of three miles from Madinah. This is certainly not a condition for the start of shortening prayers. It happened as needed. What appears to us when we study his travels is that the Prophet used not to start his travel close to the time of a prayer that may be shortened and would be close to Madinah when such a prayer fell due, opting then to pray it in full. What he normally did was to start his travel when there was still much time before such a prayer. It would then fall due when he was at a distance of three miles or more and he would offer it then. The general statements of the relevant hadiths and the apparent meaning of the Qur'an confirm that prayers may be shortened once the traveller has left his hometown or village. It is then that he is called a traveller, and God knows best.

The text of hadith No. 1339 goes as follows: 'I went with Shuraḥbīl ibn al-Simṭ to a village, which was seventeen or eighteen miles away. He offered his prayer in two *rakʿahs*. I spoke to him and he said: "I saw ʿUmar praying in two *rakʿahs* at Dhul-Hulayfah". I questioned him and he said: "I am doing as I saw God's Messenger (peace be upon him) do".' This hadith may be thought to provide evidence for the Ẓāhirī scholars' view that shortening prayers is permissible even during short travels. This is wrong because what is attributed to the Prophet and ʿUmar is that they shortened the prayer at Dhul-Hulayfah, which was not their ultimate destination. The fact that Shuraḥbīl ibn al-Simṭ shortened his prayer at a distance of seventeen or eighteen miles does not provide any evidence. He belonged to the *tābiʿīn* generation and did something contrary to the view of the majority of scholars. Alternatively, it may be taken as something he did during his travel, not at his destination. This understanding is apparent, and it makes his argument, based on ʿUmar's action which emulates the Prophet's action, valid, but God knows best.

Hadith No. 1341 says: 'We travelled with God's Messenger (peace be upon him) from Madinah to Makkah, and he offered prayers in two *rakʿahs* each until he went back'. I asked: 'How long did he stay in Makkah?' He said: 'Ten days'. This means that he stayed in Makkah and its adjacent area, not in Makkah itself. This refers to his travel when he performed the Farewell Pilgrimage. He arrived in Makkah on the fourth of Dhul-Hijjah and stayed there on the fifth, sixth and seventh days, heading for Mina on the eighth and from there to Arafat on the ninth of Dhul-Hijjah. On the tenth day of the month he went back to Mina where he stayed on the eleventh and the twelfth, heading back to Makkah on the thirteenth and leaving it for Madinah on the fourteenth. Thus his total stay in Makkah and its surrounding area was ten days and he shortened his prayers throughout. Therefore, the hadith gives evidence that a traveller who intends to stay at a place less than four days other than his day of entry and his day of departure shortens his prayers throughout. A three-day stay is not considered as residence because the Prophet and his Muhājirīn Companions stayed in Makkah three days, which shows that such a stay is not considered residence for religious purposes. It also shows that the day of entry and the day of departure are not counted. Such say al-Shāfiʿā and the majority of scholars, but scholars of earlier generations differ widely on these points.

Transmission

The chain of transmission of hadith No. 1330 includes ʿAbdullāh ibn Bābayh. His name is variously mentioned as Ibn Bābāh and Ibn Bābī. Yaḥyā ibn Yazīd al-Hunā'ī is one of the narrators in the chain of hadith No. 1338. Al-Samʿānī said that al-Hunā'ī was affiliated to Hunā' ibn Mālik ibn Fahm.

Hadith No. 1339 includes in its chain of transmission, 'Shuʿbah narrated: from Yazīd ibn Khumayr; from Ḥabīb ibn ʿUbayd; from Jubayr ibn Nufayr. He said: "I went with Shuraḥbīl ibn al-Simṭ".' This chain of transmission includes four narrators, from Yazīd ibn Khumayr to the end, belonging to the *tābiʿīn* generation and reporting from each other. We have mentioned several cases like this and there will be more, which we will highlight at the appropriate places.

CHAPTER 2

SHORTENING PRAYERS AT MINA

[1344–16]. (Dar al-Salam 1477) Ḥarmalah ibn Yaḥyā narrated to me: Ibn Wahb narrated; ʿAmr (who is Ibn al-Ḥārith) reported to me; from Ibn Shihāb; from Sālim ibn ʿAbdullāh; from his father that **'God's Messenger (peace be upon him) prayed as a traveller in Mina and elsewhere, offering [prayers] in two *rakʿahs*. So did Abu Bakr and ʿUmar, praying only two *rakʿahs*, and so did ʿUthmān for a part of his reign. He then prayed it complete, in four *rakʿahs*'.**

وَحَدَّثَنِي حَرْمَلَةُ بْنُ يَحْيَى، حَدَّثَنَا ابْنُ وَهْبٍ، أَخْبَرَنِي عَمْرٌو (وَهُوَ ابْنُ الْحَارِثِ) عَنِ ابْنِ شِهَابٍ، عَنْ سَالِمِ بْنِ عَبْدِ اللهِ، عَنْ أَبِيهِ، عَنْ رَسُولِ اللهِ صَلَّى اللهُ عَلَيْهِ وَسَلَّمَ، أَنَّهُ صَلَّى صَلَاةَ الْمُسَافِرِ بِمِنًى وَغَيْرِهِ رَكْعَتَيْنِ، وَأَبُو بَكْرٍ وَعُمَرُ. وَعُثْمَانُ رَكْعَتَيْنِ صَدْرًا مِنْ خِلَافَتِهِ، ثُمَّ أَتَمَّهَا أَرْبَعًا.

[1345–000]. (Dar al-Salam 1478) Zuhayr ibn Ḥarb narrated: al-Walīd ibn Muslim narrated; from al-Awzāʿī [H]. Also, Isḥāq and ʿAbd ibn Ḥumayd narrated; they said: ʿAbd al-Razzāq reported; Maʿmar reported; all from al-Zuhrī; with the same chain of transmission. He said: **'in Mina' but did not say: 'and elsewhere'.**

وَحَدَّثَنَاهُ زُهَيْرُ بْنُ حَرْبٍ، حَدَّثَنَا الْوَلِيدُ بْنُ مُسْلِمٍ، عَنِ الأَوْزَاعِيِّ، ح. وَحَدَّثَنَاهُ إِسْحَاقُ وَعَبْدُ بْنُ حُمَيْدٍ، قَالا: أَخْبَرَنَا عَبْدُ الرَّزَّاقِ، أَخْبَرَنَا مَعْمَرٌ، جَمِيعًا عَنِ الزُّهْرِيِّ، بِهَذَا الإِسْنَادِ. قَالَ: بِمِنًى، وَلَمْ يَقُلْ وَغَيْرِهِ.

[1346–17]. (Dar al-Salam 1479–1480) Abu Bakr ibn Abi Shaybah narrated: Abu Usāmah narrated; ʿUbaydullāh; from Nāfiʿ; from Ibn ʿUmar. He said: **'God's Messenger (peace be upon him) prayed in Mina [shortening prayers to] two *rakʿahs* and so did Abu Bakr after him, and ʿUmar after Abu Bakr, and ʿUthmān for a part of his reign. Subsequently, ʿUthmān offered his prayers in four *rakʿahs*'. When Ibn ʿUmar prayed with the imam, he offered his prayer in four *rakʿahs*, and if he prayed alone, he prayed two *rakʿahs*.**

حَدَّثَنَا أَبُو بَكْرِ بْنُ أَبِي شَيْبَةَ، حَدَّثَنَا أَبُو أُسَامَةَ، حَدَّثَنَا عُبَيْدُ اللهِ، عَنْ نَافِعٍ، عَنِ ابْنِ عُمَرَ قَالَ: صَلَّى رَسُولُ اللهِ صَلَّى اللهُ عَلَيْهِ وَسَلَّمَ بِمِنًى رَكْعَتَيْنِ، وَأَبُو بَكْرٍ بَعْدَهُ، وَعُمَرُ بَعْدَ أَبِي بَكْرٍ. وَعُثْمَانُ صَدْرًا مِنْ خِلَافَتِهِ، ثُمَّ إِنَّ عُثْمَانَ صَلَّى بَعْدُ أَرْبَعًا.

فَكَانَ ابْنُ عُمَرَ إِذَا صَلَّى مَعَ الإِمَامِ صَلَّى أَرْبَعًا وَإِذَا صَلَّاهَا وَحْدَهُ صَلَّى رَكْعَتَيْنِ.

Ibn al-Muthannā and ʿUbaydullāh ibn Saʿīd narrated it: both said: Yaḥyā (who is al-Qaṭṭān) narrated [H]. Also, Abu Kurayb narrated it; Ibn Abi Zā'idah reported [H]. Ibn Numayr narrated; ʿUqbah ibn Khālid narrated; all of them from ʿUbaydullāh; with the same chain of transmission: **a similar text.**

وَحَدَّثَنَاهُ ابْنُ الْمُثَنَّى وَعُبَيْدُ اللهِ بْنُ سَعِيدٍ، قَالا: حَدَّثَنَا يَحْيَى (وَهُوَ الْقَطَّانُ) ح. وَحَدَّثَنَاهُ أَبُو كُرَيْبٍ، أَخْبَرَنَا ابْنُ أَبِي زَائِدَةَ، ح. وَحَدَّثَنَاهُ ابْنُ نُمَيْرٍ، حَدَّثَنَا عُقْبَةُ بْنُ خَالِدٍ، كُلُّهُمْ عَنْ عُبَيْدِ اللهِ، بِهَذَا الإِسْنَادِ: نَحْوَهُ.

[1347–18]. (Dar al-Salam 1481) ʿUbaydullāh ibn Muʿādh narrated: my father narrated; Shuʿbah narrated; from Khubayb ibn ʿAbd al-Raḥmān; he heard Ḥafṣ ibn ʿĀṣim; from Ibn ʿUmar. He said: **'The Prophet (peace be upon him) prayed in Mina the way a traveller prays, and so did Abu Bakr and ʿUmar. ʿUthmān also did for eight years, or he said six years. Ḥafṣ said: "Ibn ʿUmar used to pray two *rakʿahs* in Mina and then go to his bed." I said: "Uncle, would you rather offer two *rakʿahs* after that?" He said: "If I were to do that, I would have completed my prayer".'**

وَحَدَّثَنَا عُبَيْدُ اللهِ بْنُ مُعَاذٍ، حَدَّثَنَا أَبِي، حَدَّثَنَا شُعْبَةُ، عَنْ خُبَيْبِ بْنِ عَبْدِ الرَّحْمَنِ، سَمِعَ حَفْصَ بْنَ عَاصِمٍ، عَنِ ابْنِ عُمَرَ قَالَ: صَلَّى النَّبِيُّ صَلَّى اللهُ عَلَيْهِ وَسَلَّمَ بِمِنًى صَلاَةَ الْمُسَافِرِ، وَأَبُو بَكْرٍ وَعُمَرُ. وَعُثْمَانُ ثَمَانِيَ سِنِينَ أَوْ قَالَ سِتَّ سِنِينَ. قَالَ حَفْصٌ: وَكَانَ ابْنُ عُمَرَ يُصَلِّي بِمِنًى رَكْعَتَيْنِ ثُمَّ يَأْتِي فِرَاشَهُ. فَقُلْتُ: أَيْ عَمِّ لَوْ صَلَّيْتَ بَعْدَهَا رَكْعَتَيْنِ. قَالَ: لَوْ فَعَلْتُ لأَتْمَمْتُ الصَّلاَةَ.

[1348–000]. (Dar al-Salam 1482) Yaḥyā ibn Ḥabīb narrated: Khālid (meaning Ibn al-Ḥārith) narrated [H]. Also, Ibn al-Muthannā narrated; ʿAbd al-Ṣamad narrated to me; both said: Shuʿbah narrated; with the same chain of transmission: **the same but they did not say: 'in Mina' but said: 'prayed during travel'.**

وَحَدَّثَنَاهُ يَحْيَى بْنُ حَبِيبٍ، حَدَّثَنَا خَالِدٌ (يَعْنِي ابْنَ الْحَارِثِ)، ح. وَحَدَّثَنَا ابْنُ الْمُثَنَّى قَالَ: حَدَّثَنِي عَبْدُ الصَّمَدِ، قَالاَ: حَدَّثَنَا شُعْبَةُ، بِهَذَا الإِسْنَادِ. وَلَمْ يَقُولاَ فِي الْحَدِيثِ بِمِنًى. وَلَكِنْ قَالاَ: صَلَّى فِي السَّفَرِ.

[1349–19]. (Dar al-Salam 1483–1484) Qutaybah ibn Saʿīd narrated:[i] ʿAbd al-Wāḥid narrated from al-Aʿmash; Ibrāhīm

i. Related by al-Bukhari, 1084 and 1657; Abu Dāwūd, 1960; al-Nasāʾī, 1447 and 1448.

narrated. He said: I heard ʿAbd al-Raḥmān ibn Yazīd say: **'ʿUthmān led us in prayer in Mina, praying four *rakʿahs*. This was mentioned to ʿAbdullāh ibn Masʿūd**. He expressed regret,[i] **then said: "I prayed with God's Messenger (peace be upon him) at Mina in two *rakʿahs*, and I prayed with Abu Bakr al-Ṣiddīq at Mina in two *rakʿahs*, and I prayed with ʿUmar ibn al-Khaṭṭāb in Mina in two *rakʿahs*. I wish that I gain from four *rakʿahs* two accepted *rakʿahs*".'**

حَدَّثَنَا قُتَيْبَةُ بْنُ سَعِيدٍ، حَدَّثَنَا عَبْدُ الْوَاحِدِ، عَنِ الأَعْمَشِ، حَدَّثَنَا إِبْرَاهِيمُ قَالَ: سَمِعْتُ عَبْدَ الرَّحْمَنِ بْنَ يَزِيدَ يَقُولُ: صَلَّى بِنَا عُثْمَانُ بِمِنًى أَرْبَعَ رَكَعَاتٍ. فَقِيلَ ذَلِكَ لِعَبْدِ اللهِ بْنِ مَسْعُودٍ، فَاسْتَرْجَعَ ثُمَّ قَالَ: صَلَّيْتُ مَعَ رَسُولِ اللهِ صَلَّى اللهُ عَلَيْهِ وَسَلَّمَ بِمِنًى رَكْعَتَيْنِ، وَصَلَّيْتُ مَعَ أَبِي بَكْرٍ الصِّدِّيقِ بِمِنًى رَكْعَتَيْنِ، وَصَلَّيْتُ مَعَ عُمَرَ بْنِ الْخَطَّابِ بِمِنًى رَكْعَتَيْنِ. فَلَيْتَ حَظِّي مِنْ أَرْبَعِ رَكَعَاتٍ رَكْعَتَانِ مُتَقَبَّلَتَانِ.

Abu Bakr ibn Abi Shaybah and Abu Kurayb narrated: both said: Abu Muʿāwiyah narrated [H]. Also, ʿUthmān ibn Abi Shaybah narrated; Jarīr narrated [H]. And Isḥāq and Ibn Khashram narrated: both said: ʿĪsā reported; all from al-Aʿmash; with the same chain of transmission: **a similar text.**

حَدَّثَنَا أَبُو بَكْرِ بْنُ أَبِي شَيْبَةَ وَأَبُو كُرَيْبٍ، قَالَا: حَدَّثَنَا أَبُو مُعَاوِيَةَ، ح. وَحَدَّثَنَا عُثْمَانُ بْنُ أَبِي شَيْبَةَ قَالَ: حَدَّثَنَا جَرِيرٌ، ح. وَحَدَّثَنَا إِسْحَاقُ وَابْنُ خَشْرَمٍ، قَالَا أَخْبَرَنَا عِيسَى، كُلُّهُمْ عَنِ الأَعْمَشِ، بِهَذَا الإِسْنَادِ: نَحْوَهُ.

[1350–20]. (Dar al-Salam 1485) Yaḥyā ibn Yaḥyā and Qutaybah narrated:[ii] Abu al-Aḥwaṣ (Yaḥyā said: 'reported' and Qutaybah

i. The phrase he said is not mentioned in full in the text of the hadith, but rather referred to briefly. It is *innā lillāh wa innā ilayhi rājiʿūn*, which means 'We all belong to God and to Him we shall all return'.

ii. Related by al-Bukhari, 1083 and 1656; Abu Dāwūd, 1965; al-Tirmidhī, 882; al-Nasāʾī, 1444 and 1445.

said: 'narrated'); from Abu Isḥāq; from Ḥārithah ibn Wahb. He said: **'I prayed with God's Messenger (peace be upon him) in Mina with people never more secure nor greater in number, in two *rak'ahs*'.**

وَحَدَّثَنَا يَحْيَى بْنُ يَحْيَى وَقُتَيْبَةُ، قَالَ يَحْيَى أَخْبَرَنَا وَقَالَ قُتَيْبَةُ حَدَّثَنَا أَبُو الأَحْوَصِ، عَنْ أَبِي إِسْحَاقَ، عَنْ حَارِثَةَ بْنِ وَهْبٍ قَالَ: صَلَّيْتُ مَعَ رَسُولِ اللهِ صَلَّى اللهُ عَلَيْهِ وَسَلَّمَ بِمِنًى - آمَنَ مَا كَانَ النَّاسُ وَأَكْثَرَهُ - رَكْعَتَيْنِ.

[1351–21]. (Dar al-Salam 1486) Ahmad ibn 'Abdullāh ibn Yūnus narrated: Zuhayr narrated; Abu Isḥāq narrated; Ḥarithah ibn Wahb al-Khuzā'ī narrated to me. He said: **'I prayed behind God's Messenger (peace be upon him) in Mina with people never greater in number, and he prayed in two *rak'ahs* during the Farewell Pilgrimage'.**

Muslim said: Ḥārithah ibn Wahb al-Khuzā'ī was 'Ubaydullāh ibn 'Umar ibn al-Khaṭṭāb's half-brother, having the same mother.

حَدَّثَنَا أَحْمَدُ بْنُ عَبْدِ اللهِ بْنِ يُونُسَ، حَدَّثَنَا زُهَيْرٌ، حَدَّثَنَا أَبُو إِسْحَاقَ، حَدَّثَنِي حَارِثَةُ بْنُ وَهْبٍ الْخُزَاعِيُّ قَالَ: صَلَّيْتُ خَلْفَ رَسُولِ اللهِ صَلَّى اللهُ عَلَيْهِ وَسَلَّمَ بِمِنًى، وَالنَّاسُ أَكْثَرُ مَا كَانُوا، فَصَلَّى رَكْعَتَيْنِ فِي حَجَّةِ الْوَدَاعِ.

قَالَ مُسْلِمٌ: حَارِثَةُ بْنُ وَهْبٍ الْخُزَاعِيُّ هُوَ أَخُو عُبَيْدِ اللهِ بْنِ عُمَرَ بْنِ الْخَطَّابِ لأُمِّهِ.

Text Explanation

In hadith No. 1349, Ibn Mas'ūd says: 'I wish that I gain from four *rak'ahs* two accepted *rak'ahs*'. This statement expresses Ibn Mas'ūd's preference that 'Uthmān should have prayed two *rak'ahs*, like the Prophet, Abu Bakr, 'Umar and 'Uthmān (in the early part of his reign). This is how Ibn Masʿūd expressed his disapproval of doing what was different from the practice of the Prophet and his two closest Companions. Yet, Ibn Masʿūd considered it perfectly acceptable to offer the prayers in their full version during travel. Therefore, he used to pray with ʿUthmān when he completed the prayers. Had shortening the prayer been viewed by Ibn Masʿūd as a duty or obligatory, he would not have prayed behind anyone who abandoned it. The fact that Ibn Masʿūd expressed disapproval means that he disapproved of abandoning what was better, as we have already explained.

Transmission

In the last hadith, No. 1351 Muslim mentions that the narrator Ḥārithah ibn Wahb al-Khuzāʿī was a half-brother of ʿUbaydullāh ibn ʿUmar ibn al-Khaṭṭāb, having the same mother. In some original manuscripts, the name is given as ʿAbdullāh, but this is wrong as mentioned by many authorities, including al-Bukhari, Ibn Abi Ḥātim and Ibn ʿAbd al-Barr. Ḥārithah's mother was Mulaykah bint Jarwal al-Khuzāʿī. She married ʿUmar ibn al-Khaṭṭāb and gave him their son ʿUbaydullāh. ʿUmar earlier married Zaynab bint Maẓʿūn and she gave him his son ʿAbdullāh and his daughter Ḥafṣah, the Prophet's wife.

CHAPTER 3

PRAYING AT HOME ON RAINY DAYS

[1352–22]. (Dar al-Salam 1487) Yaḥyā ibn Yaḥyā narrated:[i] he said: I read out to Mālik; from Nāfiʿ; that **'Ibn ʿUmar called the *adhān* on a cold windy night, and he said: "Pray in your own homes". He said: "If the night was cold and rainy, God's Messenger (peace be upon him) used to instruct the person calling the *adhān* to say: 'Do pray in your homes'."'**

حَدَّثَنَا يَحْيَى بْنُ يَحْيَى قَالَ: قَرَأْتُ عَلَى مَالِكٍ عَنْ نَافِعٍ، أَنَّ ابْنَ عُمَرَ أَذَّنَ بِالصَّلاَةِ فِي لَيْلَةٍ ذَاتِ بَرْدٍ وَرِيحٍ، فَقَالَ: أَلاَ صَلُّوا فِي الرِّحَالِ. ثُمَّ قَالَ: كَانَ رَسُولُ اللهِ صَلَّى اللهُ عَلَيْهِ وَسَلَّمَ يَأْمُرُ الْمُؤَذِّنَ إِذَا كَانَتْ لَيْلَةٌ بَارِدَةٌ ذَاتُ مَطَرٍ يَقُولُ: «أَلاَ صَلُّوا فِي الرِّحَالِ».

[1353–23]. (Dar al-Salam 1488) Muhammad ibn ʿAbdullāh ibn Numayr narrated: ʿUbaydullāh narrated; Nāfiʿ narrated to me; from Ibn ʿUmar that **'He called the *adhān* for prayer on a night that was cold, windy and rainy. At the end of his *adhān* he said: "Pray in your homes! Pray at home!" He then said: "If the night was cold or rainy, during travel, God's Messenger used to instruct the one who called the *adhān* to say: 'Do pray in your places'."'**

---

i. Related by al-Bukhari, 666; Abu Dāwūd, 1063; al-Nasāʾī, 653.

حَدَّثَنَا مُحَمَّدُ بْنُ عَبْدِ اللهِ بْنِ نُمَيْرٍ، حَدَّثَنَا أَبِي، حَدَّثَنَا عُبَيْدُ اللهِ، حَدَّثَنِي نَافِعٌ، عَنِ ابْنِ عُمَرَ، أَنَّهُ نَادَى بِالصَّلَاةِ فِي لَيْلَةٍ ذَاتِ بَرْدٍ وَرِيحٍ وَمَطَرٍ، فَقَالَ فِي آخِرِ نِدَائِهِ: أَلَا صَلُّوا فِي رِحَالِكُمْ. أَلَا صَلُّوا فِي الرِّحَالِ. ثُمَّ قَالَ: إِنَّ رَسُولَ اللهِ صَلَّى اللهُ عَلَيْهِ وَسَلَّمَ كَانَ يَأْمُرُ الْـمُؤَذِّنَ، إِذَا كَانَتْ لَيْلَةٌ بَارِدَةٌ أَوْ ذَاتُ مَطَرٍ فِي السَّفَرِ، أَنْ يَقُولَ: أَلَا صَلُّوا فِي رِحَالِكُمْ.

[1354–24]. (Dar al-Salam 1489) Abu Bakr ibn Abi Shaybah narrated:[i] Abu Usāmah narrated; ʿUbaydullāh narrated; from Nāfiʿ; from Ibn ʿUmar that **'He called the *adhān* at Ḍajnān...'. He narrated the same and said: 'Pray in your homes', but he did not repeat the second phrase of what Ibn ʿUmar said: 'Pray at home'.**

وَحَدَّثَنَاهُ أَبُو بَكْرِ بْنُ أَبِي شَيْبَةَ، حَدَّثَنَا أَبُو أُسَامَةَ، حَدَّثَنَا عُبَيْدُ اللهِ، عَنْ نَافِعٍ، عَنِ ابْنِ عُمَرَ، أَنَّهُ نَادَى بِالصَّلَاةِ بِضَجْنَانَ، ثُمَّ ذَكَرَ بِمِثْلِهِ، وَقَالَ: أَلَا صَلُّوا فِي رِحَالِكُمْ. وَلَمْ يُعِدْ ثَانِيَةً: أَلَا صَلُّوا فِي الرِّحَالِ، مِنْ قَوْلِ ابْنِ عُمَرَ.

[1355–25]. (Dar al-Salam 1490) Yaḥyā ibn Yaḥyā narrated:[ii] Abu Khaythamah reported; from Abu al-Zubayr; from Jābir [H]. Also, Ahmad ibn Yūnus narrated; Zuhayr narrated; Abu al-Zubayr narrated; from Jābir. He said: **'We went with God's Messenger (peace be upon him) on a journey, and it rained. He said: "Whoever wishes to pray at his place may do so".'**

حَدَّثَنَا يَحْيَى بْنُ يَحْيَى، أَخْبَرَنَا أَبُو خَيْثَمَةَ، عَنْ أَبِي الزُّبَيْرِ، عَنْ جَابِرٍ، ح. وَحَدَّثَنَا أَحْمَدُ بْنُ يُونُسَ قَالَ: حَدَّثَنَا زُهَيْرٌ، حَدَّثَنَا أَبُو الزُّبَيْرِ، عَنْ جَابِرٍ قَالَ: خَرَجْنَا مَعَ رَسُولِ اللهِ صَلَّى اللهُ عَلَيْهِ وَسَلَّمَ فِي سَفَرٍ، فَمُطِرْنَا فَقَالَ: «لِيُصَلِّ مَنْ شَاءَ مِنْكُمْ فِي رَحْلِهِ».

---

i. Related by Abu Dāwūd, 1062.
ii. Related by Abu Dāwūd, 1065; al-Tirmidhī, 409.

[1356–26]. (Dar al-Salam 1491) ʿAlī ibn Ḥujr al-Saʿdī narrated to me:[i] Ismāʿīl narrated; from ʿAbd al-Ḥamīd, al-Ziyādī's companion; from ʿAbdullāh ibn al-Ḥārith; from ʿAbdullāh ibn ʿAbbās that **'He said to the one who called the *adhān* for him: "On a rainy day, when you have said: '*ashhadu an la ilāha illa Allah* [i.e. I bear witness that there is no deity other than God], *ashhadu anna Muhammadan rasūl Allah* [i.e. I bear witness that Muhammad is God's Messenger],' do not say: '*ḥayi ʿala al-ṣalāh* [i.e. come to prayer]'. Say instead: 'Pray in your homes'."**

He said: "It appears that people disliked this". So he said: "Do you feel this strange? It was done by one who is better than me. The Friday Prayer requires effort, and I dislike giving you the trouble of walking in mud on slippery ground".'

وَحَدَّثَنِي عَلِيُّ بْنُ حُجْرٍ السَّعْدِيُّ، حَدَّثَنَا إِسْمَاعِيلُ، عَنْ عَبْدِ الْحَمِيدِ، صَاحِبِ الزِّيَادِيِّ، عَنْ عَبْدِ اللهِ بْنِ الْحَارِثِ، عَنْ عَبْدِ اللهِ بْنِ عَبَّاسٍ أَنَّهُ قَالَ لِمُؤَذِّنِهِ فِي يَوْمٍ مَطِيرٍ: إِذَا قُلْتَ أَشْهَدُ أَنْ لاَ إِلَهَ إِلاَّ اللهُ أَشْهَدُ أَنَّ مُحَمَّدًا رَسُولُ اللهِ، فَلاَ تَقُلْ: حَيَّ عَلَى الصَّلاَةِ. قُلْ: صَلُّوا فِي بُيُوتِكُمْ.

قَالَ: فَكَأَنَّ النَّاسَ اسْتَنْكَرُوا ذَاكَ، فَقَالَ: أَتَعْجَبُونَ مِنْ ذَا؟ قَدْ فَعَلَ ذَا مَنْ هُوَ خَيْرٌ مِنِّي. إِنَّ الْجُمُعَةَ عَزْمَةٌ، وَإِنِّي كَرِهْتُ أَنْ أُحْرِجَكُمْ فَتَمْشُوا فِي الطِّينِ وَالدَّحْضِ.

[1357–27]. (Dar al-Salam 1492–1493) Abu Kāmil al-Jaḥdarī narrated it to me: Ḥammād (meaning Ibn Zayd) narrated; from ʿAbd al-Ḥamīd. He said: I heard ʿAbdullāh ibn al-Ḥārith say: **'ʿAbdullāh ibn ʿAbbās addressed us on a rainy day…'. He continued the hadith in the same meaning as Ibn ʿUlayyah's**

i. Related by al-Bukhari, 616; Abu Dāwūd, 1066; Ibn Mājah, 939.

narration but did not mention Friday Prayer but said: 'It was done by one who is better than me, meaning the Prophet (peace be upon him)'.

Abu Kāmil also said: Ḥammād narrated; from ʿĀṣim; from ʿAbdullāh ibn al-Ḥārith: **a similar text.**

وَحَدَّثَنِيهِ أَبُو كَامِلٍ الْجَحْدَرِيُّ، حَدَّثَنَا حَمَّادٌ (يَعْنِي ابْنَ زَيْدٍ)، عَنْ عَبْدِ الْحَمِيدِ قَالَ: سَمِعْتُ عَبْدَ اللهِ بْنَ الْحَارِثِ قَالَ: خَطَبَنَا عَبْدُ اللهِ بْنُ عَبَّاسٍ فِي يَوْمٍ ذِي رَدْغٍ. وَسَاقَ الْحَدِيثَ بِمَعْنَى حَدِيثِ ابْنِ عُلَيَّةَ، وَلَمْ يَذْكُرِ الْجُمُعَةَ، وَقَالَ: قَدْ فَعَلَهُ مَنْ هُوَ خَيْرٌ مِنِّي. يَعْنِي النَّبِيَّ صَلَّى اللهُ عَلَيْهِ وَسَلَّمَ.

وَقَالَ أَبُو كَامِلٍ حَدَّثَنَا حَمَّادٌ، عَنْ عَاصِمٍ، عَنْ عَبْدِ اللهِ بْنِ الْحَارِثِ: بِنَحْوِهِ.

Abu al-Rabīʿ al-ʿAtakī (who is al-Zahrānī) narrated it to me: Ḥammād (meaning Ibn Zayd) narrated; Ayyūb and ʿĀṣim al-Aḥwal narrated; with the same chain of transmission. **However, he did not mention in his narration 'meaning the Prophet (peace be upon him)'.**

وَحَدَّثَنِيهِ أَبُو الرَّبِيعِ الْعَتَكِيُّ (هُوَ الزَّهْرَانِيُّ)، حَدَّثَنَا حَمَّادٌ (يَعْنِي ابْنَ زَيْدٍ)، حَدَّثَنَا أَيُّوبُ، وَعَاصِمٌ الأَحْوَلُ، بِهَذَا الإِسْنَادِ. وَلَمْ يَذْكُرْ فِي حَدِيثِهِ: يَعْنِي النَّبِيَّ صَلَّى اللهُ عَلَيْهِ وَسَلَّمَ.

[1358–28]. (Dar al-Salam 1494) Isḥāq ibn Manṣūr narrated to me: Ibn Shumayl reported; Shuʿbah reported; ʿAbd al-Ḥamīd, al-Ziyādī's Companion narrated; he said: I heard ʿAbdullāh ibn al-Ḥārith say: **'Ibn ʿAbbās' man who called the *adhān* made the call on a rainy Friday…'. He added a similar text to Ibn ʿUlayyah's narration and said: 'I did not like that you should walk on muddy, slippery ground'.**

وَحَدَّثَنِي إِسْحَاقُ بْنُ مَنْصُورٍ، أَخْبَرَنَا ابْنُ شُمَيْلٍ، أَخْبَرَنَا شُعْبَةُ، حَدَّثَنَا عَبْدُ الْحَمِيدِ صَاحِبُ الزِّيَادِيِّ قَالَ: سَمِعْتُ عَبْدَ اللهِ بْنَ الْحَارِثِ قَالَ: أَذَّنَ مُؤَذِّنُ ابْنِ عَبَّاسٍ يَوْمَ جُمُعَةٍ فِي يَوْمٍ مَطِيرٍ. فَذَكَرَ نَحْوَ حَدِيثِ ابْنِ عُلَيَّةَ وَقَالَ وَكَرِهْتُ أَنْ تَمْشُوا فِي الدَّحْضِ وَالزَّلَلِ.

[1359–29]. (Dar al-Salam 1495) ʿAbd ibn Ḥumayd narrated it: Saʿīd ibn ʿĀmir narrated; from Shuʿbah [H]. Also, ʿAbd ibn Ḥumayd narrated; ʿAbd al-Razzāq reported; Maʿmar reported; both from ʿĀṣim al-Aḥwal; from ʿAbdullāh ibn al-Ḥārith that **'Ibn ʿAbbās instructed the man who called the *adhān* for him, in Maʿmar's narration, on a rainy Friday…' the same as their narration, but added in Maʿmar's narration: 'It was done by one who is better than me, meaning the Prophet (peace be upon him)'.**

وَحَدَّثَنَاهُ عَبْدُ بْنُ حُمَيْدٍ، حَدَّثَنَا سَعِيدُ بْنُ عَامِرٍ، عَنْ شُعْبَةَ، ح. وَحَدَّثَنَا عَبْدُ بْنُ حُمَيْدٍ، أَخْبَرَنَا عَبْدُ لرَّزَّاقِ، أَخْبَرَنَا مَعْمَرٌ، كِلاَهُمَا عَنْ عَاصِمٍ الأَحْوَلِ، عَنْ عَبْدِ اللهِ بْنِ الْحَارِثِ، أَنَّ ابْنَ عَبَّاسٍ أَمَرَ مُؤَذِّنَهُ - فِي حَدِيثِ مَعْمَرٍ - فِي يَوْمِ جُمُعَةٍ فِي يَوْمٍ مَطِيرٍ، بِنَحْوِ حَدِيثِهِمْ. وَذَكَرَ فِي حَدِيثِ مَعْمَرٍ: فَعَلَهُ مَنْ هُوَ خَيْرٌ مِنِّي، يَعْنِي النَّبِيَّ صَلَّى اللهُ عَلَيْهِ وَسَلَّمَ.

[1360–30]. (Dar al-Salam 1496) ʿAbd ibn Ḥumayd narrated: Ahmad ibn Isḥāq al-Ḥaḍramī narrated; Wuhayb narrated; Ayyūb narrated; from ʿAbdullāh ibn al-Ḥārith (Wuhayb said: he did not hear it directly from him). He said: **'Ibn ʿAbbās instructed the man who called the *adhān* for him on a rainy Friday…' a similar text.**

وَحَدَّثَنَاهُ عَبْدُ بْنُ حُمَيْدٍ، حَدَّثَنَا أَحْمَدُ بْنُ إِسْحَاقَ الْحَضْرَمِيُّ، حَدَّثَنَا وُهَيْبٌ، حَدَّثَنَا أَيُّوبُ، عَنْ عَبْدِ اللهِ بْنِ الْحَارِثِ، - قَالَ وُهَيْبٌ: لَمْ يَسْمَعْهُ مِنْهُ—قَالَ: أَمَرَ ابْنُ عَبَّاسٍ مُؤَذِّنَهُ فِي يَوْمِ جُمُعَةٍ فِي يَوْمٍ مَطِيرٍ. بِنَحْوِ حَدِيثِهِمْ.

Text Explanation

These hadiths mention that the Prophet used to instruct the person who called the *adhān* to announce to people on a rainy day that they may pray at home, and in one version he gives everyone the choice of praying at his place. In another hadith, Ibn ʿAbbās did the same on a Friday, telling his announcer to replace the phrase of 'come to prayer' by saying 'pray at home'. When people objected, he told them that it was done by one who was better than him, meaning the Prophet (peace be upon him).

These hadiths provide evidence that attending congregational prayer is waived in cases of difficulty, such as rain. Attending congregational prayer is strongly urged when there is no reason to stay away. However, it is perfectly proper if a person undertakes the trouble of attending it, even in difficult circumstances, as hadith No. 1355 says: 'Whoever wishes to pray at his place may do so'. The hadith also indicates that congregational prayers are held by people when they are travelling and that the *adhān* is also announced when travelling. In the hadiths mentioned by Ibn ʿAbbās, the announcement to pray at home is made during the *adhān*, while in the hadiths quoting Ibn ʿUmar, it is done at the end of the *adhān*. Both are perfectly acceptable, as al-Shāfiʿī mentions in the chapter on the *adhān* in his book *al-Umm*. The great majority of scholars of his school follow his lead, stating that such an announcement is perfectly acceptable during the *adhān* itself, or after it, because authentic hadiths mention both cases. However, making this announcement after the *adhān* is better so that the *adhān* is made complete first and then followed by this announcement. Some of our scholars say that it may be said only after the *adhān* has been completed, but this view is weak because it is contrary to the clear statement by Ibn ʿAbbās. There is no contradiction between the hadiths of Ibn ʿUmar and Ibn ʿAbbās because they occurred on different occasions, and both are authentic.

In hadith No. 1356, Ibn ʿAbbās says that Friday Prayer requires effort and that he disliked giving people trouble. The Arabic wording describes Friday Prayer as *ʿazmah*, and al-Nawawi says that it means that it is a binding duty. Had the person calling the *adhān* said [the usual phrase] 'come to prayer', you would have been required to come and undertake the difficulty.[i]

This hadith provides evidence that the incumbent duty of Friday Prayer is waived when there is a legitimate excuse, such as rain. This is the view of our school and others. Mālik takes the opposite view, but God knows best.

The hadith No. 1354 mentions Ḍujnān as the place where Ibn ʿUmar made this announcement. Ḍujnān is the name of a mountain some distance from Makkah.

Transmission

The second narration of hadith No. 1357 has a chain of transmission which begins with 'Abu al-Rabīʿ al-ʿAtakī (who is al-Zahrānī) narrated'. *Qadi* ʿIyāḍ said: 'This is how the name occurs here, combining al-ʿAtakī with al-Zahrānī, while Muslim normally says either al-ʿAtakī or al-Zahrānī. Al-ʿAtak and Zahrān were two cousins whose lines of ancestry met at their grandfather; they were of two different branches. They are Zahrān ibn al-Ḥajar ibn ʿImrān ibn ʿUmar and al-ʿAtak ibn Aḥad ibn ʿAmr'.

i. Other scholars disagree with al-Nawawi on this point. Al-Ismāʿīlī said: 'I do not think that this is right. Most reports quote the hadith as stating 'It requires effort', making the pronoun refer to the announcer's phrase, 'come to prayer', rather than to Friday Prayer. Had it referred to the prayer itself, the requirement is not waived by dropping the rest of the *adhān*'. Ibn Ḥajar says: 'It appears that the rest of the *adhān* was not dropped, but the words 'come to prayer' were replaced by 'pray at home'.

CHAPTER 4

PRAYING SUNNAH ON ONE'S MOUNT

[1361–31]. (Dar al-Salam 1497) Muhammad ibn ʿAbdullāh ibn Numayr narrated: my father narrated; ʿUbaydullāh ibn Nāfiʿ narrated; from Ibn ʿUmar; that **'God's Messenger used to offer his sunnah prayer [riding], no matter what direction his she-camel took'.**

حَدَّثَنَا مُحَمَّدُ بْنُ عَبْدِ اللهِ بْنِ نُمَيْرٍ، حَدَّثَنَا أَبِي، حَدَّثَنَا عُبَيْدُ اللهِ، عَنْ نَافِعٍ، عَنِ ابْنِ عُمَرَ، أَنَّ رَسُولَ اللهِ صَلَّى اللهُ عَلَيْهِ وَسَلَّمَ كَانَ يُصَلِّي سُبْحَتَهُ حَيْثُمَا تَوَجَّهَتْ بِهِ نَاقَتُهُ.

[1362–32]. (Dar al-Salam 1498) Abu Bakr ibn Abi Shaybah narrated: Abu Khālid al-Aḥmar narrated; from ʿUbaydullāh; from Nāfiʿ; from Ibn ʿUmar; that **'The Prophet (peace be upon him) used to pray on his mount in whatever direction it took'.**

وَحَدَّثَنَاهُ أَبُو بَكْرِ بْنُ أَبِي شَيْبَةَ، حَدَّثَنَا أَبُو خَالِدٍ الأَحْمَرُ، عَنْ عُبَيْدِ اللهِ، عَنْ نَافِعٍ، عَنِ ابْنِ عُمَرَ، أَنَّ النَّبِيَّ صَلَّى اللهُ عَلَيْهِ وَسَلَّمَ كَانَ يُصَلِّي عَلَى رَاحِلَتِهِ حَيْثُ تَوَجَّهَتْ بِهِ.

[1363–33]. (Dar al-Salam 1499) ʿUbaydullāh ibn ʿUmar al-Qawārīrī narrated to me:[i] Yaḥyā ibn Saʿīd narrated; from ʿAbd al-Malik ibn Abi Sulaymān; he said: Saʿīd ibn Jubayr narrated; from Ibn ʿUmar. He said: **'God's Messenger (peace**

i. Related by al-Tirmidhī in similar wording, 2958.

be upon him) used to pray, as he was coming from Makkah to Madinah, while on his she-camel, however he was facing'. He added: 'It is concerning this that God revealed: "Wherever you turn there will be the face of God" (2: 115).'

وَحَدَّثَنِي عُبَيْدُ اللهِ بْنُ عُمَرَ الْقَوَارِيرِيُّ، حَدَّثَنَا يَحْيَى بْنُ سَعِيدٍ، عَنْ عَبْدِ الْمَلِكِ بْنِ أَبِي سُلَيْمَانَ، قَالَ حَدَّثَنَا سَعِيدُ بْنُ جُبَيْرٍ، عَنِ ابْنِ عُمَرَ قَالَ: كَانَ رَسُولُ اللهِ صَلَّى اللهُ عَلَيْهِ وَسَلَّمَ يُصَلِّي وَهُوَ مُقْبِلٌ مِنْ مَكَّةَ إِلَى الْمَدِينَةِ عَلَى رَاحِلَتِهِ، حَيْثُ كَانَ وَجْهُهُ. وَفِيهِ نَزَلَت قَالَ: "فَأَيْنَمَا تُوَلُّوا فَثَمَّ وَجْهُ اللهِ".

[1364–34]. (Dar al-Salam 1500) Abu Kurayb narrated: Ibn al-Mubārak and Ibn Abi Zā'idah reported [H]. Also Ibn Numayr narrated; my father narrated; all of them from 'Abd al-Malik; with this same chain of transmission: **a similar text.**

In Ibn Mubārak's and Ibn Abi Zā'idah's narration: **'Then Ibn 'Umar recited: "Wherever you turn there will be the face of God" and said: "It was revealed concerning this".'**

وَحَدَّثَنَاهُ أَبُو كُرَيْبٍ، أَخْبَرَنَا ابْنُ الْمُبَارَكِ، وَابْنُ أَبِي زَائِدَةَ، ح وَحَدَّثَنَا ابْنُ نُمَيْرٍ، حَدَّثَنَا أَبِي كُلُّهُمْ، عَنْ عَبْدِ الْمَلِكِ، بِهَذَا الإِسْنَادِ نَحْوَهُ. وَفِي حَدِيثِ ابْنِ مُبَارَكٍ وَابْنِ أَبِي زَائِدَةَ ثُمَّ تَلاَ ابْنُ عُمَرَ "فَأَيْنَمَا تُوَلُّوا فَثَمَّ وَجْهُ اللهِ". وَقَالَ فِي هَذَا نَزَلَتْ.

[1365–35]. (Dar al-Salam 1501) Yaḥyā ibn Yaḥyā narrated:[i] he said: I read out to Mālik; from 'Amr ibn Yaḥyā al-Māzinī; from Sa'īd ibn Yasār; from Ibn 'Umar. He said: **'I saw God's Messenger praying while riding a donkey, heading towards Khaybar'.**

i. Related by Abu Dāwūd, 1226; al-Nasā'ī, 739.

حَدَّثَنَا يَحْيَى بْنُ يَحْيَى قَالَ: قَرَأْتُ عَلَى مَالِكٍ عَنْ عَمْرِو بْنِ يَحْيَى الْمَازِنِيِّ، عَنْ سَعِيدِ بْنِ يَسَارٍ، عَنِ ابْنِ عُمَرَ قَالَ: رَأَيْتُ رَسُولَ اللهِ صَلَّى اللهُ عَلَيْهِ وَسَلَّمَ يُصَلِّي عَلَى حِمَارٍ، وَهُوَ مُوَجِّهٌ إِلَى خَيْبَرَ.

[1366–36]. (Dar al-Salam 1502) Yaḥyā ibn Yaḥyā narrated:[i] he said: I read out to Mālik; from Abu Bakr ibn ʿUmar ibn ʿAbd al-Raḥmān ibn ʿAbdullāh ibn ʿUmar ibn al-Khaṭṭāb; from Saʿīd ibn Yasār. He said: **'I was travelling with Ibn ʿUmar on the road to Makkah when I feared that the break of dawn was close. Therefore, I dismounted and prayed Witr. I then caught up with him. Ibn ʿUmar asked me: "Where have you been?" I told him that I feared that the morning was so close that I dismounted to pray Witr. 'Abdullāh said: "Do you not have a good example in God's Messenger (peace be upon him)?" I said: "Indeed, I have". He said: "God's Messenger (peace be upon him) used to pray Witr while riding his camel".'**

وَحَدَّثَنَا يَحْيَى بْنُ يَحْيَى قَالَ: قَرَأْتُ عَلَى مَالِكٍ، عَنْ أَبِي بَكْرِ بْنِ عُمَرَ بْنِ عَبْدِ الرَّحْمَنِ بْنِ عَبْدِ اللهِ بْنِ عُمَرَ بْنِ الْخَطَّابِ، عَنْ سَعِيدِ بْنِ يَسَارٍ أَنَّهُ قَالَ: كُنْتُ أَسِيرُ مَعَ ابْنِ عُمَرَ بِطَرِيقِ مَكَّةَ. قَالَ سَعِيدٌ: فَلَمَّا خَشِيتُ الصُّبْحَ نَزَلْتُ فَأَوْتَرْتُ، ثُمَّ أَدْرَكْتُهُ، فَقَالَ لِي ابْنُ عُمَرَ: أَيْنَ كُنْتَ؟ فَقُلْتُ لَهُ: خَشِيتُ الْفَجْرَ، فَنَزَلْتُ فَأَوْتَرْتُ. فَقَالَ عَبْدُ اللهِ: أَلَيْسَ لَكَ فِي رَسُولِ اللهِ صَلَّى اللهُ عَلَيْهِ وَسَلَّمَ أُسْوَةٌ؟ فَقُلْتُ: بَلَى وَاللهِ. قَالَ: إِنَّ رَسُولَ اللهِ صَلَّى اللهُ عَلَيْهِ وَسَلَّمَ كَانَ يُوتِرُ عَلَى الْبَعِيرِ.

[1367–37]. (Dar al-Salam 1503) Yaḥyā ibn Yaḥyā narrated:[ii] he said: I read out to Mālik; from ʿAbdullāh ibn Dīnār; from Ibn

i. Related by al-Bukhari, 999; al-Tirmidhī, 472; al-Nasāʾī in a shorter version, 1687; Ibn Mājah, 1200.

ii. Related by al-Nasāʾī, 491 and 742.

ʿUmar; that he said: **'God's Messenger used to pray while riding his she-camel, however it was facing'.**

ʿAbdullāh ibn Dīnār said: **'Ibn ʿUmar used to do that'.**

وَحَدَّثَنَا يَحْيَى بْنُ يَحْيَى قَالَ: قَرَأْتُ عَلَى مَالِكٍ عَنْ عَبْدِ اللهِ بْنِ دِينَارٍ، عَنِ ابْنِ عُمَرَ أَنَّهُ قَالَ: كَانَ رَسُولُ اللهِ صَلَّى اللهُ عَلَيْهِ وَسَلَّمَ يُصَلِّي عَلَى رَاحِلَتِهِ، حَيْثُمَا تَوَجَّهَتْ بِهِ.

قَالَ عَبْدُ اللهِ بْنُ دِينَارٍ: كَانَ ابْنُ عُمَرَ يَفْعَلُ ذَلِكَ.

[1368–38]. (Dar al-Salam 1504) ʿĪsā ibn Ḥammād al-Miṣrī narrated to me: al-Layth reported; Ibn al-Hād narrated to me; from ʿAbdullāh ibn Dīnār; from ʿAbdullāh ibn ʿUmar; that he said: **'God's Messenger (peace be upon him) used to pray Witr riding his she-camel'.**

وَحَدَّثَنِي عِيسَى بْنُ حَمَّادٍ الْمِصْرِيُّ، أَخْبَرَنَا اللَّيْثُ، حَدَّثَنِي ابْنُ الْهَادِ، عَنْ عَبْدِ اللهِ بْنِ دِينَارٍ، عَنْ عَبْدِ اللهِ بْنِ عُمَرَ أَنَّهُ قَالَ: كَانَ رَسُولُ اللهِ صَلَّى اللهُ عَلَيْهِ وَسَلَّمَ يُوتِرُ عَلَى رَاحِلَتِهِ.

[1369–39]. (Dar al-Salam 1505) Ḥarmalah ibn Yaḥyā narrated to me:[i] Ibn Wahb reported; Yūnus reported to me; from Ibn Shihāb; from Sālim ibn ʿAbdullāh; from his father. He said: **'God's Messenger (peace be upon him) used to pray the sunnah riding his she-camel in whatever direction he was taking and he used to pray Witr riding it. But he never prayed an obligatory prayer while riding it'.**

وَحَدَّثَنِي حَرْمَلَةُ بْنُ يَحْيَى، أَخْبَرَنَا ابْنُ وَهْبٍ، أَخْبَرَنِي يُونُسُ، عَنِ ابْنِ شِهَابٍ، عَنْ سَالِمِ بْنِ عَبْدِ اللهِ، عَنْ أَبِيهِ قَالَ: كَانَ رَسُولُ اللهِ صَلَّى اللهُ عَلَيْهِ وَسَلَّمَ يُسَبِّحُ عَلَى الرَّاحِلَةِ، قِبَلَ أَيِّ وَجْهٍ تَوَجَّهَ، وَيُوتِرُ عَلَيْهَا. غَيْرَ أَنَّهُ لَا يُصَلِّي عَلَيْهَا الْمَكْتُوبَةَ.

i. Related by al-Bukhari, 1098; Abu Dāwūd, 1224; al-Nasāʾī, 489 and 743.

[1370–40]. (Dar al-Salam 1506) ʿAmr ibn Sawwād and Ḥarmalah narrated:[i] Ibn Wahb reported; Yūnus reported to me; from Ibn Shihāb; from ʿAbdullāh ibn ʿĀmir ibn Rabīʿah; he reported to him that his father reported to him; that **'He saw God's Messenger (peace be upon him) praying sunnah prayer at night, while on a journey, riding his she-camel, in whatever direction it took'.**

وَحَدَّثَنَا عَمْرُو بْنُ سَوَّادٍ وَحَرْمَلَةُ، قَالا: أَخْبَرَنَا ابْنُ وَهْبٍ، أَخْبَرَنِي يُونُسُ، عَنِ ابْنِ شِهَابٍ، عَنْ عَبْدِ اللهِ بْنِ عَامِرِ بْنِ رَبِيعَةَ، أَخْبَرَهُ أَنَّ أَبَاهُ أَخْبَرَهُ أَنَّهُ رَأَى رَسُولَ اللهِ صَلَّى اللهُ عَلَيْهِ وَسَلَّمَ يُصَلِّي السُّبْحَةَ بِاللَّيْلِ فِي السَّفَرِ، عَلَى ظَهْرِ رَاحِلَتِهِ حَيْثُ تَوَجَّهَتْ.

[1371–41]. (Dar al-Salam 1507) Muhammad ibn Ḥātim narrated to me:[ii] ʿAffān ibn Muslim narrated; Hammām narrated; Anas ibn Sīrīn narrated. He said: **'We received Anas ibn Mālik when he came to Syria, and we met him at ʿAyn al-Tamr. I saw him praying while riding a donkey, and his face towards this side (Hammām pointed to the left of the *qiblah*). I said to him: "I saw you praying, but not facing the *qiblah*". He said: "Had I not seen God's Messenger (peace be upon him) doing so, I would not have done it".'**

وَحَدَّثَنِي مُحَمَّدُ بْنُ حَاتِمٍ، حَدَّثَنَا عَفَّانُ بْنُ مُسْلِمٍ، حَدَّثَنَا هَمَّامٌ، حَدَّثَنَا أَنَسُ بْنُ سِيرِينَ قَالَ: تَلَقَّيْنَا أَنَسَ بْنَ مَالِكٍ حِينَ قَدِمَ الشَّامَ، فَتَلَقَّيْنَاهُ بِعَيْنِ التَّمْرِ، فَرَأَيْتُهُ يُصَلِّي عَلَى حِمَارٍ وَوَجْهُهُ ذَلِكَ الْجَانِبَ - وَأَوْمَأَ هَمَّامٌ عَنْ يَسَارِ الْقِبْلَةِ. فَقُلْتُ لَهُ: رَأَيْتُكَ تُصَلِّي لِغَيْرِ الْقِبْلَةِ. قَالَ: لَوْلاَ أَنِّي رَأَيْتُ رَسُولَ اللهِ صَلَّى اللهُ عَلَيْهِ وَسَلَّمَ يَفْعَلُهُ لَمْ أَفْعَلْهُ.

---

i. Related by al-Bukhari, 1093.
ii. Related by al-Bukhari, 1100.

Text Explanation

All these hadiths make it clear that it is permissible to pray the voluntary prayer [i.e. the sunnah] while riding during travel, irrespective of what direction one is facing. This is permissible according to the unanimous view of all Muslims. The only condition that applies here is that the journey is not intended for something sinful, such as a person travelling to perform some highway robbery, to take part in unjust fighting, travel undertaken by a son in disobedience of his parents or a wife rebelling against her husband. An exception is made in the case of a person who has no water to perform the ablution. He may do the dry ablution and pray, but, according to the correct view, he is required to repeat the prayer. All this applies to long and short travel. According to our school and the majority of other scholars, it is permissible to pray the sunnah while riding one's mount, but it is not valid in town. According to Mālik, it is only permissible during travel that permits shortening the prayers. This view is also attributed to al-Shāfiʿī, but this is rather strange.

Abu Saʿīd al-Ḥasan ibn Ahmad al-Iṣṭakhrī of the Shāfiʿī School said that it is permissible to perform the sunnah prayer on one's mount in town. This view is also reported from Anas ibn Mālik and Abu Yūsuf, Abu Ḥanīfah's disciple.

The hadiths provide evidence that it is not permissible to offer an obligatory prayer facing any direction other than the *qiblah*. Nor is it permissible to offer an obligatory prayer on a mount. This is unanimously agreed upon, except in a situation of great fear. However, if it is possible for a person to face the *qiblah*, stand up, bow and prostrate, in a mount's howdah or something similar to it, offering an obligatory prayer whilst stationary is permissible and valid according to our Shāfiʿī School. If it is moving, the prayer is invalid according to the recorded and correct view of al-Shāfiʿī. Some say that it is valid, comparing it to a ship, where it is unanimously agreed that obligatory prayer is valid.

If a person is with a travelling group and fears that should he dismount to offer his obligatory prayer he would be left alone and find himself in difficulty, then our scholars say that in such a case, he prays while riding, as well as possible, but he is required to repeat the prayer later. This is, however, a rare scenario.

The hadiths make it clear that the Prophet used to pray Witr on his mount. This is clear evidence in support of the view of our school, the Mālikī and Ḥanbalī schools, as well as the majority of scholars, that it is permissible to pray Witr while riding when travelling, however one is heading, and that Witr is a sunnah, not a duty. Abu Ḥanīfah (may God be pleased with him) said that Witr is a duty and it may not be prayed when one is riding. We say that these hadiths are the basis of our view. It may also be said to us that we argue that Witr was a personal duty for the Prophet (peace be upon him). In reply we say that even though it might have been a duty for him, it is authentically reported that he offered it while riding his she-camel. The fact that he did so shows that it was right for him. Had Witr been a duty for all Muslims, it would not have been acceptable for it to be prayed when riding, in the same way that this cannot be done for Ẓuhr Prayer. It may still be said that Ẓuhr is obligatory but Witr is a duty, and there is a difference between the two. In response we say that this difference is something you state, and the majority of scholars do not accept it. Indeed, neither religion nor the language requires it. Moreover, even if such difference is accepted, it does not provide a valid argument, but God knows best.

If a passenger on a ship wants to offer a sunnah prayer, such prayer is not valid unless the worshipper faces the *qiblah*. The only exception is for the pilot who may face a different direction if necessary. Mālik is reported to have two views: one is the same as ours and the other suggests that anyone on board may face any direction.[i]

The hadiths mention that the Prophet prayed the sunnah on his mount 'whatever direction it faced'. This means that he was

---

i. Al-Nawawi wrote his commentary at a time when ships were small and without engines, relying on sails and natural laws. Today, with much bigger ships, anyone on board can easily face any direction; hence prayer is not valid unless one faces the *qiblah*. Still, what al-Nawawi has written may apply to small boats, depending on the situation.

heading towards his destination. Our scholars say that if one is facing a point other than one's destination [i.e. one's mount is moving towards one's destination but one turns one's face differently], one's prayer is valid if one is facing the direction of the *qiblah,* otherwise it is not valid.

In the last hadith, No. 1371 Ibn Sīrīn says: 'We received Anas ibn Mālik when he arrived in Syria'. This is how the hadith is stated in all copies of Muslim's anthology. Thus, it is also mentioned in all reports of Muslim's anthology by *Qadi* 'Iyāḍ. He adds: 'It is said that this is an error because they went out from Basrah to receive him when he went there arriving from Syria'. My view is that Muslim's narration is also correct as it means that they received him on his return, arriving in Syria. The words 'his return' are not mentioned because the occasion was known, but God knows best.

Transmission

Imam al-Dāraquṭnī and other scholars discuss hadith No. 1365, in which it is stated that the Prophet prayed while riding a donkey. Al-Dāraquṭnī says: 'This is an error by [the narrator] ʿAmr ibn Yaḥyā al-Māzinī. What is known of the Prophet's prayer is that he prayed on his camel. What is right is that prayer while riding a donkey was performed by Anas, as later mentioned by him. This is why al-Bukhari does not include this hadith narrated by ʿAmr'.

This is the argument provided by al-Dāraquṭnī and scholars who agree with him. To rule that ʿAmr's narration is wrong is questionable because he is a reliable narrator mentioning what is probable. It might have been that the Prophet prayed riding a donkey once and a camel once, or on several occasions. However, it may be said that this report is 'peculiar' [i.e. *shādhdh*] because it is at variance with the narration of the majority who mention prayer when riding a camel. A peculiar narration is rejected because it is contrary to the narration by the majority, but God knows best.

CHAPTER 5

COMBINING TWO OBLIGATORY PRAYERS DURING TRAVEL

[1372–42]. (Dar al-Salam 1508) Yaḥyā ibn Yaḥyā narrated:[i] he said: I read out to Mālik; from Nāfiʿ; from Ibn ʿUmar. He said: **'When he was hard on his way, God's Messenger would combine the Maghrib and ʿIsha [Prayers]'.**

حَدَّثَنَا يَحْيَى بْنُ يَحْيَى قَالَ: قَرَأْتُ عَلَى مَالِكٍ عَنْ نَافِعٍ، عَنِ ابْنِ عُمَرَ قَالَ: كَانَ رَسُولُ اللهِ صَلَّى اللهُ عَلَيْهِ وَسَلَّمَ إِذَا عَجِلَ بِهِ السَّيْرُ جَمَعَ بَيْنَ الْمَغْرِبِ وَالْعِشَاءِ.

[1373–43]. (Dar al-Salam 1509) Muhammad ibn al-Muthannā narrated: Yaḥyā narrated; from ʿUbaydullāh; he said: Nāfiʿ reported to me that **'When Ibn ʿUmar was hard on his way, he would combine Maghrib and ʿIsha after the twilight had disappeared. He used to say that "When God's Messenger was hard on his way, he would combine Maghrib and ʿIsha".'**

وَحَدَّثَنَا مُحَمَّدُ بْنُ الْمُثَنَّى، حَدَّثَنَا يَحْيَى، عَنْ عُبَيْدِ اللهِ قَالَ: أَخْبَرَنِي نَافِعٌ، أَنَّ ابْنَ عُمَرَ كَانَ إِذَا جَدَّ بِهِ السَّيْرُ جَمَعَ بَيْنَ الْمَغْرِبِ وَالْعِشَاءِ، بَعْدَ أَنْ يَغِيبَ الشَّفَقُ. وَيَقُولُ: إِنَّ رَسُولَ اللهِ صَلَّى اللهُ عَلَيْهِ وَسَلَّمَ كَانَ إِذَا جَدَّ بِهِ السَّيْرُ جَمَعَ بَيْنَ الْمَغْرِبِ وَالْعِشَاءِ.

[1374–44]. (Dar al-Salam 1510) Yaḥyā ibn Yaḥyā, Qutaybah ibn Saʿīd, Abu Bakr ibn Abi Shaybah and ʿAmr al-Nāqid narrated:[ii]

---

i. Related by al-Nasāʾī, 597.
ii. Related by al-Bukhari, 1106; al-Nasāʾī, 599.

all of them from Ibn 'Uyaynah. 'Amr said: Sufyān narrated; from al-Zuhrī; from Sālim: from his father: **'I saw God's Messenger (peace be upon him) combining Maghrib and 'Isha prayers when he was hard on his way'.**

وَحَدَّثَنَا يَحْيَى بْنُ يَحْيَى وَقُتَيْبَةُ بْنُ سَعِيدٍ وَأَبُو بَكْرِ بْنُ أَبِي شَيْبَةَ وَعَمْرٌو النَّاقِدُ: كُلُّهُمْ عَنِ ابْنِ عُيَيْنَةَ، قَالَ عَمْرٌو: حَدَّثَنَا سُفْيَانُ، عَنِ الزُّهْرِيِّ، عَنْ سَالِمٍ، عَنْ أَبِيهِ: رَأَيْتُ رَسُولَ اللهِ صَلَّى اللهُ عَلَيْهِ وَسَلَّمَ يَجْمَعُ بَيْنَ الْمَغْرِبِ وَالْعِشَاءِ، إِذَا جَدَّ بِهِ السَّيْرُ.

[1375–45]. (Dar al-Salam 1511) Ḥarmalah ibn Yaḥyā narrated to me:[i] Ibn Wahb reported; Yūnus reported to me; from Ibn Shihāb; he said: Sālim ibn 'Abdullāh reported to me; that his father said: **'I saw God's Messenger (peace be upon him), and when he was hard on his way during travel, he would delay Maghrib so that he could combine it with 'Isha'.**

وَحَدَّثَنِي حَرْمَلَةُ بْنُ يَحْيَى، أَخْبَرَنَا ابْنُ وَهْبٍ، أَخْبَرَنِي يُونُسُ، عَنِ ابْنِ شِهَابٍ قَالَ: أَخْبَرَنِي سَالِمُ بْنُ عَبْدِ اللهِ، أَنَّ أَبَاهُ قَالَ: رَأَيْتُ رَسُولَ اللهِ صَلَّى اللهُ عَلَيْهِ وَسَلَّمَ إِذَا أَعْجَلَهُ السَّيْرُ فِي السَّفَرِ يُؤَخِّرُ صَلَاةَ الْمَغْرِبِ حَتَّى يَجْمَعَ بَيْنَهَا وَبَيْنَ صَلَاةِ الْعِشَاءِ.

[1376–46]. (Dar al-Salam 1512) Qutaybah ibn Sa'īd narrated:[ii] al-Mufaḍḍal (meaning Ibn Faḍālah) narrated; from 'Uqayl; from Ibn Shihāb; from Anas ibn Mālik. He said: **'When God's Messenger (peace be upon him) started his journey before noon, he would delay Ẓuhr Prayer until the time of 'Aṣr Prayer, and he would then stop and pray them together. If**

i. Related by al-Bukhari, 1091.
ii. Related by al-Bukhari, 1111 and 1112; Abu Dāwūd, 1218 and 1219; al-Nasā'ī in similar wording, 593 and 585.

the sun had started its decline before his departure, he would pray Ẓuhr and begin his journey'.

وَحَدَّثَنَا قُتَيْبَةُ بْنُ سَعِيدٍ، حَدَّثَنَا الْمُفَضَّلُ (يَعْنِي ابْنَ فَضَالَةَ) عَنْ عُقَيْلٍ، عَنِ ابْنِ شِهَابٍ، عَنْ أَنَسِ بْنِ مَالِكٍ قَالَ: كَانَ رَسُولُ اللهِ صَلَّى اللهُ عَلَيْهِ وَسَلَّمَ إِذَا ارْتَحَلَ قَبْلَ أَنْ تَزِيغَ الشَّمْسُ أَخَّرَ الظُّهْرَ إِلَى وَقْتِ الْعَصْرِ، ثُمَّ نَزَلَ فَجَمَعَ بَيْنَهُمَا. فَإِنْ زَاغَتِ الشَّمْسُ قَبْلَ أَنْ يَرْتَحِلَ، صَلَّى الظُّهْرَ ثُمَّ رَكِبَ.

[1377–47]. (Dar al-Salam 1513) ʻAmr al-Nāqid narrated to me: Shabābah ibn Sawwār al- Madāyinī narrated; Laythn ibn Saʻd narrated; from ʻUqayl ibn Khālid; from al-Zuhrī; from Anas. He said: **'If the Prophet (peace be upon him) wanted to combine two prayers when he was on a journey, he would delay Ẓuhr until ʻAṣr time begins, and he would pray both prayers'.**

وَحَدَّثَنِي عَمْرٌو النَّاقِدُ، حَدَّثَنَا شَبَابَةُ بْنُ سَوَّارٍ الْمَدَايِنِيُّ، حَدَّثَنَا لَيْثُ بْنُ سَعْدٍ، عَنْ عُقَيْلِ بْنِ خَالِدٍ، عَنِ الزُّهْرِيِّ، عَنْ أَنَسٍ قَالَ: كَانَ النَّبِيُّ صَلَّى اللهُ عَلَيْهِ وَسَلَّمَ إِذَا أَرَادَ أَنْ يَجْمَعَ بَيْنَ الصَّلَاتَيْنِ فِي السَّفَرِ أَخَّرَ الظُّهْرَ حَتَّى يَدْخُلَ أَوَّلُ وَقْتِ الْعَصْرِ، ثُمَّ يَجْمَعُ بَيْنَهُمَا.

[1378–48]. (Dar al-Salam 1514) Abu al-Ṭāhir and ʻAmr ibn Sawwād narrated to me: both said: Ibn Wahb reported; Jābir ibn Ismāʻīl narrated to me; from ʻUqayl; from Ibn Shihāb; from Anas; from the Prophet (peace be upon him): **'If the Prophet was hard on his way, he would delay Ẓuhr until the beginning of ʻAṣr time and combine the two prayers, and he would delay Maghrib so that he combined it with ʻIsha after the twilight had disappeared'.**

وَحَدَّثَنِي أَبُو الطَّاهِرِ وَعَمْرُو بْنُ سَوَّادٍ، قَالَا: أَخْبَرَنَا ابْنُ وَهْبٍ، حَدَّثَنِي جَابِرُ بْنُ إِسْمَاعِيلَ، عَنْ عُقَيْلٍ، عَنِ ابْنِ شِهَابٍ، عَنْ أَنَسٍ، عَنِ النَّبِيِّ صَلَّى اللهُ عَلَيْهِ وَسَلَّمَ: إِذَا

عَجِلَ عَلَيْهِ السَّفَرُ يُؤَخِّرُ الظُّهْرَ إِلَى أَوَّلِ وَقْتِ الْعَصْرِ فَيَجْمَعُ بَيْنَهُمَا، وَيُؤَخِّرُ الْـمَغْرِبَ حَتَّى يَجْمَعَ بَيْنَهَا وَبَيْنَ الْعِشَاءِ حِينَ يَغِيبُ الشَّفَقُ.

Text Explanation

Al-Shāfiʿī and the majority of scholars say that it is permissible to combine Ẓuhr and ʿAṣr prayers during the time range of either when one is on a long journey. If the journey is short, al-Shāfiʿī expresses two views on its permissibility, the more correct of which is that it is not permissible. A long journey is a distance of forty-eight Hashimite miles, which is equal to two average stages, as we mentioned earlier.

If a person has stopped during the time of the first prayer, it is preferable that he offers it and adds the second prayer, bringing it forward. If he is continuing his journey during the time of the first prayer and knows that he will be stopping before the end of the time range of the second, then he delays the first prayer to the time of the second. If a person does the opposite, it is permissible but he thus abandons the better option. The condition for combining the prayers during the time range of the first is that one prays it first and intends to combine the second with it before he finishes his first prayer. He should also pray both prayers one after the other, without a long interval. If he wants to combine the two prayers during the time of the second, he should formulate the intention to do so during the time of the first prayer, and the intention should be before its time becomes too short. There should remain at least enough of the time of the first prayer to offer it. If one delays the first prayer without the intention of combining it with the second, one is in error and the prayer would be a compensatory one, [i.e. *qaḍā'*]. If one delayed it with the intention of doing so, it is desirable to offer the first prayer first, intending combination, and to pray both prayers without leaving a long interval between them, but none of these is obligatory. This is the sum of the rules of combining prayers, but further details are provided in books of Fiqh.

It is permissible to combine prayer in rainy weather during the time of the first prayer, but not in the time of the second according to the more correct view, because it is impossible to know if the rain will continue until the second prayer becomes due. It is a condition for the validity of such a combination that rain would be falling at the time of starting the first prayer and continuing until it finishes and the start of the second prayer. This is permissible for a person who goes to attend the congregational prayer along an open road without shelter to protect him from the rain. The more correct view is that such combination is permissible only for such a person. This is the view of our Shāfiʿī School concerning combination of prayers in case of rain. It is agreed by the majority of scholars with regard to combining Ẓuhr and ʿAṣr and also combining Maghrib and ʿIsha. Mālik limits it to Maghrib and ʿIsha only.

Is combining prayers permissible for a sick person? The better-known view of the Shāfiʿī School and the majority of scholars is that it is not permissible. Ahmad and a number of Shāfiʿī scholars say that it is permissible, supported by good evidence, as we will presently explain, God willing, when commenting on the hadith narrated by Ibn ʿAbbās. Abu Ḥanīfah, on the other hand, says that combining two prayers is not permissible during travel, in rainy weather, for illness, or any other reason. The only permissible combination is to pray Ẓuhr and ʿAṣr together at Arafat, and Maghrib and ʿIsha together at Muzdalifah, but these two combinations only result from pilgrimage duties. However, the authentic hadiths in both al-Bukhari's and Muslim's *Ṣaḥīḥ* anthologies, Abu Dāwūd's *Sunan* and other anthologies provide a strong counter argument.

In hadith No. 1373, narrated by Ibn ʿUmar: 'When he was hard on his way, he would combine Maghrib and ʿIsha, after the twilight had disappeared'. This clearly states that combining two prayers during the time range of one of them is permissible in certain situations. It invalidates the Ḥanafī view that combination means delaying the first prayer to nearly the end of its time range and bringing the second forward to the beginning of its time range. The same may be said about the hadith narrated by Anas, No. 1376: 'When God's Messenger (peace be upon him) started his journey before noon, he would delay Ẓuhr Prayer until the time of ʿAṣr Prayer and he would then stop and pray them together'. This is clear, showing that the combination took place during the time range of the second prayer. The next hadith, No. 1377, is even clearer: 'When the Prophet (peace be upon him) wanted to combine two prayers when he was on a journey, he would delay Ẓuhr until ʿAṣr time begins, and he would pray both prayers'. The same may be said about the next hadith, No. 1378: 'And he would delay Maghrib so that he combined it with ʿIsha after the twilight had disappeared'.

It should be noted that Ibn ʿUmar mentioned only the combination of Maghrib with ʿIsha because he said this in explanation of something that had happened to him. He was called to attend his wife who was in trouble, and he went in haste and combined Maghrib with ʿIsha. He mentioned this because he wanted to show that his action was in accordance with the sunnah. The hadith does not suggest that Ẓuhr and ʿAṣr may not be combined. Such combination has been reported by Anas, Ibn ʿAbbās and other Companions of the Prophet.

Transmission

The chain of transmission of hadith No. 1378 starts as follows: 'Abu al-Ṭāhir and ʿAmr ibn Sawwād narrated to me: both said: Ibn Wahb reported; Jābir ibn Ismāʿīl narrated to me; from ʿUqayl'. This is how we checked it and how it occurs in the narrations of scholars of our areas, Jābir ibn Ismāʿīl. However, the name occurs in some copies as Ḥātim ibn Ismāʿīl. The same occurs in some narrations by scholars from the Maghrib areas [i.e. in North Africa and the Andalus]. But this second version is wrong. The correct and agreed name of this narrator is Jābir ibn Ismāʿīl al-Ḥaḍramī al-Miṣrī.

CHAPTER 6

COMBINING PRAYERS WHEN IN RESIDENCE

[1379–49]. (Dar al-Salam 1515) Yaḥyā ibn Yaḥyā narrated:[i] he said: I read out to Mālik; from Abu al-Zubayr; from Saʿīd ibn Jubayr; from Ibn ʿAbbās. He said: **'God's Messenger (peace be upon him) prayed Ẓuhr and ʿAṣr together and Maghrib and 'Isha together in a situation of neither fear nor travel'.**

حَدَّثَنَا يَحْيَى بْنُ يَحْيَى قَالَ: قَرَأْتُ عَلَى مَالِكٍ عَنْ أَبِي الزُّبَيْرِ، عَنْ سَعِيدِ بْنِ جُبَيْرٍ، عَنِ ابْنِ عَبَّاسٍ قَالَ: صَلَّى رَسُولُ اللهِ صَلَّى اللهُ عَلَيْهِ وَسَلَّمَ الظُّهْرَ وَالْعَصْرَ جَمِيعًا، وَالْمَغْرِبَ وَالْعِشَاءَ جَمِيعًا، فِي غَيْرِ خَوْفٍ وَلاَ سَفَرٍ.

[1380–50]. (Dar al-Salam 1516) Ahmad ibn Yūnus and ʿAwn ibn Sallām narrated; both from Zuhayr; Ibn Yūnus said: Zuhayr narrated; Abu al-Zubayr narrated; from Saʿīd ibn Jubayr; from Ibn ʿAbbās. He said: **'God's Messenger prayed Ẓuhr and ʿAṣr together in Madinah, in a situation of neither fear nor travel'.**

Abu al-Zubayr said: **'I asked Saʿīd: "Why did he do that?" He said: "I asked Ibn ʿAbbās the same question and he said: 'He wished not to put anyone from his community in difficulty'."'**

---

i. Related by Abu Dāwūd, 1210; al-Nasāʾī, 600.

وَحَدَّثَنَا أَحْمَدُ بْنُ يُونُسَ وَعَوْنُ بْنُ سَلاَّمٍ، جَمِيعًا عَنْ زُهَيْرٍ، قَالَ ابْنُ يُونُسَ: حَدَّثَنَا زُهَيْرٌ، حَدَّثَنَا أَبُو الزُّبَيْرِ، عَنْ سَعِيدِ بْنِ جُبَيْرٍ، عَنِ ابْنِ عَبَّاسٍ قَالَ: صَلَّى رَسُولُ اللهِ صَلَّى اللهُ عَلَيْهِ وَسَلَّمَ الظُّهْرَ وَالْعَصْرَ جَمِيعًا بِالْـمَدِينَةِ، فِي غَيْرِ خَوْفٍ وَلاَ سَفَرٍ.

قَالَ أَبُو الزُّبَيْرِ: فَسَأَلْتُ سَعِيدًا لِمَ فَعَلَ ذَلِكَ؟ فَقَالَ سَأَلْتُ ابْنَ عَبَّاسٍ كَمَا سَأَلْتَنِي فَقَالَ: أَرَادَ أَنْ لاَ يُحْرِجَ أَحَدًا مِنْ أُمَّتِهِ.

[1381–51]. (Dar al-Salam 1517) Yaḥyā ibn Ḥabīb al-Ḥārithī narrated: Khālid (meaning Ibn al-Ḥārith) narrated; Qurrah narrated; Abu al-Zubayr narrated; Saʿīd ibn Jubayr narrated; Ibn ʿAbbās narrated that **'God's Messenger (peace be upon him) combined prayers on a certain journey, in the Expedition of Tabuk. He combined Ẓuhr and ʿAṣr and combined Maghrib and ʿIsha'.**

Saʿīd said: **'I asked Ibn ʿAbbās: "Why did he do that?" He said: "He wished not to put his community in difficulty".'**

وَحَدَّثَنَا يَحْيَى بْنُ حَبِيبٍ الْحَارِثِيُّ، حَدَّثَنَا خَالِدٌ (يَعْنِي ابْنَ الْحَارِثِ)، حَدَّثَنَا قُرَّةُ، حَدَّثَنَا أَبُو الزُّبَيْرِ، حَدَّثَنَا سَعِيدُ بْنُ جُبَيْرٍ، حَدَّثَنَا ابْنُ عَبَّاسٍ، أَنَّ رَسُولَ اللهِ صَلَّى اللهُ عَلَيْهِ وَسَلَّمَ جَمَعَ بَيْنَ الصَّلاَةِ فِي سَفْرَةٍ سَافَرَهَا فِي غَزْوَةِ تَبُوكَ فَجَمَعَ بَيْنَ الظُّهْرِ وَالْعَصْرِ، وَالْـمَغْرِبِ وَالْعِشَاءِ.

قَالَ سَعِيدٌ فَقُلْتُ لِابْنِ عَبَّاسٍ: مَا حَمَلَهُ عَلَى ذَلِكَ؟ قَالَ: أَرَادَ أَنْ لاَ يُحْرِجَ أُمَّتَهُ.

[1382–52]. (Dar al-Salam 1518) Ahmad ibn ʿAbdullāh ibn Yūnus narrated:[i] Zuhayr narrated; Abu al-Zubayr narrated; from Abu al-Ṭufayl ʿĀmir; from Muʿādh. He said: **'We joined God's Messenger (peace be upon him) on the Expedition of**

i. Related by Abu Dāwūd, 1206 and 1208; al-Nasāʾī in a longer version, 586.

Tabūk, and he used to combine Ẓuhr and ʿAṣr together and Maghrib and ʿIsha together'.

حَدَّثَنَا أَحْمَدُ بْنُ عَبْدِ اللهِ بْنِ يُونُسَ، حَدَّثَنَا زُهَيْرٌ، حَدَّثَنَا أَبُو الزُّبَيْرِ، عَنْ أَبِي الطُّفَيْلِ عَامِرٍ، عَنْ مُعَاذٍ قَالَ: خَرَجْنَا مَعَ رَسُولِ اللهِ صَلَّى اللهُ عَلَيْهِ وَسَلَّمَ فِي غَزْوَةِ تَبُوكَ فَكَانَ يُصَلِّي الظُّهْرَ وَالْعَصْرَ جَمِيعًا، وَالْـمَغْرِبَ وَالْعِشَاءَ جَمِيعًا.

[1383–53]. (Dar al-Salam 1519) Yaḥyā ibn Ḥabīb narrated: Khālid (meaning Ibn al-ḥārith) narrated; Qurrah ibn Khālid narrated; Abu al-Zubayr narrated; ʿĀmir ibn Wāthilah Abu al-Ṭufayl narrated; Muʿādh ibn Jabal narrated. He said: **'During the Expedition of Tabuk, God's Messenger (peace be upon him) combined Ẓuhr and ʿAṣr and also Maghrib and ʿIsha'.**

I asked: 'Why did he do that?' He said: 'He did not wish to put his community in difficulty'.

حَدَّثَنَا يَحْيَى بْنُ حَبِيبٍ، حَدَّثَنَا خَالِدٌ (يَعْنِي ابْنَ الْحَارِثِ) حَدَّثَنَا قُرَّةُ بْنُ خَالِدٍ، حَدَّثَنَا أَبُو الزُّبَيْرِ، حَدَّثَنَا عَامِرُ بْنُ وَاثِلَةَ أَبُو الطُّفَيْلِ، حَدَّثَنَا مُعَاذُ بْنُ جَبَلٍ قَالَ: جَمَعَ رَسُولُ اللهِ صَلَّى اللهُ عَلَيْهِ وَسَلَّمَ فِي غَزْوَةِ تَبُوكَ بَيْنَ الظُّهْرِ وَالْعَصْرِ، وَبَيْنَ الْـمَغْرِبِ وَالْعِشَاءِ.

قَالَ فَقُلْتُ: مَا حَمَلَهُ عَلَى ذَلِكَ؟ قَالَ: فَقَالَ أَرَادَ أَنْ لاَ يُحْرِجَ أُمَّتَهُ.

[1384–54]. (Dar al-Salam 1520) Abu Bakr ibn Abi Shaybah and Abu Kurayb narrated:[i] both said: Abu Muʿāwiyah narrated [H]. Abu Kurayb and Abu Saʿīd al-Ashajj narrated (Abu Saʿīd's text); both said: Wakīʿ narrated; both from al-Aʿmash; from Ḥabīb ibn Abi Thābit; from Saʿīd ibn Jubayr; from Ibn ʿAbbās. He said: **'God's Messenger (peace be upon him) combined**

i. Related by Abu Dāwūd, 1211; al-Tirmidhī, 187; al-Nasāʾī, 601.

Ẓuhr and ʿAsr and also Maghrib and ʿIsha in Madinah in a situation of neither fear nor rain'.

In Wakīʿ's narration: **I said to Ibn ʿAbbās: 'Why did he do that?' He said: 'So as not to put his community in difficulty'.**

And in Abu Muʿāwiyah's narration: **Ibn ʿAbbās was asked: 'What was his purpose in doing so?' He said: 'He wished not to put his community in difficulty'.**

وَحَدَّثَنَا أَبُو بَكْرِ بْنُ أَبِي شَيْبَةَ وَأَبُو كُرَيْبٍ، قَالاَ: حَدَّثَنَا أَبُو مُعَاوِيَةَ، ح. وَحَدَّثَنَا أَبُو كُرَيْبٍ، وَأَبُو سَعِيدٍ الأَشَجُّ (وَاللَّفْظُ لأَبِي كُرَيْبٍ)، قَالاَ: حَدَّثَنَا وَكِيعٌ، كِلاَهُمَا عَنِ الأَعْمَشِ، عَنْ حَبِيبِ بْنِ أَبِي ثَابِتٍ، عَنْ سَعِيدِ بْنِ جُبَيْرٍ، عَنِ ابْنِ عَبَّاسٍ قَالَ: جَمَعَ رَسُولُ اللهِ صَلَّى اللهُ عَلَيْهِ وَسَلَّمَ بَيْنَ الظُّهْرِ وَالْعَصْرِ، وَالْمَغْرِبِ وَالْعِشَاءِ، بِالْمَدِينَةِ، فِي غَيْرِ خَوْفٍ وَلاَ مَطَرٍ.

فِي حَدِيثِ وَكِيعٍ قَالَ: قُلْتُ لاِبْنِ عَبَّاسٍ: لِمَ فَعَلَ ذَلِكَ؟ قَالَ كَيْ لاَ يُحْرِجَ أُمَّتَهُ. وَفِي حَدِيثِ أَبِي مُعَاوِيَةَ: قِيلَ لاِبْنِ عَبَّاسٍ مَا أَرَادَ إِلَى ذَلِكَ؟ قَالَ: أَرَادَ أَنْ لاَ يُحْرِجَ أُمَّتَهُ.

[1385–55]. (Dar al-Salam 1521) Abu Bakr ibn Abi Shaybah narrated:[i] Sufyān ibn ʿUyaynah narrated; from ʿAmr; from Jābir ibn Zayd; from Ibn ʿAbbās. He said: **'I prayed with the Prophet (peace be upon him) eight [*rakʿahs*] together and seven [*rakʿahs*] together'.**

I said: 'Abu al-Shaʿthā',[ii] I think he delayed Ẓuhr and prayed ʿAṣr early and delayed Maghrib and prayed ʿIsha early'. He said: 'I also think so'.

وَحَدَّثَنَا أَبُو بَكْرِ بْنُ أَبِي شَيْبَةَ، حَدَّثَنَا سُفْيَانُ بْنُ عُيَيْنَةَ، عَنْ عَمْرٍو، عَنْ جَابِرِ بْنِ زَيْدٍ، عَنِ ابْنِ عَبَّاسٍ قَالَ: صَلَّيْتُ مَعَ النَّبِيِّ صَلَّى اللهُ عَلَيْهِ وَسَلَّمَ ثَمَانِيًا جَمِيعًا، وَسَبْعًا جَمِيعًا.

---

i. Related by al-Bukhari, 543, 562 and 1174; Abu Dāwūd, 1214; al-Nasāʾī, 588 & 602.
ii. Abu al-Shaʿthā' is Jābir ibn Zayd (21–93 AH, 642–712 CE). He belonged to the *tābiʿīn* generation.

قُلْتُ: يَا أَبَا الشَّعْثَاءِ، أَظُنُّهُ أَخَّرَ الظُّهْرَ وَعَجَّلَ الْعَصْرَ، وَأَخَّرَ الْـمَغْرِبَ وَعَجَّلَ الْعِشَاءَ. قَالَ: وَأَنَا أَظُنُّ ذَاكَ.

[1386–56]. (Dar al-Salam 1522) Abu al-Rabīʿ al-Zahrānī narrated: Ḥammād ibn Zayd narrated; from ʿAmr ibn Dīnār; from Jābir ibn Zayd; from Ibn ʿAbbās; that **'God's Messenger (peace be upon him) prayed in Madinah seven [*rakʿahs*] and eight [*rakʿahs*]: Ẓuhr and ʿAṣr [together] and Maghrib and ʿIsha [together]'.**

وَحَدَّثَنَا أَبُو الرَّبِيعِ الزَّهْرَانِيُّ، حَدَّثَنَا حَمَّادُ بْنُ زَيْدٍ، عَنْ عَمْرِو بْنِ دِينَارٍ، عَنْ جَابِرِ بْنِ زَيْدٍ، عَنِ ابْنِ عَبَّاسٍ أَنَّ رَسُولَ اللهِ صَلَّى اللهُ عَلَيْهِ وَسَلَّمَ صَلَّى بِالْـمَدِينَةِ سَبْعًا وَثَمَانِيًا: الظُّهْرَ وَالْعَصْرَ، وَالْـمَغْرِبَ وَالْعِشَاءَ.

[1387–57]. (Dar al-Salam 1523) Abu al-Rabīʿ al-Zahrānī narrated to me: Ḥammād narrated; from al-Zubayr ibn al-Khirrīt; from ʿAbdullāh ibn Shaqīq. He said: **'One day Ibn ʿAbbās addressed us after ʿAṣr [continuing] until the sun had set and the stars appeared. People said: "Prayer! Prayer!" Then a man from the Tamīm tribe came and he continued to say: "Prayer! Prayer!" without stopping. Ibn ʿAbbās said [to him]: "Are you teaching me the sunnah, you motherless one? I saw God's Messenger (peace be upon him) combining Ẓuhr and ʿAṣr and also Maghrib and ʿIsha".'**

ʿAbdullāh ibn Shaqīq said: 'I felt uneasy about this. Therefore, I went to Abu Hurayrah and asked him. He confirmed what [Ibn ʿAbbās] said'.

وَحَدَّثَنِي أَبُو الرَّبِيعِ الزَّهْرَانِيُّ، حَدَّثَنَا حَمَّادٌ، عَنِ الزُّبَيْرِ بْنِ الْخِرِّيتِ، عَنْ عَبْدِ اللهِ بْنِ شَقِيقٍ قَالَ: خَطَبَنَا ابْنُ عَبَّاسٍ يَوْمًا بَعْدَ الْعَصْرِ حَتَّى غَرَبَتِ الشَّمْسُ وَبَدَتِ النُّجُومُ.

وَجَعَلَ النَّاسُ يَقُولُونَ: الصَّلاَةَ الصَّلاَةَ. قَالَ: فَجَاءَهُ رَجُلٌ مِنْ بَنِي تَمِيمٍ لاَ يَفْتُرُ وَلاَ يَنْثَنِي: الصَّلاَةَ، الصَّلاَةَ! فَقَالَ ابْنُ عَبَّاسٍ: أَتُعَلِّمُنِي بِالسُّنَّةِ لاَ أُمَّ لَكَ؟ ثُمَّ قَالَ: رَأَيْتُ رَسُولَ اللهِ صَلَّى اللهُ عَلَيْهِ وَسَلَّمَ جَمَعَ بَيْنَ الظُّهْرِ وَالْعَصْرِ، وَالْمَغْرِبِ وَالْعِشَاءِ.

قَالَ عَبْدُ اللهِ بْنُ شَقِيقٍ: فَحَاكَ فِي صَدْرِي مِنْ ذَلِكَ شَيْءٌ، فَأَتَيْتُ أَبَا هُرَيْرَةَ فَسَأَلْتُهُ، فَصَدَّقَ مَقَالَتَهُ.

[1388–58]. (Dar al-Salam 1524) Ibn Abi ʿUmar narrated: Wakīʿ narrated; ʿImrān ibn Ḥudayr; from ʿAbdullāh ibn Shaqīq al-ʿUqaylī. He said: **'A man said to Ibn ʿAbbās: "Prayer!" He was silent. The man said: "Prayer!" He was silent. The man [again] said: "Prayer!" He said: "You motherless one! Are you teaching us about prayer? We used to combine two prayers during God's Messenger's lifetime".'**

وَحَدَّثَنَا ابْنُ أَبِي عُمَرَ، حَدَّثَنَا وَكِيعٌ، حَدَّثَنَا عِمْرَانُ بْنُ حُدَيْرٍ، عَنْ عَبْدِ اللهِ بْنِ شَقِيقٍ الْعُقَيْلِيِّ قَالَ: قَالَ رَجُلٌ لِابْنِ عَبَّاسٍ: الصَّلاَةَ، فَسَكَتَ. ثُمَّ قَالَ الصَّلاَةَ، فَسَكَتَ. ثُمَّ قَالَ الصَّلاَةَ، فَسَكَتَ. ثُمَّ قَالَ: لاَ أُمَّ لَكَ، أَتُعَلِّمُنَا بِالصَّلاَةِ؟ وَكُنَّا نَجْمَعُ بَيْنَ الصَّلاَتَيْنِ عَلَى عَهْدِ رَسُولِ اللهِ صَلَّى اللهُ عَلَيْهِ وَسَلَّمَ.

Text Explanation

These hadiths are well documented in Muslim, and scholars have expressed different views and stated rulings concerning them. Al-Tirmidhī says at the end of his book: 'There is no hadith in my book the Muslim community has unanimously agreed to discard except Ibn ʿAbbās' hadith on combining prayers in Madinah in a situation of neither fear nor rain and the hadith advising killing the person who is to be punished for drinking intoxicants for the fourth time'. What al-Tirmidhī says concerning a habitual drunkard is certainly correct. It is an abrogated hadith and the unanimity of scholars confirm its abrogation.

As for Ibn ʿAbbās' hadith [in this chapter concerning the combination of prayers], there is no unanimity to discard it. Scholars hold different views concerning it. Some understand it as combination due to rain. This is the well-known view of a number of early scholars, but it is countered by the other narration that states that such combination of prayers was 'in a situation of neither fear nor rain'. Others understand it as being the case on an overcast day when he prayed Ẓuhr, but subsequently the sky was clear and then he realised that ʿAṣr was due and he prayed that too. This is totally wrong because if it is marginally possible for Ẓuhr and ʿAṣr, it cannot be the case for Maghrib and ʿIsha. Others still explain it as delaying the first prayer to the end of its time range, and by the time the Prophet finished it, the next prayer was due and so he prayed it. Thus, his prayer took the form of combination. This is again groundless, because it goes totally against the apparent meaning of the hadiths. Moreover, what Ibn ʿAbbās did when he addressed the people, his citing the hadith to confirm that he did right and also Abu Hurayrah's confirmation of its being right serve as clear evidence that this suggestion is unacceptable. Other scholars say that it should be understood as meaning combination due to illness or some other valid reason. This is what Ahmad ibn Ḥanbal suggests, as well as some scholars of our school like *Qadi* Ḥusayn, al-Khaṭṭābī, al-Mutawallī and al-Ruwayyānī. This is the view of choice in understanding the apparent meaning of the hadith, Ibn ʿAbbās' action, Abu Hurayrah's agreement and because it is a harder situation than rain. A number of leading scholars are also of the view that combining prayers when in residence is permissible when needed, provided that one does not make it a habit. This is the view of Ibn Sīrīn and Ashhab of the Mālikī School. It is reported by al-Khaṭṭābī to be expressed by al-Qaffāl; as also by al-Shāshī senior of the Shāfiʿī School as expressed by Abu Isḥāq al-Marwazī attributing it to a number of Hadith scholars. It is also the chosen interpretation of Ibn al-Mundhir. It is further confirmed by the apparent meaning of Ibn 'Abbās' explanation: 'He wished not to put his community in difficulty'. He did not suggest any further reason, such as illness, but God knows best.[i]

In the last two hadiths, No. 1387 and 1388, Ibn 'Abbās says to the man who interrupts him to urge attendance to prayer, 'You motherless one!' This is a phrase the Arabs used at the time, but it is never meant literally. It is no more than an expression of disapproval.

Transmission

In the chains of transmission of hadith No. 1382 and 1383, the name of Abu al-Ṭufayl 'Āmir ibn Wāthilah occurs. This is how we checked the correct pronunciation of the name, 'Āmir ibn Wāthilah, and it occurs thus in some copies in our area.[ii] Further, according to *Qadi* 'Iyāḍ, this is how it is reported by the majority of reporters of Muslim's *Ṣaḥīḥ*. In some copies, however, it occurs as 'Amr ibn Wāthilah, and it is so in many original copies in our area, particularly in hadith No. 1383. In the first of these two hadiths, No. 1382, there is no disagreement. It is 'Āmir in all copies. This means that the better-known version is 'Āmir, even though some say 'Amr. The difference in his name is mentioned by several leading scholars, including al-Bukhari in his book *Tārīkh*.

i. The fact that there are so many views on this question makes it unclear. Perhaps the view that is most appropriate in this case is the one that says that combination of prayers is permissible when needed, provided that one does not make it a habit. This ruling is particularly useful in areas where Muslims are a minority community, when days are very short in winter, or nights very short in summer.

ii. When al-Nawawi uses the expression 'our area' he means Syria and its surrounding provinces. *Qadi* 'Iyāḍ's usage of the same expression refers to North Africa and the Andalus.

CHAPTER 7

TURNING TO EITHER DIRECTION AFTER PRAYER

[1389–59]. (Dar al-Salam 1525–1526) Abu Bakr ibn Abi Shaybah narrated:[i] Abu Muʿāwiyah and Wakīʿ narrated; from al-Aʿmash; from ʿUmārah; from al-Aswad; from ʿAbdullāh. He said: **'Let none of you allow Satan a portion of himself, thinking that it is incumbent on him that he must turn to his right [when he has finished prayer]. On most occasions, I saw God's Messenger (peace be upon him) turn to his left'.**

حَدَّثَنَا أَبُو بَكْرِ بْنُ أَبِي شَيْبَةَ، حَدَّثَنَا أَبُو مُعَاوِيَةَ وَوَكِيعٌ، عَنِ الأَعْمَشِ، عَنْ عُمَارَةَ، عَنِ الأَسْوَدِ، عَنْ عَبْدِ اللهِ قَالَ: لا يَجْعَلَنَّ أَحَدُكُمْ لِلشَّيْطَانِ مِنْ نَفْسِهِ جُزْءًا، لاَ يَرَى إِلاَّ أَنَّ حَقًّا عَلَيْهِ أَنْ لاَ يَنْصَرِفَ إِلاَّ عَنْ يَمِينِهِ. أَكْثَرُ مَا رَأَيْتُ رَسُولَ اللهِ صَلَّى اللهُ عَلَيْهِ وَسَلَّمَ يَنْصَرِفُ عَنْ شِمَالِهِ.

Isḥāq ibn Ibrāhīm narrated: Jarīr and ʿĪsā ibn Yūnus reported [H]. Also ʿAlī ibn Khashram narrated; ʿĪsā reported; all from al-Aʿmash; with the same chain of transmission: **the same text.**

حَدَّثَنَا إِسْحَاقُ بْنُ إِبْرَاهِيمَ، أَخْبَرَنَا جَرِيرٌ وَعِيسَى بْنُ يُونُسَ، ح. وَحَدَّثَنَاهُ عَلِيُّ بْنُ خَشْرَمٍ، أَخْبَرَنَا عِيسَى، جَمِيعًا عَنِ الأَعْمَشِ، بِهَذَا الإِسْنَادِ مِثْلَهُ.

---

i. Related by al-Bukhari in similar wording, 852; Abu Dāwūd in similar wording, 1042; al-Nasāʾī, 1359; Ibn Mājah, 930.

[1390–60]. (Dar al-Salam 1527) Qutaybah ibn Saʿīd narrated:[i] Abu ʿAwānah narrated; from al-Suddī. He said: **'I asked Anas: "How should I turn when I have finished my prayers? To my right or to my left?" He said: "As for me, on most occasions, I saw God's Messenger turn to his right".'**

وَحدَّثَنا قُتَيْبَةُ بْنُ سَعِيدٍ، حَدَّثَنا أَبُو عَوانَةَ، عَنِ السُّدِّيِّ قالَ: سَأَلْتُ أَنَسًا كَيْفَ أَنْصَرِفُ إِذَا صَلَّيْتُ، عَنْ يَمِينِي أَوْ عَنْ يَسارِي؟ قالَ: أَمَّا أَنَا فَأَكْثَرُ مَا رَأَيْتُ رَسُولَ اللهِ صَلَّى اللهُ عَلَيْهِ وَسَلَّمَ يَنْصَرِفُ عَنْ يَمِينِه.

[1391–61]. (Dar al-Salam 1528) Abu Bakr ibn Abi Shaybah and Zuhayr ibn Ḥarb narrated: Wakīʿ narrated; from Sufyān; from al-Suddī; from Anas; that **'The Prophet (peace be upon him) used to turn to his right'.**

حَدَّثَنا أَبُو بَكْرِ بْنُ أَبِي شَيْبَةَ وَزُهَيْرُ بْنُ حَرْبٍ، قالا: حَدَّثَنا وَكِيعٌ، عَنْ سُفْيانَ، عَنِ السُّدِّيِّ، عَنْ أَنَسٍ، أَنَّ النَّبِيَّ صَلَّى اللهُ عَلَيْهِ وَسَلَّمَ كانَ يَنْصَرِفُ عَنْ يَمِينِهِ.

Text Explanation

The first hadith narrated by ʿAbdullāh ibn Masʿūd says that he saw the Prophet turning most regularly to his left after he had finished his prayers, while the other hadiths quote Anas suggesting that he saw him turning most regularly to his right. These hadiths may be reconciled when we understand that the Prophet used to do it one way at times and the other way at other times. Each of the two narrators mentioned what he believed to be the more frequent, according to his knowledge. Thus, the hadiths mean that both ways are permissible, and neither is discouraged.

What is reprehensible [i.e. *makrūh*], as suggested by Ibn Masʿūd, is not whether one turns to the right or the left, but the belief that

i. Related by al-Nasāʾī, 1358.

there is an incumbent duty in the matter. Anyone who believes that it is a duty to turn to either of the two directions is wrong. Hence, he said: 'thinking that it is incumbent on him'. The criticism applies to one who feels that there is a duty in the matter. According to our school, there is no discouragement of either way. It is desirable, however, to turn to the direction that serves one's need, whether it is to the right or to the left. If both are equal, then the right side is preferable, on the basis of the other hadiths that speak generally of the preferability of the right side. This is the correct explanation that may be said about these two hadiths. Some may say what is wrong, but God knows best.

Transmission

The chain of transmission of hadith No. 1389 is as follows: 'Abu Bakr ibn Abi Shaybah narrated: Abu Muʿāwiyah and Wakīʿ narrated; from al-Aʿmash; from ʿUmārah; from al-Aswad; from 'Abdullāh'. This entire chain consists of narrators who belonged to Kufah. Moreover, it includes three narrators from the *tābiʿīn* generation, reporting from each other. These are al-Aʿmash, ʿUmārah and al-Aswad.

CHAPTER 8

THE PREFERABILITY OF STANDING TO THE RIGHT OF THE IMAM

[1392–62]. (Dar al-Salam 1529) Abu Kurayb narrated:[i] Ibn Abi Zā'idah reported; from Mis'ar; from Thābit ibn 'Ubayd; from Ibn al-Barā'; from al-Barā'. He said: **'When we prayed behind God's Messenger (peace be upon him), we preferred to be to his right, so that he would turn to us with his face. I heard him say: "My Lord, spare me Your punishment on the Day when You resurrect (or gather) Your servants".'**

وَحَدَّثَنَا أَبُو كُرَيْبٍ، أَخْبَرَنَا ابْنُ أَبِي زَائِدَةَ، عَنْ مِسْعَرٍ، عَنْ ثَابِتِ بْنِ عُبَيْدٍ، عَنِ ابْنِ الْبَرَاءِ، عَنِ الْبَرَاءِ قَالَ: كُنَّا إِذَا صَلَّيْنَا خَلْفَ رَسُولِ اللهِ صَلَّى اللهُ عَلَيْهِ وَسَلَّمَ أَحْبَبْنَا أَنْ نَكُونَ عَنْ يَمِينِهِ، يُقْبِلُ عَلَيْنَا بِوَجْهِهِ. قَالَ: فَسَمِعْتُهُ يَقُولُ: «رَبِّ قِنِي عَذَابَكَ يَوْمَ تَبْعَثُ - أَوْ تَجْمَعُ-عِبَادَكَ».

[1393–000]. (Dar al-Salam 1530) Abu Kurayb and Zuhayr ibn Ḥarb narrated: both said: Wakī' narrated; from Mis'ar; with the same chain of transmission: **the same text but did not mention: 'he would turn to us with his face'.**

وَحَدَّثَنَاهُ أَبُو كُرَيْبٍ وَزُهَيْرُ بْنُ حَرْبٍ، قَالَا: حَدَّثَنَا وَكِيعٌ، عَنْ مِسْعَرٍ، بِهَذَا الإِسْنَادِ. وَلَمْ يَذْكُرْ يُقْبِلُ عَلَيْنَا بِوَجْهِهِ.

---

i. Related by Abu Dāwūd, 615; al-Nasā'ī in a shorter version, 821; Ibn Mājah in similar wording, 1006.

Text Explanation

Qadi ʿIyāḍ said: 'It is probable that being on the right side was preferable to them when the prayer was finished with *salām*, which is the more apparent meaning. It was the Prophet's custom when he finished his prayer to turn his face to all those with him. He perhaps moved towards them when he stood up after the prayer or when he was about to leave.'

CHAPTER 9

NO SUNNAH PRAYER WHEN THE *IQĀMAH* IS ANNOUNCED

[1394–63]. (Dar al-Salam 1531) Ahmad ibn Ḥanbal narrated to me:[i] Muhammad ibn Jaʿfar narrated; Shuʿbah narrated; from Warqā'; from ʿAmr ibn Dīnār; from ʿAṭā' ibn Yasār; from Abu Hurayrah; from the Prophet (peace be upon him): **'When the *iqāmah* is announced, no prayer may be offered other than the obligatory one'.**

This hadith was also narrated to me by Muhammad ibn Ḥatim and Ibn Rāfiʿ; both said: Shabābah narrated; Warqā' narrated; with the same chain of transmission.

وَحَدَّثَنِي أَحْمَدُ بْنُ حَنْبَلٍ، حَدَّثَنَا مُحَمَّدُ بْنُ جَعْفَرٍ، حَدَّثَنَا شُعْبَةُ، عَنْ وَرْقَاءَ، عَنْ عَمْرِو بْنِ دِينَارٍ، عَنْ عَطَاءِ بْنِ يَسَارٍ، عَنْ أَبِي هُرَيْرَةَ، عَنِ النَّبِيِّ صَلَّى اللهُ عَلَيْهِ وَسَلَّمَ قَالَ: «إِذَا أُقِيمَتِ الصَّلاَةُ فَلاَ صَلاَةَ إِلاَّ الْمَكْتُوبَةُ».

وَحَدَّثَنِيهِ مُحَمَّدُ بْنُ حَاتِمٍ وَابْنُ رَافِعٍ، قَالاَ: حَدَّثَنَا شَبَابَةُ، حَدَّثَنِي وَرْقَاءُ بِهَذَا الإِسْنَادِ.

[1395–64]. (Dar al-Salam 1532–1534) Yaḥyā ibn Ḥabīb al-Ḥārithī narrated to me: Rawḥ narrated; Zakariyyā' ibn Isḥāq narrated; ʿAmr ibn Dīnār narrated; he said: I heard ʿAṭā' ibn Yasār say; from Abu Hurayrah; from the Prophet (peace be upon him).

---

i. Related by Abu Dāwūd, 1266; al-Tirmidhī, 421; al-Nasā'ī, 864 and 865; Ibn Mājah, 1151.

He said: **'When the prayer is announced [i.e. *iqāmah*], no prayer may be offered other than the obligatory one'.**

وَحَدَّثَنِي يَحْيَى بْنُ حَبِيبٍ الْحَارِثِيُّ، حَدَّثَنَا رَوْحٌ، حَدَّثَنَا زَكَرِيَّاءُ بْنُ إِسْحَاقَ، حَدَّثَنَا عَمْرُو بْنُ دِينَارٍ قَالَ: سَمِعْتُ عَطَاءَ بْنَ يَسَارٍ، يَقُولُ عَنْ أَبِي هُرَيْرَةَ، عَنِ النَّبِيِّ صَلَّى اللهُ عَلَيْهِ وَسَلَّمَ أَنَّهُ قَالَ: «إِذَا أُقِيمَتِ الصَّلاَةُ فَلاَ صَلاَةَ إِلاَّ الْـمَكْتُوبَةُ».

'Abd ibn Ḥumayd narrated it: 'Abd al-Razzāq reported; Zakariyyā' ibn Isḥāq reported; with the same chain of transmission: **the same text.**

وَحَدَّثَنَاهُ عَبْدُ بْنُ حُمَيْدٍ، أَخْبَرَنَا عَبْدُ الرَّزَّاقِ، أَخْبَرَنَا زَكَرِيَّاءُ بْنُ إِسْحَاقَ، بِهَذَا الإِسْنَادِ: مِثْلَهُ.

Ḥasan al-Ḥulwānī narrated: Yazīd ibn Ḥārūn narrated; Ḥammād ibn Zayd reported; from Ayyūb; from 'Amr ibn Dīnār; from 'Aṭā' ibn Yasār; from Abu Hurayrah; from the Prophet (peace be upon him): **the same text**.

Ḥammād said: **'I later met 'Amr and he narrated it to me but did not attribute it to the Prophet'.**

وَحَدَّثَنَا حَسَنٌ الْحُلْوَانِيُّ، حَدَّثَنَا يَزِيدُ بْنُ هَارُونَ، أَخْبَرَنَا حَمَّادُ بْنُ زَيْدٍ، عَنْ أَيُّوبَ، عَنْ عَمْرِو بْنِ دِينَارٍ، عَنْ عَطَاءِ بْنِ يَسَارٍ، عَنْ أَبِي هُرَيْرَةَ، عَنِ النَّبِيِّ صَلَّى اللهُ عَلَيْهِ وَسَلَّمَ. بِمِثْلِهِ. قَالَ حَمَّادٌ: ثُمَّ لَقِيتُ عَمْرًا فَحَدَّثَنِي بِهِ وَلَمْ يَرْفَعْهُ.

[1396–65]. (Dar al-Salam 1535) 'Abdullāh ibn Maslamah al-Qa'nabī narrated:[i] Ibrāhīm ibn Sa'd narrated; from his father; from Ḥafṣ ibn 'Āṣim; from 'Abdullāh ibn Mālik ibn Buḥaynah; that **'God's Messenger passed by a man praying when the**

i. Related by al-Bukhari, 663; al-Nasā'ī, 866; Ibn Mājah, 1153.

iqāmah **for Fajr Prayer had been announced. He spoke to him saying something we did not know. When we finished, we gathered around him saying: "What did God's Messenger say to you?" He said: "He told me that any of you could easily pray Fajr in four** ***rakʿahs*****".'**

Al-Qaʿnabī said: '**ʿAbdullāh ibn Mālik ibn Buḥaynah; from his father'.**

Abu al-Ḥusayn Muslim said: **'It is wrong for him to say in this hadith "from his father".'**

حَدَّثَنَا عَبْدُ اللهِ بْنُ مَسْلَمَةَ الْقَعْنَبِيُّ، حَدَّثَنَا إِبْرَاهِيمُ بْنُ سَعْدٍ، عَنْ أَبِيهِ، عَنْ حَفْصِ بْنِ عَاصِمٍ، عَنْ عَبْدِ اللهِ بْنِ مَالِكٍ ابْنِ بُحَيْنَةَ، أَنَّ رَسُولَ اللهِ صَلَّى اللهُ عَلَيْهِ وَسَلَّمَ مَرَّ بِرَجُلٍ يُصَلِّي، وَقَدْ أُقِيمَتْ صَلَاةُ الصُّبْحِ، فَكَلَّمَهُ بِشَيْءٍ لَا نَدْرِي مَا هُوَ. فَلَمَّا انْصَرَفْنَا أَحَطْنَا نَقُولُ: مَاذَا قَالَ لَكَ رَسُولُ اللهِ صَلَّى اللهُ عَلَيْهِ وَسَلَّمَ؟ قَالَ قَالَ لِي: «يُوشِكُ أَنْ يُصَلِّيَ أَحَدُكُمُ الصُّبْحَ أَرْبَعًا».

قَالَ الْقَعْنَبِيُّ عَبْدُ اللهِ بْنُ مَالِكٍ ابْنُ بُحَيْنَةَ عَنْ أَبِيه.

قَالَ أَبُو الْحُسَيْنِ مُسْلِمٌ: وَقَوْلُهُ عَنْ أَبِيهِ فِي هَذَا الْحَدِيثِ خَطَأٌ.

[1397–66]. (Dar al-Salam 1536) Qutaybah ibn Saʿīd narrated: Abu ʿAwānah narrated; from Saʿd ibn Ibrāhīm; from Ḥafṣ ibn ʿĀṣim; from Ibn Buḥaynah. He said: **'The congregational Fajr Prayer was announced, and God's Messenger (peace be upon him) saw a man praying while the caller was announcing the** ***iqāmah*****. He said: "Do you pray Fajr in four** ***rakʿahs*****?".'**

حَدَّثَنَا قُتَيْبَةُ بْنُ سَعِيدٍ، حَدَّثَنَا أَبُو عَوَانَةَ، عَنْ سَعْدِ بْنِ إِبْرَاهِيمَ، عَنْ حَفْصِ بْنِ عَاصِمٍ، عَنِ ابْنِ بُحَيْنَةَ قَالَ: أُقِيمَتْ صَلَاةُ الصُّبْحِ، فَرَأَى رَسُولُ اللهِ صَلَّى اللهُ عَلَيْهِ وَسَلَّمَ رَجُلًا يُصَلِّي وَالْمُؤَذِّنُ يُقِيمُ، فَقَالَ: «أَتُصَلِّي الصُّبْحَ أَرْبَعًا»؟

[1398–67]. (Dar al-Salam 1537) Abu Kāmil al-Jaḥdarī narrated:[i] Ḥammād (meaning Ibn Zayd) narrated [H]. Also, Ḥāmid ibn ʿUmar al-Bakrāwī narrated to me; ʿAbd al-Wāḥid (meaning Ibn Ziyād) narrated [H]. And, Ibn Numayr narrated; Abu Muʿāwiyah narrated; all from ʿĀṣim [H]. Also, Zuhayr ibn Ḥarb narrated (his text); Marwān ibn Muʿāwiyah al-Fazārī narrated; from ʿĀṣim al-Aḥwal; from ʿAbdullāh ibn Sarjis. He said: **'A man entered the mosque when God's Messenger was leading the Fajr Prayer. He prayed two *rakʿahs* at the side of the mosque then joined God's Messenger (peace be upon him). When God's Messenger finished his prayer with *salām*, he said, naming him: "Which of the two prayers did you count? Your prayer alone or your prayer with us?".'**

حَدَّثَنَا أَبُو كَامِلٍ الْجَحْدَرِيُّ، حَدَّثَنَا حَمَّادٌ (يَعْنِي ابْنَ زَيْدٍ)، ح. وَحَدَّثَنِي حَامِدُ بْنُ عُمَرَ الْبَكْرَاوِيُّ، حَدَّثَنَا عَبْدُ الْوَاحِدِ (يَعْنِي ابْنَ زِيَادٍ)، ح. وَحَدَّثَنَا ابْنُ نُمَيْرٍ، حَدَّثَنَا أَبُو مُعَاوِيَةَ، كُلُّهُمْ عَنْ عَاصِمٍ، ح. وَحَدَّثَنِي زُهَيْرُ بْنُ حَرْبٍ (وَاللَّفْظُ لَهُ)، حَدَّثَنَا مَرْوَانُ بْنُ مُعَاوِيَةَ الْفَزَارِيُّ، عَنْ عَاصِمٍ الأَحْوَلِ، عَنْ عَبْدِ اللهِ بْنِ سَرْجِسَ قَالَ: دَخَلَ رَجُلٌ الْمَسْجِدَ وَرَسُولُ اللهِ صَلَّى اللهُ عَلَيْهِ وَسَلَّمَ فِي صَلَاةِ الْغَدَاةِ، فَصَلَّى رَكْعَتَيْنِ فِي جَانِبِ الْمَسْجِدِ، ثُمَّ دَخَلَ مَعَ رَسُولِ اللهِ صَلَّى اللهُ عَلَيْهِ وَسَلَّمَ، فَلَمَّا سَلَّمَ رَسُولُ اللهِ صَلَّى اللهُ عَلَيْهِ وَسَلَّمَ قَالَ: «يَا فُلَانُ، بِأَيِّ الصَّلَاتَيْنِ اعْتَدَدْتَ؟ أَبِصَلَاتِكَ وَحْدَكَ أَمْ بِصَلَاتِكَ مَعَنَا»؟

Text Explanation

These hadiths make it very clear that no sunnah prayer may be started when the congregational prayer has been announced with the *iqāmah*. This applies to all sunnah, whether it is a regular one like those of Fajr, Ẓuhr and ʿAṣr or other voluntary prayers. This is the view of the Shāfiʿī School as well as the majority of scholars. Abu

i. Related by Abu Dāwūd, 1265; al-Nasāʾī, 867; Ibn Mājah, 1152.

Ḥanīfah and scholars of his school say: 'If a person has not prayed the sunnah of Fajr he may pray it in the mosque after the *iqāmah* has been announced, unless he fears to miss the second *rakʿah* with the congregation'. Al-Thawrī said: 'unless he fears to miss the first *rakʿah*'. A number of scholars say that such a person should pray the sunnah outside the mosque, and he may not pray these two *rakʿahs* in the mosque after the *iqāmah*.

In hadith No. 1397, the Prophet asks the person who prayed the sunnah after the *iqāmah* had been announced: 'Do you pray Fajr in four *rakʿahs*?' This is a rhetorical question, which means that once the *iqāmah* has been announced, no prayer may be started other than the obligatory prayer. Therefore, if a person prays two *rakʿahs* of sunnah after the *iqāmah* and then prays two *rakʿahs* with the congregation, he is thought to be one who made the Fajr Prayer in four *rakʿahs* because he prayed four *rakʿahs* after the *iqāmah*.

Qadi ʿIyāḍ said: 'The reason for prohibiting praying sunnah after the *iqāmah* is that if it is done like that for a long period of time, it may come to be thought of as a duty'. However, this reasoning is not strong. The correct thing to say is that the reason is that every worshipper must be free to attend to the obligatory prayer from the moment of its start and to begin it immediately after the imam has started it. Were he to be preoccupied with his sunnah prayer, he will miss starting the prayer with the imam, and he will miss out on some aspects that make the obligatory prayer perfect. It is more important to attend to the obligatory prayer and ensure its perfection. *Qadi* ʿIyāḍ adds: 'Another reason for this prohibition is that it prevents disagreement with imams'.

In hadith No. 1398, the Prophet asks the man who prayed the sunnah of Fajr at one side of the mosque before joining the congregation, which was already in progress: 'Which of the two prayers did you count? Your prayer alone or your prayer with us?' This provides clear evidence that a person must not pray a sunnah prayer after the *iqāmah* of the congregational prayer has been announced, even though one thinks that he can catch up with the imam. It replies to those who allow such a sunnah if the man offering the sunnah knows that he will catch up in the first or second *rak'ah*, but God knows best.

Transmission

In the third chain of transmission of hadith No. 1395, Ḥammād says: 'I later met 'Amr and he narrated it to me but did not attribute it to the Prophet'. This statement does not detract from the authenticity of the hadith and its attribution to the Prophet because most of the narrators take it up to the Prophet (peace be upon him). Al-Tirmidhī said: 'The narration taking this hadith up to the Prophet is more authentic'. We have explained in the 'Notes' to our 'Introduction' that when a hadith is narrated with a chain of transmission that stops at the Prophet's Companion and another that goes up to the Prophet, the latter is given preference according to the correct view. This is the case even when the number of narrations going up to the Prophet is less. Needless to say, if they are the greater number, the case is that much more valid.

The chain of transmission of hadith No. 1396 includes 'Abdullāh ibn Mālik ibn Buḥaynah. Then at the end of the text of the hadith, Muslim adds that al-Qa'nabī said: ''Abdullāh ibn Mālik ibn Buhaynah; from his father' and Abu al-Ḥusayn Muslim said: 'It is wrong for him to say in this hadith "from his father".' As for Abu al-Ḥusayn, he is Muslim [ibn al-Ḥajjā al-Qushayrī] who compiled this anthology of authentic hadiths. What Muslim says here is correct according to the majority of scholars. The addition of 'from his father' is wrong. The hadith is narrated by 'Abdullāh from the Prophet. He is 'Abdullāh ibn Mālik ibn al-Qishb. Buḥaynah is his mother.

CHAPTER 10

WHAT TO SAY WHEN ENTERING A MOSQUE

[1399–68]. (Dar al-Salam 1538–1539) Yaḥyā ibn Yaḥyā narrated:[i] Sulaymān ibn Bilāl reported; from Rabīʿah ibn Abu ʿAbd al-Raḥmān; from ʿAbd al-Malik ibn Saʿīd; from Abu Ḥumayd (or from Abu Usayd). He said: **'God's Messenger (peace be upon him) said: "When any of you enters a mosque, let him say: 'My Lord, open for me the gates of Your mercy', and when he leaves, let him say: 'My Lord, I pray to You to grant me of Your bounty'."'**

Muslim said: I heard Yaḥyā ibn Yaḥyā say: **'I wrote down this hadith from Sulaymān ibn Bilāl's book'. He said: 'I have been told that Yaḥyā al-Ḥimmānī said: "And Abu Usayd".'**

حَدَّثَنَا يَحْيَى بْنُ يَحْيَى، أَخْبَرَنَا سُلَيْمَانُ بْنُ بِلَالٍ، عَنْ رَبِيعَةَ بْنِ أَبِي عَبْدِ الرَّحْمَنِ، عَنْ عَبْدِ الْـمَلِكِ بْنِ سَعِيدٍ، عَنْ أَبِي حُمَيْدٍ (أَوْ عَنْ أَبِي أُسَيْدٍ) قَالَ: قَالَ رَسُولُ اللهِ صَلَّى اللهُ عَلَيْهِ وَسَلَّمَ: «إِذَا دَخَلَ أَحَدُكُمُ الْـمَسْجِدَ فَلْيَقُلِ: اللهُمَّ افْتَحْ لِي أَبْوَابَ رَحْمَتِكَ». وَإِذَا خَرَجَ فَلْيَقُلِ: «اللَّهُمَّ إِنِّي أَسْأَلُكَ مِنْ فَضْلِكَ».

قَالَ مُسْلِمٌ: سَمِعْتُ يَحْيَى بْنَ يَحْيَى يَقُولُ: كَتَبْتُ هَذَا الْحَدِيثَ مِنْ كِتَابِ سُلَيْمَانَ بْنِ بِلَالٍ. قَالَ: بَلَغَنِي أَنَّ يَحْيَى الْحِمَّانِيَّ يَقُولُ: وَأَبِي أُسَيْدٍ.

---

i. Related by Abu Dāwūd, 465; al-Nasāʾī, 728; Ibn Mājah, 772.

Ḥāmid ibn ʿUmar al-Bakrāwī narrated: Bishr ibn al-Mufaḍḍal narrated; ʿUmārah ibn Ghaziyyah narrated; from Rabīʿah ibn ʿAbd al-Raḥmān; from ʿAbd al-Malik ibn Saʿīd ibn Suwayd al-Anṣārī; from Abu Ḥumayd or Abu Usayd; from the Prophet: **the same text.**

وَحَدَّثَنَا حَامِدُ بْنُ عُمَرَ الْبَكْرَاوِيُّ، حَدَّثَنَا بِشْرُ بْنُ الْمُفَضَّلِ، حَدَّثَنَا عُمَارَةُ بْنُ غَزِيَّةَ، عَنْ رَبِيعَةَ بْنِ أَبِي عَبْدِ الرَّحْمَنِ، عَنْ عَبْدِ الْمَلِكِ بْنِ سَعِيدِ بْنِ سُوَيْدٍ الأَنْصَارِيِّ، عَنْ أَبِي حُمَيْدٍ، أَوْ عَنْ أَبِي أُسَيْدٍ، عَنِ النَّبِيِّ صَلَّى اللهُ عَلَيْهِ وَسَلَّمَ: بِمِثْلِهِ.

Text Explanation

This hadith shows the desirability of saying this supplication when entering a mosque and when leaving. There are many supplications and glorifications to be said on these occasions, and these are mentioned in Abu Dāwūd's *Sunan* anthology. I have given a full list of these at the beginning of my book, *al-Adhkār*, and they may be summed up as follows: *'aʿūdhu billāhi al-ʿAẓīm, wa bi-wajhih al-karīm, wa sulṭānih al-qadīm min al-Shayṭān al-rajīm. Bismillāh wa alḥamd lillāh. Allāhumma ṣalli ʿalā Muhammad wa ʿalā āli Muhammad wa sallim. Allāhumma ighfirlī dhunūbī waftaḥlī abwāba raḥmatik.'* On leaving, one says the same phrases but replaces the last one with: *Allāhumma innī as'aluka min faḍlik*. The supplication on entry means: 'I seek refuge with God the Supreme, His honoured face and His eternal authority against Satan the accursed. My Lord, grant peace and blessings to Muhammad and Muhammad's household. My Lord, forgive me my sins and open to me the gates of Your mercy'. When leaving, the last sentence is replaced with: 'the gates of Your bounty'.

Transmission

After the first hadith, No. 1399, Muslim adds a note in which Yaḥyā al-Ḥimmānī is mentioned. His name stems from his tribe, the Ḥimmān, which moved to Kufah.

CHAPTER 11

GREETING THE MOSQUE

[1400–69]. (Dar al-Salam 1540) ʿAbdullāh ibn Maslamah ibn Qaʿnab and Qutaybah ibn Saʿīd narrated:[i] both said: Mālik narrated [H]. Also, Yaḥyā ibn Yaḥyā narrated: he said: I read out to Mālik; from ʿĀmir ibn ʿAbdullāh ibn al-Zubayr; from ʿAmr ibn Sulaym al-Zuraqī; from Abu Qatādah; that God's Messenger (peace be upon him) said: **'When any of you enters the mosque, let him offer two *rakʿahs* before sitting down'.**

حَدَّثَنَا عَبْدُ اللهِ بْنُ مَسْلَمَةَ بْنِ قَعْنَبٍ وَقُتَيْبَةُ بْنُ سَعِيدٍ، قَالا: حَدَّثَنَا مَالِكٌ، ح. وَحَدَّثَنَا يَحْيَى بْنُ يَحْيَى قَالَ: قَرَأْتُ عَلَى مَالِكٍ عَنْ عَامِرِ بْنِ عَبْدِ اللهِ بْنِ الزُّبَيْرِ، عَنْ عَمْرِو بْنِ سُلَيْمٍ الزُّرَقِيِّ، عَنْ أَبِي قَتَادَةَ، أَنَّ رَسُولَ اللهِ صَلَّى اللهُ عَلَيْهِ وَسَلَّمَ قَالَ: «إِذَا دَخَلَ أَحَدُكُمُ الْمَسْجِدَ فَلْيَرْكَعْ رَكْعَتَيْنِ قَبْلَ أَنْ يَجْلِسَ».

[1401–70]. (Dar al-Salam 1541) Abu Bakr ibn Abi Shaybah narrated: Ḥusayn ibn ʿAlī narrated; from Zā'idah; he said: ʿAmr ibn Yaḥyā al-Anṣārī narrated to me; Muhammad ibn Yaḥyā ibn Ḥabbān narrated to me; from ʿAmr ibn Sulaym ibn Khaldah al-Anṣārī; from Abu Qatādah, the Prophet's Companion. He said: **'I entered the mosque when God's Messenger (peace be upon him) was sitting with the people, and I sat down. God's Messenger (peace be upon him) said: "What has prevented you from offering two *rakʿahs* before sitting down?" I said:**

i. Related by al-Bukhari, 444 and 1163; Abu Dāwūd, 467 and 468; al-Tirmidhī, 316; al-Nasā'ī in a shorter version, 729; Ibn Mājah, 1013.

"Messenger of God, I saw you sitting and the people sitting." He said: "When any of you enters the mosque, let him not sit down until he has offered two *rakʿahs*".'

حَدَّثَنَا أَبُو بَكْرِ بْنُ أَبِي شَيْبَةَ، حَدَّثَنَا حُسَيْنُ بْنُ عَلِيٍّ، عَنْ زَائِدَةَ، قَالَ حَدَّثَنِي عَمْرُو بْنُ يَحْيَى الأَنْصَارِيُّ، حَدَّثَنِي مُحَمَّدُ بْنُ يَحْيَى بْنِ حَبَّانَ، عَنْ عَمْرِو بْنِ سُلَيْمٍ بْنِ خَلْدَةَ الأَنْصَارِيِّ، عَنْ أَبِي قَتَادَةَ، صَاحِبِ رَسُولِ اللهِ صَلَّى اللهُ عَلَيْهِ وَسَلَّمَ قَالَ: دَخَلْتُ الْـمَسْجِدَ وَرَسُولُ اللهِ صَلَّى اللهُ عَلَيْهِ وَسَلَّمَ جَالِسٌ بَيْنَ ظَهْرَانَيِ النَّاسِ. قَالَ: فَجَلَسْتُ. فَقَالَ رَسُولُ اللهِ صَلَّى اللهُ عَلَيْهِ وَسَلَّمَ: «مَا مَنَعَكَ أَنْ تَرْكَعَ رَكْعَتَيْنِ قَبْلَ أَنْ تَجْلِسَ»؟ قَالَ: فَقُلْتُ يَا رَسُولَ اللهِ رَأَيْتُكَ جَالِسًا وَالنَّاسُ جُلُوسٌ. قَالَ: «فَإِذَا دَخَلَ أَحَدُكُمُ الْـمَسْجِدَ فَلاَ يَجْلِسْ حَتَّى يَرْكَعَ رَكْعَتَيْنِ».

[1402–71]. (Dar al-Salam 1542) Ahmad ibn Jawwās al-Ḥanafī Abu ʿĀṣim narrated:[i] ʿUbaydullāh al-Ashjaʿī narrated; from Sufyān; from Muḥārib ibn Dithār; from Jābir ibn ʿAbdullāh. He said: **'I had a debt owed to me by the Prophet, and he repaid me and gave me more. When I entered the mosque, he said to me: "Pray two *rakʿahs*".'**

حَدَّثَنَا أَحْمَدُ بْنُ جَوَّاسٍ الْحَنَفِيُّ أَبُو عَاصِمٍ، حَدَّثَنَا عُبَيْدُ اللهِ الأَشْجَعِيُّ، عَنْ سُفْيَانَ، عَنْ مُحَارِبِ بْنِ دِثَارٍ، عَنْ جَابِرِ بْنِ عَبْدِ اللهِ قَالَ: كَانَ لِي عَلَى النَّبِيِّ صَلَّى اللهُ عَلَيْهِ وَسَلَّمَ دَيْنٌ، فَقَضَانِي وَزَادَنِي. وَدَخَلْتُ عَلَيْهِ الْـمَسْجِدَ، فَقَالَ لِي: «صَلِّ رَكْعَتَيْنِ».

Text Explanation

These hadiths speak of the desirability of greeting a mosque on entry by offering a prayer of two *rakʿahs*. This is a sunnah, according to the unanimous view of all Muslims. *Qadi* ʿIyāḍ mentions that Dāwūd

i. Related by al-Bukhari in longer versions, 443, 2394 and in shorter versions 2603, 2604, 3089 and 3090; Abu Dāwūd, 3347; al-Nasāʾī, 4604 and 4605.

and his disciples consider such a prayer a duty. The hadiths show that one is discouraged from sitting down in a mosque without first offering such a voluntary prayer. The hadiths also show that such a greeting is desirable at whatever time one enters a mosque. This is the view of our Shāfiʿī School, and it is shared by a number of scholars. However, Abu Ḥanīfah, al-Awzāʿī and al-Layth say that it is discouraged if one enters during the periods when prayer is disallowed. Our scholars respond to this view saying that what is disallowed is prayer that is not occasioned by a particular reason. The Prophet offered two *rakʿahs* of sunnah after he had prayed ʿAṣr [which is a period when voluntary prayers are disallowed] because these were in compensation for the sunnah prayer he missed when he prayed Ẓuhr. Thus, he considered the period of disallowed prayer a special period and therefore, he offered the prayer that had a particular reason. He never abandoned the greeting of the mosque in any case. On the contrary, he ordered a person who entered the mosque and sat down when he was addressing the congregation before Friday Prayer to stand up and pray two *rakʿahs*, although all prayers are disallowed during the *khuṭbah* [i.e. Friday speech] except for greeting the mosque. Had it been acceptable for such a greeting to be abandoned at any time, it would have been appropriate on this particular occasion because the man sat down and this means its time has lapsed because the greeting prayer is done before sitting down. Moreover, he was not aware of the ruling concerning it. Indeed, the Prophet interrupted his own speech to speak to the man and order him to offer this prayer. We note the great importance the Prophet attached to this prayer, which means that it is important at all times.

It is not a condition that a person should intend his prayer to be a greeting for the mosque. It is sufficient that he prays two *rakʿahs* of an obligatory or recommended prayer. If a person intends his prayer to combine both an obligatory prayer and greeting the mosque, his prayer is valid and sufficient for both. But if he offers a *Janāzah* Prayer or prostrates himself in gratitude to God for some blessing, or during his recitation of the Qur'an, or prays one *rakʿah* as greeting, this sunnah of greeting the mosque is not fulfilled, according to the correct view of our Shāfiʿī School. Some of our scholars say that this is sufficient, but it is contrary to the apparent meaning of the hadith. Their argument is that this sunnah is an act done to honour the mosque and these actions fulfil this purpose. The correct view is that it does not fulfil it.

The only exception is the Sacred Mosque in Makkah. The first thing a pilgrim does on entering the Sacred Mosque is to perform the *ṭawāf* of arrival, which is the special greeting of this mosque. After finishing, the person prays two *rakʿahs* called the *ṭawāf* sunnah.

In hadith No. 1402, the Prophet's Companion, Jābir ibn ʿAbdullāh, mentions that the Prophet owed him some money. When the Prophet repaid him, he gave him more than he owed. This suggests that it is desirable to repay more than one has borrowed,[i] but God knows best.

---

i. This extra payment must be by the debtor's own choice. It may not be agreed, or even understood, in advance or at the time the loan is given. Otherwise, it would constitute usury.

CHAPTER 12

ON RETURNING FROM A JOURNEY, A PRAYER IN A MOSQUE IS DESIRABLE

[1403–72]. (Dar al-Salam 1543) ʿUbaydullāh ibn Muʿādh narrated: my father narrated; Shuʿbah narrated; from Muḥārib; he heard Jābir ibn ʿAbdullāh say: **'God's Messenger (peace be upon him) bought a camel from me. When he arrived in Madinah, he ordered me to go to the mosque and pray two *rakʿahs*'.**

حَدَّثَنَا عُبَيْدُ اللهِ بْنُ مُعَاذٍ، حَدَّثَنَا أَبِي، حَدَّثَنَا شُعْبَةُ، عَنْ مُحَارِبٍ، سَمِعَ جَابِرَ بْنَ عَبْدِ اللهِ يَقُولُ: «اشْتَرَى مِنِّي رَسُولُ اللهِ صَلَّى اللهُ عَلَيْهِ وَسَلَّمَ بَعِيرًا، فَلَمَّا قَدِمَ الْـمَدِينَةَ أَمَرَنِي أَنْ آتِيَ الْـمَسْجِدَ فَأُصَلِّيَ رَكْعَتَيْنِ».

[1404–73]. (Dar al-Salam 1544) Muhammad ibn al-Muthannā narrated to me:[i] ʿAbd al-Wahhāb (meaning al-Thaqafī) narrated; ʿUbaydullāh narrated; from Wahb ibn Kaysān; from Jābir ibn ʿAbdullāh. He said: **'I joined God's Messenger (peace be upon him) on an expedition. My camel slowed me down and was exhausted. The Prophet arrived before me, while I did not arrive until the morning. I went to the mosque and saw him standing at the gate there. He said: "Have you just now arrived?" I said: "Yes". He said: "Leave your camel and go in to offer two *rakʿahs*". I went in and prayed, then came back'.**

i. Related by al-Bukhari in longer versions, 2097 and 2718.

وَحَدَّثَنِي مُحَمَّدُ بْنُ الْـمُثَنَّى، حَدَّثَنَا عَبْدُ الْوَهَّابِ (يَعْنِي الثَّقَفِيَّ)، حَدَّثَنَا عُبَيْدُ اللهِ، عَنْ وَهْبِ بْنِ كَيْسَانَ، عَنْ جَابِرِ بْنِ عَبْدِ اللهِ قَالَ: خَرَجْتُ مَعَ رَسُولِ اللهِ صَلَّى اللهُ عَلَيْهِ وَسَلَّمَ فِي غَزَاةٍ، فَأَبْطَأَ بِي جَمَلِي وَأَعْيَى. ثُمَّ قَدِمَ رَسُولُ اللهِ صَلَّى اللهُ عَلَيْهِ وَسَلَّمَ قَبْلِي، وَقَدِمْتُ بِالْغَدَاةِ، فَجِئْتُ الْـمَسْجِدَ، فَوَجَدْتُهُ عَلَى بَابِ الْـمَسْجِدِ. قَالَ: «الآنَ حِينَ قَدِمْتَ»؟ قُلْتُ: نَعَمْ. قَالَ: «فَدَعْ جَمَلَكَ وَادْخُلْ فَصَلِّ رَكْعَتَيْنِ». قَالَ: فَدَخَلْتُ فَصَلَّيْتُ ثُمَّ رَجَعْتُ.

[1405–74]. (Dar al-Salam 1545) Muhammad ibn al-Muthannā narrated:[i] al-Ḍaḥḥāk (meaning Abu ʿĀṣim) narrated [H]. Also, Maḥmūd ibn Ghaylān narrated to me; ʿAbd al-Razzāq narrated; both said: Ibn Jurayj reported; Ibn Shihāb reported to me; that ʿAbd al-Raḥmān ibn ʿAbdullāh ibn Kaʿb reported to him; from his father ʿAbdullāh ibn Kaʿb and his uncle ʿUbaydullāh ibn Kaʿb; from Kaʿb ibn Mālik; that **'God's Messenger (peace be upon him) never came back from a journey except during the day, at mid-morning. When he arrived, he would start by going to the mosque where he would pray two *rakʿahs* then sit down'.**

حَدَّثَنَا مُحَمَّدُ بْنُ الْـمُثَنَّى، حَدَّثَنَا الضَّحَّاكُ (يَعْنِي أَبَا عَاصِمٍ)، ح. وَحَدَّثَنِي مَحْمُودُ بْنُ غَيْلاَنَ، حَدَّثَنَا عَبْدُ الرَّزَّاقِ، قَالا جَمِيعًا: أَخْبَرَنَا ابْنُ جُرَيْجٍ، أَخْبَرَنِي ابْنُ شِهَابٍ، أَنَّ عَبْدَ الرَّحْمَنِ بْنَ عَبْدِ اللهِ بْنِ كَعْبٍ أَخْبَرَهُ، عَنْ أَبِيهِ عَبْدِ اللهِ بْنِ كَعْبٍ، وَعَنْ عَمِّهِ عُبَيْدِ اللهِ بْنِ كَعْبٍ، عَنْ كَعْبِ بْنِ مَالِكٍ، أَنَّ رَسُولَ اللهِ صَلَّى اللهُ عَلَيْهِ وَسَلَّمَ كَانَ لاَ يَقْدَمُ مِنْ سَفَرٍ إِلاَّ نَهَارًا فِي الضُّحَى. فَإِذَا قَدِمَ بَدَأَ بِالْـمَسْجِدِ فَصَلَّى فِيهِ رَكْعَتَيْنِ، ثُمَّ جَلَسَ فِيهِ.

i. Related by al-Bukhari, 3088; Abu Dāwūd, 2773 and 2781; al-Nasāʾī in a longer version, 730.

Text Explanation

These hadiths make it clear that it is desirable for anyone returning from a journey to go first to the mosque and offer two *rak'ahs*. This prayer is particularly recommended on arrival from a journey. It is not a greeting to the mosque. The hadiths make this very clear. The hadiths also show that it is preferable to arrive early in the day.

It is also desirable for a dignitary or someone whom people visit on arriving from a journey to sit at an obvious place near his home, either the local mosque or some other place, where it is easy for his visitors to meet him.

CHAPTER 13

THE DESIRABLE PRAYER IN MID-MORNING [i.e. *ḌUḤĀ*]

[1406–75]. (Dar al-Salam 1546) Yaḥyā ibn Yaḥyā narrated: Yazīd ibn Zurayʿ reported; from Saʿīd al-Jurayrī; from ʿAbdullāh ibn Shaqīq. He said: **'I asked ʿĀ'ishah: "Did the Prophet pray the Ḍuḥā Prayer?" She said: "No, except when he returned from a journey".'**

وَحَدَّثَنَا يَحْيَى بْنُ يَحْيَى، أَخْبَرَنَا يَزِيدُ بْنُ زُرَيْعٍ، عَنْ سَعِيدٍ الْجُرَيْرِيِّ، عَنْ عَبْدِ اللهِ بْنِ شَقِيقٍ قَالَ: قُلْتُ لِعَائِشَةَ: هَلْ كَانَ النَّبِيُّ صَلَّى اللهُ عَلَيْهِ وَسَلَّمَ يُصَلِّي الضُّحَى؟ قَالَتْ لا، إِلاَّ أَنْ يَجِيءَ مِنْ مَغِيبِهِ.

[1407–76]. (Dar al-Salam 1547) ʿUbaydullāh ibn Muʿādh narrated: my father narrated; Kahmas ibn al-Ḥasan al-Qaysī narrated; from ʿAbdullāh ibn Shaqīq. He said: **'I asked ʿĀ'ishah: "Did the Prophet pray the Ḍuḥā Prayer?" She said: "No, except when he returned from a journey".'**

وَحَدَّثَنَا عُبَيْدُ اللهِ بْنُ مُعَاذٍ، حَدَّثَنَا أَبِي، حَدَّثَنَا كَهْمَسُ بْنُ الْحَسَنِ الْقَيْسِيُّ، عَنْ عَبْدِ اللهِ بْنِ شَقِيقٍ قَالَ: قُلْتُ لِعَائِشَةَ: أَكَانَ النَّبِيُّ صَلَّى اللهُ عَلَيْهِ وَسَلَّمَ يُصَلِّي الضُّحَى؟ قَالَتْ لاَ، إِلاَّ أَنْ يَجِيءَ مِنْ مَغِيبِهِ.

[1408–77]. (Dar al-Salam 1548) Yaḥyā ibn Yaḥyā narrated: I read out to Mālik; from Ibn Shihāb; from ʿUrwah; from ʿĀ'ishah; that she said: **'I never saw God's Messenger (peace be upon him) praying the Ḍuḥā sunnah but I do it. God's Messenger (peace be upon him) sometimes refrained from doing something that he would have loved to do, for fear that people would do it and it would then be made obligatory on them'.**

حَدَّثَنَا يَحْيَى بْنُ يَحْيَى قَالَ: قَرَأْتُ عَلَى مَالِكٍ عَنِ ابْنِ شِهَابٍ، عَنْ عُرْوَةَ، عَنْ عَائِشَةَ أَنَّهَا قَالَتْ: مَا رَأَيْتُ رَسُولَ اللهِ صَلَّى اللهُ عَلَيْهِ وَسَلَّمَ يُصَلِّي سُبْحَةَ الضُّحَى قَطُّ. وَإِنِّي لأُسَبِّحُهَا، وَإِنْ كَانَ رَسُولُ اللهِ صَلَّى اللهُ عَلَيْهِ وَسَلَّمَ لَيَدَعُ الْعَمَلَ وَهُوَ يُحِبُّ أَنْ يَعْمَلَ بِهِ، خَشْيَةَ أَنْ يَعْمَلَ بِهِ النَّاسُ فَيُفْرَضَ عَلَيْهِمْ.

[1409–78]. (Dar al-Salam 1549) Shaybān ibn Farrūkh narrated: ʿAbd al-Wārith narrated; Yazīd (meaning al-Rishk) narrated; Muʿādhah narrated to me; that she asked ʿĀʾishah: **'How many *rakʿahs* did God's Messenger pray in the Ḍuḥā Prayer?' She said: 'Four *rakʿahs*, but he added whatever he wished'.**

حَدَّثَنَا شَيْبَانُ بْنُ فَرُّوخَ، حَدَّثَنَا عَبْدُ الْوَارِثِ، حَدَّثَنَا يَزِيدُ (يَعْنِي الرِّشْكَ)، حَدَّثَتْنِي مُعَاذَةُ، أَنَّهَا سَأَلَتْ عَائِشَةَ، رضى الله عنها: كَمْ كَانَ رَسُولُ اللهِ صَلَّى اللهُ عَلَيْهِ وَسَلَّمَ يُصَلِّي صَلاَةَ الضُّحَى؟ قَالَتْ: أَرْبَعَ رَكَعَاتٍ، وَيَزِيدُ مَا شَاءَ.

[1410–000]. (Dar al-Salam 1550) Muhammad ibn al-Muthannā and Ibn Bashshār narrated: both said: Muhammad ibn Jaʿfar narrated; Shuʿbah narrated; from Yazīd; with the same chain of transmission: **the same text. Yazīd, however, said: 'He added whatever God willed'.**

حَدَّثَنَا مُحَمَّدُ بْنُ الْـمُثَنَّى وَابْنُ بَشَّارٍ، قَالا: حَدَّثَنَا مُحَمَّدُ بْنُ جَعْفَرٍ، حَدَّثَنَا شُعْبَةُ، عَنْ يَزِيدَ، بِهَذَا الإِسْنَادِ. مِثْلَهُ، وَقَالَ: يَزِيدُ مَا شَاءَ اللهُ.

[1411–79]. (Dar al-Salam 1551–1552) Yaḥyā ibn Ḥabīb al-Ḥārithī narrated to me: Khālid ibn al-Ḥārith narrated; from Saʿīd; Qatādah narrated; that Muʿādhah al-ʿAdawiyyah narrated; from ʿĀ'ishah. She said: **'God's Messenger (peace be upon him) used to pray Ḍuḥā in four *rakʿahs* and he might add whatever God willed'.**

وَحَدَّثَنِي يَحْيَى بْنُ حَبِيبٍ الْحَارِثِيُّ، حَدَّثَنَا خَالِدُ بْنُ الْحَارِثِ، عَنْ سَعِيدٍ، حَدَّثَنَا قَتَادَةُ، أَنَّ مُعَاذَةَ الْعَدَوِيَّةَ حَدَّثَتْهُمْ عَنْ عَائِشَةَ، قَالَتْ: كَانَ رَسُولُ اللهِ صَلَّى اللهُ عَلَيْهِ وَسَلَّمَ يُصَلِّي الضُّحَى أَرْبَعًا، وَيَزِيدُ مَا شَاءَ اللهُ.

Isḥāq ibn Ibrāhīm and Ibn Bashshār narrated: both from Muʿādh ibn Hishām; he said: my father narrated to me; from Qatādah; with the same chain of transmission: **the same text.**

وَحَدَّثَنَا إِسْحَاقُ بْنُ إِبْرَاهِيمَ وَابْنُ بَشَّارٍ، جَمِيعًا عَنْ مُعَاذِ بْنِ هِشَامٍ، قَالَ حَدَّثَنِي أَبِي، عَنْ قَتَادَةَ، بِهَذَا الإِسْنَادِ مِثْلَهُ

[1412–80]. (Dar al-Salam 1553) Muhammad ibn al-Muthannā and Ibn Bashshār narrated: both said: Muhammad ibn Jaʿfar narrated; Shuʿbah narrated; from ʿAmr ibn Murrah; from ʿAbd al-Raḥmān ibn Abi Laylā. He said: **'No one told me that he saw the Prophet praying the Ḍuḥā Prayer except Umm Hāni. She narrated that the Prophet (peace be upon him) entered her home on the day when Makkah fell to Islam and he prayed eight *rakʿahs*. "I never saw him praying a lighter prayer, but his bowing and prostration were perfect".'**

Ibn Bashshār did not mention in his narration the word: ***'qaṭṭ'***.[i]

i. This word is added for emphasis and it occurs in Umm Hāni's statement 'I never saw him...' It means 'never'.

وَحَدَّثَنَا مُحَمَّدُ بْنُ الْـمُثَنَّى وَابْنُ بَشَّارٍ، قَالا: حَدَّثَنَا مُحَمَّدُ بْنُ جَعْفَرٍ، حَدَّثَنَا شُعْبَةُ، عَنْ عَمْرِو بْنِ مُرَّةَ، عَنْ عَبْدِ الرَّحْمَنِ بْنِ أَبِي لَيْلَى قَالَ: مَا أَخْبَرَنِي أَحَدٌ أَنَّهُ رَأَى النَّبِيَّ صَلَّى اللهُ عَلَيْهِ وَسَلَّمَ يُصَلِّي الضُّحَى، إِلاَّ أُمُّ هَانِئٍ، فَإِنَّهَا حَدَّثَتْ أَنَّ النَّبِيَّ صَلَّى اللهُ عَلَيْهِ وَسَلَّمَ دَخَلَ بَيْتَهَا يَوْمَ فَتْحِ مَكَّةَ، فَصَلَّى ثَمَانِيَ رَكَعَاتٍ، مَا رَأَيْتُهُ صَلَّى صَلاَةً قَطُّ أَخَفَّ مِنْهَا. غَيْرَ أَنَّهُ كَانَ يُتِمُّ الرُّكُوعَ وَالسُّجُودَ. وَلَمْ يَذْكُرِ ابْنُ بَشَّارٍ فِي حَدِيثِهِ قَوْلَهُ قَطُّ.

[1413–81]. (Dar al-Salam 1554) Ḥarmalah ibn Yaḥyā and Muhammad ibn Maslamah al-Murādī narrated to me: both said: ʿAbdullāh ibn Wahb reported; Yūnus reported to me; from Ibn Shihāb; he said: Ibn ʿAbdullāh ibn al-Ḥārith narrated to me; that his father ʿAbdullāh ibn al-Ḥārith ibn Nawfal said: **'I asked and I was keen to find someone to tell me that God's Messenger (peace be upon him) prayed the Ḍuḥā sunnah prayer, and I could find no one. However, Umm Hāni' bint Abu Ṭālib mentioned to me that God's Messenger (peace be upon him) came when the day was fully bright, on the day Makkah fell to Islam, and he was brought a robe to screen him as he took a bath. He then stood up and prayed eight *rakʿahs*. I am not sure which was longest: his standing up, bowing or prostration. All were of nearly equal lengths. She said: "I never saw him praying [this prayer] before or after that time".'**

Al-Murādī said: **'from Yūnus'**, not: **'Yūnus reported to me'**.

وَحَدَّثَنِي حَرْمَلَةُ بْنُ يَحْيَى وَمُحَمَّدُ بْنُ سَلَمَةَ الْـمُرَادِيُّ، قَالا: أَخْبَرَنَا عَبْدُ اللهِ بْنُ وَهْبٍ، أَخْبَرَنِي يُونُسُ، عَنِ ابْنِ شِهَابٍ، قَالَ حَدَّثَنِي ابْنُ عَبْدِ اللهِ بْنِ الْحَارِثِ، أَنَّ أَبَاهُ عَبْدَ اللهِ بْنَ الْحَارِثِ بْنِ نَوْفَلٍ قَالَ: سَأَلْتُ وَحَرَصْتُ عَلَى أَنْ أَجِدَ أَحَدًا مِنَ النَّاسِ يُخْبِرُنِي أَنَّ رَسُولَ اللهِ صَلَّى اللهُ عَلَيْهِ وَسَلَّمَ سَبَّحَ سُبْحَةَ الضُّحَى، فَلَمْ أَجِدْ أَحَدًا يُحَدِّثُنِي ذَلِكَ. غَيْرَ أَنَّ أُمَّ هَانِئٍ بِنْتَ أَبِي طَالِبٍ أَخْبَرَتْنِي أَنَّ رَسُولَ اللهِ صَلَّى اللهُ عَلَيْهِ وَسَلَّمَ أَتَى بَعْدَ مَا

ارْتَفَعَ النَّهَارُ يَوْمَ الْفَتْحِ، فَأُتِيَ بِثَوْبٍ فَسُتِرَ عَلَيْهِ، فَاغْتَسَلَ، ثُمَّ قَامَ فَرَكَعَ ثَمَانِيَ رَكَعَاتٍ. لاَ أَدْرِي أَقِيَامُهُ فِيهَا أَطْوَلُ أَمْ رُكُوعُهُ أَمْ سُجُودُهُ: كُلُّ ذَلِكَ مِنْهُ مُتَقَارِبٌ. قالت: فَلَمْ أَرَهُ سَبَّحَهَا قَبْلُ وَلاَ بَعْدُ. قَالَ الْـمُرَادِيُّ عَنْ يُونُس، وَلَمْ يَقُلْ أَخْبَرَنِي.

[1414–82]. (Dar al-Salam 1555) Yaḥyā ibn Yaḥyā narrated: he said: I read out to Mālik; from Abu al-Naḍr; that Abu Murrah, Umm Hāni' bint Abu Ṭālib's *mawlā*, reported to him; that he heard Umm Hāni' bint Abu Ṭālib say: **'I went to see God's Messenger (peace be upon him) in the year Makkah fell to Islam, and I found him taking a bath and his daughter Fāṭimah screening him with a robe. I greeted him with *salām*, and he said: "Who is this?" I said: "Umm Hāni' bint Abi Ṭālib". He said: "Welcome to Umm Hāni'". When he finished his bath, he stood up and prayed eight *rakʿahs*, wearing only one garment. When he finished, I said: "Messenger of God, my mother's son, ʿAlī ibn Abi Ṭālib, says that he will be killing a man to whom I extended protection, so-and-so ibn Hubayrah". God's Messenger (peace be upon him) said: "We protect the one you have protected, Umm Hāni'". Umm Hāni' said: "This was in the mid-morning".'**

حَدَّثَنَا يَحْيَى بْنُ يَحْيَى قَالَ: قَرَأْتُ عَلَى مَالِكٍ عَنْ أَبِي النَّضْرِ، أَنَّ أَبَا مُرَّةَ، مَوْلَى أُمِّ هَانِئٍ بِنْتِ أَبِي طَالِبٍ، أَخْبَرَهُ أَنَّهُ سَمِعَ أُمَّ هَانِئٍ بِنْتَ أَبِي طَالِبٍ تَقُولُ: ذَهَبْتُ إِلَى رَسُولِ اللهِ صَلَّى اللهُ عَلَيْهِ وَسَلَّمَ عَامَ الْفَتْحِ، فَوَجَدْتُهُ يَغْتَسِلُ وَفَاطِمَةُ ابْنَتُهُ تَسْتُرُهُ بِثَوْبٍ. قَالَتْ: فَسَلَّمْتُ، فَقَالَ «مَنْ هَذِهِ»؟ قُلْتُ: أُمُّ هَانِئٍ بِنْتُ أَبِي طَالِبٍ. قَالَ: «مَرْحَبًا بِأُمِّ هَانِئٍ». فَلَمَّا فَرَغَ مِنْ غُسْلِهِ قَامَ فَصَلَّى ثَمَانِيَ رَكَعَاتٍ، مُلْتَحِفًا فِي ثَوْبٍ وَاحِدٍ. فَلَمَّا انْصَرَفَ قُلْتُ: يَا رَسُولَ اللهِ، زَعَمَ ابْنُ أُمِّي عَلِيُّ بْنُ أَبِي طَالِبٍ أَنَّهُ قَاتِلٌ رَجُلاً أَجَرْتُهُ، فُلاَنُ بْنُ هُبَيْرَةَ. فَقَالَ رَسُولُ اللهِ صَلَّى اللهُ عَلَيْهِ وَسَلَّمَ: «قَدْ أَجَرْنَا مَنْ أَجَرْتِ يَا أُمَّ هَانِئٍ». قَالَتْ أُمُّ هَانِئٍ: وَذَلِكَ ضُحًى.

[1415–83]. (Dar al-Salam 1556) Ḥajjāj ibn al-Shā'ir narrated to me: Mu'allā ibn Asad narrated; Wuhayb ibn Khālid narrated; from Ja'far ibn Muhammad; from his father; from Abu Murrah, 'Aqīl's *mawlā*, from Umm Hāni'; that **'God's Messenger (peace be upon him) prayed in her home, in the year Makkah fell to Islam, eight *rak'ahs*, wearing one garment and crossing its end parts'.**

وَحَدَّثَنِي حَجَّاجُ بْنُ الشَّاعِرِ، حَدَّثَنَا مُعَلَّى بْنُ أَسَدٍ، حَدَّثَنَا وُهَيْبُ بْنُ خَالِدٍ، عَنْ جَعْفَرِ بْنِ مُحَمَّدٍ، عَنْ أَبِيهِ، عَنْ أَبِي مُرَّةَ مَوْلَى عَقِيلٍ، عَنْ أُمِّ هَانِئٍ أَنَّ رَسُولَ اللهِ صَلَّى اللهُ عَلَيْهِ وَسَلَّمَ صَلَّى فِي بَيْتِهَا عَامَ الْفَتْحِ ثَمَانِيَ رَكَعَاتٍ، فِي ثَوْبٍ وَاحِدٍ، قَدْ خَالَفَ بَيْنَ طَرَفَيْهِ.

[1416–84]. (Dar al-Salam 1557) 'Abdullāh ibn Muhammad ibn Asmā' al-Ḍuba'ī narrated: Mahdī (who is Ibn Maymūn) narrated; Wāṣil, Abu 'Uyaynah's *mawlā*, narrated; from Yaḥyā ibn 'Uqayl; from Yaḥyā ibn Ya'mar; from Abu al-Aswad al-Du'alī; from Abu Dharr; from the Prophet (peace be upon him); that he said: **'Every joint in anyone's body is required to give a *ṣadaqah* every day: every *subḥān Allah* is a *ṣadaqah*, every *alḥamd lillāh* is a *ṣadaqah*, every *lā ilāha illa Allah* is a *ṣadaqah*, every *Allah-u akbar* is a *ṣadaqah*, enjoining something good is a *ṣadaqah* and discouraging something wrong is a *ṣadaqah*. Two *rak'ahs* offered in the mid-morning are equal to all that'.**

حَدَّثَنَا عَبْدُ اللهِ بْنُ مُحَمَّدِ بْنِ أَسْمَاءَ الضُّبَعِيُّ، حَدَّثَنَا مَهْدِيٌّ (وَهُوَ ابْنُ مَيْمُونٍ) حَدَّثَنَا وَاصِلٌ مَوْلَى أَبِي عُيَيْنَةَ، عَنْ يَحْيَى بْنِ عُقَيْلٍ، عَنْ يَحْيَى بْنِ يَعْمَرَ، عَنْ أَبِي الأَسْوَدِ الدُّؤَلِيِّ، عَنْ أَبِي ذَرٍّ، عَنِ النَّبِيِّ صَلَّى اللهُ عَلَيْهِ وَسَلَّمَ أَنَّهُ قَالَ: «يُصْبِحُ عَلَى كُلِّ سُلاَمَى مِنْ أَحَدِكُمْ صَدَقَةٌ، فَكُلُّ تَسْبِيحَةٍ صَدَقَةٌ، وَكُلُّ تَحْمِيدَةٍ صَدَقَةٌ، وَكُلُّ تَهْلِيلَةٍ صَدَقَةٌ، وَكُلُّ تَكْبِيرَةٍ صَدَقَةٌ، وَأَمْرٌ بِالْمَعْرُوفِ صَدَقَةٌ، وَنَهْيٌ عَنِ الْمُنْكَرِ صَدَقَةٌ. وَيُجْزِئُ مِنْ ذَلِكَ رَكْعَتَانِ يَرْكَعُهُمَا مِنَ الضُّحَى».

[1417–85]. (Dar al-Salam 1558) Shaybān ibn Farrūkh narrated: ʿAbd al-Wārith narrated; Abu al-Tayyāḥ narrated; Abu ʿUthmān al-Nahdī narrated to me; from Abu Hurayrah. He said: **'My friend (peace be upon him) urged me to maintain three things: fasting three days in every month, praying two *rakʿahs* in the mid-morning and praying Witr before I go to bed'.**

حَدَّثَنَا شَيْبَانُ بْنُ فَرُّوخَ، حَدَّثَنَا عَبْدُ الْوَارِثِ، حَدَّثَنَا أَبُو التَّيَّاحِ، حَدَّثَنِي أَبُو عُثْمَانَ النَّهْدِيُّ، عَنْ أَبِي هُرَيْرَةَ قَالَ: «أَوْصَانِي خَلِيلِي صَلَّى اللهُ عَلَيْهِ وَسَلَّمَ بِثَلَاثٍ: بِصِيَامِ ثَلَاثَةِ أَيَّامٍ مِنْ كُلِّ شَهْرٍ، وَرَكْعَتَيِ الضُّحَى، وَأَنْ أُوتِرَ قَبْلَ أَنْ أَرْقُدَ».

[000–000]. (Dar al-Salam 1559–1560) Muhammad ibn al-Muthannā and Ibn Bashshār narrated: both said: Muhammad ibn Jaʿfar narrated; Shuʿbah narrated; from ʿAbbās al-Jurayrī and Abu Shimr al-Ḍubaʿī; both said: we heard Abu ʿUthmān al-Nahdī narrating; from Abu Hurayrah; from the Prophet (peace be upon him): **the same text**.

وَحَدَّثَنَا مُحَمَّدُ بْنُ الْمُثَنَّى وَابْنُ بَشَّارٍ، قَالَا: حَدَّثَنَا مُحَمَّدُ بْنُ جَعْفَرٍ، حَدَّثَنَا شُعْبَةُ، عَنْ عَبَّاسٍ الْجُرَيْرِيِّ وَأَبِي شِمْرٍ الضُّبَعِيِّ، قَالَا: سَمِعْنَا أَبَا عُثْمَانَ النَّهْدِيَّ، يُحَدِّثُ عَنْ أَبِي هُرَيْرَةَ، عَنِ النَّبِيِّ صَلَّى اللهُ عَلَيْهِ وَسَلَّمَ بِمِثْلِهِ.

Sulaymān ibn Maʿbad narrated to me: Muʿallā ibn Asad narrated; ʿAbd al-ʿAzīz ibn Mukhtār; from ʿAbdullāh al-Dānāj; he said: Abu Rāfiʿ al-Ṣā'igh narrated to me. He said: **'I heard Abu Hurayrah say: "My friend, Abu al-Qāsim (peace be upon him), urged me to maintain three things…".' He mentioned the same as narrated by Abu ʿUthmān from Abu Hurayrah.**

وَحَدَّثَنِي سُلَيْمَانُ بْنُ مَعْبَدٍ، حَدَّثَنَا مُعَلَّى بْنُ أَسَدٍ، حَدَّثَنَا عَبْدُ الْعَزِيزِ بْنُ مُخْتَارٍ، عَنْ عَبْدِ اللهِ الدَّانَاجِ قَالَ: حَدَّثَنِي أَبُو رَافِعٍ الصَّائِغُ قَالَ: سَمِعْتُ أَبَا هُرَيْرَةَ قَالَ: أَوْصَانِي خَلِيلِي أَبُو الْقَاسِمِ صَلَّى اللهُ عَلَيْهِ وَسَلَّمَ بِثَلَاثٍ. فَذَكَرَ مِثْلَ حَدِيثِ أَبِي عُثْمَانَ عَنْ أَبِي هُرَيْرَةَ.

[1418–86]. (Dar al-Salam 1561) Ḥarūn ibn ʿAbdullāh and Muhammad ibn Rāfiʿ narrated to me: both said: Ibn Abi Fudayk narrated; from al-Ḍaḥḥāk ibn ʿUthmān; from Ibrāhīm ibn ʿAbdullāh ibn Ḥunayn; from Abu Murrah, Umm Hāni's *mawlā*; from Abu al-Dardā'. He said: **'My beloved one (peace be upon him) urged me to maintain three things, and I will not abandon them for the rest of my life: fasting three days every month, the Ḍuḥā Prayer and that I do not go to sleep before I pray Witr'.**

وَحَدَّثَنِي هَارُونُ بْنُ عَبْدِ اللهِ وَمُحَمَّدُ بْنُ رَافِعٍ، قَالَا: حَدَّثَنَا ابْنُ أَبِي فُدَيْكٍ، عَنِ الضَّحَّاكِ بْنِ عُثْمَانَ، عَنْ إِبْرَاهِيمَ بْنِ عَبْدِ اللهِ بْنِ حُنَيْنٍ، عَنْ أَبِي مُرَّةَ مَوْلَى أُمِّ هَانِئٍ، عَنْ أَبِي الدَّرْدَاءِ قَالَ: «أَوْصَانِي حَبِيبِي صَلَّى اللهُ عَلَيْهِ وَسَلَّمَ بِثَلَاثٍ لَنْ أَدَعَهُنَّ مَا عِشْتُ: بِصِيَامِ ثَلَاثَةِ أَيَّامٍ مِنْ كُلِّ شَهْرٍ، وَصَلَاةِ الضُّحَى، وَبِأَنْ لَا أَنَامَ حَتَّى أُوتِرَ.

Text Explanation

These hadiths quote ʿĀ'ishah stating that the Prophet did not pray the Ḍuḥā Prayer except when he returned from a journey. In another hadith, she says that she offers this prayer although she never saw the Prophet doing so. Yet she reports that he used to pray it in four *rakʿahs* and add any additional number. Umm Hāni's report mentions that the Prophet offered it in eight *rakʿahs*, while it is only two *rakʿahs* in the hadiths narrated by Abu Hurayrah and Abu al-Dardā'.

According to scholars of insight, all these hadiths confirm each other and there is no disagreement between them. The message they give is that the Ḍuḥā Prayer is a regular sunnah and that it may be offered in as few as two *rakʿahs* but its most perfect version is eight *rakʿahs*. In between, it may be in four or six *rakʿahs*, but both of these are better than two *rakʿahs* and less than eight. ʿĀ'ishah gives two different statements: one says that the Prophet did not pray this prayer except when he returned from a journey, and the other mentions that he prayed it. These hadiths are reconciled on the basis that he used to pray it sometimes because of the reward it earned and he did not pray it at other times so as to ensure that it did not become obligatory, as ʿĀ'ishah herself suggests. Her statement that he did not pray it 'except when he returned from a journey' is understood to mean that she did not see him doing it except on such an occasion. This is what she said in the other report: 'I never saw God's Messenger (peace be upon him) praying the Ḍuḥā sunnah'. The reason is that the Prophet very rarely happened to be in ʿĀ'ishah's home in the mid-morning. He might be on a journey or staying in Madinah but was in the mosque or some other place. If he was with his wives, she had only one day in nine. Thus, she states a fact when she says that she did not see him offering it. She would know that he did it only if the Prophet or someone else told her. Alternatively, we may say that her statement that 'he did not pray it' means that he did not do it regularly. Thus the negative applies to regularity and consistency, not to merely offering it, but God knows best.

It is confirmed that Ibn ʿUmar said Ḍuḥā is a deviation [i.e. *bidʿah*]. This is understood to mean that to offer it in the mosque and be keen to be seen doing so is a deviation. It should be offered at home and in similar places. Alternatively, we may say that he meant offering it regularly and consistently is a deviation because the Prophet did not do so, fearing that it might become obligatory. This, however, applies to the Prophet only. It is confirmed by the hadiths narrated by Abu Hurayrah and Abu al-Dardā' that we Muslims may offer it regularly. It may also be said that Ibn ʿUmar was not aware that the Prophet offered it and encouraged offering it. Whatever the case may be, the majority of scholars say that the Ḍuḥā Prayer is desirable, but the opposite opinion is reported to have been expressed by Ibn Masʿūd and Ibn ʿUmar, and God knows best.

In hadith No. 1408, ʿĀ'ishah mentions that the Prophet might decide not to do something and yet would have loved to do it. His reason for abstaining stemmed from his fear that it might become obligatory. In other words, he refrained out of compassion and kindness for his community. When different interests clashed, he would choose the most important.

Hadith No. 1414 mentions that Umm Hāni' offered the *salām* greeting when she went to see the Prophet. This makes it clear that a woman may offer such a greeting to a man in the presence of his immediate female relatives. When the Prophet asked: 'Who is this?' She answered, stating her appellation [i.e. *kunyah*]: 'Umm Hāni''. This means that it is acceptable for a person to state his or her appellation to identify themselves if such an appellation is well known. The hadith further suggests that when a person seeks admission, the one inside may ask who the person is, and it is incumbent upon that person to identify himself.

The Prophet said to his visitor: 'Welcome to Umm Hāni'.' It is recommended, then, to say to one's visitor, welcome, or other words of kind reception. The hadith suggests that, unlike the case of answering the call of nature, it is appropriate to speak to another person when one is taking a bath or performing the ablution, but not to greet them with *salām*. It further suggests that a man may take a bath in the presence of a woman who is a close relative, i.e. a *maḥram*, if his private parts are covered, and it is permissible for such a woman to screen him with a robe or a sheet.

In hadith No. 1414, Umm Hāni' mentions that when the Prophet finished his bath 'he prayed eight *rakʿahs*, wearing one garment'. This makes it clear that it is permissible to pray wearing one garment. In the next hadith, she mentions the way the Prophet crossed its end parts. [This means that the garment was large, and a man wrapped himself with it, covering himself from above the waistline to well below his knees, bringing its right end from under his right arm and over his left shoulder. Then bringing the left end from under his left arm and over his right shoulder, thus leaving his two arms uncovered.]

When the Prophet finished his prayer, she told him: 'My mother's son, ʿAlī ibn Abi Ṭālib, says that he will be killing a man[i] to whom I extended protection, so-and-so ibn Hubayrah. God's Messenger (peace be upon him) said: "We protect the one you have protected, Umm Hāni'".' This makes it clear that one should wait until the person one wants to speak to finishes his immediate business before putting one's request, unless one fears that a delay may lead to a problem. The way Umm Hāni' put her case shows clearly that she disagreed with her brother, whom she referred to as 'my mother's son' although he was her full brother. This was done to emphasise the closeness of the two and that they were reared by the same mother. It is the same as when Aaron spoke to his brother, Moses, addressing him as 'my mother's son', as reported in the Qur'an (7: 150)

Some of our Shāfiʿī scholars and the majority of scholars cite this hadith as evidence that a Muslim woman could extend protection to other people. They say that the hadith is understood to mean that the Islamic ruling is that your protection is right and permissible. Other scholars say that the hadith does not provide such evidence because although the hadith admits this meaning, it may also be understood to refer to an initial case of protection. This disagreement among scholars is similar to their disagreement concerning the hadith that quotes the Prophet: 'Whoever kills an enemy takes his booty'. They differed as to whether this was a rule for all wars until the Day of Judgement or an exception decided by the ruler on that specific occasion. In the latter scenario, it requires the ruler's decision on every occasion. Otherwise, it does not apply. Al-Shāfiʿī and other scholars take up the first view concerning a woman's protection, while Abu Ḥanīfah and Mālik uphold the second. In support of the majority, we may say that the Prophet (peace be upon him) did not object to Umm Hāni' extending protection, nor did he tell her that

---

i. When the Muslim army moved into Makkah, the city was taken over peacefully, except for a local skirmish. The Prophet had named certain persons to be killed because of their hardened hostility to Islam and the Muslims, but most of them were subsequently pardoned, as in this case. ʿAlī wanted to kill this person in line with the Prophet's instructions, but his sister protected him, and the Prophet approved her action.

she could not do so. Had it been wrong, he would have made this clear to her so that no one would take it wrongly.

In hadith No. 1414, Umm Hāni' refers to the man she was protecting as so-and-so ibn Hubayrah. As reported in other anthologies, the narration quotes Umm Hāni' saying: 'Two men of my in-laws sought refuge with me'. In al-Zubayr ibn Bakkār's book, [*al-Nasab*], we read that so-and-so ibn Hubayrah was al-Ḥārith ibn Hishām of the Makhzūm clan of the Quraysh, while others say that he was ʿAbdullāh ibn Abi Rabīʿah. In al-Azraqī's *Tārīkh Makkah,* it is reported that she gave protection to two men: one was ʿAbdullāh ibn Abi Rabīʿah ibn al-Mughīrah and the other al-Ḥārith ibn Hishām ibn al-Mughīrah, both from the Makhzūm clan. What al-Azraqī mentions gives us the names of both and confirms all reports.

In the same hadith, Umm Hāni' mentions that this occurred mid-morning. Our scholars and the majority of scholars take this as confirming the desirability of praying the Ḍuḥā sunnah in eight *rakʿahs*, but *Qadi* ʿIyāḍ and other scholars do not accept it as evidence confirming this. They say that she only mentions the time of his prayer, not how the Prophet intended it. It might have been a prayer expressing gratitude to God for giving him Makkah. This argument is incorrect. It is indeed correct to cite the hadith as evidence confirming the Ḍuḥā Prayer. Umm Hāni' is authentically quoted as saying that the Prophet prayed Ḍuḥā in eight *rak'ahs*, finishing every two *rakʿahs* with *salām,* on the day when Makkah was taken over. In his *Sunan* anthology, Abu Dāwūd enters this hadith in this wording and an authentic chain of transmission that fulfils al-Bukhari's conditions.

In hadith No. 1416, the Prophet mentions that every day everyone needs to give a *ṣadaqah,* which means charity, for every joint in one's body. We will discuss a hadith that comes later in Muslim's *Ṣaḥīḥ* which says that 'man is created with three hundred and sixty joints, and a *ṣadaqah* is due for every joint'. In this hadith, the Prophet says that 'two *rakʿahs* offered in the mid-morning are equal to all this'. This tells us the importance of this prayer and the great reward it earns. It also shows that it is deemed fulfilled with two *rakʿahs*.

In hadith No. 1417, the narrator, Abu Hurayrah, describes the Prophet as 'my friend'. This does not contradict the Prophet's statement, 'Were I to choose anyone of my community as my friend…'. This means that the Prophet would not choose anyone as his special friend, but this does not exclude the possibility that one of the Prophet's Companions chose him as a special friend. This hadith and the one narrated by Abu al-Dardā', No. 1418, urge offering the Ḍuḥā voluntary prayer, which is acceptable in two *rak'ahs*, fasting three days every month and observing the Witr Prayer before going to bed if one fears not being able to wake up late at night to offer it. This is how these two hadiths are understood to explain what Muslim relates later, which will be discussed in due course, God willing.

Transmission

Umm Hāni''s name was generally known as Fākhitah, but she is also said to be named Hind. Her appellation came about because her son was named Hāni'.

Abu Murrah is mentioned in one hadith as the *mawlā* of Umm Hāni' and in another as the *mawlā* of 'Aqīl ibn Abi Ṭālib. He was in fact Umm Hāni''s but attached to her brother 'Aqīl because he attended him regularly.

Abu Shimr is mentioned as one of the narrators in the third chain of transmission of hadith No. 1417. His name is also pronounced as Abu Shamir. He is included among people who are known by their appellations [i.e. *kunyah*] while their names are unknown.

CHAPTER 14

THE FAJR SUNNAH PRAYER

[1419–87]. (Dar al-Salam 1562–1563) Yaḥyā ibn Yaḥyā narrated:[i] he said: I read out to Mālik; from Nāfiʿ; from Ibn ʿUmar; that Ḥafṣah, the Mother of the Believers, told him; that **'When the caller has finished the *adhān* for Fajr Prayer and the dawn has broken, God's Messenger (peace be upon him) would pray two light *rakʿahs* before the [congregational] prayer is announced [with *iqāmah*]'.**

حَدَّثَنَا يَحْيَى بْنُ يَحْيَى قَالَ: قَرَأْتُ عَلَى مَالِكٍ عَنْ نَافِعٍ، عَنِ ابْنِ عُمَرَ، أَنَّ حَفْصَةَ أُمَّ الْمُؤْمِنِينَ أَخْبَرَتْهُ أَنَّ رَسُولَ اللهِ صَلَّى اللهُ عَلَيْهِ وَسَلَّمَ كَانَ إِذَا سَكَتَ الْمُؤَذِّنُ مِنَ الأَذَانِ لِصَلاَةِ الصُّبْحِ، وَبَدَا الصُّبْحُ، رَكَعَ رَكْعَتَيْنِ خَفِيفَتَيْنِ قَبْلَ أَنْ تُقَامَ الصَّلاَةُ.

Yaḥyā ibn Yaḥyā, Qutaybah and Ibn Rumḥ narrated: from al-Layth ibn Saʿd [H]. Also, Zuhayr ibn Ḥarb and ʿUbaydullāh ibn Saʿīd narrated to me; both said: Yaḥyā narrated; from ʿUbaydullāh [H]. And, Zuhayr ibn Ḥarb narrated to me; Ismāʿīl narrated; from Ayyūb; all from Nāfiʿ; with the same chain of transmission: **the same text as Mālik's**.

وَحَدَّثَنَا يَحْيَى بْنُ يَحْيَى وَقُتَيْبَةُ وَابْنُ رُمْحٍ، عَنِ اللَّيْثِ بْنِ سَعْدٍ، ح. وَحَدَّثَنِي زُهَيْرُ بْنُ حَرْبٍ وَعُبَيْدُ اللهِ بْنُ سَعِيدٍ، قَالاَ: حَدَّثَنَا يَحْيَى، عَنْ عُبَيْدِ اللهِ، ح. وَحَدَّثَنِي زُهَيْرُ بْنُ حَرْبٍ، حَدَّثَنَا إِسْمَاعِيلُ، عَنْ أَيُّوبَ، كُلُّهُمْ عَنْ نَافِعٍ، بِهَذَا الإِسْنَادِ، كَمَا قَالَ مَالِكٌ.

---

i. Related by al-Bukhari, 618, 1173 and 1181; al-Tirmidhī, 433; al-Nasāʾī, 582, 1759 and 1775; Ibn Mājah, 1145.

[1420–88]. (Dar al-Salam 1564–1565) Ahmad ibn ʿAbdullāh ibn al-Ḥakam narrated to me: Muhammad ibn Jaʿfar narrated; Shuʿbah narrated; from Zayd ibn Muhammad; he said: I heard Nāfiʿ narrating from Ibn ʿUmar; from Ḥafṣah. She said: **'When the dawn had broken, God's Messenger (peace be upon him) did not pray more than two light *rakʿahs*'.**

وَحَدَّثَنِي أَحْمَدُ بْنُ عَبْدِ اللهِ بْنِ الْحَكَمِ، حَدَّثَنَا مُحَمَّدُ بْنُ جَعْفَرٍ، حَدَّثَنَا شُعْبَةُ، عَنْ زَيْدِ بْنِ مُحَمَّدٍ قَالَ: سَمِعْتُ نَافِعًا يُحَدِّثُ عَنِ ابْنِ عُمَرَ، عَنْ حَفْصَةَ قَالَتْ: كَانَ رَسُولُ اللهِ صَلَّى اللهُ عَلَيْهِ وَسَلَّمَ إِذَا طَلَعَ الْفَجْرُ لاَ يُصَلِّي إِلاَّ رَكْعَتَيْنِ خَفِيفَتَيْنِ.

Isḥāq ibn Ibrāhīm narrated: al-Naḍr reported; Shuʿbah narrated; with the same chain of transmission: **the same text.**

وَحَدَّثَنَاهُ إِسْحَاقُ بْنُ إِبْرَاهِيمَ، أَخْبَرَنَا النَّضْرُ، حَدَّثَنَا شُعْبَةُ، بِهَذَا الإِسْنَادِ: مِثْلَهُ.

[1421–89]. (Dar al-Salam 1566) Muhammad ibn ʿAbbād narrated; Sufyān narrated; from ʿAmr; from al-Zuhrī; from Sālim; from his father: **'Ḥafṣah reported to me that God's Messenger (peace be upon him) used to pray two *rakʿahs* when the dawn was clear before him'.**

حَدَّثَنَا مُحَمَّدُ بْنُ عَبَّادٍ، حَدَّثَنَا سُفْيَانُ، عَنْ عَمْرٍو، عَنِ الزُّهْرِيِّ، عَنْ سَالِمٍ، عَنْ أَبِيهِ: أَخْبَرَتْنِي حَفْصَةُ أَنَّ النَّبِيَّ صَلَّى اللهُ عَلَيْهِ وَسَلَّمَ كَانَ إِذَا أَضَاءَ لَهُ الْفَجْرُ صَلَّى رَكْعَتَيْنِ.

[1422–90]. (Dar al-Salam 1567) ʿAmr al-Nāqid narrated: ʿAbdah ibn Sulaymān narrated; Hishām ibn ʿUrwah narrated; from his father; from ʿĀ'ishah. She said: **'God's Messenger (peace be upon him) used to pray the two *rakʿahs* of the Fajr [sunnah] when he had heard the *adhān*, and he used to make them light'.**

حَدَّثَنَا عَمْرٌو النَّاقِدُ، حَدَّثَنَا عَبْدَةُ بْنُ سُلَيْمَانَ، حَدَّثَنَا هِشَامُ بْنُ عُرْوَةَ، عَنْ أَبِيهِ، عَنْ عَائِشَةَ قَالَتْ: كَانَ رَسُولُ اللهِ صَلَّى اللهُ عَلَيْهِ وَسَلَّمَ يُصَلِّي رَكْعَتَيِ الْفَجْرِ إِذَا سَمِعَ الأَذَانَ، وَيُخَفِّفُهُمَا.

[1423–000]. (Dar al-Salam 1568) ʿAlī ibn Ḥujr narrated: ʿAlī (meaning Ibn Mushir) narrated [H]. Also, Abu Kurayb narrated it; Abu Usāmah narrated [H]. And, Abu Bakr, Abu Kurayb and Ibn Numayr narrated it; from ʿAbdullāh ibn Numayr [H]. Also, ʿAmr al-Nāqid narrated it; Wakīʿ narrated; all from Hishām; with the same chain of transmission.

In Abu Usāmah's narration: **'After the break of dawn'.**

وَحَدَّثَنِيهِ عَلِيُّ بْنُ حُجْرٍ، حَدَّثَنَا عَلِيٌّ (يَعْنِي ابْنَ مُسْهِرٍ)، ح. وَحَدَّثَنَاهُ أَبُو كُرَيْبٍ، حَدَّثَنَا أَبُو أُسَامَةَ، ح. وَحَدَّثَنَاهُ أَبُو بَكْرٍ وَأَبُو كُرَيْبٍ وَابْنُ نُمَيْرٍ، عَنْ عَبْدِ اللهِ بْنِ نُمَيْرٍ، ح. وَحَدَّثَنَاهُ عَمْرٌو النَّاقِدُ، حَدَّثَنَا وَكِيعٌ، كُلُّهُمْ عَنْ هِشَامٍ، بِهَذَا الإِسْنَادِ. وَفِي حَدِيثِ أَبِي أُسَامَةَ إِذَا طَلَعَ الْفَجْرُ.

[1424–91]. (Dar al-Salam 1569) Muhammad ibn al-Muthannā narrated:[i] Ibn Abi ʿAdiy narrated; from Hishām; from Yaḥyā ibn Abi Salamah; from ʿĀ'ishah; that **'The Prophet (peace be upon him) used to pray two *rakʿahs* between the *adhān* and the *iqāmah* of the Fajr Prayer'.**

وَحَدَّثَنَاهُ مُحَمَّدُ بْنُ الْمُثَنَّى، حَدَّثَنَا ابْنُ أَبِي عَدِيٍّ، عَنْ هِشَامٍ، عَنْ يَحْيَى، عَنْ أَبِي سَلَمَةَ، عَنْ عَائِشَةَ أَنَّ نَبِيَّ اللهِ صَلَّى اللهُ عَلَيْهِ وَسَلَّمَ كَانَ يُصَلِّي رَكْعَتَيْنِ بَيْنَ النِّدَاءِ وَالإِقَامَةِ مِنْ صَلاَةِ الصُّبْحِ.

---

i. Related by al-Bukhari, 619.

[1425–92]. (Dar al-Salam 1570) Muhammad ibn al-Muthannā narrated:[i] ʿAbd al-Wahhāb narrated; he said: I heard Yaḥyā ibn Saʿīd say: Muhammad ibn ʿAbd al-Raḥmān reported to me; that he heard ʿAmrah narrating from ʿĀ'ishah; that she used to say: **'God's Messenger (peace be upon him) used to pray the two *rakʿahs* of the Fajr [sunnah] and he would make them so light that I wondered, has he recited the Fātiḥah in them?'.**

وَحَدَّثَنَا مُحَمَّدُ بْنُ الْمُثَنَّى، حَدَّثَنَا عَبْدُ الْوَهَّابِ قَالَ: سَمِعْتُ يَحْيَى بْنَ سَعِيدٍ قَالَ: أَخْبَرَنِي مُحَمَّدُ بْنُ عَبْدِ الرَّحْمَنِ أَنَّهُ سَمِعَ عَمْرَةَ تُحَدِّثُ عَنْ عَائِشَةَ أَنَّهَا كَانَتْ تَقُولُ: كَانَ رَسُولُ اللهِ صَلَّى اللهُ عَلَيْهِ وَسَلَّمَ يُصَلِّي رَكْعَتَيِ الْفَجْرِ فَيُخَفِّفُ حَتَّى إِنِّي أَقُولُ هَلْ قَرَأَ فِيهِمَا بِأُمِّ الْقُرْآنِ.

[1426–93]. (Dar al-Salam does not include this hadith) ʿUbaydullāh ibn Muʿādh narrated: my father narrated; Shuʿbah narrated; from Muhammad ibn ʿAbd al-Raḥmān al-Anṣārī; he heard ʿAmrah bint ʿAbd al-Raḥmān; from ʿĀ'ishah. She said: **'When the dawn had broken, God's Messenger (peace be upon him) would pray two *rakʿahs*. I would wonder whether he recited al-Fātiḥah in them'.**

حَدَّثَنَا عُبَيْدُ اللهِ بْنُ مُعَاذٍ، حَدَّثَنَا أَبِي، حَدَّثَنَا شُعْبَةُ، عَنْ مُحَمَّدِ بْنِ عَبْدِ الرَّحْمَنِ الأَنْصَارِيِّ، سَمِعَ عَمْرَةَ بِنْتَ عَبْدِ الرَّحْمَنِ، عَنْ عَائِشَةَ قَالَتْ: كَانَ رَسُولُ اللهِ صَلَّى اللهُ عَلَيْهِ وَسَلَّمَ إِذَا طَلَعَ الْفَجْرُ صَلَّى رَكْعَتَيْنِ أَقُولُ هَلْ يَقْرَأُ فِيهِمَا بِفَاتِحَةِ الْكِتَابِ.

[1427–94]. (Dar al-Salam 1571) Zuhayr ibn Ḥarb narrated to me:[ii] Yaḥyā ibn Saʿīd narrated; from Ibn Jurayj; he said: ʿAṭā'

---

i. Related by al-Bukhari, 1171; Abu Dāwūd, 1255; al-Nasā'ī, 945.
ii. Related by al-Bukhari, 1169; Abu Dāwūd, 1254.

narrated to me; from ʿUbayd ibn ʿUmayr; from ʿĀ'ishah; that **'The Prophet never attended more regularly to any sunnah prayer than the two *rakʿahs* before Fajr Prayer'.**

وَحَدَّثَنِي زُهَيْرُ بْنُ حَرْبٍ، حَدَّثَنَا يَحْيَى بْنُ سَعِيدٍ، عَنِ ابْنِ جُرَيْجٍ قَالَ: حَدَّثَنِي عَطَاءٌ، عَنْ عُبَيْدِ بْنِ عُمَيْرٍ، عَنْ عَائِشَةَ أَنَّ النَّبِيَّ صَلَّى اللهُ عَلَيْهِ وَسَلَّمَ لَمْ يَكُنْ عَلَى شَيْءٍ مِنَ النَّوَافِلِ أَشَدَّ مُعَاهَدَةً مِنْهُ عَلَى رَكْعَتَيْنِ قَبْلَ الصُّبْحِ.

[1428–95]. (Dar al-Salam 1572) Abu Bakr ibn Abi Shaybah and Ibn Numayr narrated: both from Ḥafṣ ibn Ghiyāth; Ibn Numayr said: Ḥafṣ narrated; from Ibn Jurayj; from ʿAṭā'; from ʿUbayd ibn ʿUmayr; from ʿĀ'ishah; she said: **'I never saw God's Messenger (peace be upon him) more quickly attending to any sunnah than to the two *rakʿahs* before Fajr Prayer'.**

وَحَدَّثَنَا أَبُو بَكْرِ بْنُ أَبِي شَيْبَةَ وَابْنُ نُمَيْرٍ، جَمِيعًا عَنْ حَفْصِ بْنِ غِيَاثٍ، قَالَ ابْنُ نُمَيْرٍ: حَدَّثَنَا حَفْصٌ، عَنِ ابْنِ جُرَيْجٍ، عَنْ عَطَاءٍ، عَنْ عُبَيْدِ بْنِ عُمَيْرٍ، عَنْ عَائِشَةَ قَالَتْ: مَا رَأَيْتُ رَسُولَ اللهِ صَلَّى اللهُ عَلَيْهِ وَسَلَّمَ فِي شَيْءٍ مِنَ النَّوَافِلِ أَسْرَعَ مِنْهُ إِلَى الرَّكْعَتَيْنِ قَبْلَ الْفَجْرِ.

[1429–96]. (Dar al-Salam 1573) Muhammad ibn ʿUbayd al-Ghubarī narrated:[i] Abu ʿAwānah narrated; from Qatādah; from Zurārah ibn Awfā; from Saʿd ibn Hishām; from ʿĀ'ishah; from the Prophet. He said: **'The two *rakʿahs* of Fajr are better than the whole world and all it contains'.**

حَدَّثَنَا مُحَمَّدُ بْنُ عُبَيْدٍ الْغُبَرِيُّ، حَدَّثَنَا أَبُو عَوَانَةَ، عَنْ قَتَادَةَ، عَنْ زُرَارَةَ بْنِ أَوْفَى، عَنْ سَعْدِ بْنِ هِشَامٍ، عَنْ عَائِشَةَ، عَنِ النَّبِيِّ صَلَّى اللهُ عَلَيْهِ وَسَلَّمَ قَالَ: «رَكْعَتَا الْفَجْرِ خَيْرٌ مِنَ الدُّنْيَا وَمَا فِيهَا».

i. Related by al-Tirmidhī, 416; al-Nasā'ī, 1758.

[1430–97]. (Dar al-Salam 1574) Yaḥyā ibn Ḥabīb narrated: Muʿtamir narrated; he said: my father said; Qatādah narrated; from Zurārah; from Saʿd ibn Hishām; from ʿĀ'ishah; from the Prophet (peace be upon him); that he said concerning [praying] the two *rakʿahs* after the break of dawn: **'These are dearer to me than the whole world'.**

وَحَدَّثَنَا يَحْيَى بْنُ حَبِيبٍ، حَدَّثَنَا مُعْتَمِرٌ قَالَ: قَالَ أَبِي، حَدَّثَنَا قَتَادَةُ، عَنْ زُرَارَةَ، عَنْ سَعْدِ بْنِ هِشَامٍ، عَنْ عَائِشَةَ، عَنِ النَّبِيِّ صَلَّى اللهُ عَلَيْهِ وَسَلَّمَ أَنَّهُ قَالَ فِي شَأْنِ الرَّكْعَتَيْنِ عِنْدَ طُلُوعِ الْفَجْرِ: «لَهُمَا أَحَبُّ إِلَيَّ مِنَ الدُّنْيَا جَمِيعًا».

[1431–98]. (Dar al-Salam 1575) Muhammad ibn ʿAbbād and Ibn Abi ʿUmar narrated to me:[i] both said: Marwān ibn Muʿāwiyah narrated; from Yazīd (who is Ibn Kaysān); from Abu Ḥāzim; from Abu Hurayrah; that **'God's Messenger (peace be upon him) recited in the two *rakʿahs* of Fajr [sunnah]: "Say: Unbelievers" and "Say: He is God, the One and only God".'**[ii]

حَدَّثَنِي مُحَمَّدُ بْنُ عَبَّادٍ وَابْنُ أَبِي عُمَرَ، قَالَا: حَدَّثَنَا مَرْوَانُ بْنُ مُعَاوِيَةَ، عَنْ يَزِيدَ (هُوَ ابْنُ كَيْسَانَ)، عَنْ أَبِي حَازِمٍ، عَنْ أَبِي هُرَيْرَةَ، أَنَّ رَسُولَ اللهِ صَلَّى اللهُ عَلَيْهِ وَسَلَّمَ قَرَأَ فِي رَكْعَتَيِ الْفَجْرِ: «قُلْ يَا أَيُّهَا الْكَافِرُونَ» وَ «قُلْ هُوَ اللهُ أَحَدٌ».

[1432–99]. (Dar al-Salam 1576) Qutaybah ibn Saʿīd narrated:[iii] al-Fazārī (meaning Marwān ibn Muʿāwiyah) narrated; from ʿUthmān ibn Ḥakīm al-Anṣārī; he said: Saʿīd ibn Yasār reported to me; that Ibn ʿAbbās reported to him; that **'God's Messenger (peace be upon him) used to recite in the two *rakʿahs* of Fajr**

i. Related by Abu Dāwūd, 1256; al-Nasā'ī, 944; Ibn Mājah, 1148.
ii. These are Surah 109 and 112, respectively.
iii. Related by Abu Dāwūd, 1259; al-Nasā'ī, 943.

[sunnah]: in the first of the two the verse in [the surah] The Cow that says: "Say: we believe in God and what has been revealed to us" (2: 136) and in the second of the two [the verse that says]: "We believe in God. Bear witness that we have surrendered ourselves to Him". (3: 52)'

وَحَدَّثَنَا قُتَيْبَةُ بْنُ سَعِيدٍ، حَدَّثَنَا الْفَزَارِيُّ (يَعْنِي مَرْوَانَ بْنَ مُعَاوِيَةَ)، عَنْ عُثْمَانَ بْنِ حَكِيمٍ الأَنْصَارِيِّ قَالَ: أَخْبَرَنِي سَعِيدُ بْنُ يَسَارٍ أَنَّ ابْنَ عَبَّاسٍ أَخْبَرَهُ، أَنَّ رَسُولَ اللهِ، صَلَّى اللهُ عَلَيْهِ وَسَلَّمَ، كَانَ يَقْرَأُ فِي رَكْعَتَيِ الْفَجْرِ: فِي الأُولَى مِنْهُمَا «قُولُوا آمَنَّا بِاللهِ وَمَا أُنْزِلَ إِلَيْنَا» الآيَةَ الَّتِي فِي الْبَقَرَةِ، وَفِي الآخِرَةِ مِنْهُمَا: «آمَنَّا بِاللهِ وَاشْهَدْ بِأَنَّا مُسْلِمُونَ».

[1433–100]. (Dar al-Salam 1577–1578) Abu Bakr ibn Abi Shaybah narrated: Abu Khālid al-Aḥmar narrated; from ʿUthmān ibn Ḥakīm; from Saʿīd ibn Yasār; from Ibn ʿAbbās. He said: **'God's Messenger used to recite in the two *rakʿahs* of Fajr [sunnah]: "Say: we believe in God and what has been revealed to us", and [the verse] that is in [the surah] Āl-ʿImrān: "Let us come to an agreement which is equitable between you and us". (3: 64)'**

وَحَدَّثَنَا أَبُو بَكْرِ بْنُ أَبِي شَيْبَةَ، حَدَّثَنَا أَبُو خَالِدٍ الأَحْمَرُ، عَنْ عُثْمَانَ بْنِ حَكِيمٍ، عَنْ سَعِيدِ بْنِ يَسَارٍ، عَنِ ابْنِ عَبَّاسٍ قَالَ: كَانَ رَسُولُ اللهِ صَلَّى اللهُ عَلَيْهِ وَسَلَّمَ يَقْرَأُ فِي رَكْعَتَيِ الْفَجْرِ: «قُولُوا آمَنَّا بِاللهِ وَمَا أُنْزِلَ إِلَيْنَا» وَالَّتِي فِي آلِ عِمْرَانَ «تَعَالَوْا إِلَى كَلِمَةٍ سَوَاءٍ بَيْنَنَا وَبَيْنَكُمْ».

ʿAlī ibn Khashram narrated to me: ʿĪsā ibn Yūnus reported; from ʿUthmān ibn Ḥakīm; with the same chain of transmission: **the same text as Marwān al-Fazārī's narration.**

وَحَدَّثَنِي عَلِيُّ بْنُ خَشْرَمٍ، أَخْبَرَنَا عِيسَى بْنُ يُونُسَ، عَنْ عُثْمَانَ بْنِ حَكِيمٍ، فِي هَذَا الإِسْنَادِ: بِمِثْلِ حَدِيثِ مَرْوَانَ الْفَزَارِيِّ.

Text Explanation

These hadiths speak of the importance of the sunnah prayer before the obligatory Fajr [i.e. dawn] Prayer and that it should be in two light *rakʿahs*. Hadith No. 1420 mentions that the Prophet did not pray after the break of dawn more than two light *rakʿahs*. This hadith may be cited as evidence in support of the view that prayer is discouraged once the dawn has broken, with the exception of the two *rakʿahs* of Fajr sunnah and what is due to a specific reason. Our scholars express three different views. One of them is that which we have just mentioned. *Qadi* ʿIyāḍ attributes this view to Mālik and the majority. The second view is that the time when prayer is discouraged begins after a person has completed the Fajr sunnah, while the third view considers it commences after the person has completed the obligatory Fajr Prayer. This is the correct view according to our Shāfiʿī scholars. This hadith does not provide any clear evidence of discouragement of prayer. It only tells us that the Prophet did not pray more than the two *rakʿahs* of sunnah before Fajr Prayer, but he did not disallow any prayer in addition [before offering the obligatory Fajr Prayer].

Hadith No. 1422 mentions that the Prophet used to pray the sunnah of Fajr when he heard the *adhān* and made it in two light *rakʿahs*. In another version, he prayed this sunnah 'when the dawn had broken'. This means that the Fajr sunnah does not become due until the break of dawn and that it is desirable to pray these shortly after and to make it light. This is the view of Mālik, al-Shāfiʿī and the majority of scholars. Some early scholars say that it is permissible to make these two *rakʿahs* long, but perhaps they meant that this is not forbidden, and they do not disagree that making this prayer light is desirable. Some go to extremes, however, and say, as mentioned by al-Ṭaḥāwī and *Qadi* ʿIyāḍ, that no Qur'anic recitation is needed in them. But this is wrong. It is confirmed in the authentic hadiths Muslim mentions in this chapter that God's Messenger used to recite in these two *rakʿahs*, after the *Fātiḥah*, Surah 109 and 112 respectively, and according to one narration he recited Quran 2: 136 and 3: 64. It is also confirmed in authentic hadiths that 'No prayer is valid without recitation', and 'No prayer is acceptable without reciting the *Fātiḥah*', and 'No prayer is complete unless the *Fātiḥah* is recited'.

Some Ḥanafī scholars take this hadith as evidence that the *adhān* for Fajr Prayer may not be called before the break of dawn. This is on the basis of the authentic hadith that refers to the start of the fasting day [which is when Fajr Prayer becomes due]: 'Bilāl calls the *adhān* when it is still night. You may continue to eat and drink until Ibn Umm Maktūm calls the *adhān*'. The present hadith, No. 1422, refers to this second *adhān*.

Hadith No. 1425 quotes ʿĀ'ishah who says that the Prophet made the two *rakʿahs* of Fajr sunnah so light that she wondered whether he recited the *Fātiḥah* in them. This suggests making this prayer very light, but this is in comparison to his habit of making voluntary night prayers and other sunnah prayers long. The hadith provides no evidence in support of the view of those who say that no recitation is needed in these two *rakʿahs*. We have already stated some contrary evidence which is both clear and authentic.

In hadith No. 1427, ʿĀ'ishah says that the Prophet never attended more regularly to any sunnah prayer than he did to the two *rakʿahs* before Fajr obligatory prayer. This hadith makes clear that these two *rakʿahs* are of particular importance and that they are a sunnah, not a duty. This is the view of the majority of scholars. *Qadi* ʿIyāḍ mentions that al-Ḥasan al-Baṣrī considered them a duty, but the correct view is that they are not because ʿĀ'ishah says: 'to any sunnah prayer'. Moreover, when the Bedouin asked him the duty of prayer, the Prophet said: 'Five prayers'. The Bedouin asked: 'Do I have any other as a duty?' The Prophet said: 'No, unless you wish to add more'. This hadith may be deemed to provide evidence in support of one of the two views of our Shāfiʿī School, which considers the Fajr sunnah to be more important than the Witr Prayer. But there is no such evidence in this hadith because Witr was a particular duty of the Prophet. Hence, this hadith does not apply.

Hadith No. 1429 describes the two *rakʿahs* of Fajr sunnah as better than the world and what it contains. This means that they are better than all the pleasant things in this world.

Hadith No. 1431 mentions that the Prophet recited in the Fajr sunnah Surah 109 and 112, and in the following hadiths, he recited certain verses of the Qur'an. These hadiths are cited as evidence in support of our view, which is also the view of the majority of scholars, that it is desirable to recite a surah after the *Fātiḥah* in each of the two *rak'ahs* and that it is desirable to recite these two surahs or two verses in particular. This is again a sunnah. Mālik and the majority of Mālikī scholars say that one recites the *Fātiḥah* only. As we mentioned earlier, some early scholars suggest that no recitation is made in this sunnah, but both views are contrary to the authentic sunnah.

CHAPTER 15

REGULAR SUNNAH BEFORE AND AFTER OBLIGATORY PRAYERS

[1434–101]. (Dar al-Salam 1579) Muhammad ibn ʿAbdullāh ibn Numayr narrated:[i] Abu Khālid (meaning Sulaymān ibn Ḥayyān) narrated; from Dāwūd ibn Abi Hind; from al-Nuʿmān ibn Sālim; from ʿAmr ibn Aws; he said: ʿAnbasah ibn Abi Sufyān narrated to me during his final illness a hadith that is sought after with pleasure; he said: I heard Umm Ḥabībah say: **'I heard God's Messenger (peace be upon him) say: "Whoever prays twelve *rakʿahs* during a day and night will have a home built for him in Heaven".'**

Umm Ḥabībah said: 'I have not left doing them ever since I heard them mentioned by God's Messenger (peace be upon him)'. ʿAnbasah said: 'I have not left doing them ever since I heard them mentioned by Umm Ḥabībah'. ʿAmr ibn Aws said: 'I have not left doing them ever since I heard them mentioned by ʿAnbasah'. Al-Nuʿmān ibn Sālim said: 'I have never left doing them ever since I heard them mentioned by ʿAmr ibn Aws'.

حَدَّثَنَا مُحَمَّدُ بْنُ عَبْدِ اللهِ بْنِ نُمَيْرٍ، حَدَّثَنَا أَبُو خَالِدٍ (يَعْنِي سُلَيْمَانَ بْنَ حَيَّانَ)، عَنْ دَاوُدَ بْنِ أَبِي هِنْدٍ، عَنِ النُّعْمَانِ بْنِ سَالِمٍ، عَنْ عَمْرِو بْنِ أَوْسٍ قَالَ: حَدَّثَنِي عَنْبَسَةُ بْنُ أَبِي سُفْيَانَ، فِي مَرَضِهِ الَّذِي مَاتَ فِيهِ، بِحَدِيثٍ يُتَسَارُّ إِلَيْهِ، قَالَ: سَمِعْتُ أُمَّ حَبِيبَةَ تَقُولُ:

i. Related by Abu Dāwūd, 1250.

سَمِعْتُ رَسُولَ اللهِ صَلَّى اللهُ عَلَيْهِ وَسَلَّمَ يَقُولُ: «مَنْ صَلَّى اثْنَتَى عَشْرَةَ رَكْعَةً فِي يَوْمٍ وَلَيْلَةٍ بُنِيَ لَهُ بِهِنَّ بَيْتٌ فِي الْجَنَّةِ».

قَالَتْ أُمُّ حَبِيبَةَ فَمَا تَرَكْتُهُنَّ مُنْذُ سَمِعْتُهُنَّ مِنْ رَسُولِ اللهِ صَلَّى اللهُ عَلَيْهِ وَسَلَّمَ. وَقَالَ عَنْبَسَةُ فَمَا تَرَكْتُهُنَّ مُنْذُ سَمِعْتُهُنَّ مِنْ أُمِّ حَبِيبَةَ. وَقَالَ عَمْرُو بْنُ أَوْسٍ مَا تَرَكْتُهُنَّ مُنْذُ سَمِعْتُهُنَّ مِنْ عَنْبَسَةَ. وَقَالَ النُّعْمَانُ بْنُ سَالِمٍ مَا تَرَكْتُهُنَّ مُنْذُ سَمِعْتُهُنَّ مِنْ عَمْرِو بْنِ أَوْسٍ.

[1435–102]. (Dar al-Salam 1580) Abu Ghassān al-Misma῾ī narrated: Bishr ibn al-Mufaḍḍal narrated; Dāwūd narrated; from al-Nu῾mān ibn Sālim; with the same chain of transmission: **'Whoever prays twelve *rak῾ahs* on a day, voluntarily, will have a home built for him in Heaven'.**

حَدَّثَنِي أَبُو غَسَّانَ الْمِسْمَعِيُّ، حَدَّثَنَا بِشْرُ بْنُ الْمُفَضَّلِ، حَدَّثَنَا دَاوُدُ، عَنِ النُّعْمَانِ بْنِ سَالِمٍ، بِهَذَا الإِسْنَادِ: «مَنْ صَلَّى فِي يَوْمٍ ثِنْتَى عَشْرَةَ سَجْدَةً تَطَوُّعًا بُنِيَ لَهُ بَيْتٌ فِي الْجَنَّةِ».

[1436–103]. (Dar al-Salam 1581) Muhammad ibn Bashshār narrated: Muhammad ibn Ja῾far narrated; Shu῾bah narrated; from al-Nu῾mān ibn Sālim; from ῾Amr ibn Aws; from ῾Anbasah ibn Abi Sufyān; from Umm Ḥabībah, the Prophet's wife, that she said: **'I heard God's Messenger say: "For any Muslim servant of God who prays twelve *rak῾ahs* every day, voluntarily, not part of the obligatory prayers, God will build a home in Heaven. Or, will have a home built for him in Heaven".'**

Umm Ḥabībah said: 'I continued to pray them after that'. ῾Amr said: 'I continued to pray them after that'. Al-Nu῾mān said the same.

وَحَدَّثَنَا مُحَمَّدُ بْنُ بَشَّارٍ، حَدَّثَنَا مُحَمَّدُ بْنُ جَعْفَرٍ، حَدَّثَنَا شُعْبَةُ، عَنِ النُّعْمَانِ بْنِ سَالِمٍ، عَنْ عَمْرِو بْنِ أَوْسٍ، عَنْ عَنْبَسَةَ بْنِ أَبِي سُفْيَانَ، عَنْ أُمِّ حَبِيبَةَ، زَوْجِ النَّبِيِّ صَلَّى اللهُ عَلَيْهِ

وَسَلَّمَ، أَنَّهَا قَالَتْ: سَمِعْتُ رَسُولَ اللهِ صَلَّى اللهُ عَلَيْهِ وَسَلَّمَ يَقُولُ: «مَا مِنْ عَبْدٍ مُسْلِمٍ يُصَلِّي لِلهِ كُلَّ يَوْمٍ ثِنْتَيْ عَشْرَةَ رَكْعَةً، تَطَوُّعًا غَيْرَ فَرِيضَةٍ، إِلاَّ بَنَى اللهُ لَهُ بَيْتًا فِي الْجَنَّةِ، أَوْ إِلاَّ بُنِيَ لَهُ بَيْتٌ فِي الْجَنَّةِ».

قَالَتْ أُمُّ حَبِيبَةَ فَمَا بَرِحْتُ أُصَلِّيهِنَّ بَعْدُ. وَقَالَ عَمْرٌو مَا بَرِحْتُ أُصَلِّيهِنَّ بَعْدُ. وَقَالَ النُّعْمَانُ مِثْلَ ذَلِكَ.

[1437–000]. (Dar al-Salam 1582) ʿAbd al-Raḥmān ibn Bishr and ʿAbdullāh ibn Hāshim al-ʿAbdī narrated to me: both said: Bahz narrated; Shuʿbah narrated; he said: al-Nuʿmān ibn Sālim reported to me; he said: I heard ʿAmr ibn Aws narrating from ʿAnbasah; from Umm Ḥabībah. She said: **'God's Messenger (peace be upon him) said: "Any Muslim servant of God performs the ablution well and prays to God every day…".' Adding the same text.**

وَحَدَّثَنِي عَبْدُ الرَّحْمَنِ بْنُ بِشْرٍ وَعَبْدُ اللهِ بْنُ هَاشِمٍ الْعَبْدِيُّ، قَالا: حَدَّثَنَا بَهْزٌ، حَدَّثَنَا شُعْبَةُ، قَالَ: النُّعْمَانُ بْنُ سَالِمٍ أَخْبَرَنِي قَالَ: سَمِعْتُ عَمْرَو بْنَ أَوْسٍ، يُحَدِّثُ عَنْ عَنْبَسَةَ، عَنْ أُمِّ حَبِيبَةَ قَالَتْ: قَالَ رَسُولُ اللهِ صَلَّى اللهُ عَلَيْهِ وَسَلَّمَ: «مَا مِنْ عَبْدٍ مُسْلِمٍ تَوَضَّأَ فَأَسْبَغَ الْوُضُوءَ ثُمَّ صَلَّى لِلهِ كُلَّ يَوْمٍ». فَذَكَرَ بِمِثْلِهِ.

[1438–104]. (Dar al-Salam 1583) Zuhayr ibn Ḥarb and ʿUbaydullāh ibn Saʿīd narrated to me:[i] both said: Yaḥyā (who is Ibn Saʿīd) narrated; from ʿUbaydullāh; he said: Nāfiʿ reported to me; from Ibn ʿUmar [H]. Also, Abu Bakr ibn Abi Shaybah narrated; Abu Usāmah narrated; ʿUbaydullāh, from Nāfiʿ; from Ibn ʿUmar. He said: **'I prayed with God's Messenger (peace**

---

i. Related by al-Bukhari, 1172.

be upon him) two *rakʿahs* before Ẓuhr and two after it, two *rakʿahs* after Maghrib, and two after ʿIsha, and two *rakʿahs* after Friday Prayer. And as for those of Maghrib, ʿIsha and Friday Prayer I prayed with the Prophet in his home.

وَحَدَّثَنِي زُهَيْرُ بْنُ حَرْبٍ وَعُبَيْدُ اللهِ بْنُ سَعِيدٍ، قَالَا: حَدَّثَنَا يَحْيَى (وَهُوَ ابْنُ سَعِيدٍ)، عَنْ عُبَيْدِ اللهِ، قَالَ: أَخْبَرَنِي نَافِعٌ، عَنِ ابْنِ عُمَرَ، ح. وَحَدَّثَنَا أَبُو بَكْرِ بْنُ أَبِي شَيْبَةَ، حَدَّثَنَا أَبُو أُسَامَةَ، حَدَّثَنَا عُبَيْدُ اللهِ، عَنْ نَافِعٍ، عَنِ ابْنِ عُمَرَ قَالَ: صَلَّيْتُ مَعَ رَسُولِ اللهِ صَلَّى اللهُ عَلَيْهِ وَسَلَّمَ قَبْلَ الظُّهْرِ سَجْدَتَيْنِ، وَبَعْدَهَا سَجْدَتَيْنِ، وَبَعْدَ الْمَغْرِبِ سَجْدَتَيْنِ، وَبَعْدَ الْعِشَاءِ سَجْدَتَيْنِ، وَبَعْدَ الْجُمُعَةِ سَجْدَتَيْنِ. فَأَمَّا الْمَغْرِبُ وَالْعِشَاءُ وَالْجُمُعَةُ، فَصَلَّيْتُ مَعَ النَّبِيِّ صَلَّى اللهُ عَلَيْهِ وَسَلَّمَ فِي بَيْتِهِ.

Text Explanation

The hadith narrated by Umm Ḥabībah speaks of offering twelve *rakʿahs* of sunnah during the day and night and that God builds a home in Heaven for anyone who prays these recommended prayers. The hadith narrated by Ibn ʿUmar, No. 1438, mentions two *rakʿahs* before Ẓuhr and two after it, as well as two after Maghrib, ʿIsha and the Friday Prayer. In al-Bukhari's *Ṣaḥīḥ,* two before Fajr are added, making a total of twelve *rakʿahs*. In the hadith narrated by ʿĀ'ishah [No. 1439 in the next chapter] the details of these prayers are given as four before Ẓuhr and two after Ẓuhr, Maghrib and ʿIsha, and two after the break of dawn. These are also twelve *rakʿahs*.

No mention is made of ʿAṣr in this connection in either of the two *Ṣaḥīḥ* anthologies. However, in Abu Dāwūd's *Sunan* a hadith narrated by ʿAlī with a good chain of transmission mentions that the Prophet used to pray two *rakʿahs* before ʿAṣr. In a hadith related by Abu Dāwūd and al-Tirmidhī, Ibn ʿUmar quotes the Prophet: 'May God bestow mercy on a person who prays four *rakʿahs* before ʿAṣr'. A different authentic hadith also related by al-Tirmidhī and Abu Dāwūd mentions four *rakʿahs* of sunnah after Ẓuhr. Umm Ḥabībah said that the Prophet (peace be upon him) said: 'Whoever maintains four *rak'ahs* before Ẓuhr and four after it, God will make him immune from the Fire'. Al-Bukhari enters in his *Ṣaḥīḥ* a hadith narrated by Ibn Mughaffal quoting the Prophet: 'Pray before Maghrib', repeating it three times and adding in the third 'for whoever so wishes'. A hadith also narrated by Ibn Mughaffal and related in both *Ṣaḥīḥ* anthologies quotes the Prophet saying: 'A prayer may be offered between every two *adhāns*'. This means between the *adhān* and *iqāmah*. These are some of the authentic hadiths mentioning the regular sunnah prayers that it is desirable to offer alongside the obligatory prayers.

Our Shāfiʿī School and the majority of other scholars uphold all these hadiths and consider all the prayers they recommend as desirable. There is no disagreement among scholars concerning any of them except the two *rak'ahs* before Maghrib. Our Shāfiʿī scholars express two views on this prayer, the better-known of which is that it is not recommended. The correct view upheld by scrupulous scholars is that they are desirable, based on the two hadiths narrated by Ibn Mughaffal quoted above and by the hadith that the Prophet's Companions prayed these two *rak'ahs* near the pillars in the Prophet's Mosque. This hadith is entered in both *Ṣaḥīḥ* anthologies.

Our scholars and others say that the difference in the numbers mentioned in these hadiths is understood to provide scope for choice, so as to give both smaller and more complete numbers. Fulfilling the sunnah is achieved by the smaller number, but the choice would be to do the larger and more complete number. We saw earlier the difference in the numbers mentioned in the hadiths speaking of the Ḍuḥā Prayer, and a similar difference relates to the Witr Prayer. In all these we have a small number and a larger one and a number in between the two, so as to indicate the smallest adequate number, the most perfect and the one in between, but God knows best.

After narrating hadith No. 1454, Umm Ḥabībah said: 'I have not left doing them ever since I heard them mentioned by God's Messenger (peace be upon him)'. The same was said by three other narrators in the chain of transmission. This shows that it is desirable that a scholar should say something similar, not to praise his own action, but to urge his listeners to do the same and maintain it.

Transmission

The chain of transmission of hadith No. 1434 includes: 'Abu Khālid; from Dāwūd ibn Abi Hind; from al-Nuʿmān ibn Sālim; from ʿAmr ibn Aws; from ʿAnbasah ibn Abi Sufyān'. This chain includes four narrators who belonged to the *tābiʿ*īn generation, reporting from each other. These are Dāwūd, al-Nuʿmān, ʿAmr ibn Aws and ʿAnbasah. In this chain, ʿAmr says: 'ʿAnbasah ibn Abi Sufyān narrated to me during his final illness a hadith that is sought after with pleasure'. This is due to the good news it brings, considering the easy requirements it specifies.

CHAPTER 16

SUNNAH PRAYERS MAY BE OFFERED STANDING OR SEATED

[1439–105]. (Dar al-Salam 1584) Yaḥyā ibn Yaḥyā narrated:[i] Hushaym reported; from Khālid; from ʿAbdullāh ibn Shaqīq. He said: **'I asked ʿĀ'ishah about God's Messenger's prayers, his voluntary ones. She said: "He used to pray in my home four *rakʿahs* before Ẓuhr, then he went out to lead the congregational prayer. He then came in and prayed two *rakʿahs*. He led the congregational Maghrib Prayer and came in and prayed two *rakʿahs*. He also led the congregational 'Isha Prayer then came into my home and prayed two *rakʿahs*. He also used to pray nine *rakʿahs* that included Witr. He might pray standing for a long while at night and might pray seated for a long while at night. If he recited the Qur'an standing, he would bow and prostrate himself from the standing position, and if he recited the Qur'an seated, he would bow and prostrate himself from the sitting position. When the dawn broke, he would pray two *rakʿahs*".'**

حَدَّثَنَا يَحْيَى بْنُ يَحْيَى، أَخْبَرَنَا هُشَيْمٌ، عَنْ خَالِدٍ، عَنْ عَبْدِ اللهِ بْنِ شَقِيقٍ قَالَ: سَأَلْتُ عَائِشَةَ عَنْ صَلاَةِ رَسُولِ اللهِ صَلَّى اللهُ عَلَيْهِ وَسَلَّمَ، عَنْ تَطَوُّعِهِ فَقَالَتْ: كَانَ يُصَلِّي فِي بَيْتِي قَبْلَ الظُّهْرِ أَرْبَعًا، ثُمَّ يَخْرُجُ فَيُصَلِّي بِالنَّاسِ، ثُمَّ يَدْخُلُ فَيُصَلِّي رَكْعَتَيْنِ. وَكَانَ يُصَلِّي بِالنَّاسِ الْـمَغْرِبَ ثُمَّ يَدْخُلُ فَيُصَلِّي رَكْعَتَيْنِ. وَيُصَلِّي بِالنَّاسِ الْعِشَاءَ وَيَدْخُلُ

i. Related by Abu Dāwūd, 1251; al-Tirmidhī in shorter versions, 375 and 436.

بَيْتِي فَيُصَلِّي رَكْعَتَيْنِ. وَكَانَ يُصَلِّي مِنَ اللَّيْلِ تِسْعَ رَكَعَاتٍ، فِيهِنَّ الْوِتْرُ. وَكَانَ يُصَلِّي لَيْلاً طَوِيلاً قَائِمًا، وَلَيْلاً طَوِيلاً قَاعِدًا. وَكَانَ إِذَا قَرَأَ وَهُوَ قَائِمٌ رَكَعَ وَسَجَدَ وَهُوَ قَائِمٌ. وَإِذَا قَرَأَ قَاعِدًا رَكَعَ وَسَجَدَ وَهُوَ قَاعِدٌ. وَكَانَ إِذَا طَلَعَ الْفَجْرُ صَلَّى رَكْعَتَيْنِ.

[1440–106-107]. (Dar al-Salam 1585) Qutaybah ibn Saʿīd narrated:[i] Ḥammād narrated; from Budayl and Ayyūb; from ʿAbdullāh ibn Shaqīq; from ʿĀ'ishah. She said: **'God's Messenger (peace be upon him) used to pray for a long time at night. If he prayed standing, he would bow from the standing position, and if he prayed seated, he would bow from the sitting position'.**

حَدَّثَنَا قُتَيْبَةُ بْنُ سَعِيدٍ، حَدَّثَنَا حَمَّادٌ، عَنْ بُدَيْلٍ، وَأَيُّوبَ، عَنْ عَبْدِ اللهِ بْنِ شَقِيقٍ، عَنْ عَائِشَةَ قَالَتْ: كَانَ رَسُولُ اللهِ صَلَّى اللهُ عَلَيْهِ وَسَلَّمَ يُصَلِّي لَيْلاً طَوِيلاً، فَإِذَا صَلَّى قَائِمًا رَكَعَ قَائِمًا، وَإِذَا صَلَّى قَاعِدًا رَكَعَ قَاعِدًا.

[1441–108]. (Dar al-Salam 1586) Muhammad ibn al-Muthannā narrated: Muhammad ibn Jaʿfar narrated; Shuʿbah narrated; from Budayl; from ʿAbdullāh ibn Shaqīq. He said: **'I was ill in Persia, and I prayed seated. I asked ʿĀ'ishah about this and she said: "God's Messenger (peace be upon him) used to pray standing for a long time at night…".' He narrated the hadith in full.**

وَحَدَّثَنَا مُحَمَّدُ بْنُ الْـمُثَنَّى، حَدَّثَنَا مُحَمَّدُ بْنُ جَعْفَرٍ، حَدَّثَنَا شُعْبَةُ، عَنْ بُدَيْلٍ، عَنْ عَبْدِ اللهِ بْنِ شَقِيقٍ قَالَ: كُنْتُ شَاكِيًا بِفَارِسَ، فَكُنْتُ أُصَلِّي قَاعِدًا. فَسَأَلْتُ عَنْ ذَلِكَ عَائِشَةَ، فَقَالَتْ: كَانَ رَسُولُ اللهِ صَلَّى اللهُ عَلَيْهِ وَسَلَّمَ يُصَلِّي لَيْلاً طَوِيلاً قَائِمًا. فَذَكَرَ الْحَدِيثَ

i. Related by Abu Dāwūd, 955; al-Nasā'ī, 1645.

[1442–109]. (Dar al-Salam 1587) Abu Bakr ibn Abi Shaybah narrated:[i] Muʿādh ibn Muʿādh narrated; from Ḥumayd; from ʿAbdullāh ibn Shaqīq al-ʿUqaylī. He said: **'I asked ʿĀ'ishah about God's Messenger's night prayer. She said: "He might pray standing for a long time at night or pray seated for a long time at night. If he recited the Qur'an standing, he would bow from the standing position, and if recited the Qur'an seated, he would bow from the sitting position".'**

وَحَدَّثَنَا أَبُو بَكْرِ بْنُ أَبِي شَيْبَةَ، حَدَّثَنَا مُعَاذُ بْنُ مُعَاذٍ، عَنْ حُمَيْدٍ، عَنْ عَبْدِ اللهِ بْنِ شَقِيقٍ الْعُقَيْلِيِّ قَالَ: سَأَلْتُ عَائِشَةَ عَنْ صَلاَةِ رَسُولِ اللهِ صَلَّى اللهُ عَلَيْهِ وَسَلَّمَ بِاللَّيْلِ، فَقَالَتْ: كَانَ يُصَلِّي لَيْلاً طَوِيلاً قَائِمًا، وَلَيْلاً طَوِيلاً قَاعِدًا. وَكَانَ إِذَا قَرَأَ قَائِمًا رَكَعَ قَائِمًا، وَإِذَا قَرَأَ قَاعِدًا رَكَعَ قَاعِدًا.

[1443–110]. (Dar al-Salam 1588) Yaḥyā ibn Yaḥyā narrated: Abu Muʿāwiyah reported; from Hishām ibn Ḥassān; from Muhammad ibn Sīrīn; from ʿAbdullāh ibn Shaqīq al-ʿUqaylī. He said: **'We asked ʿĀ'ishah about God's Messenger's prayer. She said: "God's Messenger (peace be upon him) used to spend much time in prayer, standing and sitting. If he started the prayer standing, he would bow from the standing position, and if he started the prayer seated, he would bow from the sitting position".'**

وَحَدَّثَنَا يَحْيَى بْنُ يَحْيَى، أَخْبَرَنَا أَبُو مُعَاوِيَةَ، عَنْ هِشَامِ بْنِ حَسَّانَ، عَنْ مُحَمَّدِ بْنِ سِيرِينَ، عَنْ عَبْدِ اللهِ بْنِ شَقِيقٍ الْعُقَيْلِيِّ، قَالَ: سَأَلْنَا عَائِشَةَ عَنْ صَلاَةِ رَسُولِ اللهِ صَلَّى اللهُ عَلَيْهِ وَسَلَّمَ، فَقَالَتْ: كَانَ رَسُولُ اللهِ صَلَّى اللهُ عَلَيْهِ وَسَلَّمَ يُكْثِرُ الصَّلاَةَ قَائِمًا وَقَاعِدًا. فَإِذَا افْتَتَحَ الصَّلاَةَ قَائِمًا رَكَعَ قَائِمًا، وَإِذَا افْتَتَحَ الصَّلاَةَ قَاعِدًا رَكَعَ قَاعِدًا.

---

i. Related by Ibn Mājah, 1228.

[1444–111]. (Dar al-Salam 1589) Abu al-Rabīʿ al-Zahrānī narrated to me: Ḥammād (meaning Ibn Zayd) narrated [H]. Also, Ḥasan ibn al-Rabīʿ narrated; Mahdī ibn Maymūn narrated [H]. And, Abu Bakr ibn Abi Shaybah narrated: Wakīʿ narrated [H]. Also, Abu Kurayb narrated; Ibn Numayr narrated; all from Hishām ibn ʿUrwah [H]. Also, Zuhayr ibn Ḥarb narrated (his text);[i] Yaḥyā ibn Saʿīd narrated; from Hishām ibn ʿUrwah; he said: my father reported to me; from ʿĀ'ishah. She said: **'I did not see God's Messenger (peace be upon him) reciting [the Qur'an] during any part of his night prayer while sitting down. But when he grew old, he recited seated. When around thirty or forty verses of the surah [he was reciting] remained, he would stand up and recite them, then bow'.**

وَحَدَّثَنِي أَبُو الرَّبِيعِ الزَّهْرَانِيُّ، أَخْبَرَنَا حَمَّادٌ (يَعْنِي ابْنَ زَيْد)، ح. قَالَ: وَحَدَّثَنَا حَسَنُ بْنُ الرَّبِيعِ، حَدَّثَنَا مَهْدِيُّ بْنُ مَيْمُونٍ، ح. وَحَدَّثَنَا أَبُو بَكْرِ بْنُ أَبِي شَيْبَةَ، حَدَّثَنَا وَكِيعٌ، ح. وَحَدَّثَنَا أَبُو كُرَيْبٍ، حَدَّثَنَا ابْنُ نُمَيْرٍ، جَمِيعًا عَنْ هِشَامِ بْنِ عُرْوَةَ، ح. وَحَدَّثَنِي زُهَيْرُ بْنُ حَرْبٍ (وَاللَّفْظُ لَهُ)، قَالَ: حَدَّثَنَا يَحْيَى بْنُ سَعِيدٍ، عَنْ هِشَامِ بْنِ عُرْوَةَ قَالَ: أَخْبَرَنِي أَبِي، عَنْ عَائِشَةَ، قَالَتْ: مَا رَأَيْتُ رَسُولَ اللهِ صَلَّى اللهُ عَلَيْهِ وَسَلَّمَ يَقْرَأُ فِي شَيْءٍ مِنْ صَلَاةِ اللَّيْلِ جَالِسًا، حَتَّى إِذَا كَبِرَ قَرَأَ جَالِسًا، حَتَّى إِذَا بَقِيَ عَلَيْهِ مِنَ السُّورَةِ ثَلَاثُونَ أَوْ أَرْبَعُونَ آيَةً، قَامَ فَقَرَأَهُنَّ ثُمَّ رَكَعَ.

[1445–112]. (Dar al-Salam 1590) Yaḥyā ibn Yaḥyā narrated:[ii] he said: I read out to Mālik; from ʿAbdullāh ibn Yazīd and Abu al-Naḍr; from Abu Salamah ibn ʿAbd al-Raḥmān; from ʿĀ'ishah; that **'God's Messenger (peace be upon him) used to pray seated and he recited the Qur'an seated. When around thirty**

i. Related by al-Bukhari, 1148.
ii. Related by al-Bukhari, 1119; Abu Dāwūd, 954, al-Tirmidhī, 374; al-Nasā'ī, 1647.

of forty verses [of the Qur'an] remained, he would stand up and recite standing. He would then bow and prostrate himself. He would do the same in the second *rak'ah*'.

وَحَدَّثَنَا يَحْيَى بْنُ يَحْيَى قَالَ: قَرَأْتُ عَلَى مَالِكٍ، عَنْ عَبْدِ اللهِ بْنِ يَزِيدَ وَأَبِي النَّضْرِ، عَنْ أَبِي سَلَمَةَ بْنِ عَبْدِ الرَّحْمَنِ، عَنْ عَائِشَةَ، أَنَّ رَسُولَ اللهِ صَلَّى اللهُ عَلَيْهِ وَسَلَّمَ كَانَ يُصَلِّي جَالِسًا، فَيَقْرَأُ وَهُوَ جَالِسٌ، فَإِذَا بَقِيَ مِنْ قِرَاءَتِهِ قَدْرُ مَا يَكُونُ ثَلَاثِينَ أَوْ أَرْبَعِينَ آيَةً، قَامَ فَقَرَأَ وَهُوَ قَائِمٌ، ثُمَّ رَكَعَ ثُمَّ سَجَدَ. ثُمَّ يَفْعَلُ فِي الرَّكْعَةِ الثَّانِيَةِ مِثْلَ ذَلِكَ.

[1446–113]. (Dar al-Salam 1591) Abu Bakr ibn Abi Shaybah and Isḥāq ibn Ibrāhīm narrated:[i] Abu Bakr said: Ismā'īl ibn 'Ulayyah narrated; from al-Walīd ibn Abi Hishām; from Abu Bakr ibn Muhammad; from 'Amrah; from 'Ā'ishah. She said: **'God's Messenger used to recite [the Qur'an in prayer] seated. When he was about to bow, he would stand up and continue to recite what was equal to forty verses'.**

حَدَّثَنَا أَبُو بَكْرِ بْنُ أَبِي شَيْبَةَ وَإِسْحَاقُ بْنُ إِبْرَاهِيمَ، قَالَ أَبُو بَكْرٍ: حَدَّثَنَا إِسْمَاعِيلُ ابْنُ عُلَيَّةَ، عَنِ الْوَلِيدِ بْنِ أَبِي هِشَامٍ، عَنْ أَبِي بَكْرِ بْنِ مُحَمَّدٍ، عَنْ عَمْرَةَ، عَنْ عَائِشَةَ، قَالَتْ: كَانَ رَسُولُ اللهِ صَلَّى اللهُ عَلَيْهِ وَسَلَّمَ يَقْرَأُ وَهُوَ قَاعِدٌ، فَإِذَا أَرَادَ أَنْ يَرْكَعَ قَامَ قَدْرَ مَا يَقْرَأُ إِنْسَانٌ أَرْبَعِينَ آيَةً.

[1447–114]. (Dar al-Salam 1592) Ibn Numayr narrated: Muhammad ibn Bishr narrated; Muhammad ibn 'Amr narrated; Muhammad ibn Ibrāhīm narrated to me; from 'Alqamah ibn Abi Waqqāṣ. He said: **'I asked 'Ā'ishah: "What did God's Messenger (peace be upon him) do when he prayed two**

i. Related by al-Nasā'ī, 1649; Ibn Mājah, 1226.

***rakʿahs* seated?" She said: "He would recite [the Qur'an] in both. When he wanted to bow [i.e. do the *rukūʿ*], he would stand up and bow".'**

وَحَدَّثَنَا ابْنُ نُمَيْرٍ، حَدَّثَنَا مُحَمَّدُ بْنُ بِشْرٍ، حَدَّثَنَا مُحَمَّدُ بْنُ عَمْرٍو، حَدَّثَنِي مُحَمَّدُ بْنُ إِبْرَاهِيمَ، عَنْ عَلْقَمَةَ بْنِ وَقَّاصٍ، قَالَ قُلْتُ لِعَائِشَةَ: كَيْفَ كَانَ يَصْنَعُ رَسُولُ اللهِ صَلَّى اللهُ عَلَيْهِ وَسَلَّمَ فِي الرَّكْعَتَيْنِ وَهُوَ جَالِسٌ؟ قَالَتْ: كَانَ يَقْرَأُ فِيهِمَا، فَإِذَا أَرَادَ أَنْ يَرْكَعَ، قَامَ فَرَكَعَ.

[1448–115]. (Dar al-Salam 1593–1594) Yaḥyā ibn Yaḥyā narrated:[i] Yazīd ibn Zurayʿ reported; from Saʿīd al-Jurayrī; from ʿAbdullāh ibn Shaqīq. He said: **'I said to ʿĀ'ishah: "Did the Prophet (peace be upon him) pray seated?" She said: "Yes, after the people had weighed him down".'**

وَحَدَّثَنَا يَحْيَى بْنُ يَحْيَى، أَخْبَرَنَا يَزِيدُ بْنُ زُرَيْعٍ، عَنْ سَعِيدٍ الْجُرَيْرِيِّ، عَنْ عَبْدِ اللهِ بْنِ شَقِيقٍ قَالَ: قُلْتُ لِعَائِشَةَ: هَلْ كَانَ النَّبِيُّ صَلَّى اللهُ عَلَيْهِ وَسَلَّمَ يُصَلِّي وَهُوَ قَاعِدٌ؟ قَالَتْ: نَعَمْ، بَعْدَ مَا حَطَمَهُ النَّاسُ.

ʿUbaydullāh ibn Muʿādh narrated: my father narrated; Kahmas narrated; from ʿAbdullāh ibn Shaqīq. He said: **'I said to ʿĀ'ishah…' mentioning the same about the Prophet (peace be upon him).**

وَحَدَّثَنَا عُبَيْدُ اللهِ بْنُ مُعَاذٍ، حَدَّثَنَا أَبِي، حَدَّثَنَا كَهْمَسٌ، عَنْ عَبْدِ اللهِ بْنِ شَقِيقٍ قَالَ: قُلْتُ لِعَائِشَةَ. فَذَكَرَ عَنِ النَّبِيِّ صَلَّى اللهُ عَلَيْهِ وَسَلَّمَ بِمِثْلِهِ.

---

i. Related by al-Nasā'ī, 1656.

[1449–116]. (Dar al-Salam 1595) Muhammad ibn Ḥātim and Ḥarūn ibn ʿAbdullāh narrated to me:[i] both said: Ḥajjāh ibn Muhammad narrated; he said: Ibn Jurayj said: ʿUthmān ibn Abi Sulaymān reported to me; that Abu Salamah ibn ʿAbd al-Raḥmān reported to him; that ʿĀ'ishah told him that **'The Prophet (peace be upon him) did not die until much of his prayer was offered with him sitting down'.**

وَحَدَّثَنِي مُحَمَّدُ بْنُ حَاتِمٍ وَهَارُونُ بْنُ عَبْدِ اللهِ، قَالَا: حَدَّثَنَا حَجَّاجُ بْنُ مُحَمَّدٍ قَالَ: قَالَ ابْنُ جُرَيْجٍ: أَخْبَرَنِي عُثْمَانُ بْنُ أَبِي سُلَيْمَانَ، أَنَّ أَبَا سَلَمَةَ بْنَ عَبْدِ الرَّحْمَنِ أَخْبَرَهُ أَنَّ عَائِشَةَ أَخْبَرَتْهُ أَنَّ النَّبِيَّ صَلَّى اللهُ عَلَيْهِ وَسَلَّمَ لَمْ يَمُتْ حَتَّى كَانَ كَثِيرٌ مِنْ صَلَاتِهِ وَهُوَ جَالِسٌ.

[1450–117]. (Dar al-Salam 1596) Muhammad ibn Ḥātim and Ḥasan al-Ḥulwānī narrated to me: both from Zayd; Ḥasan said Zayd ibn al-Ḥubāb narrated; al-Ḍaḥḥāk ibn ʿUthmān narrated to me; ʿAbdullāh ibn ʿUrwah narrated to me; from his father; from ʿĀ'ishah. She said: **'When God's Messenger (peace be upon him) was older and became heavier, he offered most of his [sunnah] prayer seated'.**

وَحَدَّثَنِي مُحَمَّدُ بْنُ حَاتِمٍ وَحَسَنٌ الْحُلْوَانِيُّ، كِلَاهُمَا عَنْ زَيْدٍ، قَالَ حَسَنٌ: حَدَّثَنَا زَيْدُ بْنُ الْحُبَابِ، حَدَّثَنِي الضَّحَّاكُ بْنُ عُثْمَانَ، حَدَّثَنِي عَبْدُ اللهِ بْنُ عُرْوَةَ، عَنْ أَبِيهِ، عَنْ عَائِشَةَ قَالَتْ: لَمَّا بَدَّنَ رَسُولُ اللهِ صَلَّى اللهُ عَلَيْهِ وَسَلَّمَ وَثَقُلَ، كَانَ أَكْثَرُ صَلَاتِهِ جَالِسًا.

[1451–118]. (Dar al-Salam 1597) Yaḥyā ibn Yaḥyā narrated:[ii] he said: I read out to Mālik; from Ibn Shihāb; from al-Sā'ib

i. Related by al-Nasā'ī, 1655.
ii. Related by al-Tirmidhī, 373; al-Nasā'ī, 1657.

ibn Yazīd; from al-Muṭṭalib ibn Abi Wadāʿah al-Sahmī; from Ḥafṣah; that she said: **'I never saw God's Messenger (peace be upon him) praying his sunnah prayer seated, until the last year before his death. He then used to pray his sunnah prayer seated. He would recite a surah so well that it would take longer than a longer surah'.**

حَدَّثَنَا يَحْيَى بْنُ يَحْيَى قَالَ: قَرَأْتُ عَلَى مَالِكٍ عَنِ ابْنِ شِهَابٍ، عَنِ السَّائِبِ بْنِ يَزِيدَ، عَنِ الْمُطَّلِبِ بْنِ أَبِي وَدَاعَةَ السَّهْمِيِّ، عَنْ حَفْصَةَ أَنَّهَا قَالَتْ: مَا رَأَيْتُ رَسُولَ اللهِ صَلَّى اللهُ عَلَيْهِ وَسَلَّمَ صَلَّى فِي سُبْحَتِهِ قَاعِدًا حَتَّى كَانَ قَبْلَ وَفَاتِهِ بِعَامٍ. فَكَانَ يُصَلِّي فِي سُبْحَتِهِ قَاعِدًا، وَكَانَ يَقْرَأُ بِالسُّورَةِ فَيُرَتِّلُهَا، حَتَّى تَكُونَ أَطْوَلَ مِنْ أَطْوَلَ مِنْهَا.

[1452–000]. (Dar al-Salam 1598) Abu al-Ṭāhir and Ḥarmalah narrated: both said: Ibn Wahb reported; Yūnus reported to me [H]. Also, Isḥāq ibn Ibrāhīm and ʿAbd ibn Ḥumayd narrated; both said: ʿAbd al-Razzāq reported; Maʿmar reported; all from al-Zuhrī; with the same chain of transmission: **the same text, except that they said: 'until one or two years...'.**

وَحَدَّثَنِي أَبُو الطَّاهِرِ وَحَرْمَلَةُ، قَالَا: أَخْبَرَنَا ابْنُ وَهْبٍ، أَخْبَرَنِي يُونُسُ، ح. وَحَدَّثَنَا إِسْحَاقُ بْنُ إِبْرَاهِيمَ وَعَبْدُ بْنُ حُمَيْدٍ، قَالا أَخْبَرَنَا عَبْدُ الرَّزَّاقِ، أَخْبَرَنَا مَعْمَرٌ، جَمِيعًا عَنِ الزُّهْرِيِّ، بِهَذَا الإِسْنَادِ. مِثْلَهُ غَيْرَ أَنَّهُمَا قَالاَ بِعَامٍ وَاحِدٍ أَوِ اثْنَيْنِ.

[1453–119]. (Dar al-Salam 1599) Abu Bakr ibn Abi Shaybah narrated: ʿUbaydullāh ibn Mūsā narrated; from Ḥasan ibn Ṣāliḥ; from Simāk; he said: Jābir ibn Samurah reported to me; that **'The Prophet (peace be upon him) did not die until he had to pray seated'.**

وَحَدَّثَنَا أَبُو بَكْرِ بْنُ أَبِي شَيْبَةَ، حَدَّثَنَا عُبَيْدُ اللهِ بْنُ مُوسَى، عَنْ حَسَنِ بْنِ صَالِحٍ، عَنْ سِمَاكٍ قَالَ: أَخْبَرَنِي جَابِرُ بْنُ سَمُرَةَ، أَنَّ النَّبِيَّ صَلَّى اللهُ عَلَيْهِ وَسَلَّمَ لَمْ يَمُتْ حَتَّى صَلَّى قَاعِدًا.

[1454–120]. (Dar al-Salam 1600–1601) Zuhayr ibn Ḥarb narrated to me:[i] Jarīr narrated; from Manṣūr; from Hilāl ibn Yasāf; from Abu Yaḥyā; from ʿAbdullāh ibn ʿAmr. He said: **'I was told that God's Messenger (peace be upon him) said: "A person's prayer seated is equal to half a prayer". I went to him and found him praying seated. I put my hand on his head. He said: "What is the matter, ʿAbdullāh ibn ʿAmr?" I said: "Messenger of God, I am told that you said, 'A person's prayer seated is equal to half a prayer,' and you pray seated!" He said: "Yes, but I am unlike any one of you".'**

وَحَدَّثَنِي زُهَيْرُ بْنُ حَرْبٍ، حَدَّثَنَا جَرِيرٌ، عَنْ مَنْصُورٍ، عَنْ هِلَالِ بْنِ يَسَافٍ، عَنْ أَبِي يَحْيَى، عَنْ عَبْدِ اللهِ بْنِ عَمْرٍو قَالَ: حُدِّثْتُ أَنَّ رَسُولَ اللهِ صَلَّى اللهُ عَلَيْهِ وَسَلَّمَ قَالَ: «صَلَاةُ الرَّجُلِ قَاعِدًا نِصْفُ الصَّلَاةِ». قَالَ: فَأَتَيْتُهُ فَوَجَدْتُهُ يُصَلِّي جَالِسًا، فَوَضَعْتُ يَدِي عَلَى رَأْسِهِ، فَقَالَ: مَا لَكَ يَا عَبْدَ اللهِ بْنَ عَمْرٍو؟ قُلْتُ: حُدِّثْتُ يَا رَسُولَ اللهِ أَنَّكَ قُلْتَ: «صَلَاةُ الرَّجُلِ قَاعِدًا عَلَى نِصْفِ الصَّلَاةِ»، وَأَنْتَ تُصَلِّي قَاعِدًا! قَالَ: «أَجَلْ، وَلَكِنِّي لَسْتُ كَأَحَدٍ مِنْكُمْ».

Abu Bakr ibn Abi Shaybah, Muhammad ibn al-Muthannā and Ibn Bashshār narrated; all from Muhammad ibn Jaʿfar; from Shuʿbah [H]. Also, Ibn al-Muthannā narrated; Yaḥyā ibn Saʿīd narrated; Sufyān narrated; both from Manṣūr; with the same chain of transmission: **the same text.**

In Shuʿbah's narration: **'from Abu Yaḥyā al-Aʿraj'.**

i. Related by Abu Dāwūd, 950; al-Nasāʾī, 1658.

وَحَدَّثَنَاهُ أَبُو بَكْرِ بْنُ أَبِي شَيْبَةَ وَمُحَمَّدُ بْنُ الْـمُثَنَّى وَابْنُ بَشَّارٍ، جَمِيعًا عَنْ مُحَمَّدِ بْنِ جَعْفَرٍ، عَنْ شُعْبَةَ، ح. وَحَدَّثَنَا ابْنُ الْـمُثَنَّى، حَدَّثَنَا يَحْيَى بْنُ سَعِيدٍ، حَدَّثَنَا سُفْيَانُ، كِلَاهُمَا عَنْ مَنْصُورٍ، بِهَذَا الإِسْنَادِ.

وَفِي رِوَايَةِ شُعْبَةَ: عَنْ أَبِي يَحْيَى الأَعْرَجِ.

Text Explanation

In hadith No. 1440, ʿĀ'ishah says that if the Prophet prayed seated, he would bow from the sitting position. This makes it clear that sunnah prayers may be offered with the worshipper seated, even though he is able to stand up. This is the unanimous view of all scholars.

In hadith No. 1441 the narrator ʿAbdullāh ibn Shaqīq says: 'I was ill in Persia and I prayed seated. I asked ʿĀ'ishah about this…'. This is how the hadith is reported by all narrators in eastern and western countries. It is reported thus by *Qadi* ʿIyāḍ according to all narrators. He adds: 'Some consider the wording wrong, saying that the correct way is to replace the words "in Persia" by the word "*naqāris*",[i] which is the name of a well-known disease. They add that ʿĀ'ishah never went to Persia; so how could he ask her there? This is clearly wrong because the hadith does not necessarily mean that the narrator asked her in Persia. He asked her in Madinah after he returned from Persia. This is the apparent meaning of the hadith, which states that he asked her about something that he did in the past and whether his action was valid or not'.

In hadith No. 1444, ʿĀ'ishah mentions that the Prophet might pray seated, reciting the Qur'an, then when about thirty or forty verses of the surah remained, he would stand up and recite them standing, then bow. This hadith makes clear that it is permissible to stand during a part of one *rakʿah* and sit during the other part. This

---

i. If Arabic letters are undotted, as was the case in old writings, this word would look exactly the same as 'in Persia' which, in Arabic, is one word.

is the view of our Shāfiʿī School, as well as the Māliki and Ḥanīfi Schools and the general view of scholars. It is the same whether a person starts standing then sits down or starts seated then stands up. Some of the early scholars say that it is not permissible, but this view is wrong. *Qadi* ʿIyāḍ says that Abu Ḥanīfah's closest disciples, Abu Yūsuf and Muhammad, as well as other scholars, disapproved of sitting down after one had started standing. If a worshipper intends to pray standing then decides to sit down, this is permissible according to our scholars and the majority. Among the Mālikī scholars, Ibn al-Qāsim approves of this while Ashhab disapproves.

The text of hadith No. 1446 is as follows: 'God's Messenger used to recite [the Qur'an in prayer] seated. When he was about to bow, he would stand up and continue to recite what is equal to reciting forty verses'. This is clear evidence of the desirability of standing up for longer in sunnah prayer and that at the time it was considered better than offering a larger number of *rakʿahs*. We have discussed this question and mentioned the different views of scholars and that the view of the Shāfiʿī School prefers longer *rakʿahs*.

In hadith No. 1448, ʿĀ'ishah mentions that the Prophet prayed seated 'after people had weighed him down'. This is explained as meaning that he looked after them, took care of them and attended to their needs and interests, which was a heavy burden. In hadith No. 1450, ʿĀ'ishah mentions that the Prophet offered much of his sunnah prayers seated when he became old. The Arabic word used here is *baddana,* and Abu ʿUbayd explains the hadith according to this usage as 'when he grew old'. He adds: 'To narrate the hadith as using the word *baduna* is inappropriate because it means "to put on weight", which is contrary to the context' [the two words are written in the same way in Arabic]. *Qadi* ʿIyāḍ said: 'According to the majority of reporters, the word is *baduna,* while al-ʿUdhrī uses *baddana* and I think this usage is to improve the meaning. But neither of the two words is inappropriate to use about the Prophet (peace be upon him)'. ʿĀ'ishah is quoted a little later in Muslim's *Ṣaḥīḥ* as saying: "When God's Messenger (peace be upon him) was older and put on weight, he prayed the Witr in seven *rak'ahs*". This is stated in more than one hadith. Ibn Abi Hālah describes him as 'well-built'. Such says *Qadi* 'Iyāḍ, and in the majority of the original manuscripts in our area, the word used is *baddana*, meaning 'grew old', but God knows best.

Hadith No. 1454 mentions that 'a person's prayer seated is equal to half a prayer'. This means that its reward is half the reward for praying standing. Thus, it is correct and valid, but its reward is diminished. This hadith is understood to refer to a sunnah prayer offered seated when one is able to stand up. If one prays sunnah prayers seated because one is unable to stand up, his reward is the same as praying standing. As for obligatory prayers, if a person prays an obligatory prayer seated when he is able to offer it standing, the prayer is invalid. It earns no reward but incurs a sin. Our scholars say that if such a person considers such action to be permissible, he is considered an unbeliever and all rulings applicable to apostates apply to him, in the same way as a person who considers adultery or usury permissible. On the other hand, a person who offers an obligatory prayer seated because he is unable to stand up or reclining because he cannot stand up or sit down, his reward is the same as praying standing. Nothing is deducted from it according to the agreed view of our scholars. Therefore, the hadith mentioning halving the reward for praying seated must be understood as referring to a sunnah prayer offered seated by one who is able to stand up.

This is the detailed view of our Shāfi'ī School. It is agreed by the majority of scholars in explaining this hadith. *Qadi* 'Iyāḍ mentions a number of leading scholars sharing this view, including Sufyān al-Thawrī and Ibn al-Mājashūn. He quotes al-Bājī, a leading Mālikī scholar, as applying the hadith to a person who prays an obligatory prayer seated for a valid reason and to one who prays a sunnah prayer seated for a reason or for no reason. *Qadi* 'Iyāḍ adds that some scholars understand it to apply to one who has a valid reason permitting praying seated in obligatory or sunnah prayer but is able to pray standing with difficulty.

The Prophet says to ʿAbdullāh ibn ʿAmr: 'I am unlike any one of you'. According to our scholars, this is something special given to the Prophet (peace be upon him), making his sunnah prayer seated the same as offering it standing. He was given certain special things which are well known and mentioned in the books of many scholars, including those of our school. I give these details in my book, *Tahdhīb al-Asmā' wal-Lughāt*.

Qadi ʿIyāḍ says that it means that 'the Prophet endured hardship due to the care he took of his community and old age, which made standing difficult for him. Therefore, his reward is given in full, unlike others who have no valid reason'. This view is suspect or wrong. Other people who pray seated for a valid reason also earn full reward for their prayers. If he is able to stand up, then he is not like one with a valid reason. Thus, his statement 'I am unlike any one of you' would not be meaningful. The correct thing is to say that his prayer seated when he was able to stand up earned the full reward for praying standing. It was a special privilege given to him, but God knows best.

Scholars differ as to the best form of sitting down in prayer. Al-Shāfiʿī mentions two ways: the more obvious of which is that one places one's left foot horizontally and sits on it, and the other suggests sitting cross-legged. Some of our scholars say that it is better to place one's left thigh on the ground, while others say it is better to put one's knee up. Whichever form of sitting is acceptable, the difference is about preferability.

The more correct view of our school is that a sunnah prayer in the reclining position is valid even if one is able to sit or stand. An authentic hadith related by al-Bukhari says: 'A person who prays lying down earns half the reward of one who prays seated'. If one reclines down on one's side when praying, one should lie on one's right side. To recline on one's left side is acceptable but contrary to what is preferable. If one lies down on one's back when one is able to recline on one side, one's prayer is invalid. Yet some say that it is preferable to lie down and that reclining is unacceptable. The first view is the correct one, but God knows best.

Transmission

The chain of transmission of hadith No. 1451 includes: 'from Ibn Shihāb; from al-Sā'ib ibn Yazīd; from al-Muṭṭalib ibn Abi Wadāʿah; from Ḥafṣah'. The last three narrators, al-Sā'ib, al-Muṭṭalib and Ḥafṣah, were all Companions of the Prophet.

CHAPTER 17

NIGHT PRAYER AND THE NUMBER OF *RAKʿAHS* THE PROPHET OFFERED

[1455–121]. (Dar al-Salam 1602) Yaḥyā ibn Yaḥyā narrated: he said:[i] I read out to Mālik; from Ibn Shihāb; from ʿUrwah; from ʿĀ'ishah; that **'God's Messenger (peace be upon him) used to pray eleven *rakʿahs* at night, offering the Witr in one *rakʿah*. When he had finished, he would lie down on his right side until the caller of the *adhān* came to him. He would then pray two light *rakʿahs*'.**

حَدَّثَنَا يَحْيَى بْنُ يَحْيَى قَالَ: قَرَأْتُ عَلَى مَالِكٍ عَنِ ابْنِ شِهَابٍ، عَنْ عُرْوَةَ، عَنْ عَائِشَةَ، أَنَّ رَسُولَ اللهِ صَلَّى اللهُ عَلَيْهِ وَسَلَّمَ كَانَ يُصَلِّي بِاللَّيْلِ إِحْدَى عَشْرَةَ رَكْعَةً، يُوتِرُ مِنْهَا بِوَاحِدَةٍ. فَإِذَا فَرَغَ مِنْهَا اضْطَجَعَ عَلَى شِقِّهِ الأَيْمَنِ، حَتَّى يَأْتِيَهُ الْمُؤَذِّنُ، فَيُصَلِّي رَكْعَتَيْنِ خَفِيفَتَيْنِ.

[1456–122]. (Dar al-Salam 1603) Ḥarmalah ibn Yaḥyā narrated to me:[ii] Ibn Wahb narrated; ʿAmr ibn al-Ḥārith reported to me; from Ibn Shihāb; from ʿUrwah ibn al-Zubayr; from ʿĀ'ishah, the Prophet's wife. She said: **'God's Messenger (peace be upon him) used to pray in between the time he finished the Isha Prayer (the one which people call 'the darkness' prayer) and dawn, eleven *rakʿahs*, ending each two *rakʿahs* with the *salām*, and he prayed Witr in one *rakʿah*. When the caller of**

i. Related by Abu Dāwūd, 1335; al-Tirmidhī, 440 and 441; al-Nasā'ī, 1695 and 1725.
ii. Related by Abu Dāwūd, 1337; al-Nasā'ī, 684 and 1327.

the *adhān* ended his call for Fajr Prayer and he had ascertained the break of dawn and the caller came to him, he would stand up and pray two light *rakʿahs*. He would then lie down on his right side, until the caller came to him for the *iqāmah*'.

وَحَدَّثَنِي حَرْمَلَةُ بْنُ يَحْيَى، حَدَّثَنَا ابْنُ وَهْبٍ، أَخْبَرَنِي عَمْرُو بْنُ الْحَارِثِ، عَنِ ابْنِ شِهَابٍ، عَنْ عُرْوَةَ بْنِ الزُّبَيْرِ، عَنْ عَائِشَةَ، زَوْجِ النَّبِيِّ صَلَّى اللهُ عَلَيْهِ وَسَلَّمَ، قَالَتْ: كَانَ رَسُولُ اللهِ صَلَّى اللهُ عَلَيْهِ وَسَلَّمَ يُصَلِّي فِيمَا بَيْنَ أَنْ يَفْرُغَ مِنْ صَلاَةِ الْعِشَاءِ - وَهِيَ الَّتِي يَدْعُو النَّاسُ الْعَتَمَةَ - إِلَى الْفَجْرِ إِحْدَى عَشْرَةَ رَكْعَةً، يُسَلِّمُ بَيْنَ كُلِّ رَكْعَتَيْنِ، وَيُوتِرُ بِوَاحِدَةٍ. فَإِذَا سَكَتَ الْمُؤَذِّنُ مِنْ صَلاَةِ الْفَجْرِ، وَتَبَيَّنَ لَهُ الْفَجْرُ، وَجَاءَهُ الْمُؤَذِّنُ، قَامَ فَرَكَعَ رَكْعَتَيْنِ خَفِيفَتَيْنِ، ثُمَّ اضْطَجَعَ عَلَى شِقِّهِ الأَيْمَنِ، حَتَّى يَأْتِيَهُ الْمُؤَذِّنُ لِلإِقَامَةِ.

[1457–000]. (Dar al-Salam 000) Ḥarmalah narrated the same to me:[i] Ibn Wahb reported; Yūnus reported to me; from Ibn Shihāb; with the same chain of transmission: **Ḥarmalah narrated the hadith in the same wording, but he did not mention: 'and he had ascertained the break of dawn and the caller came to him', nor did he mention the *iqāmah*. The rest of the hadith is exactly the same as ʿAmr's narration.**

وَحَدَّثَنِيهِ حَرْمَلَةُ، أَخْبَرَنَا ابْنُ وَهْبٍ، أَخْبَرَنِي يُونُسُ، عَنِ ابْنِ شِهَابٍ، بِهَذَا الإِسْنَادِ. وَسَاقَ حَرْمَلَةُ الْحَدِيثَ بِمِثْلِهِ، غَيْرَ أَنَّهُ لَمْ يَذْكُرْ «وَتَبَيَّنَ لَهُ الْفَجْرُ وَجَاءَهُ الْمُؤَذِّنُ»، وَلَمْ يَذْكُرِ الإِقَامَةَ. وَسَائِرُ الْحَدِيثِ بِمِثْلِ حَدِيثِ عَمْرٍو سَوَاءً.

[1458–123]. (Dar al-Salam 1604) Abu Bakr ibn Abi Shaybah and Abu Kurayb narrated:[ii] both said: ʿAbdullāh ibn Numayr narrated [H]. Also, Ibn Numayr narrated; my father narrated;

i. Related by al-Nasāʾī, 1327.
ii. Related by al-Tirmidhī, 459.

Hishām narrated; from his father; from ʿĀ'ishah. She said: **'God's Messenger used to pray thirteen *rakʿahs* at night, of which five were Witr. He would not sit down [for *tashahhud*] in any of them other than the last'.**

وَحَدَّثَنَا أَبُو بَكْرِ بْنُ أَبِي شَيْبَةَ وَأَبُو كُرَيْبٍ قَالَا: حَدَّثَنَا عَبْدُ اللهِ بْنُ نُمَيْرٍ، ح. وَحَدَّثَنَا ابْنُ نُمَيْرٍ، حَدَّثَنَا أَبِي، حَدَّثَنَا هِشَامٌ، عَنْ أَبِيهِ، عَنْ عَائِشَةَ قَالَتْ: كَانَ رَسُولُ اللهِ صَلَّى اللهُ عَلَيْهِ وَسَلَّمَ يُصَلِّي مِنَ اللَّيْلِ ثَلَاثَ عَشْرَةَ رَكْعَةً، يُوتِرُ مِنْ ذَلِكَ بِخَمْسٍ، لَا يَجْلِسُ فِي شَيْءٍ إِلَّا فِي آخِرِهَا.

[000–000]. (Dar al-Salam 1605) Abu Bakr ibn Abi Shaybah narrated:[i] ʿAbdah ibn Sulaymān narrated [H]. Abu Kurayb narrated the same: Wakīʿ and Abu Usāmah narrated; all from Hishām, with the same chain of transmission: **the same text.**

وَحَدَّثَنَا أَبُو بَكْرِ بْنُ أَبِي شَيْبَةَ، حَدَّثَنَا عَبْدَةُ بْنُ سُلَيْمَانَ، ح. وَحَدَّثَنَاهُ أَبُو كُرَيْبٍ، حَدَّثَنَا وَكِيعٌ وَأَبُو أُسَامَةَ، كُلُّهُمْ عَنْ هِشَامٍ، بِهَذَا الإِسْنَادِ.

[1459–124]. (Dar al-Salam 1606) Qutaybah ibn Saʿīd narrated:[ii] Layth narrated; from Yazīd ibn Abi Ḥabīb; from ʿIrāk ibn Mālik; from ʿUrwah; that ʿĀ'ishah told him; that **'God's Messenger (peace be upon him) used to pray thirteen *rakʿahs*, including the two *rakʿahs* of Fajr'.**

وَحَدَّثَنَا قُتَيْبَةُ بْنُ سَعِيدٍ، حَدَّثَنَا لَيْثٌ، عَنْ يَزِيدَ بْنِ أَبِي حَبِيبٍ، عَنْ عِرَاكِ بْنِ مَالِكٍ، عَنْ عُرْوَةَ، أَنَّ عَائِشَةَ أَخْبَرَتْهُ أَنَّ رَسُولَ اللهِ صَلَّى اللهُ عَلَيْهِ وَسَلَّمَ كَانَ يُصَلِّي ثَلَاثَ عَشْرَةَ رَكْعَةً، بِرَكْعَتَيِ الْفَجْرِ.

i. Related by Ibn Mājah, 1359.
ii. Related by Abu Dāwūd, 1360.

[1460–125]. (Dar al-Salam 1607) Yaḥyā ibn Yaḥyā narrated:[i] I read out to Mālik; from Saʿīd ibn Abi Saʿīd al-Maqburī; from Abu Salamah ibn ʿAbd al-Raḥmān; that he asked ʿĀ'ishah: **'What was God's Messenger's [night] prayer in Ramadan like?' She said: 'God's Messenger (peace be upon him) did not pray in Ramadan or at other times more than eleven *rakʿahs*. He would pray four [*rakʿahs*], and you need not ask about their perfection and length. He would then pray [another] four *rakʿahs*, and you need not ask about their perfection and length. He would then add another three *rakʿahs*'. ʿĀ'ishah said: 'I asked: "Messenger of God, do you sleep before you pray Witr?" He said: "ʿĀ'ishah, my eyes go to sleep, but my heart does not".'**

حَدَّثَنَا يَحْيَى بْنُ يَحْيَى قَالَ: قَرَأْتُ عَلَى مَالِكٍ، عَنْ سَعِيدِ بْنِ أَبِي سَعِيدٍ الْمَقْبُرِيِّ، عَنْ أَبِي سَلَمَةَ بْنِ عَبْدِ الرَّحْمَنِ، أَنَّهُ سَأَلَ عَائِشَةَ: كَيْفَ كَانَتْ صَلاَةُ رَسُولِ اللهِ صَلَّى اللهُ عَلَيْهِ وَسَلَّمَ فِي رَمَضَانَ؟ قَالَتْ: مَا كَانَ رَسُولُ اللهِ صَلَّى اللهُ عَلَيْهِ وَسَلَّمَ يَزِيدُ فِي رَمَضَانَ وَلاَ فِي غَيْرِهِ عَلَى إِحْدَى عَشْرَةَ رَكْعَةً. يُصَلِّي أَرْبَعًا، فَلاَ تَسْأَلْ عَنْ حُسْنِهِنَّ وَطُولِهِنَّ. ثُمَّ يُصَلِّي أَرْبَعًا، فَلاَ تَسْأَلْ عَنْ حُسْنِهِنَّ وَطُولِهِنَّ. ثُمَّ يُصَلِّي ثَلاَثًا. فَقَالَتْ عَائِشَةُ: فَقُلْتُ يَا رَسُولَ اللهِ: أَتَنَامُ قَبْلَ أَنْ تُوتِرَ؟ فَقَالَ: «يَا عَائِشَةُ إِنَّ عَيْنَيَّ تَنَامَانِ وَلاَ يَنَامُ قَلْبِي».

[1461–126]. (Dar al-Salam 1608) Muhammad ibn al-Muthannā narrated:[ii] Ibn Abi ʿAdiy narrated; Hishām narrated; from Yaḥyā; from Abu Salamah. He said: **'I asked ʿĀ'ishah about God's Messenger [night] prayer. She said: "He prayed thirteen *rakʿahs*: he prayed eight *rakʿahs* then prayed Witr.**

i. Related by al-Bukhari, 1147; 2013 and 3569; Abu Dāwūd, 1341; al-Tirmidhī, 439; al-Nasā'ī, 1696.

ii. Related by Abu Dāwūd, 1340; al-Nasā'ī, 1755 and 1779, and in similar wording 1780.

He then prayed two *rak'ahs* seated. When he wanted to bow [i.e. do the *rukū'*] he stood up and bowed. He then prayed two *rak'ahs* between the *adhān* and the *iqāmah* of Fajr".'

وَحَدَّثَنَا مُحَمَّدُ بْنُ الْمُثَنَّى، حَدَّثَنَا ابْنُ أَبِي عَدِيٍّ، حَدَّثَنَا هِشَامٌ، عَنْ يَحْيَى، عَنْ أَبِي سَلَمَةَ قَالَ: سَأَلْتُ عَائِشَةَ عَنْ صَلاَةِ رَسُولِ اللهِ صَلَّى اللهُ عَلَيْهِ وَسَلَّمَ فَقَالَتْ: كَانَ يُصَلِّي ثَلاَثَ عَشْرَةَ رَكْعَةً. يُصَلِّي ثَمَانَ رَكَعَاتٍ، ثُمَّ يُوتِرُ، ثُمَّ يُصَلِّي رَكْعَتَيْنِ وَهُوَ جَالِسٌ. فَإِذَا أَرَادَ أَنْ يَرْكَعَ قَامَ فَرَكَعَ، ثُمَّ يُصَلِّي رَكْعَتَيْنِ بَيْنَ النِّدَاءِ وَالإِقَامَةِ مِنْ صَلاَةِ الصُّبْحِ.

[1462–000]. (Dar al-Salam 1609) Zuhayr ibn Ḥarb narrated to me: Ḥusayn ibn Muhammad narrated; Shaybān narrated; from Yaḥyā; he said: I heard Abu Salamah [H]. Also, Yaḥyā ibn Bishr al-Ḥarīrī narrated to me; Mu'āwiyah (meaning Ibn Sallām) narrated; from Yaḥyā ibn Abi Kathīr. He said: **'Abu Salamah reported to me that he asked 'Ā'ishah about God's Messenger's prayer...' the same except that in their narration: 'nine *rak'ahs* standing, including Witr'.**

وَحَدَّثَنِي زُهَيْرُ بْنُ حَرْبٍ، حَدَّثَنَا حُسَيْنُ بْنُ مُحَمَّدٍ، حَدَّثَنَا شَيْبَانُ، عَنْ يَحْيَى، قَالَ سَمِعْتُ أَبَا سَلَمَةَ، ح. وَحَدَّثَنِي يَحْيَى بْنُ بِشْرٍ الْحَرِيرِيُّ، حَدَّثَنَا مُعَاوِيَةُ، (يَعْنِي ابْنَ سَلاَّمٍ)، عَنْ يَحْيَى بْنِ أَبِي كَثِيرٍ، قَالَ: أَخْبَرَنِي أَبُو سَلَمَةَ، أَنَّهُ سَأَلَ عَائِشَةَ عَنْ صَلاَةِ رَسُولِ اللهِ صَلَّى اللهُ عَلَيْهِ وَسَلَّمَ: بِمِثْلِهِ. غَيْرَ أَنَّ فِي حَدِيثِهِمَا: تِسْعَ رَكَعَاتٍ قَائِمًا يُوتِرُ مِنْهُنَّ.

[1463–127]. (Dar al-Salam 1610) 'Amr al-Nāqid narrated: Sufyān ibn 'Uyaynah; from 'Abdullāh ibn Abi Labīd. He heard Abu Salamah who said: **'I went to 'Ā'ishah and said: "Mother, tell me about God's Messenger's prayer". She said: "In Ramadan and at other times, he prayed thirteen *rak'ahs* at night, including the two of Fajr".'**

وَحَدَّثَنَا عَمْرٌو النَّاقِدُ، حَدَّثَنَا سُفْيَانُ بْنُ عُيَيْنَةَ، عَنْ عَبْدِ اللهِ بْنِ أَبِي لَبِيدٍ، سَمِعَ أَبَا سَلَمَةَ قَالَ: أَتَيْتُ عَائِشَةَ فَقُلْتُ: أَيْ أُمَّهْ، أَخْبِرِينِي عَنْ صَلاَةِ رَسُولِ اللهِ صَلَّى اللهُ عَلَيْهِ وَسَلَّمَ. فَقَالَتْ: كَانَتْ صَلاَتُهُ فِي شَهْرِ رَمَضَانَ وَغَيْرِهِ ثَلاَثَ عَشْرَةَ رَكْعَةً بِاللَّيْلِ، مِنْهَا رَكْعَتَا الْفَجْرِ.

[1464–128]. (Dar al-Salam 1611) Ibn Numayr narrated:[i] my father narrated; Ḥanẓalah narrated; from al-Qāsim ibn Muhammad. He said: **'I heard ʿĀ'ishah say: "God's Messenger's night prayer was ten *rakʿahs* and he prayed Witr one *rakʿah*. He then prayed the two *rakʿahs* of the Fajr [sunnah]. This is a total of thirteen *rakʿahs*".'**

حَدَّثَنَا ابْنُ نُمَيْرٍ، حَدَّثَنَا أَبِي، حَدَّثَنَا حَنْظَلَةُ، عَنِ الْقَاسِمِ بْنِ مُحَمَّدٍ قَالَ: سَمِعْتُ عَائِشَةَ تَقُولُ: كَانَتْ صَلاَةُ رَسُولِ اللهِ صَلَّى اللهُ عَلَيْهِ وَسَلَّمَ مِنَ اللَّيْلِ عَشَرَ رَكَعَاتٍ، وَيُوتِرُ بِسَجْدَةٍ. وَيَرْكَعُ رَكْعَتَيِ الْفَجْرِ، فَتِلْكَ ثَلاَثَ عَشْرَةَ رَكْعَةً.

[1465–129]. (Dar al-Salam 1612) Ahmad ibn Yūnus narrated:[ii] Zuhayr narrated; Abu Isḥāq narrated [H]. Also, Yaḥyā ibn Yaḥyā narrated; Abu Khaythamah reported; from Abu Isḥāq. He said: **'I asked al-Aswad ibn Yazīd about what ʿĀ'ishah reported of God's Messenger's prayer. She said: "He used to go to sleep early at night and stay up the later part in worship. If he was in need of his wife, he would have that and go to sleep. Then when it was the first *adhān* (she said) he jumped (No, by God, she did not say: he rose) and washed himself (No, by God, she did not say: he took a bath, but I know what she meant). If he was not in a state of ceremonial impurity**

i. Related by al-Bukhari, 1140; Abu Dāwūd, 1334.
ii. Related by al-Nasā'ī in a shorter version, 1639.

[i.e. *janābah*] he would perform the ablution as anyone does the ablution for prayer, and he then prayed the two *rak'ahs* [of sunnah]".'

وَحَدَّثَنَا أَحْمَدُ بْنُ يُونُسَ، حَدَّثَنَا زُهَيْرٌ، حَدَّثَنَا أَبُو إِسْحَاقَ، ح. وَحَدَّثَنَا يَحْيَى بْنُ يَحْيَى، أَخْبَرَنَا أَبُو خَيْثَمَةَ، عَنْ أَبِي إِسْحَاقَ قَالَ: سَأَلْتُ الأَسْوَدَ بْنَ يَزِيدَ عَمَّا حَدَّثَتْهُ عَائِشَةُ عَنْ صَلاَةِ رَسُولِ اللهِ صَلَّى اللهُ عَلَيْهِ وَسَلَّمَ. قَالَتْ: كَانَ يَنَامُ أَوَّلَ اللَّيْلِ وَيُحْيِي آخِرَهُ. ثُمَّ إِنْ كَانَتْ لَهُ حَاجَةٌ إِلَى أَهْلِهِ قَضَى حَاجَتَهُ، ثُمَّ يَنَامُ. فَإِذَا كَانَ عِنْدَ النِّدَاءِ الأَوَّلِ-قَالَتْ: وَثَبَ (وَلاَ وَاللهِ مَا قَالَتْ قَامَ)، فَأَفَاضَ عَلَيْهِ الْمَاءَ، (وَلاَ وَاللهِ مَا قَالَتِ اغْتَسَلَ). وَأَنَا أَعْلَمُ مَا تُرِيدُ. وَإِنْ لَمْ يَكُنْ جُنُبًا تَوَضَّأَ وُضُوءَ الرَّجُلِ لِلصَّلاَةِ ثُمَّ صَلَّى الرَّكْعَتَيْنِ.

[1466–130]. (Dar al-Salam 1613) Abu Bakr ibn Abi Shaybah and Abu Kurayb narrated: both said: Yaḥyā ibn Adam narrated; 'Ammār ibn Ruzayq narrated; from Abu Isḥāq; from al-Aswad; from 'Ā'ishah. She said: **'God's Messenger (peace be upon him) used to pray at night, making Witr the last of his prayers'.**

حَدَّثَنَا أَبُو بَكْرِ بْنُ أَبِي شَيْبَةَ وَأَبُو كُرَيْبٍ، قَالاَ: حَدَّثَنَا يَحْيَى بْنُ آدَمَ، حَدَّثَنَا عَمَّارُ بْنُ رُزَيْقٍ، عَنْ أَبِي إِسْحَاقَ، عَنِ الأَسْوَدِ، عَنْ عَائِشَةَ، قَالَتْ: كَانَ رَسُولُ اللهِ صَلَّى اللهُ عَلَيْهِ وَسَلَّمَ يُصَلِّي مِنَ اللَّيْلِ حَتَّى يَكُونَ آخِرَ صَلاَتِهِ الْوِتْرُ.

[1467–131]. (Dar al-Salam 1614) Hannād ibn al-Sariy narrated to me:[i] Abu al-Aḥwaṣ narrated; from Ash'ath; from his father; from Masrūq. He said: **'I asked 'Ā'ishah about what God's Messenger (peace be upon him) did. She said: "He loved**

i. Related by al-Bukhari, 1132 and 6461; Abu Dāwūd in similar wording, 1317; al-Nasā'ī, 1615.

what is continuous". I asked: "At what times did he pray?" She said: "When he heard the crier, he got up and prayed".'

حَدَّثَنِي هَنَّادُ بْنُ السَّرِيِّ، حَدَّثَنَا أَبُو الأَحْوَصِ، عَنْ أَشْعَثَ، عَنْ أَبِيهِ، عَنْ مَسْرُوقٍ قَالَ: سَأَلْتُ عَائِشَةَ عَنْ عَمَلِ رَسُولِ اللهِ صَلَّى اللهُ عَلَيْهِ وَسَلَّمَ فَقَالَتْ: كَانَ يُحِبُّ الدَّائِمَ. قَالَ: قُلْتُ أَيَّ حِينٍ كَانَ يُصَلِّي؟ فَقَالَتْ: كَانَ إِذَا سَمِعَ الصَّارِخَ قَامَ فَصَلَّى.

[1468–132]. (Dar al-Salam 1615) Abu Kurayb narrated:[i] Ibn Bishr reported; from Misʿar; from Saʿd; from Abu Salamah; from ʿĀ'ishah. She said: **'Never did the early part of dawn find God's Messenger (peace be upon him) in my home, or at my place, other than asleep'.**

حَدَّثَنَا أَبُو كُرَيْبٍ، أَخْبَرَنَا ابْنُ بِشْرٍ، عَنْ مِسْعَرٍ، عَنْ سَعْدٍ، عَنْ أَبِي سَلَمَةَ، عَنْ عَائِشَةَ قَالَتْ: مَا أَلْفَى رَسُولَ اللهِ صَلَّى اللهُ عَلَيْهِ وَسَلَّمَ السَّحَرُ الأَعْلَى فِي بَيْتِي، أَوْ عِنْدِي، إِلاَّ نَائِمًا.

[1469–133]. (Dar al-Salam 1616–1617) Abu Bakr ibn Abi Shaybah, Naṣr ibn ʿAlī and Ibn Abi ʿUmar narrated:[ii] Abu Bakr said: Sufyān ibn ʿUyaynah narrated: from Abu al-Naḍr; from Abu Salamah; from ʿĀ'ishah. She said: **'When the Prophet had prayed the two [sunnah] *rakʿahs* of Fajr, he would talk to me if I was awake; otherwise, he would lie down'.**

حَدَّثَنَا أَبُو بَكْرِ بْنُ أَبِي شَيْبَةَ وَنَصْرُ بْنُ عَلِيٍّ وَابْنُ أَبِي عُمَرَ، قَالَ أَبُو بَكْرٍ: حَدَّثَنَا سُفْيَانُ بْنُ عُيَيْنَةَ، عَنْ أَبِي النَّضْرِ، عَنْ أَبِي سَلَمَةَ، عَنْ عَائِشَةَ قَالَتْ: كَانَ النَّبِيُّ صَلَّى اللهُ عَلَيْهِ وَسَلَّمَ إِذَا صَلَّى رَكْعَتَيِ الْفَجْرِ، فَإِنْ كُنْتُ مُسْتَيْقِظَةً حَدَّثَنِي، وَإِلاَّ اضْطَجَعَ.

i. Related by al-Bukhari, 1133; Abu Dāwūd, 1318; Ibn Mājah, 1197.
ii. Related by al-Bukhari, 1161 and 1168; Abu Dāwūd, 1262; al-Tirmidhī in similar wording, 418.

Ibn Abi 'Umar narrated:[i] Sufyān narrated; from Ziyād ibn Sa'd; from Ibn Abi 'Attāb; from Abu Salamah; from 'Ā'ishah; from the Prophet: **the same text.**

وَحَدَّثَنَا ابْنُ أَبِي عُمَرَ، حَدَّثَنَا سُفْيَانُ، عَنْ زِيَادِ بْنِ سَعْدٍ، عَنِ ابْنِ أَبِي عَتَّابٍ، عَنْ أَبِي سَلَمَةَ، عَنْ عَائِشَةَ، عَنِ النَّبِيِّ صَلَّى اللهُ عَلَيْهِ وَسَلَّمَ: مِثْلَهُ.

[1470–134]. (Dar al-Salam 1618) Zuhayr ibn Ḥarb narrated: Jarīr narrated; from al-A'mash; from Tamīm ibn Salamah; from 'Urwah ibn al-Zubayr; from 'Ā'ishah. She said: **'God's Messenger (peace be upon him) used to pray at night. When he had finished his Witr, he would say: "Get up, 'Ā'ishah, and pray Witr".'**

وَحَدَّثَنَا زُهَيْرُ بْنُ حَرْبٍ، حَدَّثَنَا جَرِيرٌ، عَنِ الأَعْمَشِ، عَنْ تَمِيمِ بْنِ سَلَمَةَ، عَنْ عُرْوَةَ بْنِ الزُّبَيْرِ، عَنْ عَائِشَةَ قَالَتْ: كَانَ رَسُولُ اللهِ صَلَّى اللهُ عَلَيْهِ وَسَلَّمَ يُصَلِّي مِنَ اللَّيْلِ، فَإِذَا أَوْتَرَ قَالَ: «قُومِي فَأَوْتِرِي يَا عَائِشَةُ».

[1471–135]. (Dar al-Salam 1619) Ḥarūn ibn Sa'īd al-Aylī narrated to me: Ibn Wahb narrated; Sulaymān ibn Bilāl reported to me; from Rabī'ah ibn Abu 'Abd al-Raḥmān; from al-Qāsim ibn Muhammad; from 'Ā'ishah; that **'God's Messenger (peace be upon him) used to pray his night prayers and she would be lying across in front of him. When only Witr remained, he would wake her up to pray Witr'.**

وَحَدَّثَنِي هَارُونُ بْنُ سَعِيدٍ الأَيْلِيُّ، حَدَّثَنَا ابْنُ وَهْبٍ، أَخْبَرَنِي سُلَيْمَانُ بْنُ بِلَالٍ، عَنْ رَبِيعَةَ بْنِ أَبِي عَبْدِ الرَّحْمَنِ، عَنِ الْقَاسِمِ بْنِ مُحَمَّدٍ، عَنْ عَائِشَةَ، أَنَّ رَسُولَ اللهِ صَلَّى

i. Related by Abu Dāwūd, 1263.

اللهُ عَلَيْهِ وَسَلَّمَ كَانَ يُصَلِّي صَلاَتَهُ بِاللَّيْلِ وَهِيَ مُعْتَرِضَةٌ بَيْنَ يَدَيْهِ، فَإِذَا بَقِيَ الْوِتْرُ أَيْقَظَهَا فَأَوْتَرَتْ.

[1472–136]. (Dar al-Salam 1620) Yaḥyā ibn Yaḥyā narrated:[i] Sufyān ibn ʿUyaynah reported from Abu Yaʿfūr (his name is Wāqid and nickname Waqdān) [H]. Also Abu Bakr ibn Abi Shaybah and Abu Kurayb narrated; both said: Abu Muʿāwiyah narrated; from al-Aʿmash; both from Muslim; from Masrūq; from ʿĀ'ishah. She said: **'At all times of night the Prophet prayed Witr, and the last that he offered the Witr Prayer was shortly before dawn'.**

وَحَدَّثَنَا يَحْيَى بْنُ يَحْيَى، أَخْبَرَنَا سُفْيَانُ بْنُ عُيَيْنَةَ، عَنْ أَبِي يَعْفُورٍ (وَاسْمُهُ وَاقِدٌ، وَلَقَبُهُ وَقْدَانُ)، ح. وَحَدَّثَنَا أَبُو بَكْرِ بْنُ أَبِي شَيْبَةَ وَ أَبُو كُرَيْبٍ، قَالاَ: حَدَّثَنَا أَبُو مُعَاوِيَةَ، عَنِ الأَعْمَشِ، كِلاَهُمَا عَنْ مُسْلِمٍ، عَنْ مَسْرُوقٍ، عَنْ عَائِشَةَ قَالَتْ: مِنْ كُلِّ اللَّيْلِ قَدْ أَوْتَرَ رَسُولُ اللهِ صَلَّى اللهُ عَلَيْهِ وَسَلَّمَ، فَانْتَهَى وِتْرُهُ إِلَى السَّحَرِ.

[1473–137]. (Dar al-Salam 1621) Abu Bakr ibn Abi Shaybah and Zuhayr ibn Ḥarb narrated:[ii] both said: Wakīʿ narrated; from Sufyān; from Abu Ḥaṣīn; from Yaḥyā ibn Waththāb; from Masrūq; from ʿĀ'ishah. She said: **'At all times of night the Prophet prayed Witr: its early part, its middle and tail end. The last that his Witr was offered was shortly before dawn'.**

وَحَدَّثَنَا أَبُو بَكْرِ بْنُ أَبِي شَيْبَةَ وَزُهَيْرُ بْنُ حَرْبٍ، قَالاَ: حَدَّثَنَا وَكِيعٌ، عَنْ سُفْيَانَ، عَنْ أَبِي حَصِينٍ، عَنْ يَحْيَى بْنِ وَثَّابٍ، عَنْ مَسْرُوقٍ، عَنْ عَائِشَةَ قَالَتْ: مِنْ كُلِّ اللَّيْلِ قَدْ

---

i. Related by al-Bukhari, 996; Abu Dāwūd, 1435.
ii. Related by al-Tirmidhī, 456; al-Nasā'ī, 1680; Ibn Mājah, 1185.

أَوْتَرَ رَسُولُ اللهِ صَلَّى اللهُ عَلَيْهِ وَسَلَّمَ: مِنْ أَوَّلِ اللَّيْلِ، وَأَوْسَطِهِ، وَآخِرِهِ. فَانْتَهَى وِتْرُهُ إِلَى السَّحَرِ.

[1474–138]. (Dar al-Salam 1622) ʿAlī ibn Ḥujr narrated to me: Ḥassān (the judge of Kirmān) narrated; from Saʿīd ibn Masrūq; from Abu al-Ḍuḥā; from Masrūq; from ʿĀ'ishah. She said: **'God's Messenger prayed Witr at all times of night, and the last that he used to offer Witr was the tail end of the night'.**

حَدَّثَنِي عَلِيُّ بْنُ حُجْرٍ، حَدَّثَنَا حَسَّانُ، قَاضِي كِرْمَانَ، عَنْ سَعِيدِ بْنِ مَسْرُوقٍ، عَنْ أَبِي الضُّحَى، عَنْ مَسْرُوقٍ، عَنْ عَائِشَةَ قَالَتْ: كُلَّ اللَّيْلِ قَدْ أَوْتَرَ رَسُولُ اللهِ صَلَّى اللهُ عَلَيْهِ وَسَلَّمَ، فَانْتَهَى وِتْرُهُ إِلَى آخِرِ اللَّيْلِ.

Text Explanation

Qadi ʿIyāḍ discussed ʿĀ'ishah's hadith as narrated by Saʿd ibn Hishām, which mentions that 'the Prophet's night worship was nine *rakʿahs*', and her hadith narrated by ʿUrwah that the Prophet prayed 'eleven *rakʿahs* including Witr and ended each two *rakʿahs* with *salām* and that he prayed the sunnah of Fajr when the one who called the *adhān* came to him'. Also Hishām ibn ʿUrwah and others narrate from ʿUrwah; from ʿĀ'ishah: 'thirteen *rakʿahs* including the Fajr [sunnah]'. She also reported that the Prophet 'did not do more than eleven *rakʿahs* in Ramadan or at other times: four and four and three'. Also, that he 'prayed thirteen: eight followed by two seated, then the two *rakʿahs* of the sunnah of Fajr'. She explained this in another hadith that they included the two *rakʿahs* of sunnah before Fajr. Al-Bukhari enters a hadith she narrates stating that the Prophet's prayer at night was seven or nine *rakʿahs*. Al-Bukhari mentions, as does Muslim later, a hadith narrated by Ibn ʿAbbās that the Prophet's night worship was thirteen *rakʿahs* and two *rakʿahs* of the sunnah of Fajr. In the hadith narrated by Zayd ibn Khālid, the

Prophet is said to have prayed two light *rakʿahs* followed by two long ones, and he mentions at the end: 'Thus the total is thirteen'.

Qadi ʿIyāḍ said:

> Explaining these hadiths, scholars said that Ibn ʿAbbās, Zayd and ʿĀ'ishah reported what they saw. As for the differences in ʿĀ'ishah's reports, some scholars say that they are hers while others attribute them to those reporting from her. It is probable that she reported eleven *rakʿahs* as the most common practice, while other reports refer to what occurred occasionally. The highest number was fifteen *rakʿahs* including the two of Fajr, and the minimum was seven. This mentions what happened as to the time available or the length of recitation of the Qur'an in prayer, as mentioned in the hadith narrated by Hudhayfah and Ibn Masʿūd, or due to sleep or illness, etc. or when the Prophet became older, as she said: "In old age he prayed seven *rakʿahs*". At times, she might count the two light *rakʿahs* the Prophet did at the beginning of his night worship, as reported by Zayd ibn Khālid, and ʿĀ'ishah reported after that. All this is entered by Muslim. At times she counted the two *rakʿahs* of Fajr sunnah but not at other times, and she might have counted the two *rakʿahs* of sunnah after ʿIsha on certain occasions but did not do so at others.
>
> There is no disagreement that no specific number is mentioned so as to make it wrong to add to or omit from it. Night prayer is a voluntary action that earns reward, and the more done of it the greater the reward. The disagreement is centred on what the Prophet did and what he chose for himself, but God knows best.

In the first hadith, No. 1455, ʿĀ'ishah mentions that the Prophet 'offered Witr in one *rakʿah*'. This is clear evidence that the minimum for Witr is one *rakʿah* and that a single *rakʿah* is a perfectly valid prayer. This is the view of our school and the majority of scholars. Abu Ḥanīfah, however, said that praying Witr in one *rakʿah* is invalid and that a single *rak'ah* cannot be a valid prayer. The authentic hadith, though, states the contrary.

The same hadith says: 'God's Messenger (peace be upon him) used to pray eleven *rak'ahs* at night, offering Witr in one *rak'ah*. When he had finished, he would lie down on his right side until the caller of the *adhān* came to him. He would then pray two light *rak'ahs*'. *Qadi* 'Iyāḍ said: 'According to this hadith, lying down is after the night prayer, i.e. *tahajjud*, and before the Fajr sunnah. In the next hadith, No. 1456, 'Ā'ishah mentions that the Prophet lay down after praying the Fajr sunnah. In the hadith narrated by Ibn 'Abbās, lying down was after the night worship and before the Fajr sunnah. This is contrary to al-Shāfi'ī's view as he and his disciples say that lying down after the Fajr sunnah is recommended'.

He adds: 'Mālik and the majority of scholars, as well as a number of the Prophet's Companions, consider it a deviation [i.e. *bid'ah*]'. He refers to the report of lying down after praying the Fajr sunnah as the weaker report. Therefore, the report that it is before Fajr should be given preference. He says: 'No one says that lying down before the Fajr sunnah is recommended. The same applies to lying down after it. Muslim enters hadith No. 1469 quoting 'Ā'ishah: "He would talk to me if I was awake; otherwise, he would lie down". This shows that it is not a sunnah, and that the Prophet sometimes lay down before the Fajr sunnah and sometimes after it. On some occasions he did not lie down at all.'

This is what *Qadi* 'Iyāḍ says. The correct or right thing to say is that lying down is after praying the Fajr sunnah, as this is confirmed by the hadith narrated by Abu Hurayrah quoting the Prophet (peace be upon him): 'When any of you has prayed the two *rak'ahs* of Fajr [sunnah], let him lie down on his right side'. This hadith is related by Abu Dāwūd and al-Tirmidhī with an authentic chain of transmission that meets the conditions set by al-Bukhari and Muslim. Al-Tirmidhī adds that it is a 'good, authentic hadith'. This is then an authentic hadith that gives a clear order to lie down. The hadiths narrated by 'Ā'ishah mentioning lying down before and after this sunnah and the hadith narrated by Ibn 'Abbās mentioning it before the Fajr sunnah do not contradict this hadith. Lying down before offering the Fajr sunnah does not preclude doing the same after it. Perhaps the Prophet might have omitted lying down after the Fajr sunnah to show that this is permissible, but he might have lied down before and after it.

As the hadith states the order to lie down after the Fajr sunnah and there are reports that he actually did so, this must be upheld. If hadiths can be reconciled, it is not permissible to reject any of them. In this case, reconciliation is achieved in two ways: 1) that he lay down before and after it and 2) the Prophet omitted lying down after the Fajr sunnah to show that this is permissible, but God knows best.

The hadiths mention that the Prophet 'lied down on his right side'. This shows that it is desirable to do likewise when we go to bed. Scholars say that the reason is that in this position, one does not fall fast asleep because man's heart is on the left side of the body and when a person lies down on the right side, the heart's position prevents deep sleep. By contrast, sleeping on one's left side gives greater relaxation to one's heart and this helps deep sleep. In hadith No. 1456, it is mentioned that when the person who called the *adhān* came to him, the Prophet would 'stand up and pray two light *rakʿahs*'. These are the regular sunnah of Fajr. The hadith gives evidence that this sunnah is preferably light. We have explained this in the appropriate place.

The same hadith mentions that the Prophet finished every two *rakʿahs* of his night worship with *salām*. This is evidence that it is desirable to do so and to offer night worship in two *rakʿahs* at a time. In some hadiths, it is mentioned that the Prophet did the *salām* only after the last *rakʿah*. This is understood to show that this is permissible. The hadith also mentions that the Prophet prayed Witr in one *rakʿah*. This makes it clear that it is perfectly proper to pray one *rakʿah* and that one *rakʿah* is the minimum component of Witr, as we have already explained.

In hadith No. 1458, ʿĀ'ishah mentions that the Prophet 'prayed thirteen *rakʿahs* of night worship, five of which were Witr and he sat down [for *tashahhud*] only in the last *rakʿah*'. In another hadith, she mentions that he finished with *salām* after each two *rak'ahs*. In hadith No. 1460, she mentions that his prayer was four *rak'ahs*, then another four, then three, and yet in another narration he prayed eight *rak'ahs* and added Witr in one *rak'ah*. Hadith No. 1464 quotes her as saying the Prophet offered ten *rak'ahs* and added one for Witr. In the hadith narrated by Ibn 'Abbās, it is mentioned that the Prophet 'offered two *rak'ahs...*', and in Ibn 'Umar's narration, the Prophet is quoted to have said: 'Night prayer is offered two *rak'ahs* at a time'. All this gives evidence that Witr is not specifically limited to one *rak'ah*, nor is it eleven or thirteen *rak'ahs*. These figures are all permissible, as are all figures in between. It is also permissible to pray a number of *rak'ahs* with one *salām* to end them. This also shows that this is permissible, but the more preferable way is to pray two *rak'ahs* at a time, finishing them with *salām*. This is the best-known practice of God's Messenger (peace be upon him) and conforms with the order to pray night worship two *rak'ahs* at a time.

In hadith No. 1460, 'Ā'ishah says that the Prophet 'prayed four *rak'ahs*, and you need not ask about their perfection and their length'. This means that they were at the highest level of perfection and length that everyone could see, and none need ask about. In this hadith and others that come later, we have evidence in support of the view of al-Shāfi'ī and other scholars who say that standing for a long time in prayer is preferable to praying a large number of *rak'ahs* with many bowings and prostrations. A number of scholars are of the opposite view, while other scholars say that standing up longer is better in night worship, while offering many *rak'ahs* of voluntary worship is better during the day. We discussed this question and its related evidence in the chapters that explain how prayer is offered.

In the same hadith, the Prophet says: 'My eyes go to sleep, but my heart does not'. This is a special privilege given to prophets (peace be upon them all). An earlier hadith mentioned that the Prophet slept in a valley and he was unaware of the time of Fajr Prayer until the sun had risen. We explained that the break of dawn and sunrise are felt by man's eyes, not his mental faculty. The invalidation of ablution and similar matters are felt mentally. Some suggest that his mental faculty goes to sleep at times and remains awake at others. On that occasion in the valley, his sleep coincided with the time when his mental faculty was asleep. The first view is the correct one.

In hadith No. 1461 ʿĀ'ishah narrates that the Prophet 'prayed thirteen *rakʿahs*: he prayed eight *rak'ahs* then prayed Witr. He then prayed two *rakʿahs* seated. When he wanted to bow [i.e. do the *rukūʿ*] he stood up and bowed. He then prayed two *rakʿahs* between the *adhān* and the *iqāmah* of Fajr'. This hadith is taken at face value by al-Awzāʿī and Ahmad, as quoted by *Qadi* ʿIyāḍ. Thus, according to them, it is permissible to offer two *rakʿahs* in the sitting position, after having prayed Witr. Ahmad said: 'I do not do it, but I do not stop anyone doing it'. *Qadi* ʿIyāḍ mentions that Mālik rejects this. The correct view, in my opinion, is that the Prophet prayed these two *rakʿahs* after Witr in order to show that it is permissible to pray after one has prayed Witr and to demonstrate that voluntary prayer may be offered in the sitting position. The Prophet did not do this regularly but did it once or twice or on a small number of occasions.

In several of these hadiths, ʿĀ'ishah uses the word *'kāna'* in reference to the Prophet's action, but we need not attach much importance to this usage. This word is normally translated as 'used to', but the majority of meticulous scholars consider that the Arabic word does not necessarily indicate frequent or permanent action. It is merely a verb used in the past tense, indicating an action on a single occasion. If there is additional evidence indicating continuity, we accept that. If there is no such evidence, the word does not imply such continuity. ʿĀ'ishah herself uses the same verb as she mentions that she applied perfume to the Prophet when he released himself from consecration, before performing the *ṭawāf*. It is well known that the Prophet (peace be upon him) offered the pilgrimage only once after his marriage to ʿĀ'ishah, which was the Farewell Pilgrimage. This means that she used the word *'kāna'* in reference to an action done once only. It may be suggested that she might have applied such perfume when he was in a state of consecration during his ʿumrah, because a person doing ʿumrah is forbidden to apply perfume before his *ṭawāf*, and this is unanimously agreed upon. Thus, it is confirmed that she used the word *kāna* in reference to an action that she did only once.

We have expressed this understanding of the hadith mentioning the two *rakʿahs* offered by the Prophet in the sitting position because of the several hadiths entered in the two *Ṣaḥīḥ* anthologies narrated by ʿĀ'ishah, as well as the hadiths narrated by many Companions of the Prophet, and entered in the two *Ṣaḥīḥs* stating that the last thing the Prophet prayed at night was Witr. In both *Ṣaḥīḥ* anthologies, we have well known hadiths stating clearly the order to make Witr the last prayer at night, such as the hadith that says: 'Make Witr the last of your prayers at night' and 'Night prayer is two *rakʿahs* at a time. If you fear that the break of dawn is close, then pray Witr in one *rakʿah*'. Other hadiths express the same meaning. In light of these hadiths and similar ones, how can anyone think that the Prophet would continuously offer two *rakʿahs* after he had prayed Witr and make them the last of his night worship? What the aforementioned hadith indicates is its permissibility, as we have mentioned. This is the correct view.

Qadi ʿIyāḍ leans towards accepting the well-known hadiths and rejecting the hadith that mentions the two *rakʿahs* offered seated, but this is not right. If we have authentic hadiths that can be reconciled and applied, this must be done. We have, by the grace of God, reconciled these hadiths relating to this question.

In hadith No. 1465, ʿĀ'ishah says that when the Prophet heard the first *adhān*, 'he jumped'. This urges giving one's attention to worship and doing it with energy. This is implied by the authentic hadith that says: 'A strong believer is better and dearer to God than a weak believer'. At the end of this hadith, she says: 'He then prayed the two *rakʿahs*', meaning the Fajr sunnah.

ʿĀ'ishah says in hadith No. 1466: 'God's Messenger used to pray at night, making Witr the last of his prayers'. This hadith provides evidence in support of what we stated earlier that it is recommended to make the last of one's night prayer Witr, i.e. in an odd number. This is agreed upon by all scholars, and we have explained the reason for the Prophet's praying two *rakʿahs* after Witr and doing them in the sitting position.

In hadith No. 1467, ʿĀ'ishah mentions that the Prophet 'loved what is continuous'. This urges doing what is reasonable of worship and that one must not commit oneself to doing more than one can do regularly. One should then endeavour to keep this up. In the same hadith, she says that when the Prophet 'heard the crier, he got up and prayed'. The 'crier' in this instance means 'fowl' or 'cock', as agreed by all scholars. They say that it is given this nickname because of its frequent cries.

In hadith No. 1469, ʿĀ'ishah reports: 'When the Prophet had prayed the two [sunnah] *rakʿahs* of Fajr, he would talk to me if I was awake; otherwise, he would lie down'. This makes it amply clear that it is perfectly permissible to speak and discuss after offering the Fajr sunnah. This is the view of our Shāfiʿī School, Mālik and the majority of scholars. *Qadi* ʿIyāḍ says: 'The Kūfī scholars say it is discouraged, and this is reported to have been expressed by Ibn Masʿūd and some early scholars because this is a time when seeking God's forgiveness is urged. The correct view is that it is permissible, as the Prophet did it. The fact that it is a time when praying for forgiveness is desirable is no reason to prevent ordinary speech.

In hadith No. 1470, the Prophet finished his Witr prayer and then alerted ʿĀ'ishah to rise and pray Witr. In the next hadith, he would wake her up when only Witr was left for him to pray. These hadiths show that it is encouraged to pray Witr at the tail end of the night, whether one prays night worship [i.e. *tahajjud*] or not, provided that one is sure to wake up at that time of night, either by oneself or if someone else has been asked to wake one up. The order to go to sleep after one has prayed Witr applies to one who is not sure of being able to wake up, as we shall presently explain. We referred to this earlier when we mentioned the hadiths narrated by Abu Hurayrah and Abu al-Dardā'.

In hadith No. 1472, ʿĀ'ishah says: 'At all times of night the Prophet prayed Witr, and the last that he offered the Witr Prayer was shortly before dawn', and in the other hadith she mentions that he did it 'at the tail end of the night'. This makes it clear that it is permissible to pray Witr at any time of night after it becomes due. Scholars differ as to when its time starts. The correct view of our school, which is also the best-known view of al-Shāfiʿī, is that its time starts when one has finished the obligatory prayer of ʿIsha and that its time extends until the break of the second dawn. In another version, it starts when the time of ʿIsha starts, and in a different view, Witr may not be offered in a single *rakʿah* except after two *rakʿahs* of sunnah after ʿIsha. A different view suggests that the Witr time extends until Fajr Prayer, and it is also said that it extends until sunrise.

In hadith No. 1473, ʿĀ'ishah mentions that the last time that the Prophet offered Witr was 'shortly before dawn'. This means the tail end of the night, as mentioned in other narrations. It makes it clear that it is desirable to delay Witr to the tail end of the night. Several authentic hadiths confirm this.

Transmission

The chain of transmission of hadith No. 1472 includes Abu Yaʿfūr. Muslim adds that 'his name is Wāqid and nickname Waqdān'. This is the better-known knowledge, but some say the opposite, yet both agree. This narrator is Abu Yaʿfūr Junior, who belonged to the *tābiʿīn* generation and Kufah. His name is ʿAbd al-Raḥmān ibn ʿUbayd ibn Nisṭās. Another narrator known as Abu Yaʿfūr is described as Senior. The two have the same appellation [i.e. *kunyah*] and belonged to the same city. They are distinguished by their names and tribes, in addition to their titles of Junior and Senior. We mentioned both earlier in the Book of Faith when we discussed best actions.

CHAPTER 18

A TOTAL VIEW OF NIGHT PRAYERS

[1475–139]. (Dar al-Salam 1623) Muhammad ibn al-Muthannā al-ʿAnazī narrated:[i] Muhammad ibn Abi ʿAdiy narrated; from Saʿīd; from Qatādah; from Zurārah; that **'Saʿd ibn Hishām ibn ʿĀmir wanted to fight for God's cause. He went to Madinah where he wanted to sell some property he owned there and to use the proceeds to buy arms and horses so as to fight the Byzantines until he died. When he arrived in Madinah, he met some of its people and they told him not to go ahead with what he intended. They told him that six people wanted to do the same during the Prophet's lifetime, but the Prophet (peace be upon him) ordered them not to do so. He said to them: "Do you not have me as the example to follow?"**

When they told him this, he re-instated his marriage, as he had [earlier] divorced his wife, and he asked people to be witnesses to this reinstatement of his marriage. He went to Ibn ʿAbbās and asked him about the Prophet's Witr prayer. Ibn ʿAbbās said to him: "Shall I point to you the one who knows the Prophet's Witr better than the rest of mankind?" He asked: "Who is that?" [Ibn ʿAbbās] said: "ʿĀ'ishah. Go to her and ask her, then come back and tell me her reply". I went to visit her, and I stopped by Ḥakīm ibn Aflaḥ and asked him to join me. He said: "I shall not go to her because I told her not to say anything about these two groups, but she insisted on doing that". I appealed to him by God and he came with me.

i. Related by Abu Dāwūd, 1342, 1343, 1344 and 1345.

We went to ʿĀ'ishah and sought her permission to enter. She granted us permission and we entered. She said: "Is that Ḥakīm?" (recognising him). He said: "Yes". She said: "Who is with you?" He said: "Saʿd ibn Hishām". She said: "Which Hishām?" He said: "Ibn ʿĀmir". She prayed for mercy for him and said good words. (Qatādah said: He was wounded in the Battle of Uhud.)

I said: "Mother of the Believers. Tell me about God's Messenger's manners". She said: "Do you not read the Qur'an?" I said: "I do". She said: "The Prophet's manners were the Qur'an in practice". I was about to rise and ask no one else about anything until I die. Then it occurred to me and I said: "Tell me about God's Messenger's night prayer". She said: "Do you not read Surah *al-Muzammil*?"[i] I said: "I do". She said: "In the opening of this surah, God, the Mighty and Exalted, made night prayer obligatory. The Prophet and his Companions fulfilled this obligation for a year, and God retained its final verse in Heaven for twelve months, then God revealed at the end of the surah the relaxation [of this obligation]. Thus, night prayer became voluntary after it had been obligatory". I said: "Mother of the Believers, tell me about the Prophet's Witr prayer". She said: "We used to prepare for him his tooth stick [i.e. *miswāk*] and his [water for] ablution. God would alert him at night as He wished, and he would then brush his teeth and perform his ablution. He would pray nine *rakʿahs* but would not sit [for *tashahhud*] except after the eighth *rakʿah*. He would glorify, praise and pray to God, then he would rise without saying the *salām*. He would then stand up and pray the ninth *rakʿah*, then sit down, glorify, praise and pray to God. He would then say the *salām* in such a way that we heard him. He then prayed two

i. This is Surah 73, entitled 'The Enfolded One'.

rak'ahs after having said the salām, [praying] in the sitting position. These, son, are eleven rak'ahs. When the Prophet was older and put on weight, he prayed seven rak'ahs including Witr, and he did the two rak'ahs in the same way as before. These, son, are nine rak'ahs.

When the Prophet (peace be upon him) offered a [voluntary] prayer, he loved to keep it up. If he was prevented from doing his night prayer by sleep or illness, he would do twelve rak'ahs during the day. I do not know that the Prophet ever recited the Qur'an in full in one night, nor did he pray the whole night until dawn, nor did he fast a whole month other than Ramadan".

I went back to Ibn 'Abbās and related to him what she said. He said: "She is right. Were I to go near her or visit her, I would go now so that I could hear it from her". I said: "Had I known that you do not visit her, I would not have told you what she said".'[i]

حَدَّثَنَا مُحَمَّدُ بْنُ الْـمُثَنَّى الْعَنَزِيُّ، حَدَّثَنَا مُحَمَّدُ بْنُ أَبِي عَدِيٍّ، عَنْ سَعِيدٍ، عَنْ قَتَادَةَ، عَنْ زُرَارَةَ، أَنَّ سَعْدَ بْنَ هِشَامِ بْنِ عَامِرٍ، أَرَادَ أَنْ يَغْزُوَ فِي سَبِيلِ اللهِ. فَقَدِمَ الْـمَدِينَةَ، فَأَرَادَ أَنْ يَبِيعَ عَقَارًا لَهُ بِهَا فَيَجْعَلَهُ فِي السِّلَاحِ وَالْكُرَاعِ، وَيُجَاهِدَ الرُّومَ حَتَّى يَمُوتَ. فَلَمَّا قَدِمَ الْـمَدِينَةَ لَقِيَ أُنَاسًا مِنْ أَهْلِ الْـمَدِينَةِ فَنَهَوْهُ عَنْ ذَلِكَ، وَأَخْبَرُوهُ أَنَّ رَهْطًا سِتَّةً أَرَادُوا ذَلِكَ فِي حَيَاةِ نَبِيِّ اللهِ صَلَّى اللهُ عَلَيْهِ وَسَلَّمَ، فَنَهَاهُمْ نَبِيُّ اللهِ صَلَّى اللهُ عَلَيْهِ وَسَلَّمَ وَقَالَ: «أَلَيْسَ لَكُمْ فِيَّ أُسْوَةٌ»؟

فَلَمَّا حَدَّثُوهُ بِذَلِكَ رَاجَعَ امْرَأَتَهُ وَقَدْ كَانَ طَلَّقَهَا، وَأَشْهَدَ عَلَى رَجْعَتِهَا. فَأَتَى ابْنَ عَبَّاسٍ فَسَأَلَهُ عَنْ وِتْرِ رَسُولِ اللهِ صَلَّى اللهُ عَلَيْهِ وَسَلَّمَ، فَقَالَ ابْنُ عَبَّاسٍ: أَلَا أَدُلُّكَ عَلَى أَعْلَمِ

i. This a question of manners and trust. If Ibn 'Abbās would not visit 'Ā'ishah, then what is learnt from her by others should not be given to him for the asking. Hence, Sa'd said to Ibn 'Abbās that he would not have given him this information if he had known that Ibn 'Abbās did not visit her.

أَهْلِ الأَرْضِ بِوِتْرِ رَسُولِ اللهِ صَلَّى اللهُ عَلَيْهِ وَسَلَّمَ؟ قَالَ مَنْ؟ قَالَ: عَائِشَةُ، فَأْتِهَا فَاسْأَلْهَا، ثُمَّ ائْتِنِي فَأَخْبِرْنِي بِرَدِّهَا عَلَيْكَ. فَانْطَلَقْتُ إِلَيْهَا، فَأَتَيْتُ عَلَى حَكِيمِ بْنِ أَفْلَحَ فَاسْتَلْحَقْتُهُ إِلَيْهَا، فَقَالَ: مَا أَنَا بِقَارِبِهَا، لأَنِّي نَهَيْتُهَا أَنْ تَقُولَ فِي هَاتَيْنِ الشِّيعَتَيْنِ شَيْئًا، فَأَبَتْ فِيهِمَا إِلاَّ مُضِيًّا. قَالَ: فَأَقْسَمْتُ عَلَيْهِ فَجَاءَ. فَانْطَلَقْنَا إِلَى عَائِشَةَ، فَاسْتَأْذَنَّا عَلَيْهَا فَأَذِنَتْ لَنَا، فَدَخَلْنَا عَلَيْهَا. فَقَالَتْ أَحَكِيمٌ؟ فَعَرَفَتْهُ. فَقَالَ: نَعَمْ. فَقَالَتْ مَنْ مَعَكَ؟ قَالَ: سَعْدُ بْنُ هِشَامٍ. قَالَتْ: مَنْ هِشَامٌ؟ قَالَ ابْنُ عَامِرٍ: فَتَرَحَّمَتْ عَلَيْهِ وَقَالَتْ خَيْرًا. قَالَ قَتَادَةُ: وَكَانَ أُصِيبَ يَوْمَ أُحُدٍ.

فَقُلْتُ: يَا أُمَّ الْمُؤْمِنِينَ أَنْبِئِينِي عَنْ خُلُقِ رَسُولِ اللهِ صَلَّى اللهُ عَلَيْهِ وَسَلَّمَ. قَالَتْ: أَلَسْتَ تَقْرَأُ الْقُرْآنَ؟ قُلْتُ: بَلَى. قَالَتْ فَإِنَّ خُلُقَ نَبِيِّ اللهِ صَلَّى اللهُ عَلَيْهِ وَسَلَّمَ كَانَ الْقُرْآنَ. قَالَ: فَهَمَمْتُ أَنْ أَقُومَ وَلاَ أَسْأَلَ أَحَدًا عَنْ شَيْءٍ حَتَّى أَمُوتَ. ثُمَّ بَدَا لِي فَقُلْتُ: أَنْبِئِينِي عَنْ قِيَامِ رَسُولِ اللهِ صَلَّى اللهُ عَلَيْهِ وَسَلَّمَ. فَقَالَتْ: أَلَسْتَ تَقْرَأُ: "يَا أَيُّهَا الْمُزَّمِّلُ"؟ قُلْتُ: بَلَى. قَالَتْ فَإِنَّ اللهَ عَزَّ وَجَلَّ افْتَرَضَ قِيَامَ اللَّيْلِ فِي أَوَّلِ هَذِهِ السُّورَةِ، فَقَامَ نَبِيُّ اللهِ صَلَّى اللهُ عَلَيْهِ وَسَلَّمَ وَأَصْحَابُهُ حَوْلاً. وَأَمْسَكَ اللهُ خَاتِمَتَهَا اثْنَى عَشَرَ شَهْرًا فِي السَّمَاءِ، حَتَّى أَنْزَلَ اللهُ فِي آخِرِ هَذِهِ السُّورَةِ التَّخْفِيفَ. فَصَارَ قِيَامُ اللَّيْلِ تَطَوُّعًا بَعْدَ فَرِيضَةٍ. قَالَ: قُلْتُ: يَا أُمَّ الْمُؤْمِنِينَ أَنْبِئِينِي عَنْ وِتْرِ رَسُولِ اللهِ صَلَّى اللهُ عَلَيْهِ وَسَلَّمَ. فَقَالَتْ: كُنَّا نُعِدُّ لَهُ سِوَاكَهُ وَطَهُورَهُ، فَيَبْعَثُهُ اللهُ مَا شَاءَ أَنْ يَبْعَثَهُ مِنَ اللَّيْلِ، فَيَتَسَوَّكُ وَيَتَوَضَّأُ وَيُصَلِّي تِسْعَ رَكَعَاتٍ لاَ يَجْلِسُ فِيهَا إِلاَّ فِي الثَّامِنَةِ. فَيَذْكُرُ اللهَ وَيَحْمَدُهُ وَيَدْعُوهُ، ثُمَّ يَنْهَضُ وَلاَ يُسَلِّمُ، ثُمَّ يَقُومُ فَيُصَلِّي التَّاسِعَةَ. ثُمَّ يَقْعُدُ فَيَذْكُرُ اللهَ وَيَحْمَدُهُ وَيَدْعُوهُ، ثُمَّ يُسَلِّمُ تَسْلِيمًا يُسْمِعُنَا. ثُمَّ يُصَلِّي رَكْعَتَيْنِ بَعْدَ مَا يُسَلِّمُ وَهُوَ قَاعِدٌ. فَتِلْكَ إِحْدَى عَشْرَةَ رَكْعَةً يَا بُنَيَّ. فَلَمَّا أَسَنَّ نَبِيُّ اللهِ صَلَّى اللهُ عَلَيْهِ وَسَلَّمَ وَأَخَذَ اللَّحْمَ أَوْتَرَ بِسَبْعٍ، وَصَنَعَ فِي الرَّكْعَتَيْنِ مِثْلَ صَنِيعِهِ الأَوَّلِ. فَتِلْكَ تِسْعٌ يَا بُنَيَّ.

وَكَانَ نَبِيُّ اللهِ صَلَّى اللهُ عَلَيْهِ وَسَلَّمَ إِذَا صَلَّى صَلاَةً أَحَبَّ أَنْ يُدَاوِمَ عَلَيْهَا. وَكَانَ إِذَا غَلَبَهُ نَوْمٌ أَوْ وَجَعٌ عَنْ قِيَامِ اللَّيْلِ صَلَّى مِنَ النَّهَارِ ثِنْتَيْ عَشْرَةَ رَكْعَةً. وَلاَ أَعْلَمُ نَبِيَّ اللهِ

صَلَّى اللهُ عَلَيْهِ وَسَلَّمَ قَرَأَ الْقُرْآنَ كُلَّهُ فِي لَيْلَةٍ، وَلاَ صَلَّى لَيْلَةً إِلَى الصُّبْحِ، وَلاَ صَامَ شَهْرًا كَامِلاً غَيْرَ رَمَضَانَ.

فَانْطَلَقْتُ إِلَى ابْنِ عَبَّاسٍ، فَحَدَّثْتُهُ بِحَدِيثِهَا. فَقَالَ: صَدَقَتْ. لَوْ كُنْتُ أَقْرَبُهَا أَوْ أَدْخُلُ عَلَيْهَا لأَتَيْتُهَا حَتَّى تُشَافِهَنِي بِهِ. قَالَ: قُلْتُ لَوْ عَلِمْتُ أَنَّكَ لاَ تَدْخُلُ عَلَيْهَا مَا حَدَّثْتُكَ حَدِيثَهَا.

[1476–000]. (Dar al-Salam 1624) Muhammad ibn al-Muthannā narrated: Muʿādh ibn Hishām narrated; my father narrated to me; from Qatādah; from Zurārah ibn Awfā; from Saʿd ibn Hishām; that **'He divorced his wife, then went to Madinah to sell his real property…'. He added a similar text.**

وَحَدَّثَنَا مُحَمَّدُ بْنُ الْمُثَنَّى، حَدَّثَنَا مُعَاذُ بْنُ هِشَامٍ، حَدَّثَنِي أَبِي، عَنْ قَتَادَةَ، عَنْ زُرَارَةَ بْنِ أَوْفَى، عَنْ سَعْدِ بْنِ هِشَامٍ، أَنَّهُ طَلَّقَ امْرَأَتَهُ ثُمَّ انْطَلَقَ إِلَى الْمَدِينَةِ لِيَبِيعَ عَقَارَهُ. فَذَكَرَ نَحْوَهُ.

[1477–000]. (Dar al-Salam 1625) Abu Bakr ibn Abi Shaybah narrated: Muhammad ibn Bishr narrated; Saʿīd ibn Abi ʿArūbah narrated; Qatādah narrated; from Zurārah ibn Awfā; from Saʿd ibn Hishām; that he said: **'I went to ʿAbdullāh ibn ʿAbbās and asked him about Witr…'. He related the hadith with its story, mentioning in it: 'She said: "Which Hishām?" I said: "Ibn ʿĀmir". She said: "A good man ʿĀmir was. He was wounded in the Battle of Uḥud".'**

وَحَدَّثَنَا أَبُو بَكْرِ بْنُ أَبِي شَيْبَةَ، حَدَّثَنَا مُحَمَّدُ بْنُ بِشْرٍ، حَدَّثَنَا سَعِيدُ بْنُ أَبِي عَرُوبَةَ، حَدَّثَنَا قَتَادَةُ، عَنْ زُرَارَةَ بْنِ أَوْفَى، عَنْ سَعْدِ بْنِ هِشَامٍ أَنَّهُ قَالَ: انْطَلَقْتُ إِلَى عَبْدِ اللهِ بْنِ عَبَّاسٍ فَسَأَلْتُهُ عَنِ الْوِتْرِ. وَسَاقَ الْحَدِيثَ بِقِصَّتِهِ. وَقَالَ فِيهِ قَالَتْ: مَنْ هِشَامٌ؟ قُلْتُ: ابْنُ عَامِرٍ. قَالَتْ: نِعْمَ الْمَرْءُ. كَانَ عَامِرٌ أُصِيبَ يَوْمَ أُحُدٍ.

[1478–000]. (Dar al-Salam 1626) Isḥāq ibn Ibrāhīm and Muhammad ibn Rāfiʿ narrated: both from ʿAbd al-Razzāq; Maʿmar reported; from Qatādah; from Zurārah ibn Awfā; that **Saʿd ibn Hishām was his neighbour and he told him that he had divorced his wife.** He related the hadith in the same meaning as Saʿīd's narration. It included: **'She said: "Which Hishām?" He said: "Ibn ʿĀmir". She said: "A good man. He was wounded fighting with God's Messenger in the Battle of Uḥud".'** It also **mentions: 'Ḥakīm ibn Aflaḥ said: "Had I known that you do not visit her, I would not have told you what she said".'**

وَحَدَّثَنَا إِسْحَاقُ بْنُ إِبْرَاهِيمَ، وَمُحَمَّدُ بْنُ رَافِعٍ، كِلاَهُمَا عَنْ عَبْدِ الرَّزَّاقِ، أَخْبَرَنَا مَعْمَرٌ، عَنْ قَتَادَةَ، عَنْ زُرَارَةَ بْنِ أَوْفَى، أَنَّ سَعْدَ بْنَ هِشَامٍ كَانَ جَارًا لَهُ، فَأَخْبَرَهُ أَنَّهُ طَلَّقَ امْرَأَتَهُ. وَاقْتَصَّ الْحَدِيثَ بِمَعْنَى حَدِيثِ سَعِيدٍ، وَفِيهِ قَالَتْ: مَنْ هِشَامٌ؟ قَالَ: ابْنُ عَامِرٍ. قَالَتْ: نِعْمَ الْمَرْءُ كَانَ أُصِيبَ مَعَ رَسُولِ اللهِ صَلَّى اللهُ عَلَيْهِ وَسَلَّمَ يَوْمَ أُحُدٍ. وَفِيهِ فَقَالَ حَكِيمُ بْنُ أَفْلَحَ: أَمَا إِنِّي لَوْ عَلِمْتُ أَنَّكَ لاَ تَدْخُلُ عَلَيْهَا مَا أَنْبَأْتُكَ بِحَدِيثِهَا.

[1479–140]. (Dar al-Salam 1627) Saʿīd ibn Manṣūr and Qutaybah ibn Saʿīd narrated:[i] both from Abu ʿAwānah; Saʿīd said: Abu ʿAwānah narrated; from Qatādah; from Zurārah ibn Awfā; from Saʿd ibn Hishām; from ʿĀ'ishah that **'If God's Messenger (peace be upon him) missed night prayer because of illness or some reason, he would pray twelve *rakʿahs* during the day'.**

حَدَّثَنَا سَعِيدُ بْنُ مَنْصُورٍ وَقُتَيْبَةُ بْنُ سَعِيدٍ، جَمِيعًا عَنْ أَبِي عَوَانَةَ، قَالَ سَعِيدٌ: حَدَّثَنَا أَبُو عَوَانَةَ، عَنْ قَتَادَةَ، عَنْ زُرَارَةَ بْنِ أَوْفَى، عَنْ سَعْدِ بْنِ هِشَامٍ، عَنْ عَائِشَةَ أَنَّ رَسُولَ اللهِ صَلَّى اللهُ عَلَيْهِ وَسَلَّمَ كَانَ إِذَا فَاتَتْهُ الصَّلاَةُ مِنَ اللَّيْلِ، مِنْ وَجَعٍ أَوْ غَيْرِهِ، صَلَّى مِنَ النَّهَارِ ثِنْتَيْ عَشْرَةَ رَكْعَةً.

i. Related by al-Nasā'ī in similar wording, 1788; al-Tirmidhī, 445.

[1480–141]. (Dar al-Salam 1628) ʿAlī ibn Khashram narrated: ʿĪsā (who is Ibn Yūnus) reported; from Shuʿbah; from Qatādah; from Zurārah; from Saʿd ibn Hishām al-Anṣārī; from ʿĀ'ishah. She said: **'When God's Messenger (peace be upon him) did something [new], he would maintain it. If he slept through the night or was ill, he would pray twelve *rakʿahs* during the day'.**

She [also] said: 'I never saw God's Messenger (peace be upon him) pray through the night until the morning, and he never fasted a whole consecutive month except Ramadan'.

وَحَدَّثَنَا عَلِيُّ بْنُ خَشْرَمٍ، أَخْبَرَنَا عِيسَى (وَهُوَ ابْنُ يُونُسَ)، عَنْ شُعْبَةَ، عَنْ قَتَادَةَ، عَنْ زُرَارَةَ، عَنْ سَعْدِ بْنِ هِشَامٍ الأَنْصَارِيِّ، عَنْ عَائِشَةَ قَالَتْ: كَانَ رَسُولُ اللهِ صَلَّى اللهُ عَلَيْهِ وَسَلَّمَ إِذَا عَمِلَ عَمَلاً أَثْبَتَهُ. وَكَانَ إِذَا نَامَ مِنَ اللَّيْلِ أَوْ مَرِضَ، صَلَّى مِنَ النَّهَارِ ثِنْتَيْ عَشْرَةَ رَكْعَةً.

قَالَتْ: وَمَا رَأَيْتُ رَسُولَ اللهِ صَلَّى اللهُ عَلَيْهِ وَسَلَّمَ قَامَ لَيْلَةً حَتَّى الصَّبَاحِ، وَمَا صَامَ شَهْرًا مُتَتَابِعًا إِلاَّ رَمَضَانَ.

[1481–142]. (Dar al-Salam 1629) Ḥarūn ibn Maʿrūf narrated:[i] ʿAbdullāh ibn Wahb narrated [H]. Also, Abu al-Ṭāhir and Ḥarmalah narrated to me; both said Ibn Wahb reported; from Yūnus ibn Yazīd; from Ibn Shihāb; from al-Sā'ib ibn Yazīd; and ʿUbaydullāh ibn ʿAbdullāh; both reported to him from ʿAbd al-Raḥmān ibn ʿAbd al-Qāriy; he said: I heard ʿUmar ibn al-Khaṭṭāb say: **'God's Messenger (peace be upon him) said: "Whoever sleeps [omitting] his regular recitation, or a part of it, and he recites it during the time between Fajr Prayer and**

i. Related by Abu Dāwūd, 1313; al-Tirmidhī, 581; al-Nasā'ī, 1789, 1790, 1791 and 1792; Ibn Mājah, 1343.

Ẓuhr Prayer, it will be credited to him as though he recited it during the night".'

حَدَّثَنَا هَارُونُ بْنُ مَعْرُوفٍ، حَدَّثَنَا عَبْدُ اللهِ بْنُ وَهْبٍ، ح. وَحَدَّثَنِي أَبُو الطَّاهِرِ وَحَرْمَلَةُ، قَالَا: أَخْبَرَنَا ابْنُ وَهْبٍ، عَنْ يُونُسَ بْنِ يَزِيدَ، عَنِ ابْنِ شِهَابٍ، عَنِ السَّائِبِ بْنِ يَزِيدَ وَعُبَيْدِ اللهِ بْنِ عَبْدِ اللهِ، أَخْبَرَاهُ عَنْ عَبْدِ الرَّحْمَنِ بْنِ عَبْدٍ الْقَارِيِّ قَالَ: سَمِعْتُ عُمَرَ بْنَ الْخَطَّابِ يَقُولُ: قَالَ رَسُولُ اللهِ صَلَّى اللهُ عَلَيْهِ وَسَلَّمَ: «مَنْ نَامَ عَنْ حِزْبِهِ أَوْ عَنْ شَيْءٍ مِنْهُ، فَقَرَأَهُ فِيمَا بَيْنَ صَلَاةِ الْفَجْرِ وَصَلَاةِ الظُّهْرِ، كُتِبَ لَهُ كَأَنَّمَا قَرَأَهُ مِنَ اللَّيْلِ.

Text Explanation

In hadith No. 1475, Saʿd ibn Hishām asks Ibn ʿAbbās about how the Prophet prayed Witr, but instead of answering him, Ibn ʿAbbās said: 'Shall I point out to you the one who knows the Prophet's Witr better than the rest of mankind?' This shows that it is desirable for a scholar who is aware that someone else has greater knowledge of a question that is put to him to point out the fact to his questioner. Sincerity is the essence of faith. Moreover, such an attitude is one of fairness and giving others their due. It further shows real humility.

Ḥakīm ibn Aflaḥ mentions that he told ʿĀ'ishah not to say anything about two groups, but she insisted on doing so. The 'two groups' refer to the battles that took place between Muslims at the time.[i]

In answer to the question about the Prophet's manners, ʿĀ'ishah said that his manners were 'the Qur'an in practice'. This means implementing Qur'anic teachings, refraining from what it prohibits, applying its values, learning the lessons it provides through the stories and examples it gives, reflecting on its meaning and reciting it properly.

ʿĀ'ishah mentions that night worship became recommended after it was obligatory. The apparent meaning of this statement is that it

---

i. This refers mainly to the Battle of Ṣiffīn, which took place between ʿAlī and Muʿāwiyah.

became recommended to the Prophet (peace be upon him) and to all Muslims. As for Muslims generally, it is unanimously agreed upon that it is recommended, not obligatory. As for the Prophet, scholars differ with regard to whether the duty to do it was also abrogated. The more correct view according to our Shāfiʿī School is that it was abrogated. *Qadi* ʿIyāḍ mentions that some early scholars claim that the whole Muslim community has a duty to offer night worship for as little as fulfils the meaning, even as little as the time of milking a sheep. This view is wrong and refuted by the unanimity of all who preceded him, as well as the authentic statements that confirm that only the five daily prayers are obligatory.

ʿĀ'ishah mentions that the Prophet's wives prepared for him his tooth stick and water for his ablution. This shows that it is desirable to get things that are related to worship ready before prayer is due. The hadith mentions that when the Prophet woke up, he brushed his teeth and performed the ablution. This means that it is recommended to brush one's teeth when one wakes up.

In hadith No. 1479, ʿĀ'ishah mentions: 'If God's Messenger (peace be upon him) missed night prayer because of illness or some reason, he would pray twelve *rakʿahs* during the day'. This statement makes it clear that it is desirable to keep up what one does regularly of voluntary worship, and that if one misses out on them, they may be done later in compensation.

Transmission

The chain of transmission of hadith No. 1481 includes: 'from Yūnus ibn Yazīd; from Ibn Shihāb; from al-Sā'ib ibn Yazīd; and ʿUbaydullah ibn ʿAbdullāh; both reported to him from ʿAbd al-Raḥmān ibn ʿAbd al-Qāriy; he said: I heard ʿUmar ibn al-Khaṭṭāb say'. This chain of transmission and the hadith as a whole are questioned by Imam al-Dāraquṭnī. He claimed that the hadith is questioned on the basis that some narrators report it in this way, attributing it to the Prophet, while others stop at the Prophet's Companion, making it *mawqūf,* which means that it quotes the Prophet's Companion. Yet the hadith is authentic, and its transmission is also sound and authentic. We have explained this rule in the 'Notes' and in other places. As we have explained, the correct view upheld by scholars of *Fiqh* and methodology, as well as scrupulous scholars of Hadith, makes it clear that if a hadith is narrated with a complete chain of transmission going up to the Prophet and with one that is *mawqūf,* stopping at the Prophet's Companion, it is considered to have a complete chain because it represents an addition by a reliable narrator. This rule applies even when those who narrate the hadith with a complete chain are fewer in number and narrate less.

The chain of transmission also has an interesting feature in the fact that it includes a Companion of the Prophet, al-Sā'ib, narrating from one who belonged to the *tābiʿīn* generation, ʿAbd al-Raḥmān. This comes under 'seniors reporting from juniors'.

CHAPTER 19

THE *AWWĀBĪN* PRAYER

[1482–143]. (Dar al-Salam 1630) Zuhayr ibn Ḥarb and Ibn Numayr narrated: both said: Ismāʿīl (who is Ibn ʿUlayyah) narrated; from Ayyūb; from al-Qāsim al-Shaybānī; that **Zayd ibn Arqam saw some people praying during the mid-morning. He said: 'They do know that prayer at a different time is better, because God's Messenger (peace be upon him) said: "The *Awwābīn* Prayer is when the feet of young camels are scorched".'**

وَحَدَّثَنَا زُهَيْرُ بْنُ حَرْبٍ وَابْنُ نُمَيْرٍ، قَالَا: حَدَّثَنَا إِسْمَاعِيلُ (وَهُوَ ابْنُ عُلَيَّةَ) عَنْ أَيُّوبَ، عَنِ الْقَاسِمِ الشَّيْبَانِيِّ، أَنَّ زَيْدَ بْنَ أَرْقَمَ، رَأَى قَوْمًا يُصَلُّونَ مِنَ الضُّحَى، فَقَالَ: أَمَا لَقَدْ عَلِمُوا أَنَّ الصَّلَاةَ فِي غَيْرِ هَذِهِ السَّاعَةِ أَفْضَلُ. إِنَّ رَسُولَ اللهِ صَلَّى اللهُ عَلَيْهِ وَسَلَّمَ قَالَ: «صَلَاةُ الأَوَّابِينَ حِينَ تَرْمَضُ الْفِصَالُ».

[1483–144]. (Dar al-Salam 1631) Zuhayr ibn Ḥarb narrated: Yaḥyā ibn Saʿīd narrated; from Hishām ibn Abi ʿAbdullāh; he said: al-Qāsim al-Shaybānī narrated; from Zayd ibn Arqam. He said: **'God's Messenger came to the people of Qubā' when they were praying. He said: "The *Awwābīn* Prayer is when the feet of young camels are scorched".'**

حَدَّثَنَا زُهَيْرُ بْنُ حَرْبٍ، حَدَّثَنَا يَحْيَى بْنُ سَعِيدٍ، عَنْ هِشَامِ بْنِ أَبِي عَبْدِ اللهِ قَالَ: حَدَّثَنَا الْقَاسِمُ الشَّيْبَانِيُّ، عَنْ زَيْدِ بْنِ أَرْقَمَ قَالَ: خَرَجَ رَسُولُ اللهِ صَلَّى اللهُ عَلَيْهِ وَسَلَّمَ عَلَى أَهْلِ قُبَاءٍ وَهُمْ يُصَلُّونَ، فَقَالَ: «صَلَاةُ الأَوَّابِينَ إِذَا رَمِضَتِ الْفِصَالُ».

Text Explanation

This prayer is called by this name which means 'those who are obedient', or 'those who revert to obedience' [thus it is usually observed by people who are devout].

In this hadith, the Prophet gives a figurative description of the best time to offer the Ḍuḥā Prayer. He uses the verb *tarmiḍ,* which is derived from *ramḍā'*, meaning exceedingly hot sand. Thus, when young camels walk on such sand, their feet are scorched. The hadith gives a time of preference for offering voluntary prayer. Our scholars say this time is the most preferable to offer the Ḍuḥā Prayer, even though its time range is from sunrise to midday.

CHAPTER 20

NIGHT PRAYERS TWO *RAKʿAHS* AT A TIME, WITR IS ONE *RAKʿAH* LATE AT NIGHT

[1484–145]. (Dar al-Salam 1632) Yaḥyā ibn Yaḥyā narrated:[i] I read out to Mālik; from Nāfiʿ and ʿAbdullāh ibn Dīnār; from Ibn ʿUmar; that **'A man asked God's Messenger (peace be upon him) about night prayer. The Prophet said: "Night prayers are two *rakʿahs* after two. If any of you fears the break of dawn [to be close], he should pray one *rakʿah* to make the number of his prayers an odd number".'**

وَحَدَّثَنَا يَحْيَى بْنُ يَحْيَى قَالَ: قَرَأْتُ عَلَى مَالِكٍ، عَنْ نَافِعٍ وَعَبْدِ اللهِ بْنِ دِينَارٍ، عَنِ ابْنِ عُمَرَ، أَنَّ رَجُلاً سَأَلَ رَسُولَ اللهِ صَلَّى اللهُ عَلَيْهِ وَسَلَّمَ عَنْ صَلاَةِ اللَّيْلِ، فَقَالَ رَسُولُ اللهِ صَلَّى اللهُ عَلَيْهِ وَسَلَّمَ: «صَلاَةُ اللَّيْلِ مَثْنَى مَثْنَى، فَإِذَا خَشِيَ أَحَدُكُمُ الصُّبْحَ، صَلَّى رَكْعَةً وَاحِدَةً تُوتِرُ لَهُ مَا قَدْ صَلَّى.

[1485–146]. (Dar al-Salam 1633) Abu Bakr ibn Abi Shaybah, ʿAmr al-Nāqid and Zuhayr ibn Ḥarb narrated:[ii] Zuhayr said: Sufyān ibn ʿUyaynah narrated; from al-Zuhrī; from Sālim; from his father who heard the Prophet (peace be upon him) say [H]. Also, Muhammad ibn ʿAbbād narrated (his text); Sufyān narrated; ʿAmr narrated; from Ṭāwūs; from Ibn ʿUmar

i. Related by al-Bukhari, 990; Abu Dāwūd, 1326; al-Nasāʾī, 1693.
ii. Related by Ibn Mājah, 1320.

[H]. And, al-Zuhrī narrated; from Sālim; from his father; that **'A man asked the Prophet (peace be upon him) about night prayer. He said: "Two [*rakʿahs*] at a time. If you fear the break of dawn, make it odd with one *rakʿah*".'**

حَدَّثَنَا أَبُو بَكْرِ بْنُ أَبِي شَيْبَةَ وَعَمْرٌو النَّاقِدُ وَزُهَيْرُ بْنُ حَرْبٍ، قَالَ زُهَيْرٌ: حَدَّثَنَا سُفْيَانُ بْنُ عُيَيْنَةَ، عَنِ الزُّهْرِيِّ، عَنْ سَالِمٍ، عَنْ أَبِيهِ، سَمِعَ النَّبِيَّ صَلَّى اللهُ عَلَيْهِ وَسَلَّمَ يَقُولُ ح. وَحَدَّثَنَا مُحَمَّدُ بْنُ عَبَّادٍ (وَاللَّفْظُ لَهُ)، حَدَّثَنَا سُفْيَانُ، حَدَّثَنَا عَمْرٌو، عَنْ طَاوُسٍ، عَنِ ابْنِ عُمَرَ، ح. وَحَدَّثَنَا الزُّهْرِيُّ، عَنْ سَالِمٍ، عَنْ أَبِيهِ، أَنَّ رَجُلاً سَأَلَ النَّبِيَّ صَلَّى اللهُ عَلَيْهِ وَسَلَّمَ عَنْ صَلاَةِ اللَّيْلِ، فَقَالَ: «مَثْنَى مَثْنَى، فَإِذَا خَشِيتَ الصُّبْحَ فَأَوْتِرْ بِرَكْعَةٍ».

[1486–147]. (Dar al-Salam 1634) Ḥarmalah ibn Yaḥyā narrated to me:[i] ʿAbdullāh ibn Wahb narrated; ʿAmr reported to me; that Ibn Shihāb narrated to him; that Sālim ibn ʿAbdullāh ibn ʿUmar and Ḥumayd ibn ʿAbd al-Raḥmān ibn ʿAwf narrated to him; from ʿAbdullāh ibn ʿUmar ibn al-Khaṭṭāb; that he said: **'A man stood up and said: "Messenger of God, how to offer night prayer?" God's Messenger (peace be upon him) said: "Night prayer is two *rakʿahs* at a time. If you fear the break of dawn, pray Witr in one *rakʿah*".'**

وَحَدَّثَنِي حَرْمَلَةُ بْنُ يَحْيَى، حَدَّثَنَا عَبْدُ اللهِ بْنُ وَهْبٍ، أَخْبَرَنِي عَمْرٌو، أَنَّ ابْنَ شِهَابٍ حَدَّثَهُ، أَنَّ سَالِمَ بْنَ عَبْدِ اللهِ بْنِ عُمَرَ وَحُمَيْدَ بْنَ عَبْدِ الرَّحْمَنِ بْنِ عَوْفٍ حَدَّثَاهُ، عَنْ عَبْدِ اللهِ بْنِ عُمَرَ بْنِ الْخَطَّابِ أَنَّهُ قَالَ: قَامَ رَجُلٌ فَقَالَ: يَا رَسُولَ اللهِ كَيْفَ صَلاَةُ اللَّيْلِ؟ قَالَ رَسُولُ اللهِ صَلَّى اللهُ عَلَيْهِ وَسَلَّمَ: «صَلاَةُ اللَّيْلِ مَثْنَى مَثْنَى، فَإِذَا خِفْتَ الصُّبْحَ فَأَوْتِرْ بِوَاحِدَةٍ».

i. Related by al-Nasāʾī, 1672 and 1673.

[1487–148]. (Dar al-Salam 1635) Abu al-Rabīʿ al-Zahrānī narrated to me:[i] Ḥammād narrated; Ayyūb and Budayl narrated; from ʿAbdullāh ibn Shaqīq; from ʿAbdullāh ibn ʿUmar; that **'A man asked the Prophet (peace be upon him) as I was between him and the questioner. He said: "Messenger of God, how to offer night prayers?" He said: "Two *rakʿahs* at a time. When you fear the break of dawn [to be close], pray one *rakʿah*. Make the last of your prayer in an odd number". A year later a man asked him as I was in the same place close to God's Messenger (peace be upon him). I am not sure whether he was the same man or a different one. The Prophet gave him the same answer'.**

وَحَدَّثَنِي أَبُو الرَّبِيعِ الزَّهْرَانِيُّ، حَدَّثَنَا حَمَّادٌ، حَدَّثَنَا أَيُّوبُ وَبُدَيْلٌ عَنْ عَبْدِ اللهِ بْنِ شَقِيقٍ، عَنْ عَبْدِ اللهِ بْنِ عُمَرَ، أَنَّ رَجُلاً سَأَلَ النَّبِيَّ صَلَّى اللهُ عَلَيْهِ وَسَلَّمَ، وَأَنَا بَيْنَهُ وَبَيْنَ السَّائِلِ، فَقَالَ: يَا رَسُولَ اللهِ كَيْفَ صَلاَةُ اللَّيْلِ؟ قَالَ: «مَثْنَى مَثْنَى، فَإِذَا خَشِيتَ الصُّبْحَ فَصَلِّ رَكْعَةً، وَاجْعَلْ آخِرَ صَلاَتِكَ وِتْرًا». ثُمَّ سَأَلَهُ رَجُلٌ عَلَى رَأْسِ الْحَوْلِ، وَأَنَا بِذَلِكَ الْمَكَانِ مِنْ رَسُولِ اللهِ صَلَّى اللهُ عَلَيْهِ وَسَلَّمَ، فَلاَ أَدْرِي هُوَ ذَلِكَ الرَّجُلُ أَوْ رَجُلٌ آخَرُ، فَقَالَ لَهُ مِثْلَ ذَلِكَ.

[1488–000]. (Dar al-Salam 1636) Abu Kāmil narrated to me: Ḥammād narrated; Ayyūb, Budayl and ʿImrān ibn Ḥudayr narrated; from ʿAbdullāh ibn Shaqīq; from Ibn ʿUmar [H]. Also, Muhammad ibn ʿUbayd al-Ghubarī narrated; Ḥammād narrated; Ayyūb and al-Zubayr ibn al-Khirrīt narrated; from ʿAbdullāh ibn Shaqīq; from Ibn ʿUmar. He said: **'A man asked the Prophet…' both mentioned the same but they did not include in their narration: 'a year later a man asked him…' to the end of the hadith.**

i. Related by Abu Dāwūd, 1421; al-Nasāʾī in a shorter version, 1690.

وَحَدَّثَنِي أَبُو كَامِلٍ، حَدَّثَنَا حَمَّادٌ، حَدَّثَنَا أَيُّوبُ وَبُدَيْلٌ وَعِمْرَانُ بْنُ حُدَيْرٍ، عَنْ عَبْدِ اللهِ بْنِ شَقِيقٍ، عَنِ ابْنِ عُمَرَ، ح. وَحَدَّثَنَا مُحَمَّدُ بْنُ عُبَيْدٍ الْغُبَرِيُّ، حَدَّثَنَا حَمَّادٌ، حَدَّثَنَا أَيُّوبُ وَالزُّبَيْرُ بْنُ الْخِرِّيتِ، عَنْ عَبْدِ اللهِ بْنِ شَقِيقٍ، عَنِ ابْنِ عُمَرَ، قَالَ: سَأَلَ رَجُلٌ النَّبِيَّ صَلَّى اللهُ عَلَيْهِ وَسَلَّمَ. فَذَكَرَا بِمِثْلِهِ وَلَيْسَ فِي حَدِيثِهِمَا ثُمَّ سَأَلَهُ رَجُلٌ عَلَى رَأْسِ الْحَوْلِ وَمَا بَعْدَهُ.

[1489–149]. (Dar al-Salam 1637) Ḥarūn ibn Maʿrūf, Surayj ibn Yūnus and Abu Kurayb narrated: all from Ibn Abi Zā'idah; Ḥarūn said: Ibn Abi Zā'idah narrated; ʿĀṣim al-Aḥwal reported to me; from ʿAbdullāh ibn Shaqīq; from Ibn ʿUmar; that the Prophet (peace be upon him) said: **'Make sure to pray Witr before dawn break'.**

وَحَدَّثَنَا هَارُونُ بْنُ مَعْرُوفٍ وَسُرَيْجُ بْنُ يُونُسَ وَأَبُو كُرَيْبٍ، جَمِيعًا عَنِ ابْنِ أَبِي زَائِدَةَ، قَالَ هَارُونُ: حَدَّثَنَا ابْنُ أَبِي زَائِدَةَ، أَخْبَرَنِي عَاصِمٌ الأَحْوَلُ، عَنْ عَبْدِ اللهِ بْنِ شَقِيقٍ، عَنِ ابْنِ عُمَرَ، أَنَّ النَّبِيَّ صَلَّى اللهُ عَلَيْهِ وَسَلَّمَ قَالَ: «بَادِرُوا الصُّبْحَ بِالْوِتْرِ».

[1490–150]. (Dar al-Salam 1638) Qutaybah ibn Saʿīd narrated:[i] Layth narrated [H]. Also, Ibn Rumḥ narrated; al-Layth reported; from Nāfiʿ; that Ibn ʿUmar said: **'Whoever offers night prayers should make Witr the last of his prayer, as God's Messenger (peace be upon him) used to order so'.**

وَحَدَّثَنَا قُتَيْبَةُ بْنُ سَعِيدٍ، حَدَّثَنَا لَيْثٌ، ح. وَحَدَّثَنَا ابْنُ رُمْحٍ، أَخْبَرَنَا اللَّيْثُ، عَنْ نَافِعٍ، أَنَّ ابْنَ عُمَرَ قَالَ: مَنْ صَلَّى مِنَ اللَّيْلِ فَلْيَجْعَلْ آخِرَ صَلاَتِهِ وِتْرًا، فَإِنَّ رَسُولَ اللهِ صَلَّى اللهُ عَلَيْهِ وَسَلَّمَ كَانَ يَأْمُرُ بِذَلِكَ.

i. Related by al-Nasā'ī, 1681.

[1491–151]. (Dar al-Salam 1639) Abu Bakr ibn Abi Shaybah narrated:[i] Abu Usāmah narrated [H]. Also, Ibn Numayr narrated; my father narrated [H]. And, Zuhayr ibn Ḥarb and Ibn al-Muthannā narrated to me; both said: Yaḥyā narrated; all from ʿUbaydullāh; from Nāfiʿ; from Ibn ʿUmar; from the Prophet (peace be upon him). He said: **'Make Witr the last of your prayer at night'.**

وَحَدَّثَنَا أَبُو بَكْرِ بْنُ أَبِي شَيْبَةَ، حَدَّثَنَا أَبُو أُسَامَةَ، ح. وَحَدَّثَنَا ابْنُ نُمَيْرٍ، حَدَّثَنَا أَبِي ح. وَحَدَّثَنِي زُهَيْرُ بْنُ حَرْبٍ وَابْنُ الْمُثَنَّى، قَالا: حَدَّثَنَا يَحْيَى، كُلُّهُمْ عَنْ عُبَيْدِ اللهِ، عَنْ نَافِعٍ، عَنِ ابْنِ عُمَرَ، عَنِ النَّبِيِّ صَلَّى اللهُ عَلَيْهِ وَسَلَّمَ قَالَ: «اجْعَلُوا آخِرَ صَلاتِكُمْ بِاللَّيْلِ وِتْرًا».

[1492–152]. (Dar al-Salam 1640) Ḥarūn ibn ʿAbdullāh narrated to me: Ḥajjāj ibn Muhammad narrated; he said: Ibn Jurayj said: Nāfiʿ reported to me; that Ibn ʿUmar used to say: **'Whoever offers night prayers should make Witr the last of his prayers before dawn. Thus, God's Messenger used to command'.**

وَحَدَّثَنِي هَارُونُ بْنُ عَبْدِ اللهِ، حَدَّثَنَا حَجَّاجُ بْنُ مُحَمَّدٍ قَالَ: قَالَ ابْنُ جُرَيْجٍ: أَخْبَرَنِي نَافِعٌ، أَنَّ ابْنَ عُمَرَ كَانَ يَقُولُ: مَنْ صَلَّى مِنَ اللَّيْلِ فَلْيَجْعَلْ آخِرَ صَلاتِهِ وِتْرًا قَبْلَ الصُّبْحِ. كَذَلِكَ كَانَ رَسُولُ اللهِ صَلَّى اللهُ عَلَيْهِ وَسَلَّمَ يَأْمُرُهُمْ.

[1493–153]. (Dar al-Salam 1641) Shaybān ibn Farrūkh narrated:[ii] ʿAbd al-Wārith narrated; from Abu al-Tayyāḥ; he said: Abu Mijlaz narrated to me; from Ibn ʿUmar: **'God's Messenger (peace be upon him) said: "The Witr is one *rakʿah* at the tail end of the night".'**

---

i. Related by al-Bukhari, 998; Abu Dāwūd, 1438.
ii. Related by al-Nasāʾī, 1688 and 1689.

حَدَّثَنَا شَيْبَانُ بْنُ فَرُّوخَ، حَدَّثَنَا عَبْدُ الْوَارِثِ، عَنْ أَبِي التَّيَّاحِ قَالَ: حَدَّثَنِي أَبُو مِجْلَزٍ، عَنِ ابْنِ عُمَرَ قَالَ: قَالَ رَسُولُ اللهِ صَلَّى اللهُ عَلَيْهِ وَسَلَّمَ: «الْوِتْرُ رَكْعَةٌ مِنْ آخِرِ اللَّيْلِ».

[1494–154]. (Dar al-Salam 1642) Muhammad ibn al-Muthannā and Ibn Bashshār narrated: Ibn al-Muthannā said: Muhammad ibn Ja'far narrated; Shu'bah narrated; from Qatādah; from Abu Mijlaz; he said: **'I heard Ibn 'Umar narrating from the Prophet (peace be upon him) and said: "The Witr is one *rak'ah* at the tail end of the night".'**

وَحَدَّثَنَا مُحَمَّدُ بْنُ الْـمُثَنَّى وَابْنُ بَشَّارٍ، قَالَ ابْنُ الْـمُثَنَّى: حَدَّثَنَا مُحَمَّدُ بْنُ جَعْفَرٍ، حَدَّثَنَا شُعْبَةُ، عَنْ قَتَادَةَ، عَنْ أَبِي مِجْلَزٍ، قَالَ: سَمِعْتُ ابْنَ عُمَرَ يُحَدِّثُ عَنِ النَّبِيِّ صَلَّى اللهُ عَلَيْهِ وَسَلَّمَ قَالَ: «الْوِتْرُ رَكْعَةٌ مِنْ آخِرِ اللَّيْلِ».

[1495–155]. (Dar al-Salam 1643) Zuhayr ibn Ḥarb narrated to me: 'Abd al-Ṣamad narrated; Hammām narrated; Qatādah narrated; from Abu Mijlaz. He said: **'I asked Ibn 'Abbās about the Witr and he said: "I heard God's Messenger (peace be upon him) say: 'One *rak'ah* at the tail end of the night'." And I asked Ibn 'Umar and he said: "I heard God's Messenger (peace be upon him) say: 'One *rak'ah* at the tail end of the night'."'**

وَحَدَّثَنِي زُهَيْرُ بْنُ حَرْبٍ، حَدَّثَنَا عَبْدُ الصَّمَدِ، حَدَّثَنَا هَمَّامٌ، حَدَّثَنَا قَتَادَةُ، عَنْ أَبِي مِجْلَزٍ قَالَ: سَأَلْتُ ابْنَ عَبَّاسٍ عَنِ الْوِتْرِ فَقَالَ: سَمِعْتُ رَسُولَ اللهِ صَلَّى اللهُ عَلَيْهِ وَسَلَّمَ يَقُولُ: «رَكْعَةٌ مِنْ آخِرِ اللَّيْلِ». وَسَأَلْتُ ابْنَ عُمَرَ فَقَالَ: سَمِعْتُ رَسُولَ اللهِ صَلَّى اللهُ عَلَيْهِ وَسَلَّمَ يَقُولُ: «رَكْعَةٌ مِنْ آخِرِ اللَّيْلِ».

[1496–156]. (Dar al-Salam 1644) Abu Kurayb and Ḥarūn ibn 'Abdullāh narrated: both said: Abu Usāmah narrated; from al-Walīd ibn Kathīr; he said: ʿUbaydullāh ibn ʿAbdullāh ibn ʿUmar narrated to me; that Ibn ʿUmar narrated to them; that **'A man called out to the Prophet as he was in the mosque and said: "Messenger of God, how should I make night prayer an odd number [of *rakʿahs*]?" God's Messenger (peace be upon him) said: "Whoever prays [during the night] should offer his prayers two [*rakʿahs*] at a time. When he feels the break of dawn to be close, he should pray one *rakʿah* to make the number of his prayers an odd number".'**

Abu Kurayb said: **''Ubaydullāh ibn 'Abdullāh', without adding Ibn ʿUmar.**

وَحَدَّثَنَا أَبُو كُرَيْبٍ وَهَارُونُ بْنُ عَبْدِ اللهِ، قَالَا: حَدَّثَنَا أَبُو أُسَامَةَ، عَنِ الْوَلِيدِ بْنِ كَثِيرٍ قَالَ: حَدَّثَنِي عُبَيْدُ اللهِ بْنُ عَبْدِ اللهِ بْنِ عُمَرَ، أَنَّ ابْنَ عُمَرَ حَدَّثَهُمْ أَنَّ رَجُلًا نَادَى رَسُولَ اللهِ صَلَّى اللهُ عَلَيْهِ وَسَلَّمَ وَهُوَ فِي الْـمَسْجِدِ فَقَالَ: يَا رَسُولَ اللهِ كَيْفَ أُوتِرُ صَلَاةَ اللَّيْلِ؟ فَقَالَ رَسُولُ اللهِ صَلَّى اللهُ عَلَيْهِ وَسَلَّمَ: «مَنْ صَلَّى فَلْيُصَلِّ مَثْنَى مَثْنَى، فَإِنْ أَحَسَّ أَنْ يُصْبِحَ سَجَدَ سَجْدَةً، فَأَوْتَرَتْ لَهُ مَا صَلَّى».

قَالَ أَبُو كُرَيْبٍ: عُبَيْدُ اللهِ بْنُ عَبْدِ اللهِ، وَلَمْ يَقُلِ ابْنِ عُمَرَ.

[1497–157]. (Dar al-Salam 1645) Khalaf ibn Hishām and Abu Kāmil narrated:[i] both said: Ḥammād ibn Zayd narrated; from Anas ibn Sīrīn; he said: **'I asked Ibn ʿUmar saying: "Those two *rakʿahs* before the Fajr Prayer, should my recitation be long in them?" He said: "God's Messenger (peace be upon him) used to pray night worship two [*rakʿahs*] after two and add one *rakʿah* for Witr". I said: "I am not asking you about this". He said: "You are a big man! Would you not let me complete**

i. Related by al-Bukhari, 995; al-Tirmidhī, 461; Ibn Mājah in shorter versions, 1144 and 1174.

the hadith for you? God's Messenger (peace be upon him) used to pray night worship two [*rak'ahs*] after two and add one *rak'ah* for Witr, and he prayed two *rak'ahs* before the Fajr Prayer, as though he were hearing the *iqāmah* in his ears".'

Khalaf said: **'Those two *rak'ahs* before Fajr' but did not say the word 'prayer'.**

حَدَّثَنَا خَلَفُ بْنُ هِشَامٍ وَأَبُو كَامِلٍ، قَالَا: حَدَّثَنَا حَمَّادُ بْنُ زَيْدٍ، عَنْ أَنَسِ بْنِ سِيرِينَ قَالَ: سَأَلْتُ ابْنَ عُمَرَ. قُلْتُ: أَرَأَيْتَ الرَّكْعَتَيْنِ قَبْلَ صَلَاةِ الْغَدَاةِ، أَأُطِيلُ فِيهِمَا الْقِرَاءَةَ؟ قَالَ: كَانَ رَسُولُ اللهِ صَلَّى اللهُ عَلَيْهِ وَسَلَّمَ يُصَلِّي مِنَ اللَّيْلِ مَثْنَى مَثْنَى وَيُوتِرُ بِرَكْعَةٍ. قُلْتُ: إِنِّي لَسْتُ عَنْ هَذَا أَسْأَلُكَ. قَالَ: إِنَّكَ لَضَخْمٌ. أَلَا تَدَعُنِي أَسْتَقْرِئُ لَكَ الْحَدِيثَ؟ كَانَ رَسُولُ اللهِ صَلَّى اللهُ عَلَيْهِ وَسَلَّمَ يُصَلِّي مِنَ اللَّيْلِ مَثْنَى مَثْنَى وَيُوتِرُ بِرَكْعَةٍ، وَيُصَلِّي رَكْعَتَيْنِ قَبْلَ الْغَدَاةِ كَأَنَّ الْأَذَانَ بِأُذُنَيْهِ.

قَالَ خَلَفٌ: أَرَأَيْتَ الرَّكْعَتَيْنِ قَبْلَ الْغَدَاةِ، وَلَمْ يَذْكُرْ صَلَاةً.

[1498–158]. (Dar al-Salam 1646) Ibn al-Muthannā and Ibn Bashshār narrated: both said: Muhammad ibn Ja'far narrated; Shu'bah narrated; from Anas ibn Sīrīn. He said: **'I asked Ibn 'Umar…' the same text but added: 'And add one *rak'ah* for Witr at the tail end of the night'. Also in this narration: 'He said: "Bah! Bah! You are a big man!".'**

وَحَدَّثَنَا ابْنُ الْمُثَنَّى وَابْنُ بَشَّارٍ، قَالَا: حَدَّثَنَا مُحَمَّدُ بْنُ جَعْفَرٍ، حَدَّثَنَا شُعْبَةُ، عَنْ أَنَسِ بْنِ سِيرِينَ، قَالَ: سَأَلْتُ ابْنَ عُمَرَ، بِمِثْلِهِ. وَزَادَ وَيُوتِرُ بِرَكْعَةٍ مِنْ آخِرِ اللَّيْلِ. وَفِيهِ فَقَالَ: بَهْ بَهْ! إِنَّكَ لَضَخْمٌ!

[1499–159]. (Dar al-Salam 1647) Muhammad ibn al-Muthannā narrated: Muhammad ibn Ja'far narrated; Shu'bah narrated;

he said: I heard ʿUqbah ibn Ḥurayth say: I heard Ibn ʿUmar narrating; that God's Messenger (peace be upon him) said: **'Night prayers is two *rakʿahs* at a time. If you think that the break of dawn is close, pray Witr in one *rakʿah*'. Ibn ʿUmar was asked: 'What does two *rakʿahs* at a time mean?' He said: 'That one finishes with *salām* after every two *rakʿahs*'.**

حَدَّثَنَا مُحَمَّدُ بْنُ الْـمُثَنَّى، حَدَّثَنَا مُحَمَّدُ بْنُ جَعْفَرٍ، حَدَّثَنَا شُعْبَةُ قَالَ: سَمِعْتُ عُقْبَةَ بْنَ حُرَيْثٍ قَالَ: سَمِعْتُ ابْنَ عُمَرَ يُحَدِّثُ أَنَّ رَسُولَ اللهِ صَلَّى اللهُ عَلَيْهِ وَسَلَّمَ قَالَ: «صَلَاةُ اللَّيْلِ مَثْنَى مَثْنَى، فَإِذَا رَأَيْتَ أَنَّ الصُّبْحَ يُدْرِكُكَ فَأَوْتِرْ بِوَاحِدَةٍ». فَقِيلَ لِابْنِ عُمَرَ: مَا مَثْنَى مَثْنَى؟ قَالَ: أَنْ يُسَلِّمَ فِي كُلِّ رَكْعَتَيْنِ.

[1500–160]. (Dar al-Salam 1648) Abu Bakr ibn Abi Shaybah narrated:[i] ʿAbd al-Aʿlā ibn ʿAbd al-Aʿlā; from Maʿmar; from Yaḥyā ibn Abi Kathīr; from Abu Naḍrah; from Abu Saʿīd; that the Prophet said: **'Pray Witr before the break of dawn'.**

حَدَّثَنَا أَبُو بَكْرِ بْنُ أَبِي شَيْبَةَ، حَدَّثَنَا عَبْدُ الأَعْلَى بْنُ عَبْدِ الأَعْلَى، عَنْ مَعْمَرٍ، عَنْ يَحْيَى بْنِ أَبِي كَثِيرٍ، عَنْ أَبِي نَضْرَةَ، عَنْ أَبِي سَعِيدٍ أَنَّ النَّبِيَّ صَلَّى اللهُ عَلَيْهِ وَسَلَّمَ قَالَ: «أَوْتِرُوا قَبْلَ أَنْ تُصْبِحُوا».

[1501–161]. (Dar al-Salam 1649) Isḥāq ibn Manṣūr narrated to me: ʿUbaydullāh reported to me; from Shaybān; from Yaḥyā; he said: Abu Naḍrah al-ʿAwaqī reported to me; that Abu Saʿīd reported to them that they [i.e. the Prophet's Companions] asked the Prophet about Witr. He said: **'Pray Witr before the break of dawn'.**

---

i. Related by al-Tirmidhī, 468; al-Nasāʾī, 1683; Ibn Mājah, 1189.

وَحَدَّثَنِي إِسْحَاقُ بْنُ مَنْصُورٍ، أَخْبَرَنِي عُبَيْدُ اللهِ، عَنْ شَيْبَانَ، عَنْ يَحْيَى، قَالَ أَخْبَرَنِي أَبُو نَضْرَةَ الْعَوَقِيُّ، أَنَّ أَبَا سَعِيدٍ أَخْبَرَهُمْ، أَنَّهُمْ سَأَلُوا النَّبِيَّ صَلَّى اللهُ عَلَيْهِ وَسَلَّمَ عَنِ الْوِتْرِ، فَقَالَ: «أَوْتِرُوا قَبْلَ الصُّبْحِ».

Text Explanation

These hadiths confirm that voluntary night prayer is offered two *rak'ahs* at a time, and these are finished with *salām*. This is how the hadith is reported by al-Bukhari and Muslim in their authentic anthologies. Both Abu Dāwūd and al-Tirmidhī related a hadith with a sound chain of transmission that says: 'Night and day prayers are two *rak'ahs* at a time'. These hadiths are understood to indicate what is better and preferable – finishing with *salām* after each two *rak'ahs*. This applies to all voluntary prayers offered during the night and also during the day. However, if one prays several *rak'ahs* before finishing them with *salām* or prayed only one *rak'ah* in voluntary worship, it is perfectly permissible according to our school.

In hadith No. 1484, the Prophet says that if one fears the break of dawn to be very close, one should offer one *rak'ah* to make his prayer in an odd number. In another hadith the Prophet says: 'Pray Witr before the break of dawn'. This provides evidence that it is recommended [i.e. sunnah] to make Witr the last prayer at night and that its time range ends at the break of dawn. This is the better-known view of our school, and it is agreed by the majority of scholars. Yet some say that its time range extends till after the break of dawn and until one prays the obligatory Fajr Prayer. Those hadiths that mention that Witr is one *rak'ah* offered at the tail end of the night confirm that it is valid to pray Witr in one *rak'ah* and that it is desirable to offer it towards the end of the night.

In hadith No. 1597, Ibn 'Umar says to his questioner: 'You are a big man'. This expression refers to his lack of manners and poor intelligence. Some say that these are usually applicable to tall and fat people. Ibn 'Umar said this to him because he interrupted him as he was answering his question. Ibn 'Umar tells him to wait until he had told him the rest of the hadith. The hadith mentions that the Prophet 'prayed two *rak'ahs* before the Fajr Prayer, as though he were hearing the *iqāmah* in his ears' [a literal translation would have said: 'as though he were hearing the *adhān* in his ears']. *Qadi* 'Iyāḍ said: 'What is meant by the *adhān* in this instance is the *iqāmah*, and it is a reference to the need to make these two *rak'ahs* very short in relation to the rest of one's prayers'. In the next hadith, No. 1598, the words: 'Bah! Bah!' are used. It is said that this is an expression denoting an order to stop. Ibn al-Sukayt said that it suggests that the matter is serious.

Transmission

The chain of transmission of hadith No. 1501 includes a narrator called Abu Naḍrah al-'Awaqī. He belonged to al-'Awaqah, a clan of the tribe of 'Abd al-Qays. Ibn Qaraqūl, the author of *Maṭāli' al-Anwār*, says that the name is pronounced either al-'Awaqī or al-'Awqī, but the first is the correct and better-known pronunciation.

CHAPTER 21

FEARING NOT WAKING UP FOR WITR

[1502–162]. (Dar al-Salam 1650) Abu Bakr ibn Abi Shaybah narrated:[i] Ḥafṣ and Abu Muʿāwiyah narrated; from al-Aʿmash; from Abu Sufyān; from Jābir. He said: **'God's Messenger (peace be upon him) said: "Whoever fears not waking up towards the end of the night should pray Witr early at night, but whoever hopes to wake up late at night should pray Witr at the tail end of the night because prayer then is witnessed, and that is better".'**

Abu Muʿāwiyah said: **'attended' [in place of witnessed].**

حَدَّثَنَا أَبُو بَكْرِ بْنُ أَبِي شَيْبَةَ، حَدَّثَنَا حَفْصٌ وَأَبُو مُعَاوِيَةَ، عَنِ الأَعْمَشِ، عَنْ أَبِي سُفْيَانَ، عَنْ جَابِرٍ قَالَ: قَالَ رَسُولُ اللهِ صَلَّى اللهُ عَلَيْهِ وَسَلَّمَ: «مَنْ خَافَ أَنْ لَا يَقُومَ مِنْ آخِرِ اللَّيْلِ فَلْيُوتِرْ أَوَّلَهُ، وَمَنْ طَمِعَ أَنْ يَقُومَ آخِرَهُ فَلْيُوتِرْ آخِرَ اللَّيْلِ، فَإِنَّ صَلَاةَ آخِرِ اللَّيْلِ مَشْهُودَةٌ، وَذَلِكَ أَفْضَلُ».

وَقَالَ أَبُو مُعَاوِيَةَ مَحْضُورَةٌ.

[1503–163]. (Dar al-Salam 1651) Salamah ibn Shabīb narrated to me: al-Ḥasan ibn Aʿyan narrated; Miʿqal (who is Ibn ʿUbaydullāh) narrated; from Abu al-Zubayr; from Jābir. He said: **'I heard the Prophet (peace be upon him) say: "Whoever**

i. Related by al-Tirmidhī, 455; Ibn Mājah, 1187.

fears not waking up towards the end of the night should pray Witr, then go to sleep. And whoever is sure to wake up at night should pray Witr towards its end. Recitation at the tail end of the night is attended, and that is better".'

وَحَدَّثَنِي سَلَمَةُ بْنُ شَبِيبٍ، حَدَّثَنَا الْحَسَنُ بْنُ أَعْيَنَ، حَدَّثَنَا مَعْقِلٌ (وَهُوَ ابْنُ عُبَيْدِ اللهِ)، عَنْ أَبِي الزُّبَيْرِ، عَنْ جَابِرٍ قَالَ: سَمِعْتُ النَّبِيَّ صَلَّى اللهُ عَلَيْهِ وَسَلَّمَ يَقُولُ: «أَيُّكُمْ خَافَ أَنْ لاَ يَقُومَ مِنْ آخِرِ اللَّيْلِ فَلْيُوتِرْ، ثُمَّ لْيَرْقُدْ. وَمَنْ وَثِقَ بِقِيَامٍ مِنَ اللَّيْلِ فَلْيُوتِرْ مِنْ آخِرِهِ، فَإِنَّ قِرَاءَةَ آخِرِ اللَّيْلِ مَحْضُورَةٌ، وَذَلِكَ أَفْضَلُ».

Text Explanation

These two hadiths provide clear evidence that delaying the Witr prayer until the end of the night is preferable, provided that one is sure to wake up. If one is unsure of being able to wake up, then offering it early is preferable. This is the correct view. Other hadiths that speak in general terms should be understood in light of this detailed and clear statement. An example of such hadiths is the one narrated by Abu Hurayrah: 'My friend urged me not to go to sleep until I had prayed Witr'. This is understood to apply to a person who is unsure of waking up.

The Prophet says that prayer towards the end of the night is 'witnessed'. This means that it is attended by the angels of mercy. The hadith gives two clear pieces of evidence that offering Witr and other voluntary prayers at the tail end of the night is better.

CHAPTER 22

LONG NIGHT PRAYER IS THE BEST

[1504–164]. (Dar al-Salam 1652) ʿAbd ibn Ḥumayd narrated:[i] Abu ʿĀṣim reported; Ibn Jurayj reported; Abu al-Zubayr reported to me; from Jābir. He said: **'God's Messenger (peace be upon him) said: "The best prayer is to stand up for a long time".'**

حَدَّثَنَا عَبْدُ بْنُ حُمَيْدٍ، أَخْبَرَنَا أَبُو عَاصِمٍ، أَخْبَرَنَا ابْنُ جُرَيْجٍ، أَخْبَرَنِي أَبُو الزُّبَيْرِ، عَنْ جَابِرٍ قَالَ: قَالَ رَسُولُ اللهِ صَلَّى اللهُ عَلَيْهِ وَسَلَّمَ: «أَفْضَلُ الصَّلَاةِ طُولُ الْقُنُوتِ».

[1505–165]. (Dar al-Salam 1653) Abu Bakr ibn Abi Shaybah and Abu Kurayb narrated: both said: Abu Muʿāwiyah narrated; al-Aʿmash narrated; from Abu Sufyān; from Jābir. He said: **'God's Messenger (peace be upon him) was asked: "which prayer is best?" He said: "Standing up [for] long".'**

Abu Bakr said: 'Abu Muʿāwiyah narrated; from al-Aʿmash.'

وَحَدَّثَنَا أَبُو بَكْرِ بْنُ أَبِي شَيْبَةَ وَأَبُو كُرَيْبٍ، قَالَا: حَدَّثَنَا أَبُو مُعَاوِيَةَ، حَدَّثَنَا الأَعْمَشُ، عَنْ أَبِي سُفْيَانَ، عَنْ جَابِرٍ قَالَ: سُئِلَ رَسُولُ اللهِ صَلَّى اللهُ عَلَيْهِ وَسَلَّمَ: أَيُّ الصَّلَاةِ أَفْضَلُ؟ قَالَ: «طُولُ الْقُنُوتِ».

قَالَ أَبُو بَكْرٍ: حَدَّثَنَا أَبُو مُعَاوِيَةَ عَنِ الأَعْمَشِ.

---

i. Related by Ibn Mājah, 1421.

Text Explanation

The hadith uses the expression 'a long *qunūt*' [and this Arabic word normally refers to supplication before prostration in the last *rakʿah* of a prayer]. Al-Nawawī says: 'To the best of my knowledge, *qunūt* in this instance refers to standing up [when one is reciting the Qur'an]. The hadith provides evidence in support of the view of al-Shāfiʿī and other scholars that in night worship, standing up is preferable to many bowings and prostrations' [in other words, a longer recitation of the Qur'an in prayer is preferable to a larger number of shorter *rakʿahs*]. This point was discussed earlier in this volume.

CHAPTER 23

A TIME AT NIGHT WHEN SUPPLICATION IS ANSWERED

[1506–166]. (Dar al-Salam 1654) ʿUthmān ibn Abi Shaybah narrated: Jarīr narrated; from al-Aʿmash; from Abu Sufyān; from Jābir; he said: I heard the Prophet (peace be upon him) say: **'There is an hour during the night when any Muslim who happens to request God for any good thing of this life or the life to come will be granted his request. This is so every night'.**

وَحَدَّثَنَا عُثْمَانُ بْنُ أَبِي شَيْبَةَ، حَدَّثَنَا جَرِيرٌ، عَنِ الأَعْمَشِ، عَنْ أَبِي سُفْيَانَ، عَنْ جَابِرٍ قَالَ: سَمِعْتُ النَّبِيَّ صَلَّى اللهُ عَلَيْهِ وَسَلَّمَ يَقُولُ: «إِنَّ فِي اللَّيْلِ لَسَاعَةً لاَ يُوَافِقُهَا رَجُلٌ مُسْلِمٌ، يَسْأَلُ اللهَ خَيْرًا مِنْ أَمْرِ الدُّنْيَا وَالآخِرَةِ، إِلاَّ أَعْطَاهُ إِيَّاهُ. وَذَلِكَ كُلَّ لَيْلَةٍ».

[1507–167]. (Dar al-Salam 1655) Salamah ibn Shabīb narrated to me: al-Ḥasan ibn Aʿyan narrated; Maʿqil narrated; from Abu al-Zubayr; from Jābir; that God's Messenger (peace be upon him) said: **'There is an hour during the night when any Muslim who happens to request God for any good thing will be granted his request'.**

وَحَدَّثَنِي سَلَمَةُ بْنُ شَبِيبٍ، حَدَّثَنَا الْحَسَنُ بْنُ أَعْيَنَ، حَدَّثَنَا مَعْقِلٌ، عَنْ أَبِي الزُّبَيْرِ، عَنْ جَابِرٍ، أَنَّ رَسُولَ اللهِ صَلَّى اللهُ عَلَيْهِ وَسَلَّمَ قَالَ: «إِنَّ مِنَ اللَّيْلِ سَاعَةً لاَ يُوَافِقُهَا عَبْدٌ مُسْلِمٌ يَسْأَلُ اللهَ خَيْرًا إِلاَّ أَعْطَاهُ إِيَّاهُ».

Text Explanation

This hadith confirms that there is a time when supplication is answered and that this is on every night. The hadith urges us to appeal to God and to supplicate at all hours of the night hoping that our supplication coincides with this particular time.

CHAPTER 24

SUPPLICATION AND GLORIFICATION AT THE TAIL END OF THE NIGHT

[1508–168]. (Dar al-Salam 1656) Yaḥyā ibn Yaḥyā narrated:[i] he said: I read out to Mālik; from Ibn Shihāb; from Abu ʿAbdullāh al-Agharr; and also from Abu Salamah ibn ʿAbd al-Raḥmān; from Abu Hurayrah; that God's Messenger (peace be upon him) said: **'Every night our Lord, Blessed and Exalted, descends to the nearest Heaven when the last third of the night remains, and He says: "Whoever is praying to Me, I will answer them and whoever is requesting Me, I will grant them and whoever is seeking My forgiveness, I will forgive them".'**

حَدَّثَنَا يَحْيَى بْنُ يَحْيَى قَالَ: قَرَأْتُ عَلَى مَالِكٍ، عَنِ ابْنِ شِهَابٍ، عَنْ أَبِي عَبْدِ اللهِ الأَغَرِّ، وَعَنْ أَبِي سَلَمَةَ بْنِ عَبْدِ الرَّحْمَنِ، عَنْ أَبِي هُرَيْرَةَ، أَنَّ رَسُولَ اللهِ صَلَّى اللهُ عَلَيْهِ وَسَلَّمَ قَالَ: «يَنْزِلُ رَبُّنَا تَبَارَكَ وَتَعَالَى كُلَّ لَيْلَةٍ إِلَى السَّمَاءِ الدُّنْيَا، حِينَ يَبْقَى ثُلُثُ اللَّيْلِ الآخِرُ، فَيَقُولُ: مَنْ يَدْعُونِي فَأَسْتَجِيبَ لَهُ؟ وَمَنْ يَسْأَلُنِي فَأُعْطِيَهُ؟ وَمَنْ يَسْتَغْفِرُنِي فَأَغْفِرَ لَهُ»؟

[1509–169]. (Dar al-Salam 1657) Qutaybah ibn Saʿīd narrated:[ii] Yaʿqūb (who is Ibn ʿAbd al-Raḥmān al-Qariy) narrated; from Suhayl ibn Abi Ṣāliḥ; from his father; from Abu Hurayrah;

---

i. Related by al-Bukhari, 7494, 6321 and 1145; Abu Dāwūd, 1315 and 4733; al-Tirmidhī, 3498.

ii. Related by al-Tirmidhī, 446.

from God's Messenger (peace be upon him). He said: **'God descends to the nearest heaven every night when the first third of the night has gone, and He says: "I am the Sovereign, I am the Sovereign. Who is the one to pray to Me and I will answer him? Who is the one to request Me and I will grant him? and who is the one to seek My forgiveness and I will forgive him?" This will continue until dawn sheds its light'.**

وَحَدَّثَنَا قُتَيْبَةُ بْنُ سَعِيدٍ، حَدَّثَنَا يَعْقُوبُ (وَهُوَ ابْنُ عَبْدِ الرَّحْمَنِ الْقَارِيُّ)، عَنْ سُهَيْلِ بْنِ أَبِي صَالِحٍ، عَنْ أَبِيهِ، عَنْ أَبِي هُرَيْرَةَ، عَنْ رَسُولِ اللهِ صَلَّى اللهُ عَلَيْهِ وَسَلَّمَ قَالَ: «يَنْزِلُ اللهُ إِلَى السَّمَاءِ الدُّنْيَا كُلَّ لَيْلَةٍ، حِينَ يَمْضِي ثُلُثُ اللَّيْلِ الأَوَّلُ، فَيَقُولُ: أَنَا الْمَلِكُ، أَنَا الْمَلِكُ. مَنْ ذَا الَّذِي يَدْعُونِي فَأَسْتَجِيبَ لَهُ؟ مَنْ ذَا الَّذِي يَسْأَلُنِي فَأُعْطِيَهُ؟ مَنْ ذَا الَّذِي يَسْتَغْفِرُنِي فَأَغْفِرَ لَهُ؟ فَلاَ يَزَالُ كَذَلِكَ حَتَّى يُضِيءَ الْفَجْرُ».

[1510–170]. (Dar al-Salam 1658) Isḥāq ibn Manṣūr narrated: Abu al-Mughīrah reported; al-Awzāʿī narrated; Yaḥyā narrated; Abu Salamah ibn ʿAbd al-Raḥmān narrated; from Abu Hurayrah. He said: **'God's Messenger (peace be upon him) said: "When half of the night or its two thirds have gone, God, Blessed and Exalted, descends to the nearest Heaven and says: 'Is there anyone making a request to be granted? Is there anyone saying a prayer to be answered? Is there anyone seeking forgiveness to be forgiven?' Until the break of dawn".'**

حَدَّثَنَا إِسْحَاقُ بْنُ مَنْصُورٍ، أَخْبَرَنَا أَبُو الْمُغِيرَةِ، حَدَّثَنَا الأَوْزَاعِيُّ، حَدَّثَنَا يَحْيَى، حَدَّثَنَا أَبُو سَلَمَةَ بْنُ عَبْدِ الرَّحْمَنِ، عَنْ أَبِي هُرَيْرَةَ قَالَ: قَالَ رَسُولُ اللهِ صَلَّى اللهُ عَلَيْهِ وَسَلَّمَ: «إِذَا مَضَى شَطْرُ اللَّيْلِ أَوْ ثُلُثَاهُ، يَنْزِلُ اللهُ تَبَارَكَ وَتَعَالَى إِلَى السَّمَاءِ الدُّنْيَا فَيَقُولُ: هَلْ مِنْ سَائِلٍ يُعْطَى؟ هَلْ مِنْ دَاعٍ يُسْتَجَابُ لَهُ؟ هَلْ مِنْ مُسْتَغْفِرٍ يُغْفَرُ لَهُ؟ حَتَّى يَنْفَجِرَ الصُّبْحُ».

[1511–171]. (Dar al-Salam 1659) Ḥajjāj ibn al-Shāʿir narrated to me: Muḥāḍir Abu al-Muwarriʿ narrated; Saʿd ibn Saʿīd narrated; Ibn Marjānah reported to me; he said: I heard Abu Hurayrah say: **'God's Messenger (peace be upon him) said: "God descends to the nearest heaven when half the night has gone or at the last third of the night, and He says: 'Who will pray to Me and I will answer them or who will put a request to Me and I will grant them?' He then says: 'Who will lend to the One who is neither poor nor unfair?'".'**

Muslim said: Ibn Marjānah is Saʿīd ibn ʿAbdullāh. Marjānah is his mother.

حَدَّثَنِي حَجَّاجُ بْنُ الشَّاعِرِ، حَدَّثَنَا مُحَاضِرٌ أَبُو الْمُوَرِّعِ، حَدَّثَنَا سَعْدُ بْنُ سَعِيدٍ، قَالَ أَخْبَرَنِي ابْنُ مَرْجَانَةَ قَالَ: سَمِعْتُ أَبَا هُرَيْرَةَ يَقُولُ: قَالَ رَسُولُ اللهِ صَلَّى اللهُ عَلَيْهِ وَسَلَّمَ: «يَنْزِلُ اللهُ فِي السَّمَاءِ الدُّنْيَا لِشَطْرِ اللَّيْلِ أَوْ لِثُلُثِ اللَّيْلِ الآخِرِ فَيَقُولُ: مَنْ يَدْعُونِي فَأَسْتَجِيبَ لَهُ، أَوْ يَسْأَلُنِي فَأُعْطِيَهُ؟ ثُمَّ يَقُولُ: مَنْ يُقْرِضُ غَيْرَ عَدِيمٍ وَلاَ ظَلُومٍ»؟

قَالَ مُسْلِمٌ: ابْنُ مَرْجَانَةَ هُوَ سَعِيدُ بْنُ عَبْدِ اللهِ وَمَرْجَانَةُ أُمُّهُ.

[1512–000]. (Dar al-Salam[i]) Ḥarūn ibn Saʿīd al-Aylī narrated: Ibn Wahb narrated; he said: Sulaymān ibn Bilāl reported to me; from Saʿd ibn Saʿīd; with the same chain of transmission: **He added: 'Then He, Blessed and Exalted, stretches out His hands and says: "Who will lend to the One who is neither poor nor unfair?".'**

حَدَّثَنَا هَارُونُ بْنُ سَعِيدٍ الأَيْلِيُّ، حَدَّثَنَا ابْنُ وَهْبٍ، قَالَ: أَخْبَرَنِي سُلَيْمَانُ بْنُ بِلاَلٍ، عَنْ سَعْدِ بْنِ سَعِيدٍ، بِهَذَا الإِسْنَادِ، وَزَادَ: «ثُمَّ يَبْسُطُ يَدَيْهِ تَبَارَكَ وَتَعَالَى يَقُولُ: مَنْ يُقْرِضُ غَيْرَ عَدُومٍ وَلاَ ظَلُومٍ»؟

i. Dar al-Salam's edition attaches this hadith to the previous one.

[1513–172]. (Dar al-Salam 1660–1661) ʿUthmān and Abu Bakr, sons of Abu Shaybah and Isḥāq ibn Ibrāhīm al-Ḥanẓalī narrated (ʿUthmān's and Abu Bakr's text): Jarīr (Isḥāq said: 'reported' and the other two said: 'narrated'); from Manṣūr; from Abu Isḥāq; from al-Agharr Abi Muslim; narrating it from Abu Saʿīd and Abu Hurayrah: both said: **'God's Messenger (peace be upon him) said: "God gives respite, then in the first third of the night He descends to the nearest heaven and says: 'Is there anyone seeking forgiveness? Is there anyone turning in repentance? Is there anyone making a request? Is there anyone supplicating?' until the break of dawn".'**

حَدَّثَنَا عُثْمَانُ وَأَبُو بَكْرٍ ابْنَا أَبِي شَيْبَةَ وَإِسْحَاقُ بْنُ إِبْرَاهِيمَ الْحَنْظَلِيُّ (وَاللَّفْظُ لِابْنَيْ أَبِي شَيْبَةَ)، قَالَ إِسْحَاقُ أَخْبَرَنَا وَقَالَ الآخَرَانِ حَدَّثَنَا جَرِيرٌ، عَنْ مَنْصُورٍ، عَنْ أَبِي إِسْحَاقَ، عَنِ الأَغَرِّ أَبِي مُسْلِمٍ، يَرْوِيهِ عَنْ أَبِي سَعِيدٍ وَأَبِي هُرَيْرَةَ، قَالا: قَالَ رَسُولُ اللهِ صَلَّى اللهُ عَلَيْهِ وَسَلَّمَ: «إِنَّ اللهَ يُمْهِلُ، حَتَّى إِذَا ذَهَبَ ثُلُثُ اللَّيْلِ الأَوَّلُ نَزَلَ إِلَى السَّمَاءِ الدُّنْيَا فَيَقُولُ: هَلْ مِنْ مُسْتَغْفِرٍ؟ هَلْ مِنْ تَائِبٍ؟ هَلْ مِنْ سَائِلٍ؟ هَلْ مِنْ دَاعٍ؟ حَتَّى يَنْفَجِرَ الْفَجْرُ».

Muhammad ibn al-Muthannā and Ibn Bashshār narrated: both said: Muhammad ibn Jaʿfar narrated; Shuʿbah narrated; from Abu Isḥāq; with the same chain of transmission; **but Manṣūr's narration is more complete and longer.**

وَحَدَّثَنَاهُ مُحَمَّدُ بْنُ الْمُثَنَّى وَابْنُ بَشَّارٍ، قَالا: حَدَّثَنَا مُحَمَّدُ بْنُ جَعْفَرٍ، حَدَّثَنَا شُعْبَةُ، عَنْ أَبِي إِسْحَاقَ، بِهَذَا الإِسْنَاد. غَيْرَ أَنَّ حَدِيثَ مَنْصُورٍ أَتَمُّ وَأَكْثَرُ.

Text Explanation

Hadith No. 1508 says that 'our Lord descends to the nearest heaven and says: "Whoever is praying to Me, I will answer them".' This is one of the hadiths that mention God's attributes. Scholars have two well-known ways of understanding these hadiths, and we explained these in the Book of Faith. Here, we mention them in brief. The first is the view of the majority of the early scholars and some scholars of theology. These attributes should be believed in as true and that they apply in the way that is suited to God, the Exalted. Their apparent form that is known to us is not what is intended. We may not try to explain them, but we must believe that God is unlike what applies to created beings, including changing places, movement and all other qualities of created beings. The second view is upheld by the majority of scholars of theology and a number of early scholars. We state it here as expressed by Mālik and al-Awzāʿī: that they are understood according to what is suited to them in their different contexts. In this light, they understand this hadith in two different ways. The first is expressed by Mālik ibn Anas and others, and it means that what descends is God's mercy and angels. It is like when we say that the king did so-and-so, but it was rather his officials who did so by his orders. The second is that it is a metaphor, which means that He turns to His supplicating servants with kindness and answers their supplication. But God knows best.

In hadith No. 1508, the Prophet mentions that God descends 'when the last third of the night remains', and in hadith No. 1509: 'when the first third of the night has gone', and in No. 1510: 'when half or two thirds of the night have gone'. *Qadi* 'Iyāḍ says: 'The correct narration is "when the last third of the night remains". Thus say the leading Hadith scholars based on various clearly stated reports… It is possible that the descending is what is meant by "after the first third of the night", and that He says, "who will pray to Me", in the last third'. This is what *Qadi* 'Iyāḍ said, but it might have been that the Prophet (peace be upon him) was informed of one of the two things at one time and he stated the information he was given. He might have been given the other information at some other time and stated that too. Abu Hurayrah might have heard the two pieces of information and reported them both, while

Abu Saʿīd heard only the information relating to the first third of the night and he reported it with Abu Hurayrah, as Muslim mentions in hadith No. 1513. This is clear and it negates what *Qadi* ʿIyāḍ said claiming that this narration about the first third of the night is lacking authenticity. How can he say this when it is entered by Muslim in his *Ṣaḥīḥ* with an unblemished chain of transmitters, going up to two Companions of the Prophet, Abu Saʿīd and Abu Hurayrah? But God knows best.

Hadith No. 1509 mentions that God says: 'I am the Sovereign, I am the Sovereign'. This is how it is stated in the narrations and manuscripts. The repetition gives special emphasis.

In the same hadith, the Prophet says: 'This will continue until the dawn sheds its light'. This gives us evidence that the time of divine mercy and perfect blessing extends until dawn has spread its light. It urges that supplication and seeking God's forgiveness is maintained throughout this time. The Prophet's statement also explains that the last part of the night is preferable to its early part for prayer, supplication and seeking God's forgiveness and other aspects of worship, but God knows best.

In hadith No. 1511 God is quoted as saying: 'Who will lend to the One who is neither poor nor unfair?' What is meant by lending – and God knows best – is every act of worship, and it equally includes giving charity, i.e. *ṣadaqah*, prayer, fasting, glorifying God, etc. God describes these as a loan given to Him so as to put it in a friendly way to His servants, urging them to attend to such acts of worship. A loan is given by someone the borrower knows, and there is a degree of love and friendship between the two. Hence, when the borrower makes his request, the lender gives him what he wants. He is pleased that the borrower considers him worthy of giving a loan and mentioning his need.

In hadith No. 1512, God is said to stretch out His hands. This refers to bestowing His mercy on all, as well as His generous bounty and inexhaustible blessings.

Transmission

The chain of transmission of hadith No. 1511 includes Muḥāḍir Abu al-Muwarriʿ. This is how his name occurs in all copies, but he is most frequently mentioned in books of hadith as Ibn al-Muwarriʿ. Both versions are correct because he is the son of al-Muwarriʿ, and his appellation is Abu al-Muwarriʿ.

Al-Agharr Abi Muslim is included in the chain of transmission of hadith No. 1513. Al-Agharr is his nickname, but his name is Salmān.

CHAPTER 25

NIGHT WORSHIP DURING RAMADAN: *TARĀWĪḤ*

[1514–173]. (Dar al-Salam 1662) Yaḥyā ibn Yaḥyā narrated: he said:[i] I read out to Mālik; from Ibn Shihāb; from Ḥumayd ibn ʿAbd al-Raḥmān; from Abu Hurayrah; that God's Messenger (peace be upon him) said: **'Whoever attends to night worship during Ramadan, out of faith and in true devotion, shall have all his past sins forgiven'.**

حَدَّثَنَا يَحْيَى بْنُ يَحْيَى قَالَ: قَرَأْتُ عَلَى مَالِكٍ، عَنِ ابْنِ شِهَابٍ، عَنْ حُمَيْدِ بْنِ عَبْدِ الرَّحْمَنِ، عَنْ أَبِي هُرَيْرَةَ، أَنَّ رَسُولَ اللهِ صَلَّى اللهُ عَلَيْهِ وَسَلَّمَ قَالَ: «مَنْ قَامَ رَمَضَانَ إِيمَانًا وَاحْتِسَابًا غُفِرَ لَهُ مَا تَقَدَّمَ مِنْ ذَنْبِهِ».

[1515–174]. (Dar al-Salam 1663) ʿAbd ibn Ḥumayd narrated:[ii] ʿAbd al-Razzāq reported; Maʿmar reported; from al-Zuhrī; from Abu Salamah; from Abu Hurayrah. He said: **'God's Messenger (peace be upon him) encouraged night worship in Ramadan without giving an order of duty. He would say: "Whoever attends to night worship during Ramadan, out of faith and in true devotion, shall have all his past sins forgiven". The matter was such until God's Messenger (peace be upon him)**

---

i. Related by al-Bukhari, 37 and 2009; al-Nasāʾī, 1601, 2198, 2199, 2200, 5040 and 5041.

ii. Related by Abu Dāwūd, 1371; al-Tirmidhī, 808; al-Nasāʾī, 2103 and 2197.

passed away, then it continued as such during Abu Bakr's reign and for a part of 'Umar's reign'.

وَحَدَّثَنَا عَبْدُ بْنُ حُمَيْدٍ، أَخْبَرَنَا عَبْدُ الرَّزَّاقِ، أَخْبَرَنَا مَعْمَرٌ، عَنِ الزُّهْرِيِّ، عَنْ أَبِي سَلَمَةَ، عَنْ أَبِي هُرَيْرَةَ قَالَ: كَانَ رَسُولُ اللهِ صَلَّى اللهُ عَلَيْهِ وَسَلَّمَ يُرَغِّبُ فِي قِيَامِ رَمَضَانَ، مِنْ غَيْرِ أَنْ يَأْمُرَهُمْ فِيهِ بِعَزِيمَةٍ، فَيَقُولُ: «مَنْ قَامَ رَمَضَانَ إِيمَانًا وَاحْتِسَابًا غُفِرَ لَهُ مَا تَقَدَّمَ مِنْ ذَنْبِهِ». فَتُوُفِّيَ رَسُولُ اللهِ صَلَّى اللهُ عَلَيْهِ وَسَلَّمَ وَالأَمْرُ عَلَى ذَلِكَ، ثُمَّ كَانَ الأَمْرُ عَلَى ذَلِكَ فِي خِلَافَةِ أَبِي بَكْرٍ، وَصَدْرًا مِنْ خِلَافَةِ عُمَرَ عَلَى ذَلِكَ.

[1516–175]. (Dar al-Salam 1664) Zuhayr ibn Ḥarb narrated to me:[i] Muʿādh ibn Hishām narrated; my father narrated; from Yaḥyā ibn Abi Kathīr; he said: Abu Salamah ibn ʿAbd al-Raḥmān narrated; that Abu Hurayrah narrated to them; that God's Messenger (peace be upon him) said: **'Whoever fasts during Ramadan, out of faith and in true devotion, shall have all his past sins forgiven, and whoever attends to night worship on the Night of Power, out of faith and in true devotion, shall have all his past sins forgiven'.**

وَحَدَّثَنِي زُهَيْرُ بْنُ حَرْبٍ، حَدَّثَنَا مُعَاذُ بْنُ هِشَامٍ، حَدَّثَنِي أَبِي، عَنْ يَحْيَى بْنِ أَبِي كَثِيرٍ قَالَ: حَدَّثَنَا أَبُو سَلَمَةَ بْنُ عَبْدِ الرَّحْمَنِ، أَنَّ أَبَا هُرَيْرَةَ حَدَّثَهُمْ أَنَّ رَسُولَ اللهِ صَلَّى اللهُ عَلَيْهِ وَسَلَّمَ قَالَ: «مَنْ صَامَ رَمَضَانَ إِيمَانًا وَاحْتِسَابًا غُفِرَ لَهُ مَا تَقَدَّمَ مِنْ ذَنْبِهِ، وَمَنْ قَامَ لَيْلَةَ الْقَدْرِ إِيمَانًا وَاحْتِسَابًا غُفِرَ لَهُ مَا تَقَدَّمَ مِنْ ذَنْبِهِ».

[1517–176]. (Dar al-Salam 1665) Muhammad ibn Rāfiʿ narrated to me: Shabābah narrated; Warqā' narrated to me; from Abu al-Zinād; from al-Aʿraj; from Abu Hurayrah; from the Prophet

i. Related by al-Bukhari, 1901.

(peace be upon him). He said: **'Whoever attends to night worship on the Night of Power and it is actually the Night, (I think he said:) out of faith and in true devotion, shall have his sins forgiven'.**

حَدَّثَنِي مُحَمَّدُ بْنُ رَافِعٍ، حَدَّثَنَا شَبَابَةُ، حَدَّثَنِي وَرْقَاءُ، عَنْ أَبِي الزِّنَادِ، عَنِ الأَعْرَجِ، عَنْ أَبِي هُرَيْرَةَ، عَنِ النَّبِيِّ صَلَّى اللهُ عَلَيْهِ وَسَلَّمَ قَالَ: «مَنْ يَقُمْ لَيْلَةَ الْقَدْرِ فَيُوَافِقُهَا - أُرَاهُ قَالَ - إِيمَانًا وَاحْتِسَابًا غُفِرَ لَهُ».

[1518–177]. (Dar al-Salam 1666) Yaḥyā ibn Yaḥyā narrated:[i] he said: I read out to Mālik; from Ibn Shihāb; from 'Urwah; from 'Ā'ishah; that **'God's Messenger (peace be upon him) prayed one night in the mosque, and some people joined him in his prayer. He then prayed the following night and more people joined. Then they gathered on the third or the fourth night, but God's Messenger (peace be upon him) did not go out to join them. In the morning he said to them: "I saw what you did. Nothing prevented me from coming out to join you except that I feared that it would become a duty for you".'**

He said: 'This was during Ramadan'.

حَدَّثَنَا يَحْيَى بْنُ يَحْيَى قَالَ: قَرَأْتُ عَلَى مَالِكٍ، عَنِ ابْنِ شِهَابٍ، عَنْ عُرْوَةَ، عَنْ عَائِشَةَ، أَنَّ رَسُولَ اللهِ صَلَّى اللهُ عَلَيْهِ وَسَلَّمَ صَلَّى فِي الْمَسْجِدِ ذَاتَ لَيْلَةٍ، فَصَلَّى بِصَلاَتِهِ نَاسٌ. ثُمَّ صَلَّى مِنَ الْقَابِلَةِ، فَكَثُرَ النَّاسُ. ثُمَّ اجْتَمَعُوا مِنَ اللَّيْلَةِ الثَّالِثَةِ أَوِ الرَّابِعَةِ. فَلَمَّا أَصْبَحَ قَالَ: «قَدْ رَأَيْتُ الَّذِي صَنَعْتُمْ، فَلَمْ يَمْنَعْنِي مِنَ الْخُرُوجِ إِلَيْكُمْ إِلاَّ أَنِّي خَشِيتُ أَنْ تُفْرَضَ عَلَيْكُمْ».

قَالَ: وَذَلِكَ فِي رَمَضَانَ.

---

i. Related by al-Bukhari, 1129 and 2011; Abu Dāwūd, 1373.

[1519–178]. (Dar al-Salam 1667) Ḥarmalah ibn Yaḥyā narrated to me:[i] ʿAbdullāh ibn Wahb reported; Yūnus ibn Yazīd reported to me; from Ibn Shihāb; he said: ʿUrwah ibn al-Zubayr reported to me; that ʿĀ'ishah reported to him; that **'God's Messenger (peace be upon him) went out in the middle of the night and prayed in the mosque. A number of men joined him in prayer. In the morning, people were talking about this, and more people gathered. God's Messenger (peace be upon him) went out on the second night and they joined him in prayer. Again, people spoke about this in the morning. The people in the mosque were numerous on the third night. He went out and they joined him in prayer. On the fourth night, the mosque was overcrowded, but God's Messenger (peace be upon him) did not go out to join them. Some men among them called out: "Prayer!", but God's Messenger (peace be upon him) did not go out to join them until he went out for the Fajr Prayer. When he finished the Fajr Prayer, he turned to the people and said the declaration. He then said: "Meanwhile, I was not unaware of what you were doing last night, but I feared that night prayer would become obligatory to you and you will not be able to maintain it".'**

وَحَدَّثَنِي حَرْمَلَةُ بْنُ يَحْيَى، أَخْبَرَنَا عَبْدُ اللهِ بْنُ وَهْبٍ، أَخْبَرَنِي يُونُسُ بْنُ يَزِيدَ، عَنِ ابْنِ شِهَابٍ قَالَ: أَخْبَرَنِي عُرْوَةُ بْنُ الزُّبَيْرِ، أَنَّ عَائِشَةَ أَخْبَرَتْهُ، أَنَّ رَسُولَ اللهِ صَلَّى اللهُ عَلَيْهِ وَسَلَّمَ خَرَجَ مِنْ جَوْفِ اللَّيْلِ فَصَلَّى فِي الْـمَسْجِدِ، فَصَلَّى رِجَالٌ بِصَلَاتِهِ. فَأَصْبَحَ النَّاسُ يَتَحَدَّثُونَ بِذَلِكَ، فَاجْتَمَعَ أَكْثَرُ مِنْهُمْ، فَخَرَجَ رَسُولُ اللهِ صَلَّى اللهُ عَلَيْهِ وَسَلَّمَ فِي اللَّيْلَةِ الثَّانِيَةِ فَصَلَّوْا بِصَلَاتِهِ. فَأَصْبَحَ النَّاسُ يَذْكُرُونَ ذَلِكَ، فَكَثُرَ أَهْلُ الْـمَسْجِدِ مِنَ اللَّيْلَةِ الثَّالِثَةِ فَخَرَجَ فَصَلَّوْا بِصَلَاتِهِ. فَلَمَّا كَانَتِ اللَّيْلَةُ الرَّابِعَةُ عَجَزَ الْـمَسْجِدُ عَنْ

i. Related by al-Bukhari, 924; al-Nasā'ī, 2192.

أَهْلِهِ، فَلَمْ يَخْرُجْ إِلَيْهِمْ رَسُولُ اللهِ صَلَّى اللهُ عَلَيْهِ وَسَلَّمَ، فَطَفِقَ رِجَالٌ مِنْهُمْ يَقُولُونَ: الصَّلَاةَ! فَلَمْ يَخْرُجْ إِلَيْهِمْ رَسُولُ اللهِ صَلَّى اللهُ عَلَيْهِ وَسَلَّمَ، حَتَّى خَرَجَ لِصَلَاةِ الْفَجْرِ. فَلَمَّا قَضَى الْفَجْرَ، أَقْبَلَ عَلَى النَّاسِ ثُمَّ تَشَهَّدَ فَقَالَ: «أَمَّا بَعْدُ فَإِنَّهُ لَمْ يَخْفَ عَلَيَّ شَأْنُكُمُ اللَّيْلَةَ، وَلَكِنِّي خَشِيتُ أَنْ تُفْرَضَ عَلَيْكُمْ صَلَاةُ اللَّيْلِ فَتَعْجِزُوا عَنْهَا».

[1520–179]. (Dar al-Salam 1668) Muhammad ibn Mihrān al-Rāzī narrated:[i] al-Walīd ibn Muslim narrated; al-Awzāʿī narrated; ʿAbdah narrated to me; from Zirr; he said: I heard Ubayy ibn Kaʿb say: (He was told that ʿAbdullāh ibn Masʿūd said: whoever offers night worship throughout the year will certainly include the Night of Power). Ubayy said: **'By God other than whom there is no deity, it is during Ramadan (He swore without adding 'God willing'). By God, I know on which night it is. It is the night God's Messenger (peace be upon him) ordered us to spend in worship. It is the night before day twenty-seven. Its sign is that the sun rises on the morning following it, white without rays'.**

حَدَّثَنَا مُحَمَّدُ بْنُ مِهْرَانَ الرَّازِيُّ، حَدَّثَنَا الْوَلِيدُ بْنُ مُسْلِمٍ، حَدَّثَنَا الأَوْزَاعِيُّ، حَدَّثَنِي عَبْدَةُ، عَنْ زِرٍّ قَالَ: سَمِعْتُ أُبَيَّ بْنَ كَعْبٍ يَقُولُ: - وَقِيلَ لَهُ إِنَّ عَبْدَ اللهِ بْنَ مَسْعُودٍ يَقُولُ: مَنْ قَامَ السَّنَةَ أَصَابَ لَيْلَةَ الْقَدْرِ - فَقَالَ أُبَيٌّ: وَاللهِ الَّذِي لاَ إِلَهَ إِلاَّ هُوَ إِنَّهَا لَفِي رَمَضَانَ - يَحْلِفُ مَا يَسْتَثْنِي - وَوَاللهِ إِنِّي لأَعْلَمُ أَيُّ لَيْلَةٍ هِيَ. هِيَ اللَّيْلَةُ الَّتِي أَمَرَنَا بِهَا رَسُولُ اللهِ صَلَّى اللهُ عَلَيْهِ وَسَلَّمَ بِقِيَامِهَا. هِيَ لَيْلَةُ صَبِيحَةِ سَبْعٍ وَعِشْرِينَ، وَأَمَارَتُهَا أَنْ تَطْلُعَ الشَّمْسُ فِي صَبِيحَةِ يَوْمِهَا بَيْضَاءَ لاَ شُعَاعَ لَهَا.

[1521–180]. (Dar al-Salam 1669–1670) Muhammad ibn al-Muthannā narrated: Muhammad ibn Jaʿfar narrated; Shuʿbah

---

i. Related by Abu Dāwūd in similar wording, 1378; al-Nasāʾī, 793.

narrated; he said: I heard ʿAbdah ibn Abi Lubābah narrating; from Zirr ibn Ḥubaysh; from Ubayy ibn Kaʿb. He said: **'Ubayy said about the Night of Power: "By God, I know it. My best knowledge is that it is the night God's Messenger (peace be upon him) ordered us to spend in worship. It is the night of twenty-seven".**

Shuʿbah only doubted this word: **'It is the night God's Messenger ordered us [to mark]'. He said: 'a friend of his mentioned it to me reporting from him.'**

حَدَّثَنَا مُحَمَّدُ بْنُ الْـمُثَنَّى، حَدَّثَنَا مُحَمَّدُ بْنُ جَعْفَرٍ، حَدَّثَنَا شُعْبَةُ قَالَ: سَمِعْتُ عَبْدَةَ بْنَ أَبِي لُبَابَةَ، يُحَدِّثُ عَنْ زِرِّ بْنِ حُبَيْشٍ، عَنْ أُبَيِّ بْنِ كَعْبٍ، قَالَ أُبَيٌّ فِي لَيْلَةِ الْقَدْرِ: وَاللهِ إِنِّي لَأَعْلَمُهَا وَأَكْثَرُ عِلْمِي هِيَ اللَّيْلَةُ الَّتِي أَمَرَنَا رَسُولُ اللهِ صَلَّى اللهُ عَلَيْهِ وَسَلَّمَ بِقِيَامِهَا، هِيَ لَيْلَةُ سَبْعٍ وَعِشْرِينَ. وَإِنَّمَا شَكَّ شُعْبَةُ فِي هَذَا الْحَرْفِ: هِيَ اللَّيْلَةُ الَّتِي أَمَرَنَا بِهَا رَسُولُ اللهِ صَلَّى اللهُ عَلَيْهِ وَسَلَّمَ. قَالَ: وَحَدَّثَنِي بِهَا صَاحِبٌ لِي عَنْهُ.

ʿUbaydullāh ibn Muʿādh narrated to me: my father narrated; Shuʿbah narrated; with the same chain of transmission: **a similar text but did not mention [the point] that Shuʿbah doubted and what came after it.**

وَحَدَّثَنِي عُبَيْدُ اللهِ بْنُ مُعَاذٍ، حَدَّثَنَا أَبِي، حَدَّثَنَا شُعْبَةُ، بِهَذَا الإِسْنَادِ: نَحْوَهُ. وَلَمْ يَذْكُرْ إِنَّمَا شَكَّ شُعْبَةُ، وَمَا بَعْدَهُ.

Text Explanation

Hadith No. 1534 says: 'Whoever attends to night worship during Ramadan, out of faith and in true devotion, shall have all his past sins forgiven'. The meaning of 'out of faith' is that the worshipper believes that it is right and hopes for receiving the benefit of it. 'In true devotion' means that he dedicates his worship to God alone, caring nothing for being known or seen or anything else that is contrary to sincere devotion. Night worship during Ramadan means the prayer known as Tarāwīḥ. Scholars agree that it is desirable and recommended, but they differ as to whether it is preferable to be offered alone at home or in a congregation in the mosque. Al-Shāfiʿī and the majority of scholars of his school, Abu Ḥanīfah, Ahmad, a number of Mālikī scholars and others say that it is preferable to offer it in congregation, as done by ʿUmar ibn al-Khaṭṭāb and the Prophet's Companions and as is continued to be done by Muslims. It is one of the main public aspects of Islamic worship, and as such it is similar to the Eid Prayer. On the other hand, Mālik, Abu Yūsuf, a number of Shāfiʿī scholars and others say that it is preferable to offer it individually at home, as the Prophet says: 'The best prayer is for a person to pray at home, except for obligatory prayers'.

In this hadith, the Prophet says: 'shall have all his past sins forgiven'. According to scholars, this refers in particular to minor sins, not major ones. Some scholars say that it may also mean that major sins may be reduced if minor ones are not committed.

Hadith No. 1515 says: 'God's Messenger (peace be upon him) encouraged night worship during Ramadan without giving an order of duty. He would say: "Whoever attends to night worship during Ramadan, out of faith and in true devotion, shall have all his past sins forgiven".' The expression 'without giving an order of duty' means that he did not make this obligatory on them. He only gave them a recommendation and encouraged them to do it. This is explained by the rest of the hadith. The way it is phrased shows that it is definitely a recommendation. The Muslim community is unanimously agreed that night worship during Ramadan is not obligatory but recommended.

Hadith No. 1515 mentions 'The matter was such until God's Messenger (peace be upon him) passed away, then it continued such during Abu Bakr's reign and for a part of ʿUmar's reign'. This means that everyone offered the night prayer during Ramadan at his own home and this continued for some time into ʿUmar's reign. ʿUmar then organised the prayer in a congregation and appointed

Ubayy ibn Kaʿb to lead the prayer. It has continued to be offered in congregation ever since. This addition occurs in al-Bukhari's *Ṣaḥīḥ* in the Book of Fasting.

Hadith No. 1516 quotes the Prophet: 'Whoever attends to night worship on the Night of Power, out of faith and in true devotion, shall have all his past sins forgiven'. The earlier hadith, No. 1514, says: 'Whoever attends to night worship during Ramadan, out of faith and in true devotion, shall have all his past sins forgiven'. It may be said that either one is sufficient and makes the other of little value. In answer, we may say that attending to night worship during Ramadan without knowing the Night of Power is enough to have one's sins forgiven. At the same time, when a person spends the Night of Power in worship, knowing it, this is a good reason for such forgiveness, even if a person does not attend to worship on any other night.

Hadith No. 1517 says: 'Whoever attends to night worship on the Night of Power and it is the Night…'. This means that such a person offers night prayer knowing that it is the Night of Power.

Hadith No. 1518 mentions that one night the Prophet (peace be upon him) offered his prayer in the mosque and some people joined him in his prayer. This hadith makes it clear that voluntary and recommended prayers may be offered in a congregation, although the preference is to offer them individually, except for certain prayers which are the Eid Prayer, the prayer at the time of an eclipse and the prayer for rain. The same applies to Tarāwīḥ Prayer, according to the majority of scholars, as explained earlier. The hadith also shows that recommended prayers may be offered in the mosque, even though they are better offered at home. It may be that the Prophet prayed this prayer in the mosque to show that it is permissible, and perhaps he was in *iʿtikāf*, which means spending some days in the mosque.

The hadith further shows that it is permissible to join someone in prayer even though he did not intend to be an imam leading a prayer. This is the correct view according to what is best known in our school and among the majority of scholars. However, when some people join someone in prayer and he then intends to lead them, the greater reward of congregational prayer is earned by both the imam and the people joining him. If he does not make the additional intention of leading them, the greater reward applies to them but not to him because 'actions are but by intention' and he has not made the intention while they have done so.

The hadith confirms that if two beneficial options are in conflict or if a benefit is in conflict with fear of an adverse outcome, the more important option is given preference. The Prophet (peace be upon him) saw a certain benefit in offering this prayer in the mosque, as we have mentioned. However, this was subsequently opposed out of fear that this prayer would become obligatory, and he did not come out. He thought of the harm that would result from believers' inability to fulfil such an obligation. The hadith also indicates that if the leader of a community does something that is contrary to what his community expects and he has a reason for it, he should explain his reason to them, so as to reassure them and prevent some contrary and ill thoughts, but God knows best.

Hadith No. 1519 concludes with the following: 'When he finished the Fajr Prayer, he turned to the people and said the declaration. He then said: "Meanwhile, I was not unaware of what you were doing last night...'. There are several points of interest here. The first is that it is desirable to start one's speech or admonition with the declaration, [i.e. saying: I bear witness that there is no deity other than God and I bear witness that Muhammad is God's servant and Messenger]. A hadith related in Abu Dāwūd's *Sunan* anthology says: 'A speech [i.e. *khuṭbah*] that does not include the declaration is like a hand affected by leprosy'. Another point is that it is advisable to say 'meanwhile' in a speech. This is mentioned in several authentic hadiths. Al-Bukhari includes in his *Ṣaḥīḥ* a chapter on starting one's speech with 'meanwhile'. It includes several hadiths. A further point is to face the people when one is giving a speech or saying some admonition.

Hadith No. 1520 and 1521 mention that Ubayy ibn Kaʿb used to swear that the Night of Power is the night of the 27th of Ramadan. This is one view. The majority of scholars are of the view that it is an undefined night during the last third of Ramadan, but the odd nights are more probable, and the ones that are most probable are the nights of the 27th, 23rd and 21st. The majority of scholars maintain that it is a fixed night and that it does not change. Scrupulous scholars say that it changes so that it is on the 27th of Ramadan one year, on the 23rd on another year and the 21st on yet another, and it could even be on a different night. This is more likely, as it reconciles the different hadiths speaking about it. We shall discuss this more fully at the end of the Book of Fasting, God willing.

CHAPTER 26

SUPPLICATION DURING NIGHT PRAYER AND WORSHIP

[1522–181]. (Dar al-Salam 1671) ʿAbdullāh ibn Hāshim ibn Ḥayyān al-ʿAbdī narrated to me: ʿAbd al-Raḥmān (meaning Ibn Mahdī) narrated; Sufyān narrated; from Salamah ibn Kuhayl; from Kurayb; from Ibn ʿAbbās. He said: **'One night I slept at my maternal aunt Maymūnah's home. The Prophet (peace be upon him) woke up and relieved himself. He then washed his face and hands, then slept. He woke up [again] and he went up to the waterskin, undid its string and performed a good ablution, in between the two extremes. He did not use much water but did his ablution perfectly. He then stood up and prayed. I rose and stretched myself so that he would not notice that I was watching him. I performed my ablution and he stood up in prayer. I stood on his left side. He took my hand and moved me to his right. God's Messenger completed his night worship in thirteen *rakʿahs*, then he lay down and slept, breathing soundly. He used to breath soundly when he slept. Bilāl came over and informed him that it was time for prayer. He got up and prayed without performing the ablution [again]. He said in his supplication: "My Lord, place in my heart light, in my sight light, in my hearing light, to my right light, to my left light, above me light, beneath me light, in front of me light, behind me light, and increase my light".**

Kurayb said: **'And seven in the chest. I met one of al-'Abbās' descendants and he narrated them to me, mentioning my nerves, flesh, blood, hair and skin, adding two others.'**

حَدَّثَنِي عَبْدُ اللهِ بْنُ هَاشِمِ بْنِ حَيَّانَ الْعَبْدِيُّ، حَدَّثَنَا عَبْدُ الرَّحْمَنِ (يَعْنِي ابْنَ مَهْدِيٍّ)، حَدَّثَنَا سُفْيَانُ، عَنْ سَلَمَةَ بْنِ كُهَيْلٍ، عَنْ كُرَيْبٍ، عَنِ ابْنِ عَبَّاسٍ قَالَ: بِتُّ لَيْلَةً عِنْدَ خَالَتِي مَيْمُونَةَ، فَقَامَ النَّبِيُّ صَلَّى اللهُ عَلَيْهِ وَسَلَّمَ مِنَ اللَّيْلِ فَأَتَى حَاجَتَهُ، ثُمَّ غَسَلَ وَجْهَهُ وَيَدَيْهِ، ثُمَّ نَامَ. ثُمَّ قَامَ فَأَتَى الْقِرْبَةَ، فَأَطْلَقَ شِنَاقَهَا، ثُمَّ تَوَضَّأَ وُضُوءًا بَيْنَ الْوُضُوءَيْنِ، وَلَمْ يُكْثِرْ وَقَدْ أَبْلَغَ. ثُمَّ قَامَ فَصَلَّى. فَقُمْتُ فَتَمَطَّيْتُ كَرَاهِيَةَ أَنْ يَرَى أَنِّي كُنْتُ أَنْتَبِهُ لَه، فَتَوَضَّأْتُ. فَقَامَ فَصَلَّى، فَقُمْتُ عَنْ يَسَارِهِ، فَأَخَذَ بِيَدِي فَأَدَارَنِي عَنْ يَمِينِهِ. فَتَتَامَّتْ صَلَاةُ رَسُولِ اللهِ صَلَّى اللهُ عَلَيْهِ وَسَلَّمَ مِنَ اللَّيْلِ ثَلَاثَ عَشْرَةَ رَكْعَةً. ثُمَّ اضْطَجَعَ فَنَامَ حَتَّى نَفَخَ. وَكَانَ إِذَا نَامَ نَفَخَ. فَأَتَاهُ بِلَالٌ فَآذَنَهُ بِالصَّلَاةِ فَقَامَ فَصَلَّى وَلَمْ يَتَوَضَّأْ وَكَانَ فِي دُعَائِهِ «اللَّهُمَّ اجْعَلْ فِي قَلْبِي نُورًا وَفِي بَصَرِي نُورًا وَفِي سَمْعِي نُورًا وَعَنْ يَمِينِي نُورًا وَعَنْ يَسَارِي نُورًا وَفَوْقِي نُورًا وَتَحْتِي نُورًا وَأَمَامِي نُورًا وَخَلْفِي نُورًا وَعَظِّمْ لِي نُورًا». قَالَ كُرَيْبٌ وَسَبْعًا فِي التَّابُوتِ فَلَقِيتُ بَعْضَ وَلَدِ الْعَبَّاسِ فَحَدَّثَنِي بِهِنَّ فَذَكَرَ عَصَبِي وَلَحْمِي وَدَمِي وَشَعَرِي وَبَشَرِي وَذَكَرَ خَصْلَتَيْنِ .

[1523–182]. (Dar al-Salam 1672) Yaḥyā ibn Yaḥyā narrated:[i] he said: I read out to Mālik; from Makhramah ibn Sulaymān; from Kurayb, Ibn 'Abbās's *mawlā*; that **Ibn 'Abbās told him that he stayed one night at Maymūnah's, the Mother of the Believers, who was his maternal aunt. He [Ibn 'Abbās] said: 'I lay down on the side of the pillow, while God's Messenger and his wife used its long side. God's Messenger slept. When it was midnight, or a little before it, or shortly after it, God's Messenger (peace be upon him) woke up. He rubbed**

i. Related by al-Bukhari, 183, 992, 1198, 4570, 4571, 4572 and 698; Abu Dāwūd, 1364 and 1367; al-Nasā'ī, 1619; Ibn Mājah, 1362.

the sleep off his face with his hand, then recited the last ten verses of Surah [3] Āl ʿImrān. He then walked to a hanging old waterskin and performed the ablution with its water. He perfected his ablution, then stood up and prayed'.

Ibn ʿAbbās said: 'I rose and did the same as God's Messenger (peace be upon him), walked over and stood to his side. God's Messenger placed his right hand on my head and twisted my right ear. He prayed two *rakʿahs*, then two, then two, then two, then two, then two, then prayed Witr. He then lay down until the caller came over. He prayed two light *rakʿahs* and went out and prayed the Fajr Prayer'.

حَدَّثَنَا يَحْيَى بْنُ يَحْيَى قَالَ: قَرَأْتُ عَلَى مَالِكٍ، عَنْ مَخْرَمَةَ بْنِ سُلَيْمَانَ، عَنْ كُرَيْبٍ مَوْلَى ابْنِ عَبَّاسٍ، أَنَّ ابْنَ عَبَّاسٍ أَخْبَرَهُ، أَنَّهُ بَاتَ لَيْلَةً عِنْدَ مَيْمُونَةَ أُمِّ الْمُؤْمِنِينَ، وَهِيَ خَالَتُهُ. قَالَ: فَاضْطَجَعْتُ فِي عَرْضِ الْوِسَادَةِ، وَاضْطَجَعَ رَسُولُ اللهِ صَلَّى اللهُ عَلَيْهِ وَسَلَّمَ وَأَهْلُهُ فِي طُولِهَا، فَنَامَ رَسُولُ اللهِ صَلَّى اللهُ عَلَيْهِ وَسَلَّمَ حَتَّى انْتَصَفَ اللَّيْلُ، أَوْ قَبْلَهُ بِقَلِيلٍ أَوْ بَعْدَهُ بِقَلِيلٍ اسْتَيْقَظَ رَسُولُ اللهِ صَلَّى اللهُ عَلَيْهِ وَسَلَّمَ، فَجَعَلَ يَمْسَحُ النَّوْمَ عَنْ وَجْهِهِ بِيَدِهِ. ثُمَّ قَرَأَ الْعَشْرَ الآيَاتِ الْخَوَاتِمَ مِنْ سُورَةِ آلِ عِمْرَانَ. ثُمَّ قَامَ إِلَى شَنٍّ مُعَلَّقَةٍ، فَتَوَضَّأَ مِنْهَا فَأَحْسَنَ وُضُوءَهُ، ثُمَّ قَامَ فَصَلَّى. قَالَ ابْنُ عَبَّاسٍ: فَقُمْتُ فَصَنَعْتُ مِثْلَ مَا صَنَعَ رَسُولُ اللهِ صَلَّى اللهُ عَلَيْهِ وَسَلَّمَ، ثُمَّ ذَهَبْتُ فَقُمْتُ إِلَى جَنْبِهِ، فَوَضَعَ رَسُولُ اللهِ صَلَّى اللهُ عَلَيْهِ وَسَلَّمَ يَدَهُ الْيُمْنَى عَلَى رَأْسِي، وَأَخَذَ بِأُذُنِي الْيُمْنَى يَفْتِلُهَا. فَصَلَّى رَكْعَتَيْنِ، ثُمَّ رَكْعَتَيْنِ، ثُمَّ رَكْعَتَيْنِ، ثُمَّ رَكْعَتَيْنِ، ثُمَّ رَكْعَتَيْنِ، ثُمَّ رَكْعَتَيْنِ. ثُمَّ أَوْتَرَ، ثُمَّ اضْطَجَعَ حَتَّى جَاءَ الْمُؤَذِّنُ، فَقَامَ فَصَلَّى رَكْعَتَيْنِ خَفِيفَتَيْنِ، ثُمَّ خَرَجَ فَصَلَّى الصُّبْحَ.

[1524–183]. (Dar al-Salam 1673) Muhammad ibn Salamah al-Murādī narrated to me: ʿAbdullāh ibn Wahb narrated; from ʿIyāḍ ibn ʿAbdullāh al-Fihrī; from Makhramah ibn Sulaymān; with the same chain of transmission: **adding: 'He then used an**

old waterskin, brushed his teeth and performed the ablution, making it perfect but used only little water. He then moved me, and I got up'. The rest of the hadith is the same as Mālik's narration.

وَحَدَّثَنِي مُحَمَّدُ بْنُ سَلَمَةَ الْـمُرَادِيُّ، حَدَّثَنَا عَبْدُ اللهِ بْنُ وَهْبٍ، عَنْ عِيَاضِ بْنِ عَبْدِ اللهِ الْفِهْرِيِّ، عَنْ مَخْرَمَةَ بْنِ سُلَيْمَانَ، بِهَذَا الإِسْنَادِ، وَزَادَ: ثُمَّ عَمَدَ إِلَى شَجْبٍ مِنْ مَاءٍ، فَتَسَوَّكَ وَتَوَضَّأَ وَأَسْبَغَ الْوُضُوءَ، وَلَمْ يُهْرِقْ مِنَ الْـمَاءِ إِلاَّ قَلِيلاً، ثُمَّ حَرَّكَنِي فَقُمْتُ. وَسَائِرُ الْحَدِيثِ نَحْوُ حَدِيثِ مَالِكٍ.

[1525–184]. (Dar al-Salam 1674) Ḥarūn ibn Saʿīd al-Aylī narrated to me: Ibn Wahb narrated; ʿAmr narrated; from ʿAbd Rabbih ibn Saʿīd; from Makhramah ibn Sulaymān; from Kurayb, Ibn ʿAbbas's *mawlā*; from Ibn ʿAbbās; that he said: **'I stayed one night at Maymūnah's, the Prophet's wife, when the Prophet was at her home that night. God's Messenger (peace be upon him) performed the ablution then stood up and prayed. I stood to his left, but he moved me and placed me to his right. He prayed thirteen *rakʿahs* that night, then he slept, breathing soundly. When he slept he would breathe soundly. Then the caller came to him and he went out and led the prayer but did not perform a fresh ablution'.**

ʿAmr said: **'I narrated this hadith to Bukayr ibn al-Ashajj, and he told me that Kurayb narrated it to him'.**

حَدَّثَنِي هَارُونُ بْنُ سَعِيدٍ الأَيْلِيُّ، حَدَّثَنَا ابْنُ وَهْبٍ، حَدَّثَنَا عَمْرٌو، عَنْ عَبْدِ رَبِّهِ بْنِ سَعِيدٍ، عَنْ مَخْرَمَةَ بْنِ سُلَيْمَانَ، عَنْ كُرَيْبٍ، مَوْلَى ابْنِ عَبَّاسٍ، عَنِ ابْنِ عَبَّاسٍ أَنَّهُ قَالَ: نِمْتُ عِنْدَ مَيْمُونَةَ، زَوْجِ النَّبِيِّ صَلَّى اللهُ عَلَيْهِ وَسَلَّمَ، وَرَسُولُ اللهِ صَلَّى اللهُ عَلَيْهِ وَسَلَّمَ عِنْدَهَا تِلْكَ اللَّيْلَةَ. فَتَوَضَّأَ رَسُولُ اللهِ صَلَّى اللهُ عَلَيْهِ وَسَلَّمَ ثُمَّ قَامَ فَصَلَّى. فَقُمْتُ عَنْ

يَسَارِهِ، فَأَخَذَنِي فَجَعَلَنِي عَنْ يَمِينِهِ. فَصَلَّى فِي تِلْكَ اللَّيْلَةِ ثَلَاثَ عَشْرَةَ رَكْعَةً. ثُمَّ نَامَ رَسُولُ اللهِ صَلَّى اللهُ عَلَيْهِ وَسَلَّمَ حَتَّى نَفَخَ، وَكَانَ إِذَا نَامَ نَفَخَ. ثُمَّ أَتَاهُ الْمُؤَذِّنُ، فَخَرَجَ فَصَلَّى وَلَمْ يَتَوَضَّأْ.

قَالَ عَمْرٌو: فَحَدَّثْتُ بِهِ بُكَيْرَ بْنَ الأَشَجِّ فَقَالَ: حَدَّثَنِي كُرَيْبٌ بِذَلِكَ.

[1526–185]. (Dar al-Salam 1675) Muhammad ibn Rāfiʿ narrated: Ibn Abi Fudayk narrated; al-Ḍaḥḥāk reported; from Makhramah ibn Sulaymān; from Kurayb, Ibn ʿAbbas's *mawlā*; from Ibn ʿAbbās. He said: **'One night I stayed at my maternal aunt's home, Maymūnah bint al-Ḥārith. I said to her: "Wake me up when God's Messenger (peace be upon him) offers his night prayer". God's Messenger (peace be upon him) stood up for his night prayer and I stood to his left side. He took me by the hand and placed me to his right. Whenever I was dozing off, he held the tip of my ear. He prayed eleven *rakʿahs*, then he gathered his knees to his chest, and I could hear his breathing as he slept. When he realised that the dawn had broken, he prayed two light *rakʿahs*'.**

وَحَدَّثَنَا مُحَمَّدُ بْنُ رَافِعٍ، حَدَّثَنَا ابْنُ أَبِي فُدَيْكٍ، أَخْبَرَنَا الضَّحَّاكُ، عَنْ مَخْرَمَةَ بْنِ سُلَيْمَانَ، عَنْ كُرَيْبٍ، مَوْلَى ابْنِ عَبَّاسٍ، عَنِ ابْنِ عَبَّاسٍ قَالَ: بِتُّ لَيْلَةً عِنْدَ خَالَتِي مَيْمُونَةَ بِنْتِ الْحَارِثِ، فَقُلْتُ لَهَا إِذَا قَامَ رَسُولُ اللهِ صَلَّى اللهُ عَلَيْهِ وَسَلَّمَ فَأَيْقِظِينِي. فَقَامَ رَسُولُ اللهِ صَلَّى اللهُ عَلَيْهِ وَسَلَّمَ، فَقُمْتُ إِلَى جَنْبِهِ الأَيْسَرِ، فَأَخَذَ بِيَدِي فَجَعَلَنِي مِنْ شِقِّهِ الأَيْمَنِ. فَجَعَلْتُ إِذَا أَغْفَيْتُ يَأْخُذُ بِشَحْمَةِ أُذُنِي. قَالَ: فَصَلَّى إِحْدَى عَشْرَةَ رَكْعَةً، ثُمَّ احْتَبَى. حَتَّى إِنِّي لأَسْمَعُ نَفَسَهُ رَاقِدًا. فَلَمَّا تَبَيَّنَ لَهُ الْفَجْرُ صَلَّى رَكْعَتَيْنِ خَفِيفَتَيْنِ.

[1527–186]. (Dar al-Salam 1676) Ibn Abi ʿUmar and Muhammad ibn Ḥātim narrated:[i] from Ibn ʿUyaynah; Ibn Abi ʿUmar said: Sufyān narrated; from ʿAmr ibn Dīnār; from Kurayb, Ibn ʿAbbās's *mawlā*; from Ibn ʿAbbās; that **'He stayed one night at Maymūnah's, his maternal aunt. God's Messenger (peace be upon him) woke up during the night and he performed a light ablution using a hanged old waterskin. (He described his ablution showing it to be light, using little water.) Ibn ʿAbbās said: "I rose and did the same as the Prophet (peace be upon him) did. I then came over and stood to his left. He moved me behind him and placed me to his right and prayed. He then lay down and slept until he breathed soundly. Then Bilāl came over and announced the prayer to him. He went out and led the Fajr Prayer without performing a fresh ablution".'**

Sufyān said: **'This is a special concession for the Prophet because we have learnt that his eyes go to sleep but not his heart'.**

حَدَّثَنَا ابْنُ أَبِي عُمَرَ وَمُحَمَّدُ بْنُ حَاتِمٍ، عَنِ ابْنِ عُيَيْنَةَ. قَالَ ابْنُ أَبِي عُمَرَ: حَدَّثَنَا سُفْيَانُ، عَنْ عَمْرِو بْنِ دِينَارٍ، عَنْ كُرَيْبٍ، مَوْلَى ابْنِ عَبَّاسٍ، عَنِ ابْنِ عَبَّاسٍ، أَنَّهُ بَاتَ عِنْدَ خَالَتِهِ مَيْمُونَةَ، فَقَامَ رَسُولُ اللهِ صَلَّى اللهُ عَلَيْهِ وَسَلَّمَ مِنَ اللَّيْلِ، فَتَوَضَّأَ مِنْ شَنٍّ مُعَلَّقٍ وُضُوءًا خَفِيفًا. قَالَ: وَصَفَ وُضُوءَهُ وَجَعَلَ يُخَفِّفُهُ وَيُقَلِّلُهُ. قَالَ ابْنُ عَبَّاسٍ: فَقُمْتُ فَصَنَعْتُ مِثْلَ مَا صَنَعَ النَّبِيُّ صَلَّى اللهُ عَلَيْهِ وَسَلَّمَ، ثُمَّ جِئْتُ فَقُمْتُ عَنْ يَسَارِهِ، فَأَخْلَفَنِي فَجَعَلَنِي عَنْ يَمِينِهِ. فَصَلَّى، ثُمَّ اضْطَجَعَ فَنَامَ حَتَّى نَفَخَ. ثُمَّ أَتَاهُ بِلَالٌ فَآذَنَهُ بِالصَّلَاةِ، فَخَرَجَ فَصَلَّى الصُّبْحَ وَلَمْ يَتَوَضَّأْ.

قَالَ سُفْيَانُ: وَهَذَا لِلنَّبِيِّ صَلَّى اللهُ عَلَيْهِ وَسَلَّمَ خَاصَّةً، لِأَنَّهُ بَلَغَنَا أَنَّ النَّبِيَّ صَلَّى اللهُ عَلَيْهِ وَسَلَّمَ تَنَامُ عَيْنَاهُ وَلَا يَنَامُ قَلْبُهُ.

---

i. Related by al-Bukhari, 138, 726 and 859; al-Tirmidhī, 232; al-Nasā'ī in a shorter version, 441; Ibn Mājah in a shorter version, 423.

[1528–187]. (Dar al-Salam 1677) Muhammad ibn Bashshār narrated: Muhammad (who is Ibn Jaʿfar) narrated; Shuʿbah narrated; from Salamah; from Kurayb; from Ibn ʿAbbās. He said: **'I stayed one night at the home of my maternal aunt, Maymūnah, and I kept watch to see how God's Messenger performed his night prayer. He urinated, then washed his hands and face. He went up to the large waterskin and untied it. He poured water in a container, tilting the mouth of the waterskin over it with his hand. He then performed a good ablution, in between the two extremes. He then stood up and prayed. I stood next to him, taking my position to his left. He moved me and stood me to his right. God's Messenger completed his night worship in thirteen *rakʿahs* then he went to sleep, breathing soundly. We knew that he was asleep by his audible breathing. Then he went out for the [Fajr] Prayer and prayed. He said in his prayer or in his prostration: "My Lord, place in my heart light, in my hearing light, in my sight light, to my right light, to my left light, in front of me light, behind me light, above me light, beneath me light and grant me light," or "and make me light".'**

حَدَّثَنَا مُحَمَّدُ بْنُ بَشَّارٍ، حَدَّثَنَا مُحَمَّدٌ (وَهُوَ ابْنُ جَعْفَرٍ)، حَدَّثَنَا شُعْبَةُ، عَنْ سَلَمَةَ، عَنْ كُرَيْبٍ، عَنِ ابْنِ عَبَّاسٍ قَالَ: بِتُّ فِي بَيْتِ خَالَتِي مَيْمُونَةَ، فَبَقَيْتُ كَيْفَ يُصَلِّي رَسُولُ اللهِ صَلَّى اللهُ عَلَيْهِ وَسَلَّمَ. قَالَ: فَقَامَ فَبَالَ، ثُمَّ غَسَلَ وَجْهَهُ وَكَفَّيْهِ ثُمَّ نَامَ. ثُمَّ قَامَ إِلَى الْقِرْبَةِ فَأَطْلَقَ شِنَاقَهَا، ثُمَّ صَبَّ فِي الْجَفْنَةِ أَوِ الْقَصْعَةِ فَأَكَبَّهُ بِيَدِهِ عَلَيْهَا. ثُمَّ تَوَضَّأَ وُضُوءًا حَسَنًا بَيْنَ الْوُضُوءَيْنِ، ثُمَّ قَامَ يُصَلِّي. فَجِئْتُ فَقُمْتُ إِلَى جَنْبِهِ، فَقُمْتُ عَنْ يَسَارِهِ. قَالَ: فَأَخَذَنِي فَأَقَامَنِي عَنْ يَمِينِهِ. فَتَكَامَلَتْ صَلَاةُ رَسُولِ اللهِ صَلَّى اللهُ عَلَيْهِ وَسَلَّمَ ثَلَاثَ عَشْرَةَ رَكْعَةً، ثُمَّ نَامَ حَتَّى نَفَخَ. وَكُنَّا نَعْرِفُهُ إِذَا نَامَ بِنَفْخِهِ. ثُمَّ خَرَجَ إِلَى الصَّلَاةِ فَصَلَّى، فَجَعَلَ يَقُولُ فِي صَلَاتِهِ أَوْ فِي سُجُودِهِ: «اللَّهُمَّ اجْعَلْ فِي قَلْبِي نُورًا، وَفِي سَمْعِي نُورًا،

وَفِي بَصَرِي نُورًا، وَعَنْ يَمِينِي نُورًا، وَعَنْ شِمَالِي نُورًان وَأَمَامِي نُورًا، وَخَلْفِي نُورًا، وَفَوْقِي نُورًا، وَتَحْتِي نُورًا، وَاجْعَلْ لِي نُورًا. أَوْ قَالَ وَاجْعَلْنِي نُورًا.

[1529–000]. (Dar al-Salam 1678) Isḥāq ibn Manṣūr narrated to me: al-Naḍr ibn Shumayl narrated; Shuʿbah reported; Salamah ibn Kuhayl narrated; from Bukayr; from Kurayb; from Ibn ʿAbbās. Salamah said: I met Kurayb and he said: Ibn ʿAbbās said: **'I was at my maternal aunt Maymūnah's. God's Messenger (peace be upon him) came in...'. He reported the same as Ghundar's narration and said: 'Make me light', expressing no doubt.**

وَحَدَّثَنِي إِسْحَاقُ بْنُ مَنْصُورٍ، حَدَّثَنَا النَّضْرُ بْنُ شُمَيْلٍ، أَخْبَرَنَا شُعْبَةُ، حَدَّثَنَا سَلَمَةُ بْنُ كُهَيْلٍ، عَنْ بُكَيْرٍ، عَنْ كُرَيْبٍ، عَنِ ابْنِ عَبَّاسٍ. قَالَ سَلَمَةُ: فَلَقِيتُ كُرَيْبًا، فَقَالَ: قَالَ ابْنُ عَبَّاسٍ: كُنْتُ عِنْدَ خَالَتِي مَيْمُونَةَ، فَجَاءَ رَسُولُ اللهِ صَلَّى اللهُ عَلَيْهِ وَسَلَّمَ. ثُمَّ ذَكَرَ بِمِثْلِ حَدِيثِ غُنْدَرٍ. وَقَالَ: «وَاجْعَلْنِي نُورًا». وَلَمْ يَشُكَّ.

[1530–188]. (Dar al-Salam 1679) Abu Bakr ibn Abi Shaybah and Hannād ibn al-Sariy narrated: both said: Abu al-Aḥwaṣ narrated; from Saʿīd ibn Masrūq; from Salmah ibn Kuhayl; from Abu Rishdīn, Ibn ʿAbbās's *mawlā*; from Ibn ʿAbbās. He said: **'One night I stayed at my maternal aunt Maymūnah's...' He narrated the hadith, but did not mention [the Prophet's] washing his face and hands but said: 'He went up to the waterskin and untied it. He performed the ablution in a way that is in between the two extremes. He then went to his bed and slept. Then he rose once more and went up to the waterskin and untied it. He then performed the ablution, which was a perfect one, and said: "Give me magnificent light", but did not mention, "make me light".'**

وَحَدَّثَنَا أَبُو بَكْرِ بْنُ أَبِي شَيْبَةَ وَهَنَّادُ بْنُ السَّرِيِّ، قَالا: حَدَّثَنَا أَبُو الأَحْوَصِ، عَنْ سَعِيدِ بْنِ مَسْرُوقٍ، عَنْ سَلَمَةَ بْنِ كُهَيْلٍ، عَنْ أَبِي رِشْدِينٍ مَوْلَى ابْنِ عَبَّاسٍ، عَنِ ابْنِ عَبَّاسٍ قَالَ: بِتُّ عِنْدَ خَالَتِي مَيْمُونَةَ. وَاقْتَصَّ الْحَدِيثَ وَلَمْ يَذْكُرْ غَسْلَ الْوَجْهِ وَالْكَفَّيْنِ. غَيْرَ أَنَّهُ قَالَ: ثُمَّ أَتَى الْقِرْبَةَ فَحَلَّ شِنَاقَهَا، فَتَوَضَّأَ وُضُوءًا بَيْنَ الْوُضُوءَيْنِ، ثُمَّ أَتَى فِرَاشَهُ فَنَامَ، ثُمَّ قَامَ قَوْمَةً أُخْرَى، فَأَتَى الْقِرْبَةَ فَحَلَّ شِنَاقَهَا، ثُمَّ تَوَضَّأَ وُضُوءًا هُوَ الْوُضُوءُ، وَقَالَ: «أَعْظِمْ لِي نُورًا». وَلَمْ يَذْكُرْ: «وَاجْعَلْنِي نُورًا».

[1531–189]. (Dar al-Salam 1680) Abu al-Ṭāhir narrated to me: Ibn Wahb narrated; from ʿAbd al-Raḥmān ibn Salmān al-Ḥajrī; from ʿUqayl ibn Khālid; that Salamah ibn Kuhayl narrated to him; that Kurayb narrated to him; that **Ibn ʿAbbās stayed one night at God's Messenger's home. He said: 'God's Messenger (peace be upon him) went up to the waterskin, poured out some water and performed the ablution. He neither used much water nor made his ablution imperfect…'. He continued the hadith, adding: 'In his supplication, God's Messenger included nineteen phrases.'**

Salamah said: **'Kurayb narrated these to me, and I memorised twelve of these and forgot the others. God's Messenger (peace be upon him) said: "My Lord, give me light in my heart, light in my tongue, light in my hearing, light in my sight, light from above me, light beneath me, light to my right, light to my left, light in front of me, light behind me, give me light in my soul and increase my light".'**

وَحَدَّثَنِي أَبُو الطَّاهِرِ، حَدَّثَنَا ابْنُ وَهْبٍ، عَنْ عَبْدِ الرَّحْمَنِ بْنِ سَلْمَانَ الْحَجْرِيِّ، عَنْ عُقَيْلِ بْنِ خَالِدٍ، أَنَّ سَلَمَةَ بْنَ كُهَيْلٍ حَدَّثَهُ، أَنَّ كُرَيْبًا حَدَّثَهُ، أَنَّ ابْنَ عَبَّاسٍ بَاتَ لَيْلَةً عِنْدَ رَسُولِ اللهِ صَلَّى اللهُ عَلَيْهِ وَسَلَّمَ. قَالَ: فَقَامَ رَسُولُ اللهِ صَلَّى اللهُ عَلَيْهِ وَسَلَّمَ إِلَى الْقِرْبَةِ، فَسَكَبَ مِنْهَا فَتَوَضَّأَ وَلَمْ يُكْثِرْ مِنَ الْمَاءِ، وَلَمْ يُقَصِّرْ فِي الْوُضُوءِ. وَسَاقَ الْحَدِيثَ

وَفِيهِ قَالَ: وَدَعَا رَسُولُ اللهِ صَلَّى اللهُ عَلَيْهِ وَسَلَّمَ لَيْلَتَئِذٍ تِسْعَ عَشْرَةَ كَلِمَةً. قَالَ سَلَمَةُ حَدَّثَنِيهَا كُرَيْبٌ فَحَفِظْتُ مِنْهَا ثِنْتَيْ عَشْرَةَ، وَنَسِيتُ مَا بَقِيَ. قَالَ رَسُولُ اللهِ صَلَّى اللهُ عَلَيْهِ وَسَلَّمَ: «اللَّهُمَّ اجْعَلْ لِي فِي قَلْبِي نُورًا، وَفِي لِسَانِي نُورًا، وَفِي سَمْعِي نُورًا، وَفِي بَصَرِي نُورًا، وَمِنْ فَوْقِي نُورًا، وَمِنْ تَحْتِي نُورًا، وَعَنْ يَمِينِي نُورًا، وَعَنْ شِمَالِي نُورًا، وَمِنْ بَيْنِ يَدَيَّ نُورًا، وَمِنْ خَلْفِي نُورًا، وَاجْعَلْ فِي نَفْسِي نُورًا، وَأَعْظِمْ لِي نُورًا».

[1532–190]. (Dar al-Salam 1681) Abu Bakr ibn Isḥāq narrated to me:[i] Ibn Abi Maryam reported; Muhammad ibn Ja'far reported; Sharīk ibn Abi Namir reported to me; from Kurayb; from Ibn 'Abbās. He said: **'I slept at Maymūnah's home on a night when the Prophet was at her place, so as to watch how the Prophet (peace be upon him) offered his night prayer. The Prophet conversed with his wife for a while then went to sleep…' He then narrated the hadith, mentioning in it: 'He woke up, performed the ablution and brushed his teeth'.**

وَحَدَّثَنِي أَبُو بَكْرِ بْنُ إِسْحَاقَ، أَخْبَرَنَا ابْنُ أَبِي مَرْيَمَ، أَخْبَرَنَا مُحَمَّدُ بْنُ جَعْفَرٍ، أَخْبَرَنِي شَرِيكُ بْنُ أَبِي نَمِرٍ، عَنْ كُرَيْبٍ، عَنِ ابْنِ عَبَّاسٍ أَنَّهُ قَالَ: رَقَدْتُ فِي بَيْتِ مَيْمُونَةَ لَيْلَةَ كَانَ النَّبِيُّ صَلَّى اللهُ عَلَيْهِ وَسَلَّمَ عِنْدَهَا، لأَنْظُرَ كَيْفَ صَلاةُ النَّبِيِّ صَلَّى اللهُ عَلَيْهِ وَسَلَّمَ بِاللَّيْلِ. قَالَ: فَتَحَدَّثَ النَّبِيُّ صَلَّى اللهُ عَلَيْهِ وَسَلَّمَ مَعَ أَهْلِهِ سَاعَةً ثُمَّ رَقَدَ. وَسَاقَ الْحَدِيثَ، وَفِيهِ: ثُمَّ قَامَ فَتَوَضَّأَ وَاسْتَنَّ.

[1533–191]. (Dar al-Salam 1682) Wāṣil ibn 'Abd al-A'lā narrated:[ii] Muhammad ibn Fuḍayl narrated; from Ḥuṣayn ibn 'Abd al-Raḥmān; from Ḥabīb ibn Abi Thābit; from Muhammad

i. Related by al-Bukhari, 4569, 7452 and in similar wording, 6215.
ii. Related by Abu Dāwūd, 58, 1353 and 1354; al-Nasā'ī, 1703 and in a shorter version 1704.

ibn ʿAlī ibn ʿAbdullāh ibn ʿAbbās; from his father; from ʿAbdullāh ibn ʿAbbās; that **'He slept at God's Messenger's home, and he [i.e. the Prophet] woke up. He brushed his teeth and performed the ablution, reciting: "In the creation of the Heavens and the earth, and in the succession of night and day, there are indeed signs for men endowed with insight", (3: 190) and continued to the end of the surah. He then stood up and prayed two *rakʿahs*, making his standing up, bowing and prostration long in both of them. He then went back to sleep and breathed soundly. He then did this three times, praying six *rakʿahs*. At each time he brushed his teeth, performed the ablution and recited these verses. He then prayed Witr in three *rakʿahs*. The caller called the *adhān* and the Prophet went out for the prayer, saying: "My Lord, give me light in my heart, light in my tongue, light in my hearing, light in my sight, light behind me, light in front of me, light from above me, light beneath me. My Lord, give me light".'**

حَدَّثَنَا وَاصِلُ بْنُ عَبْدِ الأَعْلَى، حَدَّثَنَا مُحَمَّدُ بْنُ فُضَيْلٍ، عَنْ حُصَيْنِ بْنِ عَبْدِ الرَّحْمَنِ، عَنْ حَبِيبِ بْنِ أَبِي ثَابِتٍ، عَنْ مُحَمَّدِ بْنِ عَلِيِّ بْنِ عَبْدِ اللهِ بْنِ عَبَّاسٍ، عَنْ أَبِيهِ، عَنْ عَبْدِ اللهِ بْنِ عَبَّاسٍ، أَنَّهُ رَقَدَ عِنْدَ رَسُولِ اللهِ صَلَّى اللهُ عَلَيْهِ وَسَلَّمَ، فَاسْتَيْقَظَ فَتَسَوَّكَ وَتَوَضَّأَ وَهُوَ يَقُولُ: "إِنَّ فِي خَلْقِ السَّمَوَاتِ وَالأَرْضِ وَاخْتِلَافِ اللَّيْلِ وَالنَّهَارِ لَآيَاتٍ لِأُولِي الأَلْبَابِ"، فَقَرَأَ هَؤُلَاءِ الآيَاتِ حَتَّى خَتَمَ السُّورَةَ. ثُمَّ قَامَ فَصَلَّى رَكْعَتَيْنِ، فَأَطَالَ فِيهِمَا الْقِيَامَ وَالرُّكُوعَ وَالسُّجُودَ، ثُمَّ انْصَرَفَ فَنَامَ حَتَّى نَفَخَ. ثُمَّ فَعَلَ ذَلِكَ ثَلَاثَ مَرَّاتٍ، سِتَّ رَكَعَاتٍ: كُلَّ ذَلِكَ يَسْتَاكُ وَيَتَوَضَّأُ وَيَقْرَأُ هَؤُلَاءِ الآيَاتِ. ثُمَّ أَوْتَرَ بِثَلَاثٍ، فَأَذَّنَ الْمُؤَذِّنُ فَخَرَجَ إِلَى الصَّلَاةِ وَهُوَ يَقُولُ: "اللَّهُمَّ اجْعَلْ فِي قَلْبِي نُورًا، وَفِي لِسَانِي نُورًا، وَاجْعَلْ فِي سَمْعِي نُورًا، وَاجْعَلْ فِي بَصَرِي نُورًا، وَاجْعَلْ مِنْ خَلْفِي نُورًا، وَمِنْ أَمَامِي نُورًا، وَاجْعَلْ مِنْ فَوْقِي نُورًا، وَمِنْ تَحْتِي نُورًا. اللَّهُمَّ أَعْطِنِي نُورًا".

[1534–192]. (Dar al-Salam 1683) Muhammad ibn Ḥātim narrated to me: Muhammad ibn Bakr narrated; Ibn Jurayj reported; ʿAṭā' reported to me; from Ibn ʿAbbās. He said: **'I spent one night at my maternal aunt Maymūnah's home. The Prophet (peace be upon him) got up to offer voluntary prayer at night. The Prophet went up to the waterskin and performed the ablution, then stood up and prayed. When I saw him doing this, I rose and performed the ablution from the waterskin. I stood by his left side, and he held my hand from behind his back to correct my position, moving me behind his back to his right side'. I said: 'Was this in voluntary prayer?' He said: 'Yes'.**

وَحَدَّثَنِي مُحَمَّدُ بْنُ حَاتِمٍ، حَدَّثَنَا مُحَمَّدُ بْنُ بَكْرٍ، أَخْبَرَنَا ابْنُ جُرَيْجٍ، أَخْبَرَنِي عَطَاءٌ، عَنِ ابْنِ عَبَّاسٍ، قَالَ: بِتُّ ذَاتَ لَيْلَةٍ عِنْدَ خَالَتِي مَيْمُونَةَ: فَقَامَ النَّبِيُّ صَلَّى اللهُ عَلَيْهِ وَسَلَّمَ يُصَلِّي مُتَطَوِّعًا مِنَ اللَّيْلِ. فَقَامَ النَّبِيُّ صَلَّى اللهُ عَلَيْهِ وَسَلَّمَ إِلَى الْقِرْبَةِ فَتَوَضَّأَ، فَقَامَ فَصَلَّى. فَقُمْتُ لَمَّا رَأَيْتُهُ صَنَعَ ذَلِكَ فَتَوَضَّأْتُ مِنَ الْقِرْبَةِ، ثُمَّ قُمْتُ إِلَى شِقِّهِ الأَيْسَرِ، فَأَخَذَ بِيَدِي مِنْ وَرَاءِ ظَهْرِهِ يَعْدِلُنِي كَذَلِكَ، مِنْ وَرَاءِ ظَهْرِهِ إِلَى الشِّقِّ الأَيْمَنِ. قُلْتُ: أَفِي التَّطَوُّعِ كَانَ ذَلِكَ؟ قَالَ: نَعَمْ.

[1535–193]. (Dar al-Salam 1684) Ḥarūn ibn ʿAbdullāh and Muhammad ibn Rāfiʿ narrated to me: both said: Wahb ibn Jarīr narrated; my father reported to me; he said: I heard Qays ibn Saʿd narrating from ʿAṭā'; from Ibn ʿAbbās. He said: **'Al-ʿAbbās sent me to the Prophet (peace be upon him) when he was at my maternal aunt Maymūnah's home. I stayed that night at his place. He rose up to offer his night prayers. I stood to his left, but he held me from behind his back and moved me to his right'.**

وَحَدَّثَنِي هَارُونُ بْنُ عَبْدِ اللهِ وَمُحَمَّدُ بْنُ رَافِعٍ، قَالا: حَدَّثَنَا وَهْبُ بْنُ جَرِيرٍ، أَخْبَرَنِي أَبِي قَالَ: سَمِعْتُ قَيْسَ بْنَ سَعْدٍ، يُحَدِّثُ عَنْ عَطَاءٍ، عَنِ ابْنِ عَبَّاسٍ قَالَ: بَعَثَنِي الْعَبَّاسُ إِلَى النَّبِيِّ صَلَّى اللهُ عَلَيْهِ وَسَلَّمَ، وَهُوَ فِي بَيْتِ خَالَتِي مَيْمُونَةَ، فَبِتُّ مَعَهُ تِلْكَ اللَّيْلَةَ، فَقَامَ يُصَلِّي مِنَ اللَّيْلِ، فَقُمْتُ عَنْ يَسَارِهِ، فَتَنَاوَلَنِي مِنْ خَلْفِ ظَهْرِهِ فَجَعَلَنِي عَلَى يَمِينِهِ

[1536–000]. (Dar al-Salam 1685) Ibn Numayr narrated: my father narrated:[i] ʿAbd al-Malik narrated; from ʿAṭā'; from Ibn ʿAbbās. He said: **'I stayed one night at my maternal aunt Maymūnah's…' a similar text to Ibn Jurayj's and Qays ibn Saʿd's narrations.**

وَحَدَّثَنَا ابْنُ نُمَيْرٍ، حَدَّثَنَا أَبِي، حَدَّثَنَا عَبْدُ الْـمَلِكِ، عَنْ عَطَاءٍ، عَنِ ابْنِ عَبَّاسٍ قَالَ: بِتُّ عِنْدَ خَالَتِي مَيْمُونَةَ. نَحْوَ حَدِيثِ ابْنِ جُرَيْجٍ وَقَيْسِ بْنِ سَعْدٍ.

[1537–194]. (Dar al-Salam 1686) Abu Bakr ibn Abi Shaybah narrated:[ii] Ghundar narrated; from Shuʿbah [H]. Also, Ibn al-Muthannā and Ibn Bashshār narrated; both said: Muhammad ibn Jaʿfar narrated; Shuʿbah narrated; from Abu Jamrah; he said: I heard Ibn ʿAbbās say: **'God's Messenger (peace be upon him) used to pray thirteen *rakʿahs* during the night'.**

حَدَّثَنَا أَبُو بَكْرِ بْنُ أَبِي شَيْبَةَ، حَدَّثَنَا غُنْدَرٌ، عَنْ شُعْبَةَ، ح. وَحَدَّثَنَا ابْنُ الْـمُثَنَّى وَابْنُ بَشَّارٍ، قَالا: حَدَّثَنَا مُحَمَّدُ بْنُ جَعْفَرٍ، حَدَّثَنَا شُعْبَةُ، عَنْ أَبِي جَمْرَةَ قَالَ: سَمِعْتُ ابْنَ عَبَّاسٍ يَقُولُ: كَانَ رَسُولُ اللهِ صَلَّى اللهُ عَلَيْهِ وَسَلَّمَ يُصَلِّي مِنَ اللَّيْلِ ثَلاثَ عَشْرَةَ رَكْعَةً.

[1538–195]. (Dar al-Salam 1687) Qutaybah ibn Saʿīd narrated:[iii] from Mālik ibn Anas; from ʿAbdullāh ibn Abi Bakr; from his

---

i. Related by Abu Dāwūd, 610.
ii. Related by al-Bukhari, 1138; al-Tirmidhī, 442.
iii. Related by Abu Dāwūd, 1366; Ibn Mājah, 1362.

father; that ʿAbdullāh ibn Qays ibn Makhramah reported to him; from Zayd ibn Khālid al-Juhanī; that he said: **'I shall watch God's Messenger's prayer tonight. He prayed two *rakʿahs*, then he prayed two *rakʿahs* which were very long, very long, very long, then he prayed two *rakʿahs* that were shorter than the ones before them, then he prayed two *rakʿahs* that were shorter than the ones before them, then he prayed two *rakʿahs* that were shorter than the ones before them, then he prayed two *rakʿahs* that were shorter than the ones before them, then he prayed Witr. This was a total of thirteen *rak'ahs*'.**

وَحَدَّثَنَا قُتَيْبَةُ بْنُ سَعِيدٍ، عَنْ مَالِكِ بْنِ أَنَسٍ، عَنْ عَبْدِ اللهِ بْنِ أَبِي بَكْرٍ، عَنْ أَبِيهِ، أَنَّ عَبْدَ اللهِ بْنَ قَيْسِ بْنِ مَخْرَمَةَ أَخْبَرَهُ، عَنْ زَيْدِ بْنِ خَالِدٍ الْجُهَنِيِّ أَنَّهُ قَالَ: لأَرْمُقَنَّ صَلاَةَ رَسُولِ اللهِ صَلَّى اللهُ عَلَيْهِ وَسَلَّمَ اللَّيْلَةَ. فَصَلَّى رَكْعَتَيْنِ خَفِيفَتَيْنِ، ثُمَّ صَلَّى رَكْعَتَيْنِ طَوِيلَتَيْنِ، طَوِيلَتَيْنِ، طَوِيلَتَيْنِ. ثُمَّ صَلَّى رَكْعَتَيْنِ وَهُمَا دُونَ اللَّتَيْنِ قَبْلَهُمَا. ثُمَّ صَلَّى رَكْعَتَيْنِ وَهُمَا دُونَ اللَّتَيْنِ قَبْلَهُمَا. ثُمَّ صَلَّى رَكْعَتَيْنِ وَهُمَا دُونَ اللَّتَيْنِ قَبْلَهُمَا. ثُمَّ صَلَّى رَكْعَتَيْنِ وَهُمَا دُونَ اللَّتَيْنِ قَبْلَهُمَا. ثُمَّ أَوْتَرَ، فَذَلِكَ ثَلاَثَ عَشْرَةَ رَكْعَةً.

[1539–196]. (Dar al-Salam 1688) Ḥajjāj ibn al-Shāʿir narrated to me: Muhammad ibn Jaʿfar al-Madā'inī Abu Jaʿfar narrated to me; Warqā' narrated; from Muhammad ibn al-Munkadir; from Jābir ibn ʿAbdullāh. He said: **'I was with God's Messenger (peace be upon him) on a journey, and we came to a watering place. He said: "Jābir, do you need water?" I said: "Yes". God's Messenger (peace be upon him) dismounted and I went to the water. He went to relieve himself and I placed water for him to perform the ablution. He came and performed the ablution. He stood up and prayed wearing one garment,**

bringing its two sides from opposite sides over his shoulders and tying the two ends. I stood behind him and he caught my ear, moving me to his right'.

وَحَدَّثَنِي حَجَّاجُ بْنُ الشَّاعِرِ، حَدَّثَنِي مُحَمَّدُ بْنُ جَعْفَرٍ الْـمَدَائِنِيُّ أَبُو جَعْفَرٍ، حَدَّثَنَا وَرْقَاءُ، عَنْ مُحَمَّدِ بْنِ الْـمُنْكَدِرِ، عَنْ جَابِرِ بْنِ عَبْدِ اللهِ قَالَ: «كُنْتُ مَعَ رَسُولِ اللهِ صَلَّى اللهُ عَلَيْهِ وَسَلَّمَ فِي سَفَرٍ، فَانْتَهَيْنَا إِلَى مَشْرَعَةٍ، فَقَالَ: «أَلاَ تُشْرِعُ يَا جَابِرُ»؟ قُلْتُ: بَلَى. قَالَ: فَنَزَلَ رَسُولُ اللهِ صَلَّى اللهُ عَلَيْهِ وَسَلَّمَ، وَأَشْرَعْتُ. قَالَ: ثُمَّ ذَهَبَ لِحَاجَتِهِ، وَوَضَعْتُ لَهُ وَضُوءًا. قال: فَجَاءَ فَتَوَضَّأَ، ثُمَّ قَامَ فَصَلَّى فِي ثَوْبٍ وَاحِدٍ خَالَفَ بَيْنَ طَرَفَيْهِ. فَقُمْتُ خَلْفَهُ، فَأَخَذَ بِأُذُنِي فَجَعَلَنِي عَنْ يَمِينِهِ».

[1540–197]. (Dar al-Salam 1689) Yaḥyā ibn Yaḥyā and Abu Bakr ibn Abi Shaybah narrated: both from Hushaym; Abu Bakr said: Hushaym narrated; Abu Ḥurrah reported; from al-Ḥasan; from Saʿd ibn Hishām; from ʿĀʾishah. She said: **'When God's Messenger (peace be upon him) woke up to offer his night prayer, he would start with two light *rakʿahs*'.**

حَدَّثَنَا يَحْيَى بْنُ يَحْيَى وَأَبُو بَكْرِ بْنُ أَبِي شَيْبَةَ، جَمِيعًا عَنْ هُشَيْمٍ. قَالَ أَبُو بَكْرٍ: حَدَّثَنَا هُشَيْمٌ، أَخْبَرَنَا أَبُو حُرَّةَ، عَنِ الْحَسَنِ، عَنْ سَعْدِ بْنِ هِشَامٍ، عَنْ عَائِشَةَ قَالَتْ: كَانَ رَسُولُ اللهِ صَلَّى اللهُ عَلَيْهِ وَسَلَّمَ إِذَا قَامَ مِنَ اللَّيْلِ لِيُصَلِّيَ افْتَتَحَ صَلاَتَهُ بِرَكْعَتَيْنِ خَفِيفَتَيْنِ.

[1541–198]. (Dar al-Salam 1690) Abu Bakr ibn Abi Shaybah narrated: Abu Usāmah narrated; from Hishām; from Muhammad; from Abu Hurayrah; from the Prophet (peace be upon him). He said: **'When any of you offers night prayer, let him start his prayer with two light *rakʿahs*'.**

وَحَدَّثَنَا أَبُو بَكْرِ بْنُ أَبِي شَيْبَةَ، حَدَّثَنَا أَبُو أُسَامَةَ، عَنْ هِشَامٍ، عَنْ مُحَمَّدٍ، عَنْ أَبِي هُرَيْرَةَ، عَنِ النَّبِيِّ صَلَّى اللهُ عَلَيْهِ وَسَلَّمَ قَالَ: «إِذَا قَامَ أَحَدُكُمْ مِنَ اللَّيْلِ فَلْيَفْتَتِحْ صَلَاتَهُ بِرَكْعَتَيْنِ خَفِيفَتَيْنِ».

[1542–199]. (Dar al-Salam 1691) Qutaybah ibn Saʿīd narrated:[i] from Mālik ibn Anas; from Abu al-Zubayr; from Ṭāwūs; from Ibn ʿAbbās; that **'When God's Messenger (peace be upon him) woke up to pray in the middle of the night, he used to say: "All praise is due to You, my Lord. You are the light of the Heavens and the earth. To You all praise is due, for You are the Master of the Heavens and the earth. Praise belongs to You, for You are the Lord of the Heavens and the earth and all who are in them. You are the Truth. Your promise is true, the meeting with You is true, Heaven is true, Hell is true and the Last Hour is true. My Lord, to You I surrender myself, and in You I believe and place my trust. To You I turn, and Your case I plead, and to You I turn for judgement. Forgive me for what I did in the past and what I may do in the future, what I have done in secret and in the open. You are my Lord. There is no deity other than You".'**

حَدَّثَنَا قُتَيْبَةُ بْنُ سَعِيدٍ، عَنْ مَالِكِ بْنِ أَنَسٍ، عَنْ أَبِي الزُّبَيْرِ، عَنْ طَاوُسٍ، عَنِ ابْنِ عَبَّاسٍ، أَنَّ رَسُولَ اللهِ صَلَّى اللهُ عَلَيْهِ وَسَلَّمَ كَانَ يَقُولُ إِذَا قَامَ إِلَى الصَّلَاةِ مِنْ جَوْفِ اللَّيْلِ: «اللَّهُمَّ لَكَ الْحَمْدُ، أَنْتَ نُورُ السَّمَوَاتِ وَالأَرْضِ. وَلَكَ الْحَمْدُ أَنْتَ قَيَّامُ السَّمَوَاتِ وَالأَرْضِ. وَلَكَ الْحَمْدُ أَنْتَ رَبُّ السَّمَوَاتِ وَالأَرْضِ وَمَنْ فِيهِنَّ. أَنْتَ الْحَقُّ، وَوَعْدُكَ الْحَقُّ، وَقَوْلُكَ الْحَقُّ، وَلِقَاؤُكَ حَقٌّ، وَالْجَنَّةُ حَقٌّ، وَالنَّارُ حَقٌّ، وَالسَّاعَةُ حَقٌّ. اللَّهُمَّ لَكَ أَسْلَمْتُ، وَبِكَ آمَنْتُ، وَعَلَيْكَ تَوَكَّلْتُ، وَإِلَيْكَ أَنَبْتُ، وَبِكَ خَاصَمْتُ، وَإِلَيْكَ حَاكَمْتُ، فَاغْفِرْ لِي مَا قَدَّمْتُ وَأَخَّرْتُ، وَأَسْرَرْتُ وَأَعْلَنْتُ. أَنْتَ إِلَهِي، لَا إِلَهَ إِلَّا أَنْتَ».

i. Related by Abu Dāwūd, 771; al-Tirmidhī, 3418.

[1543–000]. (Dar al-Salam 1692–1693) ʿAmr al-Nāqid, Ibn Numayr and Ibn Abi ʿUmar narrated:[i] they said: Sufyān narrated [H]. Also, Muhammad ibn Rāfiʿ narrated; ʿAbd al-Razzāq narrated; Ibn Jurayj reported; both from Sulaymān al-Aḥwal; from Ṭāwūs; from Ibn ʿAbbās; from the Prophet (peace be upon him): **Ibn Jurayj's narration is the same as Mālik's [in hadith No. 1542] differing only in two words [without affecting the meaning]. [Sufyān] ibn ʿUyaynah's narration includes some addition and differs with Mālik's and Ibn Jurayj's narrations in a few words.**

حَدَّثَنَا عَمْرٌو النَّاقِدُ وَابْنُ نُمَيْرٍ وَابْنُ أَبِي عُمَرَ، قَالُوا: حَدَّثَنَا سُفْيَانُ، ح. وَحَدَّثَنَا مُحَمَّدُ بْنُ رَافِعٍ، قَالَ حَدَّثَنَا عَبْدُ الرَّزَّاقِ، أَخْبَرَنَا ابْنُ جُرَيْجٍ، كِلاَهُمَا عَنْ سُلَيْمَانَ الأَحْوَلِ، عَنْ طَاوُسٍ، عَنِ ابْنِ عَبَّاسٍ، عَنِ النَّبِيِّ صَلَّى اللهُ عَلَيْهِ وَسَلَّمَ. أَمَّا حَدِيثُ ابْنِ جُرَيْجٍ فَاتَّفَقَ لَفْظُهُ مَعَ حَدِيثِ مَالِكٍ، لَمْ يَخْتَلِفَا إِلاَّ فِي حَرْفَيْنِ. قَالَ ابْنُ جُرَيْجٍ مَكَانَ قَيَّامُ قَيِّمُ وَقَالَ وَمَا أَسْرَرْتُ. وَأَمَّا حَدِيثُ ابْنِ عُيَيْنَةَ فَفِيهِ بَعْضُ زِيَادَةٍ، وَيُخَالِفُ مَالِكًا وَابْنَ جُرَيْجٍ فِي أَحْرُفٍ.

Shaybān ibn Farrūkh narrated:[ii] Mahdī (who is Ibn Maymūn) narrated; ʿImrān al-Qaṣīr narrated; from Qays ibn Saʿd; from Ṭāwūs; from Ibn ʿAbbās; from the Prophet: **the same text (with slight differences).**

وَحَدَّثَنَا شَيْبَانُ بْنُ فَرُّوخَ، حَدَّثَنَا مَهْدِيٌّ (وَهُوَ ابْنُ مَيْمُونٍ)، حَدَّثَنَا عِمْرَانُ الْقَصِيرُ، عَنْ قَيْسِ بْنِ سَعْدٍ، عَنْ طَاوُسٍ، عَنِ ابْنِ عَبَّاسٍ، عَنِ النَّبِيِّ صَلَّى اللهُ عَلَيْهِ وَسَلَّمَ، بِهَذَا الْحَدِيثِ. وَاللَّفْظُ قَرِيبٌ مِنْ أَلْفَاظِهِمْ.

---

i. Related by al-Bukhari, 1120, 6317, 7385, 7442 and 7499; al-Nasāʾī, 1618; Ibn Mājah, 1355.
ii. Related by Abu Dāwūd, 772.

[1544–200]. (Dar al-Salam 1694) Muhammad ibn al-Muthannā, Muhammad ibn Ḥātim, ʿAbd ibn Ḥumayd and Abu Maʿn al-Raqāshī narrated:[i] they said: ʿUmar ibn Yūnus narrated; ʿIkrimah ibn ʿAmmār narrated; Yaḥyā ibn Abi Kathīr narrated; Abu Salamah ibn ʿAbd al-Raḥmān ibn ʿAwf narrated to me. He said: **'I asked ʿĀ'ishah, the Mother of the Believers: "How did the Prophet open his worship when he woke up for night prayer?" She said: "When he woke up at night, he started his worship by saying: 'My Lord, the Lord of Gabriel, Michael and Isrāfīl, You are the Originator of the Heavens and the earth! You have knowledge of all that is beyond anyone's perception and all that anyone may witness. It is You who will judge between Your servants concerning all that over which they differ. Guide me, by Your will, to the truth concerning which they had differed. For certain, You guide whom You will to the straight path'".'**

حَدَّثَنَا مُحَمَّدُ بْنُ الْـمُثَنَّى وَمُحَمَّدُ بْنُ حَاتِمٍ وَعَبْدُ بْنُ حُمَيْدٍ وَأَبُو مَعْنٍ الرَّقَاشِيُّ، قَالُوا: حَدَّثَنَا عُمَرُ بْنُ يُونُسَ، حَدَّثَنَا عِكْرِمَةُ بْنُ عَمَّارٍ، حَدَّثَنَا يَحْيَى بْنُ أَبِي كَثِيرٍ، حَدَّثَنِي أَبُو سَلَمَةَ بْنُ عَبْدِ الرَّحْمَنِ بْنِ عَوْفٍ قَالَ: سَأَلْتُ عَائِشَةَ، أُمَّ الْـمُؤْمِنِينَ: بِأَيِّ شَيْءٍ كَانَ نَبِيُّ اللهِ صَلَّى اللهُ عَلَيْهِ وَسَلَّمَ يَفْتَتِحُ صَلاَتَهُ إِذَا قَامَ مِنَ اللَّيْلِ؟ قَالَتْ: كَانَ إِذَا قَامَ مِنَ اللَّيْلِ افْتَتَحَ صَلاَتَهُ: «اللَّهُمَّ رَبَّ جِبْرَائِيلَ وَمِيكَائِيلَ وَإِسْرَافِيلَ، فَاطِرَ السَّمَوَاتِ وَالأَرْضِ، عَالِمَ الْغَيْبِ وَالشَّهَادَةِ، أَنْتَ تَحْكُمُ بَيْنَ عِبَادِكَ فِيمَا كَانُوا فِيهِ يَخْتَلِفُونَ. اهْدِنِي لِمَا اخْتُلِفَ فِيهِ مِنَ الْحَقِّ بِإِذْنِكَ. إِنَّكَ تَهْدِي مَنْ تَشَاءُ إِلَى صِرَاطٍ مُسْتَقِيمٍ».

[1545–201]. (Dar al-Salam 1695) Muhammad ibn Abi Bakr al-Muqaddamī narrated:[ii] Yūsuf al-Mājishūn narrated; my father

i. Related by Abu Dāwūd, 767 and 768; al-Tirmidhī, 3420; al-Nasā'ī, 1624; Ibn Mājah, 1357.

ii. Related by Abu Dāwūd, 744, 760, 761 and 1509; al-Tirmidhī, 266, 3421 3422 and 3423; al-Nasā'ī, 896, 1049 and 1125; Ibn Mājah, 864.

narrated to me; from ʿAbd al-Raḥmān al-Aʿraj; from ʿUbaydullāh ibn Abi Rāfiʿ; from ʿAlī ibn Abi Ṭālib; from God's Messenger (peace be upon him); that **'When he stood up to pray, he said: "I have turned my face with pure and complete devotion to Him who brought the Heavens and the earth into being. I am not one of those who associate partners with God. My prayers, my worship, my living and my dying are for God alone, the Lord of all worlds. He has no partner. Thus have I been commanded, and I am one of those who surrender themselves to Him. My Lord, You are the Sovereign; there is no deity other than You. You are my Lord and I am your servant. I have wronged myself and I admit my sin. Forgive me all my sins, for none but You forgives sins. Guide me to the best of manners, for none but You guides to their best, and turn me away from the worst of manners, for none but You turns away from their worst. I respond to You. All goodness is in Your hand, while evil is not Yours. I exist by Your will and return to You. You are blessed and exalted. I pray for Your forgiveness and turn to You in repentance". When he bowed in prayer he said: "My Lord, to You I bow, in You I believe, to You I submit. My hearing, sight, brain, bones and nerves all submit to You." When he stood up [after bowing], he said: "Our Lord, praise be to You, the fill of the Heavens and the earth and all in between them, and the fill of whatever You wish beyond them". When he prostrated himself, he said: "My Lord, to You I prostrate myself, in You I believe, to You I submit myself. My face is prostrated to the One who has created and fashioned it, placing in it hearing and sight. Blessed is God, the best of all creators". What he said between the *tashahhud* and finishing his prayer with *salām* included: "My Lord, forgive me what I did in the past and what I may do in the future, what I do in secret and in**

the open and what You know better than me. You are the One who brings forward and sets back. There is no deity other than You".'

حَدَّثَنَا مُحَمَّدُ بْنُ أَبِي بَكْرٍ الْـمُقَدَّمِيُّ، حَدَّثَنَا يُوسُفُ الْـمَاجِشُونُ، حَدَّثَنِي أَبِي، عَنْ عَبْدِ الرَّحْمَنِ الأَعْرَجِ عَنْ عُبَيْدِ اللهِ بْنِ أَبِي رَافِعٍ، عَنْ عَلِيِّ بْنِ أَبِي طَالِبٍ، عَنْ رَسُولِ اللهِ صَلَّى اللهُ عَلَيْهِ وَسَلَّمَ، أَنَّهُ كَانَ إِذَا قَامَ إِلَى الصَّلاَةِ قَالَ: «وَجَّهْتُ وَجْهِيَ لِلَّذِي فَطَرَ السَّمَوَاتِ وَالأَرْضَ حَنِيفًا وَمَا أَنَا مِنَ الْـمُشْرِكِينَ. إِنَّ صَلاَتِي وَنُسُكِي وَمَحْيَاىَ وَمَمَاتِي للهِ رَبِّ الْعَالَـمِينَ. لاَ شَـرِيكَ لَهُ وَبِذَلِكَ أُمِـرْتُ وَأَنَا مِنَ الْـمُسْلِمِينَ. اللَّهُمَّ أَنْتَ الْـمَلِكُ لاَ إِلَهَ إِلاَّ أَنْتَ. أَنْتَ رَبِّي وَأَنَا عَبْدُكَ، ظَلَمْتُ نَفْسِي وَاعْتَرَفْتُ بِذَنْبِي، فَاغْفِرْ لِي ذُنُوبِي جَمِيعًا، إِنَّهُ لاَ يَغْفِرُ الذُّنُوبَ إِلاَّ أَنْتَ. وَاهْدِنِي لأَحْسَـنِ الأَخْلاَقِ، لاَ يَهْدِي لأَحْسَـنِهَا إِلاَّ أَنْتَ. وَاصْرِفْ عَنِّي سَيِّئَهَا، لاَ يَصْرِفُ عَنِّي سَيِّئَهَا إِلاَّ أَنْتَ. لَبَّيْكَ وَسَعْدَيْكَ، وَالْخَيْرُ كُلُّهُ فِي يَدَيْكَ، وَالشَّرُّ لَيْسَ إِلَيْكَ. أَنَا بِكَ وَإِلَيْكَ، تَبَارَكْتَ وَتَعَالَيْتَ، أَسْتَغْفِرُكَ وَأَتُوبُ إِلَيْكَ». وَإِذَا رَكَعَ قَالَ: «اللَّهُمَّ لَكَ رَكَعْتُ، وَبِكَ آمَنْتُ، وَلَكَ أَسْلَمْتُ. خَشَعَ لَكَ سَمْعِي وَبَصَرِي، وَمُخِّي وَعَظْمِي وَعَصَبِي». وَإِذَا رَفَعَ قَالَ: «اللَّهُمَّ رَبَّنَا لَكَ الْحَمْدُ، مِلْءَ السَّمَوَاتِ وَمِلْءَ الأَرْضِ، وَمِلْءَ مَا بَيْنَهُمَا، وَمِلْءَ مَا شِئْتَ مِنْ شَيْءٍ بَعْدُ». وَإِذَا سَجَدَ قَالَ: «اللَّهُمَّ لَكَ سَجَدْتُ، وَبِكَ آمَنْتُ، وَلَكَ أَسْلَمْتُ. سَجَدَ وَجْهِي لِلَّذِي خَلَقَهُ وَصَوَّرَهُ، وَشَقَّ سَمْعَهُ وَبَصَرَهُ. تَبَارَكَ اللهُ أَحْسَنُ الْخَالِقِينَ». ثُمَّ يَكُونُ مِنْ آخِرِ مَا يَقُولُ بَيْنَ التَّشَهُّدِ وَالتَّسْلِيمِ: «اللَّهُمَّ اغْفِرْ لِي مَا قَدَّمْتُ وَمَا أَخَّرْتُ، وَمَا أَسْرَرْتُ وَمَا أَعْلَنْتُ وَمَا أَسْرَفْتُ، وَمَا أَنْتَ أَعْلَمُ بِهِ مِنِّي. أَنْتَ الْـمُقَدِّمُ وَأَنْتَ الْـمُؤَخِّرُ، لاَ إِلَهَ إِلاَّ أَنْتَ».

[1546–202]. (Dar al-Salam 1696) Zuhayr ibn Ḥarb narrated the same hadith: ʿAbd al-Raḥmān ibn Mahdī narrated [H]. Also, Isḥāq ibn Ibrāhīm narrated; Abu al-Naḍr reported; both said: ʿAbd al-ʿAzīz ibn ʿAbdullāh ibn Abi Salamah narrated; from his paternal uncle al-Mājishūn ibn Abi Salamah; from al-Aʿraj; with the same chain of transmission. He said: **'When God's**

Messenger (peace be upon him) started his prayer he said: "*Allah-u akbar*", then he said: "I have turned my face...", and he would say "I am the first of those who surrender themselves".' He said: 'When he lifted his head after bowing, he said: "May God answer whoever praises Him. You are our Lord and to You belongs all praise".' He also said: 'and fashioned it perfecting its appearance'. And he said: 'After he finished with *salām*, he said: "My Lord, forgive me what I did in the past...".' to the end of the hadith, but did not say it between the *tashahhud* and finishing his prayer with *salām*.

وَحَدَّثَنَاهُ زُهَيْرُ بْنُ حَرْبٍ، حَدَّثَنَا عَبْدُ الرَّحْمَنِ بْنُ مَهْدِيٍّ، ح. وَحَدَّثَنَا إِسْحَاقُ بْنُ إِبْرَاهِيمَ، أَخْبَرَنَا أَبُو النَّضْرِ، قَالا: حَدَّثَنَا عَبْدُ الْعَزِيزِ بْنُ عَبْدِ اللهِ بْنِ أَبِي سَلَمَةَ، عَنْ عَمِّهِ الْـمَاجِشُونِ بْنِ أَبِي سَلَمَةَ، عَنِ الأَعْرَجِ، بِهَذَا الإِسْنَادِ. وَقَالَ: كَانَ رَسُولُ اللهِ صَلَّى اللهُ عَلَيْهِ وَسَلَّمَ إِذَا اسْتَفْتَحَ الصَّلاَةَ كَبَّرَ، ثُمَّ قَالَ: «وَجَّهْتُ وَجْهِي»... وَقَالَ: «وَأَنَا أَوَّلُ الْـمُسْلِمِينَ». وَقَالَ: وَإِذَا رَفَعَ رَأْسَهُ مِنَ الرُّكُوعِ قَالَ: «سَمِعَ اللهُ لِمَنْ حَمِدَهُ، رَبَّنَا وَلَكَ الْحَمْدُ». وَقَالَ: «وَصَوَّرَهُ فَأَحْسَنَ صُورَهُ». وَقَالَ: وَإِذَا سَلَّمَ قَالَ: «اللَّهُمَّ اغْفِرْ لِي مَا قَدَّمْتُ». إِلَى آخِرِ الْحَدِيثِ، وَلَمْ يَقُلْ بَيْنَ التَّشَهُّدِ وَالتَّسْلِيمِ.

Text Explanation

This chapter includes various versions of the hadith narrated by Ibn 'Abbās. In the first hadith, No. 1522, he mentions that the Prophet 'woke up, relieved himself, washed his face and hands, then went to sleep'. The wash in this instance was for cleanliness and hygiene purposes. Ibn 'Abbās mentions that he stretched himself so as to give the impression that he was not watching the Prophet. He then says that he joined the Prophet in his prayer, standing to his left side but the Prophet turned him to his right. This makes it clear that when only one worshipper joins the imam in prayer, he should stand to the right side of the imam. If he stands to his left, he should move to his right, and if he does not do it himself, the imam should move him. This also shows that little action during prayer does not invalidate it, and that prayer offered by a child is valid and that a child takes the same position as an adult. It further shows that non-obligatory prayers may be offered in congregation.

The same hadith mentions that the Prophet 'lay down and slept, breathing soundly... He then got up and prayed without performing the ablution again'. This is a special privilege given to the Prophet, which means that lying down and sleep does not invalidate his ablution because 'his eyes go to sleep but not his heart'. Unlike other people, he would have felt any discharge of wind during his sleep.

In his supplication, the Prophet prayed to God to give him light in his heart, sight, hearing, etc. Scholars said that he asked for light in his own organs and in all directions he might take. What this means is showing the truth and its light as well as guiding to it. This is why he requested light in all his senses, body, actions, positions and general situations in all six sides so that he would not miss out on the truth in any way.

In this hadith narrated by Salamah ibn Kuhayl; from Kurayb; from Ibn ʿAbbās, the supplication for light is mentioned, followed by: 'Kurayb said: "And seven in the chest. I met one of al-ʿAbbās' descendants and he narrated them to me, mentioning my nerves, flesh, blood, hair and skin, adding two others".' A literal translation is, 'and seven in the box'. Scholars say that this means that he included in the supplication seven more phrases which I forgot. 'The box' means the chest and ribs as it includes one's heart. Thus, the narrator likens the chest to a box in which some articles are placed. The meaning of his words is 'and seven that I learnt but have forgotten'. He adds: 'I met one of al-ʿAbbās' descendants...'. These are the words of Salamah ibn Kuhayl.

In hadith No. 1523, Ibn ʿAbbās says: 'I lay down on the side of the pillow, while God's Messenger and his wife used its long side'. This gives evidence that it is permissible for a man and his wife to sleep, without having sex or foreplay, in the presence of one of her *maḥrams* [i.e. relatives who are unlawful for her to marry], even if he is a grown up. *Qadi* ʿIyāḍ says:

> In some narrations of this hadith, Ibn ʿAbbās says that he slept at his aunt's home when she was having her period. Even if this added phrase cannot be established as authentic in the way it is reported, it adds very good meaning. Ibn ʿAbbās would not have wished to spend the night at a time when the Prophet might have wanted to be intimate with his wife. Nor would his father have sent him over unless he knew this, because it is taken for granted that the Prophet would not have done so in Ibn ʿAbbās' presence. Moreover, Ibn ʿAbbās wanted to watch what the Prophet did during the night, and he had only very little sleep or none at all.

The hadith mentions that the Prophet 'rubbed the sleep off his face with his hand, then recited the last ten verses of Surah [3] Āl 'Imrān'. This means that he rubbed the effect of sleep off his face, which is desirable. It also shows that reciting the Qur'an without having performed an ablution is permissible, which is unanimously agreed upon by all Muslims. Recitation is forbidden only for men in a state of ceremonial impurity [i.e. *janābah*] and women during menstruation. Reciting these last eleven verses of Surah 3 is recommended when one gets up. It is also permissible to say: 'Surah the Cow', 'Surah Āl 'Imrān' or 'Surah Women', etc. A number of early scholars discouraged this, saying that one should say 'the surah in which the cow, or Āl 'Imrān, or women are mentioned'. The correct view is the first. It is generally agreed upon by earlier and recent scholars and confirmed by authentic hadiths.

In the same hadith, Ibn ʿAbbās mentions that the Prophet twisted his right ear. This was to alert him as he felt drowsy. Some say that he did so in order that he would be more careful about how and where to stand in prayer. The first view is more accurate because it is mentioned in another narration that the Prophet held the end of Ibn ʿAbbās' ear whenever he felt sleepy.

The hadith mentions that the Prophet 'prayed two *rakʿahs*, then two, then two, then two, then two, then two, then prayed Witr. He then lay down until the caller came over. He prayed two light *rakʿahs* and went out and prayed the Fajr Prayer'. This shows that in Witr and other prayers, the preferable option is to finish with *salām* after each two *rak'ahs* and that in Witr, one brings one's prayer to an odd number by offering a single *rak'ah* apart from the two before it. This is the view of our school and the majority of scholars. Abu Ḥanīfah says that it should be a *rak'ah* added to the two before it and offered in the same way as the obligatory Maghrib Prayer. The hadith also shows that it is permissible for the caller to come to the imam and call him to start the prayer. It tells us that the sunnah before the obligatory Fajr Prayer should be light.

The number of *rak'ahs* mentioned here shows that making the Witr Prayer in thirteen *rak'ahs* is the more complete option. Our scholars express different opinions on this point. Some say that the maximum for Witr is thirteen *rak'ahs* as this hadith clearly indicates. The majority, however, say that the maximum is eleven *rak'ahs* on the basis that the first two *rak'ahs* were the sunnah of 'Isha Prayer. This view is not solid and appears to be contrary to the hadith.

In hadith No. 1528, Ibn 'Abbās mentions that he kept watch to see how the Prophet offered his night prayers. He then mentions that he performed 'a good ablution in between the two extremes'. This means that he economised in his use of water, using neither too much nor too little.

In hadith No. 1532, Ibn 'Abbās mentions that the Prophet conversed with his wife for a while before going to sleep. This means that it is permissible to have a conversation or discussion after 'Isha Prayer, if there is need or something useful to say. What is confirmed in other hadiths is that the Prophet discouraged sleeping before 'Isha and conversation after it. This applies to idle talk that serves no interest and brings about no benefit, as we explained earlier.

Hadith No. 1533 mentions: 'He then stood up and prayed two *rak'ahs*, making his standing up, bowing and prostration long in both of them. He then went back to sleep and breathed soundly. He then did this three times, praying six *rak'ahs*... He then prayed Witr in three *rak'ahs*'. This hadith is at variance with the others in that it mentions that the Prophet went to sleep after each two *rak'ahs*, and in the total number of *rak'ahs*. In the other versions, there is no mention of sleep in between prayers and the total number is given as thirteen *rak'ahs*. *Qadi* 'Iyāḍ says that this version, narrated by Ḥuṣayn, from Ḥabīb ibn Abi Thābit is one of the hadiths Muslim entered in his *Ṣaḥīḥ* but is questioned by al-Dāraquṭnī because of the uncertainty involved and the differences between narrators. Al-Dāraquṭnī says that the hadith 'is narrated in seven ways and is at variance with the majority'. In response, I say that this may not be taken against Muslim because he does not mention this hadith as a principal and independent one. He includes it by way of endorsement. As we have mentioned more than once, conditions are relaxed for endorsements, but not for principal hadiths.

Qadi 'Iyāḍ said: 'It may be that the narrator did not count the initial two light *rak'ahs* with which the Prophet used to start his night prayer, as mentioned in hadiths related by Muslim and others. He therefore said that the Prophet prayed two long *rak'ahs*. This shows that the two light ones, then the two long ones, followed by the six mentioned in the hadith and three after them make a total of thirteen *rak'ahs*, as in the other hadiths', but God knows best.

In hadith No. 1538, narrated by Zayd ibn Khālid, it is mentioned that the Prophet prayed two *rak'ahs* that were 'very long, very long, very long'. This is how the hadith is narrated, with the description 'very long' stated three times.

In the next hadith, No. 1539, the Prophet suggests to his Companion Jābir to have whatever he needed of water. Jābir mentions that the Prophet 'prayed wearing one garment, bringing its two ends from opposite sides over his shoulders and tying the two ends. I stood behind him and he caught my ear, moving me to his right'. This confirms that it is perfectly acceptable to pray wearing a single garment,[i] but it is a sunnah to take the ends of the garment and bring

i. This refers to the Arabian type of clothing at the time, which consisted of an upper and a lower garment. Islam does not prescribe any particular type of clothing and leaves it to people to decide what suits their climate. It only lays down certain principles, such as covering the area from the waistline to the knees for men and the prohibition of silk garments for men.

them over one's shoulders on opposite sides, so as to tie them on one's chest. This was discussed earlier.

In hadith No. 1540, ʿĀ'ishah mentions that when the Prophet woke up to offer his night prayer, he started with two light *rakʿahs*, and in the next hadith, the Prophet ordered us to do so. This confirms that such a start is recommended because it gives the worshipper more energy for what follows.

In hadith No. 1542, the Prophet addresses God saying: 'You are the light of the Heavens and the earth'. Scholars say that it means that God gives them light and He is the Creator of their light. Abu ʿUbayd said: 'It means that the people of the Heavens and the earth are guided by God's light'. Al-Khaṭṭābī said, explaining that light is one of God's names: 'It means that a blind person gains sight and an errant person gains guidance by His light'. He added: 'In the same way we understand the verse that says: "God is the light of the Heavens and the earth", meaning their light comes from Him. It may also mean that He is the One who has light. It is not right to say that light is an attribute of God Himself, but it is an attribute of action, which means that He creates it'. Other scholars said that the meaning of 'God is the light of the Heavens and earth' is that He is the One who controls their suns, moons and stars.

The Prophet also says in his supplication: 'You are the Master of the Heavens and the earth'. [The Prophet uses the word *qayyūm*, which is rendered as 'master', but Muslim scholars give it wider connotations.] Ibn ʿAbbās says it means 'the one who is everlasting'. Other scholars say that it means the one who is in control of everything, and who conducts the affairs of all creation. Both are acceptable in explaining the meaning of the relevant verse and hadith.

The Prophet also says: 'You are the Lord of the Heavens and the earth and all who are in them'. *Rabb* is the Arabic equivalent of 'lord'. Scholars say that *rabb* has three meanings, and it denotes 'the obeyed master'. This means that it is a condition that those who obey must have reason and intelligence. Al-Khaṭṭābī refers to this condition and says: 'It is wrong to say "the master of mountains and trees".' *Qadi* ʿIyāḍ said: 'This condition is false. All creation obeys God, the

Mighty and Exalted. In response to His command, both the Heavens and the earth said: "We do come willingly".' (41: 11)

The Prophet then adds in his address to God: 'You are the Truth'. Scholars say that in relation to God, this means His existence is true. Whatever truly and really exists is true. The Qur'an calls the Day of Resurrection 'the inevitable truth', which means that it will undoubtedly take place. Hence, the Prophet says in this hadith: 'Your promise is true, the meeting with You is true, Heaven is true, Hell is true and the Last Hour is true'. This means that all these will take place without any doubt. Other interpretations say that it means, 'Whatever You have said is absolutely true' or 'You are the master of the truth' or 'You are the one who establishes the truth' or 'You are the true God and what atheists say is false'. This last one echoes the Qur'anic verse that says: 'Thus it is because God alone is the Ultimate Truth, and all that people invoke beside Him is sheer falsehood'. (22: 62)

'Your promise is true.' This refers to meeting God which means resurrection and that it is certainly true. Some say that it means 'death', but in this case this is wrong. I am only mentioning it so that it is discarded. That it refers to resurrection is necessitated by the context in which the expression occurs. We refute the atheistic argument by referring to resurrection, not by referring to death.

The Prophet then says: 'My Lord, to You I surrender myself, and in You I believe and place my trust. To You I turn, and Your case I plead, and to You I turn for judgement. Forgive me…'. 'I surrender myself' means I submit to You and obey Your commands. 'I believe in You' means I am convinced that You are God and accept all that You have told. 'To You I turn' means I obey You and will always worship You. It is also said that I refer to You in all that I do, entrusting myself to You. 'Your case I plead' means I cite what You have given me of proofs and use my strength in opposition to whoever rejects You. I will subdue them with strong argument and all other means available to me. 'To You I turn for judgement' means that I consider You the Judge between me and anyone who denies the truth. I accept no other judgement, particularly those to whom unbelievers, of all creeds, used to refer for judgement.

The fact that the Prophet (peace be upon him) prayed for forgiveness, although God had already forgiven him all his sins, reflects his humility, submission to God and recognition of His majesty. Moreover, when people learn this hadith, they will follow his example and use the same supplication, expressing their submission to God and appealing to Him as best they can. This and other hadiths show that the Prophet used to constantly glorify God at night, supplicating, acknowledging God's right, confirming belief in what He revealed and that His promises and warnings will be fulfilled, and believing in resurrection, Heaven and Hell, etc.

In hadith No. 1544, the Prophet begins his supplication by saying: 'My Lord, the Lord of Gabriel, Michael and Isrāfīl, the Originator of the Heavens and the earth'. Scholars say that although God is the Lord of all creation, as clearly confirmed in the Qur'an and the sunnah, these three angels are specifically mentioned because of their high position. When we mention God's Lordship, we add some of His great creations, not the more humble ones. Thus, we say that He, Blessed and Exalted, is the Lord of the Heavens and the earth, the Lord of the Glorious Throne, the Lord of the angels and the Spirit, the Lord of the two risings and the Lord of the two settings, the Lord of mankind, the Lord of all the worlds, the Lord of all things, the Lord of the prophets, the Creator and the Originator of the Heavens and the earth, who appoints angels as His messengers. All such descriptions refer to His greatness, His limitless power and total sovereignty. No similar descriptions are associated with humble or despised creation. God is never referred to as 'the Lord of insects' or 'the Creator of pigs,' referring to such creatures in particular. He is referred to as the Creator of all things, and such humble creatures are, thus, included, but God knows best.

The Prophet added in his supplication: 'Guide me to the truth concerning which they had differed'. This is a prayer to steadfastly hold to the truth. It is similar to the verse in the opening surah of the Qur'an: 'Guide us to the straight path'.

Hadith No. 1545 gives a long supplication by the Prophet starting with 'I have turned my face'. This means my worship is addressed to the One who 'brought the Heavens and the earth into being', which means He initiated their creation. 'In pure and complete devotion' is the meaning of the Arabic word *ḥanīf* used here. Many scholars say that it means 'leaning towards the true faith, which is Islam'. In its pure linguistic sense, the word means 'leaning towards something' and it can be toward good or evil. Its direction is determined by the context in which the word occurs. Some scholars say that in this particular instance, the word means 'straight'. Abu ʿUbayd said that according to the Arabs, a *ḥanīf* is a person who follows Abraham's faith. Next, the Prophet said: 'I am not one of those who associate partners with God'. This is further clarification of what the word *ḥanīf* means. It is the opposite of *mushrik,* which means a person who associates partners with God. The term *mushrik* applies to all unbelievers, whether pagans, idolaters, Jews, Christians, Zoroastrians, apostates, atheists or followers of any other religion.

Next, the Prophet said: 'My prayers, my worship, my living and my dying are for God alone, the Lord of all worlds'. The words 'for God' stress two aspects: ownership and specificity. Both are intended as the supplication means that they belong specifically to God. God is described as 'the Lord of all the worlds'. The Arabic word for Lord, *rabb*, has four meanings according to scholars: the sovereign, master, conductor of affairs and sustainer. The first two are personal attributes while the last two are action attributes. When the word is preceded by the definite article, it applies to God only and to no one else. If not, it may be used for others, as we say: 'the lord of the market' or 'the lord of the manor', etc. Scholars understand the term 'world' in different ways, but according to al-Shāfiʿī and other scholars of theology as well as Qur'anic commentators, it includes all creation. Other scholars say that they refer to 'the angels, the jinn and humans', while some add 'satans'. Others still say that it refers to humans in particular, while some scholars say that it refers to this world and all that it contains. Some say that it applies specifically to beings with minds.

The Prophet added in his supplication: 'My Lord, You are the Sovereign... I am Your servant. I have wronged myself...'. This acknowledges that God is the true Master and Sovereign of all creation. 'I am Your servant' means I acknowledge that You are my Master and Sustainer and I am subject to Your will. 'I have wronged myself' is an acknowledgement of falling short of one's duty. This is stated ahead of appealing for forgiveness and it reflects fine manners. It echoes what Adam and Even said when they realised their error: 'They said: Our Lord! We have wronged ourselves, and unless You grant us forgiveness and bestow Your mercy upon us, we shall certainly be lost.' (7: 23)

'I respond to You.' This is expressed in the original in a special phrase that connotes continuity of response and obedience.

'All goodness is in Your hand, while evil is not Yours.' Al-Khaṭṭābī and other scholars said that this shows the proper way of praising God, attributing to Him only good things and not evil ones. The phrase 'evil is not Yours' needs an explanation because the view of the people of truth is that all things, good and bad, are of God's action and creation. Therefore, it has to be understood in the right way. Five alternatives are suggested: 1) Evil cannot be offered to You to gain Your acceptance. This is stated by al-Khalīl ibn Ahmad, al-Naḍr ibn Shumayl, Isḥāq ibn Rāhawayh, Yaḥyā ibn Maʿīn, Abu Bakr ibn Khuzaymah, al-Azharī and other scholars; 2) Evil cannot be attributed to You on its own. You may not be addressed as 'the Creator of pigs, the Lord of evil, etc.' but the right address is to say: 'the Creator and the Lord of all things' so as to include what is evil. This is reported by al-Ghazālī to have been said by al-Muzanī and it is expressed by other scholars; 3) Evil does not ascend to You. As the Qur'an says: 'To Him ascend all good words, and He exalts the good deed' (35: 10); 4) In relation to You, evil is not evil. You have created it in Your infinite wisdom. It is evil only in relation to created beings; and 5) Al-Khaṭṭābī says that it is like saying that someone belongs to a particular tribe or community. Hence, when we say that 'evil is not Yours' we mean that it does not belong to You.

'I exist by Your will and return to You' means that I seek Your protection and I succeed by Your will. 'You are blessed and exalted' means You deserve all praise. Some scholars say that it means that goodness stays with You. Ibn al-Anbārī said that it means that people are blessed by believing in Your oneness. But God knows best.

'Praise be to You, the fill of the Heavens and the earth and all in between them, and the fill of whatever You wish beyond them.' This means that You deserve to be praised, and had the praise due to You been in the form of physical bodies, it would have filled the Heavens and the earth and all in between.

'My face is prostrated to the One who has created and fashioned it, placing in it hearing and sight'. This part of the Prophet's supplication supports al-Zuhrī's view that one's ears are part of one's face, while some scholars say that they are part of one's head. Others say that the top of the ear is part of the head and its lower part belongs to the face, while others still say that its surface belongs to the face and its back to the head. Al-Shāfiʿī and the majority of scholars say that the ears are separate parts of one's body and they belong neither to one's face nor to one's head. Therefore, they are cleansed with fresh water during the ablution. Contrary to the view of the Shia, wiping them during the ablution is a sunnah, not a duty. A two-fold argument is cited by the majority of scholars, countering al-Zuhrī's view. The first is that 'the face' in this instance refers to the speaker's self, as in the Qur'anic verse: 'Everything is bound to perish except His face'. (28: 88) This is further supported by the fact that [the supplication refers to prostration and] other parts of the body are involved in prostration during prayer. The other argument is that in speech, a thing is identified by attachment to what is close to it, as we say 'the city's farms', but God knows best.

'Blessed is God, the best of all creators' means those who make things and fashion them.

'You are the One who brings forward and sets back.' This means that God gives a higher position to whomever He wills through obedience to Him, and He leaves others low as He in His wisdom determines. This is similar to the Qur'anic verse which says that God 'exalts whom He wills and debases whom He wills'. (3: 26)

This hadith shows that it is desirable to start one's prayer with the supplication included here, except when one is the imam leading a group of worshippers who prefer not to make their prayer long. It also shows that praise and glorification are desirable during bowing, standing up and prostration. It is also desirable to say some supplication before one finishes one's prayer with *salām*.

In hadith No. 1546, the Prophet says in his supplication, 'I am the first of those who surrender themselves'. This means that he is the first one of the Muslim community. In the other version, he says: 'I am one of those who surrender themselves'.

Transmission

The chain of transmission of hadith No. 1530 includes Abu Rishdīn, Ibn ʿAbbās' *mawlā*. Ibn Rishdīn's name is Kurayb, but he is mentioned here by his appellation as the father of his son, Rishdīn. And in the chain of the next hadith, No. 1531 one of the narrators is called ʿAbd al-Raḥmān ibn Salmān al-Ḥajrī. He belonged to Ḥajr Raʿīn, a well-known tribe.

One of the narrators of hadith No. 1540 is Abu Ḥurrah. His name is Wāṣil ibn ʿAbd al-Raḥmān. He used to recite the Qur'an in full every two nights.

Hadith No. 1545 includes in its chain of transmission the narrator Yūsuf al-Mājishūn. The surname is a foreign name, i.e. not Arabic, and means a person with a white, reddish face.

CHAPTER 27

LONG RECITATION IN NIGHT PRAYER

[1547–203]. (Dar al-Salam 1697) Abu Bakr ibn Abi Shaybah narrated: ʿAbdullāh ibn Numayr and Abu Muʿāwiyah narrated [H]. Also, Zuhayr ibn Ḥarb and Isḥāq ibn Ibrāhīm; both from Jarīr; and all from al-Aʿmash [H]. And Ibn Numayr narrated (his text); my father narrated; al-Aʿmash narrated; from Saʿd ibn ʿUbaydah; from al-Mustawrid ibn al-Aḥnaf; from Ṣilah ibn Zufar; from Ḥudhayfah. He said: **'One night I prayed with the Prophet (peace be upon him), and he started Surah [2] The Cow. I thought he would bow when he had recited 100 verses, but he went on. I thought that he would complete the surah in one *rakʿah*, but he went on. I then thought that he would bow when he had finished the surah. He then started Surah [4] Women and completed it, then he started Surah [3]** Āl ʿImrān **and completed it. He was reciting at ease. When he recited a verse that included God's glorification, he would glorify Him, and when he recited a verse with a supplication, he would say a supplication, and when he recited a prayer appealing for God's shelter, he would say the same. He then bowed and started repeating the phrase, "Limitless is my Supreme Lord in His glory". The length of his bow was close to the length of his [recitation] standing up. He then said: "May God respond to whoever praises Him", and he stood up for a long time, close to his bowing. He then prostrated himself and said: "Limitless is my Lord, the Most High in His glory". His prostration was close in length to his standing up.'**

(He added). In Jarīr's narration there is an addition. **He said: 'May God respond to whoever praises Him. Our Lord, all praise is due to You'.**

وَحَدَّثَنَا أَبُو بَكْرِ بْنُ أَبِي شَيْبَةَ، حَدَّثَنَا عَبْدُ اللهِ بْنُ نُمَيْرٍ وَأَبُو مُعَاوِيَةَ، ح. وَحَدَّثَنَا زُهَيْرُ بْنُ حَرْبٍ وَإِسْحَاقُ بْنُ إِبْرَاهِيمَ، جَمِيعًا عَنْ جَرِيرٍ، كُلُّهُمْ عَنِ الأَعْمَشِ، ح. وَحَدَّثَنَا ابْنُ نُمَيْرٍ (وَاللَّفْظُ لَه)، حَدَّثَنَا أَبِي، حَدَّثَنَا الأَعْمَشُ، عَنْ سَعْدِ بْنِ عُبَيْدَةَ، عَنِ الْـمُسْتَوْرِدِ بْنِ الأَحْنَفِ، عَنْ صِلَةَ بْنِ زُفَرَ، عَنْ حُذَيْفَةَ قَالَ: صَلَّيْتُ مَعَ النَّبِيِّ صَلَّى اللهُ عَلَيْهِ وَسَلَّمَ ذَاتَ لَيْلَةٍ، فَافْتَتَحَ الْبَقَرَةَ، فَقُلْتُ يَرْكَعُ عِنْدَ الْـمِائَةِ. ثُمَّ مَضَى فَقُلْتُ يُصَلِّي بِهَا فِي رَكْعَةٍ، فَمَضَى فَقُلْتُ يَرْكَعُ بِهَا. ثُمَّ افْتَتَحَ النِّسَاءَ فَقَرَأَهَا، ثُمَّ افْتَتَحَ آلَ عِمْرَانَ فَقَرَأَهَا، يَقْرَأُ مُتَرَسِّلاً: إِذَا مَرَّ بِآيَةٍ فِيهَا تَسْبِيحٌ سَبَّحَ، وَإِذَا مَرَّ بِسُؤَالٍ سَأَلَ، وَإِذَا مَرَّ بِتَعَوُّذٍ تَعَوَّذَ. ثُمَّ رَكَعَ، فَجَعَلَ يَقُولُ: «سُبْحَانَ رَبِّيَ الْعَظِيمِ». فَكَانَ رُكُوعُهُ نَحْوًا مِنْ قِيَامِهِ، ثُمَّ قَالَ: «سَمِعَ اللهُ لِمَنْ حَمِدَهُ». ثُمَّ قَامَ طَوِيلاً، قَرِيبًا مِمَّا رَكَعَ، ثُمَّ سَجَدَ، فَقَالَ: «سُبْحَانَ رَبِّيَ الأَعْلَى». فَكَانَ سُجُودُهُ قَرِيبًا مِنْ قِيَامِه. قَالَ: وَفِي حَدِيثِ جَرِيرٍ مِنَ الزِّيَادَةِ فَقَالَ: «سَمِعَ اللهُ لِمَنْ حَمِدَهُ، رَبَّنَا لَكَ الْحَمْدُ».

[1548–204]. (Dar al-Salam 1698–1699) ʿUthmān ibn Abi Shaybah and Isḥāq ibn Ibrāhīm narrated: both from Jarīr; ʿUthmān said: Jarīr narrated; from al-Aʿmash; from Abu Wā'il; ʿAbdullāh said: **'I prayed with God's Messenger (peace be upon him) and he made the prayer so long that I thought of doing something bad'. He was asked: 'What did you think of doing?' He said: 'I thought of sitting down leaving him [standing]'.**

وَحَدَّثَنَا عُثْمَانُ بْنُ أَبِي شَيْبَةَ وَإِسْحَاقُ بْنُ إِبْرَاهِيمَ، كِلاَهُمَا عَنْ جَرِيرٍ، قَالَ عُثْمَانُ: حَدَّثَنَا جَرِيرٌ، عَنِ الأَعْمَشِ، عَنْ أَبِي وَائِلٍ قَالَ: قَالَ عَبْدُ اللهِ: صَلَّيْتُ مَعَ رَسُولِ اللهِ صَلَّى اللهُ عَلَيْهِ وَسَلَّمَ فَأَطَالَ، حَتَّى هَمَمْتُ بِأَمْرِ سَوْءٍ. قَالَ: قِيلَ وَمَا هَمَمْتَ بِهِ؟ قَالَ: هَمَمْتُ أَنْ أَجْلِسَ وَأَدَعَهُ.

Ismāʿīl ibn al-Khalīl and Suwayd ibn Saʿīd narrated it; from ʿAlī ibn Mushir; from al-Aʿmash; with the same chain of transmission: **the same text.**

وَحَدَّثَنَاهُ إِسْمَاعِيلُ بْنُ الْخَلِيلِ وَسُوَيْدُ بْنُ سَعِيدٍ، عَنْ عَلِيِّ بْنِ مُسْهِرٍ، عَنِ الأَعْمَشِ، بِهَذَا الإِسْنَادِ: مِثْلَهُ.

Text Explanation

Hadith No. 1547 mentions the narrator Ḥudhayfah's thoughts as the Prophet went on in his recitation. He first thought that he would bow in the first *rakʿah* when he had completed 100 verses [which is about one third of the surah], but when the Prophet went on, he thought that he would recite the surah in full in the two *rakʿahs* of his prayer, but he did not and went on. Then Ḥudhayfah thought that the Prophet would bow at the end of the surah, but when he finished this surah [which is the longest in the Qur'an], 'he started Surah Women and recited it then began Surah Āl 'Imrān'. *Qadi* ʿIyāḍ said:

> This hadith provides evidence that the arrangement of the Qur'anic surahs was at the discretion of the Muslims when they wrote down the Qur'an, and that this arrangement was not by the Prophet, but rather left to his community. This is the view of Mālik and the majority of scholars and the one chosen by *Qadi* Abu Bakr al-Bāqillānī, who said: 'This is the more correct view, although both are possible'. What we say is that the arrangement of the Qur'anic surahs need not be followed in writing, prayer, study or teaching. There is no single text attributed to the Prophet on this point, nor was there an order that is forbidden to contradict. Hence, the arrangement of surahs differed in copies of the Qur'an written before ʿUthmān's standard copy. The Prophet and the Muslim community in all generations permitted disregarding the arrangement of the surahs in prayer, study and education.

Some scholars say that the arrangement of the surahs was by an order given by the Prophet and it is the same as in ʿUthmān's standard copy. They add that different copies had different arrangements because they were written before they were aware of the final arrangement, when the Prophet recited it to Gabriel for the last time. Such scholars understand the Prophet's reciting Surah 4 before Surah 3 in this prayer as having taken place before the final arrangement. These two surahs were written in this order [i.e. Surah 4, Women before Surah 3, Āl 'Imrān] in Ubayy [Ibn Kaʿb]'s copy.

There is no disagreement among scholars that it is perfectly permissible for anyone to recite, in the second *rakʿah* of his prayer, a surah that precedes the one recited in the first *rakʿah*. Such a change of order is, however, reprehensible in the same *rakʿah* and for one who is not praying. A few scholars say that even this is permissible, understanding the prohibition by early scholars of reciting the Qur'an in the wrong order to refer to reciting a single surah backwards.

There is no disagreement that the arrangement of the verses in every surah of the Qur'an is by God's order. Every surah is in the same order that it appears in the copies of the Qur'an. This is how the Muslim community learnt the surahs from the Prophet (peace be upon him).

Hadith No. 1547 says: 'When he recited a verse that included God's glorification, he would glorify Him, and when he recited a verse with a supplication, he would say a supplication, and when he recited a prayer appealing for God's shelter, he would say the same'. This means that it is desirable to do likewise for anyone reciting the Qur'an in prayer or elsewhere. According to our Shāfiʿī School, it is desirable for the imam, the congregation and individuals.

The hadith states: 'He then bowed and started repeating the phrase, "Limitless is my Supreme Lord in His glory" and the phrase "Limitless is my Lord, the Most High in His glory" in his prostration'.

This shows the desirability of repeating these phrases when one bows and prostrates oneself in prayer. This is the view of our Shāfiʿī School, as well as al-Awzāʿī, Abu Ḥanīfah, the Kūfī scholars, Ahmad and the majority of scholars. Mālik says that such desirability need not be stated.

'He then said, "May God respond to whoever praises Him", and he stood up for a long time, close to his bowing. He then prostrated himself'. This provides evidence that it is permissible to stand up for longer than one does when bowing. However, our scholars say that it is not permissible and that if done, it makes the prayer invalid.

Hadith No. 1548 mentions that the Prophet made his prayer very long, and the narrator ʿAbdullāh ibn Masʿūd said that he thought of sitting down, leaving the Prophet standing. This shows that it is important to observe good manners when one is with one's elders and leaders. They should not be contradicted by word or deed, unless what they say or do is forbidden. Scholars agree that if a person in a congregational prayer, whether obligatory or otherwise, finds standing too hard, he may sit down and continue the prayer seated. Ibn Masʿūd did not do so out of politeness. The hadith further shows that it is permissible to offer non-obligatory prayers in congregation. It also shows the desirability to make night prayer long.

Transmission

The chain of transmission of hadith No. 1547 includes al-Aʿmash narrated; from Saʿd ibn ʿUbaydah; from al-Mustawrid ibn al-Aḥnaf; from Ṣilah ibn Zufar. All these four narrators belonged to the *tābiʿīn* generation.

In the next hadith, No. 1548, the chain of transmission is as follows: ʿUthmān ibn Abi Shaybah and Isḥāq ibn Ibrāhīm narrated: both from Jarīr; ʿUthmān said: Jarīr narrated; from al-Aʿmash; from Abu Wā'il; ʿAbdullāh ibn Masʿūd. All these narrators, with the exception of Isḥāq, belonged to Kufah.

CHAPTER 28

SLEEPING INTO THE MORNING

[1549–205]. (Dar al-Salam 1700) ʿUthmān ibn Abi Shaybah and Isḥāq narrated:[i] ʿUthmān said: Jarīr narrated; from Manṣūr; from Abu Wā'il; from ʿAbdullāh. He said: **'A man who slept through the night, right into the morning, was mentioned in God's Messenger's presence. The Prophet said: "That is one in whose ears Satan has urinated" or he might have said "in whose ear".'**

حَدَّثَنَا عُثْمَانُ بْنُ أَبِي شَيْبَةَ، وَإِسْحَاقُ، قَالَ عُثْمَانُ حَدَّثَنَا جَرِيرٌ، عَنْ مَنْصُورٍ، عَنْ أَبِي وَائِلٍ، عَنْ عَبْدِ اللهِ، قَالَ ذُكِرَ عِنْدَ رَسُولِ اللهِ صَلَّى اللهُ عَلَيْهِ وَسَلَّمَ رَجُلٌ نَامَ لَيْلَةً حَتَّى أَصْبَحَ قَالَ «ذَاكَ رَجُلٌ بَالَ الشَّيْطَانُ فِي أُذُنَيْهِ». أَوْ قَالَ «فِي أُذُنِهِ» .

[1550–206]. (Dar al-Salam 1701) Qutaybah ibn Saʿīd narrated:[ii] Layth narrated; from ʿUqayl; from al-Zuhrī; from ʿAlī ibn Ḥusayn; that al-Ḥusayn ibn ʿAlī narrated; that ʿAlī ibn Abi Ṭālib mentioned that **the Prophet came one night to see him and Fāṭimah. 'He said: "Would you not rather pray?" I said: "Messenger of God, our souls are in God's hand. If He so wished, He would make us rise". God's Messenger (peace be upon him) left when I said this to him. As he turned away, I**

i. Related by al-Bukhari, 1144 and 3270; al-Nasā'ī, 1607 and 1608; Ibn Mājah, 1330.
ii. Related by al-Bukhari, 1127, 4724, 7347 and 7465; al-Nasā'ī, 1610 and 1611.

heard him striking his thigh and saying: "Man is, above all else, always given to contention [18: 54]**".'**

وَحَدَّثَنَا قُتَيْبَةُ بْنُ سَعِيدٍ، حَدَّثَنَا لَيْثٌ، عَنْ عُقَيْلٍ، عَنِ الزُّهْرِيِّ، عَنْ عَلِيِّ بْنِ حُسَيْنٍ، أَنَّ الْحُسَيْنَ بْنَ عَلِيٍّ، حَدَّثَهُ عَنْ عَلِيِّ بْنِ أَبِي طَالِبٍ، أَنَّ النَّبِيَّ صَلَّى اللهُ عَلَيْهِ وَسَلَّمَ طَرَقَهُ وَفَاطِمَةَ فَقَالَ «أَلاَ تُصَلُّونَ» . فَقُلْتُ يَا رَسُولَ اللهِ إِنَّمَا أَنْفُسُنَا بِيَدِ اللهِ فَإِذَا شَاءَ أَنْ يَبْعَثَنَا بَعَثَنَا. فَانْصَرَفَ رَسُولُ اللهِ صَلَّى اللهُ عَلَيْهِ وَسَلَّمَ حِينَ قُلْتُ لَهُ ذَلِكَ ثُمَّ سَمِعْتُهُ وَهُوَ مُدْبِرٌ يَضْرِبُ فَخِذَهُ وَيَقُولُ «وَكَانَ الإِنْسَانُ أَكْثَرَ شَيْءٍ جَدَلاً»

[1551–207]. (Dar al-Salam 1702) ʿAmr al-Nāqid and Zuhayr ibn Ḥarb narrated:[i] ʿAmr said: Sufyān ibn ʿUyaynah narrated; from Abu al-Zinād; from al-Aʿraj; from Abu Hurayrah, attributing to the Prophet (peace be upon him): **'When any of you goes to sleep, Satan ties up three knots at the back of your head, with each knot he strikes: "a long night for you". When one wakes up and mentions God's name, one knot is untied. When one performs ablution, i.e. *wuḍū'*, two knots are untied, and when one prays all knots are untied. One then finds oneself fresh with a pleasant feeling. Otherwise, one feels unfresh and unpleasant'.**

حَدَّثَنَا عَمْرٌو النَّاقِدُ، وَزُهَيْرُ بْنُ حَرْبٍ، قَالَ عَمْرٌو حَدَّثَنَا سُفْيَانُ بْنُ عُيَيْنَةَ، عَنْ أَبِي الزِّنَادِ، عَنِ الأَعْرَجِ، عَنْ أَبِي هُرَيْرَةَ، يَبْلُغُ بِهِ النَّبِيَّ صَلَّى اللهُ عَلَيْهِ وَسَلَّمَ: «يَعْقِدُ الشَّيْطَانُ عَلَى قَافِيَةِ رَأْسِ أَحَدِكُمْ ثَلاَثَ عُقَدٍ إِذَا نَامَ بِكُلِّ عُقْدَةٍ يَضْرِبُ عَلَيْكَ لَيْلاً طَوِيلاً فَإِذَا اسْتَيْقَظَ فَذَكَرَ اللهَ انْحَلَّتْ عُقْدَةٌ وَإِذَا تَوَضَّأَ انْحَلَّتْ عُقْدَتَانِ فَإِذَا صَلَّى انْحَلَّتِ الْعُقَدُ فَأَصْبَحَ نَشِيطًا طَيِّبَ النَّفْسِ وَإِلاَّ أَصْبَحَ خَبِيثَ النَّفْسِ كَسْلاَنَ» .

---

i. Related by al-Nasāʾī, 1606.

Text Explanation

In the first hadith, No. 1549, the Prophet says about a man who sleeps through the night right into the morning, that Satan has urinated in his ears. Scholars differ in explaining its meaning. Ibn Quṭaybah says it means spoiling. There is an Arabic idiom which describes ruining something as being akin to 'urinating in its ears'. Al-Muhallab, al-Ṭaḥāwī and others say that it is a metaphor referring to a person being under Satan's influence and control. Satan, thus, humiliates him and ties three knots at the back of his head. Others have said that to 'urinate in his ear' means to humiliate and despise him. It comes originally from an expression stating that an animal urinates in a lion's ear, thus looking upon the lion with contempt. Al-Ḥarbī said: 'It means overpowering and ridiculing him'. *Qadi* 'Iyāḍ said: 'It may actually mean what it says, specifying one's ears because the ears are the centre of a person's sense of alertness'.

In Hadith No. 1550, 'Alī mentions that as the Prophet left, he heard him striking his thigh and quoting the Qur'anic verse that says: 'above all else, man is always given to contention'. What this means, according to the view of choice, is that it expresses amazement at the quick answer given by 'Alī and the Prophet's disagreement with his excuse. Hence, he struck his thigh. On the other hand, it is said that the Prophet's action indicates acceptance of 'Alī's and Fāṭimah's excuse, confirming that no blame could be attached to them.

The hadith confirms the recommendation of offering night worship and that Muslims should urge their friends to do so. It also shows that leaders and elders should look after their subordinates' religious and life interests. Moreover, when a person gives advice to someone and that person appears not to heed it or gives a reason that seems unsatisfactory, then the one giving the advice should neither press hard nor make any reproaches unless that serves a clear interest.

In the last hadith, No. 1551 the Prophet says: 'When any of you goes to sleep, Satan ties up three knots at the back of your head, with each knot he strikes: "a long night for you".' Scholars differ as to the meaning of these knots. Some say that they are real, suggesting the same meaning as magical knots that prevent a person from rising. They quote the verse that appeals for God's refuge 'against the evil of the conjuror witches' (113: 4). For the conjurors' action, the verse uses a word derived from the same root as the Arabic equivalent of knots. As such, it means some words said by Satan have the effect of making the sleeper unwilling to wake up. Some say that the statement may refer to some action done in the same way as conjuror witches do. Others say that it is all mental, which means that Satan whispers to a man telling him that he has a long night to sleep.[i] Others still suggest that it is a figurative statement indicating Satan's attempt to dissuade a Muslim from attending to night worship.

The hadith then mentions: 'When one wakes up and mentions God's name, one knot is untied. When one performs ablution, i.e. *wuḍū'*, two knots are untied, and when one prays all knots are untied. One then finds oneself fresh with a pleasant feeling. Otherwise, one feels unfresh and unpleasant'. This includes several useful points, including the advice to mention God's name and glorify Him when one wakes up. There are certain supplications and glorifications recommended to say at this time, and these are well-known and mentioned in authentic anthologies of Hadith. I have devoted a chapter for these in my book *al-Adhkār*. However, it is not obligatory to stick to any particular formula of God's remembrance or glorification at this time, but using what is recommended is better.

Another useful point in this hadith is the recommendation to perform the ablution when one wakes up and to offer a prayer, even a short one. The Prophet says: 'When one performs ablution, two knots are untied'. This means a total of two knots, confirming that a second knot is untied to make up the total of two. There are similar examples in the Qur'an and hadiths. God says: 'Say: Do you indeed

i. It is perhaps more correct to say that the Prophet's description of the knots tied by Satan is figurative, describing Satan's attempt to persuade man to remain asleep, suggesting that there is still a long time before he needs to wake up. Likewise, the untying of the knots is figurative, describing man's attempt to repel Satan and counter his promptings.

disbelieve in Him who has created the earth in two days?... It is He who placed on the earth firm mountains towering above it and bestowed His blessings on it and measured out its varied provisions in four days'. (41: 9–10) This means that all this was done in two additional days, making a total of four days.

A similar example occurs in an authentic hadith related by Muslim: 'Whoever offers the funeral prayer will earn a share [of reward], and whoever joins the deceased's funeral until it is buried in its grave earns two shares'. Both al-Bukhari and Muslim relate several hadiths with different chains of transmission, giving the same meaning, suggesting that the two shares are the total reward. Thus the meaning is that a prayer for the deceased earns one share of reward and following the funeral to the graveyard earns another share. This is based on the hadith related by Muslim in his *Ṣaḥīḥ*: 'Whoever goes out with a funeral from its home and prays for the deceased, then follows the funeral until the deceased is buried will have two shares of reward, each share is as big as Mount Uhud. Whoever offers the funeral prayer and goes back will have a reward equal to Mount Uhud'. Another version is related by al-Bukhari at the beginning of his *Ṣaḥīḥ* anthology: 'Whoever follows the funeral of a deceased Muslim person, motivated by faith and dedication, and stays until the funeral prayer is done and the deceased is buried, goes back having earned two shares of reward, each of which is as big as Mount Uhud, and whoever offers the funeral prayer and returns before the deceased is buried goes back with one share of reward'. All these versions are narrated by Abu Hurayrah. A similar hadith in Muslim's *Ṣaḥīḥ* states: 'Whoever prays 'Ishā with a congregation is like one who spends half the night in worship, and whoever prays Fajr with a congregation is like one who spends the entire night in worship'. We have already explained this hadith.

The hadith mentions that the person who wakes up, glorifies God, performs the ablution and prays will find himself 'fresh having a pleasant feeling'. He is pleased with what God has enabled him to do of attending to his duties and what he is promised of reward. Moreover, God will bless him and his actions. Further, the knots tied by Satan behind his head are removed. The hadith adds: 'Otherwise, one feels unfresh and unpleasant'. This is due to the effects of what Satan did to him, causing him to slacken.

The apparent meaning of the hadith is that the one who does not do all three things, i.e. God's glorification, ablution and prayer, will be included among those who lack freshness, feeling unpleasant. There is no contradiction between this hadith and the one that prohibits saying 'I feel I am rotting'. This last hadith prohibits saying this of oneself, while the hadith we are discussing in this chapter tells of someone else.

Imam al-Bukhari devotes a chapter to this hadith, with the heading: 'Chapter on the Knots Tied by Satan on the Head of One who does not Pray'. Imam al-Māzarī criticises al-Bukhari saying that 'the hadith mentions that Satan ties the knots at the back of a person's head, even if he subsequently prays. The knots are untied by God's glorification, ablution and prayer'. Al-Māzari adds that al-Bukhari's words may be understood to mean that the knots continue to affect the one who does not pray, while the one who prays will have his knots untied, thus reverting to the same condition as one who never had such knots.

Transmission

The chain of transmission of hadith No. 1549 runs as follows: ''Uthmān ibn Abi Shaybah and Isḥāq narrated: from Jarīr; from Manṣūr; from Abu Wā'il; from 'Abdullāh'. It is thus composed of narrators who all belonged to Kufah, with the exception of Isḥāq.

Hadith No. 1550 has the following chain of transmission: 'Qutaybah ibn Sa'īd narrated: Layth narrated; from 'Uqayl; from al-Zuhrī; from 'Alī ibn Ḥusayn; that al-Ḥusayn ibn 'Alī narrated; that 'Alī ibn Abi Ṭālib mentioned'. This is how we have checked and verified it, with the name of the narrator al-Ḥusayn ibn 'Alī. It occurs so in the numerous manuscripts I have seen in our areas. However, in his book *al-Istidrākāt*, al-Dāraquṭnī mentions that in Muslim's *Ṣaḥīḥ*, the name occurs, according to Qutaybah's narration, as al-Ḥasan ibn

ʿAlī.[i] The same is agreed by Ibrāhīm ibn Naṣr al-Nahāwandī and al-Juʿafī. However, al-Nasā'ī, al-Sarrāj and Mūsā ibn Ḥarūn report it from Qutaybah as al-Ḥusayn. On the other hand, it is mentioned by Abu Ṣāliḥ, Ḥamzah ibn Ziyād and al-Walīd ibn Ṣāliḥ, reporting from Layth, as al-Ḥasan, while Yūnus al-Mu'addib, Abu al-Naḍr and others report it also from Layth as al-Ḥusayn. The same is stated by al-Zuhrī's narrators, including Ṣāliḥ ibn Kaysān, Ibn Abi ʿAtīq, Ibn Jurayj, Isḥāq ibn Rāshid, Zayd ibn Abi Anīsah, Shuʿayb, Ḥakīm ibn Ḥakam, Yaḥyā ibn Abi Anīsah, ʿAqīl narrating from Ibn Lahīʿah from al-Zuhrī, ʿAbd al-Raḥmān ibn Isḥāq, ʿUbaydullāh ibn Ziyād and others. Those who claim that Layth narrated it mentioning al-Ḥasan in his transmission are mistaken. This is what al-Dāraquṭnī said and the sum of it is that the correct narration from Layth gives the name as al-Ḥusayn ibn ʿAlī. As we have mentioned, it is thus stated in the narrations in our areas, but God knows best.

i. ʿAlī's two sons by his wife, Fāṭimah, were named al-Ḥasan and al-Ḥusayn.

CHAPTER 29

IT IS PREFERABLE TO PRAY THE SUNNAH AT HOME

[1552–208]. (Dar al-Salam 1703) Muhammad ibn al-Muthannā narrated:[i] Yaḥyā narrated; from ʿUbaydullāh; Nāfiʿ reported to me; from Ibn ʿUmar; from the Prophet (peace be upon him). He said: **'Let some of your prayers be at your homes. Do not let them be like graves'.**

حَدَّثَنَا مُحَمَّدُ بْنُ الْـمُثَنَّى، حَدَّثَنَا يَحْيَى، عَنْ عُبَيْدِ اللهِ، قَالَ أَخْبَرَنِي نَافِعٌ، عَنِ ابْنِ عُمَرَ عَنِ النَّبِيِّ صَلَّى اللهُ عَلَيْهِ وَسَلَّمَ قَالَ «اجْعَلُوا مِنْ صَلاَتِكُمْ فِي بُيُوتِكُمْ وَلاَ تَتَّخِذُوهَا قُبُورًا»

[1553–209]. (Dar al-Salam 1704) Ibn al-Muthannā narrated:[ii] ʿAbd al-Wahhāb narrated; Ayyūb reported; from Nāfiʿ; from Ibn ʿUmar; from the Prophet (peace be upon him). He said: **'Pray in your homes and do not let them be like graves'.**

وَحَدَّثَنَا ابْنُ الْـمُثَنَّى، حَدَّثَنَا عَبْدُ الْوَهَّابِ، أَخْبَرَنَا أَيُّوبُ، عَنْ نَافِعٍ، عَنِ ابْنِ عُمَرَ، عَنِ النَّبِيِّ صَلَّى اللهُ عَلَيْهِ وَسَلَّمَ قَالَ «صَلُّوا فِي بُيُوتِكُمْ وَلاَ تَتَّخِذُوهَا قُبُورًا»

[1554–210]. (Dar al-Salam 1705) Abu Bakr ibn Abi Shaybah and Abu Kurayb narrated: both said: Abu Muʿāwiyah narrated;

---

i. Related by al-Bukhari, 432; Abu Dāwūd, 1043 and 1448; Ibn Mājah in a shorter version, 1377.
ii. Related by al-Bukhari, 1187.

from al-Aʿmash; from Abu Sufyān; from Jābir; that God's Messenger (peace be upon him) said: **'When any of you has finished prayer in the mosque, let him leave a portion of his prayers for his home, as God will place goodness in his home through his prayer'.**

وَحَدَّثَنَا أَبُو بَكْرِ بْنُ أَبِي شَيْبَةَ، وَأَبُو كُرَيْبٍ قَالَا: حَدَّثَنَا أَبُو مُعَاوِيَةَ، عَنِ الأَعْمَشِ، عَنْ أَبِي سُفْيَانَ، عَنْ جَابِرٍ، قَالَ قَالَ رَسُولُ اللهِ صَلَّى اللهُ عَلَيْهِ وَسَلَّمَ: «إِذَا قَضَى أَحَدُكُمُ الصَّلَاةَ فِي مَسْجِدِهِ فَلْيَجْعَلْ لِبَيْتِهِ نَصِيبًا مِنْ صَلَاتِهِ فَإِنَّ اللهَ جَاعِلٌ فِي بَيْتِهِ مِنْ صَلَاتِهِ خَيْرًا»

[1555–211]. (Dar al-Salam 1706) ʿAbdullāh ibn Barrād al-Ashʿarī and Muhammad ibn al-ʿAlā' narrated:[i] both said: Abu Usāmah narrated; from Burayd; from Abu Burdah; from Abu Mūsā; from the Prophet (peace be upon him). He said: **'A house in which God's name is frequently mentioned and one in which God's name is not mentioned may be compared to one who is alive and one who is dead'.**

حَدَّثَنَا عَبْدُ اللهِ بْنُ بَرَّادٍ الأَشْعَرِيُّ، وَمُحَمَّدُ بْنُ الْعَلَاءِ، قَالَا حَدَّثَنَا أَبُو أُسَامَةَ، عَنْ بُرَيْدٍ، عَنْ أَبِي بُرْدَةَ، عَنْ أَبِي مُوسَى، عَنِ النَّبِيِّ صَلَّى اللهُ عَلَيْهِ وَسَلَّمَ قَالَ: «مَثَلُ الْبَيْتِ الَّذِي يُذْكَرُ اللهُ فِيهِ وَالْبَيْتِ الَّذِي لَا يُذْكَرُ اللهُ فِيهِ مَثَلُ الْحَيِّ وَالْمَيِّتِ»

[1556–212]. (Dar al-Salam 1707) Qutaybah ibn Saʿīd narrated: Yaʿqūb (who is Ibn ʿAbd al-Raḥmān al-Qāriy) narrated; from Suhayl; from his father; from Abu Hurayrah; that God's Messenger (peace be upon him) said: **'Do not let your homes be like graveyards. Satan runs away from a home where the Surah [entitled] The Cow is recited'.**

i. Related by al-Bukhari, in similar wording, 6407.

حَدَّثَنَا قُتَيْبَةُ بْنُ سَعِيدٍ، حَدَّثَنَا يَعْقُوبُ، - وَهُوَ ابْنُ عَبْدِ الرَّحْمَنِ الْقَارِيُّ - عَنْ سُهَيْلٍ، عَنْ أَبِيهِ، عَنْ أَبِي هُرَيْرَةَ، أَنَّ رَسُولَ اللهِ صَلَّى اللهُ عَلَيْهِ وَسَلَّمَ قَالَ: «لاَ تَجْعَلُوا بُيُوتَكُمْ مَقَابِرَ إِنَّ الشَّيْطَانَ يَنْفِرُ مِنَ الْبَيْتِ الَّذِي تُقْرَأُ فِيهِ سُورَةُ الْبَقَرَةِ».

[1557–213]. (Dar al-Salam 1708) Muhammad ibn al-Muthannā narrated:[i] Muhammad ibn Jaʿfar narrated; ʿAbdullāh ibn Saʿīd narrated; Sālim Abu al-Naḍr, ʿUmar ibn ʿUbaydullāh's *mawla*, narrated; from Busr ibn Saʿīd; from Zayd ibn Thābit. He said: **'God's Messenger (peace be upon him) marked out a small area with a straw mat and he went out to pray there. A few men followed him and came over to pray with him. On another night they came and attended there, but God's Messenger stayed in and did not come out to join them. They spoke aloud and threw pebbles at [his] door. God's Messenger then came out to them feeling angry and said to them: "You have continued to do this until I thought that it might become obligatory to you. Do pray in your homes, as the best of a man's prayer is that which he offers at home, except for the obligatory prayers".'**

وَحَدَّثَنَا مُحَمَّدُ بْنُ الْمُثَنَّى، حَدَّثَنَا مُحَمَّدُ بْنُ جَعْفَرٍ، حَدَّثَنَا عَبْدُ اللهِ بْنُ سَعِيدٍ، حَدَّثَنَا سَالِمٌ أَبُو النَّضْرِ، مَوْلَى عُمَرَ بْنِ عُبَيْدِ اللهِ عَنْ بُسْرِ بْنِ سَعِيدٍ، عَنْ زَيْدِ بْنِ ثَابِتٍ، قَالَ احْتَجَرَ رَسُولُ اللهِ صَلَّى اللهُ عَلَيْهِ وَسَلَّمَ حُجَيْرَةً بِخَصَفَةٍ أَوْ حَصِيرٍ فَخَرَجَ رَسُولُ اللهِ صَلَّى اللهُ عَلَيْهِ وَسَلَّمَ يُصَلِّي فِيهَا - قَالَ - فَتَتَبَّعَ إِلَيْهِ رِجَالٌ وَجَاءُوا يُصَلُّونَ بِصَلاَتِهِ - قَالَ - ثُمَّ جَاءُوا لَيْلَةً فَحَضَرُوا وَأَبْطَأَ رَسُولُ اللهِ صَلَّى اللهُ عَلَيْهِ وَسَلَّمَ عَنْهُمْ - قَالَ - فَلَمْ يَخْرُجْ إِلَيْهِمْ فَرَفَعُوا أَصْوَاتَهُمْ وَحَصَبُوا الْبَابَ فَخَرَجَ إِلَيْهِمْ رَسُولُ اللهِ صَلَّى اللهُ عَلَيْهِ وَسَلَّمَ مُغْضَبًا فَقَالَ لَهُمْ رَسُولُ اللهِ صَلَّى اللهُ عَلَيْهِ وَسَلَّمَ:

i. Related by al-Bukhari, 731, 6113 and 7290; Abu Dāwūd, 1044 in a shorter version, and 1447; al-Tirmidhī, 450 in a shorter version; al-Nasāʾī, 1598.

«مَا زَالَ بِكُمْ صَنِيعُكُمْ حَتَّى ظَنَنْتُ أَنَّهُ سَيُكْتَبُ عَلَيْكُمْ فَعَلَيْكُمْ بِالصَّلاَةِ فِي بُيُوتِكُمْ فَإِنَّ خَيْرَ صَلاَةِ الْـمَرْءِ فِي بَيْتِهِ إِلاَّ الصَّلاَةَ الْـمَكْتُوبَةَ »

[1558–214]. (Dar al-Salam 1709) Muhammad ibn Ḥātim narrated to me: Bahz narrated; Wuhayb narrated; Mūsā ibn ʿUqbah narrated; he said: I heard Abu al-Naḍr narrating from Busr ibn Saʿīd; from Zayd ibn Thābit; that **'The Prophet (peace be upon him) allocated a small compartment with a straw mat, and he prayed there for some nights, until a large group of people gathered with him...' he added a similar text and added: 'If it were to be made obligatory to you, you would not be able to fulfil it'.**

وَحَدَّثَنِي مُحَمَّدُ بْنُ حَاتِمٍ، حَدَّثَنَا بَهْزٌ، حَدَّثَنَا وُهَيْبٌ، حَدَّثَنَا مُوسَى بْنُ عُقْبَةَ، قَالَ سَمِعْتُ أَبَا النَّضْرِ، عَنْ بُسْرِ بْنِ سَعِيدٍ، عَنْ زَيْدِ بْنِ ثَابِتٍ، أَنَّ النَّبِيَّ صَلَّى اللهُ عَلَيْهِ وَسَلَّمَ اتَّخَذَ حُجْرَةً فِي الْـمَسْجِدِ مِنْ حَصِيرٍ فَصَلَّى رَسُولُ اللهِ صَلَّى اللهُ عَلَيْهِ وَسَلَّمَ فِيهَا لَيَالِيَ حَتَّى اجْتَمَعَ إِلَيْهِ نَاسٌ . فَذَكَرَ نَحْوَهُ وَزَادَ فِيهِ: « وَلَوْ كُتِبَ عَلَيْكُمْ مَا قُمْتُمْ بِهِ »

Text Explanation

The first hadith in this chapter, No. 1552, mentions that the Prophet said: 'Let some of your prayers be at your homes. Do not let them be like graves'. This encourages prayer at home, so that homes do not become bereft of prayers, like graves. The hadith refers to the sunnah, or recommended prayers. Thus, the Prophet's instruction is to offer the sunnah prayers at home. *Qadi* ʿIyāḍ said: 'some scholars say that it refers to obligatory prayers, and it means that some obligatory prayers should be offered at home, so that those in one's household who do not attend the prayers in the mosque, such as women, slaves, sick people and others, will follow your lead and pray. The majority, however, say that the instruction refers to sunnah prayers in order to keep them private. It also confirms what is mentioned in another hadith: "The best prayer is one's prayer at home, except for the obligatory prayer".'

The correct view, endorsed by all the hadiths in this chapter, is that this refers to sunnah or recommended prayers. It is incorrect to apply it to obligatory prayers. Offering the sunnah prayers at home makes them more private and keeps them free of hypocrisy. Moreover, the home will be blessed when prayers are offered in it. God's mercies are bestowed on them and angels attend, while Satan stays away from them, as mentioned in another hadith. This is what is meant in hadith No. 1554, which says: 'God will place goodness in his home through his prayer'.

Hadith No. 1555 mentions that the Prophet said: 'A house in which God's name is frequently mentioned and one in which God's name is not mentioned may be compared to one who is alive and one who is dead'. The hadith encourages mentioning God's name at home and that a Muslim's home should not be left without glorifying God. The hadith also shows that it is perfectly permissible to draw comparisons. It also says that a long life that is characterised by fulfilment of what God requires and obeying Him is a great virtue. Even when it is certain that a deceased person moves to what is better, a living person can catch up with that good deceased person and attain a better position by doing more of what pleases God.

Hadith No. 1556 mentions 'Surah The Cow', and this shows that this is permissible with no discouragement. Some scholars consider this discouraged, but they are wrong. We mentioned this earlier, and we will discuss it again presently in the chapter speaking about the excellence of the Qur'an.

Hadith No. 1557 mentions that 'God's Messenger (peace be upon him) marked out a small area with a straw mat and he went out to pray there'. This means that he placed a straw mat around this area so that it would shield him when praying there. Thus, no one would pass in front of him as he prayed. He would be able to concentrate fully on his prayer. To do so is permissible, provided that it does not inconvenience other worshippers in the mosque. The Prophet did not keep this area for himself all the time. He only did so for his night worship and then integrated the place with the rest of the mosque during the day, as mentioned by Muslim in a later hadith. Then, the Prophet stopped doing so at night and during the day. Instead, he resumed offering sunnah prayers at home.

The hadith shows that it is perfectly permissible to offer sunnah prayers in the mosque, and that it is also permissible to offer prayers that are not obligatory in congregation. It is also permissible to join in congregation someone who starts to pray without intending to be an imam leading a congregational prayer. The hadith further shows that it is right to abandon a good thing when a greater negative thing is feared as a result. The Prophet was very tender-hearted in dealing with his community, thinking always of what benefits them and serves their interests. Rulers, leaders, dignitaries and those who are followed, such as scholars, should do as he did and think of the interests of others. The hadith mentions that the Prophet's Companions threw pebbles at his door. They did so to alert him, thinking that he might have forgotten.

The Prophet told them: 'Do pray in your homes, as the best of a man's prayer is that which he offers at home, except for the obligatory prayers'. This applies to all recommended prayers, including those that are regularly offered with the obligatory prayers and the general ones, except for recommended prayers that are considered to be features of Islam, such as the Eid Prayer, the prayer at the time of a solar or lunar eclipse, the prayer for rain, as well as the Tarāwīḥ Prayer during Ramadan, according to the more correct view. Tarāwīḥ is offered in congregation at mosques, while the prayer for rain is offered in the open, and so is the Eid Prayer if the mosque is too small to accommodate the worshippers, but God knows best.

CHAPTER 30

PERMANENT VOLUNTARY WORSHIP

[1559–215]. (Dar al-Salam 1710) Muhammad ibn al-Muthannā narrated:[i] ʿAbd al-Wahhāb (meaning al-Thaqafī) narrated; ʿUbaydullāh narrated; from Saʿīd ibn Abi Saʿīd; from Abu Salamah; from ʿĀ'ishah. She said: **'God's Messenger (peace be upon him) had a straw mat and he used to make of it a small compartment where he prayed at night. People used to join him in his prayer. He would then leave it flat during the day. The people came back one night. The Prophet said [to them]: "People, do only what you can comfortably do. God is not bored until you are bored. The sort of action God loves best is what is done regularly, even though it may be little". When the people in Muhammad's household did something, they would then do it regularly'.**

يَعْنِي الثَّقَفِيَّ - حَدَّثَنَا عُبَيْدُ اللهِ، عَنْ سَعِيدِ بْنِ أَبِي سَعِيدٍ، عَنْ أَبِي سَلَمَةَ، عَنْ - وَحَدَّثَنَا
مُحَمَّدُ بْنُ الْـمُثَنَّى، حَدَّثَنَا عَبْدُ الْوَهَّابِ عَائِشَةَ، أَنَّهَا قَالَتْ: كَانَ لِرَسُولِ اللهِ صَلَّى اللهُ
عَلَيْهِ وَسَلَّمَ حَصِيرٌ وَكَانَ يُحَجِّرُهُ مِنَ اللَّيْلِ فَيُصَلِّي فِيهِ، فَجَعَلَ النَّاسُ يُصَلُّونَ بِصَلاَتِهِ
وَيَبْسُطُهُ بِالنَّهَارِ. فَثَابُوا ذَاتَ لَيْلَةٍ فَقَالَ: «يَا أَيُّهَا النَّاسُ عَلَيْكُمْ مِنَ الأَعْمَالِ مَا تُطِيقُونَ
فَإِنَّ اللهَ لاَ يَمَلُّ حَتَّى تَمَلُّوا. وَإِنَّ أَحَبَّ الأَعْمَالِ إِلَى اللهِ مَا دُووِمَ عَلَيْهِ وَإِنْ قَلَّ». وَكَانَ
آلُ مُحَمَّدٍ صَلَّى اللهُ عَلَيْهِ وَسَلَّمَ إِذَا عَمِلُوا عَمَلاً أَثْبَتُوهُ.

---

i. Related by al-Bukhari, 730 in a shorter version, and 5861; Abu Dāwūd, 1368; al-Nasā'ī, 761; Ibn Mājah, 942 in a shorter version.

[1560–216]. (Dar al-Salam 1711) Muhammad ibn al-Muthannā narrated:[i] Muhammad ibn Ja'far narrated; Shu'bah narrated; from Sa'd ibn Ibrāhīm; that he heard Abu Salamah narrating from 'Ā'ishah; that God's Messenger (peace be upon him) was asked: **'Which action does God love best?' He said: 'The one done regularly, even though it is little'.**

حَدَّثَنَا مُحَمَّدُ بْنُ الْـمُثَنَّى، حَدَّثَنَا مُحَمَّدُ بْنُ جَعْفَرٍ، حَدَّثَنَا شُعْبَةُ، عَنْ سَعْدِ بْنِ إِبْرَاهِيمَ، أَنَّهُ سَمِعَ أَبَا سَلَمَةَ، يُحَدِّثُ عَنْ عَائِشَةَ، أَنَّ رَسُولَ اللهِ صَلَّى اللهُ عَلَيْهِ وَسَلَّمَ سُئِلَ أَيُّ الْعَمَلِ أَحَبُّ إِلَى اللهِ؟ قَالَ: «أَدْوَمُهُ وَإِنْ قَلَّ».

[1561–217]. (Dar al-Salam 1712) Zuhayr ibn Ḥarb and Isḥāq ibn Ibrāhīm narrated:[ii] Zuhayr said: Jarīr narrated; from Manṣūr; from Ibrāhīm; from 'Alqamah. He said: **'I asked 'Ā'ishah, the Mother of the Believers, and said: "Mother of the Believers, how was God's Messenger's (peace be upon him) [voluntary] action? Did he do any special things on certain days?" She said: "No. His action was consistently the same, but who of you can do what God's Messenger (peace be upon him) could comfortably do?".'**

وَحَدَّثَنَا زُهَيْرُ بْنُ حَرْبٍ، وَإِسْحَاقُ بْنُ إِبْرَاهِيمَ، قَالَ زُهَيْرٌ حَدَّثَنَا جَرِيرٌ، عَنْ مَنْصُورٍ، عَنْ إِبْرَاهِيمَ، عَنْ عَلْقَمَةَ، قَالَ سَأَلْتُ أُمَّ الْـمُؤْمِنِينَ عَائِشَةَ قَالَ: قُلْتُ: يَا أُمَّ الْـمُؤْمِنِينَ كَيْفَ كَانَ عَمَلُ رَسُولِ اللهِ صَلَّى اللهُ عَلَيْهِ وَسَلَّمَ؟ هَلْ كَانَ يَخُصُّ شَيْئًا مِنَ الأَيَّامِ؟ قَالَتْ: لا. كَانَ عَمَلُهُ دِيمَةً. وَأَيُّكُمْ يَسْتَطِيعُ مَا كَانَ رَسُولُ اللهِ صَلَّى اللهُ عَلَيْهِ وَسَلَّمَ يَسْتَطِيعُ.

---

i. Related by al-Bukhari, 6465.
ii. Related by al-Bukhari, 6466 and 1987; Abu Dāwūd, 1370.

[1562–218]. (Dar al-Salam 1713) Ibn Numayr narrated: my father narrated; Saʿd ibn Saʿīd narrated; al-Qāsim ibn Muhammad reported to me; from ʿĀ'ishah. She said: **'God's Messenger (peace be upon him) said: "The type of action God, the Exalted, loves best is what is done most regularly, even though it is little". He said: "When ʿĀ'ishah did some [voluntary] action, she would keep it up".'**

وَحَدَّثَنَا ابْنُ نُمَيْرٍ، حَدَّثَنَا أَبِي، حَدَّثَنَا سَعْدُ بْنُ سَعِيدٍ، أَخْبَرَنِي الْقَاسِمُ بْنُ مُحَمَّدٍ، عَنْ عَائِشَةَ، قَالَتْ: قَالَ رَسُولُ اللهِ صَلَّى اللهُ عَلَيْهِ وَسَلَّمَ: «أَحَبُّ الأَعْمَالِ إِلَى اللهِ تَعَالَى أَدْوَمُهَا وَإِنْ قَلَّ». قَالَ: وَكَانَتْ عَائِشَةُ إِذَا عَمِلَتِ الْعَمَلَ لَزِمَتْهُ.

Text Explanation

The first hadith, No. 1559, mentions that the Prophet marked out a small compartment in the mosque with a straw mat he had. This shows that the Prophet cared little for the comforts of this world. When people came back to join him in his night prayer, the Prophet told them that they should only do what they can comfortably attend to regularly, without causing themselves any hardship. The hadith thus urges people to be moderate in their worship and not to do too much. The hadith does not refer only to prayers but covers all good actions.

The hadith says that 'God is not bored until you are bored'. Scholars state that boredom, in the sense that we humans experience, does not apply to God, the Exalted. Therefore, the hadith must be understood in a special way. Some scholars have argued that this means God does not treat His servants like someone who is bored, stopping His reward, bounty and mercy, unless you stop your action. Others have said that it means that He is not bored when you are bored. This is mentioned by Ibn Qutaybah and others and is quoted by al-Khaṭṭābī and similarly others who have put their explanation into poetic form. They cite some comparable examples from Arabic literary heritage.

This hadith reflects the Prophet's compassionate care for his community. He shows the way that brings them what is best for them, which is what they can do regularly, without difficulty and without causing themselves any harm. Thus, one approaches such voluntary worship fresh and comfortable so that worship becomes perfect. This is unlike the one who commits himself to hard work, because he ultimately stops it or cuts it short, or he may do it with a shade of discomfort or unwillingness. Thus, he misses out on much benefit. In the Qur'an, God refers with disapproval to people who took their worship to extremes. He said: 'As for monastic asceticism, We did not enjoin it upon them. They invented it themselves out of a desire for God's goodly acceptance. Even so, they did not observe it as it should properly be observed' (57: 27). ʿAbdullāh ibn ʿAmr ibn al-ʿĀṣ regretted the fact that he did not accept the Prophet's advice to reduce his voluntary worship and instead committed himself to hard work.

The hadith mentions that 'the sort of action God loves best is what is done regularly, even though it may be little'. This encourages keeping up voluntary worship so that one does it regularly. It says that even a little that is done consistently and regularly is better than much more of it, if it is stopped. The little and regular is better than more which is stopped because the regularity of the first ensures continuous good action as well as sincerity of intention and eagerness to earn God's pleasure. Indeed, the regular little yields much greater reward than what is larger in volume but does not last.

The hadith then says: 'When the people in Muhammad's household did something, they would then do it regularly'. This means that they kept it up. It seems that in this instance, 'the people of Muhammad's household' refers to his close relatives, such as his wives and family.

CHAPTER 31

FEELING DROWSY DURING PRAYER

[1563–219]. (Dar al-Salam 1714–1715) Abu Bakr ibn Abi Shaybah narrated:[i] Ibn ʿUlayyah narrated [H]. Also, Zuhayr ibn Ḥarb narrated to me; Ismāʿīl narrated; from ʿAbd al-ʿAzīz ibn Ṣuhayb; from Anas. He said: **'God's Messenger (peace be upon him) came into the mosque and saw a rope tied to two pillars. He asked: "What is this for?" They said: "It is for Zaynab, when she prays. If she felt lazy or sleepy, she would hold on to it". The Prophet said: "Take it off. Let everyone of you pray when he is fresh. If he feels lazy or sleepy, he sits down".'**

In Zuhayr's narration: **'He should sit down'.**

وَحَدَّثَنَا أَبُو بَكْرِ بْنُ أَبِي شَيْبَةَ، حَدَّثَنَا ابْنُ عُلَيَّةَ، ح وَحَدَّثَنِي زُهَيْرُ بْنُ حَرْبٍ، حَدَّثَنَا إِسْمَاعِيلُ، عَنْ عَبْدِ الْعَزِيزِ بْنِ صُهَيْبٍ، عَنْ أَنَسٍ، قَالَ: دَخَلَ رَسُولُ اللهِ صَلَّى اللهُ عَلَيْهِ وَسَلَّمَ الْمَسْجِدَ وَحَبْلٌ مَمْدُودٌ بَيْنَ سَارِيَتَيْنِ فَقَالَ: «مَا هَذَا؟» . قَالُوا: لِزَيْنَبَ تُصَلِّي فَإِذَا كَسِلَتْ أَوْ فَتَرَتْ أَمْسَكَتْ بِهِ . فَقَالَ: «حُلُّوهُ لِيُصَلِّ أَحَدُكُمْ نَشَاطَهُ، فَإِذَا كَسِلَ أَوْ فَتَرَ قَعَدَ». وَفِي حَدِيثِ زُهَيْرٍ «فَلْيَقْعُدْ»

Shaybān ibn Farrūkh narrated:[ii] ʿAbd al-Wārith narrated; from ʿAbd al-ʿAzīz; from Anas; from the Prophet (peace be upon him): **the same text.**

---

i. Related by Abu Dāwūd, 1312.
ii. Related by al-Bukhari, 1150; al-Nasāʾī, 1642; Ibn Mājah, 1371.

وَحَدَّثَنَاهُ شَيْبَانُ بْنُ فَرُّوخَ، حَدَّثَنَا عَبْدُ الْوَارِثِ، عَنْ عَبْدِ الْعَزِيزِ، عَنْ أَنَسٍ، عَنِ النَّبِيِّ صَلَّى اللهُ عَلَيْهِ وَسَلَّمَ: مِثْلَهُ .

[1564–220]. (Dar al-Salam 1716) Ḥarmalah ibn Yaḥyā and Muhammad ibn Salamah al-Murādī narrated to me: Ibn Wahb narrated; from Yūnus; from Ibn Shihāb; he said: ʿUrwah ibn al-Zubayr reported to me; that ʿĀ'ishah, the Prophet's wife, mentioned to him that **al-Ḥawlā' bint Tuwayt ibn Ḥabīb ibn Asad ibn ʿAbd al-ʿUzzā passed by her when God's Messenger (peace be upon him) was with her. 'I [i.e. ʿĀ'ishah] said: "This is al-Ḥawlā' bint Tuwayt. They claim that she does not go to sleep at night". God's Messenger (peace be upon him) said: "She does not go to sleep at night! Do only what you can comfortably attend to. By God, God is not bored until you are bored".'**

وَحَدَّثَنِي حَرْمَلَةُ بْنُ يَحْيَى، وَمُحَمَّدُ بْنُ سَلَمَةَ الْمُرَادِيُّ، قَالا: حَدَّثَنَا ابْنُ وَهْبٍ، عَنْ يُونُسَ، عَنِ ابْنِ شِهَابٍ، قَالَ أَخْبَرَنِي عُرْوَةُ بْنُ الزُّبَيْرِ، أَنَّ عَائِشَةَ، زَوْجَ النَّبِيِّ صَلَّى اللهُ عَلَيْهِ وَسَلَّمَ أَخْبَرَتْهُ أَنَّ الْحَوْلاَءَ بِنْتَ تُوَيْتِ بْنِ حَبِيبِ بْنِ أَسَدِ بْنِ عَبْدِ الْعُزَّى مَرَّتْ بِهَا وَعِنْدَهَا رَسُولُ اللهِ صَلَّى اللهُ عَلَيْهِ وَسَلَّمَ فَقُلْتُ هَذِهِ الْحَوْلاَءُ بِنْتُ تُوَيْتٍ وَزَعَمُوا أَنَّهَا لاَ تَنَامُ اللَّيْلَ فَقَالَ رَسُولُ اللهِ صَلَّى اللهُ عَلَيْهِ وَسَلَّمَ «لاَ تَنَامُ اللَّيْلَ؟ خُذُوا مِنَ الْعَمَلِ مَا تُطِيقُونَ، فَوَاللهِ لاَ يَسْأَمُ اللهُ حَتَّى تَسْأَمُوا»

[1565–221]. (Dar al-Salam 1717) Abu Bakr ibn Abi Shaybah and Abu Kurayb narrated:[i] both said: Abu Usāmah narrated; from Hishām ibn ʿUrwah [H]. Also, Zuhayr ibn Ḥarb narrated

i. Abu Bakr ibn Abi Shaybah's narration is related by Ibn Mājah, 4238. Zuhayr ibn Ḥarb's narration is related by al-Bukhari, 43; al-Nasā'ī, 1641 and 5050.

to me (his text); Yaḥyā ibn Saʿīd narrated; from Hishām; he said: my father reported to me; from ʿĀ'ishah. She said: **'God's Messenger (peace be upon him) came in when I had a female visitor. He asked: "Who is this one?" I said: "A woman. She does not sleep, but she prays". He said: "Do of [voluntary] action what you can comfortably do. By God, God is not bored until you are bored". What the best of religion [i.e. the Prophet] loved best is what a person does regularly'.**

In Abu Usāmah's narration: **she was a woman from the Asad tribe.**

حَدَّثَنَا أَبُو بَكْرِ بْنُ أَبِي شَيْبَةَ، وَأَبُو كُرَيْبٍ قَالَ حَدَّثَنَا أَبُو أُسَامَةَ، عَنْ هِشَامِ بْنِ عُرْوَةَ ح وَحَدَّثَنِي زُهَيْرُ بْنُ حَرْبٍ، - وَاللَّفْظُ لَهُ - حَدَّثَنَا يَحْيَى بْنُ سَعِيدٍ، عَنْ هِشَامٍ، قَالَ: أَخْبَرَنِي أَبِي، عَنْ عَائِشَةَ، قَالَتْ: دَخَلَ عَلَيَّ رَسُولُ اللهِ صَلَّى اللهُ عَلَيْهِ وَسَلَّمَ وَعِنْدِي امْرَأَةٌ فَقَالَ: « مَنْ هَذِهِ؟» . فَقُلْتُ امْرَأَةٌ لاَ تَنَامُ تُصَلِّي . قَالَ: «عَلَيْكُمْ مِنَ الْعَمَلِ مَا تُطِيقُونَ فَوَاللهِ لاَ يَمَلُّ اللهُ حَتَّى تَمَلُّوا » . وَكَانَ أَحَبَّ الدِّينِ إِلَيْهِ مَا دَاوَمَ عَلَيْهِ صَاحِبُهُ وَفِي حَدِيثِ أَبِي أُسَامَةَ أَنَّهَا امْرَأَةٌ مِنْ بَنِي أَسَدٍ .

[1566–222]. (Dar al-Salam 1718) Abu Bakr ibn Abi Shaybah narrated:[i] ʿAbdullāh ibn Numayr narrated [H]. Also, Abu Kurayb narrated; Abu Usāmah narrated; all from Hishām ibn ʿUrwah [H]. And, Qutaybah ibn Saʿīd narrated (his text); from Mālik ibn Anas; from Hishām ibn ʿUrwah; from his father; from ʿĀ'ishah; that the Prophet (peace be upon him) said: **'If any of you feels drowsy when he is praying, let him sleep until his drowsiness is gone. If any of you is praying while he is sleepy, he might try to pray for forgiveness, but he would abuse himself instead'.**

i. Abu Bakr ibn Abi Shaybah's and Ibn Numayr's narrations are related by Ibn Mājah, 1370; Qutaybah's narration is related by al-Bukhari, 212; Abu Dāwūd, 1310.

حَدَّثَنَا أَبُو بَكْرِ بْنُ أَبِي شَيْبَةَ، حَدَّثَنَا عَبْدُ اللهِ بْنُ نُمَيْرٍ، ح وَحَدَّثَنَا ابْنُ نُمَيْرٍ، حَدَّثَنَا أَبِي ح، وَحَدَّثَنَا أَبُو كُرَيْبٍ، حَدَّثَنَا أَبُو أُسَامَةَ، جَمِيعًا عَنْ هِشَامِ بْنِ عُرْوَةَ، ح وَحَدَّثَنَا قُتَيْبَةُ، بْنُ سعيد - واللَّفْظُ لَهُ - عَنْ مَالِكِ بْنِ أَنَسٍ، عَنْ هِشَامِ بْنِ عُرْوَةَ، عَنْ أَبِيهِ، عَنْ عَائِشَةَ، أَنَّ النَّبِيَّ صَلَّى اللهُ عَلَيْهِ وَسَلَّمَ قَالَ «إِذَا نَعَسَ أَحَدُكُمْ فِي الصَّلاَةِ فَلْيَرْقُدْ حَتَّى يَذْهَبَ عَنْهُ النَّوْمُ. فَإِنَّ أَحَدَكُمْ إِذَا صَلَّى وَهُوَ نَاعِسٌ، لَعَلَّهُ يَذْهَبُ يَسْتَغْفِرُ فَيَسُبُّ نَفْسَهُ» .

[1567–223]. (Dar al-Salam 1719) Muhammad ibn Rāfiʿ narrated:[i] ʿAbd al-Razzāq narrated; Maʿmar narrated; from Hammām ibn Munabbih; he said: This is what Abu Hurayrah narrated to us from Muhammad, God's Messenger (peace be upon him). He mentioned several hadiths, including: and **'God's Messenger (peace be upon him) said: "If any of you rises to pray during the night and he feels that he is not pronouncing the Qur'an well and he does not realise what he is saying, he should lie down".'**

وَحَدَّثَنَا مُحَمَّدُ بْنُ رَافِعٍ، حَدَّثَنَا عَبْدُ الرَّزَّاقِ، حَدَّثَنَا مَعْمَرٌ، عَنْ هَمَّامِ بْنِ مُنَبِّهٍ، قَالَ: هَذَا مَا حَدَّثَنَا أَبُو هُرَيْرَةَ، عَنْ مُحَمَّدٍ، رَسُولِ اللهِ صَلَّى اللهُ عَلَيْهِ وَسَلَّمَ، فَذَكَرَ أَحَادِيثَ مِنْهَا وَقَالَ رَسُولُ اللهِ صَلَّى اللهُ عَلَيْهِ وَسَلَّمَ: «إِذَا قَامَ أَحَدُكُمْ مِنَ اللَّيْلِ فَاسْتَعْجَمَ الْقُرْآنُ عَلَى لِسَانِهِ، فَلَمْ يَدْرِ مَا يَقُولُ، فَلْيَضْطَجِعْ».

Text Explanation

In hadith No. 1566, the Prophet says: 'If any of you feels drowsy when he is praying, let him sleep until his drowsiness is gone'. The hadith urges that prayer should be approached with a calm feeling, proper attention and freshness. It includes an order to anyone feeling sleepy or drowsy to go to sleep or do whatever expels drowsiness.

---

i. Related by Abu Dāwūd, 1311.

This is a general order that applies to obligatory and recommended prayers, whether done during the night or during the day. This is the view of our school and the majority of scholars. However, one should not let oneself miss an obligatory prayer through such sleep. *Qadi* ʿIyāḍ said that Mālik and a number of scholars understand the hadith to refer to voluntary night worship because it is at night that people normally sleep.

In the same hadith, the Prophet said: 'If any of you is praying while he is sleepy, he might try to pray for forgiveness, but he would abuse himself instead'. *Qadi* ʿIyāḍ said: 'In this instance, "pray for forgiveness" means supplication'.

In hadith No. 1567, the Prophet mentions the case of one who 'feels that he is not pronouncing the Qur'an well'. This refers to anyone who seems to have a block preventing them from vocalising the words correctly because of feeling very sleepy.

CHAPTER 32 AND 33

THE QUR'AN AND ITS MEMORISATION

[1568–224]. (Dar al-Salam 1720) Abu Bakr ibn Abi Shaybah and Abu Kurayb narrated:[i] both said: Abu Usāmah narrated; from Hishām; from his father; from ʿĀ'ishah; that **'The Prophet (peace be upon him) heard someone reciting [the Qur'an] in the night. He said: "May God bestow mercy on him. He reminded me of such-and-such, a verse from surah so-and-so which I had left out".'**

حَدَّثَنَا أَبُو بَكْرِ بْنُ أَبِي شَيْبَةَ، وَأَبُو كُرَيْبٍ قَالا: حَدَّثَنَا أَبُو أُسَامَةَ، عَنْ هِشَامٍ، عَنْ أَبِيهِ، عَنْ عَائِشَةَ أَنَّ النَّبِيَّ صَلَّى اللهُ عَلَيْهِ وَسَلَّمَ سَمِعَ رَجُلاً يَقْرَأُ مِنَ اللَّيْلِ فَقَالَ: «يَرْحَمُهُ اللهُ لَقَدْ أَذْكَرَنِي كَذَا وَكَذَا آيَةً كُنْتُ أَسْقَطْتُهَا مِنْ سُورَةِ كَذَا وَكَذَا».

[1569–225]. (Dar al-Salam 1721) Ibn Numayr narrated:[ii] ʿAbdah and Abu Muʿāwiyah narrated; from Hishām; from his father; from ʿĀ'ishah. She said: **'The Prophet was listening to the recitation of someone in the mosque. He said: "May God bestow mercy on him. He reminded me of a verse which I was made to forget".'**

---

i. Related by al-Bukhari, 5038.
ii. Related by al-Bukhari, 6335.

وَحَدَّثَنَا ابْنُ نُمَيْرٍ، حَدَّثَنَا عَبْدَةُ وَأَبُو مُعَاوِيَةَ عَنْ هِشَامٍ، عَنْ أَبِيهِ، عَنْ عَائِشَةَ قَالَتْ: كَانَ النَّبِيُّ صَلَّى اللهُ عَلَيْهِ وَسَلَّمَ يَسْتَمِعُ قِرَاءَةَ رَجُلٍ فِي الْمَسْجِدِ . فَقَالَ: « رَحِمَهُ اللهُ لَقَدْ أَذْكَرَنِي آيَةً كُنْتُ أُنْسِيتُهَا » .

[1570–226]. (Dar al-Salam 1722) Yaḥyā ibn Yaḥyā narrated:[i] I read out to Mālik; from Nāfiʿ; from ʿAbdullāh ibn ʿUmar; that God's Messenger (peace be upon him) said: **'A person who learns the Qur'an is like the owner of tied up camels; if he attends to them, he holds them, but if he lets them loose, they will go away'.**

حَدَّثَنَا يَحْيَى بْنُ يَحْيَى، قَالَ قَرَأْتُ عَلَى مَالِكٍ عَنْ نَافِعٍ، عَنْ عَبْدِ اللهِ بْنِ عُمَرَ، أَنَّ رَسُولَ اللهِ صَلَّى اللهُ عَلَيْهِ وَسَلَّمَ قَالَ: « إِنَّمَا مَثَلُ صَاحِبِ الْقُرْآنِ كَمَثَلِ الإِبِلِ الْمُعَقَّلَةِ: إِنْ عَاهَدَ عَلَيْهَا أَمْسَكَهَا وَإِنْ أَطْلَقَهَا ذَهَبَتْ » .

[1571–227]. (Dar al-Salam 1723) Zuhayr ibn Ḥarb, Muhammad ibn al-Muthannā and ʿUbaydullāh ibn Saʿīd narrated: they said: Yaḥyā (who is al-Qaṭṭān) narrated [H]. Also, Abu Bakr ibn Abi Shaybah narrated; Abu Khālid al-Aḥmar narrated [H]. And, Ibn Numayr narrated; my father narrated; all of them from ʿUbaydullāh [H]. Also, Ibn Abi ʿUmar narrated; ʿAbd al-Razzāq narrated; Maʿmar reported; from Ayyūb [H]. Further, Qutaybah ibn Saʿīd narrated; Yaʿqūb (meaning Ibn ʿ Abd al-Raḥmān) narrated [H]. Also, Muhammad ibn Isḥāq al-Musayyibī narrated; Anas (meaning Ibn ʿIyāḍ) narrated; all from Mūsā ibn ʿUqbah; and all these from Nāfiʿ; from Ibn ʿUmar; from the Prophet (peace be upon him): **the same meaning as the text narrated by Mālik**.

i. Related by al-Bukhari, 5031; al-Nasā'ī, 941.

In Mūsā ibn ʿUqbah's narration, there is the following addition: **'If the one who memorises the Qur'an rises and recites it at night and during the day, he will retain it in memory. If he does not, he will forget it'.**

حَدَّثَنَا زُهَيْرُ بْنُ حَرْبٍ، وَمُحَمَّدُ بْنُ الْـمُثَنَّى، وَعُبَيْدُ اللهِ بْنُ سَعِيدٍ، قَالُوا: حَدَّثَنَا يَحْيَى، وَهُوَ الْقَطَّانُ ح. وَحَدَّثَنَا أَبُو بَكْرِ بْنُ أَبِي شَيْبَةَ، حَدَّثَنَا أَبُو خَالِدٍ الأَحْمَرُ، ح. وَحَدَّثَنَا ابْنُ نُمَيْرٍ، حَدَّثَنَا أَبِي كُلُّهُمْ، عَنْ عُبَيْدِ اللهِ، ح. وَحَدَّثَنَا ابْنُ أَبِي عُمَرَ، حَدَّثَنَا عَبْدُ الرَّزَّاقِ، أَخْبَرَنَا مَعْمَرٌ، عَنْ أَيُّوبَ، ح. وَحَدَّثَنَا قُتَيْبَةُ بْنُ سَعِيدٍ، حَدَّثَنَا يَعْقُوبُ يَعْنِي ابْنَ عَبْدِ الرَّحْمَنِ، ح. وَحَدَّثَنَا مُحَمَّدُ بْنُ إِسْحَاقَ الْـمُسَيَّبِيُّ حَدَّثَنَا أَنَسٌ - يَعْنِي ابْنَ عِيَاضٍ. جَمِيعًا عَنْ مُوسَى بْنِ عُقْبَةَ، كُلُّ هَؤُلاَءِ عَنْ نَافِعٍ، عَنِ ابْنِ عُمَرَ، عَنِ النَّبِيِّ. بِمَعْنَى حَدِيثِ مَالِكٍ، وَزَادَ فِي حَدِيثِ مُوسَى بْنِ عُقْبَةَ: « وَإِذَا قَامَ صَاحِبُ الْقُرْآنِ فَقَرَأَهُ بِاللَّيْلِ وَالنَّهَارِ ذَكَرَهُ، وَإِذَا لَمْ يَقُمْ بِهِ نَسِيَهُ».

[1572–228]. (Dar al-Salam 1724) Zuhayr ibn Ḥarb, ʿUthmān ibn Abi Shaybah and Isḥāq ibn Ibrāhīm narrated:[i] Jarīr (Isḥāq said: 'reported', and the other two said: 'narrated'); from Manṣūr; from Abu Wā'il; from ʿAbdullāh. He said: **'God's Messenger (peace be upon him) said: "It is bad of anyone to say: 'I have forgotten such-and-such verse'. He is in fact made to forget it. Revise the Qur'an regularly, for it is quicker to drop out of people's memory than tied camels getting loose".'**

وَحَدَّثَنَا زُهَيْرُ بْنُ حَرْبٍ، وَعُثْمَانُ بْنُ أَبِي شَيْبَةَ، وَإِسْحَاقُ بْنُ إِبْرَاهِيمَ. قَالَ إِسْحَاقُ أَخْبَرَنَا وَقَالَ الآخَرَانِ حَدَّثَنَا جَرِيرٌ، عَنْ مَنْصُورٍ، عَنْ أَبِي وَائِلٍ، عَنْ عَبْدِ اللهِ قَالَ: قَالَ رَسُولُ اللهِ صَلَّى اللهُ عَلَيْهِ وَسَلَّمَ: «بِئْسَمَا لأَحَدِهِمْ يَقُولُ نَسِيتُ آيَةَ كَيْتَ وَكَيْتَ بَلْ هُوَ نُسِّيَ. اسْتَذْكِرُوا الْقُرْآنَ، فَلَهُوَ أَشَدُّ تَفَصِّيًا مِنْ صُدُورِ الرِّجَالِ مِنَ النَّعَمِ بِعُقُلِهَا».

---

i. Related by al-Bukhari, 5032 and in a shorter version, 5039; al-Tirmidhī, 2942; al-Nasā'ī, 942.

[1573–229]. (Dar al-Salam 1725) Ibn Numayr narrated: my father and Abu Muʿāwiyah narrated [H]. Also, Yaḥyā ibn Yaḥyā narrated (his text); he said: Abu Muʿāwiyah reported; from al-Aʿmash; from Shaqīq; he said: ʿAbdullāh said: **'Revise these books, or perhaps he said the Qur'an. For, it is quicker to drop out of people's memory than tied camels getting loose'. And God's Messenger (peace be upon him) said: 'Let none of you say: I have forgotten such-and-such verse. He is only made to forget it'.**

حَدَّثَنَا ابْنُ نُمَيْرٍ، حَدَّثَنَا أَبِي وَأَبُو مُعَاوِيَةَ ح. وَحَدَّثَنَا يَحْيَى بْنُ يَحْيَى، - وَاللَّفْظُ لَهُ - قَالَ أَخْبَرَنَا أَبُو مُعَاوِيَةَ، عَنِ الأَعْمَشِ، عَنْ شَقِيقٍ قَالَ: قَالَ عَبْدُ اللهِ: تَعَاهَدُوا هَذِهِ الْمَصَاحِفَ - وَرُبَّمَا قَالَ الْقُرْآنَ - فَلَهُوَ أَشَدُّ تَفَصِّيًا مِنْ صُدُورِ الرِّجَالِ مِنَ النَّعَمِ مِنْ عُقُلِهِ. قَالَ: وَقَالَ رَسُولُ اللهِ صَلَّى اللهُ عَلَيْهِ وَسَلَّمَ: «لاَ يَقُلْ أَحَدُكُمْ نَسِيتُ آيَةَ كَيْتَ وَكَيْتَ بَلْ هُوَ نُسِّيَ».

[1574–230]. (Dar al-Salam 1726) Muhammad ibn Ḥātim narrated to me:[i] Muhammad ibn Bakr narrated; Ibn Jurayj reported; ʿAbdah ibn Abi Lubābah narrated to me; from Shaqīq ibn Salamah; he said: I heard Ibn Masʿūd say: I heard God's Messenger (peace be upon him) say: **'It is bad of a man to say: "I have forgotten surah so-and-so, or I have forgotten verse such-and-such". He is only made to forget it'.**

وَحَدَّثَنِي مُحَمَّدُ بْنُ حَاتِمٍ، حَدَّثَنَا مُحَمَّدُ بْنُ بَكْرٍ، أَخْبَرَنَا ابْنُ جُرَيْجٍ، حَدَّثَنِي عَبْدَةُ بْنُ أَبِي لُبَابَةَ عَنْ شَقِيقِ بْنِ سَلَمَةَ، قَالَ: سَمِعْتُ ابْنَ مَسْعُودٍ يَقُولُ سَمِعْتُ رَسُولَ اللهِ صَلَّى اللهُ عَلَيْهِ وَسَلَّمَ يَقُولُ: «بِئْسَمَا لِلرَّجُلِ أَنْ يَقُولَ نَسِيتُ سُورَةَ كَيْتَ وَكَيْتَ أَوْ نَسِيتُ آيَةَ كَيْتَ وَكَيْتَ بَلْ هُوَ نُسِّيَ».

i. Related by al-Bukhari, 5032.

[1575–231]. (Dar al-Salam 1727) ʿAbdullāh ibn Barrād al-Ashʿarī and Abu Kurayb narrated:[i] both said: Abu Usāmah narrated; from Burayd; from Abu Burdah; from Abu Mūsā; from the Prophet (peace be upon him). He said: **'Keep revising this Qur'an. By Him who holds Muhammad's soul in His hand, it is more likely to skip out of memory than tied up camels'.**

The text of the hadith is Ibn Barrād's.

حَدَّثَنَا عَبْدُ اللهِ بْنُ بَرَّادٍ الأَشْعَرِيُّ، وَأَبُو كُرَيْبٍ قَالا: حَدَّثَنَا أَبُو أُسَامَةَ، عَنْ بُرَيْدٍ، عَنْ أَبِي بُرْدَةَ، عَنْ أَبِي مُوسَى، عَنِ النَّبِيِّ صَلَّى اللهُ عَلَيْهِ وَسَلَّمَ قَالَ: «تَعَاهَدُوا هَذَا الْقُرْآنَ فَوَالَّذِي نَفْسُ مُحَمَّدٍ بِيَدِهِ لَهُوَ أَشَدُّ تَفَلُّتًا مِنَ الإِبِلِ فِي عُقُلِهَا». وَلَفْظُ الْحَدِيثِ لِابْنِ بَرَّادٍ.

Text Explanation

In hadith No. 1568, 'The Prophet (peace be upon him) heard someone reciting [the Qur'an] in the night. He said: "May God bestow mercy on him. He reminded me of such-and-such, a verse from surah so-and-so which I had left out".' And in hadith No. 1568, 'The Prophet was listening to the recitation of someone in the mosque. He said: "May God bestow mercy on him. He reminded me of a verse which I was made to forget".' And in a subsequent hadith, No. 1572, the Prophet says: 'It is bad of anyone to say: "I have forgotten such-and-such verse". He is, in fact, made to forget it'.

These narrations give us a number of useful points, including that it is permissible to recite the Qur'an aloud at night and in the mosque. There is no discouragement in the matter if it does not inconvenience anyone else and does not lead to showing off or seeking admiration and praise, etc. Another point is to pray for someone who has caused us some benefit, even though it was unintended by that person. It also makes clear that listening to the Qur'an is a sunnah. The hadiths

---

i. Related by al-Bukhari, 5033.

also show that it is permissible to say surah so-and-so, such as saying Surah The Cow. No attention need be given to anyone who disagrees with this, since several authentic hadiths use this formula.

The hadiths discourage saying 'I have forgotten' this verse of the Qur'an, and this is of the mild type of discouragement, but it is acceptable to say: 'I was made to forget it'. The first is discouraged because it implies negligence and overlooking one's duty. God says in the Qur'an: 'Our revelations were brought to you, but you were oblivious of them' (20: 126). *Qadi* ʿIyāḍ said: 'The best that may be said concerning understanding of the hadith is a criticism of the scenario, not the words. To say: "I have forgotten" describes the situation of one who learnt the Qur'an by heart but then neglected its revision until he had forgotten it'.

The fact that the Prophet said, 'a verse which I was made to forget', shows that the Prophet could forget something that he had delivered to his community. We mentioned when we spoke about prostration to rectify errors in prayer, the areas where the Prophet could forget things and those where he could not. *Qadi* ʿIyāḍ said: 'The majority of meticulous scholars agree that the Prophet might forget something that was not part of what he needed to deliver of his message. As for what he needed to deliver and teach, their views differed. Those who said that he could forget added that he would not be left in that condition. He would be reminded or he would remember. They further differed as to whether the reminder or the remembrance would be immediate or at some later time, but before his death. Forgetting what he had already delivered, as in this hadith, is possible. We have already discussed how the Prophet forgot during his prayer. Some Sufis and their followers have claimed that forgetfulness did not apply to him in anything whatsoever, but it might have occurred in form only. This is a clear contradiction, which is unacceptable. No scholar worthy of name said it, except Abu al-Muẓaffar Shāhfūr al-Isfarāyīnī, a prominent Shāfiʿī scholar, who leaned towards this view. It remains unsupportable and self-contradictory.

In hadith No. 1570, the Prophet gives the following simile: 'A person who learns the Qur'an is like the owner of tied up camels: if he attends to them, he holds them, but if he lets them loose, they will go away'. This hadith urges the frequent revision of what one has learnt by heart of the Qur'an and reciting it so as not to forget. The Prophet uses the expression *ṣāḥib al-Qur'an,* which means 'one who has got the Qur'an'. *Qadi* 'Iyāḍ says that the word *ṣāḥib* refers to one who knows it well as a result of frequent association. Linguistically, the word means 'friend or Companion', and in this instance, it means the one who always recites the Qur'an.

In several of these hadiths, the Prophet brings home to his listeners the need to frequently revise what they have memorised of the Qur'an, particularly those who know it all by heart. He repeatedly mentioned that it is easy to forget, citing the example of camels that need to have their legs tied at their knees to prevent their breaking loose. He tells us that the Qur'an is easier to drop out of one's memory than untied camels breaking loose. It is well-known that a camel breaks loose at the first opportunity.

CHAPTER 34

IMPROVING ONE'S VOICE WHEN RECITING THE QUR'AN

[1576–232]. (Dar al-Salam 1728) ʿAmr al-Nāqid and Zuhayr ibn Ḥarb narrated to me:[i] both said: Sufyān ibn ʿUyaynah narrated; from al-Zuhrī; from Abu Salamah; from Abu Hurayrah quoting the Prophet (peace be upon him): **'God does not listen to anything as well as He listens to a prophet chanting the Qur'an'.**

حَدَّثَنِي عَمْرٌو النَّاقِدُ، وَزُهَيْرُ بْنُ حَرْبٍ، قَالا: حَدَّثَنَا سُفْيَانُ بْنُ عُيَيْنَةَ، عَنِ الزُّهْرِيِّ، عَنْ أَبِي سَلَمَةَ، عَنْ أَبِي هُرَيْرَةَ، يَبْلُغُ بِهِ النَّبِيَّ صَلَّى اللهُ عَلَيْهِ وَسَلَّمَ قَالَ: « مَا أَذِنَ اللهُ لِشَيْءٍ مَا أَذِنَ لِنَبِيٍّ يَتَغَنَّى بِالْقُرْآنِ » .

[1577–000]. (Dar al-Salam 1729) Ḥarmalah ibn Yaḥyā narrated to me: Ibn Wahb reported; Yunus reported to me [H]. Also, Yūnus ibn ʿAbd al-Aʿlā narrated to me; Ibn Wahb reported; ʿAmr reported to me; both from Ibn Shihāb; with the same chain of transmission. He said: **'In the same way as He listens to a prophet chanting the Qur'an'.**

وَحَدَّثَنِي حَرْمَلَةُ بْنُ يَحْيَى، أَخْبَرَنَا ابْنُ وَهْبٍ، أَخْبَرَنِي يُونُسُ، ح. وَحَدَّثَنِي يُونُسُ بْنُ عَبْدِ الأَعْلَى أَخْبَرَنَا ابْنُ وَهْبٍ، أَخْبَرَنِي عَمْرٌو، كِلاهُمَا عَنِ ابْنِ شِهَابٍ، بِهَذَا الإِسْنَادِ قَالَ: « كَمَا يَأْذَنُ لِنَبِيٍّ يَتَغَنَّى بِالْقُرْآنِ ».

i. Related by al-Bukhari, 5024; al-Nasā'ī, 1017

[1578–233]. (Dar al-Salam 1730–1731) Bishr ibn al-Ḥakam narrated to me:[i] ʿAbd al-ʿAzīz ibn Muhammad narrated; Yazīd (who is Ibn al-Hād) narrated; from Muhammad ibn Ibrāhīm; from Abu Salamah; from Abu Hurayrah; that he heard God's Messenger (peace be upon him) say: **'God has not listened to anything more than He does to a prophet with a sweet voice, chanting the Qur'an, reciting it aloud'.**

حَدَّثَنِي بِشْرُ بْنُ الْحَكَمِ، حَدَّثَنَا عَبْدُ الْعَزِيزِ بْنُ مُحَمَّدٍ، حَدَّثَنَا يَزِيدُ - وَهُوَ ابْنُ الْهَادِ - عَنْ مُحَمَّدِ بْنِ إِبْرَاهِيمَ، عَنْ أَبِي سَلَمَةَ، عَنْ أَبِي هُرَيْرَةَ، أَنَّهُ سَمِعَ رَسُولَ اللهِ صَلَّى اللهُ عَلَيْهِ وَسَلَّمَ يَقُولُ: «مَا أَذِنَ اللهُ لِشَيْءٍ مَا أَذِنَ لِنَبِيٍّ حَسَنِ الصَّوْتِ يَتَغَنَّى بِالْقُرْآنِ يَجْهَرُ بِهِ»

Ibn Wahb's nephew narrated to me: my paternal uncle ʿAbdullāh ibn Wahb narrated; ʿUmar ibn Mālik and Ḥaywah ibn Shurayḥ reported to me; from Ibn al-Hād, with the same chain of transmission: **exactly the same text, except that [Abu Hurayrah said]: 'God's Messenger (peace be upon him) said', and not that 'he heard God's Messenger say'.**

وَحَدَّثَنِي ابْنُ أَخِي ابْنِ وَهْبٍ، حَدَّثَنَا عَمِّي عَبْدُ اللهِ بْنُ وَهْبٍ، أَخْبَرَنِي عُمَرُ بْنُ مَالِكٍ وَحَيْوَةُ بْنُ شُرَيْحٍ عَنِ ابْنِ الْهَادِ، بِهَذَا الإِسْنَادِ. مِثْلَهُ سَوَاءً وَقَالَ إِنَّ رَسُولَ اللهِ صَلَّى اللهُ عَلَيْهِ وَسَلَّمَ. وَلَمْ يَقُلْ سَمِعَ.

[1579–234]. (Dar al-Salam 1732) al-Ḥakam ibn Mūsā narrated: Hiql narrated; from al-Awzāʿī; from Yaḥyā ibn Abi Kathīr; from Abu Salamah; from Abu Hurayrah. He said: **'God's Messenger (peace be upon him) said: "God has not listened to anything in the same way as He does to a prophet chanting the Qur'an, reciting it aloud".'**

---

i. Related by al-Bukhari, 7544; Abu Dāwūd, 1473; al-Nasāʾī, 1016.

وَحَدَّثَنَا الْحَكَمُ بْنُ مُوسَى، حَدَّثَنَا هِقْلٌ، عَنِ الأَوْزَاعِيِّ، عَنْ يَحْيَى بْنِ أَبِي كَثِيرٍ، عَنْ أَبِي سَلَمَةَ، عَنْ أَبِي هُرَيْرَةَ قَالَ: قَالَ رَسُولُ اللهِ صَلَّى اللهُ عَلَيْهِ وَسَلَّمَ: « مَا أَذِنَ اللهُ لِشَيْءٍ كَأَذَنِهِ لِنَبِيٍّ يَتَغَنَّى بِالْقُرْآنِ يَجْهَرُ بِهِ».

[1580–000]. (Dar al-Salam 1733) Yaḥyā ibn Ayyūb, Qutaybah ibn Saʿīd and Ibn Ḥujr narrated: they said: Ismāʿīl (who is Ibn Jaʿfar) narrated; from Muhammad ibn ʿAmr; from Abu Salamah; from Abu Hurayrah; from the Prophet: **the same text as narrated by Yaḥyā ibn Abi Kathīr, except that Ibn Ayyūb used in his narration a variant of one word but with the same meaning.**

وَحَدَّثَنَا يَحْيَى بْنُ أَيُّوبَ، وَقُتَيْبَةُ بْنُ سَعِيدٍ، وَابْنُ حُجْرٍ قَالُوا: حَدَّثَنَا إِسْمَاعِيلُ، - وَهُوَ ابْنُ جَعْفَرٍ - عَنْ مُحَمَّدِ بْنِ عَمْرٍو، عَنْ أَبِي سَلَمَةَ، عَنْ أَبِي هُرَيْرَةَ، عَنِ النَّبِيِّ صَلَّى اللهُ عَلَيْهِ وَسَلَّمَ . مِثْلَ حَدِيثِ يَحْيَى بْنِ أَبِي كَثِيرٍ، غَيْرَ أَنَّ ابْنَ أَيُّوبَ قَالَ فِي رِوَايَتِهِ: «كَإِذْنِهِ».

[1581–235]. (Dar al-Salam 1734) Abu Bakr ibn Abi Shaybah narrated: ʿAbdullāh ibn Numayr narrated [H]. Ibn Numayr narrated; my father narrated; Mālik (who is Ibn Mighwal) narrated; from ʿAbdullāh ibn Buraydah; from his father who said: **'God's Messenger (peace be upon him) said: "ʿAbdullāh ibn Qays, or al-Ashʿarī, has been given a voice like those of David's household".'**

حَدَّثَنَا أَبُو بَكْرِ بْنُ أَبِي شَيْبَةَ، حَدَّثَنَا عَبْدُ اللهِ بْنُ نُمَيْرٍ، ح وَحَدَّثَنَا ابْنُ نُمَيْرٍ، حَدَّثَنَا أَبِي، حَدَّثَنَا مَالِكٌ، - وَهُوَ ابْنُ مِغْوَلٍ - عَنْ عَبْدِ اللهِ بْنِ بُرَيْدَةَ، عَنْ أَبِيهِ، قَالَ قَالَ رَسُولُ اللهِ صَلَّى اللهُ عَلَيْهِ وَسَلَّمَ «إِنَّ عَبْدَ اللهِ بْنَ قَيْسٍ أَوِ الأَشْعَرِيَّ أُعْطِيَ مِزْمَارًا مِنْ مَزَامِيرِ آلِ دَاوُدَ »

[1582–236]. (Dar al-Salam 1735) Dāwūd ibn Rushayd narrated: Yaḥyā ibn Saʿīd narrated; Ṭalḥah narrated; from Abu Burdah; from Abu Mūsā. He said: **'God's Messenger (peace be upon him) said to Abu Mūsā: "I wish you had seen me as I listened to your recitation last night. You have been given a voice like those of David's household".'**

وَحَدَّثَنَا دَاوُدُ بْنُ رُشَيْدٍ، حَدَّثَنَا يَحْيَى بْنُ سَعِيدٍ، حَدَّثَنَا طَلْحَةُ، عَنْ أَبِي بُرْدَةَ، عَنْ أَبِي مُوسَى قَالَ: قَالَ رَسُولُ اللهِ صَلَّى اللهُ عَلَيْهِ وَسَلَّمَ لِأَبِي مُوسَى: «لَوْ رَأَيْتَنِي وَأَنَا أَسْتَمِعُ لِقِرَاءَتِكَ الْبَارِحَةَ. لَقَدْ أُوتِيتَ مِزْمَارًا مِنْ مَزَامِيرِ آلِ دَاوُدَ».

Text Explanation

In hadith No. 1576, the Prophet says: 'God does not listen to anything as well as He listens to a prophet chanting the Qur'an'. In its essential linguistic meaning, the Arabic word, *adhina*, means 'to listen'. Scholars say that this word, as used in these hadiths, must not be understood in its linguistic meaning, i.e. listening, because it cannot apply to God. It is used in a figurative sense, which means that He approves of the reciter and gives him rich reward. God's hearing is not subject to variation. Hence, a different understanding is needed.

The hadiths also use the word *yataghannā*, which means 'to chant, sing, etc.' According to al-Shāfiʿī and the majority of scholars of different disciplines, it means using one's best voice. However, Sufyān ibn ʿUyaynah takes the word in its other sense, which makes the meaning of the hadith as 'to consider the Qur'an as sufficient for oneself so as to be in no need of anyone'. It is also said that it means 'to consider oneself in no need of other books or discourses'. *Qadi* ʿIyāḍ said that both meanings have been reported from Ibn ʿUyaynah. Al-Shāfiʿī and those who share his view say that it means to give the recitation a 'soft and sad tone'. They cite the other hadith which says: 'Add to [the meanings] of the Qur'an with your voices'. Al-Harawī said: 'chanting the Qur'an' refers to reciting it aloud'. Al-Ṭabarī disapproves of interpreting it as meaning to consider it sufficient for oneself. He adds that it is wrong from the linguistic viewpoint and the particular sense of the hadiths. The same difference of views applies to the other hadith which says: 'A person who does not chant the Qur'an does not belong to us'. The correct meaning is that it refers to using one's best voice. This is endorsed by the other hadith saying: 'chanting the Qur'an, reciting it aloud'.

In hadith No. 1580, we read: 'except that Ibn Ayyūb used in his narration a variant of one word but with the same meaning'. The word that is varied is *adhina*, which primarily means 'to listen'. The variant used by Ibn Ayyūb is *idhn*, which means 'permission'. *Qadi* 'Iyāḍ said that according to this narration, the hadith encourages reciting the Qur'an aloud and chanting it.

In reference to Abu Mūsā al-Ash'arī [whose name is 'Abdullāh ibn Qays], the Prophet says in hadith No. 1581 and 1582 that he was given 'a voice like those of David's household'. The expression 'David's household' refers to Prophet David himself. This is recognised usage in Arabic. Prophet David had a very sweet voice. In No. 1582, the Prophet said to Abu Mūsā: 'I wish you had seen me as I listened to your recitation last night. You have been given a voice like those of David's household'. In the hadith that follows in the next chapter, the Prophet recited and repeated in his recitation. *Qadi* 'Iyāḍ said: 'Scholars are unanimous that it is desirable to try to improve one's voice as one recites the Qur'an and to make one's recitation properly understood'. Abu 'Ubayd said: 'The hadiths that speak of this are understood to mean adding a tinge of sadness and emotion when one recites'. He adds that scholars differ as to the desirability of using musical tones in one's recitation. Mālik and the majority of scholars discourage this because they consider it inconsistent with the Qur'an and with reflection on its meanings. Abu Ḥanīfah and a number of early scholars say that it is permissible because musical tone helps to soften hearts and adds to fearing God. It makes people eager to listen to the Qur'an. At one place, al-Shāfi'ī says that he dislikes using musical tones when reciting the Qur'an, but he says in another place that he does not dislike it. Our scholars say that he did not have two different opinions on this point. It is a view that looks at two different situations. If the reciter uses unacceptable elongations and causes the words to give different senses, adding to or omitting some of their meanings, elongating what should not be long or assimilating what should not be assimilated, then this is unacceptable. On the other hand, if using musical tones does not alter the sense of the words and sentences, it is acceptable, but God knows best.

CHAPTER 35

THE PROPHET'S RECITATION OF SURAH AL-FATḤ ON THE DAY MAKKAH FELL TO ISLAM

[1583–237]. (Dar al-Salam 1736) Abu Bakr ibn Abi Shaybah narrated:[i] ʿAbdullāh ibn Idrīs and Wakīʿ narrated; from Shuʿbah; from Muʿāwiyah ibn Qurrah; he said: I heard ʿAbdullāh ibn Mughaffal al-Muzanī say: **'The Prophet (peace be upon him) recited Surah al-Fatḥ [i.e. Surah 47, Victory] as he was riding his she-camel in the year of the fall of Makkah, and he chanted, repeating in his recitation'.**

Muʿāwiyah said: 'Were it not for my fear that people will gather around me, I would have imitated his recitation'.

حَدَّثَنَا أَبُو بَكْرِ بْنُ أَبِي شَيْبَةَ، حَدَّثَنَا عَبْدُ اللهِ بْنُ إِدْرِيسَ وَوَكِيعٌ، عَنْ شُعْبَةَ، عَنْ مُعَاوِيَةَ بْنِ قُرَّةَ، قَالَ: سَمِعْتُ عَبْدَ اللهِ بْنَ مُغَفَّلٍ الْمُزَنِيَّ يَقُولُ: قَرَأَ النَّبِيُّ صَلَّى اللهُ عَلَيْهِ وَسَلَّمَ عَامَ الْفَتْحِ فِي مَسِيرٍ لَهُ سُورَةَ الْفَتْحِ عَلَى رَاحِلَتِهِ، فَرَجَّعَ فِي قِرَاءَتِهِ .

قَالَ مُعَاوِيَةُ: لَوْلاَ أَنِّي أَخَافُ أَنْ يَجْتَمِعَ عَلَيَّ النَّاسُ لَحَكَيْتُ لَكُمْ قِرَاءَتَهُ.

[1584–238]. (Dar al-Salam 1737) Muhammad ibn al-Muthannā and Muhammad ibn Bashshār narrated: Ibn al-Muthannā said: Muhammad ibn Jaʿfar narrated; Shuʿbah narrated; from Muʿāwiyah ibn Qurrah; he said: I heard ʿAbdullāh ibn

i. Related by al-Bukhari, 4281 4835 and 7540; Abu Dāwūd, 1467.

Mughaffal say: **'I saw God's Messenger (peace be upon him) on the day of the fall of Makkah, riding his she-camel, reciting Surah al-Fatḥ'. Ibn Mughaffal recited and chanted.**

Muʿāwiyah said: 'Except for the fact that people are around, I would have done the same as what Ibn Mughaffal reported of the Prophet (peace be upon him)'.

وَحَدَّثَنَا مُحَمَّدُ بْنُ الْـمُثَنَّى، وَمُحَمَّدُ بْنُ بَشَّارٍ، قَالَ ابْنُ الْـمُثَنَّى حَدَّثَنَا مُحَمَّدُ بْنُ جَعْفَرٍ، حَدَّثَنَا شُعْبَةُ: عَنْ مُعَاوِيَةَ بْنِ قُرَّةَ، قَالَ سَمِعْتُ عَبْدَ اللهِ بْنَ مُغَفَّلٍ قَالَ: رَأَيْتُ رَسُولَ اللهِ صَلَّى اللهُ عَلَيْهِ وَسَلَّمَ يَوْمَ فَتْحِ مَكَّةَ عَلَى نَاقَتِهِ يَقْرَأُ سُورَةَ الْفَتْحِ. قَالَ: فَقَرَأَ ابْنُ مُغَفَّلٍ وَرَجَّعَ .

فَقَالَ مُعَاوِيَةُ: لَوْلاَ النَّاسُ لأَخَذْتُ لَكُمْ بِذَلِكَ الَّذِي ذَكَرَهُ ابْنُ مُغَفَّلٍ عَنِ النَّبِيِّ صَلَّى اللهُ عَلَيْهِ وَسَلَّمَ.

[1585–239]. (Dar al-Salam 1738) Yaḥyā ibn Ḥabīb al-Ḥārithī narrated it: Khālid ibn al-Ḥārith narrated [H]. Also, ʿUbaydullāh ibn Muʿādh narrated; my father narrated; both said: Shuʿbah narrated; with the same chain of transmission: **a similar text**.

In Khālid ibn al-Ḥārith's narration: **'Riding his she-camel as he was reciting Surah al-Fatḥ'.**

وَحَدَّثَنَاهُ يَحْيَى بْنُ حَبِيبٍ الْحَارِثِيُّ، حَدَّثَنَا خَالِدُ بْنُ الْحَارِثِ، ح. وَحَدَّثَنَا عُبَيْدُ اللهِ بْنُ مُعَاذٍ، حَدَّثَنَا أَبِي قَالاَ: حَدَّثَنَا شُعْبَةُ، بِهَذَا الإِسْنَادِ نَحْوَهُ. وَفِي حَدِيثِ خَالِدِ بْنِ الْحَارِثِ قَالَ: عَلَى رَاحِلَةٍ يَسِيرُ وَهُوَ يَقْرَأُ سُورَةَ الْفَتْحِ.

Note: As these hadiths are self-explanatory, Imam al-Nawawī does not add any explanation.

CHAPTER 36

QUR'ANIC RECITATION IMPARTS SERENITY

[1586–240]. (Dar al-Salam 1739) Yaḥyā ibn Yaḥyā narrated:[i] Abu Khaythamah reported; from Abu Isḥāq; from al-Barā'. He said: **'A man was reciting Surah The Cave, and near him was a mare tied with two ropes. A cloud came over him and it turned and drew nearer. His mare was agitated because of it. In the morning he came to see the Prophet and told him what happened. The Prophet said: "That is serenity, bestowed for [the recitation of] the Qur'an".'**

وَحَدَّثَنَا يَحْيَى بْنُ يَحْيَى، أَخْبَرَنَا أَبُو خَيْثَمَةَ، عَنْ أَبِي إِسْحَاقَ، عَنِ الْبَرَاءِ، قَالَ: كَانَ رَجُلٌ يَقْرَأُ سُورَةَ الْكَهْفِ وَعِنْدَهُ فَرَسٌ مَرْبُوطٌ بِشَطَنَيْنِ، فَتَغَشَّتْهُ سَحَابَةٌ، فَجَعَلَتْ تَدُورُ وَتَدْنُو، وَجَعَلَ فَرَسُهُ يَنْفِرُ مِنْهَا. فَلَمَّا أَصْبَحَ أَتَى النَّبِيَّ صَلَّى اللهُ عَلَيْهِ وَسَلَّمَ فَذَكَرَ ذَلِكَ لَهُ فَقَالَ: «تِلْكَ السَّكِينَةُ تَنَزَّلَتْ لِلْقُرْآنِ».

[1587–241]. (Dar al-Salam 1740) Ibn al-Muthannā and Ibn Bashshār narrated (Ibn al-Muthannā's text):[ii] both said: Muhammad ibn Ja'far narrated; Shu'bah narrated; from Abu Isḥāq; he said: I heard al-Barā' say: **'A man recited [Surah] The Cave, and an animal was at home. It became agitated. He looked up and saw that a cloud was covering him. He mentioned this to**

i. Related by al-Bukhari, 5011.
ii. Related by al-Bukhari, 2614; al-Tirmidhī, 2885.

the Prophet (peace be upon him). The Prophet said: "Recite [adding his name]. It is serenity, bestowed when the Qur'an was recited. Or, bestowed for [the recitation of] the Qur'an".'

وَحَدَّثَنَا ابْنُ الْـمُثَنَّى، وَابْنُ، بَشَّارٍ - وَاللَّفْظُ لِابْنِ الْـمُثَنَّى - قَالا: حَدَّثَنَا مُحَمَّدُ بْنُ، جَعْفَرٍ، حَدَّثَنَا شُعْبَةُ، عَنْ أَبِي إِسْحَاقَ، قَالَ: سَمِعْتُ الْبَرَاءَ يَقُولُ: قَرَأَ رَجُلٌ الْكَهْفَ وَفِي الدَّارِ دَابَّةٌ، فَجَعَلَتْ تَنْفِرُ، فَنَظَرَ فَإِذَا ضَبَابَةٌ أَوْ سَحَابَةٌ قَدْ غَشِيَتْهُ. قَالَ: فَذَكَرَ ذَلِكَ لِلنَّبِيِّ صَلَّى اللهُ عَلَيْهِ وَسَلَّمَ فَقَالَ: «اقْرَأْ فُلَانُ فَإِنَّهَا السَّكِينَةُ تَنَزَّلَتْ عِنْدَ الْقُرْآنِ أَوْ تَنَزَّلَتْ لِلْقُرْآنِ».

[1588–000]. (Dar al-Salam 1741) Ibn al-Muthannā narrated: ʿAbd al-Raḥmān ibn Mahdī and Abu Dāwūd narrated; both said: Shuʿbah narrated; from Abu Isḥāq; he said: I heard al-Barā' say: **they mentioned a similar text but said [that the horse was] perturbed.**

وَحَدَّثَنَا ابْنُ الْـمُثَنَّى، حَدَّثَنَا عَبْدُ الرَّحْمَنِ بْنُ مَهْدِيٍّ وَأَبُو دَاوُدَ قَالا: حَدَّثَنَا شُعْبَةُ، عَنْ أَبِي إِسْحَاقَ، قَالَ: سَمِعْتُ الْبَرَاءَ يَقُولُ. فَذَكَرَا نَحْوَهُ غَيْرَ أَنَّهُمَا قَالاَ تَنْقُزُ.

[1589–242]. (Dar al-Salam 1742) Ḥasan ibn ʿAlī al-Ḥulwānī and Ḥajjāj ibn al-Shāʿir narrated to me (in largely similar wording): they said: Yaʿqūb ibn Ibrāhīm narrated; my father narrated; Yazīd ibn al-Hād narrated; that ʿAbdullāh ibn Khabbāb narrated to him; that Abu Saʿīd al-Khudrī narrated to him; that **'As Usayd ibn Ḥuḍayr was one night reciting at his stable, his mare was agitated. He went on reciting and again she was agitated. He continued his recitation, and she was agitated. Usayd said: "I feared that she might step over Yaḥyā, and I went up to her. I saw something like a canopy over my head and there were in it what looked like lanterns. It went up**

in the air and I could hardly see it. In the morning I went to God's Messenger (peace be upon him) and said: 'Messenger of God, as I was last night reciting in my stable, my mare was agitated'. God's Messenger said: 'Recite, Ibn Ḥuḍayr'. I recited, then it was again agitated. God's Messenger said: 'Recite, Ibn Ḥuḍayr'. I recited, then it was further agitated. God's Messenger said: 'Recite, Ibn Ḥuḍayr'. I left. Yaḥyā was close to her and I feared that she might step over him. I saw something like a canopy over my head and there were in it what looked like lanterns. It went up in the air and I could hardly see it. God's Messenger (peace be upon him) said: 'These were angels listening to you. Had you continued to recite, they would be seen by people and they would not be hidden from [people]'."'

وَحدَّثَنِي حَسَنُ بْنُ عَلِيٍّ الْحُلْوَانِيُّ، وَحَجَّاجُ بْنُ الشَّاعِرِ، - وَتَقَارَبَا فِي اللَّفْظِ - قَالاَ حَدَّثَنَا يَعْقُوبُ بْنُ إِبْرَاهِيمَ، حَدَّثَنَا أَبِي، حَدَّثَنَا يَزِيدُ بْنُ الْهَادِ، أَنَّ عَبْدَ اللهِ بْنَ خَبَّابٍ، حَدَّثَهُ أَنَّ أَبَا سَعِيدٍ الْخُدْرِيَّ حَدَّثَهُ أَنَّ أُسَيْدَ بْنَ حُضَيْرٍ بَيْنَمَا هُوَ لَيْلَةً يَقْرَأُ فِي مِرْبَدِهِ إِذْ جَالَتْ فَرَسُهُ فَقَرَأَ. ثُمَّ جَالَتْ أُخْرَى فَقَرَأَ. ثُمَّ جَالَتْ أَيْضًا. قَالَ أُسَيْدٌ: فَخَشِيتُ أَنْ تَطَأَ يَحْيَى فَقُمْتُ إِلَيْهَا فَإِذَا مِثْلُ الظُّلَّةِ فَوْقَ رَأْسِي فِيهَا أَمْثَالُ السُّرُجِ عَرَجَتْ فِي الْجَوِّ حَتَّى مَا أَرَاهَا. قَالَ: فَغَدَوْتُ عَلَى رَسُولِ اللهِ صَلَّى اللهُ عَلَيْهِ وَسَلَّمَ فَقُلْتُ يَا رَسُولَ اللهِ بَيْنَمَا أَنَا الْبَارِحَةَ مِنْ جَوْفِ اللَّيْلِ أَقْرَأُ فِي مِرْبَدِي إِذْ جَالَتْ فَرَسِي. فَقَالَ رَسُولُ اللهِ صَلَّى اللهُ عَلَيْهِ وَسَلَّمَ «اقْرَإِ ابْنَ حُضَيْرٍ». قَالَ فَقَرَأْتُ ثُمَّ جَالَتْ أَيْضًا . فَقَالَ رَسُولُ اللهِ صَلَّى اللهُ عَلَيْهِ وَسَلَّمَ «اقْرَإِ ابْنَ حُضَيْرٍ». قَالَ فَقَرَأْتُ ثُمَّ جَالَتْ أَيْضًا . فَقَالَ رَسُولُ اللهِ صَلَّى اللهُ عَلَيْهِ وَسَلَّمَ «اقْرَإِ ابْنَ حُضَيْرٍ». قَالَ فَانْصَرَفْتُ. وَكَانَ يَحْيَى قَرِيبًا مِنْهَا خَشِيتُ أَنْ تَطَأَهُ فَرَأَيْتُ مِثْلَ الظُّلَّةِ فِيهَا أَمْثَالُ السُّرُجِ عَرَجَتْ فِي الْجَوِّ حَتَّى مَا أَرَاهَا فَقَالَ رَسُولُ اللهِ صَلَّى اللهُ عَلَيْهِ وَسَلَّمَ «تِلْكَ الْمَلاَئِكَةُ كَانَتْ تَسْتَمِعُ لَكَ وَلَوْ قَرَأْتَ لأَصْبَحَتْ يَرَاهَا النَّاسُ مَا تَسْتَتِرُ مِنْهُمْ».

Text Explanation

Hadith No. 1586 mentions that a cloud came over the man reciting the Qur'an. 'It turned and drew nearer... The Prophet said: "That is serenity, bestowed for [the recitation of] the Qur'an".' In the last hadith, No. 1589, the Prophet explains to his Companion: 'These were angels listening to you. Had you continued to recite, they would be seen by people and they would not be hidden from [people]'.

Here, 'serenity', or *sakīnah* in Arabic, is given different meanings, and the meaning of choice is that it is something of God's creation that imparts reassurance and mercy and that it is attended by angels, but God knows best. These hadiths confirm that it is possible for individual Muslims to see angels. The hadiths also stress the great merit of reciting the Qur'an and that it is a cause for bestowing grace and mercy and for the attendance of angels. The hadiths also stress the merit of listening to the Qur'an.

In hadith No. 1587, the Prophet tells his Companion to recite, and in hadith No. 1589, he repeats this three times. This means that Ibn Ḥuḍayr should have continued to recite, making the best of what happened, as serenity was bestowed and angels were in attendance. He should have recited more and more as this would have ensured they stayed with him.

CHAPTER 37

THE STATUS OF ONE WHO MEMORISES THE QUR'AN

[1590–243]. (Dar al-Salam 1743) Qutaybah ibn Saʿīd and Abu Kāmil al-Jaḥdarī narrated:[i] both from Abu ʿAwānah. Qutaybah said: Abu ʿAwānah narrated; from Qatādah; from Anas; from Abu Mūsā al-Ashʿarī. He said: **'God's Messenger (peace be upon him) said: "A believer who recites the Qur'an is like a citrus fruit: its smell is fine, and its taste is fine. A believer who does not recite the Qur'an is like a date: it has no smell but has a fine taste. A hypocrite who recites the Qur'an is like basil which has a fine smell but a bitter taste. A hypocrite who does not recite the Qur'an is like colocynth which has a bitter taste and no smell".'**

حَدَّثَنَا قُتَيْبَةُ بْنُ سَعِيدٍ، وَأَبُو كَامِلٍ الْجَحْدَرِيُّ كِلاَهُمَا عَنْ أَبِي عَوَانَةَ، قَالَ قُتَيْبَةُ: حَدَّثَنَا أَبُو عَوَانَةَ، عَنْ قَتَادَةَ، عَنْ أَنَسٍ، عَنْ أَبِي مُوسَى الأَشْعَرِيِّ قَالَ: قَالَ رَسُولُ اللهِ صَلَّى اللهُ عَلَيْهِ وَسَلَّمَ: «مَثَلُ الْمُؤْمِنِ الَّذِي يَقْرَأُ الْقُرْآنَ مَثَلُ الأُتْرُجَّةِ رِيحُهَا طَيِّبٌ وَطَعْمُهَا طَيِّبٌ، وَمَثَلُ الْمُؤْمِنِ الَّذِي لاَ يَقْرَأُ الْقُرْآنَ مَثَلُ التَّمْرَةِ: لاَ رِيحَ لَهَا وَطَعْمُهَا حُلْوٌ. وَمَثَلُ الْمُنَافِقِ الَّذِي يَقْرَأُ الْقُرْآنَ مَثَلُ الرَّيْحَانَةِ رِيحُهَا طَيِّبٌ وَطَعْمُهَا مُرٌّ. وَمَثَلُ الْمُنَافِقِ الَّذِي لاَ يَقْرَأُ الْقُرْآنَ كَمَثَلِ الْحَنْظَلَةِ لَيْسَ لَهَا رِيحٌ وَطَعْمُهَا مُرٌّ.

i. Related by al-Bukhari, 5020, 5059 and 7560; Abu Dāwūd, 4830; al-Tirmidhī, 2865; al-Nasā'ī, 5053; Ibn Mājah, 214.

[1591–000]. (Dar al-Salam 1744) Haddāb ibn Khālid narrated: Hammām narrated [H]. Also, Muhammad ibn al-Muthannā narrated; Yaḥyā ibn Saʿīd narrated; from Shuʿbah; both from Qatādah; with this chain of transmission: **the same text, except that in Hammām's narration 'hypocrite' is replaced by 'wicked'.**

وَحَدَّثَنَا هَدَّابُ بْنُ خَالِدٍ، حَدَّثَنَا هَمَّامٌ، ح. وَحَدَّثَنَا مُحَمَّدُ بْنُ الْـمُثَنَّى، حَدَّثَنَا يَحْيَى بْنُ سَعِيدٍ عَنْ شُعْبَةَ، كِلاَهُمَا عَنْ قَتَادَةَ، بِهَذَا الإِسْنَادِ: مِثْلَهُ غَيْرَ أَنَّ فِي حَدِيثِ هَمَّامٍ بَدَلَ الْـمُنَافِقِ الْفَاجِرِ.

Text Explanation

This hadith highlights the merit of a person who memorises the Qur'an. It also shows the desirability of using similes to explain meanings and ideas.

Note: This is all that Imam al-Nawawī says about this hadith. We may add that the Prophet used the word *utrujj* for the citrus fruit he meant. This name is used in different forms in different countries but hardly ever pronounced in the same way the Prophet used. It is a citrus fruit which is larger than oranges, but with a slightly lighter colour. It is used in medicine and apparently called *citrus medica* in scientific circles. It has also had various uses in traditional medicine.

CHAPTER 38

THE STATUS OF RECITERS OF THE QUR'AN

[1592–244]. (Dar al-Salam 1745) Qutaybah ibn Saʿīd and Muhammad ibn ʿUbayd al-Ghubarī narrated:[i] both from Abu ʿAwānah. Ibn ʿUbayd said: Abu ʿAwānah narrated; from Qatādah; from Zurārah ibn Awfā; from Saʿd ibn Hishām; from ʿĀʾishah. She said: **'God's Messenger (peace be upon him) said: "The one who excels in the Qur'an is with the noble and devout messengers, and the one who recites the Qur'an stumbling as he recites and finds it hard, earns double reward".'**

حَدَّثَنَا قُتَيْبَةُ بْنُ سَعِيدٍ، وَمُحَمَّدُ بْنُ عُبَيْدٍ الْغُبَرِيُّ، جَمِيعًا عَنْ أَبِي عَوَانَةَ، - قَالَ ابْنُ عُبَيْدٍ حَدَّثَنَا أَبُو عَوَانَةَ، - عَنْ قَتَادَةَ، عَنْ زُرَارَةَ بْنِ أَوْفَى، عَنْ سَعْدِ بْنِ هِشَامٍ، عَنْ عَائِشَةَ قَالَتْ: قَالَ رَسُولُ اللهِ صَلَّى اللهُ عَلَيْهِ وَسَلَّمَ: « الْمَاهِرُ بِالْقُرْآنِ مَعَ السَّفَرَةِ الْكِرَامِ الْبَرَرَةِ، وَالَّذِي يَقْرَأُ الْقُرْآنَ وَيَتَتَعْتَعُ فِيهِ وَهُوَ عَلَيْهِ شَاقٌّ لَهُ أَجْرَانِ».

[1593–000]. (Dar al-Salam 1746) Muhammad ibn al-Muthannā narrated: Ibn Abi ʿAdiy narrated; from Saʿīd [H]. Also, Abu Bakr ibn Abi Shaybah narrated; Wakīʿ narrated; from Hishām al-Dastawāʾī; both from Qatādah; with the same chain of transmission: in Wakīʿ's narration: **'And the one who recites and finds it hard receives double reward'.**

---

i. Related by al-Bukhari, 4937; Abu Dāwūd, 1454; al-Tirmidhī, 2904; Ibn Mājah, 3779.

وَحَدَّثَنَا مُحَمَّدُ بْنُ الْـمُثَنَّى، حَدَّثَنَا ابْنُ أَبِي عَدِيٍّ، عَنْ سَعِيدٍ، ح. وَحَدَّثَنَا أَبُو بَكْرِ بْنُ أَبِي شَيْبَةَ حَدَّثَنَا وَكِيعٌ، عَنْ هِشَامٍ الدَّسْتَوَائِيِّ، كِلَاهُمَا عَنْ قَتَادَةَ، بِهَذَا الإِسْنَادِ . وَقَالَ فِي حَدِيثِ وَكِيعٍ: «وَالَّذِي يَقْرَأُ وَهُوَ يَشْتَدُّ عَلَيْهِ لَهُ أَجْرَانِ».

Text Explanation

In hadith No. 1592, the Prophet says that a person who excels in the Qur'an is 'with the noble and devout messengers'. The Arabic word used by the Prophet is *safarah*, which is the plural form of *sāfir*, meaning messenger. The word refers to God's messengers who deliver God's messages to mankind. It is also said that the word *safarah* means 'scribes'. The Prophet uses this description which occurs in verses 15–16 of Surah 80. They are described as 'devout' because of their obedience.

This status belongs to one who 'excels in the Qur'an'. This is one who completes the memorisation of the Qur'an and does not find any difficulty in reciting it because of his excellence in memorisation and recitation. *Qadi* 'Iyāḍ says:

> The hadith may be understood to refer to such a person as being with angels. It may thus mean that in the life to come such a person may be given a grade that makes him a companion of angel messengers, as he portrays some of their qualities, being a bearer of God's Book. The hadith may also mean that such a person does what such angels do and follows their example. The one who stumbles while reciting the Qur'an is one who hesitates because his memorisation is not so good. He earns a double reward: one for its recitation and one for the hardship he finds in reciting it. This does not mean that his reward is greater than the one who excels in the Qur'an. The latter is of a superior status and receives greater reward because he is with the messengers and earns numerous rewards. This status is not mentioned as belonging to any other group. How can a

person who has not given the necessary attention and effort to memorising the Qur'an and perfecting its recitation so as to achieve excellence in it catch up with the one who excels in its memorisation and recitation?

CHAPTER 39

RECITING THE QUR'AN TO ONE WHO EXCELS IN IT EVEN IF THE RECITER IS OF A HIGHER STATUS

[1594–245]. (Dar al-Salam 1747) Haddāb ibn Khālid narrated:[i] Hammām narrated; Qatādah narrated; from Anas ibn Mālik; that **'God's Messenger (peace be upon him) said to Ubayy: "God has commanded me to recite to you". Ubayy said: "Has God named me to you?" The Prophet said: "God has named you to me". Ubayy was in tears'.**

حَدَّثَنَا هَدَّابُ بْنُ خَالِدٍ، حَدَّثَنَا هَمَّامٌ، حَدَّثَنَا قَتَادَةُ، عَنْ أَنَسِ بْنِ مَالِكٍ، أَنَّ رَسُولَ اللهِ صَلَّى اللهُ عَلَيْهِ وَسَلَّمَ قَالَ لأُبَيٍّ: «إِنَّ اللهَ أَمَرَنِي أَنْ أَقْرَأَ عَلَيْكَ». قَالَ: آللهُ سَمَّانِي لَكَ؟ قَالَ: «اللهُ سَمَّاكَ لِي». قَالَ فَجَعَلَ أُبَيٌّ يَبْكِي.

[1595–246]. (Dar al-Salam 1748–1749) Muhammad ibn al-Muthannā and Ibn Bashshār narrated:[ii] both said: Muhammad ibn Jaʿfar narrated; Shuʿbah narrated; he said: I heard Qatādah narrating from Anas: **'God's Messenger (peace be upon him) said to Ubayy ibn Kaʿb: "God has commanded me to recite to you [the surah starting with]: 'It is inconceivable that the unbelievers...'." [Ubayy] said: "And He named me to you?" The Prophet said: "Yes". He was in tears'.**

---

i. Related by al-Bukhari, 4960.
ii. Related by al-Bukhari, 3809 and 4959.

حَدَّثَنَا مُحَمَّدُ بْنُ الْمُثَنَّى، وَابْنُ بَشَّارٍ قَالا حَدَّثَنَا مُحَمَّدُ بْنُ جَعْفَرٍ، حَدَّثَنَا شُعْبَةُ، قَالَ: سَمِعْتُ قَتَادَةَ يُحَدِّثُ عَنْ أَنَسٍ قَالَ: قَالَ رَسُولُ اللهِ صَلَّى اللهُ عَلَيْهِ وَسَلَّمَ لأُبَيِّ بْنِ كَعْبٍ: «إِنَّ اللهَ أَمَرَنِي أَنْ أَقْرَأَ عَلَيْكَ لَمْ يَكُنِ الَّذِينَ كَفَرُوا». قَالَ: وَسَمَّانِي لَكَ؟ قَالَ: «نَعَمْ». قَالَ فَبَكَى.

Yaḥyā ibn Ḥabīb al-Ḥārithī narrated: Khālid (meaning Ibn al-Ḥārith) narrated; Shuʿbah narrated; from Qatādah; I heard Anas say: **'God's Messenger said to Ubayy…' the same text.**

حَدَّثَنَا يَحْيَى بْنُ حَبِيبٍ الْحَارِثِيُّ، حَدَّثَنَا خَالِدٌ، يَعْنِي ابْنَ الْحَارِثِ، حَدَّثَنَا شُعْبَةُ، عَنْ قَتَادَةَ قَالَ: سَمِعْتُ أَنَسًا يَقُولُ: قَالَ رَسُولُ اللهِ صَلَّى اللهُ عَلَيْهِ وَسَلَّمَ لأُبَيٍّ بِمِثْلِهِ.

Text Explanation

This hadith gives us several very interesting points. One of these is the desirability to recite the Qur'an before people who excel in its recitation, even when the one who is reciting is better and of a higher status than the one who is listening.[i] Another point is the special status given to Ubayy ibn Kaʿb, as the Prophet recited the Qur'an to him. It is not known that anyone else held the same status as Ubayy. Another point of excellence given to Ubayy is that God named him as deserving this superior status. A further point is shedding tears of joy when one is given very happy news.

In hadith No. 1594, Ubayy asks the Prophet: 'Has God named me to you?' The question suggests that it might have been that God ordered the Prophet to recite the Qur'an to a person in his community, without naming Ubayy. Ubayy wanted to make sure whether he

i. The Prophet was certainly the best reciter of the Qur'an and all excellent reciters among his Companions learnt from him. The fact that God commanded him to recite before Ubayy was a gesture of honour to Ubayy and a clear indication to all Muslims that an excellent reciter should not hesitate to recite before all people.

was named specifically or just that any man was mentioned. This tells us that it is better to make sure when different possibilities may be suggested.

Scholars differ as to the reason for the Prophet's recitation to Ubayy. The preferred view is that it sets an example encouraging recitation before those who are known to be excellent in the Qur'an. Moreover, the Muslim community thus learns the manners to be observed when reciting the Qur'an. No one should disdain to do so. It is also suggested that the order to the Prophet was to indicate Ubayy's high status and his being worthy of learning from. In fact, after the Prophet, Ubayy ibn Kaʿb was the leading scholar, or one of the leading scholars, in teaching the Qur'an. The hadith also includes one of the Prophet's miracles.

The reason for specifying this surah, which is Surah 98, The Clear Proof, is that it is a short surah that outlines a number of the essentials and details of the Islamic faith, sincerity of belief, and making sure one has a clear and pure heart. Reciting a short surah was particularly useful at the time, but God knows best.

Transmission

The chain of transmission of hadith No. 1594 runs as follows: 'Haddāb ibn Khālid narrated: Hammām narrated; Qatādah narrated; from Anas ibn Mālik'. The second hadith, No. 1595, features in its chain of transmission: 'Muhammad ibn al-Muthannā and Ibn Bashshār narrated: Muhammad ibn Jaʿfar narrated; Shuʿbah narrated; he said: I heard Qatādah narrating from Anas'. The last of these three hadiths has the following chain of transmission: 'Yaḥyā ibn Ḥabīb al-Ḥārithī narrated: Khālid (meaning Ibn al-Ḥārith) narrated; Shuʿbah narrated; from Qatādah; I heard Anas'. All narrators in these three chains of transmission belonged to Basrah. This is very interesting because these are three consecutive chains of transmission, occurring coincidently, yet all their narrators belong to the same city. We have pointed out on several occasions that Shuʿbah was from Wāsiṭ, but he moved to Basrah and settled there. The last chain of transmission gives an additional point of interest because, in this instance, Qatādah states that he actually heard the hadith from Anas, while in the other two chains he does not express it in the same way. Qatādah is graded as a 'misleading narrator' but the fact that he clearly states his hearing the hadith makes it more reliable.

CHAPTER 40

LISTENING TO THE QUR'AN

[1596–247]. (Dar al-Salam 1750) Abu Bakr ibn Abi Shaybah and Abu Kurayb narrated:[i] both from Ḥafṣ; Abu Bakr said: Ḥafṣ ibn Ghiyāth narrated; from al-Aʿmash; from Ibrāhīm; from ʿUbaydah; from ʿAbdullāh. He said: **'God's Messenger (peace be upon him) said to me: "Recite the Qur'an to me". I said: "Messenger of God, how can I recite to you when it is to you that it was revealed?" He said: "I love to hear it from someone else". I started [the Surah] Women. When I reached the verse that says: "How will it be [on Judgement Day] when We shall bring a witness from every community and call you as a witness against these people?" (4: 41) I lifted my head, or a man next to me poked me in my side and I lifted my head. I saw that he was in tears'.**

وَحَدَّثَنَا أَبُو بَكْرِ بْنُ أَبِي شَيْبَةَ، وَأَبُو كُرَيْبٍ جَمِيعًا عَنْ حَفْصٍ، قَالَ أَبُو بَكْرٍ حَدَّثَنَا حَفْصُ بْنُ غِيَاثٍ، عَنِ الأَعْمَشِ، عَنْ إِبْرَاهِيمَ، عَنْ عُبَيْدَةَ، عَنْ عَبْدِ اللهِ قَالَ: قَالَ لِي رَسُولُ اللهِ صَلَّى اللهُ عَلَيْهِ وَسَلَّمَ: « اقْرَأْ عَلَيَّ الْقُرْآنَ ». قَالَ: فَقُلْتُ يَا رَسُولَ اللهِ، أَقْرَأُ عَلَيْكَ وَعَلَيْكَ أُنْزِلَ؟ قَالَ: « إِنِّي أَشْتَهِي أَنْ أَسْمَعَهُ مِنْ غَيْرِي ». فَقَرَأْتُ النِّسَاءَ حَتَّى إِذَا بَلَغْتُ: « فَكَيْفَ إِذَا جِئْنَا مِنْ كُلِّ أُمَّةٍ بِشَهِيدٍ وَجِئْنَا بِكَ عَلَى هَؤُلاَءِ شَهِيدًا » رَفَعْتُ رَأْسِي، أَوْ غَمَزَنِي رَجُلٌ إِلَى جَنْبِي فَرَفَعْتُ رَأْسِي، فَرَأَيْتُ دُمُوعَهُ تَسِيلُ.

i. Related by al-Bukhari, 5049, 5050, 5055, 5056 and 4582; Abu Dāwūd, 3668; al-Tirmidhī, 3024 and 3025.

[1597–000]. (Dar al-Salam 1751) Hannād ibn al-Sariy and Minjāb ibn al-Ḥārith al-Tamīmī narrated: both from ʿAlī ibn Mushir; from al-Aʿmash; with this chain of transmission: **the same text, but Hannād added in his narration: 'As he was on the platform [i.e. minbar], God's Messenger (peace be upon him) said to me: "Recite to me".'**

حَدَّثَنَا هَنَّادُ بْنُ السَّرِيِّ، وَمِنْجَابُ بْنُ الْحَارِثِ التَّمِيمِيُّ، جَمِيعًا عَنْ عَلِيِّ بْنِ مُسْهِرٍ، عَنِ الأَعْمَشِ، بِهَذَا الإِسْنَادِ. وَزَادَ هَنَّادٌ فِي رِوَايَتِهِ: قَالَ لِي رَسُولُ اللهِ صَلَّى اللهُ عَلَيْهِ وَسَلَّمَ وَهُوَ عَلَى الْـمِنْبَرِ: اقْرَأْ عَلَيَّ.

[1598–248]. (Dar al-Salam 1752) Abu Bakr ibn Abi Shaybah and Abu Kurayb narrated: both said: Abu Usāmah narrated; Misʿar narrated to me; and Abu Kurayb said: from Misʿar; from ʿAmr ibn Murrah; from Ibrāhīm. He said: **'The Prophet (peace be upon him) said to ʿAbdullāh ibn Masʿūd: "Recite to me". He said: "How can I recite to you when it is to you that it was revealed?" He said: "I love to hear it from someone else". He recited to him from the beginning of Surah Women up to the verse that says: "How will it be [on Judgement Day] when We shall bring a witness from every community and call you as a witness against these people?" (4: 41) He was in tears'.**

Misʿar said: Maʿn narrated to me; from Jaʿfar ibn ʿAmr ibn Ḥurayth; from his father; from Ibn Masʿūd; that the Prophet (peace be upon him) said: **'A witness against them for as long as I am living with them, or as I am among them'.** (It is Misʿar who was uncertain.)

وَحَدَّثَنَا أَبُو بَكْرِ بْنُ أَبِي شَيْبَةَ، وَأَبُو كُرَيْبٍ قَالَا: حَدَّثَنَا أَبُو أُسَامَةَ، حَدَّثَنِي مِسْعَرٌ، وَقَالَ أَبُو كُرَيْبٍ عَنْ مِسْعَرٍ، عَنْ عَمْرِو بْنِ مُرَّةَ، عَنْ إِبْرَاهِيمَ قَالَ: قَالَ النَّبِيُّ صَلَّى اللهُ

عَلَيْهِ وَسَلَّمَ لِعَبْدِ اللهِ بْنِ مَسْعُودٍ «اقْرَأْ عَلَيَّ». قَالَ: أَقْرَأُ عَلَيْكَ وَعَلَيْكَ أُنْزِلَ؟ قَالَ: «إِنِّي أُحِبُّ أَنْ أَسْمَعَهُ مِنْ غَيْرِي». قَالَ: فَقَرَأَ عَلَيْهِ مِنْ أَوَّلِ سُورَةِ النِّسَاءِ إِلَى قَوْلِهِ: «فَكَيْفَ إِذَا جِئْنَا مِنْ كُلِّ أُمَّةٍ بِشَهِيدٍ وَجِئْنَا بِكَ عَلَى هَؤُلَاءِ شَهِيدًا»، فَبَكَى.

قَالَ مِسْعَرٌ فَحَدَّثَنِي مَعْنٌ عَنْ جَعْفَرِ بْنِ عَمْرِو بْنِ حُرَيْثٍ عَنْ أَبِيهِ عَنِ ابْنِ مَسْعُودٍ قَالَ: قَالَ النَّبِيُّ صَلَّى اللهُ عَلَيْهِ وَسَلَّمَ: «شَهِيدًا عَلَيْهِمْ مَا دُمْتُ فِيهِمْ أَوْ مَا كُنْتُ فِيهِمْ». شَكَّ مِسْعَرٌ

[1599–249]. (Dar al-Salam 1753) ʿUthmān ibn Abi Shaybah narrated:[i] Jarīr narrated; from al-Aʿmash; from Ibrāhīm; from ʿAlqamah; from ʿAbdullāh. He said: **'I was in Ḥoms when some people said to me: "Recite to us". I recited Surah Yūsuf to them. A man from among them said: "By God, it was not revealed like this". I said: "Woe to you. By God, I recited it to God's Messenger (peace be upon him) and he said to me: 'Well done'."**

As I was speaking to him, I smelled wine. I said: "Do you drink wine and deny the Book? You shall not move until I have punished you". I flogged him the mandatory punishment'.

حَدَّثَنَا عُثْمَانُ بْنُ أَبِي شَيْبَةَ، حَدَّثَنَا جَرِيرٌ، عَنِ الأَعْمَشِ، عَنْ إِبْرَاهِيمَ، عَنْ عَلْقَمَةَ، عَنْ عَبْدِ اللهِ، قَالَ: كُنْتُ بِحِمْصَ فَقَالَ لِي بَعْضُ الْقَوْمِ اقْرَأْ عَلَيْنَا. فَقَرَأْتُ عَلَيْهِمْ سُورَةَ يُوسُفَ. قَالَ: فَقَالَ رَجُلٌ مِنَ الْقَوْمِ: وَاللهِ مَا هَكَذَا أُنْزِلَتْ. قَالَ: قُلْتُ وَيْحَكَ وَاللهِ لَقَدْ قَرَأْتُهَا عَلَى رَسُولِ اللهِ صَلَّى اللهُ عَلَيْهِ وَسَلَّمَ، فَقَالَ لِي: «أَحْسَنْتَ».

فَبَيْنَمَا أَنَا أُكَلِّمُهُ إِذْ وَجَدْتُ مِنْهُ رِيحَ الْخَمْرِ. قَالَ: فَقُلْتُ أَتَشْرَبُ الْخَمْرَ وَتُكَذِّبُ بِالْكِتَابِ؟ لَا تَبْرَحُ حَتَّى أَجْلِدَكَ. قَالَ: فَجَلَدْتُهُ الْحَدَّ.

---

i. Related by al-Bukhari, 5001.

[1600–000]. (Dar al-Salam 1754) Isḥāq ibn Ibrāhīm and ʿAlī ibn Khashram narrated: ʿĪsā ibn Yūnus reported [H]. Also, Abu Bakr ibn Abi Shaybah and Abu Kurayb narrated; both said: Abu Muʿāwiyah narrated; all from al-Aʿmash; with this chain of transmission: **the same, but Abu Muʿāwiyah's narration does not include: 'And he said to me: "well done".'**

وَحَدَّثَنَا إِسْحَاقُ بْنُ إِبْرَاهِيمَ، وَعَلِيُّ بْنُ خَشْرَمٍ قَالَا: أَخْبَرَنَا عِيسَى بْنُ يُونُسَ، ح. وَحَدَّثَنَا أَبُو بَكْرِ بْنُ أَبِي شَيْبَةَ، وَأَبُو كُرَيْبٍ قَالَا: حَدَّثَنَا أَبُو مُعَاوِيَةَ، جَمِيعًا عَنِ الأَعْمَشِ، بِهَذَا الإِسْنَادِ. وَلَيْسَ فِي حَدِيثِ أَبِي مُعَاوِيَةَ فَقَالَ لِي: «أَحْسَنْتَ».

Text Explanation

This hadith narrated by Ibn Masʿūd, in its various versions, contains several useful points. One of these is the desirability of listening attentively to the Qur'an and weeping and reflecting on the meaning of the verses. It is also desirable to request another person to recite the Qur'an so that one may listen to it. This may be more conducive to understanding the meaning and reflecting on it than one's own recitation. The hadith shows the humility of scholars and noble people, even with their own subordinates.

Hadith No. 1599 mentions that Ibn Masʿūd smelled wine and he inflicted the mandatory punishment on the man. This is understood to indicate that Ibn Masʿūd had such jurisdiction for administering mandatory punishments because he was a deputy appointed by the leader, or that his jurisdiction was limited to administering mandatory punishment, or perhaps in that particular area, or that he requested and was given the necessary authority to do so. It is also understood to mean that the man confessed to drinking wine with no valid excuse. Unless the situation is so, the mandatory punishment may not be enforced simply on the basis of the smell of wine because the scenario could be one of forgetting, or suspicion, or coercion, etc. This is the view of our school and others as well.

Ibn Mas'ūd says to the man: 'Do you drink wine and deny the Book'? This means that you deny some of it on the basis of ignorance. It does not mean absolute denial of the Qur'an because that would have meant that the man was an unbeliever and an apostate who deserved the death penalty. Scholars are unanimous that a person who denies a single letter of the Qur'an which enjoys unanimous recognition as belonging to the Qur'an is an unbeliever to whom apply all rulings applicable to apostates, but God knows best.

Transmission

The chain of transmission of hadith No. 1596 runs as follows: 'Abu Bakr ibn Abi Shaybah and Abu Kurayb narrated: both from Ḥafṣ; Abu Bakr said: Ḥafṣ ibn Ghiyāth narrated; from al-A'mash; from Ibrāhīm; from 'Ubaydah; from 'Abdullāh'. The next hadith has the following chain of transmission: 'Hannād ibn al-Sariy and Minjāb ibn al-Ḥārith al-Tamīmī narrated: both from 'Alī ibn Mushir; from al-A'mash'. And hadith No. 1598 begins with the following chain of transmission: 'Abu Bakr ibn Abi Shaybah and Abu Kurayb narrated: both said: Abu Usāmah narrated; Mis'ar narrated to me; and Abu Kurayb said: from Mis'ar; from 'Amr ibn Murrah; from Ibrāhīm'. Then hadith No. 1599 features the following chain of transmission: ''Uthmān ibn Abi Shaybah narrated: Jarīr narrated; from al-A'mash; from Ibrāhīm; from 'Alqamah; from 'Abdullāh'. The narrators in all these four chains of transmission belonged to Kufah. However, Jarīr also belonged to al-Rayy. These chains also show two cases of three narrators from the *tābi'īn* generation reporting from each other. These are al-A'mash, Ibrāhīm al-Nakha'ī and 'Ubaydah al-Salmānī in the first case, and al-A'mash, Ibrāhīm and 'Alqamah in the second.

CHAPTER 41

RECITING THE QUR'AN IN PRAYER AND LEARNING IT

[1601–250]. (Dar al-Salam 1755) Abu Bakr ibn Abi Shaybah and Abu Saʿīd al-Ashajj narrated:[i] both said: Wakīʿ narrated; from al-Aʿmash; from Abu Ṣāliḥ; from Abu Hurayrah. He said: **'God's Messenger (peace be upon him) said: "When any of you go back home, would he love to find there three big, fat and pregnant camels?" We said: "Yes". He said: "To recite three verses [of the Qur'an] in your prayer is better for you than three big, fat and pregnant camels".'**

حَدَّثَنَا أَبُو بَكْرِ بْنُ أَبِي شَيْبَةَ، وَأَبُو سَعِيدٍ الأَشَجُّ قَالا: حَدَّثَنَا وَكِيعٌ، عَنِ الأَعْمَشِ، عَنْ أَبِي صَالِحٍ، عَنْ أَبِي هُرَيْرَةَ قَالَ: قَالَ رَسُولُ اللهِ صَلَّى اللهُ عَلَيْهِ وَسَلَّمَ: « أَيُحِبُّ أَحَدُكُمْ إِذَا رَجَعَ إِلَى أَهْلِهِ أَنْ يَجِدَ فِيهِ ثَلَاثَ خَلِفَاتٍ عِظَامٍ سِمَانٍ؟» قُلْنَا: نَعَمْ. قَالَ: «فَثَلَاثُ آيَاتٍ يَقْرَأُ بِهِنَّ أَحَدُكُمْ فِي صَلَاتِهِ خَيْرٌ لَهُ مِنْ ثَلَاثِ خَلِفَاتٍ عِظَامٍ سِمَانٍ».

[1602–251]. (Dar al-Salam 1756) Abu Bakr ibn Abi Shaybah narrated:[ii] al-Faḍl ibn Dukayn narrated; from Mūsā ibn ʿAlī; he said: I heard my father narrating from ʿUqbah ibn ʿĀmir. He said: **'God's Messenger (peace be upon him) came out as we were at al-Ṣuffah, and he said to us: "Who of you would love to go every day to Buṭḥān or al-ʿAqīq and get two she-camels**

---

i. Related by Ibn Mājah, 3782.
ii. Related by Abu Dāwūd, 1456.

with large humps, without committing any sin or severance of family relations?" We said: "Messenger of God, we would certainly love that". He said: "Then why would not any of you go to the mosque and learn or recite two verses from God's Book? That is better for him than two she-camels, and three verses are better than three camels and four better than four and their equal number of camels".'

وَحَدَّثَنَا أَبُو بَكْرِ بْنُ أَبِي شَيْبَةَ، حَدَّثَنَا الْفَضْلُ بْنُ دُكَيْنٍ، عَنْ مُوسَى بْنِ عُلَيٍّ قَالَ: سَمِعْتُ أَبِي يُحَدِّثُ عَنْ عُقْبَةَ بْنِ عَامِرٍ قَالَ: خَرَجَ رَسُولُ اللهِ صَلَّى اللهُ عَلَيْهِ وَسَلَّمَ وَنَحْنُ فِي الصُّفَّةِ فَقَالَ: «أَيُّكُمْ يُحِبُّ أَنْ يَغْدُوَ كُلَّ يَوْمٍ إِلَى بُطْحَانَ أَوْ إِلَى الْعَقِيقِ فَيَأْتِيَ مِنْهُ بِنَاقَتَيْنِ كَوْمَاوَيْنِ، فِي غَيْرِ إِثْمٍ وَلاَ قَطْعِ رَحِمٍ». فَقُلْنَا: يَا رَسُولَ اللهِ نُحِبُّ ذَلِكَ. قَالَ: «أَفَلاَ يَغْدُو أَحَدُكُمْ إِلَى الْمَسْجِدِ فَيَعْلَمَ أَوْ يَقْرَأَ آيَتَيْنِ مِنْ كِتَابِ اللهِ عَزَّ وَجَلَّ خَيْرٌ لَهُ مِنْ نَاقَتَيْنِ، وَثَلاَثٌ خَيْرٌ لَهُ مِنْ ثَلاَثٍ، وَأَرْبَعٌ خَيْرٌ لَهُ مِنْ أَرْبَعٍ، وَمِنْ أَعْدَادِهِنَّ مِنَ الإِبِلِ».

Note: The hadiths in this chapter and the next two chapters will be explained together after the texts of the hadiths included in these three chapters have been stated.

CHAPTER 42

RECITING THE QUR'AN AND SURAH AL-BAQARAH (THE COW)

[1603–252]. (Dar al-Salam 1757) Al-Ḥasan ibn ʿAlī al-Ḥulwānī narrated to me: Abu Tawbah (who is al-Rabīʿ ibn Nāfiʿ) narrated; Muʿāwiyah (meaning Ibn Sallām) narrated; from Zayd; that he heard Abu Sallām say: Abu Umāmah al-Bāhilī narrated to me; he said: I heard God's Messenger (peace be upon him) say: **'Recite the Qur'an. For it will intercede for its people on the Day of Judgement. Recite the two bright ones: The Cow and Surah Āl-ʿImrān. On the Day of Judgement, they will be like two clouds, or canopies, or two flocks of birds with their wings spread out. They will argue for their people. Recite Surah The Cow. To learn it is a blessing, to abandon it is a great sorrow. It is beyond the people of falsehood'.**

Muʿāwiyah said: **'I am told that "the people of falsehood" means the sorcerers'**.

حَدَّثَنِي الْحَسَنُ بْنُ عَلِيٍّ الْحُلْوَانِيُّ، حَدَّثَنَا أَبُو تَوْبَةَ، - وَهُوَ الرَّبِيعُ بْنُ نَافِعٍ - حَدَّثَنَا مُعَاوِيَةُ، يَعْنِي ابْنَ سَلاَّمٍ - عَنْ زَيْدٍ، أَنَّهُ سَمِعَ أَبَا سَلاَّمٍ، يَقُولُ حَدَّثَنِي أَبُو أُمَامَةَ الْبَاهِلِيُّ قَالَ: سَمِعْتُ رَسُولَ اللَّهِ صَلَّى اللَّهُ عَلَيْهِ وَسَلَّمَ يَقُولُ: «اقْرَءُوا الْقُرْآنَ فَإِنَّهُ يَأْتِي يَوْمَ الْقِيَامَةِ شَفِيعًا لأَصْحَابِهِ. اقْرَءُوا الزَّهْرَاوَيْنِ الْبَقَرَةَ وَسُورَةَ آلِ عِمْرَانَ، فَإِنَّهُمَا تَأْتِيَانِ يَوْمَ الْقِيَامَةِ كَأَنَّهُمَا غَمَامَتَانِ أَوْ كَأَنَّهُمَا غَيَايَتَانِ، أَوْ كَأَنَّهُمَا فِرْقَانِ مِنْ طَيْرٍ صَوَافَّ، تُحَاجَّانِ عَنْ أَصْحَابِهِمَا. اقْرَءُوا سُورَةَ الْبَقَرَةِ فَإِنَّ أَخْذَهَا بَرَكَةٌ، وَتَرْكَهَا حَسْرَةٌ، وَلاَ تَسْتَطِيعُهَا الْبَطَلَةُ». قَالَ مُعَاوِيَةُ بَلَغَنِي أَنَّ الْبَطَلَةَ السَّحَرَةُ

[1604–000]. (Dar al-Salam 1758) ʿAbdullāh ibn ʿAbd al-Raḥmān al-Dārimī narrated: Yaḥyā (meaning Ibn Ḥassān) reported; Muʿāwiyah narrated; with the same chain of transmission: **the same text, except that he said: 'they will be like' in both instances. Nor did he mention Muʿāwiyah's statement: 'I am told…'.**

وَحَدَّثَنَا عَبْدُ اللهِ بْنُ عَبْدِ الرَّحْمَنِ الدَّارِمِيُّ، أَخْبَرَنَا يَحْيَى، - يَعْنِي ابْنَ حَسَّانَ - حَدَّثَنَا مُعَاوِيَةُ، بِهَذَا الإِسْنَادِ: مِثْلَهُ، غَيْرَ أَنَّهُ قَالَ "وَكَأَنَّهُمَا"، فِي كِلَيْهِمَا. وَلَمْ يَذْكُرْ قَوْلَ مُعَاوِيَةَ: بَلَغَنِي

[1605–253]. (Dar al-Salam 1759) Isḥāq ibn Manṣūr narrated:[i] Yazīd ibn ʿAbd Rabbih reported; al-Walīd ibn Muslim narrated; from Muhammad ibn Muhājir; from al-Walīd ibn ʿAbd al-Raḥmān al-Jurashī; from Jubayr ibn Nufayr; he said: I heard al-Nawwās ibn Samʿān al-Kilābī say: **'I heard the Prophet (peace be upon him) say: "The Qur'an will be brought forward with its people who implemented it, with Surahs The Cow and Āl ʿImrān right in front". God's Messenger described them in three similes which I have not forgotten. He said: "They are like two clouds, or two black canopies with bright light between them, or they are like flocks of birds with their wings spread out. They will argue for their people".'**

حَدَّثَنِي إِسْحَاقُ بْنُ مَنْصُورٍ، أَخْبَرَنَا يَزِيدُ بْنُ عَبْدِ رَبِّهِ، حَدَّثَنَا الْوَلِيدُ بْنُ مُسْلِمٍ، عَنْ مُحَمَّدِ بْنِ مُهَاجِرٍ، عَنِ الْوَلِيدِ بْنِ عَبْدِ الرَّحْمَنِ الْجُرَشِيِّ، عَنْ جُبَيْرِ بْنِ نُفَيْرٍ، قَالَ: سَمِعْتُ النَّوَّاسَ بْنَ سَمْعَانَ الْكِلَابِيَّ يَقُولُ: سَمِعْتُ النَّبِيَّ صَلَّى اللهُ عَلَيْهِ وَسَلَّمَ يَقُولُ: «يُؤْتَى بِالْقُرْآنِ يَوْمَ الْقِيَامَةِ وَأَهْلِهِ الَّذِينَ كَانُوا يَعْمَلُونَ بِهِ، تَقْدُمُهُ سُورَةُ الْبَقَرَةِ وَآلُ عِمْرَانَ». وَضَرَبَ لَهُمَا رَسُولُ اللهِ صَلَّى اللهُ عَلَيْهِ وَسَلَّمَ ثَلَاثَةَ أَمْثَالٍ مَا نَسِيتُهُنَّ بَعْدُ، قَالَ: «كَأَنَّهُمَا غَمَامَتَانِ، أَوْ ظُلَّتَانِ سَوْدَاوَانِ بَيْنَهُمَا شَرْقٌ، أَوْ كَأَنَّهُمَا حِزْقَانِ مِنْ طَيْرٍ صَوَافَّ، تُحَاجَّانِ عَنْ صَاحِبِهِمَا».

i. Related by al-Tirmidhī, 2883.

CHAPTER 43

RECITING AL-FĀTIḤAH AND THE END OF SURAH AL-BAQARAH (THE COW)

[1606–254]. (Dar al-Salam 1760) Ḥasan ibn al-Rabīʿ and Ahmad ibn Jawwās al-Ḥanafī narrated: both said: Abu al-Aḥwaṣ narrated; from ʿAmmār ibn Ruzayq; from ʿAbdullāh ibn ʿĪsā; from Saʿīd ibn Jubayr; from Ibn ʿAbbās. He said: **'As Gabriel was sitting with the Prophet (peace be upon him), he heard the noise of a door opening above him. He lifted his head and said: "This is a door in heaven which has been opened today. It was never opened until today. An angel came down through it. Here is an angel descending to the earth. He never came down until today". He made a greeting and said: "Rejoice for being given two lights that were never given to a prophet before you: the Book's opening surah and the final verses of Surah The Cow. You shall be granted every word of these you recite".'**

حَدَّثَنَا حَسَنُ بْنُ الرَّبِيعِ، وَأَحْمَدُ بْنُ جَوَّاسٍ الْحَنَفِيُّ، قَالا: حَدَّثَنَا أَبُو الأَحْوَصِ، عَنْ عَمَّارِ بْنِ رُزَيْقٍ، عَنْ عَبْدِ اللهِ بْنِ عِيسَى، عَنْ سَعِيدِ بْنِ جُبَيْرٍ، عَنِ ابْنِ عَبَّاسٍ قَالَ: بَيْنَمَا جِبْرِيلُ قَاعِدٌ عِنْدَ النَّبِيِّ صَلَّى اللهُ عَلَيْهِ وَسَلَّمَ سَمِعَ نَقِيضًا مِنْ فَوْقِهِ، فَرَفَعَ رَأْسَهُ فَقَالَ «هَذَا بَابٌ مِنَ السَّمَاءِ فُتِحَ الْيَوْمَ، لَمْ يُفْتَحْ قَطُّ إِلاَّ الْيَوْمَ. فَنَزَلَ مِنْهُ مَلَكٌ، فَقَالَ هَذَا مَلَكٌ نَزَلَ إِلَى الأَرْضِ لَمْ يَنْزِلْ قَطُّ إِلاَّ الْيَوْمَ»، فَسَلَّمَ وَقَالَ: «أَبْشِرْ بِنُورَيْنِ أُوتِيتَهُمَا لَمْ يُؤْتَهُمَا نَبِيٌّ قَبْلَكَ: فَاتِحَةُ الْكِتَابِ وَخَوَاتِيمُ سُورَةِ الْبَقَرَةِ. لَنْ تَقْرَأَ بِحَرْفٍ مِنْهُمَا إِلاَّ أُعْطِيتَهُ».

[1607–255]. (Dar al-Salam 1761–1762) Ahmad ibn Yūnus narrated:[i] Zuhayr narrated; Manṣūr narrated; from Ibrāhīm; from ʿAbd al-Raḥmān ibn Yazīd. He said: **'I met Abu Masʿūd at the Kaʿbah and said to him: "I am told of a hadith you have narrated concerning the two verses of Surah The Cow". He said: "Indeed. God's Messenger (peace be upon him) said: 'The two verses at the end of Surah The Cow - whoever recites them at night, they shall be sufficient for him'."'**

وَحَدَّثَنَا أَحْمَدُ بْنُ يُونُسَ، حَدَّثَنَا زُهَيْرٌ، حَدَّثَنَا مَنْصُورٌ، عَنْ إِبْرَاهِيمَ، عَنْ عَبْدِ الرَّحْمَنِ، بْنِ يَزِيدَ قَالَ: لَقِيتُ أَبَا مَسْعُودٍ عِنْدَ الْبَيْتِ فَقُلْتُ: حَدِيثٌ بَلَغَنِي عَنْكَ فِي الآيَتَيْنِ فِي سُورَةِ الْبَقَرَةِ. فَقَالَ: نَعَمْ. قَالَ رَسُولُ اللهِ صَلَّى اللهُ عَلَيْهِ وَسَلَّمَ: «الآيَتَانِ مِنْ آخِرِ سُورَةِ الْبَقَرَةِ مَنْ قَرَأَهُمَا فِي لَيْلَةٍ كَفَتَاهُ».

Isḥāq ibn Ibrāhīm narrated: Jarīr reported [H]. Also, Muhammad ibn al-Muthannā and Ibn Bashshār narrated; both said: Muhammad ibn Jaʿfar narrated; Shuʿbah narrated; both from Manṣūr; with this chain of transmission: **the same text.**

وَحَدَّثَنَاهُ إِسْحَاقُ بْنُ إِبْرَاهِيمَ، أَخْبَرَنَا جَرِيرٌ، ح. وَحَدَّثَنَا مُحَمَّدُ بْنُ الْمُثَنَّى، وَابْنُ بَشَّارٍ قَالا: حَدَّثَنَا مُحَمَّدُ بْنُ جَعْفَرٍ، حَدَّثَنَا شُعْبَةُ، كِلاَهُمَا عَنْ مَنْصُورٍ، بِهَذَا الإِسْنَادِ.

[1608–256]. (Dar al-Salam 1763–1765) Minjāb ibn al-Ḥārith al-Tamīmī narrated: Ibn Mushir reported; from al-Aʿmash; from Ibrāhīm; from ʿAbd al-Raḥmān ibn Yazīd; from ʿAlqamah ibn Qays; from Abu Masʿūd al-Anṣārī. He said: **'God's Messenger (peace be upon him) said: "Whoever recites these two verses**

i. Related by al-Bukhari, 5008, 5009, 5040 and 5051; Abu Dāwūd, 1397; al-Tirmidhī, 2881; Ibn Mājah, 1368 and 1369.

at the end of Surah The Cow on any night, they shall be sufficient for him".'

'Abd al-Raḥmān said: "I met Abu Mas'ūd as he was performing the *ṭawāf* at the Ka'bah. I asked him and he narrated the hadith to me from the Prophet (peace be upon him)".

حَدَّثَنَا مِنْجَابُ بْنُ الْحَارِثِ التَّمِيمِيُّ، أَخْبَرَنَا ابْنُ مُسْهِرٍ، عَنِ الأَعْمَشِ، عَنْ إِبْرَاهِيمَ، عَنْ عَبْدِ الرَّحْمَنِ بْنِ يَزِيدَ، عَنْ عَلْقَمَةَ بْنِ قَيْسٍ، عَنْ أَبِي مَسْعُودٍ الأَنْصَارِيِّ قَالَ: قَالَ رَسُولُ اللهِ صَلَّى اللهُ عَلَيْهِ وَسَلَّمَ: «مَنْ قَرَأَ هَاتَيْنِ الآيَتَيْنِ مِنْ آخِرِ سُورَةِ الْبَقَرَةِ فِي لَيْلَةٍ كَفَتَاهُ». قَالَ عَبْدُ الرَّحْمَنِ: فَلَقِيتُ أَبَا مَسْعُودٍ وَهُوَ يَطُوفُ بِالْبَيْتِ، فَسَأَلْتُهُ فَحَدَّثَنِي بِهِ عَنِ النَّبِيِّ صَلَّى اللهُ عَلَيْهِ وَسَلَّمَ.

'Alī ibn Khashram narrated to me: 'Īsā (meaning Ibn Yūnus) reported [H]. Also, Abu Bakr ibn Abi Shaybah narrated; 'Abdullāh ibn Numayr narrated; both from al-A'mash; from Ibrāhīm; from 'Alqamah and 'Abd al-Raḥmān ibn Yazīd; from Abu Mas'ūd; from the Prophet (peace be upon him): **the same text.**

وَحَدَّثَنِي عَلِيُّ بْنُ خَشْرَمٍ، أَخْبَرَنَا عِيسَى يَعْنِي ابْنَ يُونُسَ، ح. وَحَدَّثَنَا أَبُو بَكْرِ بْنُ أَبِي شَيْبَةَ حَدَّثَنَا عَبْدُ اللهِ بْنُ نُمَيْرٍ، جَمِيعًا عَنِ الأَعْمَشِ، عَنْ إِبْرَاهِيمَ، عَنْ عَلْقَمَةَ، وَعَبْدِ الرَّحْمَنِ بْنِ يَزِيدَ عَنْ أَبِي مَسْعُودٍ، عَنِ النَّبِيِّ صَلَّى اللهُ عَلَيْهِ وَسَلَّمَ مِثْلَهُ.

Abu Bakr ibn Abi Shaybah narrated: Ḥafṣ and Abu Mu'āwiyah narrated; from al-A'mash; from Ibrāhīm; from 'Abd al-Raḥmān ibn Yazīd; from Abu Mas'ūd; from the Prophet (peace be upon him): **the same text.**

وَحَدَّثَنَا أَبُو بَكْرِ بْنُ أَبِي شَيْبَةَ، حَدَّثَنَا حَفْصٌ وَأَبُو مُعَاوِيَةَ عَنِ الأَعْمَشِ، عَنْ إِبْرَاهِيمَ، عَنْ عَبْدِ الرَّحْمَنِ بْنِ يَزِيدَ، عَنْ أَبِي مَسْعُودٍ، عَنِ النَّبِيِّ صَلَّى اللهُ عَلَيْهِ وَسَلَّمَ مِثْلَهُ

Text Explanation

In hadith No. 1601 the Prophet mentions that reciting three verses of the Qur'an during prayer is better for a person than having three big, fat and pregnant camels. The Prophet uses the word *khalifah* for describing the pregnant camel. This word refers to a she-camel in the first half of its pregnancy.[i] Buṭḥān was a place near Madinah [and al-ʿAqīq was a valley with sweet water sources near Madinah.]

Hadith No. 1603 includes the Prophet's advice to recite 'the two bright ones: The Cow and Surah Āl ʿImrān'. These two long surahs are called 'the bright ones' because of the light and guidance they provide and the rich reward they earn for anyone who recites them. The hadith makes clear that it is perfectly permissible to say Surah Āl ʿImrān, or Surah Women, or Surah The Repast, etc. There is nothing to suggest discouragement of saying so, even though some early scholars expressed such a view. They advised that one should say 'the surah in which so-and-so is mentioned'. The first view is the correct one because the meaning is clear.

In this hadith, the Prophet mentions that these two surahs will be like two clouds or canopies to give shade to the one who frequently recites them. Some scholars say that what is meant is that the reward for reciting them will be given like two clouds. The other simile the Prophet gives for them is that they will be like two flocks of birds with their wings spread out. In hadith No. 1605, the Prophet gives further details of his simile, saying that the two surahs will be 'like two black canopies with bright light between them'. This means that their blackness will not prevent sight because of the bright light that is between them.

Hadith No. 1607 and 1608 quote the Prophet saying that reciting the last two verses of Surah 2, The Cow, at night will be sufficient for anyone. It is said that this means that they will be sufficient as night worship. It is also said that they will be sufficient protection from

---

i. This was the type of camel the Arabs loved best, and if she was big and fat, then it was considered a generous source of provision and income.

Satan or from adversities. However, it may be that they are sufficient in all these respects.

[**Note**: we may add that in hadith No. 1606, the angel says to the Prophet that he will be granted every word he recites of the opening surah of the Qur'an, i.e. al-Fātiḥah and the final verses of Surah 2, The Cow. This means that he and every one of his community will be given whatever is included in every sentence therein: if it is a supplication, it will be answered, and if it is a glorification, it will be rewarded.]

Transmission

In the chain of transmission of hadith No. 1605, al-Nawwās ibn Sam'ān is mentioned as the narrator from the Prophet. His father's name is pronounced as Sam'ān or Sim'ān.

CHAPTER 44

SURAH 18, THE CAVE AND THE VERSE OF THE THRONE

[1609–257]. (Dar al-Salam 1766) Muhammad ibn al-Muthannā narrated:[i] Muʿādh ibn Hishām narrated; my father narrated to me; from Qatādah; from Sālim ibn Abi al-Jaʿd al-Ghaṭafānī; from Maʿdān ibn Abi Ṭalḥah al-Yaʿmarī; from Abu al-Dardā'; that the Prophet (peace be upon him) said: **'Whoever memorises ten verses from the beginning of Surah The Cave shall be protected from the Impostor'.**

وَحَدَّثَنَا مُحَمَّدُ بْنُ الْـمُثَنَّى، حَدَّثَنَا مُعَاذُ بْنُ هِشَامٍ، حَدَّثَنِي أَبِي، عَنْ قَتَادَةَ، عَنْ سَالِمِ بْنِ أَبِي الْـجَعْدِ الْغَطَفَانِيِّ، عَنْ مَعْدَانَ بْنِ أَبِي طَلْحَةَ الْيَعْمَرِيِّ، عَنْ أَبِي الدَّرْدَاءِ، أَنَّ النَّبِيَّ صَلَّى اللهُ عَلَيْهِ وَسَلَّمَ قَالَ: «مَنْ حَفِظَ عَشْرَ آيَاتٍ مِنْ أَوَّلِ سُورَةِ الْكَهْفِ عُصِمَ مِنَ الدَّجَّالِ».

[1610–000]. (Dar al-Salam 1767) Muhammad ibn al-Muthannā and Ibn Bashshār narrated: Muhammad ibn Jaʿfar narrated; Shuʿbah narrated [H]. Also, Zuhayr ibn Ḥarb narrated to me; ʿAbd al-Raḥmān ibn Mahdī narrated; Hammām narrated; both from Qatādah; with this chain of transmission. **Shuʿbah said: 'From the end of Surah The Cave', but Hammām said: 'From the beginning of Surah The Cave', like Hishām.**

---

i. Related by Abu Dāwūd, 4323; al-Tirmidhī, 2886.

وَحدَّثنا مُحَمَّدُ بْنُ الْـمُثَنَّى وَابْن بَشَّارٍ قَالا: حَدَّثنا مُحَمَّدُ بْنُ جَعْفَرٍ، حَدَّثَنَا شُعْبَةُ، ح. وَحَدَّثَنِي زُهَيْرُ بْنُ حَرْبٍ، حَدَّثَنَا عَبْدُ الرَّحْمَنِ بْنُ مَهْدِيٍّ، حَدَّثَنَا هَمَّامٌ، جَمِيعًا عَنْ قَتَادَةَ، بِهَذَا الإِسْنَادِ. قَالَ شُعْبَةُ مِنْ آخِرِ الْكَهْفِ. وَقَالَ هَمَّامٌ مِنْ أَوَّلِ الْكَهْفِ، كَمَا قَالَ هِشَامٌ.

[1611–258]. (Dar al-Salam 1768) Abu Bakr ibn Abi Shaybah narrated:[i] ʿAbd al-Aʿlā ibn ʿAbd al-Aʿlā narrated; from al-Jurayrī; from Abu al-Salīl; from ʿAbdullāh ibn Rabāḥ al-Anṣārī; from Ubayy ibn Kaʿb. He said: **'God's Messenger (peace be upon him) said: "Abu al-Mundhir, do you know which is the greatest verse of God's Book that is with you?" I said: "God and His Messenger know best". He said: "Abu al-Mundhir, do you know which is the greatest verse of God's Book that is with you?" I said: "God: there is no deity but Him, the Ever-Living, the Eternal Master of all". He patted me on my chest and said: "By God! Congratulations to you on your knowledge, Abu al-Mundhir".'**

حَدَّثَنَا أَبُو بَكْرِ بْنُ أَبِي شَيْبَةَ، حَدَّثَنَا عَبْدُ الأَعْلَى بْنُ عَبْدِ الأَعْلَى، عَنِ الْجُرَيْرِيِّ، عَنْ أَبِي السَّلِيلِ، عَنْ عَبْدِ اللهِ بْنِ رَبَاحٍ الأَنْصَارِيِّ، عَنْ أُبَيِّ بْنِ كَعْبٍ قَالَ: قَالَ رَسُولُ اللهِ صَلَّى اللهُ عَلَيْهِ وَسَلَّمَ: «يَا أَبَا الْـمُنْذِرِ، أَتَدْرِي أَيُّ آيَةٍ مِنْ كِتَابِ اللهِ مَعَكَ أَعْظَمُ؟» قَالَ: قُلْتُ اللهُ وَرَسُولُهُ أَعْلَمُ. قَالَ «يَا أَبَا الْـمُنْذِرِ أَتَدْرِي أَيُّ آيَةٍ مِنْ كِتَابِ اللهِ مَعَكَ أَعْظَمُ؟». قَالَ: قُلْتُ: «اللهُ لاَ إِلَهَ إِلاَّ هُوَ الْحَيُّ الْقَيُّومُ». قَالَ: فَضَرَبَ فِي صَدْرِي وَقَالَ: «وَاللهِ لِيَهْنِكَ الْعِلْمُ أَبَا الْـمُنْذِرِ».

Text Explanation

In hadith No. 1609, the Prophet says that a person who memorises the first ten verses of Surah 18, The Cave, will be protected from

i. Related by Abu Dāwūd, 1460.

the Impostor. Another version says the last ten verses of this surah. It is said that the former is due to what the surah includes at the beginning of wonderful meanings and signs. Whoever reflects on its meanings and understands them will not be deceived by the Impostor and what he alleges. The same may be said about its end, from the verse that says: 'Do the unbelievers think that they could take My creatures for patrons against Me? We have indeed readied hell as a dwelling place for the unbelievers'. (18: 102)

In hadith No. 1611 the Prophet says to Ubayy ibn Ka'b: 'Congratulations to you on your knowledge, Abu al-Mundhir'. This is a statement that Ubayy was of great merit, and it shows that he had great knowledge. It also shows that it is appropriate for a scholar to praise those who have special merit among his associates and to address them by their appellation, i.e. *kunyah*, which is considered a mark of respect by the Arabs. It also tells us that it is permissible to praise someone to his face, if this serves a good purpose and is unlikely to make such a person conceited because he is a person of true piety.

The Prophet asked Ubayy: 'Abu al-Mundhir, do you know which verse of God's Book which is with you is the greatest?' He said: 'God: there is no deity but Him, the Ever-Living, the Eternal Master of all'. [This is the beginning of Verse 255 of Surah 2, which is known as the Verse of the Throne.] *Qadi* 'Iyāḍ says that this provides argument for suggesting that some parts of the Qur'an are better or greater than others and that the Qur'an is better than God's other books. However, scholars differ on this point. Abu al-Ḥasan 'Alī ibn 'Umar al-Ash'arī and Abu Bakr Muhammad al-Bāqillānī, as well as a number of leading scholars, say that it is not permissible because to say that some of it is greater than the rest means that the other parts are deficient. None of God's words are deficient. These scholars understand words such as 'better' or 'greater' describing some verses and surahs as meaning 'good' or 'great'. On the other hand, Isḥāq ibn Rāhawayh and other scholars say that it is permissible and that it refers to the greater reward a person receives by reciting such verses and surahs. The view of choice is that it is permissible to say that such-and-such verse or surah is greater or better, meaning that the reward given for it is greater, which is the meaning of the hadith, but God knows best.

Scholars say that the Verse of the Throne is distinguished by being greatest because of what it combines of God's names and attributes: Godhead, oneness, eternal life, absolute knowledge, dominion, power and will. These seven are the most essentials of God's fine names and attributes, but God knows best.

Transmission

Abu al-Salīl is one of the narrators included in the chain of transmission of hadith No. 1611. His name is Ḍurayb ibn Nuqayr, but he is also mentioned as being Ḍurayb ibn Nufayr or Nafīl.

CHAPTER 45

RECITING SURAH 112

[1612–259]. (Dar al-Salam 1769) Zuhayr ibn Ḥarb and Muhammad ibn Bashshār narrated to me: Zuhayr said: Yaḥyā ibn Saʿīd narrated; from Shuʿbah; from Qatādah; from Sālim ibn Abi al-Jaʿd; from Maʿdān ibn Abi Ṭalḥah; from Abu al-Dardā'; from the Prophet (peace be upon him). He said: **'Is it beyond any of you to recite one third of the Qur'an in one night?' People asked: 'How can one recite one third of the Qur'an?' He said: '[The surah starting with] "Say: He is God, the One and only God" equals one third of the Qur'an'.**

وَحَدَّثَنِي زُهَيْرُ بْنُ حَرْبٍ، وَمُحَمَّدُ بْنُ بَشَّارٍ، قَالَ زُهَيْرٌ: حَدَّثَنَا يَحْيَى بْنُ سَعِيدٍ، عَنْ شُعْبَةَ، عَنْ قَتَادَةَ، عَنْ سَالِمِ بْنِ أَبِي الْجَعْدِ، عَنْ مَعْدَانَ بْنِ أَبِي طَلْحَةَ، عَنْ أَبِي الدَّرْدَاءِ، عَنِ النَّبِيِّ صَلَّى اللهُ عَلَيْهِ وَسَلَّمَ قَالَ: «أَيَعْجِزُ أَحَدُكُمْ أَنْ يَقْرَأَ فِي لَيْلَةٍ ثُلُثَ الْقُرْآنِ؟» قَالُوا: وَكَيْفَ يَقْرَأُ ثُلُثَ الْقُرْآنِ؟ قَالَ: « قُلْ هُوَ اللهُ أَحَدٌ » يَعْدِلُ ثُلُثَ الْقُرْآنِ.

[1613–260]. (Dar al-Salam 1770) Isḥāq ibn Ibrāhīm narrated: Muhammad ibn Bakr reported; Saʿīd ibn Abi ʿArūbah narrated [H]. Also, Abu Bakr ibn Abi Shaybah narrated; ʿAffān narrated; Abān al-ʿAṭṭār narrated; both from Qatādah; with this chain of transmission: **the same but their hadith adds that the Prophet said: 'God has divided the Qur'an into three parts, making [the surah starting with] "Say: He is God, the One and only God" one of the parts of the Qur'an'.**

وَحَدَّثَنَا إِسْحَاقُ بْنُ إِبْرَاهِيمَ، أَخْبَرَنَا مُحَمَّدُ بْنُ بَكْرٍ، حَدَّثَنَا سَعِيدُ بْنُ أَبِي عَرُوبَةَ، ح. وَحَدَّثَنَا أَبُو بَكْرِ بْنُ أَبِي شَيْبَةَ، حَدَّثَنَا عَفَّانُ، حَدَّثَنَا أَبَانُ الْعَطَّارُ، جَمِيعًا عَنْ قَتَادَةَ، بِهَذَا الإِسْنَاد. وَفِي حَدِيثِهِمَا مِنْ قَوْلِ النَّبِيِّ صَلَّى اللهُ عَلَيْهِ وَسَلَّمَ قَالَ: «إِنَّ اللهَ جَزَّأَ الْقُرْآنَ ثَلاَثَةَ أَجْزَاءٍ، فَجَعَلَ قُلْ هُوَ اللهُ أَحَدٌ جُزْءًا مِنْ أَجْزَاءِ الْقُرْآنِ».

[1614–261]. (Dar al-Salam 1771) Muhammad ibn Ḥātim and Ya ʿqūb ibn Ibrāhīm narrated to me:[i] both from Yaḥyā; Ibn Ḥātim said: Yaḥyā ibn Saʿīd narrated; Yazīd ibn Kaysān narrated; Abu Ḥāzim narrated; from Abu Hurayrah. He said: **'God's Messenger (peace be upon him) said: "Gather. I shall recite to you one third of the Qur'an". People gathered around. The Prophet of God came out and recited [the surah starting with] "Say: He is God, the One and only God". He then went back home. We said to one another: "I think that this is some revelation that has come to him from on high. It must be what made him go back home". Then the Prophet came out and said: "I said to you that I will be reciting to you one third of the Qur'an. Indeed it is equal to one third of the Qur'an".'**

وَحَدَّثَنِي مُحَمَّدُ بْنُ حَاتِمٍ، وَيَعْقُوبُ بْنُ إِبْرَاهِيمَ، جَمِيعًا عَنْ يَحْيَى، - قَالَ ابْنُ حَاتِمٍ حَدَّثَنَا يَحْيَى بْنُ سَعِيدٍ، - حَدَّثَنَا يَزِيدُ بْنُ كَيْسَانَ، حَدَّثَنَا أَبُو حَازِمٍ، عَنْ أَبِي هُرَيْرَةَ قَالَ: قَالَ رَسُولُ اللهِ صَلَّى اللهُ عَلَيْهِ وَسَلَّمَ: «احْشِدُوا فَإِنِّي سَأَقْرَأُ عَلَيْكُمْ ثُلُثَ الْقُرْآنِ». فَحَشَدَ مَنْ حَشَدَ، ثُمَّ خَرَجَ نَبِيُّ اللهِ صَلَّى اللهُ عَلَيْهِ وَسَلَّمَ فَقَرَأَ «قُلْ هُوَ اللهُ أَحَدٌ»، ثُمَّ دَخَلَ. فَقَالَ بَعْضُنَا لِبَعْضٍ إِنِّي أُرَى هَذَا خَبَرٌ جَاءَهُ مِنَ السَّمَاءِ، فَذَاكَ الَّذِي أَدْخَلَهُ. ثُمَّ خَرَجَ نَبِيُّ اللهِ صَلَّى اللهُ عَلَيْهِ وَسَلَّمَ، فَقَالَ: «إِنِّي قُلْتُ لَكُمْ سَأَقْرَأُ عَلَيْكُمْ ثُلُثَ الْقُرْآنِ. أَلاَ إِنَّهَا تَعْدِلُ ثُلُثَ الْقُرْآنِ».

---

i. Related by al-Tirmidhī, 2900.

[1615–262]. (Dar al-Salam 1772) Wāṣil ibn ʿAbd al-Aʿlā narrated: Ibn Fuḍayl narrated; from Bashīr Abu Ismāʿīl; from Abu Ḥāzim; from Abu Hurayrah. He said: **'God's Messenger (peace be upon him) came out to us and said: "I shall recite to you one third of the Qur'an", and he recited [the surah]: "Say: He is God, the One and only God, the Eternal, the Absolute" to its end'.**

وَحَدَّثَنَا وَاصِلُ بْنُ عَبْدِ الأَعْلَى، حَدَّثَنَا ابْنُ فُضَيْلٍ، عَنْ بَشِيرٍ أَبِي إِسْمَاعِيلَ، عَنْ أَبِي حَازِمٍ، عَنْ أَبِي هُرَيْرَةَ قَالَ: خَرَجَ إِلَيْنَا رَسُولُ اللهِ صَلَّى اللهُ عَلَيْهِ وَسَلَّمَ، فَقَالَ: «أَقْرَأُ عَلَيْكُمْ ثُلُثَ الْقُرْآنِ». فَقَرَأَ: «قُلْ هُوَ اللهُ أَحَدٌ اللهُ الصَّمَدُ» حَتَّى خَتَمَهَا.

[1616–263]. (Dar al-Salam 1773) Ahmad ibn ʿAbd al-Raḥmān ibn Wahb narrated:[i] my uncle ʿAbdullāh ibn Wahb narrated; ʿAmr ibn al-Ḥārith narrated; from Saʿīd ibn Abi Hilāl; that Abu al-Rijāl Muhammad ibn ʿAbd al-Raḥmān narrated to him; from his mother ʿAmrah bint ʿAbd al-Raḥmān who was looked after by ʿĀ'ishah, the Prophet's wife, from ʿĀ'ishah; that **'God's Messenger (peace be upon him) sent a man as a commander of an expedition, and this man was reciting the Qur'an as he led the prayer with his Companions and he always finished with "Say: He is God, the One and only God". When they came back, this was mentioned to God's Messenger (peace be upon him). He said: "Ask him why he does this". They asked him and he said: "Because it describes God, the Lord of Grace. I love to recite it". God's Messenger (peace be upon him) said to them: "Tell him that God loves him".'**

i. Related by al-Bukhari, 7375; al-Nasāʾī, 992.

حَدَّثَنَا أَحْمَدُ بْنُ عَبْدِ الرَّحْمَنِ بْنِ وَهْبٍ، حَدَّثَنَا عَمِّي عَبْدُ اللهِ بْنُ وَهْبٍ، حَدَّثَنَا عَمْرُو بْنُ الْحَارِثِ، عَنْ سَعِيدِ بْنِ أَبِي هِلَالٍ، أَنَّ أَبَا الرِّجَالِ مُحَمَّدَ بْنَ عَبْدِ الرَّحْمَنِ حَدَّثَهُ عَنْ أُمِّهِ، عَمْرَةَ بِنْتِ عَبْدِ الرَّحْمَنِ، وَكَانَتْ فِي حَجْرِ عَائِشَةَ زَوْجِ النَّبِيِّ صَلَّى اللهُ عَلَيْهِ وَسَلَّمَ، عَنْ عَائِشَةَ أَنَّ رَسُولَ اللهِ صَلَّى اللهُ عَلَيْهِ وَسَلَّمَ بَعَثَ رَجُلاً عَلَى سَرِيَّةٍ وَكَانَ يَقْرَأُ لأَصْحَابِهِ فِي صَلَاتِهِمْ فَيَخْتِمُ بِـ «قُلْ هُوَ اللهُ أَحَدٌ»، فَلَمَّا رَجَعُوا ذُكِرَ ذَلِكَ لِرَسُولِ اللهِ صَلَّى اللهُ عَلَيْهِ وَسَلَّمَ فَقَالَ: «سَلُوهُ لأَيِّ شَيْءٍ يَصْنَعُ ذَلِكَ؟» فَسَأَلُوهُ، فَقَالَ: لأَنَّهَا صِفَةُ الرَّحْمَنِ فَأَنَا أُحِبُّ أَنْ أَقْرَأَ بِهَا. فَقَالَ رَسُولُ اللهِ صَلَّى اللهُ عَلَيْهِ وَسَلَّمَ: «أَخْبِرُوهُ أَنَّ اللهَ يُحِبُّهُ».

[**Note**: The hadiths in this chapter will be explained together with the hadiths in the next chapter.]

CHAPTER 46

RECITING THE LAST TWO SURAHS

[1617–264]. (Dar al-Salam 1774) Qutaybah ibn Saʿīd narrated:[i] Jarīr narrated; from Bayān; from Qays ibn Abi Ḥāzim; from ʿUqbah ibn ʿĀmir. He said: **'God's Messenger (peace be upon him) said: "Have you not seen that tonight certain verses have been revealed, the like of which have never been known? [They are the surahs starting with]: 'Say: I seek refuge in the Lord of the daybreak', and 'Say: I seek refuge in the Lord of mankind'."'**

وَحَدَّثَنَا قُتَيْبَةُ بْنُ سَعِيدٍ، حَدَّثَنَا جَرِيرٌ، عَنْ بَيَانٍ، عَنْ قَيْسِ بْنِ أَبِي حَازِمٍ، عَنْ عُقْبَةَ بْنِ عَامِرٍ، قَالَ قَالَ رَسُولُ اللهِ صَلَّى اللهُ عَلَيْهِ وَسَلَّمَ «أَلَمْ تَرَ آيَاتٍ أُنْزِلَتِ اللَّيْلَةَ لَمْ يُرَ مِثْلُهُنَّ قَطُّ: «قُلْ أَعُوذُ بِرَبِّ الْفَلَقِ» وَ «قُلْ أَعُوذُ بِرَبِّ النَّاسِ».

[1618–265]. (Dar al-Salam 1775–1776) Muhammad ibn ʿAbdullāh ibn Numayr narrated to me: my father narrated; Ismāʿīl ibn Qays narrated; from ʿUqbah ibn ʿĀmir. He said: **'God's Messenger (peace be upon him) said to me: "Certain verses have been revealed to me, the like of which have never been known: *al-Muʿawwidhatayn* [i.e. the two surahs seeking refuge]".'**

i. Related by al-Tirmidhī, 2902; al-Nasāʾī, 953.

وَحَدَّثَنِي مُحَمَّدُ بْنُ عَبْدِ اللهِ بْنِ نُمَيْرٍ، حَدَّثَنَا أَبِي، حَدَّثَنَا إِسْمَاعِيلُ، عَنْ قَيْسٍ، عَنْ عُقْبَةَ بْنِ عَامِرٍ قَالَ: قَالَ لِي رَسُولُ اللهِ صَلَّى اللهُ عَلَيْهِ وَسَلَّمَ: «أُنْزِلَ - أَوْ أُنْزِلَتْ - عَلَيَّ آيَاتٌ لَمْ يُرَ مِثْلُهُنَّ قَطُّ: الْمُعَوِّذَتَيْنِ»

Abu Bakr ibn Abi Shaybah narrated: Wakīʿ narrated [H]. Also, Muhammad ibn Rāfiʿ narrated to me; Abu Usāmah narrated; both from Ismāʿīl; with this chain of transmission: **the same text.**

In Abu Usāmah's narration from ʿUqbah ibn ʿĀmir al-Juhanī, it is added: **'And he was one of the leading Companions of Muhammad (peace be upon him)'.**

وَحَدَّثَنَاهُ أَبُو بَكْرِ بْنُ أَبِي شَيْبَةَ، حَدَّثَنَا وَكِيعٌ، ح. وَحَدَّثَنِي مُحَمَّدُ بْنُ رَافِعٍ، حَدَّثَنَا أَبُو أُسَامَةَ، كِلَاهُمَا عَنْ إِسْمَاعِيلَ، بِهَذَا الإِسْنَادِ: مِثْلَهُ . وَفِي رِوَايَةِ أَبِي أُسَامَةَ عَنْ عُقْبَةَ بْنِ عَامِرٍ الْجُهَنِيِّ، وَكَانَ مِنْ رُفَعَاءِ أَصْحَابِ مُحَمَّدٍ صَلَّى اللهُ عَلَيْهِ وَسَلَّمَ.

Text Explanation

The Prophet says in hadith No. 1612 that Surah 112 equals one third of the Qur'an, and in the following hadith he says that God divided the Qur'an into three parts, making this surah one part. *Qadi* ʿIyāḍ quotes Imam al-Māzarī in saying that scholars interpreted this as the Qur'an tackles three main themes: stories, rulings and God's attributes. This surah, 112, starting 'Say: He is God, the One and only God' is purely concerned with God's attributes. As such, it is one of three parts. It is also said that the reward for reciting it is multiplied up to the reward of reciting one third of the Qur'an, provided that the reward for that one third is not multiplied. However, God generally grants His reward in multiples.

The Prophet was told about the man who finished his recitation in prayer by reciting Surah 112, Purity of Faith. The man said that it states the attributes of God, the Lord of Grace, and he loved to recite it for that reason. The Prophet said: 'Tell him that God loves him'. Imam al-Māzarī said: 'God's love of His servants is His will to reward them and to bestow fine bounties on them'. Others said: 'His love of His servants is rewarding them and bestowing bounties on them, not the will to do so'. *Qadi* 'Iyāḍ said: 'Their love of God may be their inclination towards Him, but He is above feeling inclined to anyone'. It is also said that their love of God is continuing to obey Him. Some also say that such continuity is the fruit of their love, while their love of God is their inclination towards Him because He deserves love in all its aspects.

In hadith No. 1617, the Prophet says: 'Have you not seen that tonight certain verses have been revealed, the like of which have never been known? [They are the surahs starting with]: "Say: I seek refuge in the Lord of the daybreak", and "Say: I seek refuge in the Lord of mankind".' This shows the great importance of these two surahs. We have already mentioned the difference of views among scholars regarding whether any part of the Qur'an is considered greater than other parts.

This hadith provides clear evidence that these two surahs are part of the Qur'an. It refutes the claim attributed to 'Abdullāh ibn Mas'ūd stating something different is said. The hadith also proves that the word 'say' is included in the Qur'an as the first word of each of these two surahs. The Muslim community is unanimous that this is so.

CHAPTER 47

THE MERIT OF ONE WHO RECITES AND TEACHES THE QUR'AN

[1619–266]. (Dar al-Salam 1777) Abu Bakr ibn Abi Shaybah, ʿAmr al-Nāqid and Zuhayr ibn Ḥarb narrated:[i] all from Ibn ʿUyaynah. Zuhayr said: Sufyān ibn ʿUyaynah narrated: al-Zuhrī narrated; from Sālim; from his father; from the Prophet (peace be upon him). He said: **'No envy is acceptable except in two things: a person to whom God has given the Qur'an and he recites in [all] hours of night and day and a person to whom God has granted money and he donates of it at night and day'.**

حَدَّثَنَا أَبُو بَكْرِ بْنُ أَبِي شَيْبَةَ، وَعَمْرٌو النَّاقِدُ، وَزُهَيْرُ بْنُ حَرْبٍ، كُلُّهُمْ عَنِ ابْنِ عُيَيْنَةَ، - قَالَ زُهَيْرٌ حَدَّثَنَا سُفْيَانُ بْنُ عُيَيْنَةَ، - حَدَّثَنَا الزُّهْرِيُّ، عَنْ سَالِمٍ، عَنْ أَبِيهِ، عَنِ النَّبِيِّ صَلَّى اللهُ عَلَيْهِ وَسَلَّمَ قَالَ: «لاَ حَسَدَ إِلاَّ فِي اثْنَتَيْنِ: رَجُلٌ آتَاهُ اللهُ الْقُرْآنَ فَهُوَ يَقُومُ بِهِ آنَاءَ اللَّيْلِ وَآنَاءَ النَّهَارِ، وَرَجُلٌ آتَاهُ اللهُ مَالاً فَهُوَ يُنْفِقُهُ آنَاءَ اللَّيْلِ وَآنَاءَ النَّهَارِ».

[1620–267]. (Dar al-Salam 1778) Ḥarmalah ibn Yaḥyā narrated to me: Ibn Wahb reported; Yūnus reported to me; from Ibn Shihāb; he said: Sālim ibn ʿAbdullāh ibn ʿUmar reported to me; from his father. He said: **'God's Messenger (peace be upon him) said: "No envy is acceptable except in two things: a person to whom God has given this book and he recites it in [all] hours of the**

i. Related by al-Bukhari, 7529; al-Tirmidhī, 1936; Ibn Mājah, 4209.

night and day and a person to whom God has granted money and he is charitable with it at night and day".'

وَحَدَّثَنِي حَرْمَلَةُ بْنُ يَحْيَى، أَخْبَرَنَا ابْنُ وَهْبٍ، أَخْبَرَنِي يُونُسُ، عَنِ ابْنِ شِهَابٍ، قَالَ أَخْبَرَنِي سَالِمُ بْنُ عَبْدِ اللهِ بْنِ عُمَرَ، عَنْ أَبِيهِ قَالَ: قَالَ رَسُولُ اللهِ صَلَّى اللهُ عَلَيْهِ وَسَلَّمَ: «لاَ حَسَدَ إِلاَّ عَلَى اثْنَتَيْنِ: رَجُلٌ آتَاهُ اللهُ هَذَا الْكِتَابَ فَقَامَ بِهِ آنَاءَ اللَّيْلِ وَآنَاءَ النَّهَارِ، وَرَجُلٌ آتَاهُ اللهُ مَالاً فَتَصَدَّقَ بِهِ آنَاءَ اللَّيْلِ وَآنَاءَ النَّهَارِ».

[1621–268]. (Dar al-Salam 1779) Abu Bakr ibn Abi Shaybah narrated:[i] Wakīʿ narrated; from Ismāʿīl; from Qays; he said: ʿAbdullāh ibn Masʿūd said: [H]. Also, Ibn Numayr narrated; my father and Muhammad ibn Bishr narrated; they said: Ismāʿīl narrated; from Qays; he said: I heard ʿAbdullāh ibn Masʿūd say: **'God's Messenger (peace be upon him) said: "No envy is acceptable except in two things: a person to whom God has granted money and enabled him to spend it in what is right and a person to whom God has granted wisdom and he rules according to it and teaches it".'**

وَحَدَّثَنَا أَبُو بَكْرِ بْنُ أَبِي شَيْبَةَ، حَدَّثَنَا وَكِيعٌ، عَنْ إِسْمَاعِيلَ، عَنْ قَيْسٍ قَالَ: قَالَ عَبْدُ اللهِ بْنُ مَسْعُودٍ ح. وَحَدَّثَنَا ابْنُ نُمَيْرٍ، حَدَّثَنَا أَبِي وَمُحَمَّدُ بْنُ بِشْرٍ، قَالاَ: حَدَّثَنَا إِسْمَاعِيلُ، عَنْ قَيْسٍ، قَالَ: سَمِعْتُ عَبْدَ اللهِ بْنَ مَسْعُودٍ يَقُولُ: قَالَ رَسُولُ اللهِ صَلَّى اللهُ عَلَيْهِ وَسَلَّمَ: «لاَ حَسَدَ إِلاَّ فِي اثْنَتَيْنِ: رَجُلٌ آتَاهُ اللهُ مَالاً فَسَلَّطَهُ عَلَى هَلَكَتِهِ فِي الْحَقِّ، وَرَجُلٌ آتَاهُ اللهُ حِكْمَةً فَهُوَ يَقْضِي بِهَا وَيُعَلِّمُهَا».

[1622–269]. (Dar al-Salam 1780) Zuhayr ibn Ḥarb narrated to me:[ii] Yaʿqūb ibn Ibrāhīm narrated; my father narrated to me;

i. Related by al-Bukhari, 73, 1409, 7141 and 7316; Ibn Mājah, 4208.
ii. Related by Ibn Mājah, 218.

from Ibn Shihāb; from ʿĀmir ibn Wāthilah; that **ʻNāfiʿ ibn ʿAbd al-Ḥārith met ʿUmar at ʿUsfān. ʿUmar had appointed him Governor of Makkah. [ʿUmar] asked him: "Whom did you appoint over the people of this valley?" [Nāfiʿ] said: "Ibn Abzā". [ʿUmar] asked: "And who is Ibn Abzā?" He said: "One of our *mawlas*". [ʿUmar] said: "You appointed a *mawla* as their ruler?" [Nāfiʿ] said: "He has learnt God's Book, the Mighty and Exalted, by heart and he is well versed in the discipline of division of inheritance". [ʿUmar] said: "Your Prophet (peace be upon him) said: 'God elevates some people by means of this Book and brings down others'."'**

وَحَدَّثَنِي زُهَيْرُ بْنُ حَرْبٍ، حَدَّثَنَا يَعْقُوبُ بْنُ إِبْرَاهِيمَ، حَدَّثَنِي أَبِي، عَنِ ابْنِ شِهَابٍ، عَنْ عَامِرِ بْنِ وَاثِلَةَ، أَنَّ نَافِعَ بْنَ عَبْدِ الْحَارِثِ، لَقِيَ عُمَرَ بِعُسْفَانَ، وَكَانَ عُمَرُ يَسْتَعْمِلُهُ عَلَى مَكَّةَ، فَقَالَ: مَنِ اسْتَعْمَلْتَ عَلَى أَهْلِ الْوَادِي؟ فَقَالَ: ابْنَ أَبْزَى. قَالَ: وَمَنِ ابْنُ أَبْزَى؟ قَالَ: مَوْلًى مِنْ مَوَالِينَا. قَالَ: فَاسْتَخْلَفْتَ عَلَيْهِمْ مَوْلًى؟ قَالَ: إِنَّهُ قَارِئٌ لِكِتَابِ اللهِ عَزَّ وَجَلَّ، وَإِنَّهُ عَالِمٌ بِالْفَرَائِضِ. قَالَ عُمَرُ: أَمَا إِنَّ نَبِيَّكُمْ صَلَّى اللهُ عَلَيْهِ وَسَلَّمَ قَدْ قَالَ: «إِنَّ اللهَ يَرْفَعُ بِهَذَا الْكِتَابِ أَقْوَامًا وَيَضَعُ بِهِ آخَرِينَ».

[000–000]. (Dar al-Salam 1781) ʿAbdullāh ibn ʿAbd al-Raḥmān al-Dārimī and Abu Bakr ibn Isḥāq narrated to me: both said: Abu al-Yamān reported; Shuʿayb reported; from al-Zuhrī; he said: ʿĀmir ibn Wāthilah al-Laythī narrated to me; that **ʻNāfiʿ ibn ʿAbd al-Ḥārith al-Khuzāʿī met ʿUmar ibn al-Khaṭṭāb at ʿUsfān…' the same text as narrated by Ibrāhīm ibn Saʿd from al-Zuhrī.**

وَحَدَّثَنِي عَبْدُ اللهِ بْنُ عَبْدِ الرَّحْمَنِ الدَّارِمِيُّ، وَأَبُو بَكْرِ بْنُ إِسْحَاقَ قَالَا: أَخْبَرَنَا أَبُو الْيَمَانِ، أَخْبَرَنَا شُعَيْبٌ، عَنِ الزُّهْرِيِّ قَالَ: حَدَّثَنِي عَامِرُ بْنُ وَاثِلَةَ اللَّيْثِيُّ، أَنَّ نَافِعَ بْنَ عَبْدِ الْحَارِثِ الْخُزَاعِيَّ لَقِيَ عُمَرَ بْنَ الْخَطَّابِ بِعُسْفَانَ. بِمِثْلِ حَدِيثِ إِبْرَاهِيمَ بْنِ سَعْدٍ عَنِ الزُّهْرِيِّ.

Text Explanation

The Prophet says in these hadiths that envy is only acceptable in two things. Scholars say that envy is of two types: real and figurative. The real is to wish that a person may be deprived of a blessing he or she is given. This is forbidden according to the unanimous view of the Muslim community and authentic texts. The figurative is called *ghibṭah* in Arabic, which means to wish to have a blessing like that given to others without wishing that those who have it are deprived of it. If that blessing is of worldly matters, such a feeling is permissible, and if it is an act of piety and obedience of God, it is desirable. Thus, the hadith means that the only desirable *ghibṭah* is in these two things.

In hadith No. 1621 the Prophet says: 'a person to whom God has granted money and enabled him to spend it in what is right'. This means spending it in ways that are acceptable to God and please Him. The Prophet adds: 'and a person to whom God has granted wisdom and he rules according to it and teaches it'. This means he acts on it and teaches it to others, hoping only for God's reward. Wisdom in this context means whatever prevents ignorance and stops evil action.

[**Note**: The last two hadiths in this chapter mention a conversation between 'Umar ibn al-Khaṭṭāb, the second caliph, and his governor of Makkah and Taif, Nāfi' ibn 'Abd al-Ḥārith. 'Umar's question sought to know whom Nāfi' had appointed as his deputy during his absence as he travelled to meet the caliph. When he was informed about the deputy, he expressed his surprise that Nāfi' felt it appropriate to appoint a *mawla*, i.e. a former slave, as his deputy, ruling over the people of the Quraysh and Thaqīf, the two leading tribes of Arabia. Yet he recognised the merit of the man, as he achieved it through learning the Qur'an and memorising it, acquiring further knowledge of its rulings.]

CHAPTER 48

THE QUR'AN IS REVEALED IN SEVEN PRONUNCIATIONS [i.e. *ḤARFS*]

[1623–270]. (Dar al-Salam 1782) Yaḥyā ibn Yaḥyā narrated:[i] he said: I read out to Mālik; from Ibn Shihāb; from ʿUrwah ibn al-Zubayr; from ʿAbd al-Raḥmān ibn ʿAbd al-Qāriy; he said: I heard ʿUmar ibn al-Khaṭṭāb say: **'I heard Hishām ibn Ḥakīm ibn Ḥizām reciting Surah al-Furqān in a different way from how I recite it. It was God's Messenger (peace be upon him) who taught it to me. I was about to stop him short but then I let him continue until he finished [his prayer], and then I held him with the top of his robe around his neck and took him to God's Messenger (peace be upon him). I said: "Messenger of God, I heard this one reciting Surah al-Furqān in a different way from how you taught me". God's Messenger (peace be upon him) said: "Release him. Recite". He recited in the same way I heard him reciting earlier. The Prophet said: "This is how it was revealed". He then said to me: "Recite". I recited and he said: "This is how it was revealed. This Qur'an has been revealed in seven ways of pronunciation [i.e. *ḥarfs*]. Recite it as [you find] easy".'**

حَدَّثَنَا يَحْيَى بْنُ يَحْيَى، قَالَ قَرَأْتُ عَلَى مَالِكٍ عَنِ ابْنِ شِهَابٍ، عَنْ عُرْوَةَ بْنِ الزُّبَيْرِ، عَنْ عَبْدِ الرَّحْمَنِ بْنِ عَبْدٍ الْقَارِيِّ قَالَ: سَمِعْتُ عُمَرَ بْنَ الْخَطَّابِ يَقُولُ: سَمِعْتُ هِشَامَ

i. Related by al-Bukhari, 2419, 4992, 5041 6936 and 7550; Abu Dāwūd, 1475; al-Tirmidhī, 2943; al-Nasāʾī, 935, 936 and 937.

بْنَ حَكِيمِ بْنِ حِزَامٍ يَقْرَأُ سُورَةَ الْفُرْقَانِ عَلَى غَيْرِ مَا أَقْرَؤُهَا، وَكَانَ رَسُولُ اللهِ صَلَّى اللهُ عَلَيْهِ وَسَلَّمَ أَقْرَأَنِيهَا. فَكِدْتُ أَنْ أَعْجَلَ عَلَيْهِ، ثُمَّ أَمْهَلْتُهُ حَتَّى انْصَرَفَ. ثُمَّ لَبَّبْتُهُ بِرِدَائِهِ، فَجِئْتُ بِهِ رَسُولَ اللهِ صَلَّى اللهُ عَلَيْهِ وَسَلَّمَ فَقُلْتُ: يَا رَسُولَ اللهِ إِنِّي سَمِعْتُ هَذَا يَقْرَأُ سُورَةَ الْفُرْقَانِ عَلَى غَيْرِ مَا أَقْرَأْتَنِيهَا. فَقَالَ رَسُولُ اللهِ صَلَّى اللهُ عَلَيْهِ وَسَلَّمَ: «أَرْسِلْهُ. اقْرَأْ». فَقَرَأَ الْقِرَاءَةَ الَّتِي سَمِعْتُهُ يَقْرَأُ، فَقَالَ رَسُولُ اللهِ صَلَّى اللهُ عَلَيْهِ وَسَلَّمَ: «هَكَذَا أُنْزِلَتْ». ثُمَّ قَالَ لِيَ: «اقْرَأْ»، فَقَرَأْتُ فَقَالَ: «هَكَذَا أُنْزِلَتْ. إِنَّ هَذَا الْقُرْآنَ أُنْزِلَ عَلَى سَبْعَةِ أَحْرُفٍ فَاقْرَءُوا مَا تَيَسَّرَ مِنْهُ».

[1624–271]. (Dar al-Salam 1783–1784) Ḥarmalah ibn Yaḥyā narrated to me: Ibn Wahb reported; Yūnus reported to me; from Ibn Shihāb; ʿUrwah ibn al-Zubayr reported to me; that al-Miswar ibn Makhramah and ʿAbd al-Raḥmān ibn ʿAbd al-Qāriy reported to him; that they heard ʿUmar ibn al-Khaṭṭāb say: **'I heard Hishām ibn Ḥakīm reciting Surah al-Furqān during God's Messenger's lifetime...'. He narrated the same text, adding: 'I was about to jump at him while he was praying, but I held back until he finished his prayer'.**

وَحَدَّثَنِي حَرْمَلَةُ بْنُ يَحْيَى، أَخْبَرَنَا ابْنُ وَهْبٍ، أَخْبَرَنِي يُونُسُ، عَنِ ابْنِ شِهَابٍ، أَخْبَرَنِي عُرْوَةُ بْنُ الزُّبَيْرِ، أَنَّ الْمِسْوَرَ بْنَ مَخْرَمَةَ، وَعَبْدَ الرَّحْمَنِ بْنَ عَبْدٍ الْقَارِيَّ، أَخْبَرَاهُ أَنَّهُمَا سَمِعَا عُمَرَ بْنَ الْخَطَّابِ يَقُولُ: سَمِعْتُ هِشَامَ بْنَ حَكِيمٍ، يَقْرَأُ سُورَةَ الْفُرْقَانِ فِي حَيَاةِ رَسُولِ اللهِ صَلَّى اللهُ عَلَيْهِ وَسَلَّمَ. وَسَاقَ الْحَدِيثَ بِمِثْلِهِ، وَزَادَ: فَكِدْتُ أُسَاوِرُهُ فِي الصَّلَاةِ فَتَصَبَّرْتُ حَتَّى سَلَّمَ.

Isḥāq ibn Ibrāhīm and ʿAbd ibn Ḥumayd narrated: ʿAbd al-Razzāq reported; Maʿmar reported; from al-Zuhrī: **the same text as narrated by Yūnus with his chain of transmission.**

حَدَّثَنَا إِسْحَاقُ بْنُ إِبْرَاهِيمَ وَعَبْدُ بْنُ حُمَيْدٍ، قَالا: أَخْبَرَنَا عَبْدُ الرَّزَّاقِ، أَخْبَرَنَا مَعْمَرٌ، عَنِ الزُّهْرِيِّ، كَرِوَايَةِ يُونُسَ بِإِسْنَادِهِ

[1625–272]. (Dar al-Salam 1785) Ḥarmalah ibn Yaḥyā narrated to me:[i] Ibn Wahb reported; Yūnus reported to me; from Ibn Shihāb; ʿUbaydullāh ibn ʿAbdullāh ibn ʿUtbah narrated to me; that Ibn ʿAbbās narrated to him; that God's Messenger (peace be upon him) said: **'Gabriel (peace be upon him) taught me to recite in one pronunciation [i.e. *ḥarf*], but I requested more. I continued to request more, and he gave me until he completed it into seven pronunciations'.**

Ibn Shihāb said: **'I have been told that these seven pronunciations apply to a single matter, that does not differ as to being permissible or forbidden'.**

وَحَدَّثَنِي حَرْمَلَةُ بْنُ يَحْيَى، أَخْبَرَنَا ابْنُ وَهْبٍ، أَخْبَرَنِي يُونُسُ، عَنِ ابْنِ شِهَابٍ، حَدَّثَنِي عُبَيْدُ اللهِ بْنُ عَبْدِ اللهِ بْنِ عُتْبَةَ، أَنَّ ابْنَ عَبَّاسٍ، حَدَّثَهُ أَنَّ رَسُولَ اللهِ صَلَّى اللهُ عَلَيْهِ وَسَلَّمَ قَالَ: «أَقْرَأَنِي جِبْرِيلُ عَلَيْهِ السَّلَامُ عَلَى حَرْفٍ فَرَاجَعْتُهُ، فَلَمْ أَزَلْ أَسْتَزِيدُهُ فَيَزِيدُنِي، حَتَّى انْتَهَى إِلَى سَبْعَةِ أَحْرُفٍ».

قَالَ ابْنُ شِهَابٍ: بَلَغَنِي أَنَّ تِلْكَ السَّبْعَةَ الأَحْرُفَ إِنَّمَا هِيَ فِي الأَمْرِ الَّذِي يَكُونُ وَاحِدًا لاَ يَخْتَلِفُ فِي حَلاَلٍ وَلاَ حَرَامٍ

[000–000]. (Dar al-Salam 1786) ʿAbd ibn Ḥumayd narrated: ʿAbd al-Razzāq reported; Maʿmar reported; from al-Zuhrī; with the same chain of transmission: **the same text.**

وَحَدَّثَنَاهُ عَبْدُ بْنُ حُمَيْدٍ، أَخْبَرَنَا عَبْدُ الرَّزَّاقِ، أَخْبَرَنَا مَعْمَرٌ، عَنِ الزُّهْرِيِّ، بِهَذَا الإِسْنَادِ

---

i. Related by al-Bukhari, 4991.

[1626–273]. (Dar al-Salam 1787) Muhammad ibn ʿAbdullāh ibn Numayr:[i] my father narrated; Ismāʿīl ibn Abi Khālid narrated; from ʿAbdullāh ibn ʿĪsā ibn ʿAbd al-Raḥmān ibn Abi Laylā; from his grandfather; from Ubayy ibn Kaʿb. He said: **'I was in the mosque, and one man came in and prayed. He recited in a way that I disapproved of. Then another man came in and recited in a way different from that of his friend. When we finished the prayer, we went together to God's Messenger (peace be upon him) and I said: "This man recited in a way that I thought wrong, and another man came in and recited in a way different from that of his friend". God's Messenger ordered them [to recite], and they recited. The Prophet commended their recitations. I experienced some thoughts of denial, but nothing like what it was like before Islam. When God's Messenger (peace be upon him) saw what happened to me, he struck me on the chest, and I profusely perspired, as if I was beholding God, the Mighty and Exalted, and I was in terrible fear. He said to me: "Ubayy, I was given a message to read the Qur'an in one way of pronunciation. I answered Him to please make it easier for my community. He came back to me the second time to recite the Qur'an in two ways of pronunciation. I answered Him to please make it easier for my community. He came back to me the third time to 'recite the Qur'an in seven ways of pronunciation. For every time I have given you an answer, you shall have a request to put to Me'. I said: 'My Lord, forgive my community. My Lord, forgive my community'. I retained the third, keeping it for a day when all creation will come to request of me, even Abraham (peace be upon him)".'**

---

i. Related by Abu Dāwūd in a shorter version, 1478; al-Nasā'ī in similar wording, 938.

حَدَّثَنَا مُحَمَّدُ بْنُ عَبْدِ اللهِ بْنِ نُمَيْرٍ، حَدَّثَنَا أَبِي، حَدَّثَنَا إِسْمَاعِيلُ بْنُ أَبِي خَالِدٍ، عَنْ عَبْدِ اللهِ بْنِ عِيسَى بْنِ عَبْدِ الرَّحْمَنِ بْنِ أَبِي لَيْلَى، عَنْ جَدِّهِ، عَنْ أُبَيِّ بْنِ كَعْبٍ قَالَ: كُنْتُ فِي الْـمَسْجِدِ فَدَخَلَ رَجُلٌ يُصَلِّي، فَقَرَأَ قِرَاءَةً أَنْكَرْتُهَا عَلَيْهِ. ثُمَّ دَخَلَ آخَرُ فَقَرَأَ قِرَاءَةً سِوَى قِرَاءَةِ صَاحِبِهِ. فَلَمَّا قَضَيْنَا الصَّلاَةَ دَخَلْنَا جَمِيعًا عَلَى رَسُولِ اللهِ صَلَّى اللهُ عَلَيْهِ وَسَلَّمَ فَقُلْتُ: إِنَّ هَذَا قَرَأَ قِرَاءَةً أَنْكَرْتُهَا عَلَيْهِ وَدَخَلَ آخَرُ فَقَرَأَ سِوَى قِرَاءَةِ صَاحِبِهِ. فَأَمَرَهُمَا رَسُولُ اللهِ صَلَّى اللهُ عَلَيْهِ وَسَلَّمَ فَقَرَءَا، فَحَسَّنَ النَّبِيُّ صَلَّى اللهُ عَلَيْهِ وَسَلَّمَ شَأْنَهُمَا، فَسُقِطَ فِي نَفْسِي مِنَ التَّكْذِيبِ وَلاَ إِذْ كُنْتُ فِي الْجَاهِلِيَّةِ. فَلَمَّا رَأَى رَسُولُ اللهِ صَلَّى اللهُ عَلَيْهِ وَسَلَّمَ مَا قَدْ غَشِيَنِي ضَرَبَ فِي صَدْرِي، فَفِضْتُ عَرَقًا، وَكَأَنَّمَا أَنْظُرُ إِلَى اللهِ عَزَّ وَجَلَّ فَرَقًا. فَقَالَ لِي: «يَا أُبَيُّ، أُرْسِلَ إِلَيَّ أَنِ اقْرَإِ الْقُرْآنَ عَلَى حَرْفٍ، فَرَدَدْتُ إِلَيْهِ أَنْ هَوِّنْ عَلَى أُمَّتِي. فَرَدَّ إِلَيَّ الثَّانِيَةَ: اقْرَأْهُ عَلَى حَرْفَيْنِ. فَرَدَدْتُ إِلَيْهِ أَنْ هَوِّنْ عَلَى أُمَّتِي. فَرَدَّ إِلَيَّ الثَّالِثَةَ: اقْرَأْهُ عَلَى سَبْعَةِ أَحْرُفٍ، فَلَكَ بِكُلِّ رَدَّةٍ رَدَدْتُكَهَا مَسْأَلَةٌ تَسْأَلُنِيهَا. فَقُلْتُ اللَّهُمَّ اغْفِرْ لأُمَّتِي. اللَّهُمَّ اغْفِرْ لأُمَّتِي. وَأَخَّرْتُ الثَّالِثَةَ لِيَوْمٍ يَرْغَبُ إِلَيَّ الْخَلْقُ كُلُّهُمْ، حَتَّى إِبْرَاهِيمُ صَلَّى اللهُ عَلَيْهِ وَسَلَّمَ.

[1627–000]. (Dar al-Salam 1788) Abu Bakr ibn Abi Shaybah narrated: Muhammad ibn Bishr narrated; Ismāʿīl ibn Abi Khālid narrated to me; ʿAbdullāh ibn ʿĪsā narrated to me; from ʿAbd al-Raḥmān ibn Abi Laylā; Ubayy ibn Kaʿb reported to me; that he **'was sitting in the mosque when a man came in and prayed. He recited in a way…'. He narrated the hadith with the same text as Ibn Numayr's.**

حَدَّثَنَا أَبُو بَكْرِ بْنُ أَبِي شَيْبَةَ، حَدَّثَنَا مُحَمَّدُ بْنُ بِشْرٍ، حَدَّثَنِي إِسْمَاعِيلُ بْنُ أَبِي خَالِدٍ، حَدَّثَنِي عَبْدُ اللهِ بْنُ عِيسَى، عَنْ عَبْدِ الرَّحْمَنِ بْنِ أَبِي لَيْلَى، أَخْبَرَنِي أُبَيُّ بْنُ كَعْبٍ، أَنَّهُ كَانَ جَالِسًا فِي الْـمَسْجِدِ إِذْ دَخَلَ رَجُلٌ فَصَلَّى فَقَرَأَ قِرَاءَةً، وَاقْتَصَّ الْحَدِيثَ بِمِثْلِ حَدِيثِ ابْنِ نُمَيْرٍ

[1628–274]. (Dar al-Salam 1789–1790) Abu Bakr ibn Abi Shaybah narrated: Ghundar narrated [H]. Also, Ibn al-Muthannā and Ibn Bashshār narrated it; Ibn al-Muthannā said: Muhammad ibn Jaʿfar narrated; Shuʿbah narrated; from al-Ḥakam; from Mujāhid; from Ibn Abi Laylā; from Ubayy ibn Kaʿb; that **'The Prophet was at the water of the Ghifār tribe when Gabriel (peace be upon him) came to him. He said: "God commands you that your community should recite the Qur'an in one way of pronunciation [i.e. *ḥarf*]". He said: "I pray to God for His pardon and forgiveness. My community cannot do that". He came to him a second time and said: "God commands you that your community should recite the Qur'an in two ways of pronunciation". He said: "I pray to God for His pardon and forgiveness. My community cannot do that". He came to him a third time and said: "God commands you that your community should recite the Qur'an in three ways of pronunciation". He said: "I pray to God for His pardon and forgiveness. My community cannot do that". He came to him a fourth time and said: "God commands you that your community should recite the Qur'an in seven ways of pronunciation. Whichever pronunciation they recite shall be correct".'**

وَحَدَّثَنَا أَبُو بَكْرِ بْنُ أَبِي شَيْبَةَ، حَدَّثَنَا غُنْدَرٌ، عَنْ شُعْبَةَ، ح. وَحَدَّثَنَاهُ ابْنُ الْمُثَنَّى وَابْنُ بَشَّارٍ: قَالَ ابْنُ الْمُثَنَّى حَدَّثَنَا مُحَمَّدُ بْنُ جَعْفَرٍ، حَدَّثَنَا شُعْبَةُ، عَنِ الْحَكَمِ، عَنْ مُجَاهِدٍ، عَنِ ابْنِ أَبِي لَيْلَى، عَنْ أُبَيِّ بْنِ كَعْبٍ، أَنَّ النَّبِيَّ صَلَّى اللهُ عَلَيْهِ وَسَلَّمَ كَانَ عِنْدَ أَضَاةِ بَنِي غِفَارٍ. قَالَ: فَأَتَاهُ جِبْرِيلُ عَلَيْهِ السَّلاَمُ فَقَالَ إِنَّ اللهَ يَأْمُرُكَ أَنْ تَقْرَأَ أُمَّتُكَ الْقُرْآنَ عَلَى حَرْفٍ . فَقَالَ: "أَسْأَلُ اللهَ مُعَافَاتَهُ وَمَغْفِرَتَهُ. وَإِنَّ أُمَّتِي لاَ تُطِيقُ ذَلِكَ". ثُمَّ أَتَاهُ الثَّانِيَةَ فَقَالَ: إِنَّ اللهَ يَأْمُرُكَ أَنْ تَقْرَأَ أُمَّتُكَ الْقُرْآنَ عَلَى حَرْفَيْنِ فَقَالَ: "أَسْأَلُ اللهَ مُعَافَاتَهُ وَمَغْفِرَتَهُ. وَإِنَّ أُمَّتِي لاَ تُطِيقُ ذَلِكَ". ثُمَّ جَاءَهُ الثَّالِثَةَ فَقَالَ: إِنَّ اللهَ يَأْمُرُكَ أَنْ تَقْرَأَ أُمَّتُكَ الْقُرْآنَ عَلَى ثَلاَثَةِ أَحْرُفٍ. فَقَالَ: "أَسْأَلُ اللهَ مُعَافَاتَهُ وَمَغْفِرَتَهُ. وَإِنَّ أُمَّتِي

لاَ تُطِيقُ ذَلِكَ". ثُمَّ جَاءَهُ الرَّابِعَةَ فَقَالَ: إِنَّ اللهَ يَأْمُرُكَ أَنْ تَقْرَأَ أُمَّتُكَ الْقُرْآنَ عَلَى سَبْعَةِ أَحْرُفٍ، فَأَيُّمَا حَرْفٍ قَرَءُوا عَلَيْهِ فَقَدْ أَصَابُوا.

ʿUbaydullāh ibn Muʿādh narrated: my father narrated; Shuʿbah narrated; with this chain of transmission: **the same text.**

وَحَدَّثَنَاهُ عُبَيْدُ اللهِ بْنُ مُعَاذٍ، حَدَّثَنَا أَبِي، حَدَّثَنَا شُعْبَةُ، بِهَذَا الإِسْنَادِ مِثْلَهُ.

Text Explanation

In the first hadith, No. 1623, ʿUmar says that he held Hishām with the top of his robe around his neck. This means that ʿUmar actually held the top of Hishām's robe and pulled him. This indicates how careful the Prophet's Companions were about the Qur'an and eager to defend it from any distortion. They wanted to recite it exactly as they learnt it from the Prophet, without allowing variants, even though they were acceptable from a linguistic point of view. However, the Prophet ordered ʿUmar to let go of Hishām because he had no evidence that Hishām deserved any punishment. ʿUmar simply told the Prophet the fact that he was reciting the Qur'an differently from what he, ʿUmar, had been taught by the Prophet. The Prophet knew all the variants that were acceptable in reciting the Qur'an, while ʿUmar did not know all these. Moreover, Hishām needed to be comfortable in order to recite at his ease.

In the same hadith, the Prophet says: 'This Qur'an has been revealed in seven ways of pronunciation [i.e. *ḥarfs*]. Recite it as [you find] easy'. Scholars say that the reason for revealing it in seven ways was to make it easier for people. Hence, the Prophet made his appeal to God, as stated in hadith No. 1626: 'Please make it easier for my community'. Scholars differed as to what 'seven *ḥarfs*' meant. *Qadi* ʿIyāḍ said:

> It is said that it is to make an allowance that would ensure its being easier to recite. It is not intended as seven only.

The majority of scholars said that the number is definitely seven, not more. It is also said that these were seven in meaning, such as promise or warning, precise or equivocal, permissible or forbidden, stories, similes, orders and prohibitions. Further, scholars differ in their selections of seven. Others said that it relates to how recitation is made and how individual words are pronounced: what applies to them of assimilation, realisation, velarisation, diphthongisation and elongation. Arabic dialects differed in such aspects of pronunciation. Therefore, God made it easier for them so that everyone could recite the Qur'an according to what they were used to in their own dialects.

Other scholars said that it refers to words and sounds. This is what Ibn Shihāb refers to as he is quoted by Muslim in hadith No. 1625. These scholars also differ with some saying that the term refers to seven variants and possibilities. Abu 'Ubayd said: it refers to seven Arabic tongues, Yemenī and Ma'iddī, and these are the most eloquent of Arabic dialects. It is further said that all seven *ḥarfs* belonged to the major tribe of Muḍar,[i] and they are all used in the Qur'an and cannot be grouped together in one word. Some say that they are found together in some words, such as 'those who worship false gods' (5: 60), 'Our Lord, make our journeys longer' (34: 19), 'he may enjoy himself and play' (12: 12), 'dreadful suffering' (7: 165) and similar ones.

Qadi Abu Bakr al-Bāqillānī said:

'The correct view is that these seven ways of pronunciation were well known and widely used as taught by the Prophet. Scholars received them accurately, and 'Uthmān and his

i. Muḍar was one of the major Arabian tribes from which several large tribes branched out. As these had different accents and dialects, the comment that all seven *ḥarfs* belonged to Muḍar means that there were other ways of Arabic pronunciation, but these were not included in how the Qur'an is recited.

scribes recorded them in the master copies of the Qur'an, stating their authenticity. They only left out what was not proven to be of the recurrent [i.e. *mutawātir*] grade of authenticity. These *ḥarfs* may differ in meaning at times and in pronunciation at other times, but they do not conflict and are not mutually exclusive.

Al-Ṭaḥāwī said that recitation of the Qur'an in the seven ways of pronunciation was particularly needed during the early period because of the different Arabic dialects and the difficulty of imposing one way of pronunciation on all groups at the outset. When the numbers of people and scribes increased and the necessity was no longer felt, only one way of pronunciation was retained.

Al-Dāwūdī said: 'The seven variant readings [i.e. *qirā'āt*] which people use in their recitations today do not correspond to the seven ways of pronunciation, in the sense that each variant represents one *ḥarf* or way of pronunciation. They may be spread in all of them'. Abu 'Ubaydullāh ibn Abi Ṣufrah said: 'These seven *qirā'āt*, or variant readings, belong to one of the seven ways of pronunciation mentioned in the hadith. This is the *ḥarf* 'Uthmān used in the master copy of the Qur'an. This is what is stated by al-Naḥḥās and other scholars'. Other scholars said: 'It is not possible to use the seven *ḥarfs* mentioned in the hadith in reciting the Qur'an once from start to finish. Nor is it known which of the variant readings, or *qirā'āt*, was the one used the last time the Prophet recited the Qur'an to Gabriel'. All of these are widely learnt from the Prophet and were meticulously learnt and taught within the Muslim community. Every one of them was attributed to the Prophet's Companion who used it most. Moreover, every one of the seven *qirā'āt* is attributed to one of the seven main reciters who taught it.

Imam al-Māzarī said: 'The view that what is meant is seven different meanings, such as rulings, similes, stories, etc. is wrong. The Prophet (peace be upon him) pointed out

> that it is permissible to recite the Qur'an using every one of the seven ways of pronunciation and to replace one way by another. It is well established that it is absolutely forbidden for a verse citing a simile to be replaced by one stating a ruling, etc. Moreover, it is wrong to claim that the hadith refers to the endings of verses, such as replacing an ending stating: 'God is Much-Forgiving, Ever-Merciful' by one that says: 'God hears all and knows all'. Again, the Muslim community is unanimous that no change is permissible in the Qur'an'.

This is the sum of what *Qadi* ʿIyāḍ mentioned on this point.

In hadith No. 1625, the Prophet says: 'Gabriel (peace be upon him) taught me to recite in one pronunciation [i.e. *ḥarf*], but I requested more. I continued to request more and he gave me until he completed it into seven pronunciations'. This means that the Prophet requested Gabriel to pray to God to give him more than one way of pronunciation, to make it easier for his community. Gabriel put the Prophet's request to God, and He increased the number, until they were complete in seven.

In hadith No. 1626, Ubayy ibn Kaʿb mentions that when the Prophet commended the two people's recitations, which were different from what he learnt from the Prophet, he 'experienced some thoughts of denial, but nothing like what it was like before Islam'. This means that Satan raised in him some thoughts of denying the prophethood and that this was harder for him than it was before Islam. Prior to becoming a Muslim he was unaware of the truth, or doubtful about it. Now, Satan raised in him thoughts of denying prophethood altogether, and this was harder. Commenting on Ubayy's statement, *Qadi* ʿIyāḍ said: ' "I experienced some thoughts" means that he felt amazed and perplexed, and "nothing like what it was before Islam" means that Satan raised in him a sort of denial that he did not believe. If such thoughts are not maintained, one is not accountable for them. Al-Māzarī said: "What this means is that Ubayy ibn Kaʿb experienced an unstable situation that was raised by

Satan and that it immediately disappeared when the Prophet struck him on the chest and he profusely perspired".'

The hadith adds that Ubayy said: 'When God's Messenger (peace be upon him) saw what happened to me, he struck me on the chest, and I profusely perspired, as if I was beholding God, the Mighty and Exalted, and I was in terrible fear'. *Qadi* ʿIyāḍ said: 'The Prophet struck him in the chest when he saw that he was experiencing such ill thoughts, in order to give him reassurance'.

In hadith No. 1626, the Prophet says to Ubayy: 'I was given a message to read the Qur'an in one way of pronunciation. I answered Him to please make it easier for my community. He came back to me the second time to recite the Qur'an in two ways of pronunciation. I answered Him to please make it easier for my community. He came back to me the third time to recite the Qur'an in seven ways of pronunciation'. This is how this hadith occurs in most original manuscripts. In some, there are some words added, but they do not affect the meaning. In No. 1628, we have a different narration by Abu Bakr ibn Abi Shaybah, stating that the Prophet was first required to recite the Qur'an in one way of pronunciation, and this was made two ways the second time, and three the third time, then the seven ways of pronunciation were granted the fourth time. This may be problematic, particularly in reconciling the two texts. The easiest way to reconcile them is to say that when in the first narration it is stated: 'he came back to me the third time to recite the Qur'an in seven ways of pronunciation', the 'third' in this instance means the 'last', which actually was the fourth. Thus, it is called the 'third' figuratively. What encourages this understanding is that the second narration clearly states that the seven pronunciations were granted the fourth time, which was the last. This understanding of the hadith supposes that the first narrations overlook some of the requests.

This is further supported by the text of the first narration as it adds: 'For every time I have given you an answer, you shall have a request to put to Me'. This shows that this narration does not mention some of these three answers, as they are clear in the second narration. That the Prophet is given such requests means that they are certainly answered. Other prayers are hoped to be answered but not absolutely certain. We have already discussed this aspect in the Book of Faith.

In the last hadith, Gabriel says to the Prophet: 'God commands you that your community should recite the Qur'an in seven ways of pronunciation. Whichever pronunciation they recite shall be correct'. This means that they must not exceed seven ways of pronunciation, and they have a choice within these seven. They must transmit the seven to future generations, with the allowed choice between them, and the condition that they may not be exceeded, but God knows best.

CHAPTER 49

THE PROPER, NOT TOO FAST, RECITATION

[1629–275]. (Dar al-Salam 11791) Abu Bakr ibn Abi Shaybah and Ibn Numayr narrated:[i] both from Wakīʿ; Abu Bakr said: Wakīʿ narrated; from al-Aʿmash; from Abu Wā'il. He said: **'A man called Nahīk ibn Sinān came to ʿAbdullāh. He said: "Abu ʿAbd al-Raḥmān, how do you read this word? Does it start with a long 'a' or a 'y' sound: *min mā'in ghayri āsin* or *min mā'in ghayri yāsin*?" ʿAbdullāh said: "Have you perfected the entire Qur'an except this [one word]?" The man said: "I recite *al-Mufaṣṣal*[ii] in one *rakʿah*". ʿAbdullāh said: "Very fast, like poetry? Some people recite the Qur'an, but it does not go beyond their throats. Yet when it is felt at heart and is established there, it yields its benefit. The best of prayer is bowing and prostration. I know the twin surahs which the Prophet used to recite together, two surahs in each *rakʿah*". Then ʿAbdullāh stood up and went in. ʿAlqamah followed him inside. Then he came out and said: "He told me about these".'**

Ibn Numayr said in his narration: **'A man from the Bajīylah tribe came to ʿAbdullāh', but he did not mention 'Nahīk ibn Sinān'.**

---

i. Related by al-Bukhari, 4996; al-Tirmidhī, 602; al-Nasā'ī in a shorter version and similar wording, 1003.

ii. *Al-Mufaṣṣal* is the end part of the Qur'an which is generally agreed to include Surahs 50-114. There will be more explanation of this in the commentary.

حَدَّثَنَا أَبُو بَكْرِ بْنُ أَبِي شَيْبَةَ وَابْنُ نُمَيْرٍ جَمِيعًا عَنْ وَكِيعٍ، - قَالَ أَبُو بَكْرٍ حَدَّثَنَا وَكِيعٌ - عَنِ الأَعْمَشِ، عَنْ أَبِي وَائِلٍ قَالَ: جَاءَ رَجُلٌ يُقَالُ لَهُ نَهِيكُ بْنُ سِنَانٍ إِلَى عَبْدِ اللهِ فَقَالَ: يَا أَبَا عَبْدِ الرَّحْمَنِ كَيْفَ تَقْرَأُ هَذَا الْحَرْفَ أَلِفًا تَجِدُهُ أَمْ يَاءً؟ مِنْ مَاءٍ غَيْرِ آسِنٍ، أَوْ مِنْ مَاءٍ غَيْرِ يَاسِنٍ؟ قَالَ: فَقَالَ عَبْدُ اللهِ: وَكُلَّ الْقُرْآنِ قَدْ أَحْصَيْتَ غَيْرَ هَذَا؟ قَالَ: إِنِّي لأَقْرَأُ الْـمُفَصَّلَ فِي رَكْعَةٍ. فَقَالَ عَبْدُ اللهِ: هَذًّا كَهَذِّ الشِّعْرِ! إِنَّ أَقْوَامًا يَقْرَءُونَ الْقُرْآنَ لاَ يُجَاوِزُ تَرَاقِيَهُمْ، وَلَكِنْ إِذَا وَقَعَ فِي الْقَلْبِ فَرَسَخَ فِيهِ نَفَعَ. إِنَّ أَفْضَلَ الصَّلاَةِ الرُّكُوعُ وَالسُّجُودُ. إِنِّي لأَعْلَمُ النَّظَائِرَ الَّتِي كَانَ رَسُولُ اللهِ صَلَّى اللهُ عَلَيْهِ وَسَلَّمَ يَقْرُنُ بَيْنَهُنَّ: سُورَتَيْنِ فِي كُلِّ رَكْعَةٍ. ثُمَّ قَامَ عَبْدُ اللهِ، فَدَخَلَ عَلْقَمَةُ فِي إِثْرِهِ ثُمَّ خَرَجَ، فَقَالَ قَدْ أَخْبَرَنِي بِهَا.

قَالَ ابْنُ نُمَيْرٍ فِي رِوَايَتِهِ جَاءَ رَجُلٌ مِنْ بَنِي بَجِيلَةَ إِلَى عَبْدِ اللهِ وَلَمْ يَقُلْ نَهِيكُ بْنُ سِنَانٍ.

[1630–276]. (Dar al-Salam 1792) Abu Kurayb narrated: Abu Muʿāwiyah narrated; from al-Aʿmash; from Abu Wā'il. He said: **'A man called Nahīk ibn Sinān came to ʿAbdullāh...'. He narrated the same as Wakīʿ's hadith, except that he said: 'ʿAlqamah stood to follow him. We said to him: "Ask him about the twin surahs the Prophet used to recite in one *rakʿah*". He went inside, following him, then came out to us and said: "Twenty surahs from *al-Mufaṣṣal*, according to ʿAbdullāh's arrangement".'**

وَحَدَّثَنَا أَبُو كُرَيْبٍ، حَدَّثَنَا أَبُو مُعَاوِيَةَ، عَنِ الأَعْمَشِ، عَنْ أَبِي وَائِلٍ قَالَ: جَاءَ رَجُلٌ إِلَى عَبْدِ اللهِ يُقَالُ لَهُ نَهِيكُ بْنُ سِنَانٍ. بِمِثْلِ حَدِيثِ وَكِيعٍ، غَيْرَ أَنَّهُ قَالَ: فَجَاءَ عَلْقَمَةُ لِيَدْخُلَ عَلَيْهِ، فَقُلْنَا لَهُ: سَلْهُ عَنِ النَّظَائِرِ الَّتِي كَانَ رَسُولُ اللهِ صَلَّى اللهُ عَلَيْهِ وَسَلَّمَ يَقْرَأُ بِهَا فِي رَكْعَةٍ. فَدَخَلَ عَلَيْهِ فَسَأَلَهُ ثُمَّ خَرَجَ عَلَيْنَا، فَقَالَ: عِشْرُونَ سُورَةً مِنَ الْـمُفَصَّلِ فِي تَأْلِيفِ عَبْدِ اللهِ.

[1631–277]. (Dar al-Salam 1793) Isḥāq ibn Ibrāhīm narrated it to us: ʿĪsā ibn Yūnus reported; al-Aʿmash narrated; with this chain of transmission: **a similar text to their narrations. He said: 'I know the twin surahs God's Messenger (peace be upon him) used to recite: two surahs in one *rakʿah* and twenty surahs in ten *rakʿahs*'.**

وَحَدَّثَنَاهُ إِسْحَاقُ بْنُ إِبْرَاهِيمَ، أَخْبَرَنَا عِيسَى بْنُ يُونُسَ، حَدَّثَنَا الأَعْمَشُ، فِي هَذَا الإِسْنَادِ. بِنَحْوِ حَدِيثِهِمَا وَقَالَ: إِنِّي لأَعْرِفُ النَّظَائِرَ الَّتِي كَانَ يَقْرَأُ بِهِنَّ رَسُولُ اللهِ صَلَّى اللهُ عَلَيْهِ وَسَلَّمَ اثْنَتَيْنِ فِي رَكْعَةٍ: عِشْرِينَ سُورَةً فِي عَشْرِ رَكَعَاتٍ.

[1632–278]. (Dar al-Salam 1794) Shaybān ibn Farrūkh narrated:[i] Mahdī ibn Maymūn narrated; Wāṣil al-Aḥdab narrated; from Abu Wā'il. He said: **'We went to ʿAbdullāh ibn Masʿūd one day after we had prayed the Fajr Prayer. We greeted him at the door, and he permitted us to enter, but we stayed at the door for a short while. A maid came out and said: "Are you not coming in?" We went in. He was seated, glorifying God. He said: "What stopped your entry when you were given permission?" We said: "Nothing, except that we thought that some people might be asleep". He said: "Then you thought that some of Umm ʿAbd's son's family might be negligent?" He then continued to glorify God until he thought that the sun had risen. He said: "Maid! Look out – has the sun risen?" She did, but the sun had not risen yet. He continued to glorify God, until he thought that it was sunrise. He said: "Maid! Look out - has the sun come out?" She did, and the sun had risen. He said: "All praise be to God who has given us life on this day of ours". (Mahdī said: 'and I think he also said:**

i. Related by al-Bukhari in a shorter version, 5043.

"and did not destroy us for our sins…".') One man in the group said: "I recited all *al-Mufaṣṣal* last night". 'Abdullāh said: "Very fast, like poetry? We have heard the twin surahs. I know the similar surahs God's Messenger (peace be upon him) used to recite: eighteen surahs from *al-Mufaṣṣal* and two surahs of those starting with *Ḥa Mīm*".'

حَدَّثَنَا شَيْبَانُ بْنُ فَرُّوخَ، حَدَّثَنَا مَهْدِيُّ بْنُ مَيْمُونٍ، حَدَّثَنَا وَاصِلٌ الأَحْدَبُ، عَنْ أَبِي وَائِلٍ قَالَ: غَدَوْنَا عَلَى عَبْدِ اللهِ بْنِ مَسْعُودٍ يَوْمًا بَعْدَ مَا صَلَّيْنَا الْغَدَاةَ، فَسَلَّمْنَا بِالْبَابِ فَأَذِنَ لَنَا. قَالَ: فَمَكَثْنَا بِالْبَابِ هُنَيَّةً. قَالَ: فَخَرَجَتِ الْجَارِيَةُ فَقَالَتْ: أَلاَ تَدْخُلُونَ؟ فَدَخَلْنَا فَإِذَا هُوَ جَالِسٌ يُسَبِّحُ، فَقَالَ: مَا مَنَعَكُمْ أَنْ تَدْخُلُوا وَقَدْ أُذِنَ لَكُمْ؟ فَقُلْنَا: لاَ، إِلاَّ أَنَّا ظَنَنَّا أَنَّ بَعْضَ أَهْلِ الْبَيْتِ نَائِمٌ. قَالَ: ظَنَنْتُمْ بِآلِ ابْنِ أُمِّ عَبْدٍ غَفْلَةً. قَالَ: ثُمَّ أَقْبَلَ يُسَبِّحُ حَتَّى ظَنَّ أَنَّ الشَّمْسَ قَدْ طَلَعَتْ فَقَالَ: يَا جَارِيَةُ، انْظُرِي هَلْ طَلَعَتْ. قَالَ: فَنَظَرَتْ فَإِذَا هِيَ لَمْ تَطْلُعْ، فَأَقْبَلَ يُسَبِّحُ حَتَّى إِذَا ظَنَّ أَنَّ الشَّمْسَ قَدْ طَلَعَتْ، قَالَ: يَا جَارِيَةُ انْظُرِي هَلْ طَلَعَتْ. فَنَظَرَتْ فَإِذَا هِيَ قَدْ طَلَعَتْ. فَقَالَ: الْحَمْدُ للهِ الَّذِي أَقَالَنَا يَوْمَنَا هَذَا. فَقَالَ مَهْدِيٌّ: وَأَحْسِبُهُ قَالَ وَلَمْ يُهْلِكْنَا بِذُنُوبِنَا. قَالَ: فَقَالَ رَجُلٌ مِنَ الْقَوْمِ: قَرَأْتُ الْمُفَصَّلَ الْبَارِحَةَ كُلَّهُ. قَالَ: فَقَالَ عَبْدُ اللهِ: هَذًّا كَهَذِّ الشِّعْرِ! إِنَّا لَقَدْ سَمِعْنَا الْقَرَائِنَ، وَإِنِّي لأَحْفَظُ الْقَرَائِنَ الَّتِي كَانَ يَقْرَؤُهُنَّ رَسُولُ اللهِ صَلَّى اللهُ عَلَيْهِ وَسَلَّمَ: ثَمَانِيَةَ عَشَرَ مِنَ الْمُفَصَّلِ وَسُورَتَيْنِ مِنْ آلِ حم.

[1633–279]. (Dar al-Salam 1795) 'Abd ibn Ḥumayd narrated: Ḥusayn ibn 'Alī al-Ju'fī narrated; from Zā'idah; from Manṣūr; from Shaqīq. He said: **'A man from the Bajīlah tribe, called Nahīk ibn Sinān, came to see 'Abdullāh. He said: "I recite *al-Mufaṣṣal* in one *rak'ah*". 'Abdullāh said: "Too fast, like poetry? I know the twin surahs which God's Messenger (peace be upon him) used to recite: two surahs in each *rak'ah*".'**

حَدَّثَنَا عَبْدُ بْنُ حُمَيْدٍ، حَدَّثَنَا حُسَيْنُ بْنُ عَلِيٍّ الْجُعْفِيُّ، عَنْ زَائِدَةَ، عَنْ مَنْصُورٍ، عَنْ شَقِيقٍ قَالَ: جَاءَ رَجُلٌ مِنْ بَنِي بَجِيلَةَ يُقَالُ لَهُ نَهِيكُ بْنُ سِنَانٍ إِلَى عَبْدِ اللهِ فَقَالَ: إِنِّي أَقْرَأُ الْـمُفَصَّلَ فِي رَكْعَةٍ. فَقَالَ عَبْدُ اللهِ: هَذًّا كَهَذِّ الشِّعْرِ! لَقَدْ عَلِمْتُ النَّظَائِرَ الَّتِي كَانَ رَسُولُ اللهِ صَلَّى اللهُ عَلَيْهِ وَسَلَّمَ يَقْرَأُ بِهِنَّ سُورَتَيْنِ فِي رَكْعَةٍ.

[1634–000]. (Dar al-Salam 1796) Muhammad ibn al-Muthannā and Ibn Bashshār narrated:[i] Ibn al-Muthannā said: Muhammad ibn Jaʿfar narrated; Shuʿbah narrated; from ʿAmr ibn Murrah; that he heard Abu Wā'il narrating; that **'A man came to Ibn Masʿūd and said: "I recited the whole of *al-Mufaṣṣal* last night in one *rakʿah*". ʿAbdullāh said: "Too fast, like poetry?" ʿAbdullāh said: "But I know the twin surahs the Prophet used to recite in pairs". He mentioned twenty surahs from *al-Mufaṣṣal*: two surahs in each *rakʿah*'.**

حَدَّثَنَا مُحَمَّدُ بْنُ الْـمُثَنَّى وَابْنُ بَشَّارٍ. قَالَ ابْنُ الْـمُثَنَّى: حَدَّثَنَا مُحَمَّدُ بْنُ جَعْفَرٍ، حَدَّثَنَا شُعْبَةُ، عَنْ عَمْرِو بْنِ مُرَّةَ، أَنَّهُ سَمِعَ أَبَا وَائِلٍ يُحَدِّثُ أَنَّ رَجُلاً، جَاءَ إِلَى ابْنِ مَسْعُودٍ فَقَالَ: إِنِّي قَرَأْتُ الْـمُفَصَّلَ اللَّيْلَةَ كُلَّهُ فِي رَكْعَةٍ. فَقَالَ عَبْدُ اللهِ: هَذًّا كَهَذِّ الشِّعْرِ! فَقَالَ عَبْدُ اللهِ: لَقَدْ عَرَفْتُ النَّظَائِرَ الَّتِي كَانَ رَسُولُ اللهِ صَلَّى اللهُ عَلَيْهِ وَسَلَّمَ يَقْرُنُ بَيْنَهُنَّ. قَالَ: فَذَكَرَ عِشْرِينَ سُورَةً مِنَ الْـمُفَصَّلِ سُورَتَيْنِ سُورَتَيْنِ فِي كُلِّ رَكْعَةٍ.

Text Explanation

In hadith No. 1629, the man asks Ibn Masʿūd about the word *āsin* and how it should be pronounced. However, Ibn Masʿūd asks him whether he understood the entire Qur'an except this word. This is understood to mean that Ibn Masʿūd realised that the man was not seeking information. Had he been seeking to learn, an answer must

i. Related by al-Bukhari, 775; al-Nasā'ī, 1004.

be given, and what he was told was not an answer to his question. The man said: 'I recite *al-Mufaṣṣal* in one *rak'ah*'. Ibn Mas'ūd said: 'Very fast, like poetry?' Thus, the man states that he knows much of the Qur'an by heart and that his memorisation is perfect. Ibn Mas'ūd's comment was that he recited it too fast and implied disapproval of such recitation. One should recite well, reflecting on the meanings of what one is reciting. This is the view of the majority of scholars. *Qadi* 'Iyāḍ said: 'A small number of scholars say that fast recitation is permissible'.

Ibn Mas'ūd compares fast recitation to poetry. This refers to how poetry is memorised and reported, not to how it is usually delivered and chanted. He further said: 'Some people recite the Qur'an, but it does not go beyond their throats. Yet when it is felt at heart and is established there, it yields its benefit'. This means that some people get nothing out of reciting the Qur'an more than uttering it. It is merely a superficial recitation that is not felt at heart. What is required is to understand what one is reciting and to reflect on its meaning. It is only then that one truly interacts with the Qur'an.

Ibn Mas'ūd adds that 'the best prayer is bowing and prostration'. This is his view. We spoke earlier about the hadith that quotes the Prophet saying: 'The best prayer is to recite the Qur'an at length' and the other hadith that says: 'The closest that a person draws to his Lord is when he is in prostration'. We explained the different views stated by scholars on this point.

'Abdullāh ibn Mas'ūd further said: 'I know the twin surahs which the Prophet used to recite together, two surahs in each *rak'ah*'. This is explained in the next hadith, No. 1630, as: 'Twenty surahs from *al-Mufaṣṣal*, according to 'Abdullāh's arrangement'. *Qadi* 'Iyāḍ said: 'This is correct and agrees with the reports given by 'Ā'ishah and Ibn 'Abbās stating that the Prophet's night worship was eleven *rak'ahs* including the Witr Prayer. This was the length of his recitation in most cases. That his night prayer was long, as clearly reported, means that it was so because of his slow recitation and his reflection on the meanings of what he recited. What is reported about his reciting [the three longest surahs] The Cow, Women and Āl ʿImrān was on rare occasions'.

The twenty surahs the Prophet used to recite in his night worship are given in detail in a hadith entered in Abu Dāwūd's *Sunan* anthology. These are the surahs entitled 'The Lord of Grace' and 'The Star' [Surah 55 and 53] in one *rakʿah*, 'The Moon' and 'The Inevitable Truth' [Surah 54 and 69] in one *rakʿah*, 'Mount Sinai' and 'The Scattering Winds' [Surah 52 and 51] in one *rakʿah*, 'The Inevitable Event' and 'The Pen' [Surah 56 and 68] in one *rakʿah*, 'Ways of Ascent' and 'The Pluckers' [Surah 70 and 79] in one *rakʿah*, 'The Stinters' and 'The Frowning' [Surah 83 and 80] in one *rakʿah*, 'Wrapped in Cloak' and 'The Enfolded One' [Surah 74 and 73] in one *rakʿah*, 'Man' and 'The Resurrection' [Surah 76 and 75] in one *rakʿah*, 'The Tidings' and 'Sent Forth' [Surah 78 and 77] in one *rakʿah* and 'Smoke' and 'The Darkening' [Surah 44 and 81] in one *rakʿah*. This part of the Qur'an is called *al-Mufaṣṣal* because its surahs are short and they follow each other in quick succession.

In hadith No. 1632, the relevant surahs are said to be eighteen from *al-Mufaṣṣal* and two of those starting with the two separate letters *Ḥa Mīm*, while earlier he said twenty surahs from *al-Mufaṣṣal*. There is no contradiction here, because he meant that most of the twenty surahs belonged to the part of the Qur'an known as *al-Mufaṣṣal*. Scholars say that the Qur'an begins with the seven longest surahs, then the surahs that include one hundred verses each or close to that, then those whose verses are in double figures, then *al-Mufaṣṣal*. We mentioned the different views about the beginning of *al-Mufaṣṣal*. Some say that it starts with Surah 47, entitled Muhammad, and others say it starts with Surah 49, The Private Apartments, and others still say it begins with Surah 50, Qāf.

In hadith No. 1629, Ibn Masʿūd said that the Prophet used to recite these surahs together, 'two surahs in each *rakʿah*'. This makes it clear that it is perfectly permissible to recite two surahs in one *rakʿah*.

In hadith No. 1632, Ibn Masʿūd asked his visitors: 'What stopped your entry when you were given permission?' We said: 'Nothing, except that we thought that some people might be asleep'. He said:

'Then you thought that some of Umm ʿAbd's son's family might be negligent?' This means that they only thought that some members of the family were still asleep. This suggests that such a thought just occurred to them, but not in the sense scholars suggest, meaning 'strong belief'. The hadith shows that it is the duty of the head of the family to take care that his family and others in his household observe their religious duties.

Ibn Masʿūd asks his maid to check whether the sun has risen. This makes it clear that it is acceptable to act on the basis of information given by one person, and by one woman, and also to act on the basis of unconfirmed information, even though certainty is possible. Ibn Masʿūd acted on the maid's information, which is considered as 'unconfirmed', although he was able to see for himself whether the sun had risen.

Transmission

The chain of transmission of the first hadith in this chapter, No. 1629, is as follows: 'Abu Bakr ibn Abi Shaybah and Ibn Numayr narrated: both from Wakīʿ; Abu Bakr said: Wakīʿ narrated; from al-Aʿmash; from Abu Wā'il; from Ibn Masʿūd'. And in the next hadith, No. 1630, we have a chain that includes: 'Abu Kurayb narrated: Abu Muʿāwiyah narrated; from al-Aʿmash'. Both chains of transmission include narrators who all belonged to Kufah.

CHAPTER 50

ON VARIANT RECITATIONS

[1635–280]. (Dar al-Salam 1797) Ahmad ibn ʿAbdullāh ibn Yūnus narrated:[i] Zuhayr narrated; Abu Isḥāq narrated. He said: **'I saw a man asking al-Aswad ibn Yazīd, as he was teaching the Qur'an in the mosque: "How do you pronounce this verse, *'fahal min muddakir'*? Is it with 'dd' or with 'dhdh'?" He said: "With 'dd'. I heard ʿAbdullāh ibn Masʿūd say: 'I heard God's Messenger (peace be upon him) say *muddakir* with dd'."'**

حَدَّثَنَا أَحْمَدُ بْنُ عَبْدِ اللهِ بْنِ يُونُسَ، حَدَّثَنَا زُهَيْرٌ، حَدَّثَنَا أَبُو إِسْحَاقَ قَالَ: رَأَيْتُ رَجُلاً سَأَلَ الأَسْوَدَ بْنَ يَزِيدَ وَهُوَ يُعَلِّمُ الْقُرْآنَ فِي الْمَسْجِدِ فَقَالَ: كَيْفَ تَقْرَأُ هَذِهِ الآيَةَ «فَهَلْ مِنْ مُدَّكِرٍ» أَدَالاً أَمْ ذَالاً؟ قَالَ: بَلْ دَالاً، سَمِعْتُ عَبْدَ اللهِ بْنَ مَسْعُودٍ يَقُولُ سَمِعْتُ رَسُولَ اللهِ صَلَّى اللهُ عَلَيْهِ وَسَلَّمَ يَقُولُ «مُدَّكِرٍ»، دَالاً.

[1636–281]. (Dar al-Salam 1798) Muhammad ibn al-Muthannā and Ibn Bashshār narrated: Ibn al-Muthannā said: Muhammad ibn Jaʿfar narrated; Shuʿbah narrated; from Abu Isḥāq; from al-Aswad; from ʿAbdullāh; from the Prophet (peace be upon him): that **'He used to recite this verse *"fahal min muddakir"*.'**

---

i. Related by al-Bukhari, 4869, 4870, 4871, 4872, 4873, 4874, 3341 and 3345; Abu Dāwūd, 3994; al-Tirmidhī, 2937.

وَحَدَّثَنَا مُحَمَّدُ بْنُ الْمُثَنَّى وَابْنُ بَشَّارٍ. قَالَ ابْنُ الْمُثَنَّى حَدَّثَنَا مُحَمَّدُ بْنُ جَعْفَرٍ، حَدَّثَنَا شُعْبَةُ، عَنْ أَبِي إِسْحَاقَ، عَنِ الأَسْوَدِ، عَنْ عَبْدِ اللهِ، عَنِ النَّبِيِّ صَلَّى اللهُ عَلَيْهِ وَسَلَّمَ: أَنَّهُ كَانَ يَقْرَأُ هَذَا الْحَرْفَ «فَهَلْ مِنْ مُدَّكِرٍ».

[1637–282]. (Dar al-Salam 1799) Abu Bakr ibn Abi Shaybah and Abu Kurayb narrated (Abu Bakr's text):[i] both said: Abu Muʿāwiyah narrated; from al-Aʿmash; from Ibrāhīm; from ʿAlqamah. He said: **'We arrived in Syria. Abu al-Dardā' came to see us. He said: "Does any of you recite the Qur'an as ʿAbdullāh recited?" I said: "Yes, I do". He said: "How did you hear ʿAbdullāh reciting this surah: 'By the night when she lets fall its darkness'?" He said: "I heard him reciting: 'By the night when she lets fall its darkness and by the male and female'." He said: "By God, and I heard God's Messenger (peace be upon him) reciting it thus, but these people want me to recite: 'By Him who created the male and female'. I shall not do as they say".'**

وَحَدَّثَنَا أَبُو بَكْرِ بْنُ أَبِي شَيْبَةَ وَأَبُو كُرَيبٍ، (وَاللَّفْظُ لأَبِي بَكْرٍ) قَالا: حَدَّثَنَا أَبُو مُعَاوِيَةَ عَنِ الأَعْمَشِ، عَنْ إِبْرَاهِيمَ، عَنْ عَلْقَمَةَ، قَالَ: قَدِمْنَا الشَّامَ فَأَتَانَا أَبُو الدَّرْدَاءِ فَقَالَ: أَفِيكُمْ أَحَدٌ يَقْرَأُ عَلَى قِرَاءَةِ عَبْدِ اللهِ؟ فَقُلْتُ: نَعَمْ، أَنَا. قَالَ: فَكَيْفَ سَمِعْتَ عَبْدَ اللهِ يَقْرَأُ هَذِهِ الآيَةَ "وَاللَّيْلِ إِذَا يَغْشَى" قَالَ سَمِعْتُهُ يَقْرَأُ: "وَاللَّيْلِ إِذَا يَغْشَى، وَالذَّكَرِ وَالأُنْثَى". قَالَ: وَأَنَا وَاللهِ هَكَذَا سَمِعْتُ رَسُولَ اللهِ صَلَّى اللهُ عَلَيْهِ وَسَلَّمَ يَقْرَؤُهَا، وَلَكِنْ هَؤُلَاءِ يُرِيدُونَ أَنْ أَقْرَأَ "وَمَا خَلَقَ". فَلاَ أُتَابِعُهُمْ.

[1638–283]. (Dar al-Salam 1800) Qutaybah ibn Saʿīd narrated: Jarīr narrated; from Mughīrah; from Ibrāhīm. He said: '**ʿAlqamah**

---

i. Related by al-Bukhari, 4943 and 4944; al-Tirmidhī, 2939.

arrived in Syria, and he went into a mosque and prayed there. He then joined a circle. Then a man came, and I noted how people sat apart from him. He sat next to me then said: "Do you remember how ʿAbdullāh used to recite?".' He added the same.

وَحَدَّثَنَا قُتَيْبَةُ بْنُ سَعِيدٍ، حَدَّثَنَا جَرِيرٌ، عَنْ مُغِيرَةَ، عَنْ إِبْرَاهِيمَ قَالَ: أَتَى عَلْقَمَةُ الشَّامَ فَدَخَلَ مَسْجِدًا فَصَلَّى فِيهِ ثُمَّ قَامَ إِلَى حَلْقَةٍ فَجَلَسَ فِيهَا. قَالَ: فَجَاءَ رَجُلٌ فَعَرَفْتُ فِيهِ تَحَوُّشَ الْقَوْمِ وَهَيْئَتَهُمْ. فَجَلَسَ إِلَى جَنْبِي ثُمَّ قَالَ: أَتَحْفَظُ كَمَا كَانَ عَبْدُ اللهِ يَقْرَأُ؟ فَذَكَرَ بِمِثْلِهِ.

[1639–284]. (Dar al-Salam 1801–1802) ʿAlī ibn Ḥujr al-Saʿdī narrated: Ismāʿīl ibn Ibrāhīm narrated; from Dāwūd ibn Abi Hind; from al-Shaʿbī; from ʿAlqamah. He said: **'I met Abu al-Dardā', and he said to me: "To which people do you belong?" I said: "I am from the people of Iraq". He said: "From whom among them?" I said: "From the people of Kufah". He said: "Do you recite as ʿAbdullāh ibn Masʿūd recited?" I said: "Yes". He said: "Recite [the surah starting with]: 'By the night when she lets fall its darkness'." I recited: "By the night when she lets fall its darkness, by the day in full splendour, and the male and female". He smiled, then said: "I heard God's Messenger (peace be upon him) reciting it thus".'**

حَدَّثَنَا عَلِيُّ بْنُ حُجْرٍ السَّعْدِيُّ، حَدَّثَنَا إِسْمَاعِيلُ بْنُ إِبْرَاهِيمَ، عَنْ دَاوُدَ بْنِ أَبِي هِنْدٍ، عَنِ الشَّعْبِيِّ، عَنْ عَلْقَمَةَ، قَالَ: لَقِيتُ أَبَا الدَّرْدَاءِ، فَقَالَ لِي: مِمَّنْ أَنْتَ؟ قُلْتُ: مِنْ أَهْلِ الْعِرَاقِ. قَالَ: مِنْ أَيِّهِمْ؟ قُلْتُ: مِنْ أَهْلِ الْكُوفَةِ. قَالَ: هَلْ تَقْرَأُ عَلَى قِرَاءَةِ عَبْدِ اللهِ بْنِ مَسْعُودٍ؟ قَالَ: قُلْتُ نَعَمْ. قَالَ فَاقْرَأْ "وَاللَّيْلِ إِذَا يَغْشَى". قَالَ: فَقَرَأْتُ "وَاللَّيْلِ إِذَا يَغْشَى، وَالنَّهَارِ إِذَا تَجَلَّى، وَالذَّكَرِ وَالأُنْثَى". قَالَ: فَضَحِكَ ثُمَّ قَالَ: هَكَذَا سَمِعْتُ رَسُولَ اللهِ صَلَّى اللهُ عَلَيْهِ وَسَلَّمَ يَقْرَؤُهَا.

Muhammad ibn al-Muthannā narrated: ʿAbd al-Aʿlā narrated to me; Dāwūd narrated; from ʿĀmir; from ʿAlqamah. He said: **'I arrived in Syria and I met Abu al-Dardā'...'. He mentioned the same text as the hadith narrated by Ibn ʿUlayyah.**

وَحَدَّثَنَا مُحَمَّدُ بْنُ الْـمُثَنَّى، حَدَّثَنِي عَبْدُ الأَعْلَى، حَدَّثَنَا دَاوُدُ، عَنْ عَامِرٍ، عَنْ عَلْقَمَةَ، قَالَ: أَتَيْتُ الشَّامَ فَلَقِيتُ أَبَا الدَّرْدَاءِ، فَذَكَرَ بِمِثْلِ حَدِيثِ ابْنِ عُلَيَّةَ.

Text Explanation

These hadiths mention that ʿAbdullāh ibn Masʿūd and Abu al-Dardā' recited this surah stating: 'and by the male and the female', [while it is in the Qur'an]: 'By Him who created the male and female'. *Qadi* ʿIyāḍ said that al-Māzarī said: 'This report and other similar ones must be understood so as to believe that this was how the Qur'an was but subsequently abrogated. It is not known that anyone held any view other than such abrogation, and thus the latest version remained'. He added that:

> 'Perhaps some of these reports took place before they were aware of ʿUthmān's standard version that was unanimously approved. It is unlikely that anyone contradicted it.
>
> There are many reports attributed to Ibn Masʿūd, and some of these are considered as 'not authentic' by scholars who verify reports. Whatever is authentic of these reports and contradicts what we have said is taken to mean that he used to write in his copy of the Qur'an some rulings and interpretations, knowing that they were not part of the Qur'an. He did not believe that it was forbidden to do so. He treated it as a scroll in which he could write whatever he wanted. ʿUthmān and the majority of the Prophet's Companions disapproved of this, fearing that with the passage of time some may come to think that such writings were part of the Qur'an. Thus, the controversy focuses

on a point of Fiqh, namely: is it permissible to add some interpretation in a copy of the Qur'an?

It is probable that the report that the last two surahs were not included in Ibn Mas'ūd's copy was due to his belief that he was not required to write the entire Qur'an and that he left them out because they were universally known. He might have added something other than the Qur'an instead, but God knows best.

Transmission

The chain of transmission of hadith No. 1635 runs as follows: 'Abu Bakr ibn Abi Shaybah and Abu Kurayb narrated: Abu Mu'āwiyah narrated; from al-A'mash; from Ibrāhīm; from 'Alqamah'. All the narrators in this chain belonged to Kufah, and the chain includes three narrators from the *tābi'īn* generation. These are al-A'mash, Ibrāhīm and 'Alqamah.

CHAPTER 51

TIMES WHEN PRAYER IS DISCOURAGED

[1640–285]. (Dar al-Salam 1803) Yaḥyā ibn Yaḥyā narrated:[i] he said: I read out to Mālik; from Muhammad ibn Yaḥyā ibn Ḥabbān; from al-Aʿraj; from Abu Hurayrah; that **'God's Messenger discouraged prayer after ʿAṣr until the sun has set and prayer after Fajr until the sun has risen'.**

حَدَّثَنَا يَحْيَى بْنُ يَحْيَى، قَالَ قَرَأْتُ عَلَى مَالِكٍ عَنْ مُحَمَّدِ بْنِ يَحْيَى بْنِ حَبَّانَ، عَنِ الأَعْرَجِ، عَنْ أَبِي هُرَيْرَةَ، أَنَّ رَسُولَ اللهِ صَلَّى اللهُ عَلَيْهِ وَسَلَّمَ نَهَى عَنِ الصَّلاَةِ بَعْدَ الْعَصْرِ حَتَّى تَغْرُبَ الشَّمْسُ، وَعَنِ الصَّلاَةِ بَعْدَ الصُّبْحِ حَتَّى تَطْلُعَ الشَّمْسُ.

[1641–286]. (Dar al-Salam 1804) Dāwūd ibn Rushayd and Ismāʿīl ibn Sālim narrated:[ii] both from Hushaym. Dāwūd said: Hushaym narrated; Manṣūr reported; from Qatādah; he said: Abu al-ʿĀliyah reported; from Ibn ʿAbbās. He said: **'I heard more than one of God's Messenger's Companions, including ʿUmar ibn al-Khaṭṭāb whom I loved best, that God's Messenger (peace be upon him) discouraged prayer after Fajr until the sun has risen and after ʿAṣr until the sun has set'.**

---

i. Related by al-Nasāʾī, 560.

ii. Related by al-Bukhari, 581; Abu Dāwūd in similar wording, 1276; al-Tirmidhī, 183; al-Nasāʾī, 561; Ibn Mājah, 1250.

وَحَدَّثَنَا دَاوُدُ بْنُ رُشَيْدٍ وَإِسْمَاعِيلُ بْنُ سَالِمٍ، جَمِيعًا عَنْ هُشَيْمٍ، - قَالَ دَاوُدُ حَدَّثَنَا هُشَيْمٌ، أَخْبَرَنَا مَنْصُورٌ، عَنْ قَتَادَةَ، قَالَ أَخْبَرَنَا أَبُو الْعَالِيَةِ، عَنِ ابْنِ عَبَّاسٍ، قَالَ: سَمِعْتُ غَيْرَ وَاحِدٍ مِنْ أَصْحَابِ رَسُولِ اللهِ صَلَّى اللهُ عَلَيْهِ وَسَلَّمَ، مِنْهُمْ عُمَرُ بْنُ الْخَطَّابِ وَكَانَ أَحَبَّهُمْ إِلَيَّ، أَنَّ رَسُولَ اللهِ صَلَّى اللهُ عَلَيْهِ وَسَلَّمَ نَهَى عَنِ الصَّلَاةِ بَعْدَ الْفَجْرِ حَتَّى تَطْلُعَ الشَّمْسُ وَبَعْدَ الْعَصْرِ حَتَّى تَغْرُبَ الشَّمْسُ

[1642–287]. (Dar al-Salam[i]) Zuhayr ibn Ḥarb narrated it: Yaḥyā ibn Saʿīd narrated; from Shuʿbah [H]. Also, Abu Ghassān al-Mismaʿī narrated to me; ʿAbd al-Aʿlā narrated; Saʿīd narrated [H]. And, Isḥāq ibn Ibrāhīm narrated; Muʿādh ibn Hishām reported; my father narrated to me; all of them from Qatādah; with this chain of transmission: **except that in Saʿīd's and Hishām's narration: 'after Fajr until sunrise'.**

وَحَدَّثَنِيهِ زُهَيْرُ بْنُ حَرْبٍ، حَدَّثَنَا يَحْيَى بْنُ سَعِيدٍ، عَنْ شُعْبَةَ، ح. وَحَدَّثَنِي أَبُو غَسَّانَ الْمِسْمَعِيُّ حَدَّثَنَا عَبْدُ الأَعْلَى، حَدَّثَنَا سَعِيدٌ، ح. وَحَدَّثَنَا إِسْحَاقُ بْنُ إِبْرَاهِيمَ، أَخْبَرَنَا مُعَاذُ بْنُ هِشَامٍ حَدَّثَنِي أَبِي: كُلُّهُمْ عَنْ قَتَادَةَ، بِهَذَا الإِسْنَادِ، غَيْرَ أَنَّ فِي حَدِيثِ سَعِيدٍ وَهِشَامٍ بَعْدَ الصُّبْحِ حَتَّى تَشْرُقَ الشَّمْسُ

[1643–288]. (Dar al-Salam 1805) Ḥarmalah ibn Yaḥyā narrated to me:[ii] Ibn Wahb reported; Yūnus reported to me; that Ibn Shihāb reported to him; he said: ʿAṭā' ibn Yazīd al-Laythī reported to me; that he heard Abu Saʿīd al-Khudrī say: **'God's Messenger (peace be upon him) said: "No prayer may be offered after the obligatory ʿAṣr Prayer until sunset, and no prayer may be offered after the obligatory Fajr Prayer until sunrise".'**

---

i. Dar al-Salam joins this hadith to the one before it.
ii. Related by al-Bukhari in similar wording, 586; al-Nasā'ī, 566.

وَحَدَّثَنِي حَرْمَلَةُ بْنُ يَحْيَى، أَخْبَرَنَا ابْنُ وَهْبٍ، أَخْبَرَنِي يُونُسُ، أَنَّ ابْنَ شِهَابٍ أَخْبَرَهُ قَالَ: أَخْبَرَنِي عَطَاءُ بْنُ يَزِيدَ اللَّيْثِيُّ، أَنَّهُ سَمِعَ أَبَا سَعِيدٍ الْخُدْرِيَّ يَقُولُ: قَالَ رَسُولُ اللهِ صَلَّى اللهُ عَلَيْهِ وَسَلَّمَ: «لا صَلاَةَ بَعْدَ صَلاَةِ الْعَصْرِ حَتَّى تَغْرُبَ الشَّمْسُ، وَلا صَلاَةَ بَعْدَ صَلاَةِ الْفَجْرِ حَتَّى تَطْلُعَ الشَّمْسُ».

[1644–289]. (Dar al-Salam 1806) Yaḥyā ibn Yaḥyā narrated:[i] he said: I read out to Mālik; from Nāfiʿ; from Ibn ʿUmar; that God's Messenger (peace be upon him) said: **'Let none of you make an effort to pray at the time of sunrise or sunset'.**

حَدَّثَنَا يَحْيَى بْنُ يَحْيَى قَالَ: قَرَأْتُ عَلَى مَالِكٍ عَنْ نَافِعٍ، عَنِ ابْنِ عُمَرَ أَنَّ رَسُولَ اللهِ صَلَّى اللهُ عَلَيْهِ وَسَلَّمَ قَالَ: «لاَ يَتَحَرَّى أَحَدُكُمْ فَيُصَلِّيَ عِنْدَ طُلُوعِ الشَّمْسِ وَلاَ عِنْدَ غُرُوبِهَا».

[1645–290]. (Dar al-Salam 1807) Abu Bakr ibn Abi Shaybah narrated:[ii] Wakīʿ narrated [H]. Muhammad ibn ʿAbdullāh ibn Numayr narrated; my father and Muhammad ibn Bishr narrated; both said: Hishām narrated; from his father; from Ibn ʿUmar that God's Messenger (peace be upon him) said: **'Do not make your prayer at sunrise or at sunset because it rises with Satan's two horns'.**

وَحَدَّثَنَا أَبُو بَكْرِ بْنُ أَبِي شَيْبَةَ، حَدَّثَنَا وَكِيعٌ، ح. وَحَدَّثَنَا مُحَمَّدُ بْنُ عَبْدِ اللهِ بْنِ نُمَيْرٍ، حَدَّثَنَا أَبِي وَمُحَمَّدُ بْنُ بِشْرٍ، قَالا جَمِيعًا: حَدَّثَنَا هِشَامٌ، عَنْ أَبِيهِ، عَنِ ابْنِ عُمَرَ قَالَ: قَالَ رَسُولُ اللهِ صَلَّى اللهُ عَلَيْهِ وَسَلَّمَ: «لاَ تَحَرَّوْا بِصَلاَتِكُمْ طُلُوعَ الشَّمْسِ وَلاَ غُرُوبَهَا فَإِنَّهَا تَطْلُعُ بِقَرْنَىْ شَيْطَانٍ».

---

i. Related by al-Bukhari in similar wording, 582 and 585.
ii. Related by al-Bukhari in a shorter version, 3272; al-Nasāʾī, 570.

[1646–291]. (Dar al-Salam 1808) Abu Bakr ibn Abi Shaybah narrated: Wakīʿ narrated [H]. Muhammad ibn ʿAbdullāh ibn Numayr narrated; my father and Muhammad ibn Bishr narrated; both said: Hishām narrated; from his father; from Ibn ʿUmar that God's Messenger (peace be upon him) said: **'When the sun's eyebrow appears, delay prayers until it has well risen, and when the sun's eyebrow disappears, delay prayers until the sun has set'.**

وَحَدَّثَنَا أَبُو بَكْرِ بْنُ أَبِي شَيْبَةَ، حَدَّثَنَا وَكِيعٌ ح. وَحَدَّثَنَا مُحَمَّدُ بْنُ عَبْدِ اللهِ بْنِ نُمَيْرٍ، حَدَّثَنَا أَبِي وَابْنُ بِشْرٍ، قَالُوا جَمِيعًا: حَدَّثَنَا هِشَامٌ، عَنْ أَبِيهِ، عَنِ ابْنِ عُمَرَ قَالَ: قَالَ رَسُولُ اللهِ صَلَّى اللهُ عَلَيْهِ وَسَلَّمَ: «إِذَا بَدَا حَاجِبُ الشَّمْسِ فَأَخِّرُوا الصَّلَاةَ حَتَّى تَبْرُزَ، وَإِذَا غَابَ حَاجِبُ الشَّمْسِ فَأَخِّرُوا الصَّلَاةَ حَتَّى تَغِيبَ».

[1647–292]. (Dar al-Salam 1809–1810) Qutaybah ibn Saʿīd narrated:[i] Layth narrated; from Khayr ibn Nuʿaym al-Ḥaḍramī; from Ibn Hubayrah; from Abu Tamīm al-Jayshānī; from Abu Baṣrah al-Ghifārī. He said: **'God's Messenger (peace be upon him) led us in ʿAṣr Prayer at al-Mukhammaṣ. He said: "This prayer was offered to communities before you, but they neglected it. Whoever maintains it shall have his reward doubled. No prayer is offered after it until the witness has risen".' (The witness is the star.)**

وَحَدَّثَنَا قُتَيْبَةُ بْنُ سَعِيدٍ، حَدَّثَنَا لَيْثٌ، عَنْ خَيْرِ بْنِ نُعَيْمٍ الْحَضْرَمِيِّ، عَنِ ابْنِ هُبَيْرَةَ، عَنْ أَبِي تَمِيمٍ الْجَيْشَانِيِّ، عَنْ أَبِي بَصْرَةَ الْغِفَارِيِّ، قَالَ: صَلَّى بِنَا رَسُولُ اللهِ صَلَّى اللهُ عَلَيْهِ وَسَلَّمَ الْعَصْرَ بِالْمُخَمَّصِ، فَقَالَ: «إِنَّ هَذِهِ الصَّلَاةَ عُرِضَتْ عَلَى مَنْ كَانَ

i. Related by al-Nasāʾī, 520.

قَبْلَكُمْ فَضَيَّعُوهَا، فَمَنْ حَافَظَ عَلَيْهَا كَانَ لَهُ أَجْرُهُ مَرَّتَيْنِ. وَلاَ صَلاَةَ بَعْدَهَا حَتَّى يَطْلُعَ الشَّاهِدُ». وَالشَّاهِدُ النَّجْمُ.

Zuhayr ibn Ḥarb narrated to me: Ya'qūb ibn Ibrāhīm narrated; my father narrated; from Ibn Isḥāq; he said: Yazīd ibn Abi Ḥabīb narrated to me; from Khayr ibn Nu'aym al-Ḥaḍramī; from 'Abdullāh ibn Hubayrah al-Sabā'ī (and he was reliable); from Abu Tamīm al-Jayshānī; from Abu Baṣrah al-Ghifārī. He said: **'God's Messenger led us in 'Aṣr Prayer...' the same text.**

وَحَدَّثَنِي زُهَيْرُ بْنُ حَرْبٍ، حَدَّثَنَا يَعْقُوبُ بْنُ إِبْرَاهِيمَ، حَدَّثَنَا أَبِي، عَنِ ابْنِ إِسْحَاقَ، قَالَ: حَدَّثَنِي يَزِيدُ بْنُ أَبِي حَبِيبٍ، عَنْ خَيْرِ بْنِ نُعَيْمٍ الْحَضْرَمِيِّ، عَنْ عَبْدِ اللهِ بْنِ هُبَيْرَةَ السَّبَائِيِّ - وَكَانَ ثِقَةً - عَنْ أَبِي تَمِيمٍ الْجَيْشَانِيِّ، عَنْ أَبِي بَصْرَةَ الْغِفَارِيِّ قَالَ: صَلَّى بِنَا رَسُولُ اللهِ صَلَّى اللهُ عَلَيْهِ وَسَلَّمَ الْعَصْرَ. بِمِثْلِهِ.

[1648–293]. (Dar al-Salam 1811) Yaḥyā ibn Yaḥyā narrated:[i] 'Abdullāh ibn Wahb narrated; from Mūsā ibn 'Ulayy; from his father; he said: I heard 'Uqbah ibn 'Āmir al-Juhanī say: **'God's Messenger (peace be upon him) used to point out three periods of time when we should not pray or bury our dead: when the sun appears rising until it has well risen, when it is midday noon until the sun has started to decline and when the sun begins to set until it has fully set'.**

وَحَدَّثَنَا يَحْيَى بْنُ يَحْيَى، حَدَّثَنَا عَبْدُ اللهِ بْنُ وَهْبٍ، عَنْ مُوسَى بْنِ عُلَيٍّ، عَنْ أَبِيهِ، قَالَ: سَمِعْتُ عُقْبَةَ بْنَ عَامِرٍ الْجُهَنِيَّ يَقُولُ: ثَلاَثُ سَاعَاتٍ كَانَ رَسُولُ اللهِ صَلَّى اللهُ عَلَيْهِ وَسَلَّمَ يَنْهَانَا أَنْ نُصَلِّيَ فِيهِنَّ، أَوْ أَنْ نَقْبُرَ فِيهِنَّ مَوْتَانَا: حِينَ تَطْلُعُ الشَّمْسُ بَازِغَةً

i. Related by Abu Dāwūd, 3192; al-Tirmidhī, 1030; al-Nasāī, 559, 564 and 2012; Ibn Mājah, 1519.

حَتَّى تَرْتَفِعَ، وَحِينَ يَقُومُ قَائِمُ الظَّهِيرَةِ حَتَّى تَمِيلَ الشَّمْسُ، وَحِينَ تَضَيَّفُ الشَّمْسُ لِلْغُرُوبِ حَتَّى تَغْرُبَ.

Text Explanation

The hadiths included in this chapter confirm that the Prophet spoke against offering prayers after one has offered the obligatory ʿAṣr Prayer until the sun has set, after offering Fajr Prayer until the sun has well risen, at midday until it has started on its decline and when it becomes yellow until it has set. The Muslim community is unanimous that prayer that has no specific reason requiring it should not be offered at these times. However, they agree that obligatory prayers are permissible to offer at these times. Scholars differ concerning sunnah, or voluntary, prayer that has a specific reason, such as the prayer of greeting the mosque when one enters a mosque, a prostration when reciting certain verses of the Qur'an or a prostration expressing gratitude to God, the Eid Prayer, a prayer at a solar eclipse, a funeral prayer and offering a missed obligatory prayer. Al-Shāfiʿī and a number of scholars are of the view that all these prayers are permissible, and no discouragement is attached to them. Abu Ḥanīfah and a number of other scholars take the view that all these are included in the discouragement because it is expressed in general terms. Al-Shāfiʿī and those who concur with his view argue that it is confirmed that the Prophet compensated for his regular sunnah, which he normally offered after Ẓuhr Prayer but missed on a particular occasion, by offering it after ʿAṣr. This is clear in compensation for a missed sunnah prayer. The sunnah prayer that becomes due at these times is more likely to be permissible. A missed obligatory prayer also has a greater claim to be offered at these times, and so does a funeral prayer. This is the sum of the rulings that are relevant to this chapter. There are points of detail which we shall discuss as we consider the different hadiths.

What is meant by 'until the sun has risen' is its rising well into the sky, not merely its appearance. Its light should be clear and widespread. This is stated by *Qadi* ʿIyāḍ and it is correct and valid. It fits with all the hadiths and cannot be ignored.

In hadith No. 1645, the Prophet says: 'Do not make your prayer at sunrise or at sunset because it rises with Satan's two horns'. This is how the hadith is expressed, 'with Satan's two horns'. In another authentic hadith: 'it rises in between Satan's two horns'. It is said that Satan's two horns mean his followers, and it is also said that it refers to his main force and the spread of his corruption. However, it is also said that the two horns mean the two sides of his head and that the hadith should be understood literally. This is clearly preferable. It means that Satan brings his head closer to the sun at these times so that those unbelievers who worship the sun and prostrate before it will superficially appear as if they were prostrating themselves before him. Thus, it appears as if he and his offspring have clear power and that they can confuse worshippers and spoil their worship. Therefore, Muslims are discouraged from praying at these times so as to keep prayer safe from Satan's falsehood. The same is the case with prayer in places frequented by Satan. In Abu Dāwūd's and al-Nasā'ī's narrations of the hadith concerning ʿAmr ibn ʿAbasah, the hadith says that the sun 'rises in between Satan's two horns and the unbelievers will be praying to it'.

In hadith No. 1646, the Prophet's instructions: 'When the sun's eyebrow appears, delay prayers until it has well risen'. The sun's eyebrow means its edge. 'Until it has well risen' means that it becomes fully apparent and high in the sky. Hadith No. 1647 mentions that the ʿAṣr Prayer was offered to earlier communities but they neglected it. It promises double reward to those who maintain it and fulfil it at its time. This is clear in stating the great benefit that results from regularly offering this prayer on time so that it remains an important aspect of Islamic worship. Muslims are urged to maintain it without fail.

The last hadith in this chapter, No. 1648, mentions that the Prophet pointed out three periods of time when prayer and burying the dead are discouraged. Some scholars suggest that what is discouraged is the funeral prayer, not the actual burial. But this view lacks solid argument because the funeral prayer is not discouraged at these times, according to the unanimous view. It is not right to explain a hadith in a way that is contrary to the unanimous view. The correct meaning is that it is discouraged to deliberately delay the burial until these times, just like delaying the ʿAṣr Prayer until the sun has become yellow for no valid reason. This is the sort of prayer hypocrites do, as stated in an authentic hadith.

Transmission

Ibn Hubayrah is a narrator in the chain of transmission of hadith No. 1647. He is ʿAbdullāh ibn Hubayrah al-Ḥaḍramī al-Miṣrī, and his name is mentioned in full in the next hadith. Abu Tamīm al-Jayshānī is called by his tribal affiliation as he belonged to the Yemenī tribe of Jayshān. His name is ʿAbdullāh ibn Mālik.

Mūsā ibn ʿUlayy is mentioned in the chain of transmission of hadith No. 1648. He is better known as Ibn ʿUlayy, but some mention him as Ibn ʿAlī. The two versions are written in the same way in Arabic. His full name is Mūsā ibn ʿUlayy ibn Rabāḥ al-Lakhmī.

CHAPTER 52

ʿAMR IBN ʿABASAH EMBRACES ISLAM

[1649–294]. (Dar al-Salam 1812) Ahmad ibn Jaʿfar al-Maʿqiriy narrated to me: al-Naḍr ibn Muhammad narrated; ʿIkrimah ibn ʿAmmār narrated; Shaddād ibn ʿAbdullāh, Abu ʿAmmār and Yaḥyā ibn Kathīr narrated; from Abu Umāmah. (ʿIkrimah said: Shaddād met Abu Umāmah and Wāthilah and accompanied Anas on his journey to Syria and he spoke highly of him); from Abu Umāmah; he said: ʿAmr ibn ʿAbasah al-Sulamī said: **'In pre-Islamic days I used to think that people were in error and that their beliefs had no basis as they worshipped idols. I then heard of a man in Makkah relating things, so I mounted my camel and went to him. I realised that God's Messenger (peace be upon him) was hiding and his people were openly abusive to him. I resorted to subtle ways until I managed to see him in Makkah. I asked him: "What are you?" He said: "I am a Prophet." I said: "What is a Prophet?" He said: "God has given me a message." I asked: "What is your message?" He said: "He sent me to urge kindness to relatives, ensure the breaking of idols and that people should believe in God's oneness, associating no partners with Him." I asked: "Who supports you in this?" He said: "A free man and a slave." With him on that day were Abu Bakr and Bilāl. I said to him: "I shall follow you". He said: "You cannot do this today. Do you not see my situation and the people's situation? Go back to your people. When you hear that I am in a position of strength, come back to me". I returned to my people.**

Then, while I was with my people, the Prophet migrated to Madinah. I looked for news and kept asking people when he was in Madinah. Then some people from Yathrib, i.e. Madinah, came over and I asked them: "How is this man who migrated to Madinah doing?" They said: "People are turning to him fast. His people tried to assassinate him, but they failed". I travelled to Madinah and went to him. I said: "Messenger of God, do you recognise me?" He said: "Yes, you came to meet me in Makkah". I said: "Indeed. Prophet, tell me about the things God has taught you and I am ignorant of. Tell me about prayer". He said: "Pray the dawn [i.e. Fajr] prayer, then do not pray until the sun has risen well in the sky. When it comes up it does so in between two horns of Satan.[i] At that time, unbelievers prostrate themselves before it. You may pray after that, and prayer will be witnessed until the shadow is straight [i.e. at noon] when you should not pray. At this time, Hell is burnt fiercely. When the shadows begin to extend, then you pray, for prayer will be witnessed until you have prayed ʿAṣr. Then stop praying until the sun has set because it sets in between the horns of Satan. At that time, unbelievers prostrate themselves for it".

I said: "Prophet of God, tell me about the ablution." He said: "When any of you brings forward his water and rinses his mouth and blows his nose, the sins he committed with his face, mouth and nose drop away. Then, when he washes his face as God has commanded, the sins of his face drop off his beard with the water. He then washes his arms up to his elbows and the sins of his hands drop off through his

i. This is because Satan stands parallel to the sun so when it rises it appears between the two sides of his head. When a believer prostrates, Satan deludes himself that it is for him and that he is being worshipped. God's Messenger has forbidden us helping Satan with his delusion.

fingers with the water. He then wipes his head and the sins of his head drop off through the ends of his hair with the water. He then washes his feet up to his ankles and the sins of his legs drop off through his toes with the water. When he then stands up and prays, praising God and glorifying Him as He should be praised and glorified and turning his heart towards God, he will end up free of all sin, as he was on the day when his mother gave birth to him".'

'Amr ibn 'Abasah narrated this hadith to Abu Umāmah, the Prophet's Companion. Abu Umāmah said to him: '**'Amr ibn 'Abasah, consider what you are saying - a man is given [all] this in one situation?' 'Amr said: 'Abu Umāmah, I am growing old and my bones are less strong and my life is drawing to an end. I do not need to lie to God or His Messenger. I would not have related this hadith to anyone if I heard it from God's Messenger once, twice or three times (counting up to seven times), but I heard it more than that'.**

حَدَّثَنِي أَحْمَدُ بْنُ جَعْفَرٍ الْـمَعْقِرِيُّ، حَدَّثَنَا النَّضْرُ بْنُ مُحَمَّدٍ، حَدَّثَنَا عِكْرِمَةُ بْنُ عَمَّارٍ، حَدَّثَنَا شَدَّادُ بْنُ عَبْدِ اللهِ، أَبُو عَمَّارٍ، وَيَحْيَى بْنُ أَبِي كَثِيرٍ، عَنْ أَبِي أُمَامَةَ، - قَالَ عِكْرِمَةُ: وَلَقِيَ شَدَّادٌ أَبَا أُمَامَةَ وَوَاثِلَةَ وَصَحِبَ أَنَسًا إِلَى الشَّامِ وَأَثْنَى عَلَيْهِ فَضْلاً وَخَيْراً. عَنْ أَبِي أُمَامَةَ قَالَ: قَالَ عَمْرُو بْنُ عَبَسَةَ السُّلَمِيُّ: كُنْتُ وَأَنَا فِي الْجَاهِلِيَّةِ أَظُنُّ أَنَّ النَّاسَ عَلَى ضَلاَلَةٍ، وَأَنَّهُمْ لَيْسُوا عَلَى شَيْءٍ وَهُمْ يَعْبُدُونَ الأَوْثَانَ. فَسَمِعْتُ بِرَجُلٍ بِمَكَّةَ يُخْبِرُ أَخْبَارًا، فَقَعَدْتُ عَلَى رَاحِلَتِي فَقَدِمْتُ عَلَيْهِ، فَإِذَا رَسُولُ اللهِ صَلَّى اللهُ عَلَيْهِ وَسَلَّمَ مُسْتَخْفِيًا، جُرَءَاءُ عَلَيْهِ قَوْمُهُ. فَتَلَطَّفْتُ حَتَّى دَخَلْتُ عَلَيْهِ بِمَكَّةَ، فَقُلْتُ لَهُ: مَا أَنْتَ؟ قَالَ: «أَنَا نَبِيٌّ». فَقُلْتُ وَمَا نَبِيٌّ؟ قَالَ: «أَرْسَلَنِي اللهُ». فَقُلْتُ: وَبِأَيِّ شَيْءٍ أَرْسَلَكَ؟ قَالَ: «أَرْسَلَنِي بِصِلَةِ الأَرْحَامِ، وَكَسْرِ الأَوْثَانِ، وَأَنْ يُوَحَّدَ اللهُ لاَ يُشْرَكُ بِهِ شَيْءٌ». قُلْتُ لَهُ: فَمَنْ مَعَكَ عَلَى هَذَا؟ قَالَ: «حُرٌّ وَعَبْدٌ». قَالَ: وَمَعَهُ يَوْمَئِذٍ أَبُو بَكْرٍ وَبِلاَلٌ مِمَّنْ آمَنَ بِهِ. فَقُلْتُ: إِنِّي مُتَّبِعُكَ. قَالَ: «إِنَّكَ لاَ تَسْتَطِيعُ ذَلِكَ يَوْمَكَ هَذَا. أَلاَ تَرَى

حَالِي وَحَالَ النَّاسِ؟ وَلَكِنِ ارْجِعْ إِلَى أَهْلِكَ، فَإِذَا سَمِعْتَ بِي قَدْ ظَهَرْتُ فَأْتِنِي». قَالَ: فَذَهَبْتُ إِلَى أَهْلِي. وَقَدِمَ رَسُولُ اللهِ صَلَّى اللهُ عَلَيْهِ وَسَلَّمَ الْـمَدِينَةَ، وَكُنْتُ فِي أَهْلِي.

فَجَعَلْتُ أَتَخَبَّرُ الأَخْبَارَ، وَأَسْأَلُ النَّاسَ حِينَ قَدِمَ الْـمَدِينَةَ، حَتَّى قَدِمَ عَلَيَّ نَفَرٌ مِنْ أَهْلِ يَثْرِبَ مِنْ أَهْلِ الْـمَدِينَةِ، فَقُلْتُ: مَا فَعَلَ هَذَا الرَّجُلُ الَّذِي قَدِمَ الْـمَدِينَةَ؟ فَقَالُوا: النَّاسُ إِلَيْهِ سِرَاعٌ، وَقَدْ أَرَادَ قَوْمُهُ قَتْلَهُ فَلَمْ يَسْتَطِيعُوا ذَلِكَ. فَقَدِمْتُ الْـمَدِينَةَ، فَدَخَلْتُ عَلَيْهِ فَقُلْتُ: يَا رَسُولَ اللهِ أَتَعْرِفُنِي؟ قَالَ: «نَعَمْ، أَنْتَ الَّذِي لَقِيتَنِي بِمَكَّةَ». قَالَ: فَقُلْتُ بَلَى. فَقُلْتُ: يَا نَبِيَّ اللهِ أَخْبِرْنِي عَمَّا عَلَّمَكَ اللهُ وَأَجْهَلُهُ. أَخْبِرْنِي عَنِ الصَّلاَةِ. قَالَ: «صَلِّ صَلاَةَ الصُّبْحِ ثُمَّ أَقْصِرْ عَنِ الصَّلاَةِ حَتَّى تَطْلُعَ الشَّمْسُ حَتَّى تَرْتَفِعَ، فَإِنَّهَا تَطْلُعُ حِينَ تَطْلُعُ بَيْنَ قَرْنَيْ شَيْطَانٍ، وَحِينَئِذٍ يَسْجُدُ لَهَا الْكُفَّارُ. ثُمَّ صَلِّ فَإِنَّ الصَّلاَةَ مَشْهُودَةٌ مَحْضُورَةٌ حَتَّى يَسْتَقِلَّ الظِّلُّ بِالرُّمْحِ. ثُمَّ أَقْصِرْ عَنِ الصَّلاَةِ فَإِنَّ حِينَئِذٍ تُسْجَرُ جَهَنَّمُ. فَإِذَا أَقْبَلَ الْفَيْءُ فَصَلِّ، فَإِنَّ الصَّلاَةَ مَشْهُودَةٌ مَحْضُورَةٌ حَتَّى تُصَلِّيَ الْعَصْرَ. ثُمَّ أَقْصِرْ عَنِ الصَّلاَةِ حَتَّى تَغْرُبَ الشَّمْسُ فَإِنَّهَا تَغْرُبُ بَيْنَ قَرْنَيْ شَيْطَانٍ، وَحِينَئِذٍ يَسْجُدُ لَهَا الْكُفَّارُ».

قَالَ: فَقُلْتُ يَا نَبِيَّ اللهِ، فَالْوُضُوءُ حَدِّثْنِي عَنْهُ. قَالَ: «مَا مِنْكُمْ رَجُلٌ يُقَرِّبُ وَضُوءَهُ فَيَتَمَضْمَضُ وَيَسْتَنْشِقُ فَيَنْتَثِرُ إِلاَّ خَرَّتْ خَطَايَا وَجْهِهِ وَفِيهِ وَخَيَاشِيمِهِ، ثُمَّ إِذَا غَسَلَ وَجْهَهُ كَمَا أَمَرَهُ اللهُ إِلاَّ خَرَّتْ خَطَايَا وَجْهِهِ مِنْ أَطْرَافِ لِحْيَتِهِ مَعَ الْـمَاءِ، ثُمَّ يَغْسِلُ يَدَيْهِ إِلَى الْـمِرْفَقَيْنِ إِلاَّ خَرَّتْ خَطَايَا يَدَيْهِ مِنْ أَنَامِلِهِ مَعَ الْـمَاءِ، ثُمَّ يَمْسَحُ رَأْسَهُ إِلاَّ خَرَّتْ خَطَايَا رَأْسِهِ مِنْ أَطْرَافِ شَعْرِهِ مَعَ الْـمَاءِ، ثُمَّ يَغْسِلُ قَدَمَيْهِ إِلَى الْكَعْبَيْنِ إِلاَّ خَرَّتْ خَطَايَا رِجْلَيْهِ مِنْ أَنَامِلِهِ مَعَ الْـمَاءِ. فَإِنْ هُوَ قَامَ فَصَلَّى فَحَمِدَ اللهَ وَأَثْنَى عَلَيْهِ وَمَجَّدَهُ بِالَّذِي هُوَ لَهُ أَهْلٌ، وَفَرَّغَ قَلْبَهُ لِلَّهِ، إِلاَّ انْصَرَفَ مِنْ خَطِيئَتِهِ كَهَيْئَتِهِ يَوْمَ وَلَدَتْهُ أُمُّهُ».

فَحَدَّثَ عَمْرُو بْنُ عَبَسَةَ بِهَذَا الْحَدِيثِ أَبَا أُمَامَةَ صَاحِبَ رَسُولِ اللهِ صَلَّى اللهُ عَلَيْهِ وَسَلَّمَ، فَقَالَ لَهُ أَبُو أُمَامَةَ: يَا عَمْرُو بْنَ عَبَسَةَ، انْظُرْ مَا تَقُولُ فِي مَقَامٍ وَاحِدٍ يُعْطَى هَذَا الرَّجُلُ. فَقَالَ عَمْرٌو: يَا أَبَا أُمَامَةَ، لَقَدْ كَبِرَتْ سِنِّي وَرَقَّ عَظْمِي وَاقْتَرَبَ أَجَلِي، وَمَا بِي حَاجَةٌ أَنْ أَكْذِبَ عَلَى اللهِ وَلاَ عَلَى رَسُولِ اللهِ. لَوْ لَمْ أَسْمَعْهُ مِنْ رَسُولِ اللهِ صَلَّى اللهُ عَلَيْهِ

وَسَلَّمَ إِلاَّ مَرَّةً أَوْ مَرَّتَيْنِ أَوْ ثَلاَثًا - حَتَّى عَدَّ سَبْعَ مَرَّاتٍ - مَا حَدَّثْتُ بِهِ أَبَدًا، وَلَكِنِّي سَمِعْتُهُ أَكْثَرَ مِنْ ذَلِكَ.

Text Explanation

When ʿAmr met the Prophet, he asked him 'What are you'? He did not say: 'Who are you?' He was questioning him about his status, not about his name and tribe. ʿAmr asks the Prophet about his message and he tells him that God 'sent me to urge kindness to relatives, ensure the breaking of idols and that people should believe in God's oneness, associating no partners with Him'. This clearly encourages kindness to one's kinsfolk and relatives. The Prophet highlights it together with belief in God's oneness. He did not mention to him any matter of detail but stressed the important aspects and started with kindness to relatives. ʿAmr mentions that with the Prophet were Abu Bakr and Bilāl. This stresses their high status, and some may argue that they were the first to embrace Islam, according to this hadith.

ʿAmr says to the Prophet: 'I shall follow you'. He said: 'You cannot do this today. Do you not see my situation and the people's situation? Go back to your people. When you hear that I am in a position of strength, come back to me'. This means that ʿAmr wanted to follow the Prophet and declare himself a Muslim and stay with the Prophet. The Prophet tells him that this was not feasible because of the state of weakness the Muslims were in. They would not be able to support him, and they feared what the unbelievers might do to him. This suggests that he gained his reward for accepting Islam. The Prophet advised him to go back to his people and maintain his belief in Islam. When he had heard that the Prophet had gained the upper hand, he should return to him. This was one of the Prophet's miracles, informing ʿAmr at that early stage that he was sure to triumph.

ʿAmr mentions that when he went to Madinah to meet the Prophet, he said to him: 'Messenger of God, do you recognise me?' He said: 'Yes, you came to meet me in Makkah'. I said: 'Indeed. Prophet, tell me about the things God has taught you and I am ignorant of. Tell me about prayer'. This is how ʿAmr put his question: 'Tell me about…', not 'Tell me what…'. This means that he was asking about its status and how to fulfil it. Hence, the Prophet tells him about the prayer: 'Pray the dawn [i.e. Fajr] prayer, then do not pray until the sun has risen well in the sky'. This makes it clear that the time of discouragement of prayer is not only at sunrise but extends until the sun has risen well in the sky. We explained this earlier. When the sun is high, prayer is valid, and the Prophet says that it is witnessed. This means that angels attend the prayer. Thus, it is more likely to be accepted and earn grace. This continues 'until the shadow is straight [i.e. at noon] when you should not pray. At this time, Hell is burnt fiercely. When the shadows begin to extend, then you pray, for prayer will be witnessed'. 'The shadow is straight' means that the shadow of an object faces it to the north, leaning neither to the east nor to the west. This is the straight state. The hadith makes clear that prayer should not be offered at this time, until the sun starts its decline. This is the view of al-Shāfiʿī and the great majority of scholars. Al-Shāfiʿī makes an exception for Friday.[i]

The Prophet explains that this period of discouragement of prayer extends 'until you have prayed ʿAṣr'. This makes clear that the period of discouragement does not begin when ʿAṣr is due, nor when anyone else has prayed it. It begins for everyone after one prays ʿAṣr. If one delays it, one may offer voluntary prayers before one prays the obligatory ʿAṣr.

The Prophet speaks about sins dropping off when one performs the ablution. The sins meant here are the minor ones, provided that major sins are avoided, as we have explained in the Book of Cleansing.

---

i. Imam al-Nawawī adds here: '*Qadi* ʿIyāḍ (may God bestow mercy on him) says some strange things in interpreting the hadith and the views of scholars. I am referring to it here only so that readers do not take it as correct'. I preferred to put this in a footnote as al-Nawawī does not give the details of what *Qadi* ʿIyāḍ says, but merely says that it is strange.

In explaining the ablution, the Prophet says: 'He then washes his feet'. This serves as evidence in support of the view of all scholars that what is a duty in ablution is to wash one's feet. The Shia claim that the duty is to wipe one's feet. Ibn Jarīr says that a person has a choice to wash or wipe. Some of the Ẓāhirī scholars claim that the duty is to wash and wipe one's feet.

At the end of the hadith, ʻAmr says to Abu Umāmah, 'I would not have related this hadith to anyone if I heard it from God's Messenger once, twice or three times (counting up to seven times), but I heard it more than that'. This may sound problematic because it appears to mean that one should not narrate any hadith unless one has heard it more than seven times. It is well known that a person who has heard a hadith once may narrate it. Indeed, he must if he is the only one who knows it. However, what ʻAmr means here is that he would not have narrated this hadith unless he was absolutely certain of what he was narrating. That he mentions the number of times he heard it is merely to state his own condition, not to suggest that this is a condition for narrating, but God knows best.

Transmission

The first narrator of this hadith is called Ahmad ibn Jaʻfar al-Maʻqiriy. He belonged to Maʻqir, an area in Yemen.

CHAPTER 53

PRAYER AT SUNRISE AND SUNSET

[1650–295]. (Dar al-Salam 1813) Muhammad ibn Ḥātim narrated:[i] Bahz narrated; Wuhayb narrated; ʿAbdullāh ibn Ṭāwūs narrated; from his father, from ʿĀ'ishah; that she said: **'ʿUmar misunderstood. God's Messenger (peace be upon him) only prohibited that one should deliberately seek [to pray at] sunrise and sunset'.**

حَدَّثَنَا مُحَمَّدُ بْنُ حَاتِمٍ، حَدَّثَنَا بَهْزٌ، حَدَّثَنَا وُهَيْبٌ، حَدَّثَنَا عَبْدُ اللهِ بْنُ طَاوُسٍ، عَنْ أَبِيهِ، عَنْ عَائِشَةَ، أَنَّهَا قَالَتْ: وَهِمَ عُمَرُ إِنَّمَا نَهَى رَسُولُ اللهِ صَلَّى اللهُ عَلَيْهِ وَسَلَّمَ أَنْ يُتَحَرَّى طُلُوعُ الشَّمْسِ وَغُرُوبُهَا.

[1651–296]. (Dar al-Salam 1814) Ḥasan al-Ḥulwānī narrated: ʿAbd al-Razzāq narrated; Maʿmar reported; from Ibn Ṭāwūs; from his father; from ʿĀ'ishah; that she said: **'God's Messenger (peace be upon him) did not abandon the two *rakʿahs* after ʿAṣr'.**

And ʿĀ'ishah said: 'God's Messenger (peace be upon him) said: "Do not seek the time of sunrise and sunset to pray then".'

i. Related by al-Nasā'ī, 569.

وَحَدَّثَنَا حَسَنٌ الْحُلْوَانِيُّ، حَدَّثَنَا عَبْدُ الرَّزَّاقِ، أَخْبَرَنَا مَعْمَرٌ، عَنِ ابْنِ طَاوُسٍ، عَنْ أَبِيهِ، عَنْ عَائِشَةَ، أَنَّهَا قَالَتْ: لَمْ يَدَعْ رَسُولُ اللهِ صَلَّى اللهُ عَلَيْهِ وَسَلَّمَ الرَّكْعَتَيْنِ بَعْدَ الْعَصْرِ. قَالَ: فَقَالَتْ عَائِشَةُ قَالَ رَسُولُ اللهِ صَلَّى اللهُ عَلَيْهِ وَسَلَّمَ: «لاَ تَتَحَرَّوْا طُلُوعَ الشَّمْسِ وَلاَ غُرُوبَهَا فَتُصَلُّوا عِنْدَ ذَلِكَ».

Text Explanation

In the first hadith, No. 1650, ʿĀ'ishah says that ʿUmar misunderstood. She was referring to his report that prayer after ʿAṣr is discouraged in all cases, while she is stating that what is prohibited is to deliberately seek to pray at these times. *Qadi* ʿIyāḍ said: 'ʿĀ'ishah said this because she saw the Prophet (peace be upon him) offering prayers of two *rakʿahs* after he had offered the obligatory ʿAṣr Prayer. What ʿUmar reported was also reported by Abu Saʿīd al-Khudrī and Abu Hurayrah. Ibn ʿAbbās is quoted in Muslim's *Ṣaḥīḥ* saying that he was informed of it by more than one person'.

The two reports are easily reconciled. The one concerning deliberate praying at these times is understood as referring to delaying the obligatory prayer until these times. While the other report, giving a general order of discouragement, is understood to refer to prayer that is not required for a specific reason.

CHAPTER 54

THE TWO *RAKʿAHS* THE PROPHET OFFERED AFTER ʿAṢR

[1652–297]. (Dar al-Salam 1815) Ḥarmalah ibn Yaḥyā al-Tujībī narrated to me:[i] ʿAbdullāh ibn Wahb narrated; ʿAmr (who is Ibn al-Ḥārith) reported to me; from Ibn Bukayr; from Kurayb, Ibn ʿAbbās's *mawla*; that ʿAbdullāh ibn ʿAbbās, ʿAbd al-Raḥmān ibn Azhar and al-Miswar ibn Makhramah sent him to ʿĀ'ishah, the Prophet's wife, and said to him: **'Give her the *salām* greeting from all of us and ask her about the two *rakʿahs* offered after ʿAṣr, and say that we are informed that you offer these, while we have learnt that God's Messenger (peace be upon him) discouraged them'. Ibn ʿAbbās said: 'I used to be with ʿUmar ibn al-Khaṭṭāb when he beat people for offering these two *rakʿahs*'. Kurayb said: 'I went to her and gave her the message they charged me with. She said: "Ask Umm Salamah". I left and told them what she said. They sent me to Umm Salamah with the same message as they sent me to ʿĀ'ishah. Umm Salamah said: "I had heard God's Messenger (peace be upon him) discouraging offering them but then I saw him praying these two *rakʿahs*. On that occasion when he prayed them, he had prayed ʿAṣr and came in. With me were some women from the Ḥarām clan of the Anṣār. He prayed these two *rakʿahs*. I sent him the maid and said to her: "Stand beside him and say to him: "Umm**

i. Related by al-Bukhari, 1223 and 4372; Abu Dāwūd, 1273.

Salamah says: 'Messenger of God, I hear you discouraging praying these two *rak'ahs* but now I am seeing you offering them'. If he signals with his hand, move back". The maid did that, and he signalled with his hand and she stepped back.

When he finished, he said: "O Daughter of Abu Umayyah! You are asking about the two *rak'ahs* after 'Aṣr. A delegation from [the tribe of] 'Abd al-Qays came to see me, speaking to me on behalf of their people about Islam. They kept me from offering the two *rak'ahs* after the obligatory Ẓuhr Prayer. These compensate for those".'

حَدَّثَنِي حَرْمَلَةُ بْنُ يَحْيَى التُّجِيبِيُّ، حَدَّثَنَا عَبْدُ اللهِ بْنُ وَهْبٍ، أَخْبَرَنِي عَمْرٌو، وَهُوَ ابْنُ الْحَارِثِ، عَنْ بُكَيْرٍ، عَنْ كُرَيْبٍ، مَوْلَى ابْنِ عَبَّاسٍ أَنَّ عَبْدَ اللهِ بْنَ عَبَّاسٍ وَعَبْدَ الرَّحْمَنِ بْنَ أَزْهَرَ وَالْـمِسْوَرَ بْنَ مَخْرَمَةَ أَرْسَلُوهُ إِلَى عَائِشَةَ، زَوْجِ النَّبِيِّ صَلَّى اللهُ عَلَيْهِ وَسَلَّمَ، فَقَالُوا اقْرَأْ عَلَيْهَا السَّلَامَ مِنَّا جَمِيعًا، وَسَلْهَا عَنِ الرَّكْعَتَيْنِ بَعْدَ الْعَصْرِ، وَقُلْ: إِنَّا أُخْبِرْنَا أَنَّكِ تُصَلِّينَهُمَا وَقَدْ بَلَغَنَا أَنَّ رَسُولَ اللهِ صَلَّى اللهُ عَلَيْهِ وَسَلَّمَ نَهَى عَنْهُمَا. قَالَ ابْنُ عَبَّاسٍ وَكُنْتُ أَصْرِفُ مَعَ عُمَرَ بْنِ الْخَطَّابِ النَّاسَ عَنْهَا . قَالَ كُرَيْبٌ فَدَخَلْتُ عَلَيْهَا وَبَلَّغْتُهَا مَا أَرْسَلُونِي بِهِ. فَقَالَتْ: سَلْ أُمَّ سَلَمَةَ. فَخَرَجْتُ إِلَيْهِمْ فَأَخْبَرْتُهُمْ بِقَوْلِهَا، فَرَدُّونِي إِلَى أُمِّ سَلَمَةَ بِمِثْلِ مَا أَرْسَلُونِي بِهِ إِلَى عَائِشَةَ. فَقَالَتْ أُمُّ سَلَمَةَ: سَمِعْتُ رَسُولَ اللهِ صَلَّى اللهُ عَلَيْهِ وَسَلَّمَ يَنْهَى عَنْهُمَا، ثُمَّ رَأَيْتُهُ يُصَلِّيهِمَا. أَمَّا حِينَ صَلَّاهُمَا فَإِنَّهُ صَلَّى الْعَصْرَ ثُمَّ دَخَلَ وَعِنْدِي نِسْوَةٌ مِنْ بَنِي حَرَامٍ مِنَ الأَنْصَارِ فَصَلَّاهُمَا. فَأَرْسَلْتُ إِلَيْهِ الْجَارِيَةَ فَقُلْتُ: قُومِي بِجَنْبِهِ فَقُولِي لَهُ: تَقُولُ أُمُّ سَلَمَةَ يَا رَسُولَ اللهِ إِنِّي أَسْمَعُكَ تَنْهَى عَنْ هَاتَيْنِ الرَّكْعَتَيْنِ وَأَرَاكَ تُصَلِّيهِمَا فَإِنْ أَشَارَ بِيَدِهِ فَاسْتَأْخِرِي عَنْهُ. قال: فَفَعَلَتِ الْجَارِيَةُ، فَأَشَارَ بِيَدِهِ. فَاسْتَأْخَرَتْ عَنْهُ.

فَلَمَّا انْصَرَفَ قَالَ: «يَا بِنْتَ أَبِي أُمَيَّةَ، سَأَلْتِ عَنِ الرَّكْعَتَيْنِ بَعْدَ الْعَصْرِ. إِنَّهُ أَتَانِي نَاسٌ مِنْ عَبْدِ الْقَيْسِ بِالإِسْلَامِ مِنْ قَوْمِهِمْ، فَشَغَلُونِي عَنِ الرَّكْعَتَيْنِ اللَّتَيْنِ بَعْدَ الظُّهْرِ، فَهُمَا هَاتَانِ».

[1653–298]. (Dar al-Salam 1816) Yaḥyā ibn Ayyūb, Qutaybah and ʿAlī ibn Ḥujr narrated:[i] Ibn Ayyūb said: Ismāʿīl (who is Ibn Jaʿfar) narrated; Muhammad (who is Ibn Abi Ḥarmalah) reported to me; he said: Abu Salamah reported to me; that **he asked ʿĀ'ishah about the two *rakʿahs* the Prophet used to pray after ʿAṣr Prayer. She said: 'He used to pray them before ʿAṣr, but on some occasion he was preoccupied or he might have forgotten them, and he prayed them after ʿAṣr. He then kept praying them. When he offered a particular prayer, he used to keep it up'.**

Yaḥyā ibn Ayyūb said: Ismāʿīl said: **'She meant that he would continue to pray it'.**

حَدَّثَنَا يَحْيَى بْنُ أَيُّوبَ، وَقُتَيْبَةُ، وَعَلِيُّ بْنُ حُجْرٍ، قَالَ ابْنُ أَيُّوبَ: حَدَّثَنَا إِسْمَاعِيلُ – وَهُوَ ابْنُ جَعْفَرٍ – أَخْبَرَنِي مُحَمَّدٌ – وَهُوَ ابْنُ أَبِي حَرْمَلَةَ–قَالَ: أَخْبَرَنِي أَبُو سَلَمَةَ، أَنَّهُ سَأَلَ عَائِشَةَ عَنِ السَّجْدَتَيْنِ اللَّتَيْنِ كَانَ رَسُولُ اللهِ صَلَّى اللهُ عَلَيْهِ وَسَلَّمَ يُصَلِّيهِمَا بَعْدَ الْعَصْرِ، فَقَالَتْ: كَانَ يُصَلِّيهِمَا قَبْلَ الْعَصْرِ، ثُمَّ إِنَّهُ شُغِلَ عَنْهُمَا أَوْ نَسِيَهُمَا، فَصَلاَّهُمَا بَعْدَ الْعَصْرِ ثُمَّ أَثْبَتَهُمَا. وَكَانَ إِذَا صَلَّى صَلاَةً أَثْبَتَهَا.

قَالَ يَحْيَى بْنُ أَيُّوبَ قَالَ إِسْمَاعِيلُ: تَعْنِي دَاوَمَ عَلَيْهَا.

[1654–299]. (Dar al-Salam 1817) Zuhayr ibn Ḥarb narrated: Jarīr narrated [H]. Also, Ibn Numayr narrated; my father narrated; both from Hishām ibn ʿUrwah; from his father; from ʿĀ'ishah. She said: **'God's Messenger (peace be upon him) never left praying two *rakʿahs* after ʿAṣr at my place'.**

i. Related by al-Nasā'ī, 577.

حَدَّثَنَا زُهَيْرُ بْنُ حَرْبٍ، حَدَّثَنَا جَرِيرٌ، ح. وَحَدَّثَنَا ابْنُ نُمَيْرٍ، حَدَّثَنَا أَبِي، جَمِيعًا عَنْ هِشَامِ بْنِ عُرْوَةَ، عَنْ أَبِيهِ، عَنْ عَائِشَةَ قَالَتْ: مَا تَرَكَ رَسُولُ اللهِ صَلَّى اللهُ عَلَيْهِ وَسَلَّمَ رَكْعَتَيْنِ بَعْدَ الْعَصْرِ عِنْدِي قَطُّ

[1655–300]. (Dar al-Salam 1818) Abu Bakr ibn Abi Shaybah narrated:[i] ʿAlī ibn Mushir narrated [H]. Also, ʿAlī ibn Ḥujr narrated (his text); ʿAlī ibn Mushir reported; Abu Isḥāq al-Shaybānī reported; from ʿAbd al-Raḥmān ibn al-Aswad; from his father; from ʿĀ'ishah. She said: **'God's Messenger never left offering two prayers in my home, privately or publicly: two *rakʿahs* before Fajr and two *rakʿahs* after ʿAṣr'.**

وَحَدَّثَنَا أَبُو بَكْرِ بْنُ أَبِي شَيْبَةَ، حَدَّثَنَا عَلِيُّ بْنُ مُسْهِرٍ، ح. وَحَدَّثَنَا عَلِيُّ بْنُ حُجْرٍ، (وَاللَّفْظُ لَهُ)، أَخْبَرَنَا عَلِيُّ بْنُ مُسْهِرٍ، أَخْبَرَنَا أَبُو إِسْحَاقَ الشَّيْبَانِيُّ، عَنْ عَبْدِ الرَّحْمَنِ بْنِ الأَسْوَدِ عَنْ أَبِيهِ، عَنْ عَائِشَةَ قَالَتْ: صَلاَتَانِ مَا تَرَكَهُمَا رَسُولُ اللهِ صَلَّى اللهُ عَلَيْهِ وَسَلَّمَ فِي بَيْتِي قَطُّ سِرًّا وَلاَ عَلاَنِيَةً، رَكْعَتَيْنِ قَبْلَ الْفَجْرِ وَرَكْعَتَيْنِ بَعْدَ الْعَصْرِ.

[1656–301]. (Dar al-Salam 1819) Ibn al-Muthannā and Ibn Bashshār narrated:[ii] Ibn al-Muthannā said: Muhammad ibn Jaʿfar narrated; Shuʿbah narrated; from Abu Isḥāq; from al-Aswad and Masrūq. Both said: **'We testify that ʿĀ'ishah said: "Whenever it was his day that he would be with me, God's Messenger (peace be upon him) offered these two in my home". She meant the two *rakʿahs* after ʿAṣr'.**

i. Related by al-Bukhari, 592; al-Nasā'ī, 576.
ii. Related by al-Bukhari, 593; Abu Dāwūd, 1279; al-Nasā'ī in similar wording, 575.

وَحَدَّثَنَا ابْنُ الْمُثَنَّى وَابْنُ بَشَّارٍ. قَالَ ابْنُ الْمُثَنَّى: حَدَّثَنَا مُحَمَّدُ بْنُ جَعْفَرٍ، حَدَّثَنَا شُعْبَةُ، عَنْ أَبِي إِسْحَاقَ، عَنِ الأَسْوَدِ، وَمَسْرُوقٍ، قَالا: نَشْهَدُ عَلَى عَائِشَةَ أَنَّهَا قَالَتْ: مَا كَانَ يَوْمُهُ الَّذِي كَانَ يَكُونُ عِنْدِي إِلاَّ صَلاَّهُمَا رَسُولُ اللهِ صَلَّى اللهُ عَلَيْهِ وَسَلَّمَ فِي بَيْتِي. تَعْنِي الرَّكْعَتَيْنِ بَعْدَ الْعَصْرِ.

Text Explanation

In hadith No. 1652, Ibn ʿAbbās says: 'I used to be with ʿUmar ibn al-Khaṭṭāb when he beat people for offering them'. This is how it is stated in some original manuscripts. In others, it is stated: 'I used to tell people not to offer them'. Both are correct and they are not contradictory. He might have beaten up some people on some occasions and on other occasions he only told them not to offer them. Or he might have done both on some occasions. Alternatively, he might have beaten a person who was aware of the discouragement and only spoken to those who were unaware of it. In Muslim, it is reported that ʿUmar used to beat people with his whip if he saw them offering these two *rakʿahs*. This is an aspect of the ruler taking care of his subjects, preventing them from deviation from the right course in their faith and punishing them for doing what is unlawful to them.

In the same hadith, Kurayb says: 'I went to her and gave her the message they charged me with. She said: "Ask Umm Salamah". I left and told them what she said. They sent me to Umm Salamah with the same message'. This shows that it is desirable for a scholar who has been asked to ascertain an important issue to refer it to someone else with better knowledge of it or its origin, if this is possible. It also shows the importance of acknowledging people's distinguished status. It also suggests that a messenger should observe the proper manners concerning his message. He may not take action on his own initiative, without prior permission. Kurayb did not act independently and go to Umm Salamah because he was sent to ʿĀ'ishah to put the question to her. When ʿĀ'ishah sent him to Umm Salamah, he went back to those who sent him and informed them of what she said. Therefore, they sent him to Umm Salamah.

In her explanation, Umm Salamah said that when she saw the Prophet praying the two *rakʿahs* after ʿAṣr, 'I sent him the maid'. This shows that information delivered by one person, man or woman, is sufficient and may be acted upon, even in a situation like that of Umm Salamah's, when she could apply directly to the Prophet for that information. She said to the maid: 'Stand beside him and say to him: "Umm Salamah says: 'Messenger of God, I hear you discouraging praying these two *rakʿahs* but now I am seeing you offering them'."' We note that Umm Salamah used her own appellation. She did not use her name, Hind, because she was better known by her appellation. It is appropriate that one should use one's appellation if one is better known by it. She was given this appellation, or *kunyah,* as the mother of her own son Salamah ibn Abi Salamah, who was a Companion of the Prophet.

She said: 'I hear you discouraging praying these two *rakʿahs* but now I am seeing you offering them'. She uses the present tense but means that she heard him earlier. Her enquiry makes clear that a subordinate who sees his superior doing something contrary to his usual practice should ask his superior gently about it. If it is a matter of forgetfulness, this will serve as a reminder. If it is done deliberately, for a particular reason, the subordinate will learn about it. If it is a special condition, it will be known. In addition, when such an enquiry is put, no ill thoughts of an action contradicting a declared standpoint will be entertained by the subordinate.

The hadith mentions that the Prophet signalled with his hand. This makes clear that a hand signal and similar actions do not invalidate prayer.

The Prophet explained to his wife about these two *rakʿahs* he offered: 'A delegation from [the tribe of] ʿAbd al-Qays came to see me, speaking to me on behalf of their people about Islam. They kept me from offering the two *rakʿahs* after the obligatory Ẓuhr Prayer. These compensate for those'. This explanation gives us some very interesting points. The first is the confirmation that two *rakʿahs* of sunnah are offered after the obligatory Ẓuhr Prayer. Another point is that if a regular sunnah is missed, it is desirable to compensate for it. This is the correct view, according to our school. A further point is that a prayer that is done for a particular reason is not discouraged during the periods when prayer is discouraged. What is discouraged is a prayer that has no particular reason. This hadith is the basis on which our scholars base their view. We do not have any evidence with more authentic import. Its meaning is clear. They may say that the Prophet continued to offer this prayer, but our scholars do not advocate this. We respond by saying that scholars of our school have two views on this point. The first is that a person who offers a regular sunnah and he misses it once and then prays it at a time of discouragement, may continue to pray it at that time afterwards. The second view, which is more correct and more widely known, is that this is not open to him because it is a special privilege granted to the Prophet. Doing the missed prayer at the time of discouragement is valid on the same day. If it is suggested that such compensation is also special for the Prophet, we respond by saying that the normal way is to follow his example and that it is not treated as special unless there is some evidence that it is so. On the contrary, there is clear evidence that it is not special for him, which is his explanation that it is the Ẓuhr sunnah. He did not say that this action is specific to me. This fact makes it clear that following his example is valid. A further interesting point is that sunnah prayer during the day is offered two *rakʿahs* at a time, in the same way as night worship. This is the view of our school and the majority of scholars. Furthermore, when tasks and duties move in different directions, the more important one is done first. The Prophet started by talking to those people about Islam, leaving the Ẓuhr sunnah till later, even till its normal time had lapsed, because providing guidance to those people so that they and their people might become Muslims was more important.

In hadith No. 1654, ʿĀ'ishah says: 'God's Messenger (peace be upon him) never left praying two *rakʿahs* after ʿAṣr at my place'. She meant that he never omitted praying them after the day he met the ʿAbd al-Qays delegation.

In hadith No. 1653, the narrator says: 'I asked 'Ā'ishah about the two *rak'ahs* the Prophet used to pray after 'Aṣr Prayer. She said: "He used to pray them before 'Aṣr, but on some occasion, he was preoccupied or he might have forgotten them, and he prayed them after 'Aṣr'. It is clear that the reference here is to the 'Aṣr sunnah that is offered before the obligatory prayer. *Qadi* 'Iyāḍ said: 'It should be interpreted as the Ẓuhr sunnah, as in Umm Salamah's hadith, so that the two hadiths are consistent with each other. It is right to describe the Ẓuhr sunnah as offered before 'Aṣr'.

CHAPTER 55

TWO *RAK'AHS* BEFORE MAGHRIB

[1657–302]. (Dar al-Salam 1820) Abu Bakr ibn Abi Shaybah and Abu Kurayb narrated:[i] both from Ibn Fuḍayl. Abu Bakr said: Muhammad ibn Fuḍayl narrated; from Mukhtār ibn Fulful. He said: **'I asked Anas ibn Mālik about voluntary prayer after 'Aṣr. He said: "'Umar used to slap people on their hands for praying after the 'Aṣr [obligatory] Prayer. During the Prophet's lifetime, we used to pray two *rak'ahs* after sunset, before Maghrib". I said to him: "Did God's Messenger (peace be upon him) pray these?" He said: "He saw us praying them, and he neither ordered nor forbade us to pray them".'**

وَحَدَّثَنَا أَبُو بَكْرِ بْنُ أَبِي شَيْبَةَ، وَأَبُو كُرَيْبٍ جَمِيعًا عَنِ ابْنِ فُضَيْلٍ، - قَالَ أَبُو بَكْرٍ حَدَّثَنَا مُحَمَّدُ بْنُ فُضَيْلٍ، - عَنْ مُخْتَارِ بْنِ فُلْفُلٍ، قَالَ: سَأَلْتُ أَنَسَ بْنَ مَالِكٍ عَنِ التَّطَوُّعِ بَعْدَ الْعَصْرِ. فَقَالَ: كَانَ عُمَرُ يَضْرِبُ الأَيْدِي عَلَى صَلاَةٍ بَعْدَ الْعَصْرِ، وَكُنَّا نُصَلِّي عَلَى عَهْدِ النَّبِيِّ صَلَّى اللهُ عَلَيْهِ وَسَلَّمَ رَكْعَتَيْنِ بَعْدَ غُرُوبِ الشَّمْسِ قَبْلَ صَلاَةِ الْـمَغْرِبِ. فَقُلْتُ لَهُ: أَكَانَ رَسُولُ اللهِ صَلَّى اللهُ عَلَيْهِ وَسَلَّمَ صَلاَّهُمَا؟ قَالَ: كَانَ يَرَانَا نُصَلِّيهِمَا. فَلَمْ يَأْمُرْنَا وَلَمْ يَنْهَنَا.

[1658–303]. (Dar al-Salam 1821) Shaybān ibn Farrūkh narrated: 'Abd al-Wārith narrated; from 'Abd al-'Azīz (who is Ibn

i. Related by Abu Dāwūd in a shorter version, 1282.

Ṣuhayb); from Anas ibn Mālik. He said: **'We were in Madinah. When the caller said the *adhān* for Maghrib Prayer, they would face the pillars. They would pray two *rakʿahs,* two *rakʿahs.* A stranger who enters the mosque may think that the [obligatory] prayer has finished because of the large number of people offering them'.**[i]

وَحَدَّثَنَا شَيْبَانُ بْنُ فَرُّوخَ، حَدَّثَنَا عَبْدُ الْوَارِثِ، عَنْ عَبْدِ الْعَزِيزِ، - وَهُوَ ابْنُ صُهَيْبٍ - عَنْ أَنَسِ بْنِ مَالِكٍ قَالَ: كُنَّا بِالْمَدِينَةِ فَإِذَا أَذَّنَ الْمُؤَذِّنُ لِصَلاَةِ الْمَغْرِبِ ابْتَدَرُوا السَّوَارِيَ، فَيَرْكَعُونَ رَكْعَتَيْنِ رَكْعَتَيْنِ. حَتَّى إِنَّ الرَّجُلَ الْغَرِيبَ لَيَدْخُلُ الْمَسْجِدَ فَيَحْسِبُ أَنَّ الصَّلاَةَ قَدْ صُلِّيَتْ مِنْ كَثْرَةِ مَنْ يُصَلِّيهِمَا.

---

i. These hadiths will be explained together with the hadiths in the next chapter.

CHAPTER 56

A PRAYER IN BETWEEN EVERY TWO CALLS

[1659–304]. (Dar al-Salam 1822) Abu Bakr ibn Abi Shaybah narrated:[i] Abu Usāmah and Wakīʿ narrated; from Kahmas; he said: ʿAbdullāh ibn Buraydah narrated; from ʿAbdullāh ibn Mughaffal al-Muzanī. He said: **'God's Messenger (peace be upon him) said: "There is a prayer in between every two calls". He said it three times and said in the third: "For whoever wishes".'**

وَحَدَّثَنَا أَبُو بَكْرِ بْنُ أَبِي شَيْبَةَ، حَدَّثَنَا أَبُو أُسَامَةَ وَوَكِيعٌ، عَنْ كَهْمَسٍ قَالَ: حَدَّثَنَا عَبْدُ اللهِ بْنُ بُرَيْدَةَ، عَنْ عَبْدِ اللهِ بْنِ مُغَفَّلٍ الْـمُزَنِيِّ قَالَ: قَالَ رَسُولُ اللهِ صَلَّى اللهُ عَلَيْهِ وَسَلَّمَ: «بَيْنَ كُلِّ أَذَانَيْنِ صَلاَةٌ - قَالَهَا ثَلاَثًا، قَالَ فِي الثَّالِثَةِ - لِـمَنْ شَاءَ».

[1660–000]. (Dar al-Salam 1823) Abu Bakr ibn Abi Shaybah narrated: ʿAbd al-Aʿlā narrated; from al-Jurayrī; from ʿAbdullāh ibn Buraydah; from ʿAbdullāh ibn Mughaffal; from the Prophet (peace be upon him): **the same text, except that he said on the fourth time: 'For whoever wishes'.**

وَحَدَّثَنَا أَبُو بَكْرِ بْنُ أَبِي شَيْبَةَ، حَدَّثَنَا عَبْدُ الأَعْلَى، عَنِ الْجُرَيْرِيِّ، عَنْ عَبْدِ اللهِ، بْنِ بُرَيْدَةَ عَنْ عَبْدِ اللهِ بْنِ مُغَفَّلٍ، عَنِ النَّبِيِّ صَلَّى اللهُ عَلَيْهِ وَسَلَّمَ. مِثْلَهُ إِلاَّ أَنَّهُ قَالَ فِي الرَّابِعَةِ «لِمَنْ شَاءَ».

---

i. Related by al-Bukhari, 624 and 627; Abu Dāwūd, 1283; al-Tirmidhī, 185; al-Nasā'ī, 680; Ibn Mājah, 1162.

Text Explanation

Here we have the hadith that mentions that the Prophet's Companions prayed two *rakʿahs* of sunnah after sunset and before offering Maghrib Prayer. In another version: 'they prayed these after the *adhān* had been called'. In another hadith: 'There is a prayer in between every two calls'. What is meant by the two calls is the *adhān* and the *iqāmah*. These hadiths make it desirable to pray two voluntary *rakʿahs* between the *adhān* of Maghrib and offering the obligatory Maghrib Prayer. This question is given two views by our scholars, the better known of which is that it is not desirable. However, the more correct view according to meticulous scholars is that in view of these hadiths, it is desirable.

There are two different views expressed by the early scholars. A number of the Prophet's Companions, the *tābiʿīn* and later scholars, such as Ahmad and Isḥāq, said that they are desirable. However, Abu Bakr, ʿUmar, ʿUthmān, ʿAlī, other Companions of the Prophet, Mālik and the majority of Fiqh scholars disapprove of them. Al-Nakhaʿī said that they are a *bidʿah*, or deviation. Their argument is that to say that they are desirable will lead to delaying Maghrib a little. Some of them respond to these hadiths by claiming that they have been abrogated. The view of choice is that, in view of these clear hadiths, they are desirable. A hadith related by al-Bukhari quotes the Prophet saying: 'Pray before Maghrib, pray before Maghrib, pray before Maghrib. He added in the third: for whoever wishes'. As for their claim that this leads to delaying Maghrib, this is a far-fetched suggestion that is contrary to the sunnah. No attention need be paid to it. However, it is a very short delay and the prayer is not delayed from the beginning of its time.

The claim that these hadiths are abrogated is a wild one. Abrogation is not considered unless we cannot provide a reasonable understanding of the hadiths that will reconcile them and we know the dates of the relevant hadiths. None of which exists in the present scenario, but God knows best.

CHAPTER 57

PRAYER IN A STATE OF FEAR

[1661–305]. (Dar al-Salam 1824) ʿAbd ibn Ḥumayd narrated:[i] ʿAbd al-Razzāq reported; Maʿmar reported; from al-Zuhrī; from Sālim; from Ibn ʿUmar. He said: **'God's Messenger (peace be upon him) led the prayer in the state of fear. He led one group during one *rakʿah* while the other group were facing the enemy. They [i.e. the first group] completed their prayer and took the positions of their brethren, facing the enemy. The others then came over and the Prophet led them in one *rakʿah*. The Prophet finished with *salām* and each group completed another *rakʿah*'.**

حَدَّثَنَا عَبْدُ بْنُ حُمَيْدٍ، أَخْبَرَنَا عَبْدُ الرَّزَّاقِ، أَخْبَرَنَا مَعْمَرٌ، عَنِ الزُّهْرِيِّ، عَنْ سَالِمٍ، عَنِ ابْنِ عُمَرَ قَالَ: صَلَّى رَسُولُ اللهِ صَلَّى اللهُ عَلَيْهِ وَسَلَّمَ صَلاَةَ الْخَوْفِ، بِإِحْدَى الطَّائِفَتَيْنِ رَكْعَةً وَالطَّائِفَةُ الأُخْرَى مُوَاجِهَةُ الْعَدُوِّ. ثُمَّ انْصَرَفُوا وَقَامُوا فِي مَقَامِ أَصْحَابِهِمْ، مُقْبِلِينَ عَلَى الْعَدُوِّ. وَجَاءَ أُولَئِكَ ثُمَّ صَلَّى بِهِمُ النَّبِيُّ صَلَّى اللهُ عَلَيْهِ وَسَلَّمَ رَكْعَةً، ثُمَّ سَلَّمَ النَّبِيُّ صَلَّى اللهُ عَلَيْهِ وَسَلَّمَ، ثُمَّ قَضَى هَؤُلاَءِ رَكْعَةً وَهَؤُلاَءِ رَكْعَةً.

[1662–000]. (Dar al-Salam[ii]) Abu al-Rabīʿ al-Zahrānī narrated it to me: Fulayḥ narrated; from al-Zuhrī; from Sālim ibn ʿAbdul-

i. Related by al-Bukhari, 4133; Abu Dāwūd, 1243; al-Tirmidhī, 564; al-Nasāʾī, 1537.
ii. Dar al-Salam attaches this hadith to the previous one, giving it no number.

lāh ibn ʿUmar; from his father; that he used to explain God's Messenger's prayer when in a state of fear. He said: **'I prayed them with God's Messenger (peace be upon him)...' adding the same meaning.**

وَحَدَّثَنِيهِ أَبُو الرَّبِيعِ الزَّهْرَانِيُّ، حَدَّثَنَا فُلَيْحٌ، عَنِ الزُّهْرِيِّ، عَنْ سَالِمِ بْنِ عَبْدِ اللهِ بْنِ عُمَرَ، عَنْ أَبِيهِ، أَنَّهُ كَانَ يُحَدِّثُ عَنْ صَلَاةِ رَسُولِ اللهِ صَلَّى اللهُ عَلَيْهِ وَسَلَّمَ فِي الْخَوْفِ، وَيَقُولُ: صَلَّيْتُهَا مَعَ رَسُولِ اللهِ صَلَّى اللهُ عَلَيْهِ وَسَلَّمَ. بِهَذَا الْمَعْنَى.

[1663–306]. (Dar al-Salam 1825) Abu Bakr ibn Abi Shaybah narrated:[i] Yaḥyā ibn Adam narrated; from Sufyān; from Mūsā ibn ʿUqbah; from Nāfiʿ; from Ibn ʿUmar. He said: **'God's Messenger (peace be upon him) prayed on some occasions as in a state of fear. A group joined him and another faced the enemy. He led those who joined him in one *rakʿah*, then they left. The others took over and he led them in one *rakʿah*. Each of the two groups then completed their prayers with one *rakʿah* each'.**

Ibn ʿUmar added: 'If there is greater fear, you may pray riding, or standing, merely making signals'.

وَحَدَّثَنَا أَبُو بَكْرِ بْنُ أَبِي شَيْبَةَ، حَدَّثَنَا يَحْيَى بْنُ آدَمَ، عَنْ سُفْيَانَ، عَنْ مُوسَى بْنِ عُقْبَةَ، عَنْ نَافِعٍ، عَنِ ابْنِ عُمَرَ قَالَ: صَلَّى رَسُولُ اللهِ صَلَّى اللهُ عَلَيْهِ وَسَلَّمَ صَلَاةَ الْخَوْفِ فِي بَعْضِ أَيَّامِهِ، فَقَامَتْ طَائِفَةٌ مَعَهُ وَطَائِفَةٌ بِإِزَاءِ الْعَدُوِّ، فَصَلَّى بِالَّذِينَ مَعَهُ رَكْعَةً ثُمَّ ذَهَبُوا. وَجَاءَ الْآخَرُونَ فَصَلَّى بِهِمْ رَكْعَةً، ثُمَّ قَضَتِ الطَّائِفَتَانِ رَكْعَةً رَكْعَةً. قَالَ: وَقَالَ ابْنُ عُمَرَ: فَإِذَا كَانَ خَوْفٌ أَكْثَرَ مِنْ ذَلِكَ، فَصَلِّ رَاكِبًا أَوْ قَائِمًا تُومِئُ إِيمَاءً.

i. Related by al-Bukhari, 943; al-Nasāʾī, 1541.

[1664–307]. (Dar al-Salam 1826) Muhammad ibn ʿAbdullāh ibn Numayr narrated:[i] my father narrated; ʿAbd al-Malik ibn Abi Sulaymān narrated; from ʿAṭā'; from Jābir ibn ʿAbdullāh. He said: **'I offered the prayer in a state of fear with God's Messenger (peace be upon him). He placed us in two rows: one row behind God's Messenger and the enemy was between us and the *qiblah*. The Prophet started with the *takbīr* and all of us said: *"Allah-u akbar"*. He then bowed and we all bowed. When he lifted his head from bowing, we all lifted our heads. He then went down prostrating himself, together with the front row immediately behind him. The rear row remained standing facing the enemy. When the Prophet completed his prostration and the front row behind him stood up, the rear row went down and prostrated themselves, and then stood up. Then the rear row stepped forward and the front row stepped back. The Prophet then bowed, and we all bowed. He then lifted his head and we all lifted our heads. He then went down prostrating himself together with the row behind him which was the rear row in the first *rakʿah*. The present rear row faced the enemy. When the Prophet and the row behind him completed their prostration, the rear row performed their prostration. The Prophet then finished with *salām*, and we all said the *salām* [finishing our prayer]'.**

Jābir said: 'Just as these guards of yours do with their leaders'.

حَدَّثَنَا مُحَمَّدُ بْنُ عَبْدِ اللهِ بْنِ نُمَيْرٍ، حَدَّثَنَا أَبِي، حَدَّثَنَا عَبْدُ الْمَلِكِ بْنُ أَبِي سُلَيْمَانَ، عَنْ عَطَاءٍ، عَنْ جَابِرِ بْنِ عَبْدِ اللهِ قَالَ: شَهِدْتُ مَعَ رَسُولِ اللهِ صَلَّى اللهُ عَلَيْهِ وَسَلَّمَ صَلَاةَ الْخَوْفِ. فَصَفَّنَا صَفَّيْنِ: صَفٌّ خَلْفَ رَسُولِ اللهِ صَلَّى اللهُ عَلَيْهِ وَسَلَّمَ، وَالْعَدُوُّ بَيْنَنَا

i. Related by al-Nasā'ī, 1546.

وَبَيْنَ الْقِبْلَةِ، فَكَبَّرَ النَّبِيُّ صَلَّى اللهُ عَلَيْهِ وَسَلَّمَ وَكَبَّرْنَا جَمِيعًا، ثُمَّ رَكَعَ وَرَكَعْنَا جَمِيعًا، ثُمَّ رَفَعَ رَأْسَهُ مِنَ الرُّكُوعِ وَرَفَعْنَا جَمِيعًا. ثُمَّ انْحَدَرَ بِالسُّجُودِ وَالصَّفُّ الَّذِي يَلِيهِ، وَقَامَ الصَّفُّ الْمُؤَخَّرُ فِي نَحْرِ الْعَدُوِّ. فَلَمَّا قَضَى النَّبِيُّ صَلَّى اللهُ عَلَيْهِ وَسَلَّمَ السُّجُودَ وَقَامَ الصَّفُّ الَّذِي يَلِيهِ، انْحَدَرَ الصَّفُّ الْمُؤَخَّرُ بِالسُّجُودِ وَقَامُوا. ثُمَّ تَقَدَّمَ الصَّفُّ الْمُؤَخَّرُ وَتَأَخَّرَ الصَّفُّ الْمُقَدَّمُ ثُمَّ رَكَعَ النَّبِيُّ صَلَّى اللهُ عَلَيْهِ وَسَلَّمَ وَرَكَعْنَا جَمِيعًا، ثُمَّ رَفَعَ رَأْسَهُ مِنَ الرُّكُوعِ وَرَفَعْنَا جَمِيعًا، ثُمَّ انْحَدَرَ بِالسُّجُودِ وَالصَّفُّ الَّذِي يَلِيهِ الَّذِي كَانَ مُؤَخَّرًا فِي الرَّكْعَةِ الأُولَى، وَقَامَ الصَّفُّ الْمُؤَخَّرُ فِي نُحُورِ الْعَدُوِّ. فَلَمَّا قَضَى النَّبِيُّ صَلَّى اللهُ عَلَيْهِ وَسَلَّمَ السُّجُودَ وَالصَّفُّ الَّذِي يَلِيهِ، انْحَدَرَ الصَّفُّ الْمُؤَخَّرُ بِالسُّجُودِ فَسَجَدُوا. ثُمَّ سَلَّمَ النَّبِيُّ صَلَّى اللهُ عَلَيْهِ وَسَلَّمَ وَسَلَّمْنَا جَمِيعًا. قَالَ جَابِرٌ كَمَا يَصْنَعُ حَرَسُكُمْ هَؤُلَاءِ بِأُمَرَائِهِمْ

[1665–308]. (Dar al-Salam 1827) Ahmad ibn ʿAbdullāh ibn Yūnus narrated: Zuhayr narrated; Abu al-Zubayr narrated; from Jābir. He said: **'We went to war with God's Messenger (peace be upon him) against a tribe from Juhaynah. They fought us very hard. When we prayed Ẓuhr, the unbelievers said: "Had we attacked them, we would have wiped them out". Gabriel informed God's Messenger of this and God's Messenger (peace be upon him) informed us of it and that they said: "It will soon be time for a prayer that is dearer to them than their children". When it was time for ʿAṣr Prayer, he stood us in two rows, and the unbelievers were between us and the *qiblah*. The Prophet glorified God [to start the prayer] and we did the same. He bowed, and we also bowed. Then he prostrated himself and the first row prostrated with him. When they stood up, the second row prostrated themselves. Then the first row stepped back and the second row stepped forward and replaced the first row. The Prophet glorified God and we did the same. Then he**

bowed, and we bowed. He then prostrated himself and the first row prostrated themselves with him while the second row stood up. When the second row did their prostration, all sat down together. Then God's Messenger (peace be upon him) said the *salām* for all of them'.

Abu al-Zubayr said: **'Then Jābir made a point of saying: "as your present leaders pray".'**

حَدَّثَنَا أَحْمَدُ بْنُ عَبْدِ اللهِ بْنِ يُونُسَ، حَدَّثَنَا زُهَيْرٌ، حَدَّثَنَا أَبُو الزُّبَيْرِ، عَنْ جَابِرٍ قَالَ: غَزَوْنَا مَعَ رَسُولِ اللهِ صَلَّى اللهُ عَلَيْهِ وَسَلَّمَ قَوْمًا مِنْ جُهَيْنَةَ، فَقَاتَلُونَا قِتَالاً شَدِيدًا، فَلَمَّا صَلَّيْنَا الظُّهْرَ قَالَ الْـمُشْرِكُونَ: لَوْ مِلْنَا عَلَيْهِمْ مَيْلَةً لاَقْتَطَعْنَاهُمْ. فَأَخْبَرَ جِبْرِيلُ رَسُولَ اللهِ صَلَّى اللهُ عَلَيْهِ وَسَلَّمَ ذَلِكَ، فَذَكَرَ ذَلِكَ لَنَا رَسُولُ اللهِ صَلَّى اللهُ عَلَيْهِ وَسَلَّمَ. قَالَ: وَقَالُوا إِنَّهُ سَتَأْتِيهِمْ صَلاَةٌ هِيَ أَحَبُّ إِلَيْهِمْ مِنَ الأَوْلاَدِ. فَلَمَّا حَضَرَتِ الْعَصْرُ - قَالَ - صَفَّنَا صَفَّيْنِ، وَالْـمُشْرِكُونَ بَيْنَنَا وَبَيْنَ الْقِبْلَةِ -قَالَ: فَكَبَّرَ رَسُولُ اللهِ صَلَّى اللهُ عَلَيْهِ وَسَلَّمَ وَكَبَّرْنَا، وَرَكَعَ فَرَكَعْنَا، ثُمَّ سَجَدَ وَسَجَدَ مَعَهُ الصَّفُّ الأَوَّلُ. فَلَمَّا قَامُوا سَجَدَ الصَّفُّ الثَّانِي، ثُمَّ تَأَخَّرَ الصَّفُّ الأَوَّلُ وَتَقَدَّمَ الصَّفُّ الثَّانِي، فَقَامُوا مَقَامَ الأَوَّلِ فَكَبَّرَ رَسُولُ اللهِ صَلَّى اللهُ عَلَيْهِ وَسَلَّمَ وَكَبَّرْنَا، وَرَكَعَ فَرَكَعْنَا، ثُمَّ سَجَدَ وَسَجَدَ مَعَهُ الصَّفُّ الأَوَّلُ وَقَامَ الثَّانِي. فَلَمَّا سَجَدَ الصَّفُّ الثَّانِي، ثُمَّ جَلَسُوا جَمِيعًا سَلَّمَ عَلَيْهِمْ رَسُولُ اللهِ صَلَّى اللهُ عَلَيْهِ وَسَلَّمَ. قَالَ أَبُو الزُّبَيْرِ ثُمَّ خَصَّ جَابِرٌ أَنْ قَالَ كَمَا يُصَلِّي أُمَرَاؤُكُمْ هَؤُلاَءِ.

[1666–309]. (Dar al-Salam 1828) ʿUbaydullāh ibn Muʿādh al-ʿAnbarī narrated:[i] my father narrated; Shuʿbah narrated; from ʿAbd al-Raḥmān ibn al-Qāsim; from his father; from Ṣāliḥ ibn Khawwāt ibn Jubayr; from Sahl ibn Abi Ḥathmah; that **'God's Messenger (peace be upon him) led his Companions in a prayer in a state of fear. He stood them in two rows behind him. He**

i. Related by al-Bukhari in longer versions, 4129 and 4131; Abu Dāwūd, 1237, 1238 and 1239; al-Tirmidhī in a longer version, 565; al-Nasā'ī, 1535; Ibn Mājah in a longer version, 1259.

led the ones immediately behind him in one *rakʿah,* then he stood up and remained standing until those who were behind them completed one *rakʿah.* They then stepped forward and the ones who were in front stepped backward. He led them in one *rakʿah,* then he sat down until those who stayed behind prayed one *rakʿah,* then finished the prayer with *salām.*

حَدَّثَنَا عُبَيْدُ اللهِ بْنُ مُعَاذٍ الْعَنْبَرِيُّ، حَدَّثَنَا أَبِي، حَدَّثَنَا شُعْبَةُ، عَنْ عَبْدِ الرَّحْمَنِ بْنِ الْقَاسِمِ، عَنْ أَبِيهِ، عَنْ صَالِحِ بْنِ خَوَّاتِ بْنِ جُبَيْرٍ، عَنْ سَهْلِ بْنِ أَبِي حَثْمَةَ، أَنَّ رَسُولَ اللهِ صَلَّى اللهُ عَلَيْهِ وَسَلَّمَ صَلَّى بِأَصْحَابِهِ فِي الْخَوْفِ، فَصَفَّهُمْ خَلْفَهُ صَفَّيْنِ، فَصَلَّى بِالَّذِينَ يَلُونَهُ رَكْعَةً، ثُمَّ قَامَ فَلَمْ يَزَلْ قَائِمًا حَتَّى صَلَّى الَّذِينَ خَلْفَهُمْ رَكْعَةً، ثُمَّ تَقَدَّمُوا وَتَأَخَّرَ الَّذِينَ كَانُوا قُدَّامَهُمْ فَصَلَّى بِهِمْ رَكْعَةً، ثُمَّ قَعَدَ حَتَّى صَلَّى الَّذِينَ تَخَلَّفُوا رَكْعَةً ثُمَّ سَلَّمَ.

[1667–310]. (Dar al-Salam 1829) Yaḥyā ibn Yaḥyā narrated: he said: I read out to Mālik; from Yazīd ibn Rūmān; from Ṣāliḥ ibn Khawwāt; from one who prayed with God's Messenger the prayer in a state of fear, on the day of the Battle of Dhāt al-Riqāʿ; that **'One group was with him in rank while another group was facing the enemy. He led the group that was with him in one *rakʿah,* then stood up while they completed their prayer separately. They then left the prayer and stood in rank facing the enemy while the other group joined the Prophet and he led them in the *rakʿah* that remained [of his prayer], then he remained in the seated position while they completed their prayer. He then finished his prayer with them'.**

حَدَّثَنَا يَحْيَى بْنُ يَحْيَى، قَالَ: قَرَأْتُ عَلَى مَالِكٍ عَنْ يَزِيدَ بْنِ رُومَانَ، عَنْ صَالِحِ بْنِ خَوَّاتٍ، عَمَّنْ صَلَّى مَعَ رَسُولِ اللهِ صَلَّى اللهُ عَلَيْهِ وَسَلَّمَ يَوْمَ ذَاتِ الرِّقَاعِ صَلَاةَ الْخَوْفِ: أَنَّ طَائِفَةً صَفَّتْ مَعَهُ وَطَائِفَةٌ وِجَاهَ الْعَدُوِّ. فَصَلَّى بِالَّذِينَ مَعَهُ رَكْعَةً ثُمَّ ثَبَتَ قَائِمًا، وَأَتَمُّوا لأَنْفُسِهِمْ. ثُمَّ انْصَرَفُوا فَصَفُّوا وِجَاهَ الْعَدُوِّ، وَجَاءَتِ الطَّائِفَةُ الأُخْرَى فَصَلَّى بِهِمُ الرَّكْعَةَ الَّتِي بَقِيَتْ، ثُمَّ ثَبَتَ جَالِسًا وَأَتَمُّوا لأَنْفُسِهِمْ، ثُمَّ سَلَّمَ بِهِمْ.

[1668–311]. (Dar al-Salam 1830) Abu Bakr ibn Abi Shaybah narrated:[i] ʿAffān narrated; Abān ibn Yazīd narrated; Yaḥyā ibn Abi Kathīr narrated; from Abu Salamah; from Jābir. He said: **'We travelled with God's Messenger (peace be upon him) until we reached Dhāt al-Riqāʿ. And it was our practice that where there was a tree with good shade, we would leave it for God's Messenger (peace be upon him). An unbeliever came as God's Messenger's sword was hanging from a tree. He took the Prophet's sword and drew it out. He said to God's Messenger (peace be upon him): "Do you fear me?" He said: "No". He said: "Who will protect you from me?" The Prophet said: "God will protect me from you". God's Messenger's Companions threatened him, and he placed the sword in its sheath and hung it back up. Then the prayer was called. The Prophet led one group in two *rakʿahs,* then they stepped back and he led the other group in two *rakʿahs.* Thus, [the prayer] was in four *rakʿahs* for God's Messenger and in two *rakʿahs* for the rest'.**

حَدَّثَنَا أَبُو بَكْرِ بْنُ أَبِي شَيْبَةَ، حَدَّثَنَا عَفَّانُ، حَدَّثَنَا أَبَانُ بْنُ يَزِيدَ، حَدَّثَنَا يَحْيَى بْنُ أَبِي كَثِيرٍ، عَنْ أَبِي سَلَمَةَ، عَنْ جَابِرٍ قَالَ: أَقْبَلْنَا مَعَ رَسُولِ اللهِ صَلَّى اللهُ عَلَيْهِ وَسَلَّمَ، حَتَّى إِذَا كُنَّا بِذَاتِ الرِّقَاعِ، قَالَ: كُنَّا إِذَا أَتَيْنَا عَلَى شَجَرَةٍ ظَلِيلَةٍ تَرَكْنَاهَا لِرَسُولِ اللهِ صَلَّى اللهُ عَلَيْهِ وَسَلَّمَ. قَالَ: فَجَاءَ رَجُلٌ مِنَ الْمُشْرِكِينَ وَسَيْفُ رَسُولِ اللهِ صَلَّى اللهُ عَلَيْهِ وَسَلَّمَ مُعَلَّقٌ بِشَجَرَةٍ، فَأَخَذَ سَيْفَ نَبِيِّ اللهِ صَلَّى اللهُ عَلَيْهِ وَسَلَّمَ فَاخْتَرَطَهُ، فَقَالَ لِرَسُولِ اللهِ صَلَّى اللهُ عَلَيْهِ وَسَلَّمَ: أَتَخَافُنِي؟ قَالَ: «لَا». قَالَ: فَمَنْ يَمْنَعُكَ مِنِّي؟ قَالَ: «اللهُ يَمْنَعُنِي مِنْكَ». قَالَ: فَتَهَدَّدَهُ أَصْحَابُ رَسُولِ اللهِ صَلَّى اللهُ عَلَيْهِ وَسَلَّمَ، فَأَغْمَدَ السَّيْفَ وَعَلَّقَهُ. قَالَ: فَنُودِيَ بِالصَّلَاةِ فَصَلَّى بِطَائِفَةٍ رَكْعَتَيْنِ ثُمَّ تَأَخَّرُوا، وَصَلَّى بِالطَّائِفَةِ الْأُخْرَى رَكْعَتَيْنِ. قَالَ: فَكَانَتْ لِرَسُولِ اللهِ صَلَّى اللهُ عَلَيْهِ وَسَلَّمَ أَرْبَعُ رَكَعَاتٍ وَلِلْقَوْمِ رَكْعَتَانِ.

---

i. Related by al-Bukhari, 4139.

[1669–312]. (Dar al-Salam 1831) ʿAbdullāh ibn ʿAbd al-Raḥmān al-Dārimī narrated: Yaḥyā (meaning Ibn Ḥassān) reported; Muʿāwiyah (who is Ibn Sallām) narrated; Yaḥyā reported to me; Abu Salamah ibn ʿAbd al-Raḥmān reported to me; that Jābir reported to him; that **'He prayed with God's Messenger (peace be upon him) the prayer in a state of fear. God's Messenger led one group in two *rakʿahs*, then led the other group in two *rakʿahs*. Thus, God's Messenger (peace be upon him) prayed four *rakʿahs*, leading each group in two *rakʿahs*'.**

وَحَدَّثَنَا عَبْدُ اللهِ بْنُ عَبْدِ الرَّحْمَنِ الدَّارِمِيُّ، أَخْبَرَنَا يَحْيَى - يَعْنِي ابْنَ حَسَّانَ - حَدَّثَنَا مُعَاوِيَةُ، وَهُوَ ابْنُ سَلَّامٍ - أَخْبَرَنِي يَحْيَى، أَخْبَرَنِي أَبُو سَلَمَةَ بْنُ عَبْدِ الرَّحْمَنِ، أَنَّ جَابِرًا أَخْبَرَهُ أَنَّهُ صَلَّى مَعَ رَسُولِ اللهِ صَلَّى اللهُ عَلَيْهِ وَسَلَّمَ صَلَاةَ الْخَوْفِ. فَصَلَّى رَسُولُ اللهِ صَلَّى اللهُ عَلَيْهِ وَسَلَّمَ بِإِحْدَى الطَّائِفَتَيْنِ رَكْعَتَيْنِ، ثُمَّ صَلَّى بِالطَّائِفَةِ الْأُخْرَى رَكْعَتَيْنِ، فَصَلَّى رَسُولُ اللهِ صَلَّى اللهُ عَلَيْهِ وَسَلَّمَ أَرْبَعَ رَكَعَاتٍ، وَصَلَّى بِكُلِّ طَائِفَةٍ رَكْعَتَيْنِ.

Text Explanation

In this chapter, Muslim (may God bestow mercy on him) mentions four hadiths [with different versions]. The first is the one narrated by Ibn ʿUmar [No. 1661–1663] stating that 'the Prophet led one of the two groups in one *rakʿah*, while the other faced the enemy. They then left and took the positions of the other group while these joined the Prophet who led them in one *rakʿah*. He then finished his prayer and each group completed their prayer adding one *rakʿah*'. This hadith is upheld by al-Awzāʿī and Ashhab al-Mālikī. It is valid according to al-Shāfiʿī. It is further said that both groups completed their remaining *rakʿah* together, and it is also said that they did that individually, which is the correct view.

The second hadith is narrated by Ibn Abi Ḥathmah [No. 1666]. It is similar, except that it says that the Prophet led the first group in one *rakʿah* and stood in his position while they completed their prayer. They then left and stood facing the enemy while the others joined the Prophet who led them in one *rakʿah* and remained seated until they completed their other *rakʿah* and he finished his prayer with them. This is upheld by Mālik, al-Shāfiʿī, Abu Thawr and others. In his *Sunan* anthology, Abu Dāwūd relates from the same narrator a different form, stating that the Prophet stood his Companions in two rows, leading the first row in one *rakʿah*, then stood in his position while those who were behind prayed one *rakʿah*, then they stepped forward and the ones who were ahead of them stepped back. He led the new ones in one *rakʿah*. He then sat down until those who were now behind completed one *rakʿah*, then he finished the prayer. In one version: 'he finished the prayer with all of them together'.

The third hadith is narrated by Jābir [No. 1664–1665]. It mentions that the Prophet stood his Companions in two rows behind him, while the enemy was between them and the *qiblah*. He bowed with them all, but only the rear row prostrated themselves with him. When they stood up, they stepped forward while the front row stepped back and faced the enemy. When he finished his prostration, the front row prostrated themselves. Jābir mentioned the same arrangement in the second *rakʿah*. A hadith narrated by Ibn ʿAbbās is similar to Jābir's narration but does not mention one row stepping forward and the other stepping back. This hadith is upheld by al-Shāfiʿī, Ibn Abi Laylā and Abu Yūsuf, if the enemy is positioned in the direction of the *qiblah*. According to al-Shāfiʿī, it is acceptable that the second-row steps forward and the first-row steps back as in Jābir's narration, and it is also acceptable that they remain in their respective positions, as appears in Ibn ʿAbbās' version.

The fourth hadith is also narrated by Jābir [No. 1668–1669], and it mentions that the Prophet led each group in two *rakʿahs*. In Abu Dāwūd's *Sunan* and other anthologies, a hadith narrated by Abu Bakrah mentions that the Prophet led each group in two *rakʿahs* and finished with *salām*. Thus, the second group were giving their obligatory prayer [i.e. *farḍ*] behind an imam who was doing a sunnah prayer. This is upheld by al-Shāfiʿī and it is reported that al-Ḥasan al-Baṣrī endorsed it. Al-Ṭaḥāwī, however, claimed that this is abrogated, but his claim is unacceptable as there is no evidence in support.

These are six different methods of how prayer is conducted when Muslims are facing an enemy and they fear that the enemy may attack them. Ibn Masʿūd and Abu Hurayrah report a seventh form, stating that the Prophet (peace be upon him) led one group in one *rakʿah* and they left him without finishing their prayer with *salām*. They stood facing the enemy while the others came forward and the Prophet led them in one *rakʿah*, then said the *salām*. These completed their remaining *rakʿah* and finished with *salām*. They went forward and replaced the other group who stepped back and added one *rakʿah*, then finished. This is upheld by Abu Ḥanīfah.

Abu Dāwūd and others report other methods of offering prayers during a state of fear, and the different methods complete sixteen in total. Ibn al-Qaṣṣār of the Mālikī School said that the Prophet offered this prayer on ten different occasions. The view of choice is that all these methods are valid, according to circumstances. Numerous details are given in books of Fiqh. Al-Khaṭṭābī said: 'Prayer in a state of fear takes different forms. The Prophet used it on different occasions and in different forms. In each he chose what was more appropriate for the prayer and what provided better guard. As such, all followed the same concept, despite its different forms'.

According to all scholars, prayer in a state of fear is valid today[i] as it originally was. However, Abu Yūsuf and al-Muzanī said that it did not apply after the Prophet had passed away because the Qur'anic verse that speaks of it starts with: 'When you are with the believers and about to lead them in prayer…' (4: 102). The majority of scholars reject this view, arguing that the Prophet's Companions continued to perform it after the Prophet had passed away. The verse does not mean this is applicable to the Prophet only. It is authentically confirmed that he said: 'Pray as you have seen me pray'.

The expedition called Dhāt al-Riqāʿ is well known. It took place in the fifth year after the Prophet's migration to Madinah, and it was in the Ghaṭafān's area of Najd. It is given this name because the

i. 'Today' in this instance means the commentator's time when war was still conducted face to face, and hand to hand. Modern warfare is totally different.

Muslims travelled on hard terrain which caused cuts to their feet. Therefore, they wrapped their feet with pieces of cloth [i.e. *riqāʿ*]. This is the correct view of the reason for giving it this name. It is confirmed in authentic anthologies, as narrated by Abu Mūsā al-Ashʿarī. It is also so called after a mountain in that area called al-Riqāʿ, and it is given this name because it has white, red and black patches.[i] It is further said that the name stems from a certain tree that grew in that area called *dhāt al-riqāʿ*, and it is further suggested that the reason for calling it thus was that the believers had to patch up their torn flags. It is possible that all these cases applied in this expedition.

Prayer in a state of fear was legislated during an expedition other than Dhāt al-Riqāʿ. It is said that it was instigated during the siege of the al-Naḍīr tribe. In the Qur'anic verse that mentions it, reference is made to two groups. The word 'group' refers to a collective that can be either small or large. Al-Shāfiʿī said: 'I dislike that a group offering the prayer in a state of fear be less than three people. With the imam there should be a group of three or more and the group facing the enemy should be of similar number'. He based his argument on the fact that the Qur'anic verse uses the plural pronoun throughout. Plural in Arabic applies to a minimum of three, as Arabic has a dual form when the reference is to two only.

In hadith No. 1668, 'The Prophet led one group in two *rakʿahs*, then they stepped back and he led the other group in two *rakʿahs*. Thus, [the prayer] was in four *rakʿahs* for God's Messenger and in two *rakʿahs* for the rest'. This means that he led the first group in a prayer of two *rakʿahs* and they all, including the Prophet, finished the prayer with *salām*. He did the same with the second group. Thus, in his second prayer, the Prophet was doing a sunnah prayer while those joining him were doing their obligatory prayer. Al-Shāfiʿī and his disciples take this as evidence that it is perfectly appropriate for a person offering an obligatory prayer to be led by an imam doing a sunnah prayer, but God knows best.

---

i. In Arabic, a patch is called *ruqʿah* and its plural form is *riqāʿ*. The word also refers to pieces of cloth.

BOOK OF FRIDAY PRAYER

[1670–1]. (Dar al-Salam 1832) Yaḥyā ibn Yaḥyā al-Tamīmī and Muhammad ibn Rumḥ ibn al-Muhājir narrated: both said: al-Layth reported [H]. Also, Qutaybah narrated; Layth narrated; from Nāfiʿ; from ʿAbdullāh. He said: **'I heard God's Messenger (peace be upon him) say: "When any of you aims to join the Friday Prayer, he should take a bath".'**

حَدَّثَنَا يَحْيَى بْنُ يَحْيَى التَّمِيمِيُّ وَمُحَمَّدُ بْنُ رُمْحِ بْنِ الْـمُهَاجِرِ، قَالا: أَخْبَرَنَا اللَّيْثُ، ح. وَحَدَّثَنَا قُتَيْبَةُ، حَدَّثَنَا لَيْثٌ، عَنْ نَافِعٍ، عَنْ عَبْدِ اللهِ، قَالَ: سَمِعْتُ رَسُولَ اللهِ صَلَّى اللهُ عَلَيْهِ وَسَلَّمَ يَقُولُ: «إِذَا أَرَادَ أَحَدُكُمْ أَنْ يَأْتِيَ الْجُمُعَةَ فَلْيَغْتَسِلْ».

[1671–2]. (Dar al-Salam 1833–1835) Qutaybah ibn Saʿīd narrated:[i] Layth narrated [H]. Also, Ibn Rumḥ narrated; al-Layth reported; from Ibn Shihāb; from ʿAbdullāh ibn ʿAbdullāh ibn ʿUmar; from ʿAbdullāh ibn ʿUmar; from God's Messenger (peace be upon him) that he said as he was speaking on the platform: **'Whoever of you is joining the Friday Prayer should take a bath'.**

حَدَّثَنَا قُتَيْبَةُ بْنُ سَعِيدٍ، حَدَّثَنَا لَيْثٌ، ح. وَحَدَّثَنَا ابْنُ رُمْحٍ، أَخْبَرَنَا اللَّيْثُ، عَنِ ابْنِ شِهَابٍ عَنْ عَبْدِ اللهِ بْنِ عَبْدِ اللهِ بْنِ عُمَرَ، عَنْ عَبْدِ اللهِ بْنِ عُمَرَ، عَنْ رَسُولِ اللهِ صَلَّى اللهُ عَلَيْهِ وَسَلَّمَ أَنَّهُ قَالَ وَهُوَ قَائِمٌ عَلَى الْـمِنْبَرِ: «مَنْ جَاءَ مِنْكُمُ الْجُمُعَةَ فَلْيَغْتَسِلْ».

---

i. Related by al-Tirmidhī, 493; al-Nasāʾī, 1406.

Muhammad ibn Rāfiʿ narrated to me: ʿAbd al-Razzāq narrated; Ibn Jurayj reported; Ibn Shihāb reported to me; from Sālim and ʿAbdullāh sons of ʿAbdullāh ibn ʿUmar; from Ibn ʿUmar; from the Prophet: **the same text.**

وَحَدَّثَنِي مُحَمَّدُ بْنُ رَافِعٍ، حَدَّثَنَا عَبْدُ الرَّزَّاقِ، أَخْبَرَنَا ابْنُ جُرَيْجٍ، أَخْبَرَنِي ابْنُ شِهَابٍ، عَنْ سَالِمٍ وَعَبْدِ اللهِ، ابْنَيْ عَبْدِ اللهِ بْنِ عُمَرَ، عَنِ ابْنِ عُمَرَ، عَنِ النَّبِيِّ صَلَّى اللهُ عَلَيْهِ وَسَلَّمَ . بِمِثْلِهِ

Ḥarmalah ibn Yaḥyā narrated to me: Ibn Wahb reported; Yūnus reported to me; from Ibn Shihāb; from Sālim ibn ʿAbdullāh; from his father. He said: **'I heard God's Messenger (peace be upon him) say…' the same text.**

وَحَدَّثَنِي حَرْمَلَةُ بْنُ يَحْيَى، أَخْبَرَنَا ابْنُ وَهْبٍ، أَخْبَرَنِي يُونُسُ، عَنِ ابْنِ شِهَابٍ، عَنْ سَالِمِ بْنِ عَبْدِ اللهِ، عَنْ أَبِيهِ، قَالَ سَمِعْتُ رَسُولَ اللهِ صَلَّى اللهُ عَلَيْهِ وَسَلَّمَ يَقُولُ. بِمِثْلِهِ

[1672–3]. (Dar al-Salam 1836) Ḥarmalah ibn Yaḥyā narrated to me:[i] Ibn Wahb reported; Yūnus reported to me; from Ibn Shihāb; Sālim ibn ʿAbdullāh narrated to me; from his father; that **'As ʿUmar ibn al-Khaṭṭāb was addressing the people on Friday, one of the Prophet's Companions entered the mosque. ʿUmar called out to him: "What hour is this?" The man said: "I was busy today, and I did not return home until I heard the call [i.e. the *adhān*]. I did nothing other than perform the ablution". ʿUmar said: "And only the ablution, when you know that God's Messenger (peace be upon him) used to order taking a bath".'**

i. Related by al-Bukhari, 877.

وَحَدَّثَنِي حَرْمَلَةُ بْنُ يَحْيَى، أَخْبَرَنَا ابْنُ وَهْبٍ، أَخْبَرَنِي يُونُسُ، عَنِ ابْنِ شِهَابٍ، حَدَّثَنِي سَالِمُ بْنُ عَبْدِ اللهِ، عَنْ أَبِيهِ، أَنَّ عُمَرَ بْنَ الْخَطَّابِ، بَيْنَا هُوَ يَخْطُبُ النَّاسَ يَوْمَ الْجُمُعَةِ دَخَلَ رَجُلٌ مِنْ أَصْحَابِ رَسُولِ اللهِ صَلَّى اللهُ عَلَيْهِ وَسَلَّمَ فَنَادَاهُ عُمَرُ: أَيَّةُ سَاعَةٍ هَذِهِ؟ فَقَالَ: إِنِّي شُغِلْتُ الْيَوْمَ فَلَمْ أَنْقَلِبْ إِلَى أَهْلِي حَتَّى سَمِعْتُ النِّدَاءَ، فَلَمْ أَزِدْ عَلَى أَنْ تَوَضَّأْتُ. قَالَ عُمَرُ: وَالْوُضُوءَ أَيْضًا وَقَدْ عَلِمْتَ أَنَّ رَسُولَ اللهِ صَلَّى اللهُ عَلَيْهِ وَسَلَّمَ كَانَ يَأْمُرُ بِالْغُسْلِ؟

[1673–4]. (Dar al-Salam 1837) Isḥāq ibn Ibrāhīm narrated:[i] al-Walīd ibn Muslim reported; from al-Awzāʿī; he said: Yaḥyā ibn Abi Kathīr narrated to me; Abu Salamah ibn ʿAbd al-Raḥmān narrated to me; Abu Hurayrah narrated to me. He said: **'As ʿUmar ibn al-Khaṭṭāb was addressing the people on Friday, ʿUthmān ibn ʿAffān entered the mosque. ʿUmar said some implied criticism, saying: "Why do some people come late after the call [i.e. *adhān*]"? ʿUthmān said: "*Amīr al-Mu'minīn*,[ii] when I heard the call, I did nothing other than I performed the ablution and came". ʿUmar said: "And only the ablution! Have you not heard God's Messenger say: 'When any of you joins the Friday Prayer, he should take a bath'?"'**

حَدَّثَنَا إِسْحَاقُ بْنُ إِبْرَاهِيمَ، أَخْبَرَنَا الْوَلِيدُ بْنُ مُسْلِمٍ، عَنِ الأَوْزَاعِيِّ قَالَ: حَدَّثَنِي يَحْيَى بْنُ أَبِي كَثِيرٍ، حَدَّثَنِي أَبُو سَلَمَةَ بْنُ عَبْدِ الرَّحْمَنِ، حَدَّثَنِي أَبُو هُرَيْرَةَ قَالَ: بَيْنَمَا عُمَرُ بْنُ الْخَطَّابِ يَخْطُبُ النَّاسَ يَوْمَ الْجُمُعَةِ إِذْ دَخَلَ عُثْمَانُ بْنُ عَفَّانَ، فَعَرَّضَ بِهِ عُمَرُ فَقَالَ: مَا بَالُ رِجَالٍ يَتَأَخَّرُونَ بَعْدَ النِّدَاءِ؟ فَقَالَ عُثْمَانُ: يَا أَمِيرَ الْمُؤْمِنِينَ مَا زِدْتُ حِينَ سَمِعْتُ النِّدَاءَ أَنْ تَوَضَّأْتُ ثُمَّ أَقْبَلْتُ. فَقَالَ عُمَرُ: وَالْوُضُوءَ أَيْضًا؟ أَلَمْ تَسْمَعُوا رَسُولَ اللهِ صَلَّى اللهُ عَلَيْهِ وَسَلَّمَ يَقُولُ: «إِذَا جَاءَ أَحَدُكُمْ إِلَى الْجُمُعَةِ فَلْيَغْتَسِلْ»؟

i. Related by al-Bukhari, 882; Abu Dāwūd, 340.
ii. This was the official title of the caliph, starting from ʿUmar's reign. It means Prince of the Believers.

CHAPTER 1

A BATH ON FRIDAY IS A DUTY FOR ADULT MEN

[1674–5]. (Dar al-Salam 1838) Yaḥyā ibn Yaḥyā narrated: he said:[i] I read out to Mālik; from Ṣafwān ibn Sulaym; from ʿAṭā' ibn Yasār; from Abu Saʿīd al-Khudrī; that God's Messenger (peace be upon him) said: **'Taking a bath on Friday is a duty for every male who has attained puberty'.**

حَدَّثَنَا يَحْيَى بْنُ يَحْيَى، قَالَ قَرَأْتُ عَلَى مَالِكٍ عَنْ صَفْوَانَ بْنِ سُلَيْمٍ، عَنْ عَطَاءِ بْنِ يَسَارٍ، عَنْ أَبِي سَعِيدٍ الْخُدْرِيِّ، أَنَّ رَسُولَ اللهِ صَلَّى اللهُ عَلَيْهِ وَسَلَّمَ قَالَ: «الْغُسْلُ يَوْمَ الْجُمُعَةِ وَاجِبٌ عَلَى كُلِّ مُحْتَلِمٍ».

[1675–6]. (Dar al-Salam 1839) Ḥarūn ibn Saʿīd al-Aylī and Ahmad ibn ʿĪsā narrated to me:[ii] both said: Ibn Wahb narrated; ʿAmr reported to me; from ʿUbaydullāh ibn Abi Jaʿfar; that Muhammad ibn Jaʿfar narrated to him; from ʿUrwah ibn al-Zubayr; from ʿĀ'ishah. She said: **'People used to come every Friday from their homes in the higher villages wearing their woollen garments. Dust affected them and they would carry a smell. One man of them came to see God's Messenger (peace be upon him) as he was with me. God's Messenger said to him: "If you would do your ablutions for this day".'**

---

i. Related by al-Bukhari, 857, 895 and 2665; Abu Dāwūd, 341; al-Nasā'ī, 1376; Ibn Mājah, 1089.

ii. Related by al-Bukhari, 902; Abu Dāwūd, 1055.

حَدَّثَنِي هَارُونُ بْنُ سَعِيدٍ الأَيْلِيُّ وَأَحْمَدُ بْنُ عِيسَى، قَالا: حَدَّثَنَا ابْنُ وَهْبٍ، أَخْبَرَنِي عَمْرٌو، عَنْ عُبَيْدِ اللهِ بْنِ أَبِي جَعْفَرٍ، أَنَّ مُحَمَّدَ بْنَ جَعْفَرٍ حَدَّثَهُ عَنْ عُرْوَةَ بْنِ الزُّبَيْرِ، عَنْ عَائِشَةَ أَنَّهَا قَالَتْ: كَانَ النَّاسُ يَنْتَابُونَ الْجُمُعَةَ مِنْ مَنَازِلِهِمْ مِنَ الْعَوَالِي فَيَأْتُونَ فِي الْعَبَاءِ، وَيُصِيبُهُمُ الْغُبَارُ، فَتَخْرُجُ مِنْهُمُ الرِّيحُ. فَأَتَى رَسُولَ اللهِ صَلَّى اللهُ عَلَيْهِ وَسَلَّمَ إِنْسَانٌ مِنْهُمْ وَهُوَ عِنْدِي، فَقَالَ رَسُولُ اللهِ صَلَّى اللهُ عَلَيْهِ وَسَلَّمَ: «لَوْ أَنَّكُمْ تَطَهَّرْتُمْ لِيَوْمِكُمْ هَذَا».

[1676–000]. (Dar al-Salam 1840) Muhammad ibn Rumḥ narrated:[i] al-Layth reported; from Yaḥyā ibn Saʿīd; from ʿAmrah; from ʿĀ'ishah; that she said: **'The people used to do their work themselves, as they did not have helpers. Hence, they might carry some foul smell. They were told: "If you would take a bath on Friday".'**

وَحَدَّثَنَا مُحَمَّدُ بْنُ رُمْحٍ، أَخْبَرَنَا اللَّيْثُ، عَنْ يَحْيَى بْنِ سَعِيدٍ، عَنْ عَمْرَةَ، عَنْ عَائِشَةَ أَنَّهَا قَالَتْ: كَانَ النَّاسُ أَهْلَ عَمَلٍ، وَلَمْ يَكُنْ لَهُمْ كُفَاةٌ، فَكَانُوا يَكُونُ لَهُمْ تَفَلٌ، فَقِيلَ لَهُمْ: لَوِ اغْتَسَلْتُمْ يَوْمَ الْجُمُعَةِ.

Text Explanation

The first two hadiths give the same message, which is the need to take a bath by anyone who is attending Friday Prayer. Hadith No. 1674 mentions that taking a bath on Friday is a duty for any male who has attained puberty. Another hadith says: 'It is a duty owed to God by every Muslim that he should take a bath every seven days, in which he washes his body and his head'. Hadith No. 1675 says: 'If you would do your ablutions for this day,' and in the other version: 'If you would take a bath for Friday'. Scholars differ as to

i. Related by al-Bukhari, 903; Abu Dāwūd, 352.

the status of taking a bath on Friday. It is reported that a number of the early scholars considered it a duty. This is reported from some of the Prophet's Companions, and it is the view of the Ẓāhirī School. Ibn al-Mundhir says that it is Mālik's view, and al-Khaṭṭābī attributes it to al-Ḥasan al-Baṣrī and Mālik. On the other hand, the majority of scholars of the early and later generations, as well as the Fiqh scholars of all regions, consider it a desirable sunnah, not an incumbent duty. *Qadi* ʿIyāḍ said: 'This is the view of Mālik and his disciples'.

Scholars who consider it a duty base their argument on the surface meaning of these hadiths. The majority of scholars, on the other hand, cite other authentic hadiths, including the one mentioning the man who entered while ʿUmar was delivering his Friday speech, having performed only the ablution, but no bath. Muslim mentions him, and he is none other than ʿUthmān ibn ʿAffān, as stated in hadith No. 1673. The evidence in this hadith is the fact that ʿUthmān did it, and his action was approved by ʿUmar and all those present at Friday Prayer. They were the ones to be consulted on all important matters. Had taking a bath on Friday been a duty, ʿUthmān would not have left it undone, and they would have required him to do it. Another cited hadith is the one in which the Prophet says: 'Whoever performs the ablution does well, and whoever takes a bath, does better'. This hadith is graded as 'Good' and it is well known in the *Sunan* anthologies. Further evidence is hadith No. 1676, in which the Prophet says: 'If you would take a bath on Friday'. The phraseology suggests that it is not a duty because it means: 'If you would do it, it would be better, more perfect, etc.'. They add that the hadiths that include an order to take a bath are understood to mean a preference, not an obligation. Thus, they reconcile all the relevant hadiths. That the Prophet said in hadith No. 1674: 'Taking a bath on Friday is a duty for every male who has attained puberty', means that it applies to him. A man says to his friend: 'Your right is my duty', which means that I acknowledge it as your right. It does not mean a duty of the type that incurs punishment when left undone.

In hadith No. 1671 the Prophet said: 'as he was speaking on the platform'. The platform is the *minbar* which the Prophet had ordered to be made for him so that people could hear him. This indicates that having such a platform is recommended. If this is difficult to arrange, then the speaker should stand at a high place so that he is better heard and is not in the midst of people. His words are thus more effective. It also makes clear that the one who delivers the speech on Friday, i.e. the *khuṭbah*, or sermon, should be standing.

ʿUmar said to the man entering the mosque as he was delivering his speech: 'What hour is this?' This is meant as a reproach indicating disapproval of late coming. It shows that the ruler should inspect the situation of his people, encourage them to attend to their religious duties, express disapproval of behaviour that is at variance with the sunnah, even if the one who does it is a dignitary. It also shows that expressing disapproval of behaviour by such honourable people in the presence of a large number of others is acceptable. It further suggests that ordinary speech during the *khuṭbah* is permissible.

ʿUthmān explains: 'I was busy today, and I did not return home until I heard the call [i.e. the *adhān*]. I did nothing other than perform the ablution'. This shows the desirability to apologise to rulers and people in authority, as well as others, when one is in error. It also shows that working and attending to ordinary tasks on Friday, before the time of its prayer, is permissible. It further states that he left out taking a bath because it is only a desirable practice. He felt that going straight to join the Friday Prayer was more preferable than taking a bath, which would have caused further delay. Hence, ʿUmar did not order him to go back and take a bath.

In hadith No. 1675 and 1676, people came to attend the Friday Prayer from their villages around Madinah.[i] In cold weather, they would be wearing their top garments which were made of wool, and these attracted dust, particularly when it was windy. Moreover, they had to do their work themselves as few of them had servants and helpers. Hence, they could carry some unpleasant smells. The Prophet said to those who had such a smell: 'If you would take a

---

i. The nearest of these villages was about five kilometres away from the mosque and the farthest was nearly fourteen kilometres away.

bath for Friday Prayer'. This makes clear that a person whose circumstances give a foul smell to his body or clothing is advised to take a bath before coming to the mosque or sitting with other people.

Hadith No. 1670 quotes the Prophet: 'When any of you aims to join the Friday Prayer, he should take a bath', and hadith No. 1674 says: 'Taking a bath on Friday is a duty for every male who has attained puberty'. The first of these two hadiths makes it clear that taking a bath applies to everyone who aims to attend the Friday Prayer, whether he has attained puberty or a child who distinguishes things. The second hadith clearly applies to everyone above puberty. Other hadiths include words that make it applicable to women also, such as the hadith that says: 'Whoever takes a bath does better'. To take these hadiths together we may say that taking a bath is desirable for everyone who wants to attend the Friday Prayer, and it applies to males in a greater degree than to females because for women it is closer to wearing perfume [and women are not supposed to wear perfume when they go out]. It applies in a greater degree to males who have attained puberty than to boys. The well-known view of our Shāfiʿī School is that it is desirable for everyone who wants to join the Friday Prayer. Another view of our scholars is that it is specifically desirable for males. Another view is that it is desirable for those who are required to attend the Friday Prayer, but not to others, i.e. women, boys, slaves and travellers. Yet another view suggests that it is desirable for everyone on Friday, whether that person intends to attend the Friday Prayer or not. As such, it is like taking a bath on Eid Day, which is desirable for all. The correct view is the first, but God knows best.

CHAPTER 2

USING PERFUME AND BRUSHING ONE'S TEETH ON FRIDAY

[1677–7]. (Dar al-Salam 1841) ʿAmr ibn Sawwād al-ʿĀmirī narrated:[i] ʿAbdullāh ibn Wahb narrated; ʿAmr ibn al-Ḥārith reported; that Saʿīd ibn Abi Hilāl and Bukayr ibn al-Ashajj narrated to him; from Abu Bakr ibn al-Munkadir; from ʿAmr ibn Sulaym; from ʿAbd al-Raḥmān ibn Abi Saʿīd al-Khudrī; from his father; that God's Messenger (peace be upon him) said: **'A bath on Friday is applicable to everyone who has attained puberty, as is brushing one's teeth. He should also apply whatever perfume he can'.**

But Bukayr did not mention ʿAbd al-Raḥmān, and in reference to perfume he said: **'Even if it is feminine perfume'.**

وَحَدَّثَنَا عَمْرُو بْنُ سَوَّادٍ الْعَامِرِيُّ، حَدَّثَنَا عَبْدُ اللهِ بْنُ وَهْبٍ، أَخْبَرَنَا عَمْرُو بْنُ الْحَارِثِ أَنَّ سَعِيدَ بْنَ أَبِي هِلَالٍ وَبُكَيْرَ بْنَ الأَشَجِّ حَدَّثَاهُ عَنْ أَبِي بَكْرِ بْنِ الْمُنْكَدِرِ، عَنْ عَمْرِو بْنِ سُلَيْمٍ عَنْ عَبْدِ الرَّحْمَنِ بْنِ أَبِي سَعِيدٍ الْخُدْرِيِّ، عَنْ أَبِيهِ، أَنَّ رَسُولَ اللهِ صَلَّى اللهُ عَلَيْهِ وَسَلَّمَ قَالَ: «غُسْلُ يَوْمِ الْجُمُعَةِ عَلَى كُلِّ مُحْتَلِمٍ وَسِوَاكٌ، وَيَمَسُّ مِنَ الطِّيبِ مَا قَدَرَ عَلَيْهِ».

إِلاَّ أَنَّ بُكَيْرًا لَمْ يَذْكُرْ عَبْدَ الرَّحْمَٰنِ، وَقَالَ فِي الطِّيبِ: وَلَوْ مِنْ طِيبِ الْمَرْأَةِ.

i. Related by al-Bukhari, 880; Abu Dāwūd, 344; al-Nasāʾī, 1374 and 1382.

[1678–8]. (Dar al-Salam 1842–1843) Ḥasan al-Ḥulwānī narrated:[i] Rawḥ ibn ʿUbādah narrated; Ibn Jurayj narrated [H]. Also, Muhammad ibn Rāfiʿ narrated to me; ʿAbd al-Razzāq narrated; Ibn Jurayj reported; Ibrāhīm ibn Maysarah reported to me; from Ṭāwūs; from Ibn ʿAbbās; that he mentioned what the Prophet said about taking a bath on Friday. Ṭāwūs said: **'I said to Ibn ʿAbbās: "And should he apply some perfume or ointment if his wife has it?" He said: "I do not know that".'**

حَدَّثَنَا حَسَنٌ الْحُلْوَانِيُّ، حَدَّثَنَا رَوْحُ بْنُ عُبَادَةَ، حَدَّثَنَا ابْنُ جُرَيْجٍ، ح. وَحَدَّثَنِي مُحَمَّدُ بْنُ رَافِعٍ، حَدَّثَنَا عَبْدُ الرَّزَّاقِ، أَخْبَرَنَا ابْنُ جُرَيْجٍ، أَخْبَرَنِي إِبْرَاهِيمُ بْنُ مَيْسَرَةَ، عَنْ طَاوُسٍ، عَنِ ابْنِ عَبَّاسٍ، أَنَّهُ ذَكَرَ قَوْلَ النَّبِيِّ صَلَّى اللهُ عَلَيْهِ وَسَلَّمَ فِي الْغُسْلِ يَوْمَ الْجُمُعَةِ. قَالَ طَاوُسٌ: فَقُلْتُ لِابْنِ عَبَّاسٍ: وَيَمَسُّ طِيبًا أَوْ دُهْنًا إِنْ كَانَ عِنْدَ أَهْلِهِ؟ قَالَ: لاَ أَعْلَمُهُ.

Isḥāq ibn Ibrāhīm narrated it: Muhammad ibn Bakr reported [H]. Also, Ḥarūn ibn ʿAbdullāh narrated; al-Ḍaḥḥāk ibn Makhlad narrated; both from Ibn Jurayj; with the same chain of transmission: **the same text.**

وَحَدَّثَنَاهُ إِسْحَاقُ بْنُ إِبْرَاهِيمَ، أَخْبَرَنَا مُحَمَّدُ بْنُ بَكْرٍ، ح. وَحَدَّثَنَا هَارُونُ بْنُ عَبْدِ اللهِ، حَدَّثَنَا الضَّحَّاكُ بْنُ مَخْلَدٍ، كِلاَهُمَا عَنِ ابْنِ جُرَيْجٍ، بِهَذَا الإِسْنَادِ

[1679–9]. (Dar al-Salam 1844) Muhammad ibn Ḥātim narrated to me:[ii] Bahz narrated; Wuhayb narrated; ʿAbdullāh ibn Ṭāwūs narrated; from his father; from Abu Hurayrah; from the Prophet (peace be upon him). He said: **'It is a duty owed to God by every Muslim to take a bath every seven days, washing one's head and body'.**

---

i. Related by al-Bukhari, 885;

ii. Related by al-Bukhari, 896 and 3486; al-Nasāʾī, 1366.

وَحَدَّثَنِي مُحَمَّدُ بْنُ حَاتِمٍ، حَدَّثَنَا بَهْزٌ، حَدَّثَنَا وُهَيْبٌ، حَدَّثَنَا عَبْدُ اللهِ بْنُ طَاوُسٍ، عَنْ أَبِيهِ، عَنْ أَبِي هُرَيْرَةَ، عَنِ النَّبِيِّ صَلَّى اللهُ عَلَيْهِ وَسَلَّمَ قَالَ: «حَقٌّ للهِ عَلَى كُلِّ مُسْلِمٍ أَنْ يَغْتَسِلَ فِي كُلِّ سَبْعَةِ أَيَّامٍ، يَغْسِلُ رَأْسَهُ وَجَسَدَهُ».

[1680–10]. (Dar al-Salam 1845) Qutaybah ibn Saʿīd narrated:[i] from Mālik ibn Anas in what was read out to him; from Sumayy, Abu Bakr's *mawla;* from Abu Ṣāliḥ al-Sammān; from Abu Hurayrah; that God's Messenger (peace be upon him) said: **'Whoever takes on Friday a bath like the one required for [removing] a state of ceremonial impurity then goes is like one who gives a camel to charity, and whoever goes in the second period is like one who gives a cow to charity, and whoever goes in the third period is like one who gives a horned sheep to charity, and whoever goes in the fourth period is like one who gives a hen to charity, and whoever goes in the fifth period is like one who gives an egg to charity. When the imam comes out, the angels will attend, listening to God's glorification'.**

وَحَدَّثَنَا قُتَيْبَةُ بْنُ سَعِيدٍ، عَنْ مَالِكِ بْنِ أَنَسٍ، فِيمَا قُرِئَ عَلَيْهِ عَنْ سُمَيٍّ، مَوْلَى أَبِي بَكْرٍ، عَنْ أَبِي صَالِحٍ السَّمَّانِ، عَنْ أَبِي هُرَيْرَةَ، أَنَّ رَسُولَ اللهِ صَلَّى اللهُ عَلَيْهِ وَسَلَّمَ قَالَ: «مَنِ اغْتَسَلَ يَوْمَ الْجُمُعَةِ غُسْلَ الْجَنَابَةِ ثُمَّ رَاحَ فَكَأَنَّمَا قَرَّبَ بَدَنَةً، وَمَنْ رَاحَ فِي السَّاعَةِ الثَّانِيَةِ فَكَأَنَّمَا قَرَّبَ بَقَرَةً، وَمَنْ رَاحَ فِي السَّاعَةِ الثَّالِثَةِ فَكَأَنَّمَا قَرَّبَ كَبْشًا أَقْرَنَ، وَمَنْ رَاحَ فِي السَّاعَةِ الرَّابِعَةِ فَكَأَنَّمَا قَرَّبَ دَجَاجَةً، وَمَنْ رَاحَ فِي السَّاعَةِ الْخَامِسَةِ فَكَأَنَّمَا قَرَّبَ بَيْضَةً، فَإِذَا خَرَجَ الإِمَامُ حَضَرَتِ الْمَلائِكَةُ يَسْتَمِعُونَ الذِّكْرَ.

Text Explanation

In hadith No. 1677, the Prophet says: 'A bath on Friday is applicable to everyone who has attained puberty'. This is how it occurs in

i. Related by al-Bukhari, 881; Abu Dāwūd, 351; al-Tirmidhī, 499; al-Nasāʾī, 1387.

all original manuscripts, without mentioning that it is obligatory. The hadith adds: 'as is brushing one's teeth. He should also apply whatever perfume he can'. This means that it is also recommended that a person going to Friday Prayer should brush his teeth and apply some perfume. Speaking of perfume, the hadith says: 'whatever he can'. *Qadi* ʿIyāḍ said: 'this may mean as much as one can, or it may also serve to emphasise it so that one uses whatever is available'. This is confirmed by adding 'even if it is feminine perfume'. Such perfume, which is sensorially apparent but has a subtle smell, is normally discouraged for men. In this case, it is permissible because nothing else is available. This confirms the emphasis, but God knows best.

In hadith No. 1680, the Prophet says: 'Whoever takes on Friday a bath like the one required for [removing] a state of ceremonial impurity…'. This is the meaning of this part of the sentence. The bath should be taken in the same way as the one we employ to remove a state of ceremonial impurity. However, some of our scholars say, in books of Fiqh, that it should be a bath to remove this state as if it were an actuality. They add that it is desirable for a man to have intercourse with his wife before it, so that he would experience no sexual urge. This has no sound basis; indeed, it is false. The correct view is the one we stated first.

The hadith continues: '…then goes is like one who gives a camel to charity, and whoever goes in the second period is like one who gives a cow to charity'. The words 'then goes' are subject to well-known difference of opinion among scholars. In Arabic, the Prophet uses the word *rāḥ* for 'goes', which means going early in the day. However, Imam Mālik and many of his disciples, as well as *Qadi* Ḥusayn ibn Muhammad ibn Ahmad and Imam al-Ḥaramayn, both of whom belong to the Shāfiʿī School, say that the word *sāʿah*, translated as 'period', means, in this instance, a few moments after midday. They claim that this is the linguistic meaning of the word *rāḥ*. The view of al-Shāfiʿī, the majority of his disciples, Ibn Ḥabīb of the Mālikī School and the great majority of scholars is to go to Friday Prayer early in the morning. The periods mentioned in the hadith start, according to them, at the beginning of the day, and *rāḥ* means going at the beginning and end of the day. Al-Azharī said: 'In Arabic, *rāḥ* means to go, whether one goes early or late during the day or even at night'. This is the correct meaning indicated in the hadith and its general meaning. The Prophet (peace be upon him) tells us that the angels write down the names of those who come in the first period, and whoever does so is like one who gives a camel to charity. They then record the names who come in the second, third, fourth and fifth periods. In a version related by al-Nasā'ī, they also record those who come in the sixth period. When the imam comes in, they close their scrolls and do not write any name thereafter.

It is well known that the Prophet used to come out for the Friday Prayer shortly after midday, after the sixth period. This shows that those who come after the sun has started on the decline, shortly after midday earn no special favour. The Prophet mentions these different periods to urge people to come early, so as to earn the privilege of coming ahead of others, find a place in the first row, await the prayer and use their time in offering voluntary prayer, reciting the Qur'an, glorifying God, and similar matters. Nothing of this may be done if one goes to Friday Prayer after midday. Nothing is earned by those who come when the sun begins its decline because the *adhān* is called then and staying away from Friday Prayer after the call is forbidden, but God knows best.

Our scholars differ as to when the periods mentioned by the Prophet begin; do they begin at the break of dawn or shortly after sunrise. They consider that it is more correct to say that they begin at dawn. Moreover, the one who comes at the beginning of each period and the one who comes at its end earn the reward of giving a camel, a cow or a horned sheep to charity, but the camel of the earlier one is better and more valuable than that of the one who comes later. This is the same as offering an obligatory prayer with a congregation; it is better than praying it alone by twenty-seven degrees. It is well-known that a congregational prayer is offered by two people or by thousands. A person who prays in a congregation of ten thousand people gains twenty-seven degrees, and the one who prays with one other person gains twenty-seven degrees, but the degrees of the first one are better and more perfect. There are many similar cases. What I have mentioned answers an objection mentioned by *Qadi* ʿIyāḍ (may God bestow mercy on him).

The hadiths in this chapter urge going to Friday Prayer early, making it clear that people earn their grades in good things according to what they do. This is in conformity with God's statement: 'Truly, the noblest of you in the sight of God is the one who is most genuinely God-fearing'. (49: 13)

Hadith No. 1680 makes it clear that charity and offering apply to whatever one gives, whether it is little or plentiful. In al-Nasāʾī's version, the offerings mentioned after the horned sheep are 'a duck, a hen and an egg'. In another version: 'a hen, a sparrow and an egg'. Both these narrations have reliable chains of transmission. The hadith makes it clear that sacrificing a camel is better than sacrificing a cow because the Prophet mentions the camel first and places the cow in the second grade. Scholars are unanimous that camels are better than cows in the pilgrimage sacrifice, but they differ as to other sacrifice. According to al-Shāfiʿī, Abu Ḥanīfah and the majority, camels are best, then cows, then sheep, the same as in the pilgrimage sacrifice. Mālik, however, considers that sheep are best, then cows, then camels. This argument is based on the fact that the Prophet sacrificed two rams. The argument given by the majority of scholars is the apparent meaning of this hadith and the analogy with the pilgrimage sacrifice. That the Prophet sacrificed two rams does not give preference to sheep because it might have been that he only had sheep at the time or that he did it to show that it is permissible. Moreover, it is confirmed that he sacrificed cows on behalf of his wives.

The hadith also mentions that the angels attend so as to listen to the Friday Prayer. These angels are different from guardian angels. These are specifically charged with the task of recording the names of those attending the Friday Prayer.

CHAPTER 3

LISTENING TO THE FRIDAY SERMON [i.e. *KHUṬBAH*]

[1681–11]. (Dar al-Salam 1846–1847) Qutaybah ibn Saʿīd and Muhammad ibn Rumḥ ibn al-Muhājir narrated:[i] Ibn Rumḥ said: al-Layth reported; from ʿUqayl; from Ibn Shihāb; Saʿīd ibn al-Musayyib reported to me; that Abu Hurayrah reported to him that God's Messenger (peace be upon him) said: **'If you say to your friend on Friday, "Listen", when the imam is delivering his *khuṭbah*, you do what is unacceptable'.**

وَحَدَّثَنَا قُتَيْبَةُ بْنُ سَعِيدٍ وَمُحَمَّدُ بْنُ رُمْحِ بْنِ الْـمُهَاجِرِ، قَالَ ابْنُ رُمْحٍ أَخْبَرَنَا اللَّيْثُ، عَنْ عُقَيْلٍ، عَنِ ابْنِ شِهَابٍ، أَخْبَرَنِي سَعِيدُ بْنُ الْـمُسَيَّبِ، أَنَّ أَبَا هُرَيْرَةَ أَخْبَرَهُ أَنَّ رَسُولَ اللهِ صَلَّى اللهُ عَلَيْهِ وَسَلَّمَ قَالَ: «إِذَا قُلْتَ لِصَاحِبِكَ أَنْصِتْ، يَوْمَ الْجُمُعَةِ وَالإِمَامُ يَخْطُبُ فَقَدْ لَغَوْتَ».

ʿAbd al-Malik ibn Shuʿayb ibn al-Layth narrated to me: my father narrated to me; from my grandfather; ʿUqayl ibn Khālid narrated to me; from Ibn Shihāb; from ʿUmar ibn ʿAbd al-ʿAzīz; from ʿAbdullāh ibn Ibrāhīm ibn Qāriẓ, and from Ibn al-Musayyib; that both narrated to him that Abu Hurayrah said: I heard God's Messenger (peace be upon him) say: **the same text.**

---

i. Related by al-Bukhari, 394; al-Tirmidhī, 512; al-Nasāʾī, 1400 and 1401.

وَحَدَّثَنِي عَبْدُ الْـمَلِكِ بْنُ شُعَيْبِ بْنِ اللَّيْثِ، حَدَّثَنِي أَبِي، عَنْ جَدِّي، حَدَّثَنِي عُقَيْلُ بْنُ خَالِدٍ، عَنِ ابْنِ شِهَابٍ، عَنْ عُمَرَ بْنِ عَبْدِ الْعَزِيزِ، عَنْ عَبْدِ اللهِ بْنِ إِبْرَاهِيمَ بْنِ قَارِظٍ، وَعَنِ ابْنِ الْـمُسَيَّبِ، أَنَّهُمَا حَدَّثَاهُ أَنَّ أَبَا هُرَيْرَةَ قَالَ سَمِعْتُ رَسُولَ اللهِ صَلَّى اللهُ عَلَيْهِ وَسَلَّمَ يَقُولُ. بِمِثْلِهِ

And it is narrated to me by Muhammad ibn Ḥātim: Muhammad ibn Bakr narrated; Ibn Jurayj reported; Ibn Shihāb reported to me; with both chains of transmission of this hadith: **the same text, except that Ibn Jurayj said: 'Ibrāhīm ibn ʿAbdullāh ibn Qāriẓ'.**

وَحَدَّثَنِيهِ مُحَمَّدُ بْنُ حَاتِمٍ، حَدَّثَنَا مُحَمَّدُ بْنُ بَكْرٍ، أَخْبَرَنَا ابْنُ جُرَيْجٍ، أَخْبَرَنِي ابْنُ شِهَابٍ بِالإِسْنَادَيْنِ جَمِيعًا فِي هَذَا الْحَدِيث. مِثْلَهُ غَيْرَ أَنَّ ابْنَ جُرَيْجٍ قَالَ إِبْرَاهِيمُ بْنُ عَبْدِ اللهِ بْنِ قَارِظٍ

[1682–12]. (Dar al-Salam 1848) Ibn Abi ʿUmar narrated: Sufyān narrated; from Abu al-Zinād; from al-Aʿraj; from Abu Hurayrah; from the Prophet (peace be upon him). He said: **'If you say to your friend on Friday, "Listen", when the imam is delivering his *khuṭbah*, you do what is unacceptable'.**[i]

وَحَدَّثَنَا ابْنُ أَبِي عُمَرَ، حَدَّثَنَا سُفْيَانُ، عَنْ أَبِي الزِّنَادِ، عَنِ الأَعْرَجِ، عَنْ أَبِي هُرَيْرَةَ، عَنِ النَّبِيِّ صَلَّى اللهُ عَلَيْهِ وَسَلَّمَ قَالَ: «إِذَا قُلْتَ لِصَاحِبِكَ أَنْصِتْ، يَوْمَ الْجُمُعَةِ وَالإِمَامُ يَخْطُبُ فَقَدْ لَغِيتَ». قَالَ أَبُو الزِّنَادِ هِيَ لُغَةُ أَبِي هُرَيْرَةَ وَإِنَّمَا هُوَ فَقَدْ لَغَوْتَ.

---

i. This hadith differs from the first one in this chapter in that it uses the word '*laghayt*' for 'say what is unacceptable, while in the first hadith it is '*laghawt*'. Abu al-Zinād commented: 'This is Abu Hurayrah's pronunciation, but the word is *laghawt*.'

Text Explanation

In this hadith, the Prophet says that to say 'listen' to someone else while the imam is giving his *khuṭbah* is wrong and unacceptable. The hadith thus means that any type of speech during the *khuṭbah* is unacceptable. The Prophet gives this example in order to include all speech. If a person says to another 'listen', he is only giving him sound advice, but the Prophet calls this 'unacceptable'. The description, then, applies to all other speech. If someone is speaking during the *khuṭbah,* the way to tell him to stop is by a signal, if he understands it. If that person does not understand, then he should be told to stop in minimum words. Scholars differ on whether speaking during the *khuṭbah* is forbidden or mildly discouraged. Al-Shāfiʿī expresses both views. *Qadi* ʿIyāḍ said: 'Mālik, Abu Ḥanīfah, al-Shāfiʿī and scholars generally say that it is a duty to listen to the *khuṭbah*. It is reported that al-Nakhaʿī, al-Shaʿbī and some early scholars said that it is not a duty unless the Qur'an is recited in it. They also differ about one who does not hear the imam [either because he is hard of hearing or sitting far]: must he listen as if he is hearing him? The majority of scholars say that he must. Al-Nakhaʿī, Ahmad and al-Shāfiʿī in one of his two views say that he need not'.

In the hadith, the Prophet mentions: 'when the imam is delivering his *khuṭbah*'. This suggests that the duty of listening and the prohibition of ordinary speech apply during the *khuṭbah*. This is our view, the view of Mālik and the majority of scholars. Abu Ḥanīfah said that listening applies when the imam comes in.

CHAPTER 4

A SPECIAL HOUR

[1683–13]. (Dar al-Salam 1849) Yaḥyā ibn Yaḥyā narrated:[i] I read out to Mālik [H]. Also, Qutaybah ibn Saʿīd narrated; from Mālik ibn Anas; from Abu al-Zinād; from al-Aʿraj; from Abu Hurayrah; that **'God's Messenger (peace be upon him) mentioned Friday and said: "Friday has a special hour. If a Muslim servant of God happens to be praying at this hour and he requests anything of God, God will certainly grant it".'**

Qutaybah added in his narration: **'And he signalled with his hand implying that it is short'.**

وَحَدَّثَنَا يَحْيَى بْنُ يَحْيَى، قَالَ قَرَأْتُ عَلَى مَالِكٍ ح. وَحَدَّثَنَا قُتَيْبَةُ بْنُ سَعِيدٍ، عَنْ مَالِكِ بْنِ أَنَسٍ، عَنْ أَبِي الزِّنَادِ، عَنِ الأَعْرَجِ، عَنْ أَبِي هُرَيْرَةَ، أَنَّ رَسُولَ اللهِ صَلَّى اللهُ عَلَيْهِ وَسَلَّمَ ذَكَرَ يَوْمَ الْجُمُعَةِ فَقَالَ: «فِيهِ سَاعَةٌ لاَ يُوَافِقُهَا عَبْدٌ مُسْلِمٌ وَهُوَ يُصَلِّي يَسْأَلُ اللهَ شَيْئًا إِلاَّ أَعْطَاهُ إِيَّاهُ».

زَادَ قُتَيْبَةُ فِي رِوَايَتِهِ وَأَشَارَ بِيَدِهِ يُقَلِّلُهَا

[1684–14]. (Dar al-Salam 1850–1852) Zuhayr ibn Ḥarb narrated:[ii] Ismāʿīl ibn Ibrāhīm narrated; Ayyūb narrated; from Muhammad; from Abu Hurayrah. He said: **'Abu al-Qāsim**[iii]

---

i. Related by al-Bukhari, 935.

ii. Related by al-Bukhari, 6400; al-Nasāʾī, 1431.

iii. Abu al-Qāsim is Prophet Muhammad (peace be upon him). He was given this appellation as his first son was named al-Qāsim. All three sons of the Prophet died in infancy.

(peace be upon him) said: "On Friday, there is a special hour. If a Muslim happens to be standing in prayer at this time, requesting God to grant him something good, God will certainly grant it". He signalled with his hand that it is short, very short'.

حَدَّثَنَا زُهَيْرُ بْنُ حَرْبٍ، حَدَّثَنَا إِسْمَاعِيلُ بْنُ إِبْرَاهِيمَ، حَدَّثَنَا أَيُّوبُ، عَنْ مُحَمَّدٍ، عَنْ أَبِي هُرَيْرَةَ قَالَ: قَالَ أَبُو الْقَاسِمِ صَلَّى اللهُ عَلَيْهِ وَسَلَّمَ: «إِنَّ فِي الْجُمُعَةِ لَسَاعَةً لاَ يُوَافِقُهَا مُسْلِمٌ قَائِمٌ يُصَلِّي، يَسْأَلُ اللهَ خَيْرًا إِلاَّ أَعْطَاهُ إِيَّاهُ». وَقَالَ بِيَدِهِ يُقَلِّلُهَا، يُزَهِّدُهَا.

Ibn al-Muthannā narrated: Ibn Abi ʿAdiy narrated; from Ibn ʿAwn; from Muhammad; from Abu Hurayrah. He said: **'Abu al-Qāsim (peace be upon him) said…' the same text.**

حَدَّثَنَا ابْنُ الْـمُثَنَّى، حَدَّثَنَا ابْنُ أَبِي عَدِيٍّ، عَنِ ابْنِ عَوْنٍ، عَنْ مُحَمَّدٍ، عَنْ أَبِي هُرَيْرَةَ قَالَ: قَالَ أَبُو الْقَاسِمِ صَلَّى اللهُ عَلَيْهِ وَسَلَّمَ بِمِثْلِهِ.

Ḥumayd ibn Masʿadah al-Bāhilī narrated to me:[i] Bishr (meaning Ibn Mufaḍḍal) narrated; Salamah (who is Ibn ʿAlqamah) narrated; from Muhammad; from Abu Hurayrah. He said: **'Abu al-Qāsim (peace be upon him) said…' the same text.**

وَحَدَّثَنِي حُمَيْدُ بْنُ مَسْعَدَةَ الْبَاهِلِيُّ، حَدَّثَنَا بِشْرٌ، يَعْنِي ابْنَ مُفَضَّلٍ، حَدَّثَنَا سَلَمَةُ، وَهُوَ ابْنُ عَلْقَمَةَ، عَنْ مُحَمَّدٍ، عَنْ أَبِي هُرَيْرَةَ قَالَ: قَالَ أَبُو الْقَاسِمِ صَلَّى اللهُ عَلَيْهِ وَسَلَّمَ بِمِثْلِهِ.

[1685–15]. (Dar al-Salam 1853) ʿAbd al-Raḥmān ibn Sallām al-Jumaḥī narrated: al-Rabīʿ (meaning Ibn Muslim) narrated; from Muhammad ibn Ziyād; from Abu Hurayrah; from the

i. Related by al-Bukhari, 5294.

Prophet (peace be upon him); that he said: **'There is certainly an hour on Friday and if a Muslim happens to request God for anything good at this time, God will grant it to him'. He said: 'And it is short'.**

وَحَدَّثَنَا عَبْدُ الرَّحْمَنِ بْنُ سَلاَّمٍ الْجُمَحِيُّ، حَدَّثَنَا الرَّبِيعُ، - يَعْنِي ابْنَ مُسْلِمٍ - عَنْ مُحَمَّدِ بْنِ زِيَادٍ، عَنْ أَبِي هُرَيْرَةَ، عَنِ النَّبِيِّ صَلَّى اللهُ عَلَيْهِ وَسَلَّمَ أَنَّهُ قَالَ: «إِنَّ فِي الْجُمُعَةِ لَسَاعَةً لاَ يُوَافِقُهَا مُسْلِمٌ يَسْأَلُ اللهَ فِيهَا خَيْرًا إِلاَّ أَعْطَاهُ إِيَّاهُ». قَالَ وَهِيَ سَاعَةٌ خَفِيفَةٌ.

[1686–000]. (Dar al-Salam 1854) Muhammad ibn Rāfiʿ narrated the same to me: ʿAbd al-Razzāq narrated; from Maʿmar; from Hammām ibn Munabbih; from Abu Hurayrah; from the Prophet (peace be upon him): **but he did not say that it is short.**

وَحَدَّثَنَاهُ مُحَمَّدُ بْنُ رَافِعٍ، حَدَّثَنَا عَبْدُ الرَّزَّاقِ، حَدَّثَنَا مَعْمَرٌ، عَنْ هَمَّامِ بْنِ مُنَبِّهٍ، عَنْ أَبِي هُرَيْرَةَ، عَنِ النَّبِيِّ صَلَّى اللهُ عَلَيْهِ وَسَلَّمَ. وَلَمْ يَقُلْ: وَهِيَ سَاعَةٌ خَفِيفَةٌ.

[1687–16]. (Dar al-Salam 1855) Abu al-Ṭāhir and ʿAlī ibn Khashram narrated to me:[i] both said: Ibn Wahb reported; from Makhramah ibn Bukayr [H]. Also Ḥarūn ibn Saʿīd al-Aylī and Ahmad ibn ʿĪsā narrated; both said: Ibn Wahb narrated; Makhramah reported; from his father; from Abu Burdah ibn Abu Mūsā al-Ashʿarī. He said: **'ʿAbdullāh ibn ʿUmar asked me: "Did you hear your father narrating from God's Messenger (peace be upon him) concerning the hour on Friday?" I said: "Yes. I heard him say: 'I heard God's Messenger (peace be upon him) say: "It is in between the moment when the imam sits down until the prayer has finished".'"'**

i. Related by Abu Dāwūd, 1049.

وَحَدَّثَنِي أَبُو الطَّاهِرِ وَعَلِيُّ بْنُ خَشْرَمٍ، قَالا: أَخْبَرَنَا ابْنُ وَهْبٍ، عَنْ مَخْرَمَةَ بْنِ بُكَيْرٍ ح. وَحَدَّثَنَا هَارُونُ بْنُ سَعِيدٍ الأَيْلِيُّ وَأَحْمَدُ بْنُ عِيسَى، قَالا: حَدَّثَنَا ابْنُ وَهْبٍ، أَخْبَرَنَا مَخْرَمَةُ، عَنْ أَبِيهِ، عَنْ أَبِي بُرْدَةَ بْنِ أَبِي مُوسَى الأَشْعَرِيِّ قَالَ: قَالَ لِي عَبْدُ اللهِ بْنُ عُمَرَ: أَسَمِعْتَ أَبَاكَ يُحَدِّثُ عَنْ رَسُولِ اللهِ صَلَّى اللهُ عَلَيْهِ وَسَلَّمَ فِي شَأْنِ سَاعَةِ الْجُمُعَةِ؟ قَالَ: قُلْتُ نَعَمْ سَمِعْتُهُ يَقُولُ: سَمِعْتُ رَسُولَ اللهِ صَلَّى اللهُ عَلَيْهِ وَسَلَّمَ يَقُولُ: «هِيَ مَا بَيْنَ أَنْ يَجْلِسَ الإِمَامُ إِلَى أَنْ تُقْضَى الصَّلاَةُ».

Text Explanation

[Note: in these hadiths, the word 'hour' is not used in the modern sense of the word, which makes an hour equal to sixty minutes. It simply means 'a short period of time'.]

These hadiths confirm that there is a special time on Friday, when God answers any prayer, provided that it is a request for something good. The hadiths make clear that it is a short period of time, and the last hadith, No. 1687, defines it as the time between the imam sitting down and the end of Friday Prayer. *Qadi* ʿIyāḍ said:

> Scholars of the earlier generations differed as to the time of this hour and the meaning of the words, 'standing in prayer'. Some said: It is the period after ʿAṣr until sunset. They also said: 'in prayer' means supplicating, and that 'standing' means 'doing it regularly or consistently'. The Arabic word used here for 'standing' is *qā'im* and it is used in the Qur'an in the sense of being consistent. Others said that it is from the moment when the imam comes out to the prayer until the prayer is finished. Others still said that it is from the moment when the prayer is announced [i.e. *iqāmah*] until it is finished, and these scholars understand 'prayer' in its apparent sense, i.e. the actual prayer. It is also said that this hour extends from the moment the imam sits on the platform until he finishes the prayer. It is further said that it is the last hour on Friday. Statements

> have been attributed to the Prophet explaining all these views. It is also said that it is at midday, when the sun starts to decline. Another suggestion is that it is from the time the sun begins its decline until shadows are equal to the length of a man's arm. Some said that it happens at any time throughout the day. It is further said that it extends from the break of dawn until sunrise.
>
> These statements do not mean that the hour takes up all these times. They mean that it occurs during this time because of the statement: 'He signalled with his hand implying that it is short'.

This is what *Qadi* ʿIyāḍ said, but the correct view, indeed the right view, is what Muslim has related in the last hadith, narrated by Abu Mūsā from the Prophet: that it is 'in between the moment when the imam sits down until the prayer is finished'.

Transmission

The chain of transmission of hadith No. 1687 includes: 'Makhramah ibn Bukayr, from his father, from Abu Burdah, from his father [i.e. Abu Mūsā], from the Prophet (peace be upon him)'. This chain of transmission is questioned by al-Dāraquṭnī who says:

> No one narrates it except Makhramah from his father from Abu Burdah. Others narrate it from Abu Burdah as his own statement, while some take the chain of transmission up to Abu Mūsā, without attributing it to the Prophet. The correct view is that it is stated by Abu Burdah. It has been thus narrated by Yaḥyā al-Qaṭṭān from al-Thawrī from Abu Isḥāq from Abu Burdah. And it is similarly reported by Wāṣil al-Aḥdab and Mujālid[i] as being stated by Abu Burdah. [The

i. This name occurs as Mukhālid in some copies, but it is verified as Mujālid ibn Saʿīd.

> chain]: al-Nuʿmān ibn ʿAbd al-Salām from al-Thawrī from Abu Isḥāq from Abu Burdah from his father is a *mawqūf* chain, [i.e. stopped], and the last part, i.e. 'from his father', is not confirmed. Ahmad ibn Ḥanbal quotes Ḥammād ibn Khālid: 'I said to Makhramah: "Did you listen to your father narrating any hadiths?" He said: "No".'

This is how al-Dāraquṭnī questions the authenticity of this hadith. It is based on a rule known to him and the majority of Hadith scholars. This rule says that if a hadith is reported in two chains of transmission, one stops at the Prophet's Companion and the other quotes the Prophet, they consider the hadith as *mawqūf*, or *mursal*, as the case may be. This rule has no strong basis and it is rejected. The proper and correct method is that adopted by scholars of legal theory, Fiqh, al-Bukhari, Muslim and meticulous scholars of Hadith, stating that in such cases the hadith is considered to go up to the Prophet because the addition that he stated is given by a reliable narrator. We have clarified this in the 'Notes' to our 'Introduction' and pointed out similar cases later.

We read in al-Bayhaqī's *Sunan* the following statement by Ahmad ibn Salamah: 'I discussed this hadith narrated by Makhramah with Muslim ibn al-Ḥajjāj. Muslim said: "It is the best and most authentic hadith specifying the 'hour' on Friday".'

CHAPTER 5

FRIDAY, OUR BEST DAY

[1688–17]. (Dar al-Salam 1856) Ḥarmalah ibn Yaḥyā narrated to me:[i] Ibn Wahb reported; Yūnus reported to me; from Ibn Shihāb; ʿAbd al-Raḥmān al-Aʿraj reported to me; that he heard Abu Hurayrah say: **'God's Messenger (peace be upon him) said: "The best day on which the sun has ever risen is Friday: it is the day when Adam was created, and the day on which he was settled in Heaven and the day on which he was removed from it".'**

وَحَدَّثَنِي حَرْمَلَةُ بْنُ يَحْيَى، أَخْبَرَنَا ابْنُ وَهْبٍ، أَخْبَرَنِي يُونُسُ، عَنِ ابْنِ شِهَابٍ، أَخْبَرَنِي عَبْدُ الرَّحْمَنِ الأَعْرَجُ، أَنَّهُ سَمِعَ أَبَا هُرَيْرَةَ يَقُولُ: قَالَ رَسُولُ اللهِ صَلَّى اللهُ عَلَيْهِ وَسَلَّمَ: «خَيْرُ يَوْمٍ طَلَعَتْ عَلَيْهِ الشَّمْسُ يَوْمُ الْجُمُعَةِ: فِيهِ خُلِقَ آدَمُ، وَفِيهِ أُدْخِلَ الْجَنَّةَ، وَفِيهِ أُخْرِجَ مِنْهَا».

[1689–18]. (Dar al-Salam 1857) Qutaybah ibn Saʿīd narrated:[ii] al-Mughīrah (meaning al-Ḥizāmī) narrated; from Abu al-Zinād; from al-Aʿraj; from Abu Hurayrah; that the Prophet (peace be upon him) said: **'The best day on which the sun has ever risen is Friday: it is the day when Adam was created, and the day on which he was settled in Heaven and the day on which he was removed from it. The Last Hour will only occur on Friday'.**

i. Related by al-Nasāʾī, 1372.
ii. Related by al-Tirmidhī, 488.

وَحَدَّثَنَا قُتَيْبَةُ بْنُ سَعِيدٍ، حَدَّثَنَا الْـمُغِيرَةُ، - يَعْنِي الْحِزَامِيَّ - عَنْ أَبِي الزِّنَادِ، عَنِ الأَعْرَجِ، عَنْ أَبِي هُرَيْرَةَ، أَنَّ النَّبِيَّ صَلَّى اللهُ عَلَيْهِ وَسَلَّمَ قَالَ: «خَيْرُ يَوْمٍ طَلَعَتْ عَلَيْهِ الشَّمْسُ يَوْمُ الْجُمُعَةِ: فِيهِ خُلِقَ آدَمُ، وَفِيهِ أُدْخِلَ الْجَنَّةَ، وَفِيهِ أُخْرِجَ مِنْهَا، وَلاَ تَقُومُ السَّاعَةُ إِلاَّ فِي يَوْمِ الْجُمُعَةِ».

Text Explanation

The Prophet states that the best of our days is Friday, and he mentions that it was the day when the first human being was created and placed in Heaven. He also mentions that it was the day when Adam was removed from Heaven and the day when the Last Hour occurs. *Qadi* ʿIyāḍ said: 'It appears that these points are not stated to highlight the merits of Friday because the removal of Adam from Heaven and the Last Hour are not events to be celebrated. The hadith simply mentions some of the great events that occurred or will occur on Friday. This should alert us to do whatever good we can on Friday so as to earn God's mercy and save ourselves from His punishment'.

In his book, *ʿĀriḍat al-Aḥwadhī fi Sharḥ Sunan al-Tirmidhī*, Abu Bakr ibn al-ʿArabī said:

> All these mentioned are matters of merit. Adam's removal from Heaven was the start of the creation of mankind and the existence of his great progeny, as well as the existence of prophets, God's messengers and all devout people. Adam was not expelled from Heaven but removed so that certain matters could be accomplished and then he would return there. When the Last Hour occurs, it heralds the granting of God's reward to prophets and people who are devout and good. Their honour and noble position will be shown to all.

This hadith serves as basis for a ruling on a strange but interesting case. If a man divorces his wife, saying 'You are divorced on the best of days', our scholars [of the Mālikī School] express two views. The one which is the more correct of the two is that the divorce occurs on the day of attendance at Arafat. The other view is that the divorce occurs on Friday, and this is based on this hadith. This applies if the man did not have a specific intention. If his intention is the best day of the year, then the divorce occurs on the Day of Arafat, and if his intention is the best day of the week, then it occurs on Friday. If the man tells his wife that she is divorced on the best night, then that is the Night of Power. According to our scholars and the majority of scholars, it is one of the nights of the last third of Ramadan. If the man says this before the first of these nights is over, the divorce occurs at the beginning of the last night of Ramadan. If he says it after one or more nights of the last third of Ramadan is over, then the divorce will not occur until the start of the similar night of the following Ramadan [i.e. a year later]. According to those who say that the Night of Power is not fixed and that it moves, the divorce occurs at the beginning of the last day of Ramadan, but God knows best.

CHAPTER 6

GUIDED TO FRIDAY

[1690–19]. (Dar al-Salam 1858) ʿAmr al-Nāqid narrated: Sufyān ibn ʿUyaynah narrated; from Abu al-Zinād; from al-Aʿraj; from Abu Hurayrah. He said: **'God's Messenger (peace be upon him) said: "We are the last community, but we come first on the Day of Judgement. The fact is that every community was given the book before us and we were given it after them. Then we have this day God has prescribed for us and He has guided us to. On this, other communities come behind us: the Jews tomorrow and the Christians the day after".'**

وَحَدَّثَنَا عَمْرٌو النَّاقِدُ، حَدَّثَنَا سُفْيَانُ بْنُ عُيَيْنَةَ، عَنْ أَبِي الزِّنَادِ، عَنِ الأَعْرَجِ، عَنْ أَبِي هُرَيْرَةَ قَالَ: قَالَ رَسُولُ اللهِ صَلَّى اللهُ عَلَيْهِ وَسَلَّمَ: «نَحْنُ الآخِرُونَ وَنَحْنُ السَّابِقُونَ يَوْمَ الْقِيَامَةِ، بَيْدَ أَنَّ كُلَّ أُمَّةٍ أُوتِيَتِ الْكِتَابَ مِنْ قَبْلِنَا وَأُوتِينَاهُ مِنْ بَعْدِهِمْ، ثُمَّ هَذَا الْيَوْمُ الَّذِي كَتَبَهُ اللهُ عَلَيْنَا، هَدَانَا اللهُ لَهُ. فَالنَّاسُ لَنَا فِيهِ تَبَعٌ: الْيَهُودُ غَدًا، وَالنَّصَارَى بَعْدَ غَدٍ.

[1691–000]. (Dar al-Salam 1859) Ibn Abi ʿUmar narrated: Sufyān narrated; from Abu al-Zinād; from al-Aʿraj; from Abu Hurayrah. And also, Ibn Ṭāwūs from his father; from Abu Hurayrah. He said: **'God's Messenger (peace be upon him) said: "We are the last community, but we come first on the Day of Judgement...".' The same text.**

وَحَدَّثَنَا ابْنُ أَبِي عُمَرَ، حَدَّثَنَا سُفْيَانُ، عَنْ أَبِي الزِّنَادِ، عَنِ الأَعْرَجِ، عَنْ أَبِي هُرَيْرَةَ، وَابْنِ طَاوُسٍ عَنْ أَبِيهِ، عَنْ أَبِي هُرَيْرَةَ قَالَ: قَالَ رَسُولُ اللهِ صَلَّى اللهُ عَلَيْهِ وَسَلَّمَ: «نَحْنُ الآخِرُونَ وَنَحْنُ السَّابِقُونَ يَوْمَ الْقِيَامَةِ». بِمِثْلِهِ

[1692–20]. (Dar al-Salam 1860) Qutaybah ibn Saʿīd and Zuhayr ibn Ḥarb narrated: both said: Jarīr narrated; from al-Aʿmash; from Abu Ṣāliḥ; from Abu Hurayrah. He said: **'God's Messenger (peace be upon him) said: "We are the last and the first on the Day of Judgement, and we are the first to enter Heaven. They were given the book before us and it was given to us after them. Yet they differed. By His will, God guided us to the truth concerning that which they had differed. This is the day on which they differed, and God guided us to it." He said: "Friday, and the day is ours. Tomorrow belongs to the Jews and the day after to the Christians".'**

وَحَدَّثَنَا قُتَيْبَةُ بْنُ سَعِيدٍ وَزُهَيْرُ بْنُ حَرْبٍ، قَالا حَدَّثَنَا جَرِيرٌ، عَنِ الأَعْمَشِ، عَنْ أَبِي صَالِحٍ، عَنْ أَبِي هُرَيْرَةَ قَالَ: قَالَ رَسُولُ اللهِ صَلَّى اللهُ عَلَيْهِ وَسَلَّمَ: «نَحْنُ الآخِرُونَ الأَوَّلُونَ يَوْمَ الْقِيَامَةِ. وَنَحْنُ أَوَّلُ مَنْ يَدْخُلُ الْجَنَّةَ، بَيْدَ أَنَّهُمْ أُوتُوا الْكِتَابَ مِنْ قَبْلِنَا وَأُوتِينَاهُ مِنْ بَعْدِهِمْ، فَاخْتَلَفُوا، فَهَدَانَا اللهُ لِمَا اخْتَلَفُوا فِيهِ مِنَ الْحَقِّ. فَهَذَا يَوْمُهُمُ الَّذِي اخْتَلَفُوا فِيهِ، هَدَانَا اللهُ لَهُ - قَالَ يَوْمُ الْجُمُعَةِ - فَالْيَوْمُ لَنَا، وَغَدًا لِلْيَهُودِ، وَبَعْدَ غَدٍ لِلنَّصَارَى.

[1693–21]. (Dar al-Salam 1861) Muhammad ibn Rāfiʿ narrated: ʿAbd al-Razzāq narrated; Maʿmar reported; from Hammām ibn Munabbih, Wahb ibn Muannbih's brother; he said: This is what Abu Hurayrah narrated to us from Muhammad, God's Messenger (peace be upon him). He said: **'God's Messenger (peace be upon him) said: "We are the last and the first on the Day of Judgement. They were given the book before us and it was given to us after them. This is the day that was prescribed for them and on which they differed. God has guided us to it, and they stay behind us concerning it: the Jews tomorrow and the Christians the day after".'**

وَحَدَّثَنَا مُحَمَّدُ بْنُ رَافِعٍ، حَدَّثَنَا عَبْدُ الرَّزَّاقِ، أَخْبَرَنَا مَعْمَرٌ، عَنْ هَمَّامِ بْنِ مُنَبِّهٍ، أَخِي وَهْبِ بْنِ مُنَبِّهٍ قَالَ: هَذَا مَا حَدَّثَنَا أَبُو هُرَيْرَةَ، عَنْ مُحَمَّدٍ، رَسُولِ اللهِ صَلَّى اللهُ عَلَيْهِ وَسَلَّمَ قَالَ: قَالَ رَسُولُ اللهِ صَلَّى اللهُ عَلَيْهِ وَسَلَّمَ: «نَحْنُ الآخِرُونَ السَّابِقُونَ يَوْمَ الْقِيَامَةِ. بَيْدَ أَنَّهُمْ أُوتُوا الْكِتَابَ مِنْ قَبْلِنَا وَأُوتِينَاهُ مِنْ بَعْدِهِمْ. وَهَذَا يَوْمُهُمُ الَّذِي فُرِضَ عَلَيْهِمْ، فَاخْتَلَفُوا فِيهِ. فَهَدَانَا اللهُ لَهُ، فَهُمْ لَنَا فِيهِ تَبَعٌ، فَالْيَهُودُ غَدًا، وَالنَّصَارَى بَعْدَ غَدٍ.

[1694–22]. (Dar al-Salam 1862) Abu Kurayb and Wāṣil ibn ʿAbd al-Aʿlā narrated: both said: Ibn Fuḍayl narrated; from Abu Mālik al-Ashjaʿī; from Abu Ḥāzim; from Abu Hurayrah. And also from Ribʿī ibn Ḥirāsh; from Ḥudhayfah; both said: **'God's Messenger (peace be upon him) said: "God did not guide those before us to Friday. And thus, the Jews had their Saturday and the Christians their Sunday. God then brought us and guided us to Friday. He thus established Friday, Saturday and Sunday. Likewise, they will be behind us on the Day of Judgement. We are the last of people in this life but the first on the Day of Judgement, who will have their judgement before the rest of creation".'**

In Wāṣil's narration: **'who will have judgement between them'.**

وَحَدَّثَنَا أَبُو كُرَيْبٍ وَوَاصِلُ بْنُ عَبْدِ الأَعْلَى، قَالا حَدَّثَنَا ابْنُ فُضَيْلٍ، عَنْ أَبِي مَالِكٍ، الأَشْجَعِيِّ عَنْ أَبِي حَازِمٍ، عَنْ أَبِي هُرَيْرَةَ، وَعَنْ رِبْعِيِّ بْنِ حِرَاشٍ، عَنْ حُذَيْفَةَ، قَالا: قَالَ رَسُولُ اللهِ صَلَّى اللهُ عَلَيْهِ وَسَلَّمَ: « أَضَلَّ اللهُ عَنِ الْجُمُعَةِ مَنْ كَانَ قَبْلَنَا، فَكَانَ لِلْيَهُودِ يَوْمُ السَّبْتِ، وَكَانَ لِلنَّصَارَى يَوْمُ الأَحَدِ. فَجَاءَ اللهُ بِنَا فَهَدَانَا اللهُ لِيَوْمِ الْجُمُعَةِ. فَجَعَلَ الْجُمُعَةَ وَالسَّبْتَ وَالأَحَدَ، وَكَذَلِكَ هُمْ تَبَعٌ لَنَا يَوْمَ الْقِيَامَةِ. نَحْنُ الآخِرُونَ مِنْ أَهْلِ الدُّنْيَا، وَالأَوَّلُونَ يَوْمَ الْقِيَامَةِ الْمَقْضِيُّ لَهُمْ قَبْلَ الْخَلاَئِقِ».

وَفِي رِوَايَةِ وَاصِلٍ: الْمَقْضِيُّ بَيْنَهُمْ.

[1695–23]. (Dar al-Salam 1863) Abu Kurayb narrated: Ibn Abi Zā'idah reported; from Sa'd ibn Ṭāriq; Rib'ī ibn Ḥirāsh narrated to me; from Ḥudhayfah. He said: **'God's Messenger (peace be upon him) said: "We have been guided to Friday, while God did not guide to it those before us".' He added the same as the import of Fuḍayl's narration.**

حَدَّثَنَا أَبُو كُرَيْبٍ، أَخْبَرَنَا ابْنُ أَبِي زَائِدَةَ، عَنْ سَعْدِ بْنِ طَارِقٍ، حَدَّثَنِي رِبْعِيُّ بْنُ حِرَاشٍ، عَنْ حُذَيْفَةَ قَالَ: قَالَ رَسُولُ اللهِ صَلَّى اللهُ عَلَيْهِ وَسَلَّمَ: «هُدِينَا إِلَى الْجُمُعَةِ، وَأَضَلَّ اللهُ عَنْهَا مَنْ كَانَ قَبْلَنَا». فَذَكَرَ بِمَعْنَى حَدِيثِ ابْنِ فُضَيْلٍ.

Text Explanation

In these hadiths, the Prophet says: 'We are the last community, but we come first on the Day of Judgement'. Scholars said that it means that we are the last from the point of view of time and creation, but our merits place us ahead of others on the Day of Judgement, and we enter Heaven before all others.

In hadith No. 1690 the Prophet says: 'This day God has prescribed for us'. This serves as evidence that Friday Prayer is obligatory. Moreover, the day gives the Muslim community its merit ahead of other communities. In hadith No. 1692, the Prophet says: 'This is the day on which they differed, and God guided us to it'. *Qadi* 'Iyāḍ said:

> It appears that they were required to mark Friday as an honoured day, without specification. They were left to determine it as their knowledge could serve them in that, so that they could implement their duties on that day. However, they differed in their efforts to specify it, and God did not give them guidance on this point. However, when he assigned it to the Muslim community, it was specified for them. He did not require the Muslim community to exert effort to determine it. They were thus able to receive

> its benefits. It is also reported that Moses (peace be upon him) ordered them to mark Friday, explaining that it is the best day. They debated this with him, saying that Saturday was better. He was told to leave the choice to them. Had it been specified for them, they could not have differed on which day it was. It would have been said that they disobeyed.

We may say that they were given a specific order to mark Friday, but they differed as to whether they had to abide by that, or they could choose a different day. They changed it and that was wrong. In hadith No. 1694, the Prophet says that God did not guide earlier communities to Friday. This provides evidence in support of the view of the Sunni scholars who say that guidance, following error, good and evil are all by God's will and part of His action. This is contrary to what the Mu'tazilah claim.

CHAPTER 7

ARRIVING EARLY ON FRIDAY

[1696–24]. (Dar al-Salam 1864) Abu al-Ṭāhir, Ḥarmalah and ʿAmr ibn Sawwād al-ʿĀmirī narrated to me:[i] Ibn Wahb (Abu al-Ṭāhir said: 'narrated' and the other two said: 'reported'); Yūnus reported to me; from Ibn Shihāb; Abu ʿAbdullāh al-Agharr reported to me; that he heard Abu Hurayrah say: **'God's Messenger (peace be upon him) said: "On Friday, an angel stands at every door of the mosque to record arrivals, one after the other. When the imam sits down, they fold up their scrolls and enter to listen to God's glorification. The one who comes early is like one who donates a camel to charity, the next is like one donating a cow, then like one donating a sheep, then like one donating a hen, then like one donating an egg".'**

وَحَدَّثَنِي أَبُو الطَّاهِرِ وَحَرْمَلَةُ وَعَمْرُو بْنُ سَوَّادٍ الْعَامِرِيُّ، قَالَ أَبُو الطَّاهِرِ حَدَّثَنَا وَقَالَ الآخَرَانِ أَخْبَرَنَا ابْنُ وَهْبٍ، أَخْبَرَنِي يُونُسُ، عَنِ ابْنِ شِهَابٍ، أَخْبَرَنِي أَبُو عَبْدِ اللهِ الأَغَرُّ أَنَّهُ سَمِعَ أَبَا هُرَيْرَةَ يَقُولُ: قَالَ رَسُولُ اللهِ صَلَّى اللهُ عَلَيْهِ وَسَلَّمَ: «إِذَا كَانَ يَوْمُ الْجُمُعَةِ كَانَ عَلَى كُلِّ بَابٍ مِنْ أَبْوَابِ الْمَسْجِدِ مَلاَئِكَةٌ يَكْتُبُونَ الأَوَّلَ فَالأَوَّلَ، فَإِذَا جَلَسَ الإِمَامُ طَوَوُا الصُّحُفَ وَجَاءُوا يَسْتَمِعُونَ الذِّكْرَ. وَمَثَلُ الْمُهَجِّرِ كَمَثَلِ الَّذِي يُهْدِي الْبَدَنَةَ، ثُمَّ كَالَّذِي يُهْدِي بَقَرَةً، ثُمَّ كَالَّذِي يُهْدِي الْكَبْشَ، ثُمَّ كَالَّذِي يُهْدِي الدَّجَاجَةَ، ثُمَّ كَالَّذِي يُهْدِي الْبَيْضَةَ.

i. Related by al-Bukhari, 929 and in a shorter version, 3211; al-Nasāī, 1384.

[000–000]. (Dar al-Salam 1865) Yaḥyā ibn Yaḥyā and ʿAmr al-Nāqid narrated:[i] from Sufyān; from al-Zuhrī; from Saʿīd; from Abu Hurayrah; from the Prophet (peace be upon him): **the same text.**

حَدَّثَنَا يَحْيَى بْنُ يَحْيَى وَعَمْرٌو النَّاقِدُ، عَنْ سُفْيَانَ، عَنِ الزُّهْرِيِّ، عَنْ سَعِيدٍ، عَنْ أَبِي هُرَيْرَةَ، عَنِ النَّبِيِّ صَلَّى اللهُ عَلَيْهِ وَسَلَّمَ بِمِثْلِهِ

[1697–25]. (Dar al-Salam 1866) Qutaybah ibn Saʿīd narrated: Yaʿqūb (meaning Ibn ʿAbd al-Raḥmān) narrated; from Suhayl; from his father; from Abu Hurayrah; that God's Messenger (peace be upon him) said: **'At every door of the mosque stands an angel writing down arrivals in their respective order (giving the example of a camel before giving lesser grades, down to the example of donating an egg). When the imam sits down, the scrolls are folded up and the angels attend the glorification'.**

وَحَدَّثَنَا قُتَيْبَةُ بْنُ سَعِيدٍ، حَدَّثَنَا يَعْقُوبُ، - يَعْنِي ابْنَ عَبْدِ الرَّحْمَنِ - عَنْ سُهَيْلٍ، عَنْ أَبِيهِ، عَنْ أَبِي هُرَيْرَةَ، أَنَّ رَسُولَ اللهِ صَلَّى اللهُ عَلَيْهِ وَسَلَّمَ قَالَ: «عَلَى كُلِّ بَابٍ مِنْ أَبْوَابِ الْـمَسْجِدِ مَلَكٌ يَكْتُبُ الأَوَّلَ فَالأَوَّلَ. مَثَّلَ الْجَزُورَ ثُمَّ نَزَّلَهُمْ حَتَّى صَغَّرَ إِلَى مَثَلِ الْبَيْضَةِ. فَإِذَا جَلَسَ الإِمَامُ طُوِيَتِ الصُّحُفُ وَحَضَرُوا الذِّكْرَ.

Text Explanation

The first hadith has been explained earlier. The word used in the hadith for the one who comes early, *al-muhajjir,* is given different meanings by different scholars, with al-Farrā' and others reported to have said that it means 'one who walks when the sun is high in

i. Related by al-Nasāī, 1385; Ibn Mājah, 1092.

the sky'. The correct view is that in this instance it refers to one who comes to the mosque early.

In hadith No. 1697, the Prophet says: 'When the imam sits down, the scrolls are folded up'. It is mentioned in hadith No. 1680 that 'when the imam comes out the angels will attend, listening to God's glorification'. There is no conflict between these two hadiths. Their apparent meaning is that when the imam comes out, they attend but do not fold up their scrolls. When he sits on the platform, the scrolls are folded up. The hadith shows that it is desirable for the imam to sit down at first until the *adhān* has been called. This is desirable according to al-Shāfiʿī, Mālik and the majority of scholars. Abu Ḥanīfah and one report from Mālik suggest that it is not desirable. The majority of scholars rely on this hadith and many other hadiths in authentic anthologies for the basis of their view. The evidence that makes it clear it is not a duty is the fact that it is not part of the sermon.

CHAPTER 8

LISTENING TO THE SERMON [i.e. *KHUṬBAH*]

[1698–26]. (Dar al-Salam 1867) Umayyah ibn Bisṭām narrated: Yazīd (meaning Ibn Zurayʿ) narrated; Rawḥ narrated; from Suhayl; from his father; from Abu Hurayrah; from the Prophet (peace be upon him). He said: **'Whoever takes a bath then goes to the Friday Prayer and prays whatever he may, then listens until [the imam] finishes his *khuṭbah*, then prays with him, shall have his sins between that and the other Friday forgiven and three days more'.**

حَدَّثَنَا أُمَيَّةُ بْنُ بِسْطَامٍ، حَدَّثَنَا يَزِيدُ، - يَعْنِي ابْنَ زُرَيْعٍ - حَدَّثَنَا رَوْحٌ، عَنْ سُهَيْلٍ، عَنْ أَبِيهِ، عَنْ أَبِي هُرَيْرَةَ، عَنِ النَّبِيِّ صَلَّى اللهُ عَلَيْهِ وَسَلَّمَ قَالَ: «مَنِ اغْتَسَلَ ثُمَّ أَتَى الْجُمُعَةَ فَصَلَّى مَا قُدِّرَ لَهُ، ثُمَّ أَنْصَتَ حَتَّى يَفْرُغَ مِنْ خُطْبَتِهِ ثُمَّ يُصَلِّيَ مَعَهُ، غُفِرَ لَهُ مَا بَيْنَهُ وَبَيْنَ الْجُمُعَةِ الأُخْرَى وَفَضْلَ ثَلاَثَةِ أَيَّامٍ.

[1699–27]. (Dar al-Salam 1868) Yaḥyā ibn Yaḥyā, Abu Bakr ibn Abi Shaybah and Abu Kurayb narrated:[i] Abu Muʿāwiyah (Yaḥyā said: 'reported' but the other two said: 'narrated'); from al-Aʿmash; from Abu Ṣāliḥ; from Abu Hurayrah. He said: **'God's Messenger (peace be upon him) said: "Whoever performs the ablution well then goes to the Friday Prayer and**

---

i. Related by Abu Dāwūd, 1050; al-Tirmidhī, 498; Ibn Mājah, 1090.

hearkens and listens in silence, shall have his sins between then and [the other] Friday and three days more forgiven. To play with the pebbles is unacceptable".'

وَحَدَّثَنَا يَحْيَى بْنُ يَحْيَى وَأَبُو بَكْرِ بْنُ أَبِي شَيْبَةَ وَأَبُو كُرَيْبٍ، قَالَ يَحْيَى أَخْبَرَنَا وَقَالَ الآخَرَانِ حَدَّثَنَا أَبُو مُعَاوِيَةَ، عَنِ الأَعْمَشِ، عَنْ أَبِي صَالِحٍ، عَنْ أَبِي هُرَيْرَةَ قَالَ: قَالَ رَسُولُ اللهِ صَلَّى اللهُ عَلَيْهِ وَسَلَّمَ: «مَنْ تَوَضَّأَ فَأَحْسَنَ الْوُضُوءَ، ثُمَّ أَتَى الْجُمُعَةَ فَاسْتَمَعَ وَأَنْصَتَ، غُفِرَ لَهُ مَا بَيْنَهُ وَبَيْنَ الْجُمُعَةِ وَزِيَادَةُ ثَلاثَةِ أَيَّامٍ، وَمَنْ مَسَّ الْحَصَى فَقَدْ لَغَا.

Text Explanation

The first of these hadiths mentions that a person takes a bath before going to Friday Prayer and offers some voluntary prayers, then listens to the *khuṭbah* and prays with the imam. This person will then have his sins until the next Friday and three days more forgiven. The other hadith mentions ablution but not taking a bath. This shows that it is desirable, not a duty, to take a bath on Friday. The hadith also stresses performing the ablution well. This means washing every part three times, rubbing the parts one washes for ablution, washing more than the obligatory parts, starting with the right side and doing the recommended parts as well as the obligatory ones.

The hadith also shows that offering some voluntary prayers before the imam comes out on Friday is desirable. This is the view of our school and the majority of scholars. It further shows that voluntary prayers have no limit because the Prophet said: 'and prays whatever he may'. The hadith makes clear that people should listen to the *khuṭbah* in silence. Moreover, ordinary speech after the *khuṭbah* and before starting the prayer is acceptable.

In hadith No. 1699, the Prophet says: 'he hearkens and listens in silence'. These two are different but may occur together. To hearken is to be attentive and listening in silence means keeping quiet and silent. In the Qur'an, the two are mentioned together, as God says:

'When the Qur'an is recited, hearken to it, and listen in silence, so that you may be graced with God's mercy'. (7: 204)

In both hadiths the Prophet mentions that the reward is forgiveness of sins up to the other Friday and three days more. Scholars say that this means rewarding a good deed with ten times its worth. The Friday when these good things are done is considered as a good deed that is rewarded by ten times its worth. Some scholars of our school said that the time between the two Fridays means from the Friday Prayer and its *khuṭbah* up to the same time on the following Friday, so as to complete seven days, with neither addition nor omission, and three days more are added to complete ten days.

Hadith No. 1699 concludes with: 'To play with the pebbles is unacceptable'. This applies to any type of frivolous action during the *khuṭbah*. [The Prophet's mosque was not furnished with carpets. People prayed on the bare ground. Hence, pebbles were there, and they could always be a means of distraction. Hence, the Prophet's order.] This implies that one should pay full attention to the *khuṭbah*.

CHAPTER 9

THE TIME OF FRIDAY PRAYER

[1700–28]. (Dar al-Salam 1869) Abu Bakr ibn Abi Shaybah and Isḥāq ibn Ibrāhīm narrated:[i] Abu Bakr said: Yaḥyā ibn Adam narrated; Ḥasan ibn ʿAyyāsh narrated; from Jaʿfar ibn Muhammad; from his father; from Jābir ibn ʿAbdullāh. He said: **'We used to pray with God's Messenger (peace be upon him), then go back and give our camels rest'. Ḥasan said: 'I said to Jaʿfar: "At what time was this?" He said: "When the sun had started on the decline".'**

وَحَدَّثَنَا أَبُو بَكْرِ بْنُ أَبِي شَيْبَةَ وَإِسْحَاقُ بْنُ إِبْرَاهِيمَ، قَالَ أَبُو بَكْرٍ حَدَّثَنَا يَحْيَى بْنُ آدَمَ حَدَّثَنَا حَسَنُ بْنُ عَيَّاشٍ، عَنْ جَعْفَرِ بْنِ مُحَمَّدٍ، عَنْ أَبِيهِ، عَنْ جَابِرِ بْنِ عَبْدِ اللهِ قَالَ: كُنَّا نُصَلِّي مَعَ رَسُولِ اللهِ صَلَّى اللهُ عَلَيْهِ وَسَلَّمَ ثُمَّ نَرْجِعُ فَنُرِيحُ نَوَاضِحَنَا. قَالَ حَسَنٌ: فَقُلْتُ لِجَعْفَرٍ فِي أَيِّ سَاعَةٍ تِلْكَ؟ قَالَ: زَوَالَ الشَّمْسِ.

[1701–29]. (Dar al-Salam 1870) Al-Qāsim ibn Zakariyyā' narrated to me: Khālid ibn Makhlad narrated [H]. Also, ʿAbdullāh ibn ʿAbd al-Raḥmān al-Dārimī narrated to me; Yaḥyā ibn Ḥassān narrated; both said: Sulaymān ibn Bilāl narrated; from Jaʿfar; from his father; that he asked Jābir ibn ʿAbdullāh: **'At what time did God's Messenger (peace be upon him) pray Friday Prayer?' He said: 'He prayed. Then we went to our camels and gave them rest'.**

i. Related by al-Nasā'ī, 1389.

ʿAbdullāh adds in his narration: **'when the sun began to decline' and meaning camels used for irrigation.**

وَحَدَّثَنِي الْقَاسِمُ بْنُ زَكَرِيَّاءَ، حَدَّثَنَا خَالِدُ بْنُ مَخْلَدٍ، ح. وَحَدَّثَنِي عَبْدُ اللهِ بْنُ عَبْدِ الرَّحْمَنِ الدَّارِمِيُّ، حَدَّثَنَا يَحْيَى بْنُ حَسَّانَ، قَالَا جَمِيعًا: حَدَّثَنَا سُلَيْمَانُ بْنُ بِلَالٍ، عَنْ جَعْفَرٍ، عَنْ أَبِيهِ، أَنَّهُ سَأَلَ جَابِرَ بْنَ عَبْدِ اللهِ: مَتَى كَانَ رَسُولُ اللهِ صَلَّى اللهُ عَلَيْهِ وَسَلَّمَ يُصَلِّي الْجُمُعَةَ؟ قَالَ: كَانَ يُصَلِّي ثُمَّ نَذْهَبُ إِلَى جِمَالِنَا فَنُرِيحُهَا.

زَادَ عَبْدُ اللهِ فِي حَدِيثِهِ حِينَ تَزُولُ الشَّمْسُ. يَعْنِي النَّوَاضِحَ.

[1702–30]. (Dar al-Salam 1871) ʿAbdullāh ibn Maslamah ibn Qaʿnab, Yaḥyā ibn Yaḥyā and ʿAlī ibn Ḥujr narrated:[i] ʿAbd al-ʿAzīz ibn Abi Ḥāzim (Yaḥyā said: 'reported' and the other two said: 'narrated'); from his father; from Sahl. He said: **'We did not take a nap or have lunch until after Friday Prayer'.**

Ibn Ḥujr adds: **'during God's Messenger's lifetime'.**

وَحَدَّثَنَا عَبْدُ اللهِ بْنُ مَسْلَمَةَ بْنِ قَعْنَبٍ وَيَحْيَى بْنُ يَحْيَى وَعَلِيُّ بْنُ حُجْرٍ، قَالَ يَحْيَى أَخْبَرَنَا وَقَالَ الآخَرَانِ حَدَّثَنَا عَبْدُ الْعَزِيزِ بْنُ أَبِي حَازِمٍ، عَنْ أَبِيهِ، عَنْ سَهْلٍ قَالَ: مَا كُنَّا نَقِيلُ وَلَا نَتَغَدَّى إِلَّا بَعْدَ الْجُمُعَةِ.

زَادَ ابْنُ حُجْرٍ: فِي عَهْدِ رَسُولِ اللهِ صَلَّى اللهُ عَلَيْهِ وَسَلَّمَ.

[1703–31]. (Dar al-Salam 1872) Yaḥyā ibn Yaḥyā and Isḥāq ibn Ibrāhīm narrated:[ii] both said: Wakīʿ reported; from Yaʿlā ibn al-Ḥārith al-Muḥāribī; from Iyās ibn Salamah ibn al-Akwaʿ; from

i. Related by al-Bukhari, 939; al-Tirmidhī, 525; Ibn Mājah, 1099.
ii. Related by al-Bukhari in similar wording, 4168; Abu Dāwūd in similar wording, 1085; al-Nasāʾī in similar wording, 1390; Ibn Mājah in similar wording, 1100.

his father. He said: **'We used to pray with God's Messenger (peace be upon him) when the sun had started to decline, then go back seeking the shade'.**

وَحَدَّثَنَا يَحْيَى بْنُ يَحْيَى وَإِسْحَاقُ بْنُ إِبْرَاهِيمَ، قَالا: أَخْبَرَنَا وَكِيعٌ، عَنْ يَعْلَى بْنِ الْحَارِثِ الْمُحَارِبِيِّ، عَنْ إِيَاسِ بْنِ سَلَمَةَ بْنِ الأَكْوَعِ، عَنْ أَبِيهِ قَالَ: كُنَّا نُجَمِّعُ مَعَ رَسُولِ اللهِ صَلَّى اللهُ عَلَيْهِ وَسَلَّمَ إِذَا زَالَتِ الشَّمْسُ ثُمَّ نَرْجِعُ نَتَتَبَّعُ الْفَيْءَ.

[1704–32]. (Dar al-Salam 1873) Isḥāq ibn Ibrāhīm narrated: Hishām ibn ʿAbd al-Malik reported; Yaʿlā ibn al-Ḥārith narrated; from Iyās ibn Salamah ibn al-Akwaʿ; from his father. He said: **'We used to pray Friday Prayers with God's Messenger (peace be upon him) and go back. We could hardly find any shade of the walls to walk in'.**

وَحَدَّثَنَا إِسْحَاقُ بْنُ إِبْرَاهِيمَ، أَخْبَرَنَا هِشَامُ بْنُ عَبْدِ الْمَلِكِ، حَدَّثَنَا يَعْلَى بْنُ الْحَارِثِ، عَنْ إِيَاسِ بْنِ سَلَمَةَ بْنِ الأَكْوَعِ، عَنْ أَبِيهِ قَالَ: كُنَّا نُصَلِّي مَعَ رَسُولِ اللهِ صَلَّى اللهُ عَلَيْهِ وَسَلَّمَ الْجُمُعَةَ فَنَرْجِعُ وَمَا نَجِدُ لِلْحِيطَانِ فَيْئًا نَسْتَظِلُّ بِهِ.

Text Explanation

These hadiths give a clear picture that the Friday Prayer should be offered shortly after its time begins. Mālik, Abu Ḥanīfah, al-Shāfiʿī and the great majority of scholars from the time of the Prophet's Companions and the *tābiʿīn* generation and subsequent generations say that Friday Prayer may not be offered until shortly after midday, when the sun has started on the decline. Only Ahmad ibn Ḥanbal and Isḥāq differ, saying that it may be offered earlier. *Qadi* ʿIyāḍ said: 'Certain statements attributed to the Prophet's Companions are quoted as evidence, but none of these are authentic, except what the majority of scholars say'. The majority understand these hadiths as providing emphasis on the need not to delay Friday Prayer when it becomes due. The Prophet's Companions delayed their midday nap and taking lunch until they had prayed it because they were urged to attend early. They feared that if they were to attend to something else before it, they might miss it or miss being early.

In hadith No. 1703, the Prophet's Companion narrating it says that on their return home, they were seeking the shade. This was due to going early and to the fact that walls were low at the time. The statement means that there was a little shade. In the next hadith, the narrator says: 'We could hardly find any shade to walk in'. This is consistent with the earlier expression as it does not say that there was no shade at all. There was some shade, but not enough to provide them with what is enough to walk in. This, together with the fact that walls were low, clearly suggests that the Friday Prayer started shortly after midday.

In hadith No. 1700, the narrator mentions that they gave their camels rest. He uses a special description of those camels, stating that they were the ones used in providing water. Therefore, they gave them rest for the remainder of the day. According to *Qadi* 'Iyāḍ, the expression used here also admits the explanation that they would take those camels to graze.

CHAPTER 10

THE TWO SPEECHES BEFORE THE PRAYER

[1705–33]. (Dar al-Salam 1874) ʿUbaydullāh ibn ʿUmar al-Qawārīrī and Abu Kāmil al-Jaḥdarī narrated:[i] both from Khālid. Abu Kāmil said: Khālid ibn al-Ḥārith narrated; ʿUbaydullāh narrated; from Nāfiʿ; from Ibn ʿUmar. He said: **'God's Messenger (peace be upon him) used to deliver his speech on Friday standing. He then sat down, then stood up'. He added: 'as people do today'.**

وَحَدَّثَنَا عُبَيْدُ اللهِ بْنُ عُمَرَ الْقَوَارِيرِيُّ وَأَبُو كَامِلٍ الْجَحْدَرِيُّ جَمِيعًا عَنْ خَالِدٍ، قَالَ أَبُو كَامِلٍ حَدَّثَنَا خَالِدُ بْنُ الْحَارِثِ، حَدَّثَنَا عُبَيْدُ اللهِ، عَنْ نَافِعٍ، عَنِ ابْنِ عُمَرَ قَالَ: كَانَ رَسُولُ اللهِ صَلَّى اللهُ عَلَيْهِ وَسَلَّمَ يَخْطُبُ يَوْمَ الْجُمُعَةِ قَائِمًا ثُمَّ يَجْلِسُ ثُمَّ يَقُومُ. قَالَ كَمَا يَفْعَلُونَ الْيَوْمَ.

[1706–34]. (Dar al-Salam 1875) Yaḥyā ibn Yaḥyā, Ḥasan ibn al-Rabīʿ and Abu Bakr ibn Abi Shaybah narrated:[ii] Abu al-Aḥwaṣ (Yaḥyā said: 'reported' and the other two said: 'narrated'); from Simāk; from Jābir ibn Samurah. He said: **'The Prophet used to give two speeches and sit in between them, reciting the Qur'an and reminding people'.**

i. Related by al-Bukhari, 920; al-Tirmidhī, 506.
ii. Related by Abu Dāwūd, 1094.

وَحَدَّثَنَا يَحْيَى بْنُ يَحْيَى وَحَسَنُ بْنُ الرَّبِيعِ وَأَبُو بَكْرِ بْنُ أَبِي شَيْبَةَ، قَالَ يَحْيَى أَخْبَرَنَا وَقَالَ الآخَرَانِ حَدَّثَنَا أَبُو الأَحْوَصِ، عَنْ سِمَاكٍ، عَنْ جَابِرِ بْنِ سَمُرَةَ قَالَ: كَانَتْ لِلنَّبِيِّ صَلَّى اللهُ عَلَيْهِ وَسَلَّمَ خُطْبَتَانِ يَجْلِسُ بَيْنَهُمَا يَقْرَأُ الْقُرْآنَ وَيُذَكِّرُ النَّاسَ.

[1707–35]. (Dar al-Salam 1876) Yaḥyā ibn Yaḥyā narrated:[i] Abu Khaythamah reported; from Simāk; he said: Jābir ibn Samurah told me that **'God's Messenger (peace be upon him) used to give his speech standing, then he would sit down, then stand up and give his address standing. Whoever tells you that he used to deliver his speech seated is telling a lie. By God, I prayed with him more than two thousand prayers'.**

وَحَدَّثَنَا يَحْيَى بْنُ يَحْيَى، أَخْبَرَنَا أَبُو خَيْثَمَةَ، عَنْ سِمَاكٍ، قَالَ أَنْبَأَنِي جَابِرُ بْنُ، سَمُرَةَ أَنَّ رَسُولَ اللهِ صَلَّى اللهُ عَلَيْهِ وَسَلَّمَ كَانَ يَخْطُبُ قَائِمًا ثُمَّ يَجْلِسُ، ثُمَّ يَقُومُ فَيَخْطُبُ قَائِمًا. فَمَنْ نَبَّأَكَ أَنَّهُ كَانَ يَخْطُبُ جَالِسًا فَقَدْ كَذَبَ. فَقَدْ وَاللهِ صَلَّيْتُ مَعَهُ أَكْثَرَ مِنْ أَلْفَيْ صَلاَةٍ.

Text Explanation

The first hadith, No. 1705, mentions that the Prophet delivered his speech standing, sat down and then stood up again to continue his speech. In the next hadith, No. 1706, the Prophet gave two speeches, sitting down in between. The last hadith, No. 1707, emphasises the fact that the Prophet did not deliver his speech seated. This last hadith serves as evidence in support of the view of al-Shāfiʿī and the majority of scholars that the Friday Sermon or *khuṭbah* is not valid unless the speaker stands up, if he is able to, in both parts. Moreover, it is not valid without him sitting in between the two parts, and that Friday Prayer is not valid without two *khuṭbahs*. *Qadi* ʿIyāḍ said that the majority of scholars consider that the two *khuṭbahs* are a condition

i. Related by Abu Dāwūd, 1093.

for the validity of Friday Prayer. According to al-Ḥasan al-Baṣrī and the Ẓāhirī scholars however, as well as Ibn al-Mājashūn's report from Mālik, Friday Prayer is valid without a sermon or *khuṭbah*.

Ibn ʿAbd al-Barr says that scholars are unanimous that the *khuṭbah* must be delivered standing if the imam can stand up. Abu Ḥanīfah said that it is valid if the imam delivers it seated because standing is not a duty. Mālik said that it is a duty, and the imam does badly if he does not stand up but the Friday Prayer remains valid. Abu Ḥanīfah, Mālik and the majority of scholars say that sitting down between the two *khuṭbahs* is neither a duty nor a condition; it is a sunnah, but al-Shāfiʿī considers it a duty and a condition for the validity of the *khuṭbah*. Al-Ṭaḥāwī said that only al-Shāfiʿī expresses this opinion. Al-Shāfiʿī cites as supporting evidence the fact that this is the Prophet's confirmed practice and that he said: 'Pray as you have seen me pray'.

Hadith No. 1706 mentions that the Prophet recited the Qur'an and reminded people of their duties. This serves as evidence in support of al-Shāfiʿī's view that it is a condition that the *khuṭbah* should include admonition and quotations from the Qur'an. Al-Shāfiʿī said that the two *khuṭbahs* are not valid unless they contain praise of God, blessings for the Prophet and admonition of people. These three must be included in both *khuṭbahs*. It is also obligatory that at least one verse of the Qur'an should be recited in one of the two *khuṭbahs* and that supplication for the believers should be included in the second *khuṭbah*. Mālik, Abu Ḥanīfah and the majority of scholars argue that it is sufficient that the *khuṭbah* should be what may rightly be described as a *khuṭbah* or sermon. Abu Ḥanīfah, Abu Yūsuf and one report from Mālik mention that one praise of God, or one glorification, or one phrase stating His Oneness is sufficient. However, this is a flimsy argument because it is not called a sermon and it does not fulfil its purpose. Moreover, it is at variance with what is confirmed to be the Prophet's practice.

Jābir ibn Samurah mentions in the last hadith that he prayed with the Prophet more than 2000 prayers. He means the five obligatory prayers, not 2000 Friday prayers.

CHAPTER 11

DISTRACTION AT THE TIME OF THE *KHUṬBAH*

[1708–36]. (Dar al-Salam 1877) ʿUthmān ibn Abi Shaybah and Isḥāq ibn Ibrāhīm narrated:[i] both from Jarīr. ʿUthmān said: Jarīr narrated; from Ḥuṣayn ibn ʿAbd al-Raḥmān; from Sālim ibn Abi al-Jaʿd; from Jābir ibn ʿAbdullāh; that **'The Prophet was standing, giving his *khuṭbah* on Friday when a caravan arrived from Syria. People flocked to it so that only twelve people remained [in the mosque]. This verse in Surah Friday was revealed: "Yet when people see some trade or entertainment, they head off towards it, leaving you standing there".' (62: 11)**

حَدَّثَنَا عُثْمَانُ بْنُ أَبِي شَيْبَةَ وَإِسْحَاقُ بْنُ إِبْرَاهِيمَ، كِلاَهُمَا عَنْ جَرِيرٍ، قَالَ عُثْمَانُ حَدَّثَنَا جَرِيرٌ، عَنْ حُصَيْنِ بْنِ عَبْدِ الرَّحْمَنِ، عَنْ سَالِمِ بْنِ أَبِي الْجَعْدِ، عَنْ جَابِرِ بْنِ عَبْدِ اللهِ أَنَّ النَّبِيَّ صَلَّى اللهُ عَلَيْهِ وَسَلَّمَ كَانَ يَخْطُبُ قَائِمًا يَوْمَ الْجُمُعَةِ، فَجَاءَتْ عِيرٌ مِنَ الشَّامِ، فَانْفَتَلَ النَّاسُ إِلَيْهَا حَتَّى لَمْ يَبْقَ إِلاَّ اثْنَا عَشَرَ رَجُلاً. فَأُنْزِلَتْ هَذِهِ الآيَةُ الَّتِي فِي الْجُمُعَةِ: «وَإِذَا رَأَوْا تِجَارَةً أَوْ لَهْوًا انْفَضُّوا إِلَيْهَا وَتَرَكُوكَ قَائِمًا».

[1709–000]. (Dar al-Salam 1878) Abu Bakr ibn Abi Shaybah narrated: ʿAbdullāh ibn Idrīs narrated; from Ḥuṣayn; with the same chain of transmission: **the same text, but he said: 'as**

i. Related by al-Bukhari, 936, 2058, 2064 and 4899; al-Tirmidhī, 3311.

God's Messenger (peace be upon him) was speaking' and he did not say 'standing'.

وَحَدَّثَنَاهُ أَبُو بَكْرِ بْنُ أَبِي شَيْبَةَ، حَدَّثَنَا عَبْدُ اللهِ بْنُ إِدْرِيسَ، عَنْ حُصَيْنٍ، بِهَذَا الإِسْنَادِ. قَالَ: وَرَسُولُ اللهِ صَلَّى اللهُ عَلَيْهِ وَسَلَّمَ يَخْطُبُ. وَلَمْ يَقُلْ قَائِمًا.

[1710–37]. (Dar al-Salam 1879) Rifāʿah ibn al-Haytham al-Wāsiṭī narrated: Khālid (meaning al-Ṭaḥḥān) narrated; from Ḥuṣayn; from Sālim and Abu Sufyān; from Jābir ibn ʿAbdullāh. He said: **'We were with the Prophet (peace be upon him) on a Friday when a mini-bazaar arrived. People went out to meet it. Only twelve people, including myself, remained. God then revealed: "Yet when people see some trade or entertainment, they head off towards it, leaving you standing there. Say: 'That which is with God is far better than any entertainment or trade. God is the best of providers'."' (62: 11)**

وَحَدَّثَنَا رِفَاعَةُ بْنُ الْهَيْثَمِ الْوَاسِطِيُّ، حَدَّثَنَا خَالِدٌ، - يَعْنِي الطَّحَّانَ - عَنْ حُصَيْنٍ، عَنْ سَالِمٍ، وَأَبِي، سُفْيَانَ عَنْ جَابِرِ بْنِ عَبْدِ اللهِ، قَالَ كُنَّا مَعَ النَّبِيِّ صَلَّى اللهُ عَلَيْهِ وَسَلَّمَ يَوْمَ الْجُمُعَةِ فَقَدِمَتْ سُوَيْقَةٌ قَالَ فَخَرَجَ النَّاسُ إِلَيْهَا فَلَمْ يَبْقَ إِلاَّ اثْنَا عَشَرَ رَجُلاً أَنَا فِيهِمْ - قَالَ - فَأَنْزَلَ اللهُ: «وَإِذَا رَأَوْا تِجَارَةً أَوْ لَهْوًا انْفَضُّوا إِلَيْهَا وَتَرَكُوكَ قَائِمًا»

[1711–38]. (Dar al-Salam 1880) Ismāʿīl ibn Sālim narrated: Hushaym reported; Ḥuṣayn reported; from Abu Sufyān and Sālim ibn Abi al-Jaʿd from Jābir ibn ʿAbdullāh. He said: **'As the Prophet (peace be upon him) was standing on a Friday, a caravan arrived in Madinah. God's Messenger's Companions rushed to it so that only twelve men remained with him, including Abu Bakr and ʿUmar. Then this verse was revealed: "Yet when people see some trade or entertainment, they head off towards it".'**

وَحَدَّثَنَا إِسْمَاعِيلُ بْنُ سَالِمٍ، أَخْبَرَنَا هُشَيْمٌ، أَخْبَرَنَا حُصَيْنٌ، عَنْ أَبِي سُفْيَانَ وَسَالِمِ بْنِ أَبِي الْجَعْدِ، عَنْ جَابِرِ بْنِ عَبْدِ اللهِ قَالَ: بَيْنَا النَّبِيُّ صَلَّى اللهُ عَلَيْهِ وَسَلَّمَ قَائِمٌ يَوْمَ الْجُمُعَةِ إِذْ قَدِمَتْ عِيرٌ إِلَى الْمَدِينَةِ فَابْتَدَرَهَا أَصْحَابُ رَسُولِ اللهِ صَلَّى اللهُ عَلَيْهِ وَسَلَّمَ حَتَّى لَمْ يَبْقَ مَعَهُ إِلاَّ اثْنَا عَشَرَ رَجُلاً فِيهِمْ أَبُو بَكْرٍ وَعُمَرُ - قَالَ - وَنَزَلَتْ هَذِهِ الآيَةُ: "وَإِذَا رَأَوْا تِجَارَةً أَوْ لَهْوًا انْفَضُّوا إِلَيْهَا وَتَرَكُوكَ قَائِمًا".

[1712–39]. (Dar al-Salam 1881) Muhammad ibn al-Muthannā and Ibn Bashshār narrated:[i] both said: Muhammad ibn Jaʿfar narrated; Shuʿbah narrated; from Manṣūr; from ʿAmr ibn Murrah; from Abu ʿUbaydah; from Kaʿb ibn ʿUjrah. He said: **'He entered the mosque when ʿAbd al-Raḥmān ibn Umm al-Ḥakam was delivering the *khuṭbah* seated. He said: "Look at this wicked man delivering the *khuṭbah* seated. Yet God said: 'Yet when people see some trade or entertainment, they head off towards it, leaving you standing there'."'**

وَحَدَّثَنَا مُحَمَّدُ بْنُ الْمُثَنَّى وَابْنُ بَشَّارٍ قَالاَ: حَدَّثَنَا مُحَمَّدُ بْنُ جَعْفَرٍ، حَدَّثَنَا شُعْبَةُ، عَنْ مَنْصُورٍ، عَنْ عَمْرِو بْنِ مُرَّةَ، عَنْ أَبِي عُبَيْدَةَ، عَنْ كَعْبِ بْنِ عُجْرَةَ: قَالَ دَخَلَ الْمَسْجِدَ وَعَبْدُ الرَّحْمَنِ بْنُ أُمِّ الْحَكَمِ يَخْطُبُ قَاعِدًا فَقَالَ انْظُرُوا إِلَى هَذَا الْخَبِيثِ يَخْطُبُ قَاعِدًا وَقَالَ اللهُ تَعَالَى: "وَإِذَا رَأَوْا تِجَارَةً أَوْ لَهْوًا انْفَضُّوا إِلَيْهَا وَتَرَكُوكَ قَائِمًا"

Text Explanation

These hadiths mention that the Prophet was delivering his *khuṭbah*, or sermon, on Friday when a trade caravan arrived, and people left the mosque to meet the caravan. Most people left, leaving only twelve people with the Prophet, including Abu Bakr, ʿUmar and Jābir. The

i. Related by al-Nasāʾī, 1396.

hadiths show that these three Companions of the Prophet had greater merit. It is clear that the imam should be standing when delivering his *khuṭbah*. Moreover, the hadith provides evidence in support of Mālik's view, accepted by other scholars, that Friday Prayer is valid when twelve people are present. Al-Shāfiʿī's disciples and others sharing their view of the requirement of forty worshippers at Friday Prayer to be valid answer this claim saying that it is understood that the Prophet's Companions, or some of them, returned so as to reconvene the number to forty, and thus the Prophet was able to complete the Friday Prayer with them. In a hadith related by al-Bukhari: 'As we were praying with the Prophet (peace be upon him), a caravan arrived...'. In this hadith, 'praying' means attending the *khuṭbah* and awaiting the prayer, as in these hadiths related by Muslim.

In hadith No. 1710, what arrived is described as a 'mini-bazaar'. This means the same thing as a caravan, for what arrived were traders and their camels carrying food and other merchandise. Abu Dāwūd includes in his *mursal* reports that the sermon that the Prophet's Companions left was after the Friday Prayer and that they thought they incurred no sin by leaving. It is further mentioned that the Prophet used to deliver his speech after the prayer until this event occurred.

Qadi ʿIyāḍ said: 'This is more like the Prophet's Companions. It is unlikely that they would have left prayer with the Prophet (peace be upon him), but they might have thought that no blame would attach to them if they left after the prayer was over. However, some scholars say that the Prophet never delivered the Friday Sermon after the prayer was over'.

In hadith No. 1712, Kaʿb ibn ʿUjrah said: 'Look at this wicked man delivering the *khuṭbah* seated when God has said: "Yet when people see some trade or entertainment, they head off towards it, leaving you standing there".' His words are meant to denounce what is wrong and to correct the behaviour of rulers and governors if they do what is at variance with the Prophet's sunnah. He cites the Qur'anic verse because it states that the Prophet (peace be upon him) used to stand when he delivered his *khuṭbah*, and God says: 'In God's Messenger you have a good model for everyone'. (33: 21) God also commands that we must follow the Prophet's example. He also said: 'Whatever God's Messenger bids you, do it'. The Prophet said: 'Pray as you have seen me pray'.

CHAPTER 12

THE GRAVITY OF NEGLECTING FRIDAY PRAYER

[1713–40]. (Dar al-Salam 1882) al-Ḥasan ibn ʿAlī al-Ḥulwānī narrated to me:[i] Abu Tawbah narrated; Muʿāwiyah (who is Ibn Sallām) narrated; from Zayd (meaning his brother); that he heard Abu Sallām say: al-Ḥakam ibn Mīnā' narrated to me; that ʿAbdullāh ibn ʿUmar and Abu Hurayrah narrated to him; that they heard God's Messenger (peace be upon him) say as he was standing on the steps of his platform: **'Some people shall stop neglecting Friday Prayer or else God will seal their hearts and then they will be among the heedless'.**

وَحَدَّثَنِي الْحَسَنُ بْنُ عَلِيٍّ الْحُلْوَانِيُّ، حَدَّثَنَا أَبُو تَوْبَةَ، حَدَّثَنَا مُعَاوِيَةُ - وَهُوَ ابْنُ سَلاَّمٍ - عَنْ زَيْدٍ، يَعْنِي أَخَاهُ، أَنَّهُ سَمِعَ أَبَا سَلاَّمٍ، قَالَ حَدَّثَنِي الْحَكَمُ بْنُ مِينَاءَ، أَنَّ عبد الله بن عمر وأبا هريرة حَدَّثَاهُ أَنَّهُمَا سَمِعَا رَسُولَ اللهِ صَلَّى اللهُ عَلَيْهِ وَسَلَّمَ يَقُولُ عَلَى أَعْوَادِ مِنْبَرِهِ: «لَيَنْتَهِيَنَّ أَقْوَامٌ عَنْ وَدْعِهِمُ الْجُمُعَاتِ، أَوْ لَيَخْتِمَنَّ اللهُ عَلَى قُلُوبِهِمْ، ثُمَّ لَيَكُونُنَّ مِنَ الْغَافِلِينَ».

Text Explanation

This hadith confirms the desirability of having a platform in the mosque, and this is an agreed sunnah. The hadith also confirms that Friday Prayer is an obligatory duty for all individual adult males.

---

i. Related by al-Nasā'ī, 1369; Ibn Mājah, 794.

'Sealing their hearts' means stamping and covering them. This is like the Qur'anic verse that says: 'God has sealed their hearts'. (2: 7) This is similar to *rayn*, which is mentioned in Surah 83. Scholars say that casting *rayn* is less than sealing, and sealing is less than total closure, which is the worst degree.

Qadi 'Iyāḍ said: 'Scholars of theology differ a great deal on what this means. Some say that it means denial of kindness and other goodness. Others said that it means the creation of disbelief in their hearts. This is agreed by the majority of Sunni theologians. Others still say that it is a testimony against them. Some scholars said that it is a mark God places in their hearts so that angels will be able to recognise who is to be praised and who is not.'

CHAPTER 13

A LIGHT PRAYER AND A SHORT *KHUṬBAH*

[1714–41]. (Dar al-Salam 1883) Ḥasan ibn al-Rabīʿ and Abu Bakr ibn Abi Shaybah narrated:[i] both said: Abu al-Aḥwaṣ narrated; from Simāk; from Jābir ibn Samurah. He said: **'I used to pray with God's Messenger (peace be upon him). His prayer was moderate, and his sermon was of moderate length'.**

حَدَّثَنَا حَسَنُ بْنُ الرَّبِيعِ وَأَبُو بَكْرِ بْنُ أَبِي شَيْبَةَ قَالاَ: حَدَّثَنَا أَبُو الأَحْوَصِ، عَنْ سِمَاكٍ، عَنْ جَابِرِ بْنِ سَمُرَةَ قَالَ: كُنْتُ أُصَلِّي مَعَ رَسُولِ اللهِ صَلَّى اللهُ عَلَيْهِ وَسَلَّمَ فَكَانَتْ صَلاَتُهُ قَصْدًا وَخُطْبَتُهُ قَصْدًا.

[1715–42]. (Dar al-Salam 1884) Abu Bakr ibn Abi Shaybah and Ibn Numayr narrated: both said: Muhammad ibn Bishr narrated; Zakariyyā' narrated; Simāk ibn Ḥarb narrated to me; from Jābir ibn Samurah. He said: **'I used to pray many prayers with the Prophet (peace be upon him). His prayer was moderate, and his sermon was of moderate length'.**

In Abu Bakr's narration: **'Zakariyyā' from Simāk'.**

i. Related by al-Tirmidhī, 507; al-Nasā'ī, 1581.

وَحَدَّثَنَا أَبُو بَكْرِ بْنُ أَبِي شَيْبَةَ وَابْنُ نُمَيْرٍ قَالَا: حَدَّثَنَا مُحَمَّدُ بْنُ بِشْرٍ، حَدَّثَنَا زَكَرِيَّاءُ، حَدَّثَنِي سِمَاكُ بْنُ حَرْبٍ، عَنْ جَابِرِ بْنِ سَمُرَةَ قَالَ: كُنْتُ أُصَلِّي مَعَ النَّبِيِّ صَلَّى اللهُ عَلَيْهِ وَسَلَّمَ الصَّلَوَاتِ فَكَانَتْ صَلَاتُهُ قَصْدًا وَخُطْبَتُهُ قَصْدًا.

وَفِي رِوَايَةِ أَبِي بَكْرٍ زَكَرِيَّاءُ عَنْ سِمَاكٍ.

[1716–43]. (Dar al-Salam 1885) Muhammad ibn al-Muthannā narrated to me:[i] ʿAbd al-Wahhāb ibn ʿAbd al-Majīd narrated; from Jaʿfar ibn Muhammad; from his father; from Jābir ibn ʿAbdullāh. He said: **'When God's Messenger (peace be upon him) gave a *khuṭbah* his eyes became red, his voice was louder and he was more angry so that he became like a herald warning his people, saying that an army was about to raid you in the morning or evening. He would say: "I have been sent at a time which is as close to the Last Hour as these two", showing his index and middle fingers. He would also say: "Meanwhile, the best of discourse is God's Book, and the best guidance is Muhammad's. The worst of matters are new inventions, and every deviation is errant". He would then say: "I have more claim on every believer than his own soul. Whoever leaves behind some property, it belongs to his family, but whoever leaves unpaid debt or young children, that belongs to me".'**

وَحَدَّثَنِي مُحَمَّدُ بْنُ الْمُثَنَّى، حَدَّثَنَا عَبْدُ الْوَهَّابِ بْنُ عَبْدِ الْمَجِيدِ، عَنْ جَعْفَرِ بْنِ مُحَمَّدٍ، عَنْ أَبِيهِ، عَنْ جَابِرِ بْنِ عَبْدِ اللهِ قَالَ: كَانَ رَسُولُ اللهِ صَلَّى اللهُ عَلَيْهِ وَسَلَّمَ إِذَا خَطَبَ احْمَرَّتْ عَيْنَاهُ، وَعَلَا صَوْتُهُ، وَاشْتَدَّ غَضَبُهُ، حَتَّى كَأَنَّهُ مُنْذِرُ جَيْشٍ يَقُولُ: «صَبَّحَكُمْ وَمَسَّاكُمْ». وَيَقُولُ: «بُعِثْتُ أَنَا وَالسَّاعَةَ كَهَاتَيْنِ». وَيَقْرُنُ بَيْنَ إِصْبَعَيْهِ

i. Related by al-Nasāʾī in similar wording, 1577; Ibn Mājah, 45.

السَّبَّابَةِ وَالْوُسْطَى وَيَقُولُ: «أَمَّا بَعْدُ فَإِنَّ خَيْرَ الْحَدِيثِ كِتَابُ اللهِ، وَخَيْرُ الْهُدَى هُدَى مُحَمَّدٍ، وَشَرُّ الأُمُورِ مُحْدَثَاتُهَا، وَكُلُّ بِدْعَةٍ ضَلاَلَةٌ». ثُمَّ يَقُولُ: «أَنَا أَوْلَى بِكُلِّ مُؤْمِنٍ مِنْ نَفْسِهِ. مَنْ تَرَكَ مَالاً فَلأَهْلِهِ، وَمَنْ تَرَكَ دَيْنًا أَوْ ضَيَاعًا فَإِلَيَّ وَعَلَيَّ».

[1717–44]. (Dar al-Salam 1886) ʿAbd ibn Ḥumayd narrated: Khālid ibn Makhlad narrated; Sulaymān ibn Bilāl narrated to me; Jaʿfar ibn Muhammad narrated to me; from his father; he said: I heard Jābir ibn ʿAbdullāh say: **'The Prophet's *khuṭbah* on Friday started by extolling God's praises. He would say after that in a loud voice…'. He adds the same text.**

وَحَدَّثَنَا عَبْدُ بْنُ حُمَيْدٍ، حَدَّثَنَا خَالِدُ بْنُ مَخْلَدٍ، حَدَّثَنِي سُلَيْمَانُ بْنُ بِلاَلٍ، حَدَّثَنِي جَعْفَرُ بْنُ مُحَمَّدٍ، عَنْ أَبِيهِ قَالَ: سَمِعْتُ جَابِرَ بْنَ عَبْدِ اللهِ يَقُولُ: كَانَتْ خُطْبَةُ النَّبِيِّ صَلَّى اللهُ عَلَيْهِ وَسَلَّمَ يَوْمَ الْجُمُعَةِ: يَحْمَدُ اللهَ وَيُثْنِي عَلَيْهِ، ثُمَّ يَقُولُ عَلَى إِثْرِ ذَلِكَ وَقَدْ عَلاَ صَوْتُه. ثُمَّ سَاقَ الْحَدِيثَ بِمِثْلِهِ.

[1718–45]. (Dar al-Salam 1887) Abu Bakr ibn Abi Shaybah narrated: Wakīʿ narrated; from Sufyān; from Jaʿfar, from his father; from Jābir. He said: **'God's Messenger (peace be upon him) would address the people. He would praise God and extol His fine attributes as is suitable to Him. He would then say: "Whoever God guides none can lead astray, and whomever He leaves to stray shall have no guide. The best discourse is God's Book".' He then narrated the hadith in the same text as narrated by al-Thaqafī.**

وَحَدَّثَنَا أَبُو بَكْرِ بْنُ أَبِي شَيْبَةَ، حَدَّثَنَا وَكِيعٌ، عَنْ سُفْيَانَ، عَنْ جَعْفَرٍ، عَنْ أَبِيهِ، عَنْ جَابِرٍ قَالَ: كَانَ رَسُولُ اللهِ صَلَّى اللهُ عَلَيْهِ وَسَلَّمَ يَخْطُبُ النَّاسَ: يَحْمَدُ اللهَ وَيُثْنِي عَلَيْهِ بِمَا هُوَ أَهْلُهُ، ثُمَّ يَقُولُ: «مَنْ يَهْدِهِ اللهُ فَلاَ مُضِلَّ لَهُ وَمَنْ يُضْلِلْ فَلاَ هَادِيَ لَهُ. وَخَيْرُ الْحَدِيثِ كِتَابُ اللهِ». ثُمَّ سَاقَ الْحَدِيثَ بِمِثْلِ حَدِيثِ الثَّقَفِيِّ.

[1719–46]. (Dar al-Salam 1888) Isḥāq ibn Ibrāhīm and Muhammad ibn al-Muthannā narrated:[i] both from ʿAbd al-Aʿlā; Ibn al-Muthannā said: ʿAbd al-Aʿlā (who is Abu Hammām) narrated to me; Dāwūd narrated; from ʿAmr ibn Saʿīd; from Saʿīd ibn Jubayr; from Ibn ʿAbbās that **'Ḍimād, who was from the [Yemeni tribe of] Azd Shanū'ah, arrived in Makkah. He was a faith healer who treated people with madness. He heard some idiots in Makkah saying that Muhammad was a madman and thought: "Perhaps if I see this man, God may cure him through me". He met the Prophet and said: "Muhammad, I am a faith healer and God cures through me whomever He wills. Would you like to try?"**

The Prophet said to him: "All praise belongs to God. We praise Him and seek His support. Whoever God guides no one can lead astray and whoever He leaves to go astray shall have none to guide him. I bear witness that there is no deity other than God, the One who has no partners, and that Muhammad is God's servant and messenger." Meanwhile Ḍimād said: "Repeat what you have just said". The Prophet repeated his words three times. Ḍimād said: "I have heard what monks, sorcerers and poets say, but I have never heard anything like these words of yours. Your words go far to reach the height and depth of the sea. Give me your hand so that I can pledge you my allegiance as a Muslim". The Prophet accepted his pledge and then said to him: "And for your people?" Ḍimād said: "And for my people".

[Some time later] the Prophet sent an expedition and they passed by his people. The commander said to his troops: "Have you taken anything from these people?" One man

---

i. Related by al-Nasāʾī in a shorter version, 3278; Ibn Mājah in a shorter version, 1893.

said: "I have taken a bucket." He said: "Give it back. These are Ḍimād's people".'

وَحَدَّثَنَا إِسْحَاقُ بْنُ إِبْرَاهِيمَ وَمُحَمَّدُ بْنُ الْـمُثَنَّى، كِلاَهُمَا عَنْ عَبْدِ الأَعْلَى، - قَالَ ابْنُ الْـمُثَنَّى حَدَّثَنِي عَبْدُ الأَعْلَى، وَهُوَ أَبُو هَمَّامٍ - حَدَّثَنَا دَاوُدُ، عَنْ عَمْرِو بْنِ سَعِيدٍ، عَنْ سَعِيدِ بْنِ جُبَيْرٍ، عَنِ ابْنِ عَبَّاسٍ، أَنَّ ضِمَادًا، قَدِمَ مَكَّةَ وَكَانَ مِنْ أَزْدِ شَنُوءَةَ وَكَانَ يَرْقِي مِنْ هَذِهِ الرِّيحِ. فَسَمِعَ سُفَهَاءَ مِنْ أَهْلِ مَكَّةَ يَقُولُونَ إِنَّ مُحَمَّدًا مَجْنُونٌ. فَقَالَ لَوْ أَنِّي رَأَيْتُ هَذَا الرَّجُلَ لَعَلَّ اللهَ يَشْفِيهِ عَلَى يَدَيَّ. قَالَ: فَلَقِيَهُ، فَقَالَ يَا مُحَمَّدُ إِنِّي أَرْقِي مِنْ هَذِهِ الرِّيحِ، وَإِنَّ اللهَ يَشْفِي عَلَى يَدِي مَنْ شَاءَ، فَهَلْ لَكَ؟

فَقَالَ رَسُولُ اللهِ صَلَّى اللهُ عَلَيْهِ وَسَلَّمَ: «إِنَّ الْحَمْدَ للهِ نَحْمَدُهُ وَنَسْتَعِينُهُ. مَنْ يَهْدِهِ اللهُ فَلاَ مُضِلَّ لَهُ، وَمَنْ يُضْلِلْ فَلاَ هَادِيَ لَهُ، وَأَشْهَدُ أَنْ لاَ إِلَهَ إِلاَّ اللهُ وَحْدَهُ لاَ شَرِيكَ لَهُ، وَأَنَّ مُحَمَّدًا عَبْدُهُ وَرَسُولُهُ، أَمَّا بَعْدُ». قَالَ: فَقَالَ أَعِدْ عَلَيَّ كَلِمَاتِكَ هَؤُلاَءِ. فَأَعَادَهُنَّ عَلَيْهِ رَسُولُ اللهِ صَلَّى اللهُ عَلَيْهِ وَسَلَّمَ ثَلاَثَ مَرَّاتٍ. قَالَ: فَقَالَ لَقَدْ سَمِعْتُ قَوْلَ الْكَهَنَةِ، وَقَوْلَ السَّحَرَةِ، وَقَوْلَ الشُّعَرَاءِ فَمَا سَمِعْتُ مِثْلَ كَلِمَاتِكَ هَؤُلاَءِ وَلَقَدْ بَلَغْنَ نَاعُوسَ الْبَحْرِ. قَال: فَقَالَ هَاتِ يَدَكَ أُبَايِعْكَ عَلَى الإِسْلاَمِ. قَالَ: فَبَايَعَه. فَقَالَ رَسُولُ اللهِ صَلَّى اللهُ عَلَيْهِ وَسَلَّمَ «وَعَلَى قَوْمِكَ »؟ قال: وعلى قومي.

قَالَ: فَبَعَثَ رَسُولُ اللهِ صَلَّى اللهُ عَلَيْهِ وَسَلَّمَ سَرِيَّةً فَمَرُّوا بِقَوْمِهِ فَقَالَ صَاحِبُ السَّرِيَّةِ لِلْجَيْشِ هَلْ أَصَبْتُمْ مِنْ هَؤُلاَءِ شَيْئًا فَقَالَ رَجُلٌ مِنَ الْقَوْمِ أَصَبْتُ مِنْهُمْ مِطْهَرَةً . فَقَالَ رُدُّوهَا فَإِنَّ هَؤُلاَءِ قَوْمُ ضِمَادٍ

[1720–47]. (Dar al-Salam 1889) Surayj ibn Yūnus narrated to me: ʿAbd al-Raḥmān ibn ʿAbd al-Malik ibn Abjar; from his father; from Wāṣil ibn Ḥayyān; he said: Abu Wā'il said: **'ʿAmmār addressed us but kept his speech short and full of meaning. When he came down, we said: "Abu al-Yaqẓān, you have given us rich meanings but kept it short. Would it not**

have been better to be more relaxed?" He said: "I heard God's Messenger (peace be upon him) say: 'To make one's prayer long and one's *khuṭbah* short are marks of one's knowledge. Prolong your prayers and keep your *khuṭbah* short. Some fine speech is like magic'."

حَدَّثَنِي سُرَيْجُ بْنُ يُونُسَ، حَدَّثَنَا عَبْدُ الرَّحْمَنِ بْنُ عَبْدِ الْمَلِكِ بْنِ أَبْجَرَ، عَنْ أَبِيهِ، عَنْ وَاصِلِ بْنِ حَيَّانَ قَالَ: قَالَ أَبُو وَائِلٍ: خَطَبَنَا عَمَّارٌ، فَأَوْجَزَ وَأَبْلَغَ. فَلَمَّا نَزَلَ قُلْنَا: يَا أَبَا الْيَقْظَانِ لَقَدْ أَبْلَغْتَ وَأَوْجَزْتَ، فَلَوْ كُنْتَ تَنَفَّسْتَ. فَقَالَ: إِنِّي سَمِعْتُ رَسُولَ اللهِ صَلَّى اللهُ عَلَيْهِ وَسَلَّمَ يَقُولُ: «إِنَّ طُولَ صَلاَةِ الرَّجُلِ وَقِصَرَ خُطْبَتِهِ مَئِنَّةٌ مِنْ فِقْهِهِ، فَأَطِيلُوا الصَّلاَةَ، وَاقْصُرُوا الْخُطْبَةَ. وَإِنَّ مِنَ الْبَيَانِ سِحْرًا».

[1721–48]. (Dar al-Salam 1890) Abu Bakr ibn Abi Shaybah and Muhammad ibn ʿAbdullāh ibn Numayr narrated:[i] both said: Wakīʿ narrated; from Sufyān; from ʿAbd al-ʿAzīz ibn Rufayʿ; from Tamīm ibn Ṭarafah; from ʿAdiy ibn Ḥātim; that **a man made a speech in the presence of the Prophet (peace be upon him). He said: 'Whoever obeys God and His Messenger is well guided, and whoever disobeys them goes astray'. The Prophet said: 'What a bad speaker you are! Say: "whoever disobeys God and His Messenger".'**

حَدَّثَنَا أَبُو بَكْرِ بْنُ أَبِي شَيْبَةَ وَمُحَمَّدُ بْنُ عَبْدِ اللهِ بْنِ نُمَيْرٍ، قَالاَ: حَدَّثَنَا وَكِيعٌ، عَنْ سُفْيَانَ، عَنْ عَبْدِ الْعَزِيزِ بْنِ رُفَيْعٍ، عَنْ تَمِيمِ بْنِ طَرَفَةَ، عَنْ عَدِيِّ بْنِ حَاتِمٍ، أَنَّ رَجُلاً خَطَبَ عِنْدَ النَّبِيِّ صَلَّى اللهُ عَلَيْهِ وَسَلَّمَ فَقَالَ: مَنْ يُطِعِ اللهَ وَرَسُولَهُ فَقَدْ رَشِدَ وَمَنْ يَعْصِهِمَا فَقَدْ غَوَى. فَقَالَ رَسُولُ اللهِ صَلَّى اللهُ عَلَيْهِ وَسَلَّمَ: «بِئْسَ الْخَطِيبُ أَنْتَ. قُلْ وَمَنْ يَعْصِ اللهَ وَرَسُولَهُ». قَالَ ابْنُ نُمَيْرٍ فَقَدْ غَوِيَ

---

i. Related by Abu Dāwūd, 1099 and 4981; al-Nasāʾī, 3279.

[1722–49]. (Dar al-Salam 1891) Qutaybah ibn Saʿīd, Abu Bakr ibn Abi Shaybah and Isḥāq al-Ḥanẓalī narrated:[i] all from Ibn ʿUyaynah; Qutaybah said: Sufyān narrated; from ʿAmr; that he heard ʿAṭā' reports; from Ṣafwān ibn Yaʿlā; from his father; that he heard **'the Prophet (peace be upon him) reciting as he was on the platform the Qur'anic verse: "They will cry out: Mālik, if only…".'**

حَدَّثَنَا قُتَيْبَةُ بْنُ سَعِيدٍ وَأَبُو بَكْرِ بْنُ أَبِي شَيْبَةَ وَإِسْحَاقُ الْحَنْظَلِيُّ جَمِيعًا عَنِ ابْنِ عُيَيْنَةَ، قَالَ: قُتَيْبَةُ حَدَّثَنَا سُفْيَانُ، عَنْ عَمْرٍو، سَمِعَ عَطَاءً، يُخْبِرُ عَنْ صَفْوَانَ بْنِ يَعْلَى عَنْ أَبِيهِ، أَنَّهُ سَمِعَ النَّبِيَّ صَلَّى اللهُ عَلَيْهِ وَسَلَّمَ يَقْرَأُ عَلَى الْـمِنْبَرِ "وَنَادَوْا يَا مَالِكُ".

[1723–50]. (Dar al-Salam 1892) ʿAbdullāh ibn ʿAbd al-Raḥmān al-Dārimī narrated:[ii] Yaḥyā ibn Ḥassān reported; Sulymān ibn Bilāl narrated; from Yaḥyā ibn Saʿīd; from ʿAmrah bint ʿAbd al-Raḥmān; from a sister of ʿAmrah. She said: **'I learnt the surah [starting with] "Qaf, by the Glorious Qur'an" from God's Messenger's mouth, on Friday, as he recited it on the platform every Friday'.**

وَحَدَّثَنِي عَبْدُ اللهِ بْنُ عَبْدِ الرَّحْمَنِ الدَّارِمِيُّ، أَخْبَرَنَا يَحْيَى بْنُ حَسَّانَ، حَدَّثَنَا سُلَيْمَانُ بْنُ بِلَالٍ، عَنْ يَحْيَى بْنِ سَعِيدٍ، عَنْ عَمْرَةَ بِنْتِ عَبْدِ الرَّحْمَنِ، عَنْ أُخْتٍ لِعَمْرَةَ قَالَتْ: أَخَذْتُ "ق وَالْقُرْآنِ الْـمَجِيدِ" مِنْ فِي رَسُولِ اللهِ صَلَّى اللهُ عَلَيْهِ وَسَلَّمَ يَوْمَ الْجُمُعَةِ، وَهُوَ يَقْرَأُ بِهَا عَلَى الْـمِنْبَرِ فِي كُلِّ جُمُعَةٍ.

Abu al-Ṭāhir narrated to me: Ibn Wahb reported; from Yaḥyā ibn Ayyūb; from Yaḥyā ibn Saʿīd; from ʿAmrah; from a sister

i. Related by al-Bukhari, 3230, 3266 and 4819; Abu Dāwūd, 3992; al-Tirmidhī, 508; al-Nasā'ī, 1410.

ii. Related by Abu Dāwūd in a longer version, 1100, 1102 and 1103; al-Nasā'ī, 948.

of ʿAmrah bint ʿAbd al-Raḥmān who was older than her: **the same text as Sulaymān ibn Bilāl's narration.**

وَحَدَّثَنِيهِ أَبُو الطَّاهِرِ، أَخْبَرَنَا ابْنُ وَهْبٍ، عَنْ يَحْيَى بْنِ أَيُّوبَ، عَنْ يَحْيَى بْنِ سَعِيدٍ، عَنْ عَمْرَةَ، عَنْ أُخْتٍ لِعَمْرَةَ بِنْتِ عَبْدِ الرَّحْمَنِ كَانَتْ أَكْبَرَ مِنْهَا. بِمِثْلِ حَدِيثِ سُلَيْمَانَ بْنِ بِلَالٍ.

[1724–51]. (Dar al-Salam 1893) Muhammad ibn Bashshār narrated to me: Muhammad ibn Jaʿfar narrated; Shuʿbah narrated; from Khubayb; from ʿAbdullāh ibn Muhammad ibn Maʿn; from a daughter of Ḥārithah ibn al-Nuʿmān. She said: **'I learnt the surah [starting with] Qaf from God's Messenger's own mouth, as he made it his sermon every Friday'. She added: 'Our oven and God's Messenger's oven were [almost] one'.**

حَدَّثَنِي مُحَمَّدُ بْنُ بَشَّارٍ، حَدَّثَنَا مُحَمَّدُ بْنُ جَعْفَرٍ، حَدَّثَنَا شُعْبَةُ، عَنْ خُبَيْبٍ، عَنْ عَبْدِ اللهِ بْنِ مُحَمَّدِ بْنِ مَعْنٍ، عَنْ بِنْتٍ لِحَارِثَةَ بْنِ النُّعْمَانِ، قَالَتْ: مَا حَفِظْتُ «ق» إِلاَّ مِنْ فِي رَسُولِ اللهِ صَلَّى اللهُ عَلَيْهِ وَسَلَّمَ يَخْطُبُ بِهَا كُلَّ جُمُعَةٍ. قَالَتْ: وَكَانَ تَنُّورُنَا وَتَنُّورُ رَسُولِ اللهِ صَلَّى اللهُ عَلَيْهِ وَسَلَّمَ وَاحِدًا.

[1725–52]. (Dar al-Salam 1894) ʿAmr al-Nāqid narrated: Yaʿqūb ibn Ibrāhīm ibn Saʿd narrated; my father narrated; from Muhammad ibn Isḥāq; he said: ʿAbdullāh ibn Abi Bakr ibn Muhammad ibn ʿAmr ibn Ḥazm al-Anṣārī narrated to me; from Yaḥyā ibn ʿAbdullāh ibn ʿAbd al-Raḥmān ibn Saʿd ibn Zurārah; from Umm Hishām bint Ḥārithah ibn al-Nuʿmān. She said: **'Our oven and God's Messenger's oven were [almost] one, for two years or one year and longer, and I only learnt the surah [starting with] "Qaf, by the Glorious Qur'an"**

from God's Messenger's own mouth, as he recited it on the platform every Friday when he delivered his *khuṭbah*'.

وَحَدَّثَنَا عَمْرٌو النَّاقِدُ، حَدَّثَنَا يَعْقُوبُ بْنُ إِبْرَاهِيمَ بْنِ سَعْدٍ، حَدَّثَنَا أَبِي، عَنْ مُحَمَّدِ بْنِ إِسْحَاقَ قَالَ: حَدَّثَنِي عَبْدُ اللهِ بْنُ أَبِي بَكْرِ بْنِ مُحَمَّدِ بْنِ عَمْرِو بْنِ حَزْمٍ الأَنْصَارِيُّ، عَنْ يَحْيَى بْنِ عَبْدِ اللهِ بْنِ عَبْدِ الرَّحْمَنِ بْنِ سَعْدِ بْنِ زُرَارَةَ، عَنْ أُمِّ هِشَامٍ بِنْتِ حَارِثَةَ بْنِ النُّعْمَانِ، قَالَتْ: لَقَدْ كَانَ تَنُّورُنَا وَتَنُّورُ رَسُولِ اللهِ صَلَّى اللهُ عَلَيْهِ وَسَلَّمَ وَاحِدًا سَنَتَيْنِ أَوْ سَنَةً وَبَعْضَ سَنَةٍ وَمَا أَخَذْتُ "ق وَالْقُرْآنِ الْمَجِيدِ" إِلاَّ عَنْ لِسَانِ رَسُولِ اللهِ صَلَّى اللهُ عَلَيْهِ وَسَلَّمَ، يَقْرَؤُهَا كُلَّ يَوْمِ جُمُعَةٍ عَلَى الْمِنْبَرِ إِذَا خَطَبَ النَّاسَ.

[1726–53]. (Dar al-Salam 1895) Abu Bakr ibn Abi Shaybah narrated:[i] ʿAbdullāh ibn Idrīs narrated; from Ḥuṣayn; from ʿUmārah ibn Ru'aybah. He said: **'He saw Bishr ibn Marwān on the platform with both his hands lifted. He said: "Confound these two hands. I saw God's Messenger (peace be upon him) doing no more than pointing with his hand like this", indicating with his forefinger'.**

وَحَدَّثَنَا أَبُو بَكْرِ بْنُ أَبِي شَيْبَةَ، حَدَّثَنَا عَبْدُ اللهِ بْنُ إِدْرِيسَ، عَنْ حُصَيْنٍ، عَنْ عُمَارَةَ بْنِ رُؤَيْبَةَ قَالَ رَأَى بِشْرَ بْنَ مَرْوَانَ عَلَى الْمِنْبَرِ رَافِعًا يَدَيْهِ فَقَالَ: قَبَّحَ اللهُ هَاتَيْنِ الْيَدَيْنِ. لَقَدْ رَأَيْتُ رَسُولَ اللهِ صَلَّى اللهُ عَلَيْهِ وَسَلَّمَ مَا يَزِيدُ عَلَى أَنْ يَقُولَ بِيَدِهِ هَكَذَا. وَأَشَارَ بِإِصْبَعِهِ الْمُسَبِّحَةِ

[1727–000]. (Dar al-Salam 1896) Qutaybah ibn Saʿīd narrated: Abu ʿAwānah narrated; from Ḥuṣayn ibn ʿAbd al-Raḥmān. He said: **'I saw Bishr ibn Marwān on a Friday with his hands lifted.'**

ʿUmārah ibn Ru'aybah said: **a similar text.**

---

i. Related by Abu Dāwūd, 1104; al-Tirmidhī, 515.

وَحَدَّثَنَاهُ قُتَيْبَةُ بْنُ سَعِيدٍ، حَدَّثَنَا أَبُو عَوَانَةَ، عَنْ حُصَيْنِ بْنِ عَبْدِ الرَّحْمَنِ، قَالَ: رَأَيْتُ بِشْرَ بْنَ مَرْوَانَ يَوْمَ جُمُعَةٍ يَرْفَعُ يَدَيْهِ.

فَقَالَ عُمَارَةُ بْنُ رُؤَيْبَةَ. فَذَكَرَ نَحْوَهُ.

Text Explanation

Hadith No. 1714 and 1715 mention that the Prophet's prayer was moderate, and his sermon was of moderate length. This means that they were neither too long nor too short.

In hadith No. 1716, Jābir ibn ʿAbdullāh describes the Prophet's *khuṭbah* as follows: 'When God's Messenger (peace be upon him) gave a *khuṭbah* his eyes became red, his voice was louder and he was more angry so that he became like a herald warning his people, saying that an army was about to raid you in the morning or evening. He would say: "I have been sent at a time which is as close to the Last Hour as these two", showing his index and middle fingers. He would also say: "Meanwhile, the best of discourse is God's Book, and the best guidance is Muhammad's. The worst of matters are new inventions, and every deviation is errant". He would then say: "I have more claim on every believer than his own soul. Whoever leaves behind some property, it belongs to his family, but whoever leaves unpaid debt or young children, that belongs to me".'

This hadith includes several interesting points and important rules. The sentence, 'the best guidance is Muhammad's', may be read in two ways with the Arabic word *huda* meaning 'guidance' also pronounced as *hadi*. The two words are written in the same way when short vowels are not marked as this is very common in Arabic. If it is pronounced *hadi*, it means 'the best way is Muhammad's', and when it is *huda*, it means 'the best guidance is Muhammad's'.

Al-Qadariyyah say that wherever 'guidance' is mentioned, it is merely for explanation. This is based on the erroneous basic premise that denies God's will. Our scholars and other followers of the truth who believe in God's will respond by quoting the Qur'anic verse that differentiates between what God calls on people to do and His guidance: 'God calls to the abode of peace and guides him that wills to a straight path'.

In the same hadith, No. 1716, the Prophet says that 'every deviation is errant'. [Deviation is our translation of the word *bid'ah*[i].] Although this statement is general, it is limited, and it means most types of deviation. Linguists say that *bid'ah* refers to anything that is done without any precedent. Scholars say that *bid'ah* may be divided into five types: a duty, recommended, permissible, discouraged and forbidden. In the first type, which is a duty, we may place the arrangement and classification of arguments and evidence stated by scholars to refute the claims of unbelievers and followers of deviant creeds. Writing books explaining Islamic principles, values and practices is an example of recommended *bid'ah*, as is also building schools and border military bases for defence, etc. Cooking new dishes is an example of permissible *bid'ah*. What is discouraged and what is forbidden are well known. I explained this question with its detailed evidence in *Tahdhīb al-Asmā' wal-Lughāt*.

Bearing this in mind, we understand the earlier statement that this is a general, yet limited, statement. The same may be said about similar hadiths. This is further supported by 'Umar ibn al-Khaṭṭāb when he said after organising the Tarāwīḥ Prayer: 'This is a fine *bid'ah*'. The fact that the Prophet said that 'every deviation is errant' does not preclude the hadith being 'general, yet limited', even though the word 'every' is used. Limitation may apply in this case, as in the Qur'anic verse: 'It is a storm-wind bearing painful suffering which will destroy everything by the command of its Lord'. (46: 24–25)

The Prophet also says in hadith No. 1716: 'I have more claim on every believer than his own soul'. This is consistent with what God says in the Qur'an: 'The Prophet has more claims on the believers than they have on their own selves'. This means that his right precedes

i. *Bid'ah* is often translated as 'innovation', but this gives the wrong sense, because innovation is associated with positive and praiseworthy connotations. In matters of faith and religion, *bid'ah* is unacceptable in most cases.

theirs. Our scholars say: 'Think of a situation like this: if the Prophet needs to take the food that belongs to someone else and that person needs it for himself, the Prophet may take it and the owner must give it to him. Although this is permissible, it did not happen at any time'.

The Prophet adds: 'Whoever leaves behind some property, it belongs to his family, but whoever leaves unpaid debt or young children, that belongs to me'. This is an explanation of the earlier statement: 'I have more claim on every believer than his own soul'. It was the Prophet's practice in the early period that he did not himself offer the funeral prayer for a deceased person who had left behind a debt that could not be repaid from his estate. He did so in order to make it clear to people that they must not be lax about repaying their debts.[i] His refusal to perform the funeral prayer for them served as a strong warning. However, when God gave the Muslim community better means, the Prophet repaid such outstanding debts. Scholars of our school differ on whether the Prophet did this as a duty binding on him, or as a gesture of kindness. They considered the right view to be that it was his duty. They also differed on whether this was one of the special things that applied to the Prophet. Some said that it was a special thing and that it is not a duty of the ruler of the Muslim community to repay such outstanding debts from the state treasury if the deceased's estate cannot repay it and the treasury has ample funds which are not earmarked for something more important.

In the same hadith, No. 1716, the Prophet says: 'I have been sent at a time which is as close to the Last Hour as these two', showing his index and middle fingers. *Qadi* 'Iyāḍ said: 'This may be to show the closeness of these two fingers since there is no other finger in between them, in just the same way that there will be no further prophets between Muhammad and the Day of Judgement. It may also be to show the narrowness of time between himself and the Last

i. It also served as encouragement to the deceased's relatives to repay his debts, in order to secure that the Prophet prays for him. This actually took place on some occasions, with relatives committing themselves to repay the outstanding debt, and the Prophet then led the funeral prayer for their deceased relative.

Hour. Such separation is proportionate to the separation between the two fingers'.

Jābir ibn ʿAbdullāh describes the Prophet's attitude when he delivered his *khuṭbah*: 'When God's Messenger (peace be upon him) gave a *khuṭbah* his eyes became red, his voice was louder and he was more angry so that he became like a herald warning his people, saying that an army was about to raid you'. This suggests that it is desirable for the imam to give due importance to his sermon, speaking aloud and choosing his expressions such that they fit with his subject matter, particularly if it is encouragement or warning. He was perhaps more angry when he warned against something very serious.

The Prophet would also say: 'Meanwhile', which suggests that this is also desirable to say in speeches of admonition, Friday and Eid Prayer *Khuṭbahs*, as well as in books. In his *Ṣaḥīḥ*, al-Bukhari devotes a chapter comprising several hadiths to its desirability. Scholars differ in naming the first person to use it. The names of Prophet David, Yaʿrub ibn Qaḥṭān and Qass ibn Sāʿidah are mentioned in this connection. Some commentators on the Qur'an, or rather many of them, say that it is the 'decisive address' the Qur'an says that God gave to Prophet David. However, meticulous scholars say that this means the 'decisive judgement' between truth and falsehood.

Hadith No. 1717 says: 'The Prophet's *khuṭbah* on Friday started by extolling God's praises. He would say after that…'. This provides evidence in support of al-Shāfiʿī's view that it is obligatory to praise God in the *khuṭbah* and that it must be stated verbally and cannot be replaced by anything else.

Hadith No. 1719 mentions how Ḍimād, who was a faith healer, met the Prophet in Makkah and listened to him. The hadith states that he treated people with madness. Other versions of this hadith mention that he 'treated people affected by the jinn'. When Ḍimād listened to what the Prophet had to say, he asked him to repeat his words three times, then said: 'I have heard what monks, sorcerers and poets say, but I have never heard anything like these words of yours. Your words go far to reach the height and depth of the sea'. The original Arabic expression states that the Prophet's words reached *qāmūs al-baḥr*. We have this expression spelt differently, *nā'ūs al-baḥr*.[i] This second version is not mentioned in *al-Musnad* anthology by Isḥāq ibn Ibrāhīm, from whom Muslim enters this hadith. However, Muslim mentions that he also narrates it from Abu Mūsā Muhammad ibn al-Muthannā. It may be, then, that the word *nā'ūs* occurs in Abu Mūsā's narration. Muslim says: 'I mention such words because a person may seek them but will not find them in any book, and he will be at a loss. If he looks in my book, he will know their origin and meaning'.

In hadith No. 1720, the Prophet says: 'To make one's prayer long and one's *khuṭbah* short are marks of his knowledge. Prolong your prayers and keep your *khuṭbah* short'. This hadith is not in conflict with those well-known hadiths in which the Prophet orders that prayers should be light because the first two hadiths in this chapter mention that 'his prayer was moderate, and his *khuṭbah* was of moderate length'. What the hadith we are discussing now means is that the prayer should be long in comparison to the *khuṭbah*, but not very long so as to be hard for the congregation. When its length is in such proportion, then it is moderate. The *khuṭbah* should also be of moderate length in relation to its purpose.

The Prophet also said in this hadith: 'Some fine speech is like magic'. Abu 'Ubayd said: 'It indicates good understanding and sharp intelligence'. *Qadi* 'Iyāḍ said:

> It allows two meanings: the first is negative because it suggests winning hearts with fine words and attractive meanings. Thus, the one who uses it incurs a sin as serious as for resorting to magic. Hence, Mālik classifies it in *al-Muwaṭṭa'* under the heading of unacceptable speech. This is Mālik's way of understanding this hadith. The other meaning is a praise of such fine speech because God names among His favours that He has bestowed on His servants that He

i. The expression *qāmūs al-baḥr* means the middle and depth of the sea with the word *al-baḥr* referring to the sea. The word *nā'ūs* is a strange one, and perhaps it is no more than a wrong spelling.

> taught them the articulation of thought and speech. The Prophet compares it to magic because minds and hearts love fine speech. The original meaning of the word *siḥr*, which we use to denote magic, is 'to divert'. Fine speech diverts minds, attracting them to what it advocates.

This second meaning explained by *Qadi* ʿIyāḍ is the right meaning.

Hadith No. 1721 mentions that a man gave a speech when the Prophet was present. He said: 'Whoever obeys God and His Messenger is well guided, and whoever disobeys them goes astray'. The Prophet said: 'What a bad speaker you are! Say: whoever disobeys God and His Messenger goes astray'. *Qadi* ʿIyāḍ and a number of scholars said that the Prophet's objection was because the speaker used one pronoun to group him with God, and this presupposes equality. He ordered the speaker to separate him so as to give greater glory to God and to mention His name first. This is rather like another hadith in which the Prophet advises us: 'None of you should say whatever God wills and so-and-so wills. He should say whatever God wills, then what so-and-so wills'.

The correct reason for the Prophet's order is that in a speech one explains one's point in detail and avoids symbolic words and phrases. According to authentic hadiths, when the Prophet said something, he repeated it three times so that it would be well understood. The explanation given by *Qadi* ʿIyāḍ and others seems unsound because the Prophet used this pronoun in authentic hadiths, such as his saying: 'That God and His Messenger should be dearer to one than anyone other than them'. In this case, the Prophet uses the pronoun 'them' because he is not giving a speech of admonition; he is stating a rule. The shorter a rule is the easier it is to memorise. This is not the case with a speech that is intended for admonition, not retention in memory.

This is further confirmed by a hadith related by Abu Dāwūd in his *Sunan* anthology with a reliable chain of transmission going up to Ibn Masʿūd, who said: 'God's Messenger (peace be upon him) taught us the address to be said when appealing to God for some need: "All praise be to God. We seek His help and His forgiveness. We seek His refuge from the evil within us. Whoever God guides none can lead astray and whomever he leaves to go astray shall have no guide. I bear witness that there is no deity other than God and I bear witness that Muhammad is God's servant and messenger. He sent him with the message of the truth, to give happy news and warnings as the Last Hour is drawing close. Whoever obeys God and His Messenger is well guided and whoever disobeys them causes harm only to himself, but causes no harm to God".' But God knows best.

In hadith No. 1722, the narrator says that he heard the Prophet reciting the Qur'anic verse: 'They will cry out, Mālik…'. This hadith refers to reciting the Qur'an during the *khuṭbah,* and this is valid according to all scholars, but they differ as to whether it is obligatory or not. According to our school, the correct view is that it is a duty to include at least one verse of the Qur'an in the *khuṭbah.*

In hadith No. 1724, the narrator says that she only memorised Surah Qaf [which is Surah 50] as she heard God's Messenger (peace be upon him) reciting it in his *khuṭbah* every Friday. Scholars say that the reason for choosing this surah is that it mentions death and resurrection and includes strong admonition and clear prohibition. The hadith provides further evidence confirming the desirability of reciting Qur'anic verses in the *khuṭbah* and the desirability of reciting this surah, or parts of it, in every *khuṭbah*. She says: 'Our oven and God's Messenger's oven were almost one'. This confirms her memorisation and her knowledge of the Prophet's situation as she was his neighbour.

In hadith No. 1726, 'Umārah ibn Ru'aybah comments on seeing Bishr ibn Marwān lifting his hands during the *khuṭbah*. He says that he saw God's Messenger delivering his *khuṭbah* and doing no more than pointing with his forefinger. This hadith makes it clear that it is a sunnah not to lift one's hands during the *khuṭbah*. This is the view of Mālik and our scholars, as well as other scholars. *Qadi* 'Iyāḍ quotes some early and some Mālikī scholars saying that it is permissible because the Prophet lifted his hands when he prayed for rain. The first group respond that his lifting his hands on that occasion was for a specific reason.

Transmission

The chain of transmission of hadith No. 1720 includes: ''Abd al-Raḥmān ibn 'Abd al-Malik ibn Abjar; from his father; from Wāṣil ibn Ḥayyān; he said: Abu Wā'il said'. This chain of transmission is among the ones questioned by al-Dāraquṭnī. He said: 'Only Ibn Abjar reports it from Wāṣil; from Abu Wā'il. Al-A'mash, who is a better reporter of the hadiths narrated by Abu Wā'il, differs with this as he reports the hadith "from Abu Wā'il; from Ibn Mas'ūd".' This is how al-Dāraquṭnī questions the narration. As we stated earlier, such an objection is overruled because Ibn Abjar is a reliable narrator, which means that his reporting is acceptable.

In hadith No. 1723, the chain of transmission includes 'a sister of 'Amrah'. The fact that she is not named does not detract from the authenticity of the hadith because she is a Companion of the Prophet and all his Companions are reliable and unblemished.

The chain of transmission of hadith No. 1724 includes 'Shu'bah narrated from Khubayb'. He is Khubayb ibn 'Abd al-Raḥmān ibn Khubayb ibn Yisāf al-Anṣārī. We mentioned him on several occasions.

One of the narrators included in the chain of transmission of hadith No. 1725 is Yaḥyā ibn 'Abdullāh ibn 'Abd al-Raḥmān ibn Sa'd ibn Zurārah. The name occurs in all manuscripts as Sa'd ibn Zurārah, and this is correct. Similarly, *Qadi* 'Iyāḍ states the name in the same way, as reported by all their scholars, and adds that it is correct. However, some claim that the name is As'ad, but this is wrong. The cause of this error is the reliance on al-Ḥākim Abu 'Abdullāh, Muhammad ibn 'Abdullāh as he says in his book: 'The correct name is As'ad, but some say Sa'd'. He adds that he relies on al-Bukhari. Yet what al-Bukhari mentions in his book *Tārīkh* is the opposite, as he says that 'it is Sa'd, but some say As'ad, which is wrong'. Thus, al-Ḥākim's statement rebounds on him. As'ad ibn Zurārah was the chief of the Khazraj and his brother Sa'd was the grandfather of Yaḥyā and 'Amrah. He was alive when Islam first started, but many do not mention him among the Prophet's Companions because he was noted among the hypocrites.

CHAPTER 14

GREETING THE MOSQUE DURING THE *KHUṬBAH*

[1728–54]. (Dar al-Salam 1897) Abu al-Rabīʿ al-Zahrānī and Qutaybah ibn Saʿīd narrated:[i] both said: Ḥammād (who is Ibn Zayd) narrated; from ʿAmr ibn Dīnār; from Jābir ibn ʿAbdullāh. He said: **'As the Prophet was delivering his *khuṭbah* one Friday, a man came in. The Prophet said: "Have you [naming him] prayed"? The man said: "No". The Prophet said: "Stand up and pray".'**

وَحَدَّثَنَا أَبُو الرَّبِيعِ الزَّهْرَانِيُّ وَقُتَيْبَةُ بْنُ سَعِيدٍ، قَالا: حَدَّثَنَا حَمَّادٌ - وَ هُوَ ابْنُ زَيْدٍ - عَنْ عَمْرِو بْنِ دِينَارٍ، عَنْ جَابِرِ بْنِ عَبْدِ اللهِ قَالَ: بَيْنَا النَّبِيُّ صَلَّى اللهُ عَلَيْهِ وَسَلَّمَ يَخْطُبُ يَوْمَ الْجُمُعَةِ إِذْ جَاءَ رَجُلٌ، فَقَالَ لَهُ النَّبِيُّ صَلَّى اللهُ عَلَيْهِ وَسَلَّمَ: «أَصَلَّيْتَ يَا فُلَانُ؟» قَالَ لا. قَالَ: «قُمْ فَارْكَعْ».

[1729–000]. (Dar al-Salam 1898) Abu Bakr ibn Abi Shaybah and Yaʿqūb al-Dawraqī narrated: from Ibn ʿUlayyah; from Ayyūb; from ʿAmr; from Jābir; from the Prophet (peace be upon him): **the same text as narrated by Ḥammād but did not mention the two *rakʿahs*.**

حَدَّثَنَا أَبُو بَكْرِ بْنُ أَبِي شَيْبَةَ، وَيَعْقُوبُ الدَّوْرَقِيُّ، عَنِ ابْنِ عُلَيَّةَ، عَنْ أَيُّوبَ، عَنْ عَمْرٍو، عَنْ جَابِرٍ، عَنِ النَّبِيِّ صَلَّى اللهُ عَلَيْهِ وَسَلَّمَ: كَمَا قَالَ حَمَّادٌ، وَلَمْ يَذْكُرِ الرَّكْعَتَيْنِ.

---

i. Related by al-Bukhari, 930; Abu Dāwūd, 1115; al-Tirmidhī, 510; al-Nasāʾī, 1408.

[1730–55]. (Dar al-Salam 1899) Qutaybah ibn Saʿīd and Isḥāq ibn Ibrāhīm narrated:[i] Sufyān (Qutaybah said: 'narrated' and Isḥāq said: 'reported'); from ʿAmr; he heard Jābir ibn ʿAbdullāh say: **'A man entered the mosque as God's Messenger (peace be upon him) was delivering the *khuṭbah* one Friday. He said to him: "Have you prayed?" The man said: "No". The Prophet said: "Stand up and pray the two *rakʿahs*".'**

In Qutaybah's version: **'Pray two *rakʿahs*'.**

وَحَدَّثَنَا قُتَيْبَةُ بْنُ سَعِيدٍ وَإِسْحَاقُ بْنُ إِبْرَاهِيمَ، قَالَ قُتَيْبَةُ حَدَّثَنَا وَقَالَ إِسْحَاقُ أَخْبَرَنَا سُفْيَانُ، عَنْ عَمْرٍو، سَمِعَ جَابِرَ بْنَ عَبْدِ اللهِ يَقُولُ: دَخَلَ رَجُلٌ الْـمَسْجِدَ وَرَسُولُ اللهِ صَلَّى اللهُ عَلَيْهِ وَسَلَّمَ يَخْطُبُ يَوْمَ الْجُمُعَةِ، فَقَالَ: «أَصَلَّيْتَ؟» قَالَ لا. قَالَ: «قُمْ فَصَلِّ الرَّكْعَتَيْنِ».

وَفِي رِوَايَةِ قُتَيْبَةَ قَالَ: «صَلِّ رَكْعَتَيْنِ».

[1731–56]. (Dar al-Salam 1900) Muhammad ibn Rāfiʿ and ʿAbd ibn Ḥumayd narrated to me:[ii] Ibn Rāfiʿ said: ʿAbd al-Razzāq narrated; Ibn Jurayj reported; ʿAmr ibn Dīnār reported to me; that he heard Jābir ibn ʿAbdullāh say: **'A man came in when the Prophet (peace be upon him) was on the platform delivering the *khuṭbah* one Friday. He said to him: "Have you prayed two *rakʿahs*?" The man said: "No". The Prophet said: "Pray".'**

وَحَدَّثَنِي مُحَمَّدُ بْنُ رَافِعٍ وَعَبْدُ بْنُ حُمَيْدٍ، قَالَ ابْنُ رَافِعٍ حَدَّثَنَا عَبْدُ الرَّزَّاقِ، أَخْبَرَنَا ابْنُ جُرَيْجٍ، أَخْبَرَنِي عَمْرُو بْنُ دِينَارٍ، أَنَّهُ سَمِعَ جَابِرَ بْنَ عَبْدِ اللهِ يَقُولُ: جَاءَ رَجُلٌ وَالنَّبِيُّ

---

i. Related by al-Bukhari, 931; Ibn Mājah, 1112.
ii. Related by al-Nasāʾī, 1399.

صَلَّى اللهُ عَلَيْهِ وَسَلَّمَ عَلَى الْـمِنْبَرِ يَوْمَ الْجُمُعَةِ يَخْطُبُ، فَقَالَ لَهُ: «أَرَكَعْتَ رَكْعَتَيْنِ؟» قَالَ: لا. فقال: «اركع».

[1732–57]. (Dar al-Salam 1901) Muhammad ibn Bashshār narrated:[i] Muhammad (who is Ibn Jaʿfar) narrated; Shuʿbah narrated; from ʿAmr; he said: I heard Jābir ibn ʿAbdullāh say that the Prophet (peace be upon him) said in his *khuṭbah*: **'If any of you comes on Friday when the imam has already started, he should pray two *rakʿahs*'.**

حَدَّثَنَا مُحَمَّدُ بْنُ بَشَّارٍ، حَدَّثَنَا مُحَمَّدٌ - وَهُوَ ابْنُ جَعْفَرٍ - حَدَّثَنَا شُعْبَةُ، عَنْ عَمْرٍو قَالَ: سَمِعْتُ جَابِرَ بْنَ عَبْدِ اللهِ أَنَّ النَّبِيَّ صَلَّى اللهُ عَلَيْهِ وَسَلَّمَ خَطَبَ فَقَالَ: «إِذَا جَاءَ أَحَدُكُمْ يَوْمَ الْجُمُعَةِ وَقَدْ خَرَجَ الإِمَامُ فَلْيُصَلِّ رَكْعَتَيْنِ».

[1733–58]. (Dar al-Salam 1902) Qutaybah ibn Saʿīd narrated: Layth narrated [H]. Also, Muhammad ibn Rumḥ narrated; al-Layth reported; from Abu al-Zubayr; from Jābir. He said: **'Sulayk al-Ghaṭafānī came on Friday when God's Messenger (peace be upon him) was seated on the platform. Sulayk sat down before praying. The Prophet said to him: "Have you prayed two *rakʿahs*?" He said: "No". He said: "Stand up and offer them".'**

وَحَدَّثَنَا قُتَيْبَةُ بْنُ سَعِيدٍ، حَدَّثَنَا لَيْثٌ، ح. وَحَدَّثَنَا مُحَمَّدُ بْنُ رُمْحٍ، أَخْبَرَنَا اللَّيْثُ، عَنْ أَبِي الزُّبَيْرِ، عَنْ جَابِرٍ أَنَّهُ قَالَ: جَاءَ سُلَيْكٌ الْغَطَفَانِيُّ يَوْمَ الْجُمُعَةِ وَرَسُولُ اللهِ صَلَّى اللهُ عَلَيْهِ وَسَلَّمَ قَاعِدٌ عَلَى الْـمِنْبَرِ، فَقَعَدَ سُلَيْكٌ قَبْلَ أَنْ يُصَلِّيَ، فَقَالَ لَهُ النَّبِيُّ صَلَّى اللهُ عَلَيْهِ وَسَلَّمَ: «أَرَكَعْتَ رَكْعَتَيْنِ؟» قَالَ لا. قَالَ: «قُمْ فَارْكَعْهُمَا».

---

i. Related by al-Bukhari, 1166; al-Nasāʾī, 1394.

[1734–59]. (Dar al-Salam 1903) Isḥāq ibn Ibrāhīm and ʿAlī ibn Khashram narrated:[i] both from ʿĪsā ibn Yūnus. Ibn Khashram said: ʿĪsā reported; from al-Aʿmash; from Abu Sufyān; from Jābir ibn ʿAbdullāh. He said: **'As God's Messenger (peace be upon him) was delivering his *khuṭbah* one Friday, Sulayk al-Ghaṭafānī came in and sat down. He said to him: "Sulayk, stand up and pray two *rakʿahs,* and make them light". He then said: "If any of you comes in on Friday when the imam is delivering his sermon, let him pray two *rakʿahs* making them light".'**

وَحَدَّثَنَا إِسْحَاقُ بْنُ إِبْرَاهِيمَ وَعَلِيُّ بْنُ خَشْرَمٍ، كِلاهُمَا عَنْ عِيسَى بْنِ يُونُسَ، - قَالَ ابْنُ خَشْرَمٍ أَخْبَرَنَا عِيسَى - عَنِ الأَعْمَشِ، عَنْ أَبِي سُفْيَانَ، عَنْ جَابِرِ بْنِ عَبْدِ اللهِ قَالَ: جَاءَ سُلَيْكٌ الْغَطَفَانِيُّ يَوْمَ الْجُمُعَةِ وَرَسُولُ اللهِ صَلَّى اللهُ عَلَيْهِ وَسَلَّمَ يَخْطُبُ، فَجَلَسَ فَقَالَ لَهُ: «يَا سُلَيْكُ قُمْ فَارْكَعْ رَكْعَتَيْنِ، وَتَجَوَّزْ فِيهِمَا». ثُمَّ قَالَ: «إِذَا جَاءَ أَحَدُكُمْ يَوْمَ الْجُمُعَةِ وَالإِمَامُ يَخْطُبُ فَلْيَرْكَعْ رَكْعَتَيْنِ وَلْيَتَجَوَّزْ فِيهِمَا».

Text Explanation

All these hadiths are clear in their import, providing evidence supporting the view of al-Shāfiʿī, Ahmad, Isḥāq and scholars of Hadith and Fiqh that if a person comes into the mosque on Friday when the imam is delivering the *khuṭbah,* it is desirable for him to offer a prayer of two *rakʿahs* in greeting to the mosque. He is discouraged from sitting down before praying these two *rakʿahs*. It is further desirable that he should make them light so as to listen to the *khuṭbah* after he finishes. The same view is reported to have been expressed by al-Ḥasan al-Baṣrī and other early scholars.

Qadi ʿIyāḍ said: 'Mālik, al-Layth, Abu Ḥanīfah, al-Thawrī and the majority of early scholars among the Prophet's Companions and the

---

i. Related by Abu Dāwūd in a shorter version, 1116; Ibn Mājah, 1114.

tābiʿīn said that a latecomer should not pray these two *rakʿahs*. This view is also reported to have been expressed by ʿUmar, ʿUthmān and ʿAlī. Their argument is based on the command to listen to the imam. They understand these hadiths as meaning that the man was thinly clad. Therefore, the Prophet ordered him to stand so that people would see his condition and give him some charity'. This interpretation of the hadiths is wrong as it is refuted by the clear meaning of the Prophet's order: 'If any of you comes in on Friday when the imam is delivering his sermon, let him pray two *rakʿahs* making them light'. This is a clear statement that admits no different interpretation. I do not think that a scholar who learns this statement correctly will do anything other than what it says.

These hadiths also show that ordinary speech during the *khuṭbah* is permissible if needed and that it is permissible for the imam and others. They also include enjoining what is right and pointing out what is beneficial in all situations and at all places. They further explain that the greeting of the mosque is a prayer of two *rakʿahs* and that sunnah prayers during the day are offered in two *rakʿahs* at a time. The mosque greeting does not lapse when a person sits down, if that person is unaware of the relevant ruling. Our scholars say that the general ruling is that it lapses, but this is understood to refer to people who are aware that it is a sunnah. A person who is unaware of its ruling may do it shortly after learning the ruling, as it is clear in this hadith.

We may deduce from these hadiths that the prayer of mosque greeting is not abandoned if one enters the mosque at a time when prayer is discouraged. It is dependent on a reason and, therefore, when the reason occurs, it becomes permissible at any time. The same thus applies to all prayers that are dependent on some reason, such as compensating for an obligatory prayer. Had the prayer of mosque greeting been waived in any situation, this would be the primary reason for waiving it because the latecomer is required to listen to the *khuṭbah*. What these hadiths make clear is that the person needed to offer this prayer in preference to listening to the *khuṭbah* and that the Prophet discontinued his *khuṭbah* to tell him to do so after he had sat down. The man sat down only because he was unaware of the relevant ruling. All this confirms its importance and that it should not be abandoned at any time, but God knows best.

CHAPTER 15

TEACHING DURING THE *KHUṬBAH*

[1735–60]. (Dar al-Salam 1904) Shaybān Farrūkh narrated:[i] Sulaymān ibn al-Mughīrah narrated; Ḥumayd ibn Hilāl narrated; Abu Rifāʿah said: **'I arrived at the Prophet's (peace be upon him) when he was delivering his *khuṭbah*. I said: "Messenger of God! Here is a stranger who has come to ask about his faith. He does not know his faith". God's Messenger (peace be upon him) came towards me, abandoning his *khuṭbah*, and he faced me. He was brought a chair, and I thought that it had iron legs. God's Messenger (peace be upon him) sat on it and taught me some of what God had taught him. He then resumed his *khuṭbah* and completed its remaining part'.**

وَحَدَّثَنَا شَيْبَانُ بْنُ فَرُّوخَ، حَدَّثَنَا سُلَيْمَانُ بْنُ الْمُغِيرَةِ، حَدَّثَنَا حُمَيْدُ بْنُ هِلاَلٍ قَالَ: قَالَ أَبُو رِفَاعَةَ: انْتَهَيْتُ إِلَى النَّبِيِّ صَلَّى اللهُ عَلَيْهِ وَسَلَّمَ وَهُوَ يَخْطُبُ. قَالَ: فَقُلْتُ يَا رَسُولَ اللهِ رَجُلٌ غَرِيبٌ جَاءَ يَسْأَلُ عَنْ دِينِهِ، لاَ يَدْرِي مَا دِينُهُ. قَالَ: فَأَقْبَلَ عَلَيَّ رَسُولُ اللهِ صَلَّى اللهُ عَلَيْهِ وَسَلَّمَ، وَتَرَكَ خُطْبَتَهُ، حَتَّى انْتَهَى إِلَيَّ. فَأُتِيَ بِكُرْسِيٍّ حَسِبْتُ قَوَائِمَهُ حَدِيدًا. قال: فَقَعَدَ عليه رسول الله صَلَّى اللهُ عَلَيْهِ وَسَلَّمَ وَجَعَلَ يُعَلِّمُنِي مِمَّا عَلَّمَهُ اللهُ ثُمَّ أَتَى خُطْبَتَهُ فَأَتَمَّ آخِرَهَا.

i. Related by al-Nasāʾī, 5392.

Text Explanation

The man puts his question in this way: 'Here is a stranger who has come to ask about his faith. He does not know his faith'. This suggests that when a person asks a question of a scholar, it is recommended that he select and use his words politely. The hadith also shows the Prophet's humble approach and his compassion towards his community. It further shows that a person seeking knowledge should be answered without delay and matters should be dealt with in order of importance. Perhaps the man was asking about the basic principles of faith. Scholars agree that a person enquiring about the Islamic faith and how to embrace Islam must be answered immediately and should be taught without delay.

It is possible that the *khuṭbah* the Prophet was delivering was not the Friday Prayer *Khuṭbah*. Hence, the Prophet interrupted it for such a length of time. On the other hand, it might have been the Friday *Khuṭbah* and that he resumed it after speaking to the man. It is also possible that the interruption was not a long one. On the other hand, what the Prophet said to this stranger related to the *khuṭbah* and it thus formed part of it. Nor did the Prophet's walk during the *khuṭbah* affect it.

CHAPTER 16

WHAT TO RECITE IN FRIDAY PRAYER

[1736–61]. (Dar al-Salam 1905) ʿAbdullāh ibn Maslamah ibn Qaʿnab narrated:[i] Sulaymān (who is Ibn Bilāl) narrated; from Jaʿfar; from his father; from Abu Rāfiʿ. He said: **'Marwān appointed Abu Hurayrah as his deputy [as Governor] in Madinah and travelled to Makkah. Abu Hurayrah led us in Friday Prayer. After reciting Surah The Congregation [in the first *rakʿah*] he recited in the last *rakʿah* the surah [starting with] "When the hypocrites come to you". I caught up with Abu Hurayrah when he left and said to him: "You recited two surahs which ʿAlī ibn Abi Ṭālib used to recite in Kufah". Abu Hurayrah said: "I heard God's Messenger (peace be upon him) reciting them on Friday".'**

حَدَّثَنَا عَبْدُ اللهِ بْنُ مَسْلَمَةَ بْنِ قَعْنَبٍ، حَدَّثَنَا سُلَيْمَانُ، - وَهُوَ ابْنُ بِلاَلٍ - عَنْ جَعْفَرٍ، عَنْ أَبِيهِ، عَنِ ابْنِ أَبِي رَافِعٍ، قَالَ اسْتَخْلَفَ مَرْوَانُ أَبَا هُرَيْرَةَ عَلَى الْمَدِينَةِ وَخَرَجَ إِلَى مَكَّةَ. فَصَلَّى لَنَا أَبُو هُرَيْرَةَ الْجُمُعَةَ، فَقَرَأَ بَعْدَ سُورَةِ الْجُمُعَةِ فِي الرَّكْعَةِ الآخِرَةِ «إذا جاءَكَ الْمُنَافِقُونَ». قَالَ - فَأَدْرَكْتُ أَبَا هُرَيْرَةَ حِينَ انْصَرَفَ فَقُلْتُ لَهُ إِنَّكَ قَرَأْتَ بِسُورَتَيْنِ كَانَ عَلِيُّ بْنُ أَبِي طَالِبٍ يَقْرَأُ بِهِمَا بِالْكُوفَةِ. فَقَالَ أَبُو هُرَيْرَةَ: إِنِّي سَمِعْتُ رَسُولَ اللهِ صَلَّى اللهُ عَلَيْهِ وَسَلَّمَ يَقْرَأُ بِهِمَا يَوْمَ الْجُمُعَةِ.

i. Related by Abu Dāwūd, 1124; al-Tirmidhī, 519; Ibn Mājah, 1118.

[1737–000]. (Dar al-Salam 1906) Qutaybah ibn Saʿīd and Abu Bakr ibn Abi Shaybah narrated: both said: Ḥātim ibn Ismāʿīl narrated [H]. Also, Qutaybah narrated; ʿAbd al-ʿAzīz (meaning al-Darāwardī) narrated; both from Jaʿfar; from his father; from ʿUbaydullāh ibn Abi Rāfiʿ. He said: **'Marwān appointed Abu Hurayrah as his deputy...' the same text, except that in Ḥātim's narration: 'He recited the Surah The Congregation in the first *rakʿah* and in the last "When the hypocrites come to you".'**

ʿAbd al-ʿAzīz's narration is the same as that by Sulaymān ibn Bilāl.

وَحَدَّثَنَا قُتَيْبَةُ بْنُ سَعِيدٍ وَأَبُو بَكْرِ بْنُ أَبِي شَيْبَةَ قَالا: حَدَّثَنَا حَاتِمُ بْنُ إِسْمَاعِيلَ، ح. وَحَدَّثَنَا قُتَيْبَةُ، حَدَّثَنَا عَبْدُ الْعَزِيزِ، - يَعْنِي الدَّرَاوَرْدِيَّ - كِلاَهُمَا عَنْ جَعْفَرٍ، عَنْ أَبِيهِ، عَنْ عُبَيْدِ اللهِ بْنِ أَبِي رَافِعٍ قَالَ: اسْتَخْلَفَ مَرْوَانُ أَبَا هُرَيْرَةَ. بِمِثْلِهِ، غَيْرَ أَنَّ فِي رِوَايَةِ حَاتِمٍ: فَقَرَأَ بِسُورَةِ الْجُمُعَةِ فِي السَّجْدَةِ الأُولَى، وَفِي الآخِرَةِ «إِذَا جَاءَكَ الْمُنَافِقُونَ». وَرِوَايَةُ عَبْدِ الْعَزِيزِ مِثْلُ حَدِيثِ سُلَيْمَانَ بْنِ بِلاَلٍ.

[1738–62]. (Dar al-Salam 1907–1908) Yaḥyā ibn Yaḥyā, Abu Bakr ibn Abi Shaybah and Isḥāq narrated:[i] all from Jarīr. Yaḥyā said: Jarīr reported; from Ibrāhīm ibn Muhammad ibn al-Muntashir; from his father; from Ḥabīb ibn Sālim, al-Nuʿmān ibn Bashīr's *mawla*; from al-Nuʿmān ibn Bashīr. He said: **'God's Messenger (peace be upon him) used to recite in both Eid Prayers and Friday Prayer the surahs starting "Extol the limitless glory of the name of your Lord, the Most High" and "Have you heard the story of the Enveloper?".' He added: 'If Eid happens to be on a Friday, he would recite them in both prayers'.**

i. Related by Abu Dāwūd, 1122; al-Tirmidhī, 533; al-Nasā'ī, 1423, 1567 and 1589; Ibn Mājah 1281.

حَدَّثَنَا يَحْيَى بْنُ يَحْيَى وَأَبُو بَكْرِ بْنُ أَبِي شَيْبَةَ وَإِسْحَاقُ جَمِيعًا عَنْ جَرِيرٍ، - قَالَ يَحْيَى أَخْبَرَنَا جَرِيرٌ، عَنْ إِبْرَاهِيمَ بْنِ مُحَمَّدِ بْنِ الْمُنْتَشِرِ، عَنْ أَبِيهِ، عَنْ حَبِيبِ بْنِ سَالِمٍ مَوْلَى النُّعْمَانِ بْنِ بَشِيرٍ، عَنِ النُّعْمَانِ بْنِ بَشِيرٍ قَالَ: كَانَ رَسُولُ اللهِ صَلَّى اللهُ عَلَيْهِ وَسَلَّمَ يَقْرَأُ فِي الْعِيدَيْنِ وَفِي الْجُمُعَةِ بِـ "سَبِّحِ اسْمَ رَبِّكَ الأَعْلَى" وَ "هَلْ أَتَاكَ حَدِيثُ الْغَاشِيَةِ". قَالَ: وَإِذَا اجْتَمَعَ الْعِيدُ وَالْجُمُعَةُ فِي يَوْمٍ وَاحِدٍ يَقْرَأُ بِهِمَا أَيْضًا فِي الصَّلاَتَيْنِ

Qutaybah ibn Saʿīd narrated: Abu ʿAwānah narrated; from Ibrāhīm ibn Muhammad ibn al-Muntashir; with this chain of transmission: **the same text.**

وَحَدَّثَنَاهُ قُتَيْبَةُ بْنُ سَعِيدٍ، حَدَّثَنَا أَبُو عَوَانَةَ، عَنْ إِبْرَاهِيمَ بْنِ مُحَمَّدِ بْنِ الْمُنْتَشِرِ، بِهَذَا الإِسْنَادِ

[1739–63]. (Dar al-Salam 1909) ʿAmr al-Nāqid narrated:[i] Sufyān ibn ʿUyaynah narrated; from Ḍamrah ibn Saʿīd; from ʿUbaydullāh ibn ʿAbdullāh. He said: **'Al-Ḍaḥḥāk ibn Qays wrote to al-Nuʿmān ibn Bashīr asking: "What did God's Messenger recite on Fridays, other than the Surah The Congregation?" He told him: "He recited: 'Have you heard the story [of the Enveloper]'."'**

وَحَدَّثَنَا عَمْرٌو النَّاقِدُ، حَدَّثَنَا سُفْيَانُ بْنُ عُيَيْنَةَ، عَنْ ضَمْرَةَ بْنِ سَعِيدٍ، عَنْ عُبَيْدِ اللهِ بْنِ عَبْدِ اللهِ قَالَ: كَتَبَ الضَّحَّاكُ بْنُ قَيْسٍ إِلَى النُّعْمَانِ بْنِ بَشِيرٍ يَسْأَلُهُ: أَيَّ شَيْءٍ قَرَأَ رَسُولُ اللهِ صَلَّى اللهُ عَلَيْهِ وَسَلَّمَ يَوْمَ الْجُمُعَةِ، سِوَى سُورَةِ الْجُمُعَةِ؟ فَقَالَ: كَانَ يَقْرَأُ: «هَلْ أَتَاكَ».

i. Related by Abu Dāwūd, 1123; al-Nasāʾī in similar wording, 1422; Ibn Mājah, 1119.

Text Explanation

Hadith No. 1736 and 1737 mention that the Prophet recited in Friday Prayer Surah 62, The Congregation, in the first *rak'ah* and Surah 63, The Hypocrites, in the second. This means that it is desirable to recite both surahs in full in Friday Prayer. This is the view of our school and other scholars. Scholars say that the purpose of reciting Surah 62 is that it includes the obligation to perform the Friday Prayer and other rulings concerning it. In addition, it includes several rules and urges reliance on God and glorifying Him at all times, etc. Surah 63 is concerned with the hypocrites, and it is recited in the Friday Prayer as an indirect reproach to those of them who attend the Friday Prayer, urging them to mend their ways in addition to the relevant rules it includes. It was Friday Prayer that hypocrites attended most, in order to show themselves as believers.

The other hadiths mention that the Prophet used to recite Surah 87, the Most High, and Surah 88, the Enveloper, in the Eid and Friday prayers. This makes it clear that it is desirable to recite these two surahs in these prayers. Other hadiths mention that he recited Surah 50, Qaf, and Surah 54, The Moon, on these occasions. All these reports are correct. They mean that at different times, the Prophet recited any of these pairs of surahs.

CHAPTER 17

RECITATION IN PRAYER ON FRIDAY

[1740–64]. (Dar al-Salam 1910–1912) Abu Bakr ibn Abi Shaybah narrated:[i] ʿAbdah ibn Sulaymān narrated; from Sufyān; from Mukhawwal ibn Rāshid; from Muslim al-Baṭīn; from Saʿīd ibn Jubayr; from Ibn ʿAbbās; that **'The Prophet (peace be upon him) used to recite in the Fajr Prayer on Fridays the surah starting with "The revelation of the Book" and the surah starting with "Was there not a period of time". Also, the Prophet used to recite in the Friday Prayer the two surahs: The Congregation and The Hypocrites'.**

حَدَّثَنَا أَبُو بَكْرِ بْنُ أَبِي شَيْبَةَ، حَدَّثَنَا عَبْدَةُ بْنُ سُلَيْمَانَ، عَنْ سُفْيَانَ، عَنْ مُخَوَّلِ بْنِ رَاشِدٍ عَنْ مُسْلِمٍ الْبَطِينِ، عَنْ سَعِيدِ بْنِ جُبَيْرٍ، عَنِ ابْنِ عَبَّاسٍ أَنَّ النَّبِيَّ صَلَّى اللهُ عَلَيْهِ وَسَلَّمَ كَانَ يَقْرَأُ فِي صَلَاةِ الْفَجْرِ يَوْمَ الْجُمُعَةِ "الم تَنْزِيلُ" السَّجْدَةُ وَ "هَلْ أَتَى عَلَى الإِنْسَانِ حِينٌ مِنَ الدَّهْرِ" وَأَنَّ النَّبِيَّ صَلَّى اللهُ عَلَيْهِ وَسَلَّمَ كَانَ يَقْرَأُ فِي صَلَاةِ الْجُمُعَةِ سُورَةَ الْجُمُعَةِ وَالْمُنَافِقِينَ

Ibn Numayr narrated: my father narrated [H]. Also, Abu Kurayb narrated; Wakīʿ narrated; both from Sufyān; with this chain of transmission: **the same text.**

---

i. Related by Abu Dāwūd, 1074 and 1075; al-Tirmidhī, 520; al-Nasāʾī, 955 and 1420; Ibn Mājah, 821.

وَحَدَّثَنَا ابْنُ نُمَيْرٍ، حَدَّثَنَا أَبِي ح، وَحَدَّثَنَا أَبُو كُرَيْبٍ، حَدَّثَنَا وَكِيعٌ، كِلاَهُمَا عَنْ سُفْيَانَ، بِهَذَا الإِسْنَادِ . مِثْلَهُ

Muhammad ibn Bashshār narrated: Muhammad ibn Ja'far narrated; Shu'bah narrated; from Mukhawwal; with this chain of transmission: **the same text. In both prayers, as Sufyān said.**

وَحَدَّثَنَا مُحَمَّدُ بْنُ بَشَّارٍ، حَدَّثَنَا مُحَمَّدُ بْنُ جَعْفَرٍ، حَدَّثَنَا شُعْبَةُ، عَنْ مُخَوَّلٍ، بِهَذَا الإِسْنَاد. مِثْلَهُ فِي الصَّلاَتَيْنِ كِلْتَيْهِمَ . كَمَا قَالَ سُفْيَانُ

[1741–65]. (Dar al-Salam 1913) Zuhayr ibn Ḥarb narrated to me:[i] Wakī' narrated; from Sufyān; from Sa'd ibn Ibrāhīm; from 'Abd al-Raḥmān al-A'raj; from Abu Hurayrah; from the Prophet (peace be upon him); that **'He used to recite in the Fajr Prayer on Fridays the surah starting with "The revelation of the Book" and the surah starting with "Was there not a period of time".'**

حَدَّثَنِي زُهَيْرُ بْنُ حَرْبٍ، حَدَّثَنَا وَكِيعٌ، عَنْ سُفْيَانَ، عَنْ سَعْدِ بْنِ إِبْرَاهِيمَ، عَنْ عَبْدِ الرَّحْمَنِ الأَعْرَجِ، عَنْ أَبِي هُرَيْرَةَ، عَنِ النَّبِيِّ صَلَّى اللهُ عَلَيْهِ وَسَلَّمَ. أَنَّهُ كَانَ يَقْرَأُ فِي الْفَجْرِ يَوْمَ الْجُمُعَةِ "الم تَنْزِيلُ" وَ "هَلْ أَتَى".

[1742–66]. (Dar al-Salam 1914) Abu al-Ṭāhir narrated: Ibn Wahb narrated; from Ibrāhīm ibn Sa'd; from his father; from al-A'raj; from Abu Hurayrah; that **'The Prophet used to recite in the Fajr Prayers on Fridays the surah starting with "The revelation of the Book" in the first *rak'ah* and in the second,**

i. Related by al-Bukhari, 891 and 1068; al-Nasā'ī, 954; Ibn Mājah, 823.

the surah starting with "Was there not a period of time when man was not yet something to be thought of?".'

حَدَّثَنِي أَبُو الطَّاهِرِ، حَدَّثَنَا ابْنُ وَهْبٍ، عَنْ إِبْرَاهِيمَ بْنِ سَعْدٍ، عَنْ أَبِيهِ، عَنِ الأَعْرَجِ، عَنْ أَبِي هُرَيْرَةَ أَنَّ النَّبِيَّ صَلَّى اللهُ عَلَيْهِ وَسَلَّمَ كَانَ يَقْرَأُ فِي الصُّبْحِ يَوْمَ الْجُمُعَةِ بِـ "الم تَنْزِيلُ" فِي الرَّكْعَةِ الأُولَى، وَفِي الثَّانِيَةِ: "هَلْ أَتَى عَلَى الإِنْسَانِ حِينٌ مِنَ الدَّهْرِ لَمْ يَكُنْ شَيْئًا مَذْكُورًا".

Text Explanation

These hadiths make it clear that the Prophet used to recite in the Fajr Prayer on Fridays Surah 32, Prostration, in the first *rakʿah* and Surah 76, Man, in the second. This is clear evidence that it is desirable to recite these two surahs in the Fajr Prayer on Fridays, which is the view of our school and others. It further confirms that it is perfectly acceptable to recite verses that include prostration in prayer, and to prostrate oneself when they are recited. Mālik and others say that this is discouraged, but these authentic hadiths narrated by Abu Hurayrah and Ibn ʿAbbās refute their argument.

Transmission

In hadith No. 1740, the name of Mukhawwal ibn Rāshid is included in the chain of transmission. This is how the name is normally pronounced. However, Ibn Qarāqūl, the author of *Maṭāliʿ al-Anwār*, quotes some scholars pronouncing his name as Mikhwal. The first is the better-known version, and it is more correct.

CHAPTER 18

SUNNAH PRAYER AFTER FRIDAY PRAYER

[1743–67]. (Dar al-Salam 1915) Yaḥyā ibn Yaḥyā narrated: Khālid ibn ʿAbdullāh reported; from Suhayl; from his father; from Abu Hurayrah. He said: **'God's Messenger (peace be upon him) said: "When any of you has finished the Friday Prayer, let him pray four *rakʿahs* after it".'**

وَحَدَّثَنَا يَحْيَى بْنُ يَحْيَى، أَخْبَرَنَا خَالِدُ بْنُ عَبْدِ اللهِ، عَنْ سُهَيْلٍ، عَنْ أَبِيهِ، عَنْ أَبِي هُرَيْرَةَ قَالَ: قَالَ رَسُولُ اللهِ صَلَّى اللهُ عَلَيْهِ وَسَلَّمَ: «إِذَا صَلَّى أَحَدُكُمُ الْجُمُعَةَ فَلْيُصَلِّ بَعْدَهَا أَرْبَعًا».

[1744–68]. (Dar al-Salam 1916) Abu Bakr ibn Abi Shaybah and ʿAmr al-Nāqid narrated: both said: ʿAbdullāh ibn Idrīs narrated; from Suhayl; from his father; from Abu Hurayrah. He said: **'God's Messenger (peace be upon him) said: "If you pray after the Friday Prayer, pray four *rakʿahs*".'**

ʿAmr added in his narration: **'Ibn Idrīs said: Suhayl said: "If you are in a hurry for something, pray two *rakʿahs* in the mosque and two when you go home".'**

وَحَدَّثَنَا أَبُو بَكْرِ بْنُ أَبِي شَيْبَةَ وَعَمْرٌو النَّاقِدُ، قَالَا: حَدَّثَنَا عَبْدُ اللهِ بْنُ إِدْرِيسَ، عَنْ سُهَيْلٍ، عَنْ أَبِيهِ، عَنْ أَبِي هُرَيْرَةَ قَالَ: قَالَ رَسُولُ اللهِ صَلَّى اللهُ عَلَيْهِ وَسَلَّمَ: «إِذَا صَلَّيْتُمْ بَعْدَ الْجُمُعَةِ فَصَلُّوا أَرْبَعًا». زَادَ عَمْرٌو فِي رِوَايَتِهِ: قَالَ ابْنُ إِدْرِيسَ قَالَ سُهَيْلٌ: فَإِنْ عَجِلَ بِكَ شَيْءٌ فَصَلِّ رَكْعَتَيْنِ فِي الْمَسْجِدِ وَرَكْعَتَيْنِ إِذَا رَجَعْتَ.

[1745–69]. (Dar al-Salam 1917) Zuhayr ibn Ḥarb narrated to me: Jarīr narrated [H]. Also, ʿAmr al-Nāqid and Abu Kurayb narrated; both said: Wakīʿ narrated; from Sufyān; both from Suhayl; from his father; from Abu Hurayrah. He said: **'Whoever of you wishes to pray after Friday Prayer, let him pray four *rakʿahs*'.**

Jarīr's narration does not include the words: **'of you'.**

وَحَدَّثَنِي زُهَيْرُ بْنُ حَرْبٍ، حَدَّثَنَا جَرِيرٌ، ح. وَحَدَّثَنَا عَمْرٌو النَّاقِدُ وَأَبُو كُرَيْبٍ قَالَا: حَدَّثَنَا وَكِيعٌ، عَنْ سُفْيَانَ، كِلَاهُمَا عَنْ سُهَيْلٍ، عَنْ أَبِيهِ، عَنْ أَبِي هُرَيْرَةَ قَالَ: قَالَ رَسُولُ اللهِ صَلَّى اللهُ عَلَيْهِ وَسَلَّمَ: «مَنْ كَانَ مِنْكُمْ مُصَلِّيًا بَعْدَ الْجُمُعَةِ فَلْيُصَلِّ أَرْبَعًا».

وَلَيْسَ فِي حَدِيثِ جَرِيرٍ «مِنْكُمْ».

[1746–70]. (Dar al-Salam 1918) Yaḥyā ibn Yaḥyā and Muhammad ibn Rumḥ narrated: both said: al-Layth reported [H]. Also, Qutaybah narrated; Layth narrated; from Nāfiʿ; from ʿAbdullāh; that **'When he had finished Friday Prayer, he left and prayed two *rakʿahs* at home'. He then said: 'God's Messenger (peace be upon him) used to do that'.**

وَحَدَّثَنَا يَحْيَى بْنُ يَحْيَى وَمُحَمَّدُ بْنُ رُمْحٍ، قَالَا: أَخْبَرَنَا اللَّيْثُ، ح. وَحَدَّثَنَا قُتَيْبَةُ، حَدَّثَنَا لَيْثٌ، عَنْ نَافِعٍ، عَنْ عَبْدِ اللهِ أَنَّهُ كَانَ إِذَا صَلَّى الْجُمُعَةَ انْصَرَفَ، فَسَجَدَ سَجْدَتَيْنِ فِي بَيْتِهِ. ثُمَّ قَالَ كَانَ رَسُولُ اللهِ صَلَّى اللهُ عَلَيْهِ وَسَلَّمَ يَصْنَعُ ذَلِكَ.

[1747–71]. (Dar al-Salam 1919) Yaḥyā ibn Yaḥyā narrated: he said: I read out to Mālik; from Nāfiʿ; from ʿAbdullāh ibn ʿUmar; that he described God's Messenger's sunnah prayer and said: **'He did not pray any sunnah after Friday Prayer until he had left, when he would pray two *rakʿahs* at home'. Yaḥyā said: 'I think, or rather I am certain, that I read the words "would pray".'**

وَحَدَّثَنَا يَحْيَى بْنُ يَحْيَى، قَالَ قَرَأْتُ عَلَى مَالِكٍ عَنْ نَافِعٍ، عَنْ عَبْدِ اللهِ بْنِ عُمَرَ أَنَّهُ وَصَفَ تَطَوُّعَ صَلاَةِ رَسُولِ اللهِ صَلَّى اللهُ عَلَيْهِ وَسَلَّمَ قَالَ: فَكَانَ لاَ يُصَلِّي بَعْدَ الْجُمُعَةِ حَتَّى يَنْصَرِفَ، فَيُصَلِّي رَكْعَتَيْنِ فِي بَيْتِه. قَالَ يَحْيَى: أَظُنُّنِي قَرَأْتُ فَيُصَلِّي أَوْ أَلْبَتَّةَ

[1748–72]. (Dar al-Salam 1920) Abu Bakr ibn Abi Shaybah, Zuhayr ibn Ḥarb and Ibn Numayr narrated: Zuhayr said: Sufyān ibn ʿUyaynah narrated; ʿAmr narrated; from al-Zuhrī; from Sālim; from his father; that **'The Prophet (peace be upon him) used to pray two *rakʿahs* after Friday Prayer'.**

حَدَّثَنَا أَبُو بَكْرِ بْنُ أَبِي شَيْبَةَ وَزُهَيْرُ بْنُ حَرْبٍ وَابْنُ نُمَيْرٍ، قَالَ زُهَيْرٌ حَدَّثَنَا سُفْيَانُ بْنُ عُيَيْنَةَ، حَدَّثَنَا عَمْرٌو، عَنِ الزُّهْرِيِّ، عَنْ سَالِمٍ، عَنْ أَبِيهِ، أَنَّ النَّبِيَّ صَلَّى اللهُ عَلَيْهِ وَسَلَّمَ كَانَ يُصَلِّي بَعْدَ الْجُمُعَةِ رَكْعَتَيْنِ.

[1749–73]. (Dar al-Salam 1921) Abu Bakr ibn Abi Shaybah narrated: Ghundar narrated; from Ibn Jurayj; he said: ʿUmar ibn ʿAṭā' ibn Abi al-Khuwār reported to me; that Nāfiʿ ibn Jubayr sent him to al-Sā'ib, Namir's nephew, asking about something Muʿāwiyah saw him doing in prayer. He said: **'Yes. I prayed Friday Prayer with him in the compartment. When the imam finished with *salām*, I stood up in my place and prayed. When he went in, he sent for me and said: "Do not do this again. When you have prayed Friday Prayer, do not follow it with another prayer until you have spoken or left [the mosque]. God's Messenger (peace be upon him) ordered us that no prayer should be followed by another prayer until we have spoken or left the mosque".'**

حَدَّثَنَا أَبُو بَكْرِ بْنُ أَبِي شَيْبَةَ، حَدَّثَنَا غُنْدَرٌ، عَنِ ابْنِ جُرَيْجٍ، قَالَ: أَخْبَرَنِي عُمَرُ بْنُ عَطَاءِ بْنِ أَبِي الْخُوَارِ أَنَّ نَافِعَ بْنَ جُبَيْرٍ أَرْسَلَهُ إِلَى السَّائِبِ، ابْنِ أُخْتِ نَمِرٍ، يَسْأَلُهُ عَنْ شَيْءٍ

رَآهُ مِنْهُ مُعَاوِيَةُ فِي الصَّلاَةِ. فَقَالَ: نَعَمْ. صَلَّيْتُ مَعَهُ الْجُمُعَةَ فِي الْـمَقْصُورَةِ، فَلَمَّا سَلَّمَ الإِمَامُ قُمْتُ فِي مَقَامِي فَصَلَّيْتُ، فَلَمَّا دَخَلَ أَرْسَلَ إِلَيَّ فَقَالَ: لاَ تَعُدْ لِمَا فَعَلْتَ. إِذَا صَلَّيْتَ الْجُمُعَةَ فَلاَ تَصِلْهَا بِصَلاَةٍ حَتَّى تَكَلَّمَ أَوْ تَخْرُجَ، فَإِنَّ رَسُولَ اللهِ صَلَّى اللهُ عَلَيْهِ وَسَلَّمَ أَمَرَنَا بِذَلِكَ: أَنْ لاَ تُوصَلَ صَلاَةٌ حَتَّى نَتَكَلَّمَ أَوْ نَخْرُجَ

[1750–000]. (Dar al-Salam 1922) Ḥarūn ibn ʿAbdullāh narrated: Ḥajjāj ibn Muhammad narrated; he said: Ibn Jurayj said: ʿUmar ibn ʿAṭā' reported to me; that Nāfiʿ ibn Jubayr sent him to al-Sā'ib ibn Yazīd, Namir's nephew: **He narrated the same hadith except that he said: 'When he finished with *salām*, I stood up in my place'. He did not mention the imam.**

وَحَدَّثَنَا هَارُونُ بْنُ عَبْدِ اللهِ، حَدَّثَنَا حَجَّاجُ بْنُ مُحَمَّدٍ، قَالَ: قَالَ ابْنُ جُرَيْجٍ: أَخْبَرَنِي عُمَرُ بْنُ عَطَاءٍ أَنَّ نَافِعَ بْنَ جُبَيْرٍ، أَرْسَلَهُ إِلَى السَّائِبِ بْنِ يَزِيدَ، ابْنِ أُخْتِ نَمِرٍ. وَسَاقَ الْحَدِيثَ بِمِثْلِهِ غَيْرَ أَنَّهُ قَالَ: فَلَمَّا سَلَّمَ قُمْتُ فِي مَقَامِي، وَلَمْ يَذْكُرِ الإِمَامَ.

Text Explanation

These hadiths mention that the Prophet said that if one is to pray some sunnah prayer after having offered the Friday Prayer, one should pray four *rakʿahs*. Another hadith mentions that the Prophet (peace be upon him) used to pray two *rakʿahs* after it. These hadiths show that it is desirable to pray sunnah after Friday Prayer and that the minimum is two *rakʿahs* and the perfect number is four *rakʿahs*.

The phraseology of these hadiths is significant. The first hadith, No. 1743, says: 'When any of you has finished the Friday Prayer, let him pray four *rakʿahs*'. This is expressed in the imperative to urge that we should do it. Hadith No. 1745 says: 'Whoever of you wishes to pray after Friday Prayer'. Thus, the Prophet makes clear that it is a sunnah, not obligatory. He mentions four *rakʿahs* as it is more preferable, and he prayed only two *rakʿahs* at times to show that this is the minimum. It is well known that in most cases he offered four *rakʿahs* because he told us about them and urged us to do them. He was the keenest to do what is best.

In hadith No. 1749, the narrator mentions that he offered Friday Prayer with Muʿāwiyah, the caliph, in the compartment. This makes clear that it is permissible to allocate a compartment in the mosque if the ruler considers it to serve a clear interest. It is said that the first one to allocate such a compartment was Muʿāwiyah ibn Abi Sufyān after the man from the Khawārij had stabbed him as he was going into the mosque. *Qadi* ʿIyāḍ said:

> Scholars differed on the allocation of a compartment. Many of the scholars of the early generations said that it is permissible, and they prayed in it. These included al-Ḥasan, al-Qāsim ibn Muhammad, Sālim and others. On the other hand, Ibn ʿUmar, al-Shaʿbī, Ahmad and Isḥāq disapproved of it. Ibn ʿUmar used to leave the compartment when he was there and a prayer became due. He prayed in the mosque. It is said that Friday Prayer is valid in a compartment if entry is permissible to all. But if it is permitted for some people and denied to others, Friday Prayer is not valid in it because in this case it can no longer be considered a mosque.

In the same hadith, No. 1749, Muʿāwiyah says: 'God's Messenger (peace be upon him) ordered us that no prayer should be followed by another prayer until we have spoken or left the mosque'. This is clear evidence in support of our scholars' view that it is desirable to offer a sunnah prayer, whether a regular one or not, in a different place from where one offered the obligatory prayer. The best way is to move from the mosque to one's home. If not, then to a different place in the mosque, or some other place. Thus, one increases the number of places of one's prostration and voluntary prayers are seen to be separate from obligatory prayers.

That he said, 'until we have spoken', means that separation between obligatory and voluntary prayers is achieved by mere speech, but it is better done by changing places, as we have explained, but God knows best.

BOOK OF EID PRAYER

CHAPTER 1

THE EID PRAYER AND *KHUṬBAH*

[1751–1]. (Dar al-Salam 1923) Muhammad ibn Rāfiʿ and ʿAbd ibn Ḥumayd narrated to me:[i] both from ʿAbd al-Razzāq; Ibn Rāfiʿ said: ʿAbd al-Razzāq narrated; Ibn Jurayj reported; al-Ḥasan ibn Muslim reported to me; from Ṭāwūs; from Ibn ʿAbbās. He said: **'I attended the Prayer of Eid al-Fiṭr with the Prophet (peace be upon him) and with Abu Bakr, ʿUmar, ʿUthmān and ʿAlī. All of them offered it before the *khuṭbah*, then they would give a *khuṭbah*. The Prophet came down, and I can almost see him as he signalled to the men with his hand to sit down. He then moved through them until he reached the women, and Bilāl was with him. He said: "Prophet! When believing women come and pledge to you that they will not associate any partner with God, nor steal, nor commit adultery, nor kill their children, nor lie about who fathered their children, nor disobey you in anything reasonable, then accept their pledge of allegiance and pray to God to forgive them. God is Most Forgiving, Ever Merciful", (60: 12) reciting the verse in full. When he finished it, he said: "Are you committed to this?" One woman said: "Yes, Prophet of God". None other among them answered him, and she could not be identified then. He said: "Donate *ṣadaqah*", and Bilāl spread his robe and said:**

---

i. Related by al-Bukhari, 979, 4895 and in a shorter version, 962; Abu Dāwūd in a shorter version, 1147; Ibn Mājah in a shorter version, 1274.

"Come on, may my father and mother be sacrificed for you". They threw bracelets and rings on Bilāl's robe'.

وَحَدَّثَنِي مُحَمَّدُ بْنُ رَافِعٍ وَعَبْدُ بْنُ حُمَيْدٍ، جَمِيعًا عَنْ عَبْدِ الرَّزَّاقِ، - قَالَ ابْنُ رَافِعٍ حَدَّثَنَا عَبْدُ الرَّزَّاقِ، - أَخْبَرَنَا ابْنُ جُرَيْجٍ، أَخْبَرَنِي الْحَسَنُ بْنُ مُسْلِمٍ، عَنْ طَاوُسٍ، عَنِ ابْنِ عَبَّاسٍ قَالَ: شَهِدْتُ صَلاَةَ الْفِطْرِ مَعَ نَبِيِّ اللهِ صَلَّى اللهُ عَلَيْهِ وَسَلَّمَ وَأَبِي بَكْرٍ وَعُمَرَ وَعُثْمَانَ، فَكُلُّهُمْ يُصَلِّيهَا قَبْلَ الْخُطْبَةِ ثُمَّ يَخْطُبُ. قَالَ: فَنَزَلَ نَبِيُّ اللهِ صَلَّى اللهُ عَلَيْهِ وَسَلَّمَ كَأَنِّي أَنْظُرُ إِلَيْهِ حِينَ يُجَلِّسُ الرِّجَالَ بِيَدِهِ، ثُمَّ أَقْبَلَ يَشُقُّهُمْ، حَتَّى جَاءَ النِّسَاءَ وَمَعَهُ بِلاَلٌ فَقَالَ: "**يَا أَيُّهَا النَّبِيُّ إِذَا جَاءَكَ الْمُؤْمِنَاتُ يُبَايِعْنَكَ عَلَى أَنْ لاَ يُشْرِكْنَ بِاللهِ شَيْئًا**" فَتَلاَ هَذِهِ الآيَةَ حَتَّى فَرَغَ مِنْهَا. ثُمَّ قَالَ حِينَ فَرَغَ مِنْهَا: "أَنْتُنَّ عَلَى ذَلِكِ؟" فَقَالَتِ امْرَأَةٌ وَاحِدَةٌ لَمْ يُجِبْهُ غَيْرُهَا مِنْهُنَّ: نَعَمْ يَا نَبِيَّ اللهِ. لاَ يُدْرَى حِينَئِذٍ مَنْ هِيَ. قَالَ: "فَتَصَدَّقْنَ". فَبَسَطَ بِلاَلٌ ثَوْبَهُ ثُمَّ قَالَ: هَلُمَّ فِدًى لَكُنَّ أَبِي وَأُمِّي. فَجَعَلْنَ يُلْقِينَ الْفَتَخَ وَالْخَوَاتِمَ فِي ثَوْبِ بِلاَلٍ.

[1752–2]. (Dar al-Salam 1924) Abu Bakr ibn Abi Shaybah and Ibn Abi ʿUmar narrated:[i] Abu Bakr said: Sufyān ibn ʿUyaynah narrated; Ayyūb narrated; he said: I heard ʿAṭā'; he said: I heard Ibn ʿAbbās say: **'I bear witness that God's Messenger (peace be upon him) prayed before the *khuṭbah*, and then delivered the *khuṭbah*. When he realised that the women did not hear him, he went to them, reminding and admonishing them. He ordered them to donate *ṣadaqah*. Bilāl spread his robe and women threw rings and similar articles onto it'.**

وَحَدَّثَنَا أَبُو بَكْرِ بْنُ أَبِي شَيْبَةَ وَابْنُ أَبِي عُمَرَ، قَالَ أَبُو بَكْرٍ: حَدَّثَنَا سُفْيَانُ بْنُ عُيَيْنَةَ، حَدَّثَنَا أَيُّوبُ قَالَ: سَمِعْتُ عَطَاءً قَالَ: سَمِعْتُ ابْنَ عَبَّاسٍ يَقُولُ: أَشْهَدُ عَلَى رَسُولِ

i. Related by al-Bukhari, 1449; Abu Dāwūd, 1142, 1143 and 1144; al-Nasā'ī, 1568; Ibn Mājah, 1273.

اللهِ صَلَّى اللهُ عَلَيْهِ وَسَلَّمَ لَصَلَّى قَبْلَ الْخُطْبَةِ. قَالَ: ثُمَّ خَطَبَ فَرَأَى أَنَّهُ لَمْ يُسْمِعِ النِّسَاءَ، فَأَتَاهُنَّ فَذَكَّرَهُنَّ وَوَعَظَهُنَّ وَأَمَرَهُنَّ بِالصَّدَقَةِ، وَبِلَالٌ قَائِلٌ بِثَوْبِهِ. فَجَعَلَتِ الْمَرْأَةُ تُلْقِي الْخَاتَمَ وَالْخُرْصَ وَالشَّيْءَ.

Abu al-Rabīʿ al-Zaharānī narrated: Ḥammād narrated [H]. Yaʿqūb al-Dawraqī narrated; Ismāʿīl ibn Ibrāhīm narrated; both from Ayyūb; with the same chain of transmission: **a similar text.**

وَحَدَّثَنِيهِ أَبُو الرَّبِيعِ الزَّهْرَانِيُّ، حَدَّثَنَا حَمَّادٌ، ح. وَحَدَّثَنِي يَعْقُوبُ الدَّوْرَقِيُّ، حَدَّثَنَا إِسْمَاعِيلُ بْنُ إِبْرَاهِيمَ، كِلَاهُمَا عَنْ أَيُّوبَ، بِهَذَا الإِسْنَادِ نَحْوَهُ

[1753–3]. (Dar al-Salam 1925) Isḥāq ibn Ibrāhīm and Muhammad ibn Rāfiʿ narrated:[i] Ibn Rāfiʿ said: ʿAbd al-Razzāq narrated; Ibn Jurayj reported; ʿAṭā' reported to me; from Jābir ibn ʿAbdullāh. He said: **'I heard him say: "The Prophet (peace be upon him) stood up on Eid al-Fiṭr Day and prayed. He started with the prayer before the *khuṭbah*, then he delivered his *khuṭbah*. When the Prophet (peace be upon him) finished, he came down and went to the women, reminding them. He was leaning on Bilāl's hand, while Bilāl spread his robe and the women threw their *ṣadaqah* onto it".**

I said to ʿAṭā': "Was that Zakāt al-Fiṭr?" He said: "No. It was a charitable donation they gave at the time as a *ṣadaqah*; a woman would throw her bracelet and they threw all types of things".

I said to ʿAṭā': "Is it a duty of the imam today to go to the women when he finishes his *khuṭbah* and remind them?" He

i. Related by al-Bukhari, 978 and in a shorter version, 958; Abu Dāwūd, 1141.

said: "Yes, indeed. This is indeed their duty; why are they [i.e. the imams] not doing it?".'

وَحَدَّثَنَا إِسْحَاقُ بْنُ إِبْرَاهِيمَ وَمُحَمَّدُ بْنُ رَافِعٍ، قَالَ ابْنُ رَافِعٍ: حَدَّثَنَا عَبْدُ الرَّزَّاقِ، أَخْبَرَنَا ابْنُ جُرَيْجٍ، أَخْبَرَنِي عَطَاءٌ، عَنْ جَابِرِ بْنِ عَبْدِ اللهِ، قَالَ سَمِعْتُهُ يَقُولُ: إِنَّ النَّبِيَّ صَلَّى اللهُ عَلَيْهِ وَسَلَّمَ قَامَ يَوْمَ الْفِطْرِ فَصَلَّى فَبَدَأَ بِالصَّلاَةِ قَبْلَ الْخُطْبَةِ، ثُمَّ خَطَبَ النَّاسَ. فَلَمَّا فَرَغَ نَبِيُّ اللهِ صَلَّى اللهُ عَلَيْهِ وَسَلَّمَ نَزَلَ وَأَتَى النِّسَاءَ، فَذَكَّرَهُنَّ وَهُوَ يَتَوَكَّأُ عَلَى يَدِ بِلاَلٍ، وَبِلاَلٌ بَاسِطٌ ثَوْبَهُ يُلْقِينَ النِّسَاءُ صَدَقَةً.

قُلْتُ لِعَطَاءٍ: زَكَاةَ يَوْمِ الْفِطْرِ؟ قَالَ: لا، وَلَكِنْ صَدَقَةً يَتَصَدَّقْنَ بِهَا حِينَئِذٍ، تُلْقِي الْـمَرْأَةُ فَتَخَهَا وَيُلْقِينَ وَيُلْقِينَ.

قُلْتُ لِعَطَاءٍ: أَحَقًّا عَلَى الإِمَامِ الآنَ أَنْ يَأْتِيَ النِّسَاءَ حِينَ يَفْرُغُ فَيُذَكِّرَهُنَّ؟ قَالَ: إِي لَعَمْرِي إِنَّ ذَلِكَ لَحَقٌّ عَلَيْهِمْ، وَمَا لَهُمْ لاَ يَفْعَلُونَ ذَلِكَ؟

[1754–4]. (Dar al-Salam 1926) Muhammad ibn ʿAbdullāh ibn Numayr narrated:[i] my father narrated; ʿAbd al-Malik ibn Abi Sulaymān; from ʿAṭā'; from Jābir ibn ʿAbdullāh. He said: **'I attended the prayer on the Eid Day with God's Messenger (peace be upon him). He started with the prayer before the *khuṭbah*, with neither an *adhān* nor an *iqāmah*. He then stood up, leaning on Bilāl. He ordered that people remain God-fearing and he urged obedience of God. He admonished people and reminded them. He then went to the women admonishing and reminding them. He said: "Give *ṣadaqah*, for most of you are Hell's fuel". A woman with some blackness in her cheeks in the midst of the women stood up and said: "Why is that, Messenger of God?" He said: "Because you**

---

i. Related by al-Nasā'ī, 1574.

complain much and deny your partner's kindness". They gave generously from their jewellery, throwing onto Bilāl's robe their earrings and rings'.

وَحَدَّثَنَا مُحَمَّدُ بْنُ عَبْدِ اللهِ بْنِ نُمَيْرٍ، حَدَّثَنَا أَبِي، حَدَّثَنَا عَبْدُ الْمَلِكِ بْنُ أَبِي سُلَيْمَانَ، عَنْ عَطَاءٍ، عَنْ جَابِرِ بْنِ عَبْدِ اللهِ قَالَ: شَهِدْتُ مَعَ رَسُولِ اللهِ صَلَّى اللهُ عَلَيْهِ وَسَلَّمَ الصَّلَاةَ يَوْمَ الْعِيدِ، فَبَدَأَ بِالصَّلَاةِ قَبْلَ الْخُطْبَةِ، بِغَيْرِ أَذَانٍ وَلَا إِقَامَةٍ. ثُمَّ قَامَ مُتَوَكِّئًا عَلَى بِلَالٍ، فَأَمَرَ بِتَقْوَى اللهِ وَحَثَّ عَلَى طَاعَتِهِ، وَوَعَظَ النَّاسَ وَذَكَّرَهُمْ. ثُمَّ مَضَى حَتَّى أَتَى النِّسَاءَ فَوَعَظَهُنَّ وَذَكَّرَهُنَّ، فَقَالَ: «تَصَدَّقْنَ فَإِنَّ أَكْثَرَكُنَّ حَطَبُ جَهَنَّمَ». فَقَامَتِ امْرَأَةٌ مِنْ سِطَةِ النِّسَاءِ، سَفْعَاءُ الْخَدَّيْنِ، فَقَالَتْ: لِمَ يَا رَسُولَ اللهِ؟ قَالَ: «لِأَنَّكُنَّ تُكْثِرْنَ الشَّكَاةَ، وَتَكْفُرْنَ الْعَشِيرَ». قَالَ: فَجَعَلْنَ يَتَصَدَّقْنَ مِنْ حُلِيِّهِنَّ، يُلْقِينَ فِي ثَوْبِ بِلَالٍ مِنْ أَقْرِطَتِهِنَّ وَخَوَاتِمِهِنَّ.

[1755–5]. (Dar al-Salam 1927) Muhammad ibn Rāfiʿ narrated to me:[i] ʿAbd al-Razzāq narrated; Ibn Jurayj reported; ʿAṭā' reported to me; from Ibn ʿAbbās, and from Jābir ibn ʿAbdullāh al-Anṣārī. Both said: **'No *adhān* was called on the day of Eid al-Fiṭr and the day of Eid al-Aḍḥā. I asked him about it sometime later, and he told me, saying: "Jābir ibn ʿAbdullāh al-Anṣārī told me that no *adhān* is called for the prayer on the day of Eid al-Fiṭr, neither when the imam comes out nor when he comes in. Nor was there any *iqāmah*, nor an announcement, nor anything. No announcement on that day and no *iqāmah*".'**

وَحَدَّثَنِي مُحَمَّدُ بْنُ رَافِعٍ، حَدَّثَنَا عَبْدُ الرَّزَّاقِ، أَخْبَرَنَا ابْنُ جُرَيْجٍ، أَخْبَرَنِي عَطَاءٌ، عَنِ ابْنِ عَبَّاسٍ وَعَنْ جَابِرِ بْنِ عَبْدِ اللهِ الْأَنْصَارِيِّ، قَالَا: لَمْ يَكُنْ يُؤَذَّنُ يَوْمَ الْفِطْرِ

i. Related by al-Bukhari in shorter versions, 959 and 960 as narrated by Jābir; Abu Dāwūd, 1072 as narrated by ibn ʿAbbās.

وَلاَ يَوْمَ الأَضْحَى. ثُمَّ سَأَلْتُهُ بَعْدَ حِينٍ عَنْ ذَلِكَ فَأَخْبَرَنِي قَالَ: أَخْبَرَنِي جَابِرُ بْنُ عَبْدِ اللهِ الأَنْصَارِيُّ أَنْ لاَ أَذَانَ لِلصَّلاَةِ يَوْمَ الْفِطْرِ حِينَ يَخْرُجُ الإِمَامُ، وَلاَ بَعْدَ مَا يَخْرُجُ. وَلاَ إِقَامَةَ وَلاَ نِدَاءَ وَلاَ شَيْءَ. لاَ نِدَاءَ يَوْمَئِذٍ وَلاَ إِقَامَةَ.

[1756–6]. (Dar al-Salam 1928) Muhammad ibn Rāfiʿ narrated: ʿAbd al-Razzāq narrated; Ibn Jurayj reported; ʿAṭā' reported to me; that **'Ibn ʿAbbās sent to Ibn al-Zubayr when the latter was elected that no *adhān* was called for the prayer on the day of Eid al-Fiṭr: "Do not call the *adhān* for it". Ibn al-Zubayr did not call the *adhān* then. He sent to him further: "The *khuṭbah* is after the prayer, and this was the practice". Ibn al-Zubayr led the prayer before the *khuṭbah*'.**

وَحَدَّثَنِي مُحَمَّدُ بْنُ رَافِعٍ، حَدَّثَنَا عَبْدُ الرَّزَّاقِ، أَخْبَرَنَا ابْنُ جُرَيْجٍ، أَخْبَرَنِي عَطَاءٌ، أَنَّ ابْنَ عَبَّاسٍ أَرْسَلَ إِلَى ابْنِ الزُّبَيْرِ أَوَّلَ مَا بُويِعَ لَهُ، أَنَّهُ لَمْ يَكُنْ يُؤَذَّنُ لِلصَّلاَةِ يَوْمَ الْفِطْرِ فَلاَ تُؤَذِّنْ لَهَا. قَالَ: فَلَمْ يُؤَذِّنْ لَهَا ابْنُ الزُّبَيْرِ يَوْمَهُ. وَأَرْسَلَ إِلَيْهِ مَعَ ذَلِكَ: إِنَّمَا الْخُطْبَةُ بَعْدَ الصَّلاَةِ، وَإِنَّ ذَلِكَ قَدْ كَانَ يُفْعَلُ. قَالَ: فَصَلَّى ابْنُ الزُّبَيْرِ قَبْلَ الْخُطْبَةِ.

[1757–7]. (Dar al-Salam 1929) Yaḥyā ibn Yaḥyā, Ḥasan ibn al-Rabīʿ, Qutaybah ibn Saʿīd and Abu Bakr ibn Abi Shaybah narrated:[i] Abu al-Aḥwaṣ (Yaḥyā said: 'reported' and the others said: 'narrated'); from Simāk; from Jābir ibn Samurah. He said: **'I prayed with God's Messenger (peace be upon him) the prayer on the two Eids more than once or twice, and it was without any *adhān* or *iqāmah*'.**

وَحَدَّثَنَا يَحْيَى بْنُ يَحْيَى وَحَسَنُ بْنُ الرَّبِيعِ وَقُتَيْبَةُ بْنُ سَعِيدٍ وَأَبُو بَكْرِ بْنُ أَبِي شَيْبَةَ: قَالَ يَحْيَى أَخْبَرَنَا وَقَالَ الآخَرُونَ حَدَّثَنَا أَبُو الأَحْوَصِ، عَنْ سِمَاكٍ، عَنْ جَابِرِ بْنِ سَمُرَةَ

i. Related by Abu Dāwūd, 1148; al-Tirmidhī, 532.

قَالَ: صَلَّيْتُ مَعَ رَسُولِ اللهِ صَلَّى اللهُ عَلَيْهِ وَسَلَّمَ الْعِيدَيْنِ غَيْرَ مَرَّةٍ وَلاَ مَرَّتَيْنِ، بِغَيْرِ أَذَانٍ وَلاَ إِقَامَةٍ

[1758–8]. (Dar al-Salam 1930) Abu Bakr ibn Abi Shaybah narrated:[i] ʿAbdah ibn Sulaymān and Abu Usāmah narrated; from ʿUbaydullāh; from Nāfiʿ; from Ibn ʿUmar; that **'The Prophet (peace be upon him), Abu Bakr and ʿUmar used to pray the Eid prayers before the *khuṭbah*'.**

وَحَدَّثَنَا أَبُو بَكْرِ بْنُ أَبِي شَيْبَةَ، حَدَّثَنَا عَبْدَةُ بْنُ سُلَيْمَانَ، وَأَبُو أُسَامَةَ عَنْ عُبَيْدِ اللهِ، عَنْ نَافِعٍ، عَنِ ابْنِ عُمَرَ أَنَّ النَّبِيَّ صَلَّى اللهُ عَلَيْهِ وَسَلَّمَ وَأَبَا بَكْرٍ وَعُمَرَ كَانُوا يُصَلُّونَ الْعِيدَيْنِ قَبْلَ الْخُطْبَةِ.

[1759–9]. (Dar al-Salam 1931) Yaḥyā ibn Ayyūb, Qutaybah and Ibn Ḥujr narrated: they said: Ismāʿīl ibn Jaʿfar narrated; from Dāwūd ibn Qays; from ʿIyāḍ ibn ʿAbdullāh ibn Saʿd; from Abu Saʿīd al-Khudrī: **'God's Messenger (peace be upon him) used to come out on the days of Eid al-Aḍḥā and Eid al-Fiṭr, starting with the prayer. When he completed his prayer and said the *salām,* he would address the people as they remained sitting in their prayer place. If he had an intention of sending an expedition, he would mention it to people, and if he had some other need, he would order it. He used to say: "Donate, donate, donate *ṣadaqah*". Women were the ones who donated most. He would then leave. This remained the practice until the time of Marwān ibn al-Ḥakam. I went out with Marwān hand in hand, until we reached the prayer place. I found**

i. The narration by 'Abdah ibn Sulaymān is related by al-Nasāʾī, 1563; and the one by Abu Usāmah is related by al-Bukhari, 963; al-Tirmidhī, 531; Ibn Mājah, 1276.

that Kathīr ibn al-Ṣalt had erected a platform of mud and bricks. I felt Marwān pulling my hand, as if he was pulling me towards the platform, while I was pulling him towards the prayer. When I saw what he was after, I said: "How come, when the prayer is first?" He said: "No, Abu Saʿīd. What you know has been abandoned". I said: "No. By the One who holds my soul in His hand, you cannot do better than what I know" (three times then he left).'

حَدَّثَنَا يَحْيَى بْنُ أَيُّوبَ وَقُتَيْبَةُ وَابْنُ حُجْرٍ قَالُوا: حَدَّثَنَا إِسْمَاعِيلُ بْنُ جَعْفَرٍ، عَنْ دَاوُدَ بْنِ قَيْسٍ، عَنْ عِيَاضِ بْنِ عَبْدِ اللهِ بْنِ سَعْدٍ، عَنْ أَبِي سَعِيدٍ الْخُدْرِيِّ أَنَّ رَسُولَ اللهِ صَلَّى اللهُ عَلَيْهِ وَسَلَّمَ كَانَ يَخْرُجُ يَوْمَ الأَضْحَى وَيَوْمَ الْفِطْرِ، فَيَبْدَأُ بِالصَّلاَةِ. فَإِذَا صَلَّى صَلاَتَهُ وَسَلَّمَ قَامَ فَأَقْبَلَ عَلَى النَّاسِ وَهُمْ جُلُوسٌ فِي مُصَلاَّهُمْ. فَإِنْ كَانَ لَهُ حَاجَةٌ بِبَعْثٍ ذَكَرَهُ لِلنَّاسِ، أَوْ كَانَتْ لَهُ حَاجَةٌ بِغَيْرِ ذَلِكَ أَمَرَهُمْ بِهَا. وَكَانَ يَقُولُ: «تَصَدَّقُوا، تَصَدَّقُوا، تَصَدَّقُوا». وَكَانَ أَكْثَرَ مَنْ يَتَصَدَّقُ النِّسَاءُ، ثُمَّ يَنْصَرِفُ. فَلَمْ يَزَلْ كَذَلِكَ حَتَّى كَانَ مَرْوَانُ بْنُ الْحَكَمِ. فَخَرَجْتُ مُخَاصِرًا مَرْوَانَ حَتَّى أَتَيْنَا الْـمُصَلَّى، فَإِذَا كَثِيرُ بْنُ الصَّلْتِ قَدْ بَنَى مِنْبَرًا مِنْ طِينٍ وَلَبِنٍ. فَإِذَا مَرْوَانُ يُنَازِعُنِي يَدَهُ، كَأَنَّهُ يَجُرُّنِي نَحْوَ الْـمِنْبَرِ، وَأَنَا أَجُرُّهُ نَحْوَ الصَّلاَةِ. فَلَمَّا رَأَيْتُ ذَلِكَ مِنْهُ قُلْتُ: أَيْنَ الابْتِدَاءُ بِالصَّلاَةِ؟ فَقَالَ: لا يَا أَبَا سَعِيدٍ، قَدْ تُرِكَ مَا تَعْلَمُ. قُلْتُ: كَلاَّ وَالَّذِي نَفْسِي بِيَدِهِ، لاَ تَأْتُونَ بِخَيْرٍ مِمَّا أَعْلَمُ. ثَلاَثَ مِرَارٍ ثُمَّ انْصَرَفَ.

Text Explanation

According to al-Shāfiʿī, the majority of Shāfiʿī scholars and the majority of all scholars, the Eid Prayer is a confirmed sunnah. Abu Saʿīd al-Ḥasan ibn Ahmad al-Iṣṭakhrī, who belonged to the Shāfiʿī School, said that it is a collective duty, while Abu Ḥanīfah considers it a duty. If we consider it as a collective duty and suppose that the population of a certain area refuse to hold it, they will be fought over this, as this applies to all collective duties. If we consider it a sunnah, they cannot be fought over its omission in the same way as other sunnahs. Some scholars say that they may be fought over because it is a publicised event confirming identity.

It is said that Eid is given this name, which is derived from a root signifying return, because it comes back time after time. It is also said that it is named thus because it brings back pleasure. Another suggestion is that it is an aspect of good omen that it will come back. This is the same as a caravan when it is called, in Arabic, *qāfilah*. The word means 'returning', but the caravan is given this name when it starts its journey, hoping that it will return safely.

In hadith No. 1751 Ibn ʿAbbās says: 'I attended the Prayer of Eid al-Fiṭr with the Prophet (peace be upon him) and with Abu Bakr, ʿUmar, ʿUthmān and ʿAlī. All of them offered it before the *khuṭbah*, then they would give a *khuṭbah*'. This shows evidence in support of the view of all scholars that the Eid *Khuṭbah* is after the prayer. *Qadi* ʿIyāḍ said: 'This is the agreed view of the scholars of all regions and the most distinguished scholars who are best qualified to give rulings. There is no difference on this point among distinguished scholars. It was the practice of the Prophet and the rightly-guided caliphs after him'. The only exception is the report that ʿUthmān started with the *khuṭbah* in the last part of his reign because he saw that some people missed the prayer. The same was reported to be done by ʿUmar, but this is not correct. It is said that the first one to give the *khuṭbah* first was Muʿāwiyah, while other reports suggest that it was Marwān in Madinah or Ziyād the governor of Basrah during Muʿāwiyah's reign. It is further said that Ibn al-Zuhrī did it towards the end of his life.

The Prophet signalled to the men with his hand, requiring them to remain seated, as he went over to the women. As the Prophet began his address to the women, he recited the verse stating the terms of their pledge to the Prophet and asked them whether they remained committed to it. The hadith adds that 'one woman said: "Yes, Prophet of God". None other among them answered him, and she could not be identified then'. This is how the hadith is stated in all manuscripts, 'she could not be identified then'. *Qadi* ʿIyāḍ says it is also the same in their copies. However, both he and others say that: 'it is a mistake in spelling, and the right words are "Ḥasan could not identify her".[i] In this case, the reference is to Ḥasan ibn Muslim, the narrator who narrates the hadith from Ṭāwūs, from Ibn 'Abbās. It occurs correctly in al-Bukhari's version as he relates it narrated by Isḥāq ibn Naṣr from 'Abd al-Razzāq, with the wording "Ḥasan could not identify her".' However, the other way, 'she could not be identified then', may also be correct and it means that she could not be identified because of the large number of women and they were all well clothed.

The hadith mentions that 'the Prophet (peace be upon him) came down… until he reached the women, and Bilāl was with him'. *Qadi* 'Iyāḍ said that he came down during the *khuṭbah*, but this is not so. He went to them after the Eid *Khuṭbah* was over and after he finished admonishing the men. Muslim mentions this clearly in the hadith narrated by Jābir, No. 1753: 'He started with the prayer before the *khuṭbah*, then he delivered his *khuṭbah*. When the Prophet (peace be upon him) finished, he came down and went to the women, reminding them'. This is a clear statement that he went to the women after he had finished his address to the men.

These hadiths clearly show that it is desirable to admonish women, remind them of the Day of Judgement and Islamic rulings and encourage them to make charitable donations, or *ṣadaqah*, provided that no negative effect may be caused to either the one who says the admonition or those who listen to it or anyone else. The hadiths also show that when women attend prayers with men, or sit with them, they should be separated from them so as to leave no chance for anything untoward. Further, the hadiths make clear that a voluntary *ṣadaqah* does not require a procedure of 'commitment and acceptance'. It is enough that the donor gives it. The women simply threw their donations onto Bilāl's robe, without a word

i. In Arabic, the difference between the two sentences applies to one word 'Ḥasan' instead of 'then', and there is clear similarity in the way they are written, while their positions in the sentence are the same.

being said by them, or by Bilāl or anyone else. This is the correct view of our school. However, the majority of our Iraqi scholars say that it requires the same procedure of commitment and acceptance as a gift. The first view is the correct one and it is endorsed by meticulous scholars.

In hadith No. 1751 the Prophet urges women saying: 'Donate *ṣadaqah*'. Then 'Bilāl spread his robe and said: "Come on, may my father and mother be sacrificed for you". They threw bracelets and rings onto Bilāl's robe'. This hadith shows that it is perfectly appropriate for a woman to give *ṣadaqah* out of her own money, without need for her husband's permission. This is not dependent on its being part of only one-third of her property. This is the view of our school and the majority of scholars. Mālik said that a woman may not donate more than one-third of her property without her husband's agreement. Our evidence, based on this hadith, is that the Prophet did not ask the women if they had their husband's permission to donate and whether their donations were a portion of the one-third permitted. If the ruling were to be different in such cases, the Prophet would have asked them. *Qadi* ʿIyāḍ mentions in support of the view of his Mālikī School that most probably their husbands were present, and the fact that they did not object means that they accepted what their wives did. This justification is flimsy, or even invalid, because the women were separated from them, and the men did not know who of them gave a donation and who did not and what amount they donated. Even if they were aware of all that, their non-objection does not mean permission.

In hadith No. 1751 and 1753, Bilāl spread his robe. He did so in order to collect donations on it. The Prophet would then distribute these to the needy, as he used to do with voluntary *ṣadaqah* and zakat. This may be cited as evidence that it is the ruler that is required to allocate charitable donations to their respective recipients.

Hadith No. 1753 adds: 'I said to ʿAṭā': "Is it a duty of the imam today to go to the women when he finishes his *khuṭbah* and remind them?" He said: "Yes, indeed. This is indeed their [i.e. the imams] duty; why are they not doing it?".' *Qadi* ʿIyāḍ said that ʿAṭā''s answer is not approved. But this is not so. Indeed, it is desirable that if the women cannot hear the *khuṭbah*, the imam should go to them when he has finished and admonish and remind them, provided that no negative effects result from this. This applies now and at all times in the same conditions. What reason would cause us to abandon this authentic sunnah? But God knows best.

In hadith No. 1754, Jābir mentions that the Prophet started with the prayer before the *khuṭbah* and without any *adhān* or *iqāmah*. This shows that the Eid Prayer does not require either of these. This is unanimously agreed upon by scholars today, and it is a well-known practice of the Prophet and the rightly-guided caliphs. Some views are reported from some of the early scholars suggesting that there are minor differences in various generations.

In the same hadith, reference is made to a woman standing up from in the midst of women. *Qadi* ʿIyāḍ said:

> The word here is *siṭat* and in some copies *wāsiṭat al-nisā'*, which means 'from among their best' because the centre is associated with the best qualities. However, the most excellent of our teachers claim that this word is misspelt in Muslim's book and the correct word is *siflat* [which has the opposite meaning]. It was thus related by Ibn Abi Shaybah in his *al-Musnad* and by al-Nasā'ī in his *Sunan*. In a different narration by Ibn Abi Shaybah, she is referred to as 'a woman who did not belong to their best'. This is the opposite of the first meaning, and it is supported by her description as a woman 'with some blackness in her cheeks'.

Their claim that the word is misspelt is unacceptable. It is, indeed, a correct word but does not mean that the woman was 'from among the best women', as the claim goes. It simply means that she was sitting in the midst of women. That she had some blackness in her cheeks means that this was the result of a change from her natural colour.

The Prophet explains that many women are punished in Hell because they 'complain much[i] and deny their partner's kindness'. Most scholars interpret 'partner' in this instance as referring to the woman's 'husband'. Others say that it refers to anyone who is in frequent contact. The meaning here is that they often deny what kindness other people might do them. This is taken as a criticism of anyone who does not appreciate other people's kindness.

In hadith No. 1755, Jābir, the Prophet's Companion, is quoted: 'No *adhān* is called for the prayer on the day of Eid al-Fiṭr. Nor was there any *iqāmah*, nor an announcement, nor anything'. This appears to be contrary to what our scholars and many others say whereby it is desirable to say something like *al-ṣalāt jāmiʿah*, which means 'come to prayer'. Therefore, the hadith is understood to mean that there is no *adhān, iqāmah* or anything of similar import.

In hadith No. 1759, Abu Saʿīd al-Khudrī, the Prophet's Companion, mentions that 'God's Messenger (peace be upon him) used to come out on the days of Eid al-Aḍḥā and Eid al-Fiṭr, starting with the prayer'. This provides evidence in support of the view of those who say that it is preferable to offer the Eid Prayer in an open space, rather than in the mosque. This is the practice of people in most areas. The people of Makkah have always offered it in the mosque, right from the early days of Islam. Our scholars express two views: the first, based on this hadith, makes an open space more preferable for the Eid Prayer, and the second considers the mosque more preferable, unless it cannot accommodate the people. This second view is considered by most to be the more correct. They explain that the people of Makkah offered the prayer in the mosque because it is spacious, while the Prophet went out to an open space because the mosque in Madinah could not accommodate all the people. This proves that the mosque is preferable if it is big enough.

Abu Saʿīd mentions: 'I went out with Marwān hand in hand, until we reached the prayer place… I felt Marwān pulling my hand, as if

i. This suggests that the complaints are not always reasonable.

he was pulling me towards the platform, while I was pulling him towards the prayer'. This shows that the *khuṭbah* in the Eid Prayer is after the prayer. It also urges enjoining what is right and opposing what is wrong, even if the latter is being done by a governor. It also shows that such opposition should be by hand, if possible. Verbal criticism is not enough if using one's hand is feasible.

Abu Saʿīd makes clear that prayer should be offered first, but Marwān tells him that this was abandoned. Abu Saʿīd retorts: 'You cannot do better than what I know'. What he said is certainly right because what he knew was the practice of the Prophet (peace be upon him). How could a different practice be better than that? 'He then left'. *Qadi* ʿIyāḍ said: 'This means that he turned away from the platform to go to where the prayer was to be held. It does not mean that he left the prayer place and abandoned praying with Marwān'. Indeed, one hadith related by al-Bukhari mentions that he prayed with him and spoke to him concerning the prayer after it had finished. This indicates that the Eid Prayer after the *khuṭbah* is valid. Had it not been so, Abu Saʿīd would not have joined Marwān in this prayer. Our scholars are in agreement that if the *khuṭbah* is said before the prayer, the prayer is valid, but the imam would have abandoned the sunnah and missed out on what is greatly meritorious. This is unlike the Friday Prayer, where it is a condition for the validity of the prayer that the *khuṭbah* should be before the prayer. The Friday *Khuṭbah* is obligatory, while the Eid *Khuṭbah* is recommended.

CHAPTER 2

WOMEN ATTEND THE EID PRAYER

[1760–10]. (Dar al-Salam 1932) Abu al-Rabīʿ al-Zahrānī narrated to me:[i] Ḥammād narrated; Ayyūb narrated; from Muhammad; from Umm ʿAṭiyyah. She said: **'He (meaning the Prophet, peace be upon him) ordered us to bring with us on the Eid days the young women and the ones kept at home. He commanded that those in menstruation should stay apart from the Muslims' place of prayer'.**

حَدَّثَنِي أَبُو الرَّبِيعِ الزَّهْرَانِيُّ، حَدَّثَنَا حَمَّادٌ، حَدَّثَنَا أَيُّوبُ، عَنْ مُحَمَّدٍ، عَنْ أُمِّ عَطِيَّةَ قَالَتْ: أَمَرَنَا - تَعْنِي النَّبِيَّ صَلَّى اللهُ عَلَيْهِ وَسَلَّمَ - أَنْ نُخْرِجَ فِي الْعِيدَيْنِ الْعَوَاتِقَ وَذَوَاتِ الْخُدُورِ. وَأَمَرَ الْحُيَّضَ أَنْ يَعْتَزِلْنَ مُصَلَّى الْمُسْلِمِينَ.

[1761–11]. (Dar al-Salam 1933) Yaḥyā ibn Yaḥyā narrated:[ii] Abu Khaythamah reported; from ʿĀṣim al-Aḥwal; from Ḥafṣah bint Sīrīn; from Umm ʿAṭiyyah. She said: **'We used to be commanded to come out on the Eid days, including the ones kept at home and virgins. The ones in menstruation came out and they stayed behind the people, glorifying God with the rest of the people'.**

---

i. Related by al-Bukhari in a shorter version, 974; Abu Dāwūd in a longer version and similar wording, 1136 and 1137; al-Nasāʾī, 1558; Ibn Mājah, 1308.

ii. Related by al-Bukhari, 971; Abu Dāwūd, 1138.

حَدَّثَنَا يَحْيَى بْنُ يَحْيَى، أَخْبَرَنَا أَبُو خَيْثَمَةَ، عَنْ عَاصِمٍ الأَحْوَلِ، عَنْ حَفْصَةَ بِنْتِ سِيرِينَ، عَنْ أُمِّ عَطِيَّةَ قَالَتْ: كُنَّا نُؤْمَرُ بِالْخُرُوجِ فِي الْعِيدَيْنِ، وَالْـمُخَبَّأَةُ وَالْبِكْرُ. قَالَتِ: الْحُيَّضُ يَخْرُجْنَ فَيَكُنَّ خَلْفَ النَّاسِ، يُكَبِّرْنَ مَعَ النَّاسِ.

[1762–12]. (Dar al-Salam 1934) ʿAmr al-Nāqid narrated:[i] ʿĪsā ibn Yūnus narrated; Hishām narrated; from Ḥafṣah bint Sīrīn; from Umm ʿAṭiyyah. She said: **'God's Messenger (peace be upon him) commanded that we bring them on Eid al-Fiṭr and Eid al-Aḍḥā: the young women, the ones in menstruation and the ones kept at home. The ones in menstruation stayed behind during the prayer but attended this good occasion and the Muslims' supplication. I said: "Messenger of God, some of us might not have a [suitable] frock". He said: "Let her sister give her a frock of hers to wear".'**

وَحَدَّثَنَا عَمْرٌو النَّاقِدُ، حَدَّثَنَا عِيسَى بْنُ يُونُسَ، حَدَّثَنَا هِشَامٌ، عَنْ حَفْصَةَ بِنْتِ سِيرِينَ، عَنْ أُمِّ عَطِيَّةَ قَالَتْ: أَمَرَنَا رَسُولُ اللهِ صَلَّى اللهُ عَلَيْهِ وَسَلَّمَ أَنْ نُخْرِجَهُنَّ فِي الْفِطْرِ وَالأَضْحَى، الْعَوَاتِقَ وَالْحُيَّضَ وَذَوَاتِ الْخُدُورِ. فَأَمَّا الْحُيَّضُ فَيَعْتَزِلْنَ الصَّلاَةَ، وَيَشْهَدْنَ الْخَيْرَ وَدَعْوَةَ الْـمُسْلِمِينَ. قُلْتُ يَا رَسُولَ اللهِ: إِحْدَانَا لاَ يَكُونُ لَهَا جِلْبَابٌ، قَالَ: «لِتُلْبِسْهَا أُخْتُهَا مِنْ جِلْبَابِهَا».

Text Explanation

The Prophet uses the word *ʿātiq* to refer to young women. The word means a girl that has attained puberty. Ibn Durayd said that it means a girl approaching puberty. Ibn al-Sukayt said that it refers to a woman between the time of her puberty and her becoming a

i. Related by al-Tirmidhī, 540; Ibn Mājah, 1307.

spinster, unless she gets married. A spinster is a woman who remains in her father's home, unmarried, until she is old.

Scholars of our school said that it is desirable to bring out women who are not pretty and do not have an elegant figure, but not others. When they are reminded of bringing out women kept indoors, they say that morality was much better at the time, which is not the case nowadays.[i] It is authentically reported that ʿĀ'ishah said: 'Had God's Messenger (peace be upon him) seen what women are doing, he would have stopped them from attending mosques, just like the women of the Children of Israel were prevented such attendance'.

Qadi ʿIyāḍ said: 'The early scholars differed regarding women's attendance at Eid prayers. Some said that it is their duty, and these included Abu Bakr, ʿAlī, Ibn ʿUmar and others. Some said they should not, and these included ʿUrwah, al-Qāsim, Yaḥyā al-Anṣārī, Mālik and Abu Yūsuf. Abu Ḥanīfah permitted it at one time and did not at another time'.

In hadith No. 1960, the Prophet 'commanded that those in menstruation should stay apart from the Muslims' place of prayer'. Our Shāfiʿī scholars differ concerning this order, with the majority saying that it is just a discouragement, not a strict prohibition, and that it is meant to prevent close mixing between men and women for no need or prayer. There is no prohibition here because the open space where the Eid Prayer is organised is not a mosque. Abu al-Faraj al-Dārimī, a Shāfiʿī scholar, quotes some of our scholars saying that a woman in menstruation may not stay at the open place of prayer in the same way as she may not stay in the mosque, because it is a place of prayer and as such, it is similar to a mosque. The correct view is the first one.

In hadith No. 1761 Umm ʿAṭiyyah says that the women in menstruation 'glorified God with the rest of the people'. This makes

---

i. This is something that many scholars say of their own generation, lamenting relaxed practices. There is nothing in the hadiths to suggest that particular conditions should apply before women can attend Eid Prayer, or any prayer for that matter. Hence, the order is general and applies at all times, except when special circumstances make it counterproductive.

clear that glorifying and praising God are permissible to women in menstruation and men in a state of ceremonial impurity, i.e. *janābah*. What such women may not do is to recite the Qur'an. Indeed, this hadith shows that it is desirable for everyone to glorify God at the time of Eid. This is unanimously agreed upon. Our scholars said that glorification of God, i.e. *takbīr*, is desirable during the two nights preceding the Eid days and at the time when people go out to attend the prayer. *Qadi* ʿIyāḍ said that the *takbīr* on the Eid days is done in four situations: while people are going to attend the prayer until the imam is about to start the prayer, during the prayer, during the *khuṭbah* and after the prayer. Scholars differ with regard to the *takbīr* during the first situation. A number of the Prophet's Companions and early scholars considered it desirable, and they glorified God aloud when they left their homes until they reached the place of prayer. This is endorsed by al-Awzāʿī, Mālik and al-Shāfiʿī, with the latter saying that it is desirable on the two nights preceding the Eid days. Abu Ḥanīfah said that the *takbīr* is desirable when going to the prayer of Eid al-Aḍḥā but not Eid al-Fiṭr, but his disciples differed with him, sharing the view of the majority.

Takbīr, i.e. glorifying God, with the imam during the *khuṭbah* is approved of by Mālik but rejected by other scholars. The *takbīr* included in the Eid Prayer is, according to al-Shāfiʿī, seven glorifications in the first *rakʿah*, apart from the one with which the prayer starts, and five glorifications in the second *rakʿah*, apart from the one indicating the worshipper's rise to start the second *rakʿah*. Mālik, Ahmad and Abu Thawr say the same except that they say that the first *rakʿah* has seven glorifications in total. Al-Thawrī and Abu Ḥanīfah said that they consist of five glorifications in the first *rakʿah* and four in the second, but these include the ones for starting the prayer and rising for the second *rakʿah*. The majority of scholars say that these glorifications are said consecutively, one after the other. ʿAṭā', al-Shāfiʿī and Ahmad say that it is desirable to mention God's name between every two glorifications. This is also reported from Ibn Masʿūd.

Glorifications after all prayers during the days of Eid al-Aḍḥā are subject to nearly ten different opinions expressed by early and later scholars: does it start at Fajr or Ẓuhr on the day of attendance at Arafat [which is the day before Eid] or Fajr or Ẓuhr on the day of Eid? Does it end at Ẓuhr Prayer on the first day of Eid or Ẓuhr on the third day of Eid or at Fajr, Ẓuhr or ʿAṣr Prayer on the last [i.e. fourth] day of Eid? Mālik, al-Shāfiʿī and other scholars have chosen that it starts at Ẓuhr Prayer of the first day of Eid, which is the Day of Sacrifice, and extends till Fajr Prayer on the last day of Eid. Another statement by al-Shāfiʿī says that it extends until ʿAṣr prayer on the last day of Eid, and a further statement that it begins at Fajr on the day of attendance at Arafat and extends till ʿAṣr of the last day of Eid. This last view is the one preferred by our scholars and followed in most regions.

Hadith No. 1762 says about women in menstruation going to the Eid Prayer that they thus 'attended the good occasion and the Muslims' supplication'. This makes it clear that it is desirable to attend places where people gather to do some good and supplicate to God and attend circles of study and worship.

The same hadith mentions that Umm ʿAṭiyyah, the narrator, asked the Prophet about a woman who had no suitable frock. The Arabic word used here for frock is *jilbāb*, and it is described by scholars in different ways. Al-Naḍr ibn Shumayl said that it is a dress that is shorter and wider than the *khimar,* which a woman uses to cover her head. Some say that it is a wide garment to cover a woman's chest and back, while other opinions suggest that it is the same as the *khimār*, or like a top broad garment.

The Prophet gives this answer to Umm ʿAṭiyyah: 'Let her sister give her one of her frocks to wear'. This means that she gives her a frock or a dress as a gift. The hadith urges that the Eid Prayer should be attended by all, and that Muslims should help one another to attend to worship and be more God-fearing.

CHAPTER 3

NO PRAYER BEFORE OR AFTER THE EID PRAYER

[1763–13]. (Dar al-Salam 1935) ʿUbaydullāh ibn Muʿādh al-ʿAnbarī narrated:[i] my father narrated; Shuʿbah narrated; from ʿAdiy; from Saʿīd ibn Jubayr; from Ibn ʿAbbās; that **'God's Messenger (peace be upon him) came out on the day of Eid al-Aḍḥā or Eid al-Fiṭr and prayed two *rakʿahs*. He did not do any other prayer before or after it. He then went to the women and Bilāl was with him. He urged them to give *ṣadaqah*. Women then gave their rings and necklaces'.**

وَحَدَّثَنَا عُبَيْدُ اللهِ بْنُ مُعَاذٍ الْعَنْبَرِيُّ، حَدَّثَنَا أَبِي، حَدَّثَنَا شُعْبَةُ، عَنْ عَدِيٍّ، عَنْ سَعِيدِ بْنِ جُبَيْرٍ، عَنِ ابْنِ عَبَّاسٍ، أَنَّ رَسُولَ اللهِ صَلَّى اللهُ عَلَيْهِ وَسَلَّمَ خَرَجَ يَوْمَ أَضْحَى أَوْ فِطْرٍ، فَصَلَّى رَكْعَتَيْنِ لَمْ يُصَلِّ قَبْلَهَا وَلاَ بَعْدَهَا. ثُمَّ أَتَى النِّسَاءَ وَمَعَهُ بِلاَلٌ فَأَمَرَهُنَّ بِالصَّدَقَةِ، فَجَعَلَتِ الْمَرْأَةُ تُلْقِي خُرْصَهَا وَتُلْقِي سِخَابَهَا.

ʿAmr al-Nāqid narrated to me: Ibn Idrīs narrated [H]. Also, Abu Bakr ibn Nāfiʿ and Muhammad ibn Bashshār narrated to me; both from Ghudar; both from Shuʿbah; with this chain of transmission: **a similar text.**

---

i. Related by al-Bukhari, 964, 1431, 5881 and in a shorter version, 989; Abu Dāwūd, 1159; al-Tirmidhī, 537; al-Nasāʾī, 1586; Ibn Mājah, 1291.

وَحَدَّثَنِيهِ عَمْرٌو النَّاقِدُ، حَدَّثَنَا ابْنُ إِدْرِيسَ، ح. وَحَدَّثَنِي أَبُو بَكْرِ بْنُ نَافِعٍ، وَمُحَمَّدُ بْنُ بَشَّارٍ، جَمِيعًا عَنْ غُنْدَرٍ، كِلَاهُمَا عَنْ شُعْبَةَ، بِهَذَا الإِسْنَادِ نَحْوَه.

Text Explanation

This hadith makes it clear that no sunnah prayer is offered before or after the Eid Prayer. Mālik considers the hadith as evidence indicating that such a prayer before or after the Eid Prayer is discouraged. The same view is expressed by a number of the Prophet's Companions and scholars of the *tābiʿīn* generation. However, al-Shāfiʿī and a number of the early scholars say that there is no discouragement of praying before or after the Eid Prayer. Al-Awzāʿī, Abu Ḥanīfah and other Kufi scholars say that voluntary prayer is discouraged before the Eid Prayer but not after it. The fact is that the hadith does not provide an argument in support of discouragement for such prayer because not to pray does not mean that a prayer is discouraged. The rule makes clear that no prohibition is valid without proof.

CHAPTER 4

WHAT TO RECITE IN EID PRAYER

[1764–14]. (Dar al-Salam 1936) Yaḥyā ibn Yaḥyā narrated: he said: I read out to Mālik; from Ḍamrah ibn Sa'īd al-Māzinī; from 'Ubaydullāh ibn 'Abdullāh; that 'Umar ibn al-Khaṭṭāb asked Abu Wāqid al-Laythī: **'What did God's Messenger recite in the prayers of Eid al-Aḍḥā and Eid al-Fiṭr?' He said: 'He recited in them the surahs starting "Qāf, by the glorious Qur'an" and "The Last Hour draws near, and the moon is split asunder".'**

حَدَّثَنَا يَحْيَى بْنُ يَحْيَى قَالَ: قَرَأْتُ عَلَى مَالِكٍ عَنْ ضَمْرَةَ بْنِ سَعِيدٍ الْمَازِنِيِّ، عَنْ عُبَيْدِ اللهِ بْنِ عَبْدِ اللهِ، أَنَّ عُمَرَ بْنَ الْخَطَّابِ، سَأَلَ أَبَا وَاقِدٍ اللَّيْثِيَّ: مَا كَانَ يَقْرَأُ بِهِ رَسُولُ اللهِ صَلَّى اللهُ عَلَيْهِ وَسَلَّمَ فِي الأَضْحَى وَالْفِطْرِ؟ فَقَالَ: كَانَ يَقْرَأُ فِيهِمَا بِـ «ق وَالْقُرْآنِ الْمَجِيدِ» و «اقْتَرَبَتِ السَّاعَةُ وَانْشَقَّ الْقَمَرُ».

[1765–15]. (Dar al-Salam 1937) Isḥāq ibn Ibrāhīm narrated: Abu 'Āmir al-'Aqadī reported; Fulayḥ narrated; from Ḍamrah ibn Sa'īd; from 'Ubaydullāh ibn 'Abdullāh ibn 'Utbah; from Abu Wāqid al-Laythī. He said: **''Umar ibn al-Khaṭṭāb asked me about what God's Messenger (peace be upon him) recited on the day of the Eid. I said: "[He recited] the Last Hour draws near, and Qāf, by the glorious Qur'an".'**

وَحَدَّثَنَا إِسْحَاقُ بْنُ إِبْرَاهِيمَ، أَخْبَرَنَا أَبُو عَامِرٍ الْعَقَدِيُّ، حَدَّثَنَا فُلَيْحٌ، عَنْ ضَمْرَةَ، بْنِ سَعِيدٍ عَنْ عُبَيْدِ اللهِ بْنِ عَبْدِ اللهِ بْنِ عُتْبَةَ، عَنْ أَبِي وَاقِدٍ اللَّيْثِيِّ، قَالَ: سَأَلَنِي عُمَرُ بْنُ

الْخَطَّابِ عَمَّا قَرَأَ بِهِ رَسُولُ اللهِ صَلَّى اللهُ عَلَيْهِ وَسَلَّمَ فِي يَوْمِ الْعِيدِ فَقُلْتُ بِـ "اقْتَرَبَتِ السَّاعَةُ" وَ "ق وَالْقُرْآنِ الْـمَجِيدِ"

Text Explanation

In the second hadith, No. 1765, Abu Wāqid says that ʿUmar asked him. Scholars say that ʿUmar might have had some doubts about it and he wanted to make sure, or he might have wanted to inform people about it or some other purpose. They add that it is improbable that ʿUmar did not know, given he would have offered the Eid Prayer with God's Messenger several times, and also given his closeness to him. Hence, al-Shāfiʿī and scholars who agree with him say that it is a sunnah to recite these two surahs in the Eid Prayer.

Scholars say that the reason for reciting these two surahs is that they include information about the resurrection, earlier generations and the destruction of communities that rejected the truth. The surahs also provide a comparison between people coming out to celebrate Eid and their resurrection, coming out of their graves like flocks of locusts.

Transmission

In its chain of transmission, the first hadith quotes ʿUbaydullāh saying that ʿUmar asked Abu Wāqid, while the chain of transmission of the second hadith includes: 'from ʿUbaydullāh from Abu Wāqid: ʿUmar ibn al-Khaṭṭāb asked me…'. This is how the hadiths are entered in all manuscripts and copies. The first hadith is narrated by Umm Salamah because ʿUbaydullāh never met ʿUmar. However, the hadith is undoubtedly authentic because the second chain of transmission provides the continuous sequence. Without doubt, ʿUbaydullāh met Abu Wāqid and heard his hadiths. There is no disagreement among scholars on this point. No criticism may attach to Muslim for reporting the two versions because their authenticity and continuity of transmission are well established, but God knows best.

CHAPTER 5

FUN AND ENJOYMENT DURING EID

[1766–16]. (Dar al-Salam 1938) Abu Bakr ibn Abi Shaybah narrated:[i] Abu Usāmah narrated; from Hishām; from his father; from ʿĀ'ishah. She said: **'Abu Bakr entered my home when two maids belonging to the Anṣār were with me, singing some of what the Anṣār composed about the Battle of Buʿāth'. She added: 'They were not singers. Abu Bakr said: "What! Satan's instrument in God's Messenger's home?" That was on the day of Eid. God's Messenger (peace be upon him) said: "Abu Bakr, every nation has a festive day, and this is ours".'**

حَدَّثَنَا أَبُو بَكْرِ بْنُ أَبِي شَيْبَةَ، حَدَّثَنَا أَبُو أُسَامَةَ، عَنْ هِشَامٍ، عَنْ أَبِيهِ، عَنْ عَائِشَةَ قَالَتْ: دَخَلَ عَلَيَّ أَبُو بَكْرٍ وَعِنْدِي جَارِيَتَانِ مِنْ جَوَارِي الأَنْصَارِ تُغَنِّيَانِ بِمَا تَقَاوَلَتْ بِهِ الأَنْصَارُ يَوْمَ بُعَاثٍ. قَالَتْ: وَلَيْسَتَا بِمُغَنِّيَتَيْنِ. فَقَالَ أَبُو بَكْرٍ: أَبِمَزْمُورِ الشَّيْطَانِ فِي بَيْتِ رَسُولِ اللهِ صَلَّى اللهُ عَلَيْهِ وَسَلَّمَ؟ وَذَلِكَ فِي يَوْمِ عِيدٍ. فَقَالَ رَسُولُ اللهِ صَلَّى اللهُ عَلَيْهِ وَسَلَّمَ: «يَا أَبَا بَكْرٍ إِنَّ لِكُلِّ قَوْمٍ عِيدًا وَهَذَا عِيدُنَا».

[1767–000]. (Dar al-Salam 1939) Yaḥyā ibn Yaḥyā and Abu Kurayb narrated: both from Abu Muʿāwiyah; from Hishām; with the same chain of transmission: **the same text, except that it says: 'Two maids playing the tambourine'.**

i. Related by al-Bukhari, 952; Ibn Mājah, 1897.

وَحَدَّثَنَاهُ يَحْيَى بْنُ يَحْيَى، وَأَبُو كُرَيْبٍ جَمِيعًا عَنْ أَبِي مُعَاوِيَةَ، عَنْ هِشَامٍ، بِهَذَا الإِسْنَادِ، وَفِيهِ: جَارِيَتَانِ تَلْعَبَانِ بِدُفٍّ.

[1768–17]. (Dar al-Salam 1940) Ḥarūn ibn Saʿīd al-Aylī narrated to me: Ibn Wahb narrated; ʿAmr reported to me; that Ibn Shihāb narrated to him; from ʿUrwah; from ʿĀʾishah; that **'Abu Bakr came into her home when she had two maids singing and playing [the tambourine] and this was during Mina days. God's Messenger was lying down, covered with his robe. Abu Bakr rebuked the maids. God's Messenger (peace be upon him) uncovered his face and said: "Abu Bakr, leave them alone – these are Eid days".' She also said: 'God's Messenger (peace be upon him) shielded me with his robe when I was watching the Abyssinians as they were playing. I was young. Give an allowance to a fun-loving young woman'.**

حَدَّثَنِي هَارُونُ بْنُ سَعِيدٍ الأَيْلِيُّ، حَدَّثَنَا ابْنُ وَهْبٍ، أَخْبَرَنِي عَمْرٌو، أَنَّ ابْنَ شِهَابٍ حَدَّثَهُ عَنْ عُرْوَةَ، عَنْ عَائِشَةَ، أَنَّ أَبَا بَكْرٍ دَخَلَ عَلَيْهَا، وَعِنْدَهَا جَارِيَتَانِ فِي أَيَّامِ مِنًى، تُغَنِّيَانِ وَتَضْرِبَانِ. وَرَسُولُ اللهِ صَلَّى اللهُ عَلَيْهِ وَسَلَّمَ مُسَجًّى بِثَوْبِهِ. فَانْتَهَرَهُمَا أَبُو بَكْرٍ، فَكَشَفَ رَسُولُ اللهِ صَلَّى اللهُ عَلَيْهِ وَسَلَّمَ عَنْهُ وَقَالَ: «دَعْهُمَا يَا أَبَا بَكْرٍ فَإِنَّهَا أَيَّامُ عِيدٍ». وَقَالَتْ: رَأَيْتُ رَسُولَ اللهِ صَلَّى اللهُ عَلَيْهِ وَسَلَّمَ يَسْتُرُنِي بِرِدَائِهِ، وَأَنَا أَنْظُرُ إِلَى الْحَبَشَةِ وَهُمْ يَلْعَبُونَ. وَأَنَا جَارِيَةٌ فَاقْدِرُوا قَدْرَ الْجَارِيَةِ الْعَرِبَةِ الْحَدِيثَةِ السِّنِّ.

[1769–18]. (Dar al-Salam 1941) Abu al-Ṭāhir narrated to me:[i] Ibn Wahb reported; Yūnus reported to me; from Ibn Shihāb; from ʿUrwah ibn al-Zubayr; he said: ʿĀʾishah said: **'By God, I saw God's Messenger standing by the door of my compartment**

i. Related by al-Bukhari, 455.

when the Abyssinians were playing with their spears in God's Messenger's mosque. He shielded me with his robe so that I could look at their play, and he would remain there for my sake until I chose to leave. Give an allowance to a young woman who is eager to have some fun'.

وَحَدَّثَنِي أَبُو الطَّاهِرِ، أَخْبَرَنِي ابْنُ وَهْبٍ، أَخْبَرَنِي يُونُسُ، عَنِ ابْنِ شِهَابٍ، عَنْ عُرْوَةَ بْنِ الزُّبَيْرِ قَالَ: قَالَتْ عَائِشَةُ: وَاللهِ لَقَدْ رَأَيْتُ رَسُولَ اللهِ صَلَّى اللهُ عَلَيْهِ وَسَلَّمَ يَقُومُ عَلَى بَابِ حُجْرَتِي، وَالْحَبَشَةُ يَلْعَبُونَ بِحِرَابِهِمْ فِي مَسْجِدِ رَسُولِ اللهِ صَلَّى اللهُ عَلَيْهِ وَسَلَّمَ يَسْتُرُنِي بِرِدَائِهِ لِكَيْ أَنْظُرَ إِلَى لَعِبِهِمْ. ثُمَّ يَقُومُ مِنْ أَجْلِي حَتَّى أَكُونَ أَنَا الَّتِي أَنْصَرِفُ. فَاقْدُرُوا قَدْرَ الْجَارِيَةِ الْحَدِيثَةِ السِّنِّ حَرِيصَةً عَلَى اللَّهْوِ.

[1770–19]. (Dar al-Salam 1942) Ḥarūn ibn Saʿīd al-Aylī and Yūnus ibn ʿAbd al-Aʿlā narrated to me (Ḥarūn's text):[i] both said: Ibn Wahb narrated; ʿAmr reported; that Muhammad ibn ʿAbd al-Raḥmān narrated to him; from ʿUrwah; from ʿĀ'ishah. She said: **'God's Messenger (peace be upon him) came in when I had two maids singing the songs of the Battle of Buʿāth. He lay on the bed and turned his face. Abu Bakr came in and rebuked me, saying: "Satan's instrument at God's Messenger's home?" The Prophet turned to him and said: "Leave them alone". When he was not attentive, I gave them a signal with my eye, and they left.**

And on an Eid Day, the black people played with shields and spears. Either I asked God's Messenger, or he said to me: "Would you like to watch?" I said: "Yes". He placed me behind him, with my cheek on his cheek,[ii] and he said: "Carry on, Arfidah people". When I was bored, he asked me: "Have you had enough?" I said: "Yes". He said: "You may go".'

---

i. Related by al-Bukhari, 949 and in a shorter version 2906.

ii. This means that she was behind the Prophet, putting her head on his shoulder and her cheek on his cheek.

حَدَّثَنِي هَارُونُ بْنُ سَعِيدٍ الأَيْلِيُّ، وَيُونُسُ بْنُ عَبْدِ الأَعْلَى، - وَاللَّفْظُ لِهَارُونَ-قَالا: حَدَّثَنَا ابْنُ وَهْبٍ، أَخْبَرَنَا عَمْرٌو، أَنَّ مُحَمَّدَ بْنَ عَبْدِ الرَّحْمَنِ، حَدَّثَهُ عَنْ عُرْوَةَ، عَنْ عَائِشَةَ قَالَتْ: دَخَلَ رَسُولُ اللهِ صَلَّى اللهُ عَلَيْهِ وَسَلَّمَ وَعِنْدِي جَارِيَتَانِ تُغَنِّيَانِ بِغِنَاءِ بُعَاثٍ، فَاضْطَجَعَ عَلَى الْفِرَاشِ وَحَوَّلَ وَجْهَهُ. فَدَخَلَ أَبُو بَكْرٍ فَانْتَهَرَنِي، وَقَالَ: مِزْمَارُ الشَّيْطَانِ عِنْدَ رَسُولِ اللهِ صَلَّى اللهُ عَلَيْهِ وَسَلَّمَ؟ فَأَقْبَلَ عَلَيْهِ رَسُولُ اللهِ صَلَّى اللهُ عَلَيْهِ وَسَلَّمَ فَقَالَ: «دَعْهُمَا». فَلَمَّا غَفَلَ غَمَزْتُهُمَا فَخَرَجَتَا.

وَكَانَ يَوْمَ عِيدٍ يَلْعَبُ السُّودَانُ بِالدَّرَقِ وَالْحِرَابِ، فَإِمَّا سَأَلْتُ رَسُولَ اللهِ صَلَّى اللهُ عَلَيْهِ وَسَلَّمَ وَإِمَّا قَالَ: «تَشْتَهِينَ تَنْظُرِينَ؟» فَقُلْتُ: نَعَمْ. فَأَقَامَنِي وَرَاءَهُ، خَدِّي عَلَى خَدِّهِ، وَهُوَ يَقُولُ: «دُونَكُمْ يَا بَنِي أَرْفِدَةَ». حَتَّى إِذَا مَلِلْتُ قَالَ: «حَسْبُكِ؟» قُلْتُ: نَعَمْ. قَالَ: «فَاذْهَبِي».

[1771–20]. (Dar al-Salam 1943) Zuhayr ibn Ḥarb narrated: Jarīr narrated; from Hishām; from his father; from ʿĀʾishah. She said: **'Some Abyssinians were dancing in the mosque on an Eid day. The Prophet (peace be upon him) called me and I placed my head on his shoulder, watching their play, until I was the one who chose to stop watching them'.**

حَدَّثَنَا زُهَيْرُ بْنُ حَرْبٍ، حَدَّثَنَا جَرِيرٌ، عَنْ هِشَامٍ، عَنْ أَبِيهِ، عَنْ عَائِشَةَ قَالَتْ: جَاءَ حَبَشٌ يَزْفِنُونَ فِي يَوْمِ عِيدٍ فِي الْـمَسْجِدِ فَدَعَانِي النَّبِيُّ صَلَّى اللهُ عَلَيْهِ وَسَلَّمَ، فَوَضَعْتُ رَأْسِي عَلَى مَنْكِبِهِ، فَجَعَلْتُ أَنْظُرُ إِلَى لَعِبِهِمْ. حَتَّى كُنْتُ أَنَا الَّتِي أَنْصَرِفُ عَنِ النَّظَرِ إِلَيْهِمْ.

[1772–000]. (Dar al-Salam 1944) Yaḥyā ibn Yaḥyā narrated: Yaḥyā ibn Zakariyyā' ibn Abi Zā'idah reported [H]. Muhammad ibn Bishr narrated; both from Hishām; with the same chain of transmission: **the same text, but they did not mention 'in the mosque'.**

وَحَدَّثَنَا يَحْيَى بْنُ يَحْيَى، أَخْبَرَنَا يَحْيَى بْنُ زَكَرِيَّاءَ بْنِ أَبِي زَائِدَةَ، ح. وَحَدَّثَنَا ابْنُ نُمَيْرٍ، حَدَّثَنَا مُحَمَّدُ بْنُ بِشْرٍ، كِلاَهُمَا عَنْ هِشَامٍ، بِهَذَا الإِسْنَادِ. وَلَمْ يَذْكُرَا فِي الْـمَسْجِدِ.

[1773–21]. (Dar al-Salam 1945) Ibrāhīm ibn Dīnār, ʿUqbah ibn Mukram al-ʿAmmī and ʿAbd ibn Ḥumayd narrated to me: all from Abu ʿĀṣim (ʿUqbah's text) he said: Abu ʿĀṣim narrated; from Ibn Jurayj; he said: ʿAṭā' reported to me; ʿUbayd ibn ʿUmayr reported to me; ʿĀ'ishah told me that she said in reference to the dancers: **'I wish I could watch them'. She added: 'God's Messenger (peace be upon him) stood up, and I stood near the door, looking from between his ears and shoulder as they were playing in the mosque'.**

ʿAṭā' said: **'Persians or Abyssinians?' Ibn ʿAtīq told me: 'definitely Abyssinians'.**

وَحَدَّثَنِي إِبْرَاهِيمُ بْنُ دِينَارٍ وَعُقْبَةُ بْنُ مُكْرَمٍ الْعَمِّيُّ وَعَبْدُ بْنُ حُمَيْدٍ، كُلُّهُمْ عَنْ أَبِي عَاصِمٍ (وَاللَّفْظُ لِعُقْبَةَ) قَالَ: حَدَّثَنَا أَبُو عَاصِمٍ، عَنِ ابْنِ جُرَيْجٍ، قَالَ أَخْبَرَنِي عَطَاءٌ، أَخْبَرَنِي عُبَيْدُ بْنُ عُمَيْرٍ، أَخْبَرَتْنِي عَائِشَةُ أَنَّهَا قَالَتْ لِلَعَّابِينَ: وَدِدْتُ أَنِّي أَرَاهُمْ. قَالَتْ: فَقَامَ رَسُولُ اللهِ صَلَّى اللهُ عَلَيْهِ وَسَلَّمَ، وَقُمْتُ عَلَى الْبَابِ أَنْظُرُ بَيْنَ أُذُنَيْهِ وَعَاتِقِهِ، وَهُمْ يَلْعَبُونَ فِي الْـمَسْجِدِ.

قَالَ عَطَاءٌ فُرْسٌ أَوْ حَبَشٌ. قَالَ: وَقَالَ لِي ابْنُ عَتِيقٍ: بَلْ حَبَشٌ.

[1774–22]. (Dar al-Salam 1946) Muhammad ibn Rāfiʿ and ʿAbd ibn Ḥumayd narrated to me:[i] ʿAbd al-Razzāq (ʿAbd said: 'reported' and Ibn Rāfiʿ said: 'narrated'); Maʿmar reported; from al-Zuhrī; from Ibn al-Musayyib; from Abu Hurayrah. He said: **'When the Abyssinians were at God's Messenger's playing with their spears, ʿUmar ibn al-Khaṭṭāb entered. He picked**

i. Related by al-Bukhari, 2901.

up pebbles to throw at them, but God's Messenger (peace be upon him) said to him: "Leave them alone, ʿUmar".'

وَحَدَّثَنِي مُحَمَّدُ بْنُ رَافِعٍ وَعَبْدُ بْنُ حُمَيْدٍ، قَالَ عَبْدٌ أَخْبَرَنَا وَقَالَ ابْنُ رَافِعٍ حَدَّثَنَا عَبْدُ الرَّزَّاقِ، أَخْبَرَنَا مَعْمَرٌ، عَنِ الزُّهْرِيِّ، عَنِ ابْنِ الْمُسَيَّبِ، عَنْ أَبِي هُرَيْرَةَ قَالَ: بَيْنَمَا الْحَبَشَةُ يَلْعَبُونَ عِنْدَ رَسُولِ اللهِ صَلَّى اللهُ عَلَيْهِ وَسَلَّمَ بِحِرَابِهِمْ إِذْ دَخَلَ عُمَرُ بْنُ الْخَطَّابِ، فَأَهْوَى إِلَى الْحَصْبَاءِ يَحْصِبُهُمْ بِهَا. فَقَالَ لَهُ رَسُولُ اللهِ صَلَّى اللهُ عَلَيْهِ وَسَلَّمَ: «دَعْهُمْ يَا عُمَرُ».

Text Explanation

In hadith No. 1766, ʿĀ'ishah says: 'Two maids belonging to the Anṣār were with me, singing some of what the Anṣār composed about the Battle of Buʿāth'. She added: 'They were not singers'. The Battle of Buʿāth took place between the Aws and the Khazraj, the two Arab tribes living in Madinah shortly before Islam, and it ended with victory for the Aws. ʿĀ'ishah describes the two maids as 'not singers', which means that singing was not their habit and they were not adept at it.

Scholars differ as to the ruling that applies to singing. A number of scholars from Hijaz said that it is permissible. This is also one report attributed to Mālik. On the other hand, Abu Ḥanīfah and scholars of Iraq consider it forbidden. The Shāfiʿī School considers it discouraged, or *makrūh*, and this is the better-known view of the Mālikī School. Those who consider singing permissible cite this hadith as evidence. The ones who take the opposite view say that this singing was with poetry speaking about bravery, military skills and killing the enemy and similar matters that lead to no unacceptable behaviour. This is different from singing that excites evil feelings and encourages time wasting and evil action. *Qadi* ʿIyāḍ said:

> They sang the poetry of war and made praises of bravery and victory. This does not put any evil thoughts in the maids' minds. Chanting such poetry is not a controversial matter. Differences of opinion apply to frivolous singing. Hence ʿĀ'ishah said: 'They were not singers', meaning that

> they were not like singers who sing about love, hinting about indecency, as well as descriptions of physical beauty and what excites desires. It is said: 'Singing encourages fornication'. Nor were these maids well-known singers who played on words with elongation and elaboration that excites latent feelings. And they were not professional singers. The Arabs used to describe poetry recitals as singing, but this does not belong to singing that is subject to different views. It is certainly permissible. The Prophet's Companions considered Arabic singing which is mere recital and chanting as permissible, and they permitted chanting to encourage their camels when they travelled. They did this in the Prophet's presence. All this clearly shows that this type, and whatever is similar to it, are permissible. Definitely, nothing of this type is forbidden.

When Abu Bakr entered his daughter's home and saw the maids singing, he said: 'What! Satan's instrument in God's Messenger's home?' This means that the homes and places of pious and devout people should be free of frivolity and hilarity, even if these involve no sin. Abu Bakr's action suggests that a subordinate who sees something unbecoming in the presence of his superior, may express disapproval. His action does not constitute exceeding any limits; indeed, it is an expression of care and respect of the superior, showing that the superior is above doing it himself and protecting his place from what is unbecoming. The Prophet did not censure the maids because what they did was permissible. He simply covered himself with his robe and turned his face away from their play, so that they would not feel shy and stop what was permissible. This reflected his kindness and good manners.

The Prophet said to Abu Bakr: 'Every nation has a festive day, and this is ours'. This means that playing the tambourine on a festive day, such as an Eid day or a wedding or a day of similar pleasure is permissible.

In hadith No. 1768, 'Ā'ishah mentions that this was 'in Mina days'. These are the three days that follow the day of sacrifice, which is the day of Eid al-Aḍḥā. They are also called the Tashrīq days. This signifies that these three days are included with Eid and the same rulings apply to them, such as the acceptability of a sacrifice, the prohibition of fasting, the desirability of *takbīr*, etc. ʿĀ'ishah adds: 'God's Messenger (peace be upon him) shielded me with his robe when I was watching the Abyssinians as they were playing. I was young'. In the next hadith, she says: 'I saw the Abyssinians playing with their spears in God's Messenger's mosque'. This is a clear statement showing that it is permissible to play with arms and other equipment used in war inside the mosque. The same applies to similar means that help fighters and other good ways.

Is it permissible for a woman to look at a man's face if he is a stranger? If she is looking with desire, then this is forbidden, according to all scholars. If it is not coupled with desire and no attraction is feared, then our scholars express two views, the more correct of which is that it is also forbidden, because God says: 'Tell believing women to lower their gaze'. (24: 31). In a hadith, the Prophet tells his wives Umm Salamah and Umm Ḥabībah to stay behind a screen when Ibn Umm Maktūm was with him. They said: 'But he is blind and cannot see us'. He said: 'Are you also blind? Do you not see him?' This hadith is related by al-Tirmidhī who grades it as 'good'. They give two arguments in response to this hadith narrated by ʿĀ'ishah, and the stronger of the two is that the hadith does not mention that she looked at their faces and bodies but at their play and spears. This does not necessarily mean deliberately looking at their bodies. If she happens to see them, she would immediately turn away. The other argument is that this might have been before the revelation of the verse prohibiting looking, and that she might have been young. Some scholars say that such rulings do not apply to a young person, but God knows best.[i]

i. This whole argument sounds plainly laboured. It is well known that the Prophet's wives had special rulings that did not apply to anyone else. They had to be screened from all men except their immediate relatives. Besides, the Abyssinians came to meet the Prophet in Year 7, i.e. six years after ʿĀ'ishah's marriage. Her description of herself as young is relative. She was a young woman, but not a child.

This hadith shows that the Prophet was very kind and compassionate. He treated his family and other people with kindness and understanding. ʿĀ'ishah urges people to give allowances to girls and young women who love fun and enjoyment. She thus made clear that as a young woman, she enjoyed looking at play and dancing, and she wanted to watch it as long as possible, until she got bored. Therefore, she tells Muslims to indulge their daughters and young women in such matters, and give them what they want, as love of fun is part of their nature.

The Prophet encouraged the Abyssinians to go ahead with their play and his wife continued watching. Then he asked her whether she had had enough. When she confirmed this, he told her to leave.

In hadith No. 1771 ʿĀ'ishah said that some Abyssinians 'were dancing on an Eid day in the Prophet's mosque'. Scholars understand this as meaning doing special movement with their arms and playing with their spears, and this was similar in some ways to dancing. Most of the hadiths speaking of the event say that they were playing with their spears. Therefore, the usage of the word 'dancing' in this hadith is understood to concur with the other reports mentioning playing.

Hadith No. 1773 includes that ʿAṭā' asked the question: 'Persians or Abyssinians'? and Ibn ʿAtīq said 'definitely Abyssinians'. This is how it is mentioned in all manuscripts. It means that ʿAṭā' had some doubts and asked whether they were Persians or from Abyssinia. Ibn ʿAtīq was clear and gave a definite answer that they were Abyssinians. *Qadi* ʿIyāḍ said: 'The statement, "Ibn ʿAtīq said", is how it is recorded by our teachers, but according to al-Bājī, it is "And Ibn ʿUmayr told me: he said", and in another copy, "Ibn Abi ʿAtīq said to me".' The author of *al-Mashāriq wal-Maṭāliʿ* said: 'The correct name is Ibn ʿUmayr, who is ʿUbayd ibn ʿUmayr mentioned in the chain of transmission', which is right.

In the last hadith, No. 1774, it is mentioned that when ʿUmar saw the Abyssinians playing in the mosque, he picked up some pebbles to throw at them. This is understood as meaning that ʿUmar felt that what they did was not right in the mosque and that the Prophet did not know about it, but God knows best.

BOOK OF PRAYER FOR RAIN

[1775–1]. (Dar al-Salam 1947) Yaḥyā ibn Yaḥyā narrated:[i] he said: I read out to Mālik; from ʿAbdullāh ibn Abi Bakr; that he heard ʿAbbād ibn Tamīm say: I heard ʿAbdullāh ibn Zayd al-Māzinī say: **'God's Messenger (peace be upon him) went out to the prayer place and prayed for rain. He turned his upper garment when he faced the *qiblah*'.**

وَحَدَّثَنَا يَحْيَى بْنُ يَحْيَى، قَالَ قَرَأْتُ عَلَى مَالِكٍ عَنْ عَبْدِ اللهِ بْنِ أَبِي بَكْرٍ، أَنَّهُ سَمِعَ عَبَّادَ بْنَ تَمِيمٍ يَقُولُ: سَمِعْتُ عَبْدَ اللهِ بْنَ زَيْدٍ الْـمَازِنِيَّ يَقُولُ: خَرَجَ رَسُولُ اللهِ صَلَّى اللهُ عَلَيْهِ وَسَلَّمَ إِلَى الْـمُصَلَّى فَاسْتَسْقَى، وَحَوَّلَ رِدَاءَهُ حِينَ اسْتَقْبَلَ الْقِبْلَةَ.

[1776–2]. (Dar al-Salam 1948) Yaḥyā ibn Yaḥyā narrated: Sufyān ibn ʿUyaynah reported; from ʿAbdullāh ibn Abi Bakr; from ʿAbbād ibn Tamīm; from his uncle. He said: **'The Prophet went out to the prayer place and prayed for rain. He faced the *qiblah* and turned his upper garment. He prayed two *rakʿahs*'.**

وَحَدَّثَنَا يَحْيَى بْنُ يَحْيَى، أَخْبَرَنَا سُفْيَانُ بْنُ عُيَيْنَةَ، عَنْ عَبْدِ اللهِ بْنِ أَبِي بَكْرٍ، عَنْ عَبَّادِ بْنِ تَمِيمٍ، عَنْ عَمِّهِ قَالَ: خَرَجَ النَّبِيُّ صَلَّى اللهُ عَلَيْهِ وَسَلَّمَ إِلَى الْـمُصَلَّى فَاسْتَسْقَى، وَاسْتَقْبَلَ الْقِبْلَةَ، وَقَلَبَ رِدَاءَهُ وَصَلَّى رَكْعَتَيْنِ.

---

i. Related by al-Bukhari, 1011, 1012, 1005, 1023, 1024, 1025 and 1026; Abu Dāwūd, 1161, 1162, 1163, 1164, 1166 and 1167; al-Tirmidhī, 556; al-Nasāʾī, 1504, 1506, 1508, 1509, 1510, 1511, 1518 and 1519; Ibn Mājah, 1267.

[1777–3]. (Dar al-Salam 1949) Yaḥyā ibn Yaḥyā narrated: Sulaymān ibn Bilāl reported; from Yaḥyā ibn Sa ʿīd; he said: Abu Bakr ibn Muhammad ibn ʿAmr reported to me; that ʿAbbād ibn Tamīm reported to him; that ʿAbdullāh ibn Zayd al-Anṣārī told him that **'God's Messenger (peace be upon him) went out to the prayer place to pray for rain. When he was about to start his supplication, he faced the *qiblah* and turned his garment'.**

وَحَدَّثَنَا يَحْيَى بْنُ يَحْيَى، أَخْبَرَنَا سُلَيْمَانُ بْنُ بِلَالٍ، عَنْ يَحْيَى بْنِ سَعِيدٍ قَالَ: أَخْبَرَنِي أَبُو بَكْرِ بْنُ مُحَمَّدِ بْنِ عَمْرٍو، أَنَّ عَبَّادَ بْنَ تَمِيمٍ أَخْبَرَهُ، أَنَّ عَبْدَ اللهِ بْنَ زَيْدٍ الأَنْصَارِيَّ أَخْبَرَهُ، أَنَّ رَسُولَ اللهِ صَلَّى اللهُ عَلَيْهِ وَسَلَّمَ خَرَجَ إِلَى الْـمُصَلَّى يَسْتَسْقِي. وَأَنَّهُ لَمَّا أَرَادَ أَنْ يَدْعُوَ اسْتَقْبَلَ الْقِبْلَةَ وَحَوَّلَ رِدَاءَهُ.

[1778–4]. (Dar al-Salam 1950) Abu al-Ṭāhir and Ḥarmalah narrated to me: both said: Ibn Wahb reported; Yūnus reported to me; from Ibn Shihāb; he said: ʿAbbād ibn Tamīm al-Māzinī reported to him; that he heard his uncle, who was a Companion of the Prophet (peace be upon him), say: **'God's Messenger (peace be upon him) went out one day to pray for rain. His back was to the people and he supplicated to God, facing the *qiblah*. He had turned his garment. He then prayed two *rak ʿahs*'.**

وَحَدَّثَنِي أَبُو الطَّاهِرِ وَحَرْمَلَةُ، قَالَا أَخْبَرَنَا ابْنُ وَهْبٍ، أَخْبَرَنِي يُونُسُ، عَنِ ابْنِ شِهَابٍ قَالَ: أَخْبَرَنِي عَبَّادُ بْنُ تَمِيمٍ الْـمَازِنِيُّ، أَنَّهُ سَمِعَ عَمَّهُ، وَكَانَ مِنْ أَصْحَابِ رَسُولِ اللهِ صَلَّى اللهُ عَلَيْهِ وَسَلَّمَ، يَقُولُ: خَرَجَ رَسُولُ اللهِ صَلَّى اللهُ عَلَيْهِ وَسَلَّمَ يَوْمًا يَسْتَسْقِي، فَجَعَلَ إِلَى النَّاسِ ظَهْرَهُ يَدْعُو اللهَ. وَاسْتَقْبَلَ الْقِبْلَةَ، وَحَوَّلَ رِدَاءَهُ ثُمَّ صَلَّى رَكْعَتَيْنِ.

Text Explanation

Scholars are unanimous that appealing for rain is a sunnah, but they differ on whether it is a sunnah to offer a prayer for it or not. Abu Ḥanīfah said that no prayer is recommended for it, and it is done only by supplication. The rest of the scholars of early and later generations, from the Prophet's Companions onwards, say that prayer is also recommended. Only Abu Ḥanīfah disagrees, basing his view on the hadiths that mention supplication for rain without mentioning a prayer. The majority of scholars cite the authentic hadiths entered in the two *Ṣaḥīḥ* anthologies of al-Bukhari and Muslim, as well as other anthologies, mentioning that the Prophet prayed two *rakʿahs* when he appealed to God for rain. As for the hadiths that do not mention a prayer, the omission is felt to be the result of the narrator forgetting to mention the prayer in some cases. Others mention a supplication for rain during the Friday *Khuṭbah*, or sermon, which is followed by the Friday Prayer, and the Prophet deemed it sufficient. If he did not pray at all, then he did so to show that it is permissible to supplicate for rain without performing a prayer. There is no disagreement among scholars that this is permissible. However, the hadiths that mention a prayer, are given priority because they add some information and cause no conflict.

Our scholars say that the appeal for rain is of three types: the first is to supplicate without offering a prayer, the second is to supplicate for rain during the Friday *Khuṭbah* or after an obligatory prayer – this is better than the first type – and the third, which is the best and most perfect, is to pray two *rakʿahs* and deliver two *khuṭbahs*. Prior preparation is added in the form of donating some *ṣadaqah*, or charity, or fasting, or repentance of sin, and doing some good things and avoiding all bad behaviour, etc.

Hadith No. 1775 states: 'God's Messenger (peace be upon him) went out to the prayer place and prayed for rain. He turned his upper garment when he faced the *qiblah*'. The next hadith gives the same text but adds that the Prophet prayed two *rakʿahs*. These hadiths show that it is desirable when praying for rain to go out of town because it better demonstrates humility. Moreover, it is spacious and can accommodate all comers because all people may come and no mosque can accommodate them. According to the hadiths, it is also desirable to turn one's upper garment inside out in appealing for rain. Our scholars say that the imam turns his garment inside out at about one-third of the second *khuṭbah,* which is when the imam faces the *qiblah,* i.e. the direction of prayer.

Scholars say that the imam turns his upper garment as a gesture of hope that the situation will change from draught to rain and abundance. The hadith provides evidence in support of the view of al-Shāfiʿī, Mālik, Ahmad and the great majority of scholars that turning one's garment is desirable. Abu Ḥanīfah does not approve of it. According to our school, it is also desirable for the people in the congregation to do the same as the imam. Mālik and others share this view. However, a number of scholars disagree. The hadiths make clear that prayer for rain is valid and they refute the argument of those who deny it. The hadiths make clear that the prayer for rain is in two *rakʿahs.* This is unanimously agreed upon by all those who confirm it. They differ as to whether the prayer is before or after the *khuṭbah,* with al-Shāfiʿī and the majority of scholars saying that the prayer is first. Al-Layth said that the prayer is after the *khuṭbah,* and Mālik used to say the same but then changed his views and agreed with the majority of scholars. Our scholars say that if the imam starts with the *khuṭbah* before the prayer, both are valid, but it is more preferable to start with the prayer in the same way as the Eid Prayer and its *khuṭbah.* The relevant hadiths suggest that there is no strict order. Reports from the Prophet's Companions on this point show both ways.

Scholars differ on whether this prayer starts with added glorifications, or *takbīr,* as in the Eid Prayer. Al-Shāfiʿī and Ibn Jarīr prefer it, and it is reported to be agreed upon by Ibn al-Musayyib, ʿUmar ibn ʿAbd al-ʿAzīz and Makḥūl. The majority of scholars say that no glorifications are added. In support of al-Shāfiʿī's view, scholars say that some hadiths mention that the Prophet 'prayed two *rakʿahs* as he did for Eid'. The majority of scholars understand this as meaning that the prayer is like the Eid Prayer in number, reciting the Qur'an aloud and being offered before the *khuṭbah.* Different reports are given from Ahmad on this point. Dāwūd gives the imam a choice to add glorifications or not. Reciting aloud is not mentioned in the hadiths related by Muslim, but al-Bukhari mentions it and scholars agree that it is desirable. They further agree that the prayer for rain is not preceded by an *adhān* or *iqāmah,* but it is announced with *al-ṣalāt jāmiʿah,* which means 'come to prayer'.

Hadith No. 1777 mentions that the Prophet faced the *qiblah* when he was about to start his supplication. This means that it is desirable when one supplicates. The same applies to other acts of worship, including ablution, taking a bath, dry ablution, recitation of the Qur'an, praising God and calling the *adhān,* etc. except what is not included on the basis of some evidence, such as the *khuṭbah.*

Hadith No. 1778 says: 'God's Messenger (peace be upon him) went out one day to pray for rain. His back was to the people and he supplicated to God, facing the *qiblah.* He had turned his garment. He then prayed two *rakʿahs*'. This provides a basis for the argument that the *khuṭbah* is before the prayer for rain. Our scholars interpret it as meaning that it is permissible, as stated earlier.

Transmission

The chain of transmission of hadith No. 1778 states that ''Abbād ibn Tamīm al-Māzinī reported to me that he heard his uncle'. His paternal uncle was ʿAbdullāh ibn Zayd ibn ʿĀṣim al-Anṣārī, mentioned in the previous hadiths.

CHAPTER 1

RAISING ONE'S ARMS WHEN SUPPLICATING FOR RAIN

[1779–5]. (Dar al-Salam 1951) Abu Bakr ibn Abi Shaybah narrated:[i] Yaḥyā ibn Abi Bukayr narrated; from Shuʿbah; from Thābit; from Anas. He said: **'I saw God's Messenger (peace be upon him) raising his arms when supplicating, with the whiteness of his armpits visible'.**

حَدَّثَنَا أَبُو بَكْرِ بْنُ أَبِي شَيْبَةَ، حَدَّثَنَا يَحْيَى بْنُ أَبِي بُكَيْرٍ، عَنْ شُعْبَةَ، عَنْ ثَابِتٍ، عَنْ أَنَسٍ قَالَ: رَأَيْتُ رَسُولَ اللهِ صَلَّى اللهُ عَلَيْهِ وَسَلَّمَ يَرْفَعُ يَدَيْهِ فِي الدُّعَاءِ حَتَّى يُرَى بَيَاضُ إِبْطَيْهِ.

[1780–6]. (Dar al-Salam 1952) ʿAbd ibn Ḥumayd narrated:[ii] al-Ḥasan ibn Mūsā narrated; Ḥammād ibn Salamah narrated; from Thābit; from Anas ibn Mālik; that **'The Prophet (peace be upon him) prayed for rain with the back of his palms pointing to the sky'.**

وَحَدَّثَنَا عَبْدُ بْنُ حُمَيْدٍ، حَدَّثَنَا الْحَسَنُ بْنُ مُوسَى، حَدَّثَنَا حَمَّادُ بْنُ سَلَمَةَ، عَنْ ثَابِتٍ، عَنْ أَنَسِ بْنِ مَالِكٍ أَنَّ النَّبِيَّ صَلَّى اللهُ عَلَيْهِ وَسَلَّمَ اسْتَسْقَى، فَأَشَارَ بِظَهْرِ كَفَّيْهِ إِلَى السَّمَاءِ.

---

i. Related by al-Nasāʾī 1747.
ii. Related by Abu Dāwūd, 1171.

[1781–7]. (Dar al-Salam 1953–1954) Muhammad ibn al-Muthannā narrated:[i] Ibn Abi ʿAdiy and ʿAbd al-Aʿlā narrated; from Saʿīd; from Qatādah; from Anas; that **'The Prophet (peace be upon him) did not raise his arms in any supplication other than when he supplicated for rain. [He raised them] so, that the whiteness of his two armpits was visible'.**

ʿAbd al-Aʿlā, however, said: **'that the whiteness of his armpit or armpits was visible'.**

حَدَّثَنَا مُحَمَّدُ بْنُ الْمُثَنَّى، حَدَّثَنَا ابْنُ أَبِي عَدِيٍّ وَعَبْدُ الأَعْلَى، عَنْ سَعِيدٍ، عَنْ قَتَادَةَ، عَنْ أَنَسٍ أَنَّ نَبِيَّ اللهِ صَلَّى اللهُ عَلَيْهِ وَسَلَّمَ كَانَ لاَ يَرْفَعُ يَدَيْهِ فِي شَيْءٍ مِنْ دُعَائِهِ إِلاَّ فِي الِاسْتِسْقَاءِ، حَتَّى يُرَى بَيَاضُ إِبْطَيْهِ. غَيْرَ أَنَّ عَبْدَ الأَعْلَى قَالَ يُرَى بَيَاضُ إِبْطِهِ أَوْ بَيَاضُ إِبْطَيْهِ.

Ibn al-Muthannā narrated: Yaḥyā ibn Saʿīd narrated; from Ibn Abi ʿArūbah; from Qatādah; that Anas ibn Mālik narrated to them from the Prophet (peace be upon him): **a similar text.**

وَحَدَّثَنَا ابْنُ الْمُثَنَّى، حَدَّثَنَا يَحْيَى بْنُ سَعِيدٍ، عَنِ ابْنِ أَبِي عَرُوبَةَ، عَنْ قَتَادَةَ، أَنَّ أنس بن مالك حَدَّثَهُمْ عَنِ النَّبِيِّ صَلَّى اللهُ عَلَيْهِ وَسَلَّمَ نَحْوَهُ

Text Explanation

Hadith No. 1780 says: 'The Prophet (peace be upon him) prayed for rain with the back of his palms pointing to the sky'. A number of our scholars and others say that it is a sunnah in every supplication to remove some hardship, such as a draught or shortage of provisions, that the supplicant should raise his arms and point to the sky with the back of his palms. If he is supplicating to be granted something,

i. Related by al-Bukhari, 1031 and 3565; Abu Dāwūd, 1170; al-Nasā'ī, 1512; Ibn Mājah, 1180

then the inside of his hands should be facing the sky. They cite this hadith in support of their argument.

Hadith No. 1781 quotes Anas: 'The Prophet (peace be upon him) did not raise his arms in any supplication other than when he supplicated for rain. [He raised them] so that the whiteness of his two armpits was visible'. On the surface, this hadith implies that the Prophet never raised his hands when supplicating except in the case of supplication for rain. It was not so because it is confirmed that he raised his hands when supplicating for other things on a countless number of occasions. I have put together nearly thirty hadiths on the subject, and these are related in one or both of the authentic *Ṣaḥīḥ* anthologies of al-Bukhari and Muslim. I entered them towards the end of the chapter describing prayer in my book *Sharḥ al-Muhadhdhab*. Therefore, this hadith should be understood as meaning that the Prophet did not raise his arms so high as to make the whiteness of his armpits visible except when praying for rain. Alternatively, it may be understood as the narrator, Anas, says: 'I did not see him raising his arms...'. Other people saw him doing so. These are then given preference because they are numerous, speaking about several occasions. They take priority over a single person who was not present on these occasions. The hadith must be understood as we have mentioned, but God knows best.

Transmission

The chain of transmission of hadith No. 1781 includes: 'from Qatādah from Anas', but in the other chain of transmission narrating the same hadith we have 'from Qatādah that Anas ibn Mālik narrated to them...'. This second chain of transmission confirms that Qatādah heard the hadith from Anas, using the words 'narrated to them'. We have mentioned earlier that Qatādah is graded as a 'misleading narrator'. When such a misleading narrator mentions a hadith stating that he is reporting it 'from someone', such narration is unacceptable unless it is confirmed in some other way that he heard it from that person. Hence, Muslim confirms this, stating the other chain of transmission.

CHAPTER 2

WHAT TO SAY WHEN SUPPLICATING FOR RAIN

[1782–8]. (Dar al-Salam 1955) Yaḥyā ibn Yaḥyā, Yaḥyā ibn Ayyūb, Qutaybah and Ibh Ḥujr narrated:[i] Ismāʿīl ibn Jaʿfar (Yaḥyā said: 'reported' and the others said: 'narrated'); from Sharīk ibn Abi Namir; from Anas ibn Mālik; that **'A man came into the mosque on a Friday, entering through a door close to the House of Repayment. God's Messenger (peace be upon him) was standing, delivering his speech. He faced God's Messenger standing and said: "Messenger of God, flocks have perished, and means are hard. Pray to God to save us with rain". The Prophet raised his hands and said: "Our Lord, save us with rain. Our Lord, save us with rain. Our Lord, save us with rain".' Anas said: 'By God, we could see neither thick nor single clouds in the sky, although there was neither house nor building between us and Mount Salʿ. A circular shaped cloud appeared from behind it. When it was in the middle of the sky it spread, then it poured. By God, we did not see the sun for a long while. Then a man came through the same door on the following Friday, when God's Messenger was standing, delivering his speech. He stood facing him and said: "Messenger of God, properties have been ruined and roads are unpassable. Pray to God to stop it". God's Messenger (peace**

i. Related by al-Bukhari, 1013, 1014, 1016, 1017 and 1019; Abu Dāwūd, 1175; al-Nasāʾī, 1503, 1514 and 1517.

be upon him) raised his hands and said: "Our Lord, let it be around us, not on us. Our Lord, let it be on hills and knolls, and in the bottom of valleys and where trees are grown". It stopped raining. When we left, it was sunny'.

Sharīk said: **'I asked Anas ibn Mālik: "was it the same man?" He said: "I do not know".'**

وَحَدَّثَنَا يَحْيَى بْنُ يَحْيَى وَيَحْيَى بْنُ أَيُّوبَ وَقُتَيْبَةُ وَابْنُ حُجْرٍ. قَالَ يَحْيَى أَخْبَرَنَا وَقَالَ الآخَرُونَ، حَدَّثَنَا إِسْمَاعِيلُ بْنُ جَعْفَرٍ، عَنْ شَرِيكِ بْنِ أَبِي نَمِرٍ، عَنْ أَنَسِ بْنِ مَالِكٍ، أَنَّ رجُلاً دَخَلَ الـمسجِدَ يوم جُمُعَةٍ مِنْ بَابٍ كَانَ نَحْوَ دَارِ الْقَضَاءِ، وَرَسُولُ اللهِ صَلَّى اللهُ عَلَيْهِ وَسَلَّمَ قَائِمٌ يَخْطُبُ فَاسْتَقْبَلَ رَسُولَ اللهِ صَلَّى اللهُ عَلَيْهِ وَسَلَّمَ قَائِمًا، ثُمَّ قَالَ: يَا رَسُولَ اللهِ، هَلَكَتِ الأَمْوَالُ وَانْقَطَعَتِ السُّبُلُ، فَادْعُ اللهَ يُغِثْنَا. قَالَ: فَرَفَعَ رَسُولُ اللهِ صَلَّى اللهُ عَلَيْهِ وَسَلَّمَ يَدَيْهِ، ثُمَّ قَالَ: «اللَّهُمَّ أَغِثْنَا، اللَّهُمَّ أَغِثْنَا، اللَّهُمَّ أَغِثْنَا». قَالَ أَنَسٌ: وَلاَ وَاللهِ مَا نَرَى فِي السَّمَاءِ مِنْ سَحَابٍ وَلاَ قَزَعَةٍ، وَمَا بَيْنَنَا وَبَيْنَ سَلْعٍ مِنْ بَيْتٍ وَلاَ دَارٍ. قَالَ: فَطَلَعَتْ مِنْ وَرَائِهِ سَحَابَةٌ مِثْلُ التُّرْسِ، فَلَمَّا تَوَسَّطَتِ السَّمَاءَ انْتَشَرَتْ ثُمَّ أَمْطَرَتْ. قَالَ: فَلاَ وَاللهِ مَا رَأَيْنَا الشَّمْسَ سَبْتًا. قَالَ: ثُمَّ دَخَلَ رَجُلٌ مِنْ ذَلِكَ الْبَابِ فِي الْجُمُعَةِ الْـمُقْبِلَةِ، وَرَسُولُ اللهِ صَلَّى اللهُ عَلَيْهِ وَسَلَّمَ قَائِمٌ يَخْطُبُ، فَاسْتَقْبَلَهُ قَائِمًا فَقَالَ: يَا رَسُولَ اللهِ، هَلَكَتِ الأَمْوَالُ وَانْقَطَعَتِ السُّبُلُ فَادْعُ اللهَ يُمْسِكْهَا عَنَّا. قال: فَرَفَعَ رَسُولُ اللهِ صَلَّى اللهُ عَلَيْهِ وَسَلَّمَ يَدَيْهِ، ثم قال: «اللَّهُمَّ حَوْلَنَا وَلاَ عَلَيْنَا. اللَّهُمَّ عَلَى الآكَامِ وَالظِّرَابِ وَبُطُونِ الأَوْدِيَةِ وَمَنَابِتِ الشَّجَرِ». فَانْقَلَعَتْ، وَخَرَجْنَا نَمْشِي فِي الشَّمْسِ.

قَالَ شَرِيكٌ فَسَأَلْتُ أَنَسَ بْنَ مَالِكٍ: أَهُوَ الرَّجُلُ الأَوَّلُ؟ قَالَ: لاَ أَدْرِي

[1783–9]. (Dar al-Salam 1956) Dāwūd ibn Rushayd narrated:[i] al-Walīd ibn Muslim narrated; from al-Awzāʿī; Isḥāq ibn

i. Related by al-Bukhari, 933 and in a similar version, 1033, and also 1018; al-Nasāʾī, 1527.

ʿAbdullāh ibn Abi Ṭalḥah narrated to me; from Anas ibn Mālik. He said: **'People experienced drought during the lifetime of God's Messenger (peace be upon him). As the Prophet was delivering his speech on the platform [in the mosque] on Friday, a Bedouin stood up and said: "Messenger of God, our resources are drying up and our dependants are hungry...".' He continued the hadith giving the same meaning. '[The Prophet] said: "My Lord, make it around us, not upon us". Wherever he pointed his hand towards the sky, the clouds lifted until Madinah was like a wide dry circle. The stream at the Qanah Valley was running for a month. Everyone who came from any direction spoke of the heavy rain'.**

وَحَدَّثَنَا دَاوُدُ بْنُ رُشَيْدٍ، حَدَّثَنَا الْوَلِيدُ بْنُ مُسْلِمٍ، عَنِ الأَوْزَاعِيِّ، حَدَّثَنِي إِسْحَاقُ بْنُ عَبْدِ اللهِ بْنِ أَبِي طَلْحَةَ، عَنْ أَنَسِ بْنِ مَالِكٍ قَالَ: أَصَابَتِ النَّاسَ سَنَةٌ عَلَى عَهْدِ رَسُولِ اللهِ صَلَّى اللهُ عَلَيْهِ وَسَلَّمَ، فَبَيْنَا رَسُولُ اللهِ صَلَّى اللهُ عَلَيْهِ وَسَلَّمَ يَخْطُبُ النَّاسَ عَلَى الْـمِنْبَرِ يَوْمَ الْجُمُعَةِ إِذْ قَامَ أَعْرَابِيٌّ فَقَالَ: يَا رَسُولَ اللهِ، هَلَكَ الْـمَالُ وَجَاعَ الْعِيَالُ. وَسَاقَ الْحَدِيثَ بِمَعْنَاهُ. وَفِيهِ قَالَ: «اللَّهُمَّ حَوَالَيْنَا وَلاَ عَلَيْنَا». قَالَ: فَمَا يُشِيرُ بِيَدِهِ إِلَى نَاحِيَةٍ إِلاَّ تَفَرَّجَتْ، حَتَّى رَأَيْتُ الْـمَدِينَةَ فِي مِثْلِ الْجَوْبَةِ. وَسَالَ وَادِي قَنَاةَ شَهْرًا. وَلَمْ يَجِئْ أَحَدٌ مِنْ نَاحِيَةٍ إِلاَّ أَخْبَرَ بِجَوْدٍ.

[1784–10]. (Dar al-Salam 1957) ʿAbd al-Aʿlā ibn Ḥammād and Muhammad ibn Abi Bakr al-Muqaddamī narrated:[i] both said: Muʿtamir narrated; ʿUbaydullāh narrated; from Thābit al-Bunānī; from Anas ibn Mālik. He said: **'The Prophet (peace be upon him) was delivering his *khuṭbah* on a Friday when people stood up and shouted: "Prophet of God, rain has dried**

i. Related by al-Bukhari, 1021; al-Nasāʾī, 1516.

out, trees have become red and livestock has perished"...' He added the rest of the hadith.

Added in ʿAbd al-Aʿlā's narration: **'It scattered away from Madinah and rained around it. There was no longer a single drop of rain in Madinah. I looked at Madinah and it seemed as if it was in the middle of a wreath'.**

وَحدَّثَنِي عَبْدُ الأَعْلَى بْنُ حَمَّادٍ وَمُحَمَّدُ بْنُ أَبِي بَكْرٍ الْـمُقَدَّمِيُّ، قَالا: حَدَّثَنَا مُعْتَمِرٌ، حَدَّثَنَا عُبَيْدُ اللهِ، عَنْ ثَابِتٍ الْبُنَانِيِّ، عَنْ أَنَسِ بْنِ مَالِكٍ قَالَ: كَانَ النَّبِيُّ صَلَّى اللهُ عَلَيْهِ وَسَلَّمَ يَخْطُبُ يَوْمَ الْجُمُعَةِ، فَقَامَ إِلَيْهِ النَّاسُ فَصَاحُوا، وَقَالُوا يَا نَبِيَّ اللهِ قَحِطَ الْـمَطَرُ، وَاحْمَرَّ الشَّجَرُ، وَهَلَكَتِ الْبَهَائِمُ. وَسَاقَ الْحَدِيثَ، وَفِيهِ مِنْ رِوَايَةِ عَبْدِ الأَعْلَى فَتَقَشَّعَتْ عَنِ الْـمَدِينَةِ. فَجَعَلَتْ تُمْطِرُ حَوَالَيْهَا وَمَا تُمْطِرُ بِالْـمَدِينَةِ قَطْرَةً. فَنَظَرْتُ إِلَى الْـمَدِينَةِ وَإِنَّهَا لَفِي مِثْلِ الإِكْلِيلِ.

[1785–11]. (Dar al-Salam 1958) Abu Kurayb narrated: Abu Usāmah narrated; from Sulaymān ibn al-Mughīrah; from Thābit; from Anas: **a similar text and added: 'God amassed the cloud. We stayed, and I saw even a strong man feeling uneasy about going home'.**

وَحدَّثَنَاهُ أَبُو كُرَيْبٍ، حَدَّثَنَا أَبُو أُسَامَةَ، عَنْ سُلَيْمَانَ بْنِ الْـمُغِيرَةِ، عَنْ ثَابِتٍ، عَنْ أَنَسٍ، بِنَحْوِهِ. وَزَادَ فَأَلَّفَ اللهُ بَيْنَ السَّحَابِ، وَمَكَثْنَا حَتَّى رَأَيْتُ الرَّجُلَ الشَّدِيدَ تَهُمُّهُ نَفْسُهُ أَنْ يَأْتِيَ أَهْلَهُ.

[1786–12]. (Dar al-Salam 1959) Ḥarūn ibn Saʿīd al-Aylī narrated: Ibn Wahb narrated; Usāmah narrated; that Ḥafṣ ibn ʿUbaydullāh ibn Anas ibn Mālik narrated to him; that he heard Anas ibn Mālik say: **'A Bedouin spoke to God's Messenger (peace be upon him) on a Friday when he was on**

the platform...'. He narrated the hadith and added: 'I saw the clouds splitting away like sheets being folded'.

وَحَدَّثَنَا هَارُونُ بْنُ سَعِيدٍ الأَيْلِيُّ، حَدَّثَنَا ابْنُ وَهْبٍ، حَدَّثَنِي أُسَامَةُ، أَنَّ حَفْصَ بْنَ عُبَيْدِ اللهِ بْنِ أَنَسِ بْنِ مَالِكٍ حَدَّثَهُ أَنَّهُ سَمِعَ أَنَسَ بْنَ مَالِكٍ يَقُولُ: جَاءَ أَعْرَابِيٌّ إِلَى رَسُولِ اللهِ صَلَّى اللهُ عَلَيْهِ وَسَلَّمَ يَوْمَ الْجُمُعَةِ وَهُوَ عَلَى الْمِنْبَرِ. وَاقْتَصَّ الْحَدِيثَ. وَزَادَ فَرَأَيْتُ السَّحَابَ يَتَمَزَّقُ كَأَنَّهُ الْمُلَاءُ حِينَ تُطْوَى.

[1787–13]. (Dar al-Salam 1960) Yaḥyā ibn Yaḥyā narrated:[i] Jaʿfar ibn Sulaymān reported; from Thābit al-Bunānī; from Anas. He said: **'We were with God's Messenger when it started to rain. God's Messenger (peace be upon him) folded his robe and rain fell on him. We said: "Messenger of God, why have you done that?" He said: "Because [the rain] has been recently with its Lord".'**

وَحَدَّثَنَا يَحْيَى بْنُ يَحْيَى، أَخْبَرَنَا جَعْفَرُ بْنُ سُلَيْمَانَ، عَنْ ثَابِتٍ الْبُنَانِيِّ، عَنْ أَنَسٍ قَالَ: قَالَ أَنَسٌ: أَصَابَنَا وَنَحْنُ مَعَ رَسُولِ اللهِ صَلَّى اللهُ عَلَيْهِ وَسَلَّمَ مَطَرٌ، قَالَ فَحَسَرَ رَسُولُ اللهِ صَلَّى اللهُ عَلَيْهِ وَسَلَّمَ ثَوْبَهُ حَتَّى أَصَابَهُ مِنَ الْمَطَرِ. فَقُلْنَا: يَا رَسُولَ اللهِ لِمَ صَنَعْتَ هَذَا؟ قَالَ: «لأَنَّهُ حَدِيثُ عَهْدٍ بِرَبِّهِ تَعَالَى».

Text Explanation

In hadith No. 1782, the man came into the mosque 'through a door close to the House of Repayment'. *Qadi* ʿIyāḍ said:

> This house was called the House of Repayment because it was sold to repay the debt ʿUmar ibn al-Khaṭṭāb undertook

i. Related by Abu Dāwūd, 5100.

> to repay.[i] In his will, he instructed his son ʿAbdullāh to sell all his property for the repayment of his debts. If his property was not sufficient, he should seek help from the people of the ʿAdiy clan of Quraysh [ʿUmar's own clan], and if their help was not enough, then he should seek help from the people of the Quraysh. His son sold this house and ʿUmar's other property and repaid his debts. The house was bought by Muʿāwiyah. His debt amounted to 28,000 dirhams. The house came to be known as the House of Repaying ʿUmar's Debt, then this was shortened to the House of Repayment. It then became Marwān's house. Some suggested that it was the Governor's House, but this is wrong. They learnt that it was Marwān's house and they thought it was the Governor's house because Marwān was the Governor of Madinah. What we said earlier is right.

Qadi ʿIyāḍ said that ʿUmar's debt was 28,000. This is strange – indeed, wrong. The correct and well-known figure is that it was 86,000 or around this figure. This is mentioned by al-Bukhari in his *Ṣaḥīḥ*, as also other scholars of hadith, biographies and history.

In the same hadith, the man appeals to the Prophet to pray for rain, and the Prophet raises his arms and says: 'Our Lord, save us with rain'. This shows that prayer for rain is permissible during the Friday Prayer. It is also perfectly acceptable to supplicate for rain without connecting it to the particular prayer associated with such supplication. Ḥanafī scholars make this hadith the basis of their view that supplication for rain is only done as stated in this hadith [i.e. during the Friday Prayer]. They consider going out of town to a place where people gather to pray and supplicate for rain to be a deviation [i.e. *bidʿah*]. They are wrong; it is rather a sunnah in view of the authentic hadiths we discussed earlier. We mentioned earlier that

---

i. During his reign as caliph, ʿUmar borrowed this money to help people in need, and he felt he could not charge these to the state treasury. So he burdened himself with the debt that became very considerable over the years.

supplication for rain takes different forms. Therefore, the mention of one form does not mean that other forms, which are authentically reported, are invalid, but God knows best. The Prophet repeated his supplication three times, which suggests that it is desirable that urgent supplication is so repeated.

Anas ibn Mālik, the Prophet's Companion, narrating this hadith, says: 'By God, we could see neither thick nor single clouds in the sky, although there was neither house nor building between us and Mount Salʿ.' He thus tells of this miracle God showed them at this point, confirming Prophet Muhammad's honourable position with God. He says that they could see Mount Salʿ, which is close to Madinah, as there was nothing to block their view. There was no cloud or any other natural cause, visible or invisible, suggesting that rain was forthcoming, but when the Prophet said his supplication, immediately rain started and continued for seven consecutive days.

When a man complained to the Prophet that the rain was causing damage, the Prophet said a new supplication: '"Our Lord, let it be around us, not on us. Our Lord, let it be on hills and knolls, and in the bottom of valleys and where trees are grown". It stopped raining. When we left, it was sunny'. This part of the hadith includes several useful points. The first is the clear miracle manifested in the Prophet's supplication being immediately answered. The rain stopped and by the time the prayer was over, the Prophet's Companions were walking in the sun. Another point is the Prophet's refined manners, as reflected in his supplication. He did not appeal to God to stop the rain completely but requested that it be removed from homes, roads and other facilities so that it could cause no harm to residents or travellers. He further requested that the rain should continue where it is most useful, thus it would give its benefits when it pours in the bottom of valleys and places of vegetation. The hadith shows that it is desirable to pray that homes and public facilities should be spared rain, if it continues for many days and causes damage. However, such a supplication does not require people to meet and add a prayer before or after it.

When Anas was asked whether the man who requested the Prophet to pray for stopping the rain was the same man who requested rain the week before, Anas said that he did not know. Another version of this hadith related by al-Bukhari and others confirm that he was the same man.

In hadith No. 1783, Anas says that when the Prophet appealed to God to make the rain fall 'around us, not on us', the sky was soon clear and 'wherever he pointed his hand towards the sky, the clouds lifted until Madinah was like a wide dry circle. The stream of the Qanāh Valley was running for a month'. Thus, the clouds moved away from Madinah and formed a circle around it, while inside the city, the sky was clear. The Qanāh Valley was close to Madinah and its people used it for their agriculture.

Hadith No. 1784 gives the same story and adds a vivid picture of how the Prophet's prayer to remove the rain from Madinah to its surroundings was answered: 'It scattered away from Madinah and rained around it. There was no longer a single drop of rain in Madinah. I looked at Madinah and it seemed as if it was in the middle of a wreath'.

Hadith No. 1787 speaks of a different occasion and the Prophet's action at the start of rain: 'We were with God's Messenger when it started to rain. God's Messenger (peace be upon him) folded his robe and rain fell on him. We said: "Messenger of God, why have you done that?" He said: "Because [the rain] has been recently with its Lord".' The Prophet thus exposed a part of his body to the rain, which is a manifestation of God's grace to His creation. Since it is very recently created, it carries God's blessing. This is the meaning of the Prophet's words: 'Because [the rain] has been recently with its Lord'.

The hadith provides evidence in support of our scholars' view that it is desirable to let the beginning of rain fall on one's body, except one's private parts. The hadith also shows that if someone sees his superior doing something unfamiliar, he should ask him about it, so that he learns and teaches it to others.

CHAPTER 3

REACTION TO NATURAL PHENOMENA

[1788–14]. (Dar al-Salam 1961) ʿAbdullāh ibn Maslamah ibn Qaʿnab narrated: Sulaymān (meaning Ibn Bilāl) narrated; from Jaʿfar (who is Ibn Muhammad); from ʿAṭā' ibn Abi Rabāḥ; that he heard ʿĀ'ishah, the Prophet's wife, say: **'On a windy and cloudy day, its effect was clear on the Prophet's face. He would go to and fro. If it then rained, he would be pleased and no longer agitated.' ʿĀ'ishah said: 'I asked him [about this]. He said: "I feared that it might be a punishment about to be visited on my community". When he saw it raining, he would say: "It is mercy".'**

حَدَّثَنَا عَبْدُ اللهِ بْنُ مَسْلَمَةَ بْنِ قَعْنَبٍ، حَدَّثَنَا سُلَيْمَانُ (يَعْنِي ابْنَ بِلَالٍ) عَنْ جَعْفَرٍ (وَهُوَ ابْنُ مُحَمَّدٍ) عَنْ عَطَاءِ بْنِ أَبِي رَبَاحٍ، أَنَّهُ سَمِعَ عَائِشَةَ، زَوْجَ النَّبِيِّ صَلَّى اللهُ عَلَيْهِ وَسَلَّمَ تَقُولُ: كَانَ رَسُولُ اللهِ صَلَّى اللهُ عَلَيْهِ وَسَلَّمَ إِذَا كَانَ يَوْمُ الرِّيحِ وَالْغَيْمِ عُرِفَ ذَلِكَ فِي وَجْهِهِ: أَقْبَلَ وَأَدْبَرَ. فَإِذَا مَطَرَتْ سُرَّ بِهِ، وَذَهَبَ عَنْهُ ذَلِكَ. قَالَتْ عَائِشَةُ: فَسَأَلْتُهُ فَقَالَ: «إِنِّي خَشِيتُ أَنْ يَكُونَ عَذَابًا سُلِّطَ عَلَى أُمَّتِي». وَيَقُولُ إِذَا رَأَى الْمَطَرَ: «رَحْمَةٌ».

[1789–15]. (Dar al-Salam 1962) Abu al-Ṭāhir narrated to me:[i] Ibn Wahb reported; he said: I heard Ibn Jurayj narrating to us from ʿAṭā' ibn Abi Rabāḥ; from ʿĀ'ishah, the Prophet's wife. She said: **'When wind gathered, the Prophet would say:**

i. Related by al-Tirmidhī, 3449; Ibn Mājah, 3891.

"My Lord, I appeal to You to give us of its goodness and the good that it bears and the good purpose for which it has been sent. I seek refuge with You from its evil, the evil it bears and the evil purpose it has been sent for". When thunderous clouds gathered, his colour changed. He would come in and go out, walk to and fro. If it rained, he would be at ease, and I would recognise this in his face. I asked him about it, and he said: "'Ā'ishah, it may be like what the 'Ād people said. When they saw a cloud approaching their valleys, they said: 'This cloud will bring us rain' (46: 24)."'

وَحَدَّثَنِي أَبُو الطَّاهِرِ، أَخْبَرَنَا ابْنُ وَهْبٍ، قَالَ سَمِعْتُ ابْنَ جُرَيْجٍ، يُحَدِّثُنَا عَنْ عَطَاءِ بْنِ أَبِي رَبَاحٍ، عَنْ عَائِشَةَ، زَوْجِ النَّبِيِّ صَلَّى اللهُ عَلَيْهِ وَسَلَّمَ أَنَّهَا قَالَتْ: كَانَ النَّبِيُّ صَلَّى اللهُ عَلَيْهِ وَسَلَّمَ إِذَا عَصَفَتِ الرِّيحُ قَالَ: «اللَّهُمَّ إِنِّي أَسْأَلُكَ خَيْرَهَا وَخَيْرَ مَا فِيهَا وَخَيْرَ مَا أُرْسِلَتْ بِهِ. وَأَعُوذُ بِكَ مِنْ شَرِّهَا وَشَرِّ مَا فِيهَا وَشَرِّ مَا أُرْسِلَتْ بِهِ». قَالَتْ: وَإِذَا تَخَيَّلَتِ السَّمَاءُ تَغَيَّرَ لَوْنُهُ، وَخَرَجَ وَدَخَلَ، وَأَقْبَلَ وَأَدْبَرَ، فَإِذَا مَطَرَتْ سُرِّيَ عَنْهُ، فَعَرَفْتُ ذَلِكَ فِي وَجْهِهِ. قَالَتْ عَائِشَةُ: فَسَأَلْتُهُ فَقَالَ: «لَعَلَّهُ يَا عَائِشَةُ كَمَا قَالَ قَوْمُ عَادٍ: «فَلَمَّا رَأَوْهُ عَارِضًا مُسْتَقْبِلَ أَوْدِيَتِهِمْ قَالُوا هَذَا عَارِضٌ مُمْطِرُنَا»».

[1790–16]. (Dar al-Salam 1963) Ḥarūn ibn Ma'rūf narrated to me:[i] Ibn Wahb narrated; from 'Amr ibn al-Ḥārith [H]. Also, Abu al-Ṭāhir narrated to me; 'Abdullāh ibn Wahb reported; 'Amr ibn al-Ḥārith reported; that Abu al-Naḍr narrated to him; from Sulaymān ibn Yasār; from 'Ā'ishah, the Prophet's wife, that she said: **'I never saw God's Messenger laughing heartily so as to be able to see his back palate; he only smiled. When he saw gathering clouds or when it was windy, this would be clearly visible in his face. She said: "Messenger of God, when**

i. Related by al-Bukhari, 4828, 4829 and in a shorter version, 6092; Abu Dāwūd, 5098.

people see clouds, they feel hopeful that it may bring rain. But I see your face showing dislike". He said: "ʿĀ'ishah, how can I be sure that it does not bring punishment. A certain community were punished with a storm-wind, and another community saw the forthcoming punishment and said: 'This cloud will bring us rain'."'

وَحَدَّثَنِي هَارُونُ بْنُ مَعْرُوفٍ، حَدَّثَنَا ابْنُ وَهْبٍ، عَنْ عَمْرِو بْنِ الْحَارِثِ، ح. وَحَدَّثَنِي أَبُو الطَّاهِرِ، أَخْبَرَنَا عَبْدُ اللهِ بْنُ وَهْبٍ، أَخْبَرَنَا عَمْرُو بْنُ الْحَارِثِ، أَنَّ أَبَا النَّضْرِ حَدَّثَهُ عَنْ سُلَيْمَانَ بْنِ يَسَارٍ، عَنْ عَائِشَةَ، زَوْجِ النَّبِيِّ صَلَّى اللهُ عَلَيْهِ وَسَلَّمَ أَنَّهَا قَالَتْ: مَا رَأَيْتُ رَسُولَ اللهِ صَلَّى اللهُ عَلَيْهِ وَسَلَّمَ مُسْتَجْمِعًا ضَاحِكًا حَتَّى أَرَى مِنْهُ لَهَوَاتِهِ. إِنَّمَا كَانَ يَتَبَسَّمُ. قالت: وكان إذا رَأَى غَيْمًا أَوْ رِيحًا عُرِفَ ذَلِكَ فِي وَجْهِهِ. فَقَالَتْ يَا رَسُولَ اللهِ أَرَى النَّاسَ إِذَا رَأَوُا الْغَيْمَ فَرِحُوا، رَجَاءَ أَنْ يَكُونَ فِيهِ الْمَطَرُ. وَأَرَاكَ إِذَا رَأَيْتَهُ عَرَفْتُ فِي وَجْهِكَ الْكَرَاهِيَةَ. قَالَتْ: فَقَالَ: «يَا عَائِشَةُ، مَا يُؤَمِّنُنِي أَنْ يَكُونَ فِيهِ عَذَابٌ. قَدْ عُذِّبَ قَوْمٌ بِالرِّيحِ. وَقَدْ رَأَى قَوْمٌ الْعَذَابَ فَقَالُوا: «هَذَا عَارِضٌ مُمْطِرُنَا».

[1791–17]. (Dar al-Salam 1964–1965) Abu Bakr ibn Abi Shaybah narrated:[i] Ghundar narrated; from Shuʿbah [H]. Also, Muhammad ibn al-Muthannā and Ibn Bashshār narrated; both said: Muhammad ibn Jaʿfar narrated; Shuʿbah narrated; from al-Ḥakam; from Mujāhid; from Ibn ʿAbbās; from the Prophet (peace be upon him). He said: **'I have been supported with al-Ṣabā [the eastern smooth wind], but the ʿĀd people were destroyed with al-Dabūr [the western dry and hot wind]'.**

وَحَدَّثَنَا أَبُو بَكْرِ بْنُ أَبِي شَيْبَةَ، حَدَّثَنَا غُنْدَرٌ، عَنْ شُعْبَةَ، ح. وَحَدَّثَنَا مُحَمَّدُ بْنُ الْمُثَنَّى وَابْنُ بَشَّارٍ قَالَا: حَدَّثَنَا مُحَمَّدُ بْنُ جَعْفَرٍ، حَدَّثَنَا شُعْبَةُ، عَنِ الْحَكَمِ، عَنْ مُجَاهِدٍ، عَنِ

i. Related by al-Bukhari, 1035, 3205, 3343 and 4105.

ابْنِ عَبَّاسٍ، عَنِ النَّبِيِّ صَلَّى اللهُ عَلَيْهِ وَسَلَّمَ أَنَّهُ قَالَ: «نُصِرْتُ بِالصَّبَا، وَأُهْلِكَتْ عَادٌ بِالدَّبُورِ».

Abu Bakr ibn Abi Shaybah and Abu Kurayb narrated: both said: Abu Muʿāwiyah narrated [H]. Also, ʿAbdullāh ibn ʿUmar ibn Muhammad ibn Abān al-Juʿafī; ʿAbdah (meaning Ibn Sulaymān) narrated; both from al-Aʿmash; from Masʿūd ibn Mālik; from Saʿīd ibn Jubayr; from Ibn ʿAbbās; from the Prophet (peace be upon him): **the same text.**

وَحَدَّثَنَا أَبُو بَكْرِ بْنُ أَبِي شَيْبَةَ وَأَبُو كُرَيْبٍ قَالَا: حَدَّثَنَا أَبُو مُعَاوِيَةَ، ح. وَحَدَّثَنَا عَبْدُ اللهِ بْنُ عُمَرَ بْنِ مُحَمَّدِ بْنِ أَبَانٍ الْجُعْفِيُّ، حَدَّثَنَا عَبْدَةُ، - يَعْنِي ابْنَ سُلَيْمَانَ - كِلَاهُمَا عَنِ الْأَعْمَشِ، عَنْ مَسْعُودِ بْنِ مَالِكٍ، عَنْ سَعِيدِ بْنِ جُبَيْرٍ، عَنِ ابْنِ عَبَّاسٍ، عَنِ النَّبِيِّ صَلَّى اللهُ عَلَيْهِ وَسَلَّمَ. بِمِثْلِهِ.

Text Explanation

Hadith No. 1788 mentions how the Prophet was agitated on days when winds and clouds gathered. His agitation was clearly visible, and he would walk to and fro. He would relax when it rained. This speaks of the need to be ready and to always watch God and turn to Him when things change and something is feared. The Prophet feared that his community might be punished as a result of the disobedience of wicked people. When the cause of fear was removed, his pleasure was evident.

When it rained, the Prophet said that it was a mercy, and when clouds that brought lightening and thunder gathered, he was perturbed. He explained this by mentioning the case of the ancient people of ʿĀd who rejected their prophet and his message. When they persisted in their rejection, God destroyed them. They saw clouds approaching and they thought that they would bring them rain. Instead, they brought a windstorm that caused their total destruction.

BOOK OF PRAYER AT A SOLAR ECLIPSE

CHAPTER 1

PRAYER AT THE TIME OF ECLIPSE

[1792–1]. (Dar al-Salam 1966) Qutaybah ibn Saʿīd narrated:[i] from Mālik ibn Anas; from Hishām ibn ʿUrwah; from his father; from ʿĀ'ishah [H]. Also, Abu Bakr ibn Abi Shaybah narrated (his text); he said: ʿAbdullāh ibn Numayr narrated; Hishām narrated; from his father; from ʿĀ'ishah. She said: **'The sun was eclipsed during God's Messenger's lifetime. He stood up praying and stood up for a very long time, then he bowed for a very long time, then he stood up for a very long time but less than the first standing, then he bowed for a very long time but less than the first bow. He then prostrated himself. He then stood up for a long time but less than the first standing, then he bowed for a long time but less than the first bow. He then raised his head and stood up for a long time but less than the preceding stand, then he bowed for a long time but less than the preceding bow, then he prostrated himself. God's Messenger (peace be upon him) then finished his prayer and the sun was clear. He addressed the people, starting with praising God and thanking Him. He then said: "The sun and the moon are among God's signs. They are not eclipsed for the decease or the life of anyone. If you see them, glorify God, supplicate, pray and give *ṣadaqah* [i.e. charity].**

i. Related by al-Bukhari, 1044; al-Nasā'ī, 1473.

You, Muhammad's community! [Learn that] none is more offended than God is when a servant of His, male or female, commits adultery. You, Muhammad's community! By God, were you to know what I know, you would weep much and laugh but little. Have I delivered?".'

In Mālik's narration: **"The sun and the moon are two of God's signs".**

وَحَدَّثَنَا قُتَيْبَةُ بْنُ سَعِيدٍ، عَنْ مَالِكِ بْنِ أَنَسٍ، عَنْ هِشَامِ بْنِ عُرْوَةَ، عَنْ أَبِيهِ، عَنْ عَائِشَةَ، ح. وَحَدَّثَنَا أَبُو بَكْرِ بْنُ أَبِي شَيْبَةَ، وَاللَّفْظُ لَه. قَالَ حَدَّثَنَا عَبْدُ اللهِ بْنُ نُمَيْرٍ، حَدَّثَنَا هِشَامٌ، عَنْ أَبِيهِ، عَنْ عَائِشَةَ قَالَتْ: خَسَفَتِ الشَّمْسُ فِي عَهْدِ رَسُولِ اللهِ صَلَّى اللهُ عَلَيْهِ وَسَلَّمَ، فَقَامَ رَسُولُ اللهِ صَلَّى اللهُ عَلَيْهِ وَسَلَّمَ يُصَلِّي فَأَطَالَ الْقِيَامَ جِدًّا، ثُمَّ رَكَعَ فَأَطَالَ الرُّكُوعَ جِدًّا، ثُمَّ رَفَعَ رَأْسَهُ فَأَطَالَ الْقِيَامَ جِدًّا، وَهُوَ دُونَ الْقِيَامِ الأَوَّلِ. ثُمَّ رَكَعَ فَأَطَالَ الرُّكُوعَ جِدًّا، وَهُوَ دُونَ الرُّكُوعِ الأَوَّلِ. ثُمَّ سَجَدَ، ثُمَّ قَامَ فَأَطَالَ الْقِيَامَ، وَهُوَ دُونَ الْقِيَامِ الأَوَّلِ. ثُمَّ رَكَعَ فَأَطَالَ الرُّكُوعَ، وَهُوَ دُونَ الرُّكُوعِ الأَوَّلِ. ثُمَّ رَفَعَ رَأْسَهُ، فَقَامَ فَأَطَالَ الْقِيَامَ وَهُوَ دُونَ الْقِيَامِ الأَوَّلِ. ثُمَّ رَكَعَ فَأَطَالَ الرُّكُوعَ وَهُوَ دُونَ الرُّكُوعِ الأَوَّلِ. ثُمَّ سَجَدَ، ثُمَّ انْصَرَفَ رَسُولُ اللهِ صَلَّى اللهُ عَلَيْهِ وَسَلَّمَ وَقَدْ تَجَلَّتِ الشَّمْسُ.

فَخَطَبَ النَّاسَ، فَحَمِدَ اللهَ وَأَثْنَى عَلَيْهِ، ثُمَّ قَالَ: «إِنَّ الشَّمْسَ وَالْقَمَرَ مِنْ آيَاتِ اللهِ، وَإِنَّهُمَا لاَ يَنْخَسِفَانِ لِمَوْتِ أَحَدٍ وَلاَ لِحَيَاتِهِ. فَإِذَا رَأَيْتُمُوهُمَا فَكَبِّرُوا، وَادْعُوا اللهَ وَصَلُّوا، وَتَصَدَّقُوا يَا أُمَّةَ مُحَمَّدٍ. إِنْ مِنْ أَحَدٍ أَغْيَرَ مِنَ اللهِ أَنْ يَزْنِيَ عَبْدُهُ، أَوْ تَزْنِيَ أَمَتُهُ. يَا أُمَّةَ مُحَمَّدٍ، وَاللهِ لَوْ تَعْلَمُونَ مَا أَعْلَمُ لَبَكَيْتُمْ كَثِيرًا، وَلَضَحِكْتُمْ قَلِيلاً. أَلاَ هَلْ بَلَّغْتُ؟» وَفِي رِوَايَةِ مَالِكٍ: «إِنَّ الشَّمْسَ وَالْقَمَرَ آيَتَانِ مِنْ آيَاتِ اللهِ».

[1793–2]. (Dar al-Salam 1967) Yaḥyā ibn Yaḥyā narrated the same: Abu Muʿāwiyah reported; from Hishām ibn ʿUrwah; with the same chain of transmission: **the same text, but he added: 'Meanwhile, the sun and the moon are two of God's**

signs'. He also added: 'He then lifted his arms and said: "My Lord! Have I delivered?".'

حَدَّثَنَاهُ يَحْيَى بْنُ يَحْيَى، أَخْبَرَنَا أَبُو مُعَاوِيَةَ، عَنْ هِشَامِ بْنِ عُرْوَةَ، بِهَذَا الإِسْنَادِ، وَزَادَ ثُمَّ قَالَ: «أَمَّا بَعْدُ فَإِنَّ الشَّمْسَ وَالْقَمَرَ مِنْ آيَاتِ اللَّهِ». وَزَادَ أَيْضًا ثُمَّ رَفَعَ يَدَيْهِ فَقَالَ: «اللَّهُمَّ هَلْ بَلَّغْتُ؟»

[1794–3]. (Dar al-Salam 1968) Ḥarmalah ibn Yaḥyā narrated to me:[i] Ibn Wahb reported to me; Yūnus reported to me [H]. Also, Abu al-Ṭāhir and Muhammad ibn Salamah al-Murādī narrated to me; both said: Ibn Wahb narrated; from Yūnus; from Ibn Shihāb; he said: ʿUrwah ibn al-Zubayr reported to me; from ʿĀ'ishah, the Prophet's wife. She said: **'The sun was eclipsed during God's Messenger's lifetime. God's Messenger (peace be upon him) went to the mosque, stood up, glorified God and stood the people in rows behind him. He then recited [from the Qur'an] at length, then bowed for a long time. He then lifted his head and said: "May God respond to whoever praises Him. Our Lord, all praise is due to You". He stood up and recited [from the Qur'an] at length but less than his first recitation. He then glorified God and bowed for a long time but less than his first bow. He then said: "May God respond to whoever praises Him. Our Lord, all praise is due to You". He then prostrated himself, (but Abu al-Ṭāhir did not mention: "he then prostrated himself"). He did the same in the second *rakʿah*, completing four bows [i.e. *rukūʿ*] and four prostrations [i.e. *sujūd*]. The sun was clear before he finished his prayer. He then stood up and addressed the people. He**

i. Related by al-Bukhari, 1046 and in a shorter version and similar wording 1212; Abu Dāwūd in a shorter version, 1180; al-Nasā'ī, 1471; Ibn Mājah in a shorter version, 1263.

praised God as He should be praised, then said: "The sun and the moon are two of God's signs, and they are not eclipsed for the decease or life of anyone. If you see them thus, go straight to prayer". He also said: "Pray until God removes hardship from you". God's Messenger (peace be upon him) also said: "As I stood in my place, I saw everything you have been promised. I saw myself aiming to take a bunch of [the fruit of] Heaven when you saw me moving forward. I also saw Hell raging with fire when you saw me stepping back. I saw there Ibn Luḥayy - he was the one who let she-camels loose".'

Abu al-Ṭāhir's narration ended at: **'Go straight to prayer', without adding the rest of the hadith.**

حَدَّثَنِي حَرْمَلَةُ بْنُ يَحْيَى، أَخْبَرَنِي ابْنُ وَهْبٍ، أَخْبَرَنِي يُونُسُ، ح. وَحَدَّثَنِي أَبُو الطَّاهِرِ، وَمُحَمَّدُ بْنُ سَلَمَةَ الْمُرَادِيُّ قَالا: حَدَّثَنَا ابْنُ وَهْبٍ، عَنْ يُونُسَ، عَنِ ابْنِ شِهَابٍ قَالَ: أَخْبَرَنِي عُرْوَةُ بْنُ الزُّبَيْرِ، عَنْ عَائِشَةَ، زَوْجِ النَّبِيِّ صَلَّى اللهُ عَلَيْهِ وَسَلَّمَ، قَالَتْ: خَسَفَتِ الشَّمْسُ فِي حَيَاةِ رَسُولِ اللهِ صَلَّى اللهُ عَلَيْهِ وَسَلَّمَ، فَخَرَجَ رَسُولُ اللهِ صَلَّى اللهُ عَلَيْهِ وَسَلَّمَ إِلَى الْمَسْجِدِ، فَقَامَ وَكَبَّرَ وَصَفَّ النَّاسُ وَرَاءَهُ، فَاقْتَرَأَ رَسُولُ اللهِ صَلَّى اللهُ عَلَيْهِ وَسَلَّمَ قِرَاءَةً طَوِيلَةً. ثُمَّ كَبَّرَ فَرَكَعَ رُكُوعًا طَوِيلاً، ثُمَّ رَفَعَ رَأْسَهُ فَقَالَ: «سَمِعَ اللهُ لِمَنْ حَمِدَهُ. رَبَّنَا وَلَكَ الْحَمْدُ». ثُمَّ قَامَ فَاقْتَرَأَ قِرَاءَةً طَوِيلَةً هِيَ أَدْنَى مِنَ الْقِرَاءَةِ الأُولَى، ثُمَّ كَبَّرَ فَرَكَعَ رُكُوعًا طَوِيلاً. هُوَ أَدْنَى مِنَ الرُّكُوعِ الأَوَّلِ ثُمَّ قَالَ «سَمِعَ اللهُ لِمَنْ حَمِدَهُ رَبَّنَا وَلَكَ الْحَمْدُ». ثُمَّ سَجَد. وَلَمْ يَذْكُرْ أَبُو الطَّاهِرِ ثُمَّ سَجَدَ. ثُمَّ فَعَلَ فِي الرَّكْعَةِ الأُخْرَى مِثْلَ ذَلِكَ، حَتَّى اسْتَكْمَلَ أَرْبَعَ رَكَعَاتٍ وَأَرْبَعَ سَجَدَاتٍ، وَانْجَلَتِ الشَّمْسُ قَبْلَ أَنْ يَنْصَرِفَ. ثُمَّ قَامَ فَخَطَبَ النَّاسَ، فَأَثْنَى عَلَى اللهِ بِمَا هُوَ أَهْلُهُ، ثُمَّ قَالَ: «إِنَّ الشَّمْسَ وَالْقَمَرَ آيَتَانِ مِنْ آيَاتِ اللهِ، لاَ يَخْسِفَانِ لِمَوْتِ أَحَدٍ وَلاَ لِحَيَاتِهِ. فَإِذَا رَأَيْتُمُوهَا فَافْزَعُوا لِلصَّلاَةِ». وَقَالَ أَيْضًا: «فَصَلُّوا حَتَّى يُفَرِّجَ اللهُ عَنْكُمْ». وَقَالَ رَسُولُ اللهِ صَلَّى اللهُ عَلَيْهِ وَسَلَّمَ: «رَأَيْتُ فِي مَقَامِي هَذَا كُلَّ شَيْءٍ وُعِدْتُمْ، حَتَّى لَقَدْ رَأَيْتُنِي أُرِيدُ أَنْ آخُذَ قِطْفًا

مِنَ الْـجَنَّةِ، حِينَ رَأَيْتُمُونِي جَعَلْتُ أُقَدِّمُ - وَقَالَ الْـمُرَادِيُّ أَتَقَـدَّمُ. وَلَقَـدْ رَأَيْتُ جَهَنَّمَ يَحْطِمُ بَعْضُهَـا بَعْضًـا حِـينَ رَأَيْتُمُونِي تَأَخَّرْتُ. وَرَأَيْتُ فِيهَا ابْنَ لُـحَيٍّ، وَهُوَ الَّذِي سَـيَّبَ السَّـوَائِبَ». وَانْتَهَى حَدِيثُ أَبِي الطَّاهِرِ عِنْدَ قَوْلِهِ: «فَـافْـزَعُوا لِلصَّلَاةِ». وَلَمْ يَذْكُرْ مَا بَعْدَهُ.

[1795–4]. (Dar al-Salam 1769) Muhammad ibn Mihrān al-Rāzī narrated:[i] al-Walīd ibn Muslim narrated; he said: al-Awzāʿī Abu ʿAmr and others said: I heard Ibn Shihāb al-Zuhrī reporting from ʿUrwah; from ʿĀ'ishah; that **'The sun was eclipsed during God's Messenger's lifetime and he sent a crier to call *al-ṣalat jāmiʿah* [meaning come to prayer]. They gathered. He stepped forward and glorified God. He prayed two *rakʿahs* including four bows [i.e. *rukūʿ*] and four prostrations'.**

وَحَدَّثَنَا مُحَمَّدُ بْنُ مِهْرَانَ الرَّازِيُّ، حَدَّثَنَا الْوَلِيدُ بْنُ مُسْلِمٍ قَالَ: قَالَ الأَوْزَاعِيُّ أَبُو عَمْرٍو وَغَيْرُهُ: سَمِعْتُ ابْنَ شِهَابٍ الزُّهْرِيَّ، يُخْبِرُ عَنْ عُرْوَةَ، عَنْ عَائِشَةَ، أَنَّ الشَّمْسَ خَسَفَتْ عَلَى عَهْدِ رَسُولِ اللهِ صَلَّى اللهُ عَلَيْهِ وَسَلَّمَ، فَبَعَثَ مُنَادِيًا: «الصَّلَاةَ جَامِعَةً». فَاجْتَمَعُوا، وَتَقَدَّمَ فَكَبَّرَ. وَصَلَّى أَرْبَعَ رَكَعَاتٍ فِي رَكْعَتَيْنِ وَأَرْبَعَ سَجَدَاتٍ.

[1796–5]. (Dar al-Salam 1770) Muhammad ibn Mihrān narrated:[ii] al-Walīd ibn Muslim narrated; ʿAbd al-Raḥmān ibn Namir reported; that he heard Ibn Shihāb reporting from ʿUrwah; from ʿĀ'ishah; that **'The Prophet (peace be upon him) recited aloud in the prayer at the time of the eclipse. He prayed bowing four times in two *rakʿahs* and did four prostrations'.**

---

i. Related by al-Bukhari in similar wording 1066; al-Nasā'ī, 1464 and 1472.
ii. Related by al-Bukhari in similar wording 1065; Abu Dāwūd, 1190; al-Nasā'ī, 1493 and in a longer version 1496.

وَحَدَّثَنَا مُحَمَّدُ بْنُ مِهْرَانَ، حَدَّثَنَا الْوَلِيدُ بْنُ مُسْلِمٍ، أَخْبَرَنَا عَبْدُ الرَّحْمَنِ بْنُ نَمِرٍ، أَنَّهُ سَمِعَ ابْنَ شِهَابٍ، يُخْبِرُ عَنْ عُرْوَةَ، عَنْ عَائِشَةَ، أَنَّ النَّبِيَّ صَلَّى اللهُ عَلَيْهِ وَسَلَّمَ جَهَرَ فِي صَلَاةِ الْخُسُوفِ بِقِرَاءَتِهِ، فَصَلَّى أَرْبَعَ رَكَعَاتٍ فِي رَكْعَتَيْنِ وَأَرْبَعَ سَجَدَاتٍ.

[1797–000]. (Dar al-Salam[i]) Al-Zuhrī said:[ii] Kathīr ibn ʿAbbās reported to me; from Ibn ʿAbbās; from the Prophet (peace be upon him) that **'He prayed and bowed four times in two *rak'ahs* and did four prostrations'.**

قَالَ الزُّهْرِيُّ: وَأَخْبَرَنِي كَثِيرُ بْنُ عَبَّاسٍ، عَنِ ابْنِ عَبَّاسٍ، عَنِ النَّبِيِّ صَلَّى اللهُ عَلَيْهِ وَسَلَّمَ أَنَّهُ صَلَّى أَرْبَعَ رَكَعَاتٍ فِي رَكْعَتَيْنِ وَأَرْبَعَ سَجَدَاتٍ

[1798–000]. (Dar al-Salam 1771) Ḥājib ibn al-Walīd narrated: Muhammad ibn Ḥarb narrated; Muhammad ibn al-Walīd al-Zubaydī narrated; from al-Zuhrī; he said: Kathīr ibn ʿAbbās used to narrate; that Ibn ʿAbbās narrated describing God's Messenger's prayer when the sun was eclipsed: **the same text as ʿUrwah's narration from ʿĀ'ishah.**

وَحَدَّثَنَا حَاجِبُ بْنُ الْوَلِيدِ، حَدَّثَنَا مُحَمَّدُ بْنُ حَرْبٍ، حَدَّثَنَا مُحَمَّدُ بْنُ الْوَلِيدِ الزُّبَيْدِيُّ، عَنِ الزُّهْرِيِّ قَالَ: كَانَ كَثِيرُ بْنُ عَبَّاسٍ يُحَدِّثُ أَنَّ ابْنَ عَبَّاسٍ كَانَ يُحَدِّثُ عَنْ صَلَاةِ رَسُولِ اللهِ صَلَّى اللهُ عَلَيْهِ وَسَلَّمَ يَوْمَ كَسَفَتِ الشَّمْسُ، بِمِثْلِ مَا حَدَّثَ عُرْوَةُ عَنْ عَائِشَةَ.

[1799–6]. (Dar al-Salam 1772) Isḥāq ibn Ibrāhīm narrated:[iii] Muhammad ibn Bakr reported; Ibn Jurayj reported; he said:

i. Dar al-Salam attaches this hadith to the one before it.
ii. Related by al-Bukhari in a longer version, 1046; Abu Dāwūd in a longer version with the same meaning, 1181; al-Nasā'ī, 1468.
iii. Related by Abu Dāwūd in a similar version, 1177; al-Nasā'ī in a similar version, 1469.

I heard ʿAṭāʾ say; I heard ʿUbayd ibn ʿUmayr say; the one I believe (I think he meant ʿĀʾishah) narrated; that **'The sun was eclipsed during God's Messenger's lifetime, and he stood [in prayer] for a very long time, standing up then bowing, then standing up and bowing, then standing up and bowing. He prayed two *rakʿahs*, with three bows [i.e. *rukūʿ*] [in each] and four prostrations [in all]. When he finished, the sun had cleared. When he bowed, he said: "*Allah-u akbar*", then bowed, and when he lifted his head, he said: "*samiʿ Allah liman ḥamidah*" [i.e. May God respond to whoever praises Him]. He then stood up, praised God and thanked Him. He then said: "The sun and the moon are not eclipsed for the decease or life of anyone. They are [two] of God's signs and He uses them to strike awe in His servants' hearts. When you see an eclipse, remember God until they are clear".'**

وَحَدَّثَنَا إِسْحَاقُ بْنُ إِبْرَاهِيمَ، أَخْبَرَنَا مُحَمَّدُ بْنُ بَكْرٍ، أَخْبَرَنَا ابْنُ جُرَيْجٍ، قَالَ سَمِعْتُ عَطَاءً، يَقُولُ سَمِعْتُ عُبَيْدَ بْنَ عُمَيْرٍ، يَقُولُ حَدَّثَنِي مَنْ أُصَدِّقُ، حَسِبْتُهُ يُرِيدُ عَائِشَةَ، أَنَّ الشَّمْسَ انْكَسَفَتْ عَلَى عَهْدِ رَسُولِ اللهِ صَلَّى اللهُ عَلَيْهِ وَسَلَّمَ، فَقَامَ قِيَامًا شَدِيدًا يَقُومُ قَائِمًا، ثُمَّ يَرْكَعُ، ثُمَّ يَقُومُ ثُمَّ يَرْكَعُ، ثُمَّ يَقُومُ ثُمَّ يَرْكَعُ: رَكْعَتَيْنِ فِي ثَلاَثِ رَكَعَاتٍ، وَأَرْبَعِ سَجَدَاتٍ، فَانْصَرَفَ وَقَدْ تَجَلَّتِ الشَّمْسُ. وَكَانَ إِذَا رَكَعَ قَالَ «اللهُ أَكْبَرُ»، ثُمَّ يَرْكَعُ. وَإِذَا رَفَعَ رَأْسَهُ قَالَ: «سَمِعَ اللهُ لِمَنْ حَمِدَهُ». فَقَامَ فَحَمِدَ اللهَ وَأَثْنَى عَلَيْهِ، ثُمَّ قَالَ: «إِنَّ الشَّمْسَ وَالْقَمَرَ لاَ يَكْسِفَانِ لِمَوْتِ أَحَدٍ وَلاَ لِحَيَاتِهِ، وَلَكِنَّهُمَا مِنْ آيَاتِ اللهِ يُخَوِّفُ اللهُ بِهِمَا عِبَادَهُ. فَإِذَا رَأَيْتُمْ كُسُوفًا فَاذْكُرُوا اللهَ حَتَّى يَنْجَلِيَا».

[1800–7]. (Dar al-Salam[i]) Abu Ghassān al-Mismaʿī and Muhammad ibn al-Muthannā narrated to me:[ii] Muʿādh (who

i. Dar al-Salam attaches this hadith to the one before it.
ii. Related by al-Nasāʾī, 1470.

is Ibn Hishām) narrated; my father narrated; from Qatādah; from ʿAṭāʾ ibn Rabāḥ; from ʿUbayd ibn ʿUmayr; from ʿĀʾishah; that **'The Prophet (peace be upon him) prayed doing six bows [i.e. *rukūʿ*] and four prostrations'.**

وَحَدَّثَنِي أَبُو غَسَّانَ الْـمِسْمَعِيُّ وَمُحَمَّدُ بْنُ الْـمُثَنَّى، قَالا: حَدَّثَنَا مُعَاذٌ، وَهُوَ ابْنُ هِشَام، حَدَّثَنِي أَبِي، عَنْ قَتَادَةَ، عَنْ عَطَاءِ بْنِ أَبِي رَبَاحٍ، عَنْ عُبَيْدِ بْنِ عُمَيْرٍ، عَنْ عَائِشَةَ: أَنَّ نَبِيَّ اللهِ صَلَّى اللهُ عَلَيْهِ وَسَلَّمَ صَلَّى سِتَّ رَكَعَاتٍ وَأَرْبَعَ سَجَدَاتٍ.

Text Explanation

Eclipse may affect the sun or the moon, and it means the disappearance of their light, totally or partially. Prayer at the time of an eclipse is reported in several ways. Muslim mentions some of these and Abu Dāwūd mentions a few others, while other scholars mention some other ways. Scholars are unanimous that it is a sunnah. Mālik, al-Shāfiʿī, Ahmad and the majority of scholars say that it is recommended to offer it in congregation, while Iraqi scholars say that it is offered individually. The majority's view is based on authentic hadiths related by Muslim and others.

The well-known form of the prayer at the time of an eclipse, according to the Shāfiʿī School, is that it consists of two *rakʿahs* and that each *rakʿah* includes two standings, two recitations of the Qurʾan and two bows [or *rukūʿs*]. Each *rakʿah* includes two prostrations, like other prayers. This is how it is offered, whether the eclipse takes a long time or not. The same description is agreed by Mālik, al-Layth, Ahmad, Abu Thawr, the majority of Hijazi scholars and others. Kufi scholars say that it consists of two *rakʿahs* like all other sunnah prayers. They base their view on the apparent meaning of the hadith narrated by Jābir ibn Samurah and Abu Bakrah, stating that the Prophet offered a prayer of two *rakʿahs*. The majority of scholars cite in evidence ʿĀʾishah's hadith narrated by ʿUrwah and ʿAmrah, and also the hadiths narrated by Jābir, Ibn ʿAbbās and ʿAbdullāh ibn ʿAmr ibn al-ʿĀṣ, stating that it consists of two *rakʿahs*, each of which includes two bows and two prostrations. Ibn ʿAbd al-Barr said: 'This is the most authentic narration under this heading. Other narrations giving different forms are lacking in authenticity. They also say that Ibn Samurah's hadith gives a general statement, and these hadiths explain its details'.

Muslim mentions in narrations by ʿĀ'ishah, Ibn ʿAbbās and Jābir that it consists of two *rakʿahs*, with three bows in each. One narration by Ibn ʿAbbās mentions two *rakʿahs* with four bows in each. Scholars of Hadith say that the first narrations [meaning those mentioning two bows in each *rakʿah*] are more authentic, and their narrators are better and more accurate. One hadith related by Abu Dāwūd and narrated by Ubayy ibn Kaʿb mentions a prayer of two *rakʿahs* with five bows in each. Each type is endorsed by a number of the Prophet's Companions. Some of our Shāfiʿī scholars who are well versed in Fiqh and Hadith, as well as other scholars, suggest that this difference in reports is due to differences in the eclipse events. In some cases, the eclipse took a long time before it cleared, and this led to an increase in the number of bows. In other cases, the eclipse was short, and the bows were less in number. When the eclipse was of medium duration, the number of bows was in the middle range.

Other scholars object to this argument, saying that the duration of an eclipse is not known in advance, and it cannot be known at its beginning or during the first *rakʿah*. All narrations make clear that the number of bows is the same in both *rakʿahs*, which means that it is intended right at the beginning. A number of scholars, including Isḥāq ibn Rāhawayh, Ibn Jarīr and Ibn al-Mundhir said that the prayer at an eclipse was offered at different times, and the difference in its form is understood to mean that any of these forms is correct. Therefore, it may be offered in any of these ways. This is a solid argument, but God knows best.

Scholars are in agreement that the imam recites the opening surah, al-Fātiḥah, in the first standing of each *rakʿah*, but they differ concerning reciting it in the second standing. According to our school, Mālik's School and the majority of his disciples, the prayer is invalid unless al-Fātiḥah is recited in the second standing. However,

Muhammad ibn Maslamah, a Mālikī scholar, says that it should not be recited. Scholars agree that the second standing and bow of the first *rakʿah* are shorter than the first. The same applies to the second *rakʿah*, with its second standing and bow being shorter than its first. They differ with regard to the first stand and bow of the second *rakʿah*: are they shorter than the second stand and bow of the first *rakʿah*? If so, then this is the meaning of the statement in hadith No. 1792: 'He then stood up for a long time but less than the first standing, then he bowed for a long time but less than the first bow'. Or, were these first standings and bowings in the second *rakʿah* equal to the second standing and bowing in the first *rakʿah*? In this case, 'the first standing and the first bow' refer to those first in the first *rakʿah*.

Scholars agree that a long recitation of the Qur'an and a long bow are recommended, as stated in the hadiths. If a person recites only the opening surah, al-Fātiḥah, in every standing and makes a proper bow each time, his prayer is valid, but he misses out on the additional merit. Scholars also differ on the desirability of making one's prostration long. The majority of our scholars say that it need not be elongated but kept at its normal length as in other prayers. The meticulous among our scholars say that to elongate the prostration in a similar way to the elongation of bowing is desirable. This is what is stated in al-Buwayṭī's *al-Mukhtaṣar* quoting al-Shāfiʿī. This is the correct view as stated in authentic hadiths.

When rising from every bow, or *rukūʿ*, one says: 'God responds to whoever praises Him' [i.e. *samiʿ Allah liman ḥamidah*], and follows this by saying: 'all praise is due to God, etc.' The more correct view is to say: '*aʿūdhu billāhi min al-Sayṭān al-rajīm*' before reciting al-Fātiḥah in every standing. Some say it should be said only in the first bow. Scholars also express different views on the *khuṭbah*, or sermon, during the prayer at the time of an eclipse. Al-Shāfiʿī, Isḥāq, Ibn Jarīr and the Hadith scholars who are well versed in Fiqh say that it is desirable to say two *khuṭbahs* after it. Mālik and Abu Ḥanīfah say that this is not desirable. Al-Shāfiʿī's argument is based on authentic hadiths in both *Ṣaḥīḥ* anthologies and in other Hadith anthologies, stating that the Prophet delivered a *khuṭbah* after the prayer.

Hadith No. 1792 says that the Prophet 'stood up for a very long time, then he bowed for a very long time… He then prostrated himself. He then stood up for a long time'. This is cited in support of the view of scholars who say that prostration is not elongated. Scholars who take the other view cite other hadiths that clearly state that the prostration was made long. This hadith is thus treated as a general one [on this point] and interpreted in light of the other hadiths, which are more specific.

The hadith mentions that the Prophet finished his prayer after the sun was clear, and then he addressed the people. This makes clear that the *khuṭbah* is desirable and that, unlike the prayer, its time does not lapse when the sun is clear. The Prophet started his *khuṭbah* by praising God and thanking Him. This is evidence that the *khuṭbah* should start by such praises, and al-Shāfiʿī says that the phrase *'alḥamd lillāh'* is required and may not be replaced by a different phrase with the same meaning.

The hadiths in this chapter mention that the Prophet said in his *khuṭbah* that 'the sun and the moon are two of God's signs. They are not eclipsed for the decease or the life of anyone'. In a different hadith, some people suggested that the sun was eclipsed because of the death of Ibrāhīm, the Prophet's son. The Prophet rejects what they said. Scholars said that some unbelievers used to glorify the sun and the moon. Therefore, the Prophet makes clear that they are signs created by God and that they do not do things at their own behest. They are like all creation; subject to diminution and alteration. Some misguided astrologers used to say that the sun and the moon are only eclipsed when a great person dies. The Prophet makes clear that this is false and that no one should pay heed to what they say, particularly because the solar eclipse at the time coincided with the death of Ibrāhīm, the Prophet's son.

In the same hadith, the Prophet said in his *khuṭbah* that when Muslims see a solar or lunar eclipse, they should 'glorify God, supplicate, pray and give *ṣadaqah* [i.e. charity]'. This urges us to do such acts of worship as we can. This order expresses desirability; it does not define a duty. He then said: 'You, Muhammad's community!

[Learn that] none is more offended than God is when a servant of His, male or female, commits adultery'. This means that none censures sin or hates it more than God. The Prophet adds: 'You, Muhammad's community! By God, were you to know what I know, you would pray much and laugh but little. Have I delivered?' This means that if Muslims know how severe God's punishment is and the sort of horrors that people endure on the Day of Judgement and after it, as he himself knew, and if they were to see Hell as he saw it while doing his prayer, they would have wept much and laughed but little because they would not be able to stop thinking about it. He concluded by saying, 'Have I delivered?'. This means: have I informed you of what I have been ordered to deliver of warnings and other aspects of my message? The hadith urges them to learn what he told them and keep it in mind because he is commanded to warn them.

Hadith No. 1794 mentions that at the time of an eclipse, the Prophet went to the mosque, glorified God and stood with people behind him. This confirms praying at the time of an eclipse and the desirability to offer it in a mosque where the Friday Prayer is normally offered. Our scholars say that the Prophet did not go to the prayer place out of town because he feared that its time might lapse if the sun cleared. Hence, it is recommended to offer it straightaway. The hadith further suggests that it is better to offer it in congregation, although it is permissible to offer it individually. It may be offered by women, slaves, travellers and everyone who can perform a proper prayer.

The hadith mentions that when the Prophet lifted his head after bowing, he said: *'samiʿ Allah liman ḥamidah. Rabbanā wa laka-lḥamd'* [which means: May God respond to whoever praises him. Our Lord, all praise is due to You]. It is clear that it is desirable to say these two phrases. This is the view of al-Shāfiʿī and scholars who agree with him. We discussed this point in the context of how prayer is offered in the Book of Prayer. According to our school, it is desirable for the two phrases to be said by the imam and everyone in the congregation, as well as by an individual praying alone and anyone else. This hadith shows that it is desirable to say both phrases when one lifts one's head after every bow.

In this hadith, No. 1794, the Prophet says: 'If you see them thus, go straight to prayer'. This is also quoted as: 'Pray until God removes hardship from you'. The Prophet advises us to go straight to prayer when we see an eclipse and continue praying until this situation is over because it is feared that an eclipse may foretell that some punishment is forthcoming.

The Prophet also said in this hadith: 'I also saw Hell raging with fire'. This confirms that Hell is created and exists. This is the view of the Sunni Muslims. It is raging with fire because of the intensity of its heat so as to be like sea waves. The Prophet said that he saw ʿAmr ibn Luḥayy[i] there, which confirms that some people are now being punished in Hell. May God spare us and all believers its torment. The Prophet also mentions that he stepped back. This suggests that one should stay away from places of God's punishment.

In hadith No. 1795, the Prophet 'sent a crier to call *al-ṣalat jāmiʿah*', which means 'come to prayer'. This supports the view of al-Shāfiʿī and scholars who share his view that it is desirable to call for the prayer at the time of the eclipse by saying this phrase. Scholars are unanimous that no formal *adhān* or *iqāmah* is called for it.

Hadith No. 1796 mentions that the Prophet recited the Qur'an aloud in the prayer at the time of an eclipse. This is understood by our scholars and the majority of other scholars to refer to a case of lunar eclipse. The view of our school, the Mālikī School, Abu Ḥanīfah, al-Layth ibn Saʿd and the majority of scholars is that the Qur'an is recited silently in prayer at the time of a solar eclipse and aloud during a lunar eclipse. Abu Yūsuf, Muhammad ibn al-Ḥasan, Ahmad, Isḥāq and others say that the recitation is aloud in both cases. They base their argument on this hadith, while scholars sharing the other view argue that the Prophet's Companions estimated his recitation as equal to Surah The Cow and other surahs. Had he been reciting aloud, they would have known what he recited without any

i. 'Amr ibn Luḥayy is described in the hadith as the first one 'who let she-camels loose'. This means that they were left for free pasture because they were consecrated to idols. It is also said that he was the first to introduce idolatry into Arabia.

need for estimation. Ibn Jarīr al-Ṭabarī said: 'Recitation aloud or silently are equally valid'.

In hadith No. 1799, 'the Prophet offered two *rakʿahs* with three bows and four prostrations'. This means that he did three bows, i.e. *rukūʿ*, in each *rakʿah*. The same is the meaning of the next hadith, No. 1800.

Transmission

In the chain of transmission hadith No. 1799, we read: 'I heard ʿUbayd ibn ʿUmayr say; the one I believe (I think he meant ʿĀ'ishah) narrated'. This is how the hadith is entered in the manuscripts in our regions. *Qadi* ʿIyāḍ quotes the same according to the majority, but according to some of their narrations, it occurs as 'the one I believe her narration, meaning ʿĀ'ishah'. The two are different in meaning. According to the narration of the majority, the hadith would be classified as *mursal,* which means that the chain of transmission is incomplete, if we apply to it the view of the majority of Hadith scholars that when a narrator reports from 'the one who is reliable', this reporting is unreliable.

CHAPTER 2

TORMENT IN THE GRAVE MENTIONED IN THE ECLIPSE PRAYER

[1801–8]. (Dar al-Salam 1973–1974) ʿAbdullāh ibn Maslamah al-Qaʿnabī narrated:[i] Sulaymān (meaning Ibn Bilāl) narrated; from Yaḥyā; from ʿAmrah; that **'A Jewish woman came to ʿĀ'ishah begging. She then said: "May God protect you from the torment in the grave". ʿĀ'ishah said: "I asked: 'Messenger of God, are people subjected to torment in their graves?'."' ʿAmrah said: 'ʿĀ'ishah said: "God's Messenger (peace be upon him) said: 'I seek God's refuge'."**

Then one morning God's Messenger (peace be upon him) mounted [heading somewhere], then the sun was eclipsed. ʿĀ'ishah said: "I went out with some women [walking] between the apartments in the mosque. God's Messenger came back until he reached the place where he offered his prayers. He stood up and people stood behind him [in prayer]. He stood for a long time, then he bowed. His bow was very long, then he arose and stood for a long time, but this was shorter than his standing the first time. Then he bowed for a long time but less than the other bow. Then he raised himself and the sun was clear. He said: 'I saw you being examined in the graves, like the trial of the Impostor'."'

ʿAmrah said: 'I heard ʿĀ'ishah say: "I used to hear God's Messenger (peace be upon him) after that seeking God's

i. Related by al-Bukhari, 1049 and in similar wording, 1050 and 1055; al-Nasā'ī, 1474 and 1498.

refuge from the punishment in Hell and the torment in the grave".'

وَحَدَّثَنَا عَبْدُ اللهِ بْنُ مَسْلَمَةَ الْقَعْنَبِيُّ، حَدَّثَنَا سُلَيْمَانُ، - يَعْنِي ابْنَ بِلاَلٍ - عَنْ يَحْيَى، عَنْ عَمْرَةَ، أَنَّ يَهُودِيَّةً أَتَتْ عَائِشَةَ تَسْأَلُهَا. فَقَالَتْ: أَعَاذَكِ اللهُ مِنْ عَذَابِ الْقَبْرِ! قَالَتْ عَائِشَةُ: فَقُلْتُ يَا رَسُولَ اللهِ، يُعَذَّبُ النَّاسُ فِي الْقُبُورِ؟ قَالَتْ عَمْرَةُ: فَقَالَتْ عَائِشَةُ: قَالَ رَسُولُ اللهِ صَلَّى اللهُ عَلَيْهِ وَسَلَّمَ، عَائِذًا بِاللهِ. ثُمَّ رَكِبَ رَسُولُ اللهِ صَلَّى اللهُ عَلَيْهِ وَسَلَّمَ ذَاتَ غَدَاةٍ مَرْكَبًا، فَخَسَفَتِ الشَّمْسُ. قَالَتْ عَائِشَةُ: فَخَرَجْتُ فِي نِسْوَةٍ بَيْنَ ظَهْرَيِ الْحُجَرِ فِي الْمَسْجِدِ، فَأَتَى رَسُولُ اللهِ صَلَّى اللهُ عَلَيْهِ وَسَلَّمَ مِنْ مَرْكَبِهِ، حَتَّى انْتَهَى إِلَى مُصَلاَّهُ الَّذِي كَانَ يُصَلِّي فِيهِ، فَقَامَ وَقَامَ النَّاسُ وَرَاءَهُ. قَالَتْ عَائِشَةُ: فَقَامَ قِيَامًا طَوِيلاً، ثُمَّ رَكَعَ فَرَكَعَ رُكُوعًا طَوِيلاً، ثُمَّ رَفَعَ فَقَامَ قِيَامًا طَوِيلاً، وَهُوَ دُونَ الْقِيَامِ الأَوَّلِ. ثُمَّ رَكَعَ فَرَكَعَ رُكُوعًا طَوِيلاً، وَهُوَ دُونَ ذَلِكَ الرُّكُوعِ، ثُمَّ رَفَعَ، وَقَدْ تَجَلَّتِ الشَّمْسُ فَقَالَ: «إِنِّي قَدْ رَأَيْتُكُمْ تُفْتَنُونَ فِي الْقُبُورِ كَفِتْنَةِ الدَّجَّالِ». قَالَتْ عَمْرَةُ: فَسَمِعْتُ عَائِشَةَ تَقُولُ: فَكُنْتُ أَسْمَعُ رَسُولَ اللهِ صَلَّى اللهُ عَلَيْهِ وَسَلَّمَ بَعْدَ ذَلِكَ يَتَعَوَّذُ مِنْ عَذَابِ النَّارِ وَعَذَابِ الْقَبْرِ.

Muhammad ibn al-Muthannā narrated: ʿAbd al-Wahhāb narrated [H]. Also, Ibn Abi ʿUmar narrated; Sufyān narrated; both from Yaḥyā ibn Saʿīd; with the same chain of transmission: **the same meaning as narrated by Sulaymān ibn Bilāl.**

وَحَدَّثَنَاهُ مُحَمَّدُ بْنُ الْمُثَنَّى، حَدَّثَنَا عَبْدُ الْوَهَّابِ، ح. وَحَدَّثَنَا ابْنُ أَبِي عُمَرَ، حَدَّثَنَا سُفْيَانُ، جَمِيعًا عَنْ يَحْيَى بْنِ سَعِيدٍ، فِي هَذَا الإِسْنَادِ، بِمِثْلِ مَعْنَى حَدِيثِ سُلَيْمَانَ بْنِ بِلاَلٍ.

Text Explanation

This hadith clearly shows that the Prophet's practice is that the prayer at the time of an eclipse is offered in the mosque and in congregation.

The Prophet tells his Companions that he saw them being examined in the grave. This confirms the test and the torment in the grave. This is the view of the people of the truth. When a person is examined, he is asked: 'What do you know about this man [meaning Prophet Muhammad (peace be upon him)]?' A believer will say: 'He is God's Messenger'. A hypocrite will say: 'I heard people say something and I said like they did'. This is how it is explained in an authentic hadith.

The Prophet says that the examination in the grave is 'like the trial of the Impostor'. This means that it is a very hard test. However, 'God will strengthen the believers through the true, unshakeable word'.

CHAPTER 3

WHAT THE PROPHET SAW OF HEAVEN AND HELL IN THE ECLIPSE PRAYER

[1802–9]. (Dar al-Salam 1975) Yaʿqūb ibn Ibrāhīm al-Dawraqī narrated to me:[i] Ismāʿīl ibn ʿUlayyah narrated; from Hishām al-Dastawāʾī; he said: Abu al-Zubayr narrated; from Jābir ibn ʿAbdullāh. He said: **'The sun went into eclipse during the Prophet's lifetime, on a very hot day. God's Messenger (peace be upon him) led his Companions in prayer, standing up for a long time, and some of them went down.[ii] He then bowed for a long time, then raised himself and stood for a long time, then bowed for a long time, then raised himself and stood for a long time, then he prostrated himself twice. He then stood up and did the same. Thus, there were four bows and four prostrations. He then said: "I was shown all the places where you will go. I was shown Heaven, so [near] that if I tried to take a bunch from it, I would take it (or he said: I took a bunch from it), but my hand was short of it. And I was shown Hell, and I saw in it a woman from the Children of Israel being punished for [her treatment of] a cat of hers. She tied the cat up, giving her no food and did not let her fend for herself. I saw Abu Thumāmah ʿAmr ibn Mālik[iii] dragging his intestines in the Fire. They used**

---

i. Related by Abu Dāwūd in a shorter version, 1179; al-Nasāʾī in a shorter version, 1477.

ii. They sat down as they could not stand any longer.

iii. He is the same person mentioned earlier by the name ʿAmr ibn Luḥayy.

to say that the sun and the moon do not eclipse except for the decease of a great person. They are indeed two of God's signs which He shows you. If they are eclipsed, pray until they are clear".'

وَحَدَّثَنِي يَعْقُوبُ بْنُ إِبْرَاهِيمَ الدَّوْرَقِيُّ، حَدَّثَنَا إِسْمَاعِيلُ ابْنُ عُلَيَّةَ، عَنْ هِشَامٍ الدَّسْتَوَائِيِّ، قَالَ حَدَّثَنَا أَبُو الزُّبَيْرِ، عَنْ جَابِرِ بْنِ عَبْدِ اللهِ قَالَ: كَسَفَتِ الشَّمْسُ عَلَى عَهْدِ رَسُولِ اللهِ صَلَّى اللهُ عَلَيْهِ وَسَلَّمَ، فِي يَوْمٍ شَدِيدِ الْحَرِّ. فَصَلَّى رَسُولُ اللهِ صَلَّى اللهُ عَلَيْهِ وَسَلَّمَ بِأَصْحَابِهِ، فَأَطَالَ الْقِيَامَ حَتَّى جَعَلُوا يَخِرُّونَ. ثُمَّ رَكَعَ فَأَطَالَ، ثُمَّ رَفَعَ فَأَطَالَ، ثُمَّ رَكَعَ فَأَطَالَ، ثُمَّ رَفَعَ فَأَطَالَ، ثُمَّ سَجَدَ سَجْدَتَيْنِ، ثُمَّ قَامَ فَصَنَعَ نَحْوًا مِنْ ذَاكَ. فَكَانَتْ أَرْبَعَ رَكَعَاتٍ وَأَرْبَعَ سَجَدَاتٍ. ثُمَّ قَالَ: «إِنَّهُ عُرِضَ عَلَيَّ كُلُّ شَيْءٍ تُولَجُونَهُ. فَعُرِضَتْ عَلَيَّ الْجَنَّةُ حَتَّى لَوْ تَنَاوَلْتُ مِنْهَا قِطْفًا أَخَذْتُهُ - أَوْ قَالَ تَنَاوَلْتُ مِنْهَا قِطْفًا - فَقَصُرَتْ يَدِي عَنْهُ. وَعُرِضَتْ عَلَيَّ النَّارُ، فَرَأَيْتُ فِيهَا امْرَأَةً مِنْ بَنِي إِسْرَائِيلَ تُعَذَّبُ فِي هِرَّةٍ لَهَا: رَبَطَتْهَا فَلَمْ تُطْعِمْهَا، وَلَمْ تَدَعْهَا تَأْكُلُ مِنْ خَشَاشِ الأَرْضِ. وَرَأَيْتُ أَبَا ثُمَامَةَ عَمْرَو بْنَ مَالِكٍ يَجُرُّ قُصْبَهُ فِي النَّارِ. وَإِنَّهُمْ كَانُوا يَقُولُونَ إِنَّ الشَّمْسَ وَالْقَمَرَ لاَ يَخْسِفَانِ إِلاَّ لِمَوْتِ عَظِيمٍ. وَإِنَّهُمَا آيَتَانِ مِنْ آيَاتِ اللهِ يُرِيكُمُوهُمَا، فَإِذَا خَسَفَا فَصَلُّوا حَتَّى تَنْجَلِيَ.

[1803–000]. (Dar al-Salam[i]) Abu Ghassān al-Mismaʿī narrated to me: ʿAbd al-Malik ibn al-Ṣabbāḥ narrated; from Hishām; with this chain of transmission: **the same text, except that he said: 'I saw in the Fire a tall, black woman from Ḥimyar', but did not say 'from the Children of Israel'.**

وَحَدَّثَنِيهِ أَبُو غَسَّانَ الْمِسْمَعِيُّ، حَدَّثَنَا عَبْدُ الْمَلِكِ بْنُ الصَّبَّاحِ، عَنْ هِشَامٍ، بِهَذَا الإِسْنَادِ: مِثْلَهُ، إِلاَّ أَنَّهُ قَالَ: «وَرَأَيْتُ فِي النَّارِ امْرَأَةً حِمْيَرِيَّةً سَوْدَاءَ طَوِيلَةً». وَلَمْ يَقُلْ «مِنْ بَنِي إِسْرَائِيلَ».

---

i. Dar al-Salam attaches this hadith to the one before it.

[1804–10]. (Dar al-Salam 1976) Abu Bakr ibn Abi Shaybah narrated:[i] ʿAbdullāh ibn Numayr narrated [H]. Also, Muhammad ibn ʿAbdullāh ibn Numayr narrated (in similar wording); he said: my father narrated; ʿAbd al-Malik narrated; from ʿAṭāʾ; from Jābir. He said: **'The sun was eclipsed during God's Messenger's lifetime on the day when Ibrāhīm, the son of God's Messenger, died. People said: "It is only eclipsed because of Ibrāhīm's death". The Prophet stood and led people in prayer, with six bows [i.e. *rukūʿ*] and four prostrations. He started by glorifying God. He then recited a long recitation, then bowed for nearly as long as he stood up, then he raised his head and recited [the Qur'an] a shorter recitation than the first one, then he bowed nearly as long as he stood up, then he raised his head and recited [the Qur'an] a shorter recitation than the second one, then bowed nearly as long as he stood up, then he raised his head, then he went down prostrating himself twice. He then stood up and bowed again three bows, with every time shorter than the bow preceding it. His bow was similarly as long as his prostration. He then moved backwards, and the rows moved backwards behind him until we reached the end. (Abu Bakr said: 'until we reached the women'.) He then moved forward and the people moved forward with him, until he stood back in his place. When he finished, the sun was back in its place. He said: "People, the sun and the moon are two of God's signs, and they are not eclipsed for the death of anyone. (Abu Bakr said: "for the death of any human being"). If you see something of this kind, pray until it is clear. Everything you are warned against I saw in this prayer of mine. The Fire was brought forward, and this was when you saw me moving backward, fearing that it might scorch**

i. Related by Abu Dāwūd, 1178.

me. I saw in it a man with a stick bent at its end dragging his intestine in Hell. He used to steal from pilgrims with his stick. If he was found out, he would say: 'it was accidentally caught up in my stick'. If not, he got away with it. I also saw in it a woman who tied up her cat, giving it no food and preventing it from eating from what is on earth, until it died of starvation. Then Heaven was brought forward, and this was when you saw me move forward until I stood in my place. I stretched my hand, wanting to take some of its fruit so that you can look at it, but then I thought I should not. I saw during this prayer of mine everything you are promised".'

حَدَّثَنَا أَبُو بَكْرِ بْنُ أَبِي شَيْبَةَ، حَدَّثَنَا عَبْدُ اللهِ بْنُ نُمَيْرٍ، ح. وَحَدَّثَنَا مُحَمَّدُ بْنُ عَبْدِ اللهِ بْنِ نُمَيْرٍ - وَتَقَارَبَا فِي اللَّفْظِ-قَالَ: حَدَّثَنَا أَبِي، حَدَّثَنَا عَبْدُ الْمَلِكِ، عَنْ عَطَاءٍ، عَنْ جَابِرٍ قَالَ: انْكَسَفَتِ الشَّمْسُ فِي عَهْدِ رَسُولِ اللهِ صَلَّى اللهُ عَلَيْهِ وَسَلَّمَ، يَوْمَ مَاتَ إِبْرَاهِيمُ ابْنُ رَسُولِ اللهِ صَلَّى اللهُ عَلَيْهِ وَسَلَّمَ، فَقَالَ النَّاسُ إِنَّمَا انْكَسَفَتْ لِمَوْتِ إِبْرَاهِيمَ. فَقَامَ النَّبِيُّ صَلَّى اللهُ عَلَيْهِ وَسَلَّمَ فَصَلَّى بِالنَّاسِ سِتَّ رَكَعَاتٍ بِأَرْبَعِ سَجَدَاتٍ: بَدَأَ فَكَبَّرَ، ثُمَّ قَرَأَ فَأَطَالَ الْقِرَاءَةَ ثُمَّ رَكَعَ نَحْوًا مِمَّا قَامَ، ثُمَّ رَفَعَ رَأْسَهُ مِنَ الرُّكُوعِ فَقَرَأَ قِرَاءَةً دُونَ الْقِرَاءَةِ الأُولَى ثُمَّ رَكَعَ نَحْوًا مِمَّا قَامَ، ثُمَّ رَفَعَ رَأْسَهُ مِنَ الرُّكُوعِ فَقَرَأَ قِرَاءَةً دُونَ الْقِرَاءَةِ الثَّانِيَةِ ثُمَّ رَكَعَ نَحْوًا مِمَّا قَامَ، ثُمَّ رَفَعَ رَأْسَهُ مِنَ الرُّكُوعِ. ثُمَّ انْحَدَرَ بِالسُّجُودِ فَسَجَدَ سَجْدَتَيْنِ. ثُمَّ قَامَ فَرَكَعَ أَيْضًا ثَلاَثَ رَكَعَاتٍ، لَيْسَ فِيهَا رَكْعَةٌ إِلاَّ الَّتِي قَبْلَهَا أَطْوَلُ مِنَ الَّتِي بَعْدَهَا، وَرُكُوعُهُ نَحْوًا مِنْ سُجُودِهِ. ثُمَّ تَأَخَّرَ وَتَأَخَّرَتِ الصُّفُوفُ خَلْفَهُ حَتَّى انْتَهَيْنَا - وَقَالَ أَبُو بَكْرٍ حَتَّى انْتَهَى - إِلَى النِّسَاءِ. ثُمَّ تَقَدَّمَ وَتَقَدَّمَ النَّاسُ مَعَهُ حَتَّى قَامَ فِي مَقَامِهِ. فَانْصَرَفَ حِينَ انْصَرَفَ وَقَدْ آضَتِ الشَّمْسُ، فَقَالَ: «يَا أَيُّهَا النَّاسُ، إِنَّمَا الشَّمْسُ وَالْقَمَرُ آيَتَانِ مِنْ آيَاتِ اللهِ، وَإِنَّهُمَا لاَ يَنْكَسِفَانِ لِمَوْتِ أَحَدٍ مِنَ النَّاسِ - وَقَالَ أَبُو بَكْرٍ لِمَوْتِ بَشَرٍ. فَإِذَا رَأَيْتُمْ شَيْئًا مِنْ ذَلِكَ فَصَلُّوا حَتَّى تَنْجَلِيَ. مَا مِنْ شَيْءٍ تُوعَدُونَهُ إِلاَّ قَدْ رَأَيْتُهُ فِي صَلاَتِي هَذِهِ: لَقَدْ جِيءَ بِالنَّارِ، وَذَلِكُمْ حِينَ رَأَيْتُمُونِي تَأَخَّرْتُ مَخَافَةَ أَنْ يُصِيبَنِي مِنْ لَفْحِهَا، وَحَتَّى رَأَيْتُ فِيهَا صَاحِبَ الْمِحْجَنِ يَجُرُّ قُصْبَهُ فِي النَّارِ.

كَانَ يَسْرِقُ الْحَاجَّ بِمِحْجَنِهِ، فَإِنْ فُطِنَ لَهُ قَالَ: إِنَّمَا تَعَلَّقَ بِمِحْجَنِي، وَإِنْ غُفِلَ عَنْهُ ذَهَبَ بِهِ. وَحَتَّى رَأَيْتُ فِيهَا صَاحِبَةَ الْهِرَّةِ الَّتِي رَبَطَتْهَا، فَلَمْ تُطْعِمْهَا وَلَمْ تَدَعْهَا تَأْكُلُ مِنْ خَشَاشِ الأَرْضِ، حَتَّى مَاتَتْ جُوعًا. ثُمَّ جِيءَ بِالْجَنَّةِ، وَذَلِكُمْ حِينَ رَأَيْتُمُونِي تَقَدَّمْتُ حَتَّى قُمْتُ فِي مَقَامِي. وَلَقَدْ مَدَدْتُ يَدِي وَأَنَا أُرِيدُ أَنْ أَتَنَاوَلَ مِنْ ثَمَرِهَا لِتَنْظُرُوا إِلَيْهِ. ثُمَّ بَدَا لِي أَنْ لاَ أَفْعَلَ. فَمَا مِنْ شَيْءٍ تُوعَدُونَهُ إِلاَّ قَدْ رَأَيْتُهُ فِي صَلاَتِي هَذِهِ.

[1805–11]. (Dar al-Salam 1977) Muhammad ibn al-ʿAlā' al-Hamdānī narrated:[i] Ibn Numayr narrated; Hishām narrated; from Fāṭimah; from Asmā'. She said: **'The sun was eclipsed during God's Messenger's lifetime. I went into ʿĀ'ishah's and found her praying. I said: "Why are people praying?" She pointed with her head to the sky. I said: "Is it a sign?" She answered: "Yes". God's Messenger (peace be upon him) stood up for a very long time, and I was nearly fainting. I took up a water bottle near me and I poured water over my head or on my face. God's Messenger finished his prayer with the sun having been clear. He addressed the people, praising God and thanking Him. He then said: "Meanwhile, I saw in this place of mine everything that I had not seen earlier, including Heaven and Hell. It has been revealed to me that you shall be examined in the graves, nearly or the same as the test of the False Messiah (I do not know which of the two Asmā' said). Any of you will be questioned: 'What do you know about this man?' A believer, or a man of certitude (I do not know which of the two Asmā' said) would say: 'He is Muhammad. He is God's Messenger, and he came to us with clear proof and guidance, and we accepted and obeyed', three times. He is told: 'Go to sleep. We knew that you believed**

i. Related by al-Bukhari, 86, 184, 922, 1053 and 7287, and in a shorter version, 1235.

in him. Sleep in peace'. A hypocrite, or a doubter (I do not know which of the two Asmā' said) will say: 'I do not know. I heard people say something and I said the same'."'

حَدَّثَنَا مُحَمَّدُ بْنُ الْعَلَاءِ الْهَمْدَانِيُّ، حَدَّثَنَا ابْنُ نُمَيْرٍ، حَدَّثَنَا هِشَامٌ، عَنْ فَاطِمَةَ، عَنْ أَسْمَاءَ قَالَتْ: خَسَفَتِ الشَّمْسُ عَلَى عَهْدِ رَسُولِ اللهِ صَلَّى اللهُ عَلَيْهِ وَسَلَّمَ، فَدَخَلْتُ عَلَى عَائِشَةَ وَهِيَ تُصَلِّي، فَقُلْتُ مَا شَأْنُ النَّاسِ يُصَلُّونَ؟ فَأَشَارَتْ بِرَأْسِهَا إِلَى السَّمَاءِ. فَقُلْتُ: آيَةٌ؟ قَالَتْ: نَعَمْ. فَأَطَالَ رَسُولُ اللهِ صَلَّى اللهُ عَلَيْهِ وَسَلَّمَ الْقِيَامَ جِدًّا، حَتَّى تَجَلَّانِي الْغَشْيُ، فَأَخَذْتُ قِرْبَةً مِنْ مَاءٍ إِلَى جَنْبِي، فَجَعَلْتُ أَصُبُّ عَلَى رَأْسِي أَوْ عَلَى وَجْهِي مِنَ الْمَاءِ. قَالَتْ: فَانْصَرَفَ رَسُولُ اللهِ صَلَّى اللهُ عَلَيْهِ وَسَلَّمَ وَقَدْ تَجَلَّتِ الشَّمْسُ. فَخَطَبَ رَسُولُ اللهِ صَلَّى اللهُ عَلَيْهِ وَسَلَّمَ النَّاسَ، فَحَمِدَ اللهَ وَأَثْنَى عَلَيْهِ ثُمَّ قَالَ: «أَمَّا بَعْدُ، مَا مِنْ شَيْءٍ لَمْ أَكُنْ رَأَيْتُهُ إِلَّا قَدْ رَأَيْتُهُ فِي مَقَامِي هَذَا، حَتَّى الْجَنَّةَ وَالنَّارَ. وَإِنَّهُ قَدْ أُوحِيَ إِلَيَّ أَنَّكُمْ تُفْتَنُونَ فِي الْقُبُورِ قَرِيبًا أَوْ مِثْلَ فِتْنَةِ الْمَسِيحِ الدَّجَّالِ - لَا أَدْرِي أَيَّ ذَلِكَ قَالَتْ أَسْمَاءُ. فَيُؤْتَى أَحَدُكُمْ فَيُقَالُ: مَا عِلْمُكَ بِهَذَا الرَّجُلِ؟ فَأَمَّا الْمُؤْمِنُ أَوِ الْمُوقِنُ - لَا أَدْرِي أَيَّ ذَلِكَ قَالَتْ أَسْمَاءُ—فَيَقُولُ: هُوَ مُحَمَّدٌ، هُوَ رَسُولُ اللهِ. جَاءَنَا بِالْبَيِّنَاتِ وَالْهُدَى فَأَجَبْنَا وَأَطَعْنَا. ثَلَاثَ مِرَارٍ. فَيُقَالُ لَهُ: نَمْ، قَدْ كُنَّا نَعْلَمُ إِنَّكَ لَتُؤْمِنُ بِهِ، فَنَمْ صَالِحًا. وَأَمَّا الْمُنَافِقُ أَوِ الْمُرْتَابُ - لَا أَدْرِي أَيَّ ذَلِكَ قَالَتْ أَسْمَاءُ—فَيَقُولُ: لَا أَدْرِي، سَمِعْتُ النَّاسَ يَقُولُونَ شَيْئًا فَقُلْتُ.

[1806–12]. (Dar al-Salam 1978) Abu Bakr ibn Abi Shaybah and Abu Kurayb narrated: both said: Abu Usāmah narrated; from Hishām; from Fāṭimah; from Asmā'. She said: **'I went to 'Ā'ishah and I saw people praying, and she was praying. I asked: "What is the matter with people...".' He narrated the hadith in a similar version to Ibn Numayr's narration from Hishām.**

حَدَّثَنَا أَبُو بَكْرِ بْنُ أَبِي شَيْبَةَ وَأَبُو كُرَيْبٍ قَالا: حَدَّثَنَا أَبُو أُسَامَةَ، عَنْ هِشَامٍ، عَنْ فَاطِمَةَ، عَنْ أَسْمَاءَ قَالَتْ: أَتَيْتُ عَائِشَةَ فَإِذَا النَّاسُ قِيَامٌ، وَإِذَا هِيَ تُصَلِّي. فَقُلْتُ: مَا شَأْنُ النَّاسِ؟ وَاقْتَصَّ الْحَدِيثَ بِنَحْوِ حَدِيثِ ابْنِ نُمَيْرٍ عَنْ هِشَامٍ.

[1807–13]. (Dar al-Salam[i]) Yaḥyā ibn Yaḥyā reported: Sufyān ibn ʿUyaynah reported; from al-Zuhrī; from ʿUrwah. He said: **'[When you refer to a solar eclipse] do not say: the sun *kasafat*, but *khasafat*'.**

أَخْبَرَنَا يَحْيَى بْنُ يَحْيَى، أَخْبَرَنَا سُفْيَانُ بْنُ عُيَيْنَةَ، عَنِ الزُّهْرِيِّ، عَنْ عُرْوَةَ قَالَ: لاَ تَقُلْ كَسَفَتِ الشَّمْسُ، وَلَكِنْ قُلْ خَسَفَتِ الشَّمْسُ

[1808–14]. (Dar al-Salam 1979) Yaḥyā ibn Ḥabīb al-Ḥārithī narrated: Khālid ibn al-Ḥārith narrated; Ibn Jurayj narrated; Manṣūr ibn ʿAbd al-Raḥmān narrated; from his mother Ṣafiyyah bint Shaybah; from Asmā' bint Abi Bakr; that she said: **'The Prophet rushed one day (she said: 'she meant the day when the sun was in eclipse'), and he [unwittingly] took a woman's dress, but he was sent his own top garment. He stood up for people [in prayer] for a long time; so long that if a person came in, he would not realise that he was in prayer – because of his long standing, he would not say that he was in prayer'.**

حَدَّثَنَا يَحْيَى بْنُ حَبِيبٍ الْحَارِثِيُّ، حَدَّثَنَا خَالِدُ بْنُ الْحَارِثِ، حَدَّثَنَا ابْنُ جُرَيْجٍ، حَدَّثَنِي مَنْصُورُ بْنُ عَبْدِ الرَّحْمَنِ، عَنْ أُمِّهِ صَفِيَّةَ بِنْتِ شَيْبَةَ، عَنْ أَسْمَاءَ بِنْتِ أَبِي بَكْرٍ أَنَّهَا قَالَتْ: فَزِعَ النَّبِيُّ صَلَّى اللهُ عَلَيْهِ وَسَلَّمَ يَوْمًا. قَالَتْ: تَعْنِي يَوْمَ كَسَفَتِ الشَّمْسُ. فَأَخَذَ دِرْعًا

i. Dar al-Salam attaches this hadith to the one before it.

حَتَّى أُدْرِكَ بِرِدَائِهِ، فَقَامَ لِلنَّاسِ قِيَامًا طَوِيلاً: لَوْ أَنَّ إِنْسَانًا أَتَى لَمْ يَشْعُرْ أَنَّ النَّبِيَّ صَلَّى اللهُ عَلَيْهِ وَسَلَّمَ رَكَعَ مَا حَدَّثَ أَنَّهُ رَكَعَ مِنْ طُولِ الْقِيَامِ.

[1809–15]. (Dar al-Salam 1980) Saʿīd ibn Yaḥyā al-Umawī narrated to me: my father narrated to me; Ibn Jurayj narrated; with this chain of transmission: **the same text. He said: 'Standing up for a long time; standing then bowing'. He added: 'I kept looking at this woman [realising that] she was older than me, and to the other one [realising that] she was weaker than me'.**

وَحَدَّثَنِي سَعِيدُ بْنُ يَحْيَى الأُمَوِيُّ، حَدَّثَنِي أَبِي، حَدَّثَنَا ابْنُ جُرَيْجٍ، بِهَذَا الإِسْنَادِ مِثْلَهُ. وَقَالَ: قِيَامًا طَوِيلاً يَقُومُ ثُمَّ يَرْكَعُ. وَزَادَ فَجَعَلْتُ أَنْظُرُ إِلَى الْمَرْأَةِ أَسَنَّ مِنِّي، وَإِلَى الأُخْرَى هِيَ أَسْقَمُ مِنِّي.

[1810–16]. (Dar al-Salam 1981) Ahmad ibn Saʿīd al-Dārimī narrated: Ḥabbān narrated; Wuhayb narrated; Manṣūr narrated; from his mother; from Asmā' bint Abi Bakr. She said: **'The sun was in eclipse during the Prophet's lifetime, and he rushed and unwittingly took a woman's dress, but he was later sent his own top garment. I did what I needed[i] then came and entered the mosque. I saw God's Messenger (peace be upon him) standing and I stood with him. He stayed in his standing position for a very long time so that I thought of sitting down. But then I might look at a weak woman and say to myself that this woman is weaker than me. I would then remain standing. He then bowed and stayed in the bowing position for a long time. He then raised his head and stood**

i. This means that she went home and performed her ablution.

for a long time. Had a man come in then, he would think that [the Prophet] did not bow'.

وَحَدَّثَنِي أَحْمَدُ بْنُ سَعِيدٍ الدَّارِمِيُّ، حَدَّثَنَا حَبَّانُ، حَدَّثَنَا وُهَيْبٌ، حَدَّثَنَا مَنْصُورٌ، عَنْ أُمِّهِ، عَنْ أَسْمَاءَ بِنْتِ أَبِي بَكْرٍ قَالَتْ: كَسَفَتِ الشَّمْسُ عَلَى عَهْدِ النَّبِيِّ صَلَّى اللهُ عَلَيْهِ وَسَلَّمَ، فَفَزِعَ فَأَخْطَأَ بِدِرْعٍ حَتَّى أُدْرِكَ بِرِدَائِهِ بَعْدَ ذَلِكَ. قَالَتْ: فَقَضَيْتُ حَاجَتِي، ثُمَّ جِئْتُ وَدَخَلْتُ الْمَسْجِدَ فَرَأَيْتُ رَسُولَ اللهِ صَلَّى اللهُ عَلَيْهِ وَسَلَّمَ قَائِمًا، فَقُمْتُ مَعَهُ، فَأَطَالَ الْقِيَامَ حَتَّى رَأَيْتُنِي أُرِيدُ أَنْ أَجْلِسَ، ثُمَّ أَلْتَفِتُ إِلَى الْمَرْأَةِ الضَّعِيفَةِ فَأَقُولُ هَذِهِ أَضْعَفُ مِنِّي،، فَأَقُومُ فَرَكَعَ فَأَطَالَ الرُّكُوعَ، ثُمَّ رَفَعَ رَأْسَهُ فَأَطَالَ الْقِيَامَ، حَتَّى لَوْ أَنَّ رَجُلاً جَاءَ خُيِّلَ إِلَيْهِ أَنَّهُ لَمْ يَرْكَعْ.

[1811–17]. (Dar al-Salam 1982) Suwayd ibn Saʿīd narrated:[i] Ḥafṣ ibn Maysarah narrated; Zayd ibn Aslam narrated to me; from ʿAṭā' ibn Yasār; from Ibn ʿAbbās. He said: **'The sun was in eclipse during God's Messenger's lifetime. The Prophet prayed and people prayed with him. He stood up for a long time, near to reciting Surah The Cow. He then bowed staying in [the bowing] position for a long time. He then rose and stood standing for a long time but shorter than the first standing. He then bowed for a long time but less than the first bow. He then prostrated himself. He then stood up for a long time but shorter than the first standing. He then bowed for a long time but less than the first bow. He then rose and stood standing for a long time but shorter than the first standing. He then bowed for a long time but less than the first bow. He then prostrated himself. He then finished and the sun was clear. He said: "The sun and the moon are two of God's signs.**

---

i. Related by al-Bukhari, 1052, 5197; also al-Bukhari, 29, 431, 748 and 3202; Abu Dāwūd in a shorter version, 1189; al-Nasā'ī, 1492.

They do not eclipse for the death or life of anyone. If you see such an event, glorify God". People said: "Messenger of God, we saw you picking up something while you were in your position, but then we saw you refraining from that". He said: "I saw Heaven, and I wanted to pick up a bunch of its fruit. Had I taken it, you would have eaten of it for the rest of this life. I also saw Hell, and I never saw anything [so horrible] as I saw today. I saw that the majority of its dwellers were women". They asked: "Why is that, Messenger of God?" He said: "Because of their denial". They asked: "Do they deny God?" He said: "By denying [the deeds of] their partners and by denying kindness. Were you to be kind to a woman throughout your life and she then sees you doing something [she dislikes], she would say: 'You have never done me a good thing'.""[i]

حَدَّثَنَا سُوَيْدُ بْنُ سَعِيدٍ، حَدَّثَنَا حَفْصُ بْنُ مَيْسَرَةَ، حَدَّثَنِي زَيْدُ بْنُ أَسْلَمَ، عَنْ عَطَاءِ بْنِ يَسَارٍ، عَنِ ابْنِ عَبَّاسٍ قَالَ: انْكَسَفَتِ الشَّمْسُ عَلَى عَهْدِ رَسُولِ اللهِ صَلَّى اللهُ عَلَيْهِ وَسَلَّمَ، فَصَلَّى رَسُولُ اللهِ صَلَّى اللهُ عَلَيْهِ وَسَلَّمَ وَالنَّاسُ مَعَهُ، فَقَامَ قِيَامًا طَوِيلاً قَدْرَ نَحْوِ سُورَةِ الْبَقَرَةِ. ثُمَّ رَكَعَ رُكُوعًا طَوِيلاً، ثُمَّ رَفَعَ فَقَامَ قِيَامًا طَوِيلاً وَهُوَ دُونَ الْقِيَامِ الأَوَّلِ، ثُمَّ رَكَعَ رُكُوعًا طَوِيلاً وَهُوَ دُونَ الرُّكُوعِ الأَوَّلِ، ثُمَّ سَجَدَ. ثُمَّ قَامَ قِيَامًا طَوِيلاً وَهُوَ دُونَ الْقِيَامِ الأَوَّلِ، ثُمَّ رَكَعَ رُكُوعًا طَوِيلاً وَهُوَ دُونَ الرُّكُوعِ الأَوَّلِ، ثُمَّ رَفَعَ فَقَامَ قِيَامًا طَوِيلاً وَهُوَ دُونَ الْقِيَامِ الأَوَّلِ، ثُمَّ رَكَعَ رُكُوعًا طَوِيلاً وَهُوَ دُونَ الرُّكُوعِ الأَوَّلِ، ثُمَّ سَجَدَ. ثُمَّ انْصَرَفَ وَقَدِ انْجَلَتِ الشَّمْسُ، فَقَالَ: «إِنَّ الشَّمْسَ وَالْقَمَرَ آيَتَانِ مِنْ آيَاتِ اللهِ، لاَ يَنْكَسِفَانِ لِمَوْتِ أَحَدٍ وَلاَ لِحَيَاتِهِ. فَإِذَا رَأَيْتُمْ ذَلِكَ فَاذْكُرُوا اللهَ».

---

i. Here, the Prophet is highlighting the importance of acknowledging kindness and looking at other people's behaviour with the proper perspective. The hadith does not mean that no man behaves in this way, but he is merely saying that this characteristic, which is enough to merit punishment in hell, is found more in women.

قَالُوا: يَا رَسُولَ اللهِ، رَأَيْنَاكَ تَنَاوَلْتَ شَيْئًا فِي مَقَامِكَ هَذَا، ثُمَّ رَأَيْنَاكَ كَفَفْتَ. فَقَالَ: «إِنِّي رَأَيْتُ الْجَنَّةَ فَتَنَاوَلْتُ مِنْهَا عُنْقُودًا، وَلَوْ أَخَذْتُهُ لأَكَلْتُمْ مِنْهُ مَا بَقِيَتِ الدُّنْيَا. وَرَأَيْتُ النَّارَ فَلَمْ أَرَ كَالْيَوْمِ مَنْظَرًا قَطُّ. وَرَأَيْتُ أَكْثَرَ أَهْلِهَا النِّسَاءَ». قَالُوا: بِمَ يَا رَسُولَ اللهِ؟ قَالَ: «بِكُفْرِهِنَّ». قِيلَ: أَيَكْفُرْنَ بِاللهِ؟ قَالَ: «بِكُفْرِ الْعَشِيرِ، وَبِكُفْرِ الإِحْسَانِ. لَوْ أَحْسَنْتَ إِلَى إِحْدَاهُنَّ الدَّهْرَ، ثُمَّ رَأَتْ مِنْكَ شَيْئًا قَالَتْ: مَا رَأَيْتُ مِنْكَ خَيْرًا قَطُّ.

[1812–000]. (Dar al-Salam 1983) Muhammad ibn Rāfiʿ narrated: Isḥāq (meaning Ibn ʿĪsā) narrated; Mālik reported; from Zayd ibn Aslam; with this chain of transmission: **the same text, except that he said: 'We then saw you holding back'.**

وَحَدَّثَنَاهُ مُحَمَّدُ بْنُ رَافِعٍ، حَدَّثَنَا إِسْحَاقُ، - يَعْنِي ابْنَ عِيسَى - أَخْبَرَنَا مَالِكٌ، عَنْ زَيْدِ بْنِ أَسْلَمَ، فِي هَذَا الإِسْنَادِ بِمِثْلِهِ غَيْرَ أَنَّهُ قَالَ: ثُمَّ رَأَيْنَاكَ تَكَعْكَعْتَ.

Text Explanation

In hadith No. 1802, Abu al-Zubayr reports from Jābir, the Prophet's Companion, that the Prophet 'bowed for a long time, then raised himself and stood for a long time, then he prostrated himself twice'. This appears to mean that the Prophet stood for a long time before prostrating himself. Yet this is not mentioned in the other hadiths, nor even in Jābir's narration transmitted through narrators other than Abu al-Zubayr. *Qadi* ʿIyāḍ reports that scholars are unanimous that the standing before prostration is not long. Therefore, this particular narration is considered in one of two ways: the first is that it is 'peculiar', i.e. *shādhdh,* and therefore set aside; and the second is that it means that the Prophet stayed in that position for a little longer than usual, not nearly as long as the bow [i.e. *rukū*ʿ] before it.

In this hadith, the Prophet says: 'I was shown all places where you will go', which includes Heaven, Hell, graves, the plane where people are gathered on the Day of Resurrection, etc. He adds that he was shown Heaven and Hell. *Qadi* ʿIyāḍ said that scholars said:

> It may be that he saw them physically. God would have removed whatever stood between him and them, just as he showed him Jerusalem when he described it. Thus, the Prophet's description, 'against this wall', means close to it and in its direction or is merely suggesting its closeness and full visibility. They further said that it may also be giving more detailed information, which he had not known earlier. He would thus gather more knowledge of their greatness so as to always remember them and warn against what may happen.

Hence, the Prophet said in hadith No. 1792: 'Were you to know what I know, you would weep much and laugh but little'. *Qadi* ʿIyāḍ said: 'The first meaning is better because it is closer to the wording of the hadith, which suggests real visibility, such as the Prophet's intention to pick up a bunch of fruit and his moving backwards so that he would not be scorched by the Fire'.

In the same hadith the Prophet says: 'I was shown Heaven, so [near] that if I tried to take a bunch from it, I would take it'. This means that if he stretched his hand, he would take it. This confirms that Heaven and Hell are already created and that they now exist and that there are fruits in Heaven. All this is the view of our school and all Sunni people, except the Muʿtazilah. The Prophet adds: 'And I was shown Hell, and I saw in it a woman from the Children of Israel being punished for [her treatment of] a cat of hers. She tied the cat up, giving her no food and did not let her fend for herself'. A more literal translation will render the last phrase as 'she did not let her eat of what is on earth'. This means whatever is on earth, including insects, small birds and creatures. *Qadi* ʿIyāḍ said: 'This hadith confirms that people are accountable for minor sins, but it does not say that the woman is punished by the Fire for her treatment of the cat. On the other hand, she might have been an unbeliever and her punishment is increased for this reason'. This view of *Qadi* ʿIyāḍ is not correct. The hadith clearly states that the woman is punished because of her treatment of the cat, which is a major sin. The woman tied up the cat and left her so until she died. To persist in doing a minor sin makes that sin a major one, as stated in Fiqh books and elsewhere. There is nothing in this hadith that suggests that the woman was an unbeliever.

In hadith No. 1804, the Prophet moved backwards, and the rows of the congregation moved with him until they reached the women's place, then he moved forwards and returned to his original place. This makes it clear that a few movements do not invalidate prayer. Our scholars set a limit to such movement, saying that it is less than three consecutive steps. They add that walking three consecutive steps invalidates the prayer. They explain this hadith as meaning that the steps involved were not consecutive. It may not be understood to mean only two steps because the statement that they reached the women's place contradicts that. The hadith also makes it clear that it is desirable for women to join the prayer at the time of an eclipse and that they stand behind the men's rows.

In hadith No. 1805, Asmā' mentions that she asked her sister, ʿĀ'ishah, why people were praying and that ʿĀ'ishah pointed with her head to the sky. The hadith makes clear that ordinary speech is not permissible during prayer, but a signal is appropriate when needed, and it is not discouraged. Then Asmā' said that she was nearly fainting because of standing for such a long time on a hot day. Hence, she started to pour water on her head or face. This makes clear that dizziness does not invalidate the ablution, as long as one remains well aware. That she poured on herself from a water bottle is understood to mean that she did not do many movements in succession, because several successive movements invalidate prayer.

When the angels question a person in the grave, they ask him: 'What do you know about this man?' They do not say 'What do you know about God's Messenger?' It is thus in order to keep that person in the dark, so that whoever is being questioned does not pick up a hint from the angels and praise and honour the Prophet, learning from them, rather than out of belief and conviction. Hence, a believer would say: 'He is God's Messenger', while a hypocrite would say: 'I do not know'. This confirms what God says in the Qur'an: 'God will strengthen the believers through the true, unshakeable word in both this life and the life to come'. (14: 27)

In hadiths No. 1808 and 1810, the Prophet is said to have rushed at the time of the solar eclipse. The Arabic word used for 'rush' is *faziʿa*, which indicates the sense of rushing to do something because it is felt to be urgent. It has another sense, which is 'to fear' something. On this occasion, what happened resulted from his preoccupation with the situation and a need to attend to prayer immediately, hence he unwittingly took the dress of one of the women in his household. He did not even notice his mistake. When his family realised what had happened, someone brought him his own garment.

In hadith No. 1811 the Prophet mentions the fault that leads many women to incur punishment in hell, which is their denial. The Prophet was asked: 'Do they deny God?' He said: 'By denying [the deeds of] their partners and by denying kindness'. The word the Prophet uses here for denial is *kufr*, which means 'disbelief'. Hence the Prophet is asked whether he meant denial of God. He explained that they deny kindness by their immediate relatives, particularly their husbands. This shows that this word may be used to refer to denying other people's rights, even though the person concerned is not an unbeliever.

CHAPTER 4

REPORTING EIGHT BOWS AND FOUR PROSTRATIONS

[1813–18]. (Dar al-Salam 1984) Abu Bakr ibn Abi Shaybah narrated:[i] Ismāʿīl ibn ʿUlayyah narrated; from Sufyān; from Ḥabīb; from Ṭāwūs; from Ibn ʿAbbās. He said: **'God's Messenger (peace be upon him) prayed when the sun was eclipsed, doing eight bowings [i.e. *rukūʿ*] with four prostrations'.**

ʿAlī reported the same.

حَدَّثَنَا أَبُو بَكْرِ بْنُ أَبِي شَيْبَةَ، حَدَّثَنَا إِسْمَاعِيلُ ابْنُ عُلَيَّةَ، عَنْ سُفْيَانَ، عَنْ حَبِيبٍ، عَنْ طَاوُسٍ، عَنِ ابْنِ عَبَّاسٍ قَالَ: صَلَّى رَسُولُ اللهِ صَلَّى اللهُ عَلَيْهِ وَسَلَّمَ حِينَ كَسَفَتِ الشَّمْسُ ثَمَانَ رَكَعَاتٍ فِي أَرْبَعِ سَجَدَاتٍ.

وَعَنْ عَلِيٍّ مِثْلُ ذَلِكَ

[1814–19]. (Dar al-Salam 1985) Muhammad ibn al-Muthannā and Abu Bakr ibn Khallād narrated; both from Yaḥyā al-Qaṭṭān; Ibn al-Muthannā said: Yaḥyā narrated; from Sufyān; he said: Ḥabīb narrated; from Ṭāwūs; from Ibn ʿAbbās; from the Prophet (peace be upon him): **'He prayed at the time of an eclipse: he recited then bowed, then recited and bowed, then recited and bowed, then recited and bowed, then he prostrated himself'. He added: 'And the other [*rakʿah*] the same'.**

---

i. Related by Abu Dāwūd, with the same meaning, 1183; al-Tirmidhī, 560; al-Nasāʾī in a similar text, 1466 and 1467.

وَحَدَّثَنَا مُحَمَّدُ بْنُ الْـمُثَنَّى وَأَبُو بَكْرِ بْنُ خَلاَّدٍ، كِلاَهُمَا عَنْ يَحْيَى الْقَطَّانِ، - قَالَ ابْنُ الْـمُثَنَّى حَدَّثَنَا يَحْيَى، - عَنْ سُفْيَانَ قَالَ: حَدَّثَنَا حَبِيبٌ، عَنْ طَاوُسٍ، عَنِ ابْنِ عَبَّاسٍ، عَنِ النَّبِيِّ صَلَّى اللهُ عَلَيْهِ وَسَلَّمَ أَنَّهُ صَلَّى فِي كُسُوفٍ قَرَأَ ثُمَّ رَكَعَ، ثُمَّ قَرَأَ ثُمَّ رَكَعَ، ثُمَّ قَرَأَ ثُمَّ رَكَعَ، ثُمَّ قَرَأَ ثُمَّ رَكَعَ، ثُمَّ سَجَدَ. قَالَ: وَالأُخْرَى مِثْلُهَا.

Text Explanation

What these hadiths mean is that in a prayer during the time of a solar eclipse, the Prophet prayed two *rakʿahs*, doing four bows, i.e. *rukūʿ*, in each *rakʿah*, followed by two prostrations.

CHAPTER 5

THE ANNOUNCEMENT FOR PRAYER AT AN ECLIPSE

[1815–20]. (Dar al-Salam 1986) Muhammad ibn Rāfiʿ narrated to me:[i] Abu al-Naḍr narrated; Abu Muʿāwiyah (who is Shaybān al-Naḥwī) narrated; from Yaḥyā; from Abu Salamah; from ʿAbdullāh ibn ʿAmr ibn al-ʿĀṣ [H]. Also, ʿAbdullāh ibn ʿAbd al-Raḥmān al-Dārimī narrated; Yaḥyā ibn Ḥassān reported; Muʿāwiyah ibn Sallām narrated; from Yaḥyā ibn Abi Kathīr; he said: Abu Salamah ibn ʿAbd al-Raḥmān reported to me the narration of ʿAbdullāh ibn ʿAmr ibn al-ʿĀṣ; that he said: **'When there was a solar eclipse during God's Messenger's lifetime, an announcement was made: *al-ṣalāt jāmiʿah* [i.e. come to prayer]. God's Messenger bowed twice in one *rakʿah,* then he stood up and did two bows in one *rakʿah,* then the sun was clear'. ʿĀ'ishah said: 'I never did a bow or a prostration longer than these'.**

حَدَّثَنِي مُحَمَّدُ بْنُ رَافِعٍ، حَدَّثَنَا أَبُو النَّضْرِ، حَدَّثَنَا أَبُو مُعَاوِيَةَ، - وَهُوَ شَيْبَانُ النَّحْوِيُّ - عَنْ يَحْيَى، عَنْ أَبِي سَلَمَةَ، عَنْ عَبْدِ اللهِ بْنِ عَمْرِو بْنِ الْعَاصِ، ح. وَحَدَّثَنَا عَبْدُ اللهِ بْنُ عَبْدِ الرَّحْمَنِ الدَّارِمِيُّ، أَخْبَرَنَا يَحْيَى بْنُ حَسَّانَ، حَدَّثَنَا مُعَاوِيَةُ بْنُ سَلَّامٍ، عَنْ يَحْيَى بْنِ أَبِي كَثِيرٍ، قَالَ أَخْبَرَنِي أَبُو سَلَمَةَ بْنُ عَبْدِ الرَّحْمَنِ، عَنْ خَبَرِ عَبْدِ اللهِ بْنِ عَمْرِو بْنِ الْعَاصِ أَنَّهُ قَالَ: لَمَّا انْكَسَفَتِ الشَّمْسُ عَلَى عَهْدِ رَسُولِ اللهِ صَلَّى اللهُ عَلَيْهِ وَسَلَّمَ نُودِيَ

---

i. Related by al-Bukhari, 1051 and 1045; al-Nasā'ī, 1478.

بِـ «الصَّلاَةَ جَامِعَةً»، فَرَكَعَ رَسُولُ اللهِ صَلَّى اللهُ عَلَيْهِ وَسَلَّمَ رَكْعَتَيْنِ فِي سَجْدَة، ثُمَّ قَامَ فَرَكَعَ رَكْعَتَيْنِ فِي سَجْدَةٍ، ثُمَّ جُلِّيَ عَنِ الشَّمْسِ. فَقَالَتْ عَائِشَةُ: مَا رَكَعْتُ رُكُوعًا قَطُّ وَلاَ سَجَدْتُ سُجُودًا قَطُّ كَانَ أَطْوَلَ مِنْهُ.

[1816–21]. (Dar al-Salam 1987) Yaḥyā ibn Yaḥyā narrated:[i] Hushaym reported; from Ismāʿīl; from Qays ibn Abi Ḥāzim; from Abu Masʿūd al-Anṣārī; that God's Messenger (peace be upon him) said: **'The sun and the moon are two of God's signs with which God puts fear into His servants' hearts. They are not eclipsed for the decease of any person. If you see anything of this sort, pray and supplicate until what afflicts you is removed'.**

وَحَدَّثَنَا يَحْيَى بْنُ يَحْيَى، أَخْبَرَنَا هُشَيْمٌ، عَنْ إِسْمَاعِيلَ، عَنْ قَيْسِ بْنِ أَبِي حَازِمٍ، عَنْ أَبِي مَسْعُودٍ الأَنْصَارِيِّ قَالَ: قَالَ رَسُولُ اللهِ صَلَّى اللهُ عَلَيْهِ وَسَلَّمَ: «إِنَّ الشَّمْسَ وَالْقَمَرَ آيَتَانِ مِنْ آيَاتِ اللهِ، يُخَوِّفُ اللهُ بِهِمَا عِبَادَهُ. وَإِنَّهُمَا لاَ يَنْكَسِفَانِ لِمَوْتِ أَحَدٍ مِنَ النَّاسِ. فَإِذَا رَأَيْتُمْ مِنْهَا شَيْئًا فَصَلُّوا، وَادْعُوا اللهَ حَتَّى يُكْشَفَ مَا بِكُمْ».

[1817–22]. (Dar al-Salam 1988) ʿUbaydullāh ibn Muʿādh al-ʿAnbarī and Yaḥyā ibn Ḥabīb narrated: both said: Muʿtamir narrated; from Ismāʿīl; from Qays; from Abu Masʿūd; that God's Messenger (peace be upon him) said: **'The sun and the moon are not eclipsed for the death of any human being. They are two of God's signs. When it happens, stand up and pray'.**

وَحَدَّثَنَا عُبَيْدُ اللهِ بْنُ مُعَاذٍ الْعَنْبَرِيُّ وَيَحْيَى بْنُ حَبِيبٍ، قَالاَ: حَدَّثَنَا مُعْتَمِرٌ، عَنْ إِسْمَاعِيلَ، عَنْ قَيْسٍ، عَنْ أَبِي مَسْعُودٍ، أَنَّ رَسُولَ اللهِ صَلَّى اللهُ عَلَيْهِ وَسَلَّمَ قَالَ:

---

i. Related by al-Bukhari, 1041 1057 and 3204; al-Nasāʾī, 1461; Ibn Mājah, 1261.

«إِنَّ الشَّمْسَ وَالْقَمَرَ لَيْسَ يَنْكَسِفَانِ لِمَوْتِ أَحَدٍ مِنَ النَّاسِ، وَلَكِنَّهُمَا آيَتَانِ مِنْ آيَاتِ اللهِ. فَإِذَا رَأَيْتُمُوهُ فَقُومُوا فَصَلُّوا».

[1818–23]. (Dar al-Salam 1989) Abu Bakr ibn Abi Shaybah narrated: Wakīʿ, Abu Usāmah and Ibn Numayr narrated [H]. Also, Isḥāq ibn Ibrāhīm narrated; Jarīr and Wakīʿ narrated [H]. And Ibn Abi ʿUmar narrated; Sufyān and Marwān narrated; all from Ismāʿīl, with the same chain of transmission: **the same text, adding in the narration by Sufyān and Wakīʿ: 'The sun was eclipsed on the day Ibrāhīm died. People said it was eclipsed because of Ibrāhīm's death'.**

وَحَدَّثَنَا أَبُو بَكْرِ بْنُ أَبِي شَيْبَةَ، حَدَّثَنَا وَكِيعٌ وَأَبُو أُسَامَةَ وَابْنُ نُمَيْرٍ ح. وَحَدَّثَنَا إِسْحَاقُ بْنُ إِبْرَاهِيمَ، أَخْبَرَنَا جَرِيرٌ وَوَكِيعٌ، ح. وَحَدَّثَنَا ابْنُ أَبِي عُمَرَ، حَدَّثَنَا سُفْيَانُ وَمَرْوَانُ، كُلُّهُمْ عَنْ إِسْمَاعِيلَ، بِهَذَا الإِسْنَادِ. وَفِي حَدِيثِ سُفْيَانَ وَوَكِيعٍ: انْكَسَفَتِ الشَّمْسُ يَوْمَ مَاتَ إِبْرَاهِيمُ، فَقَالَ النَّاسُ انْكَسَفَتْ لِمَوْتِ إِبْرَاهِيمَ.

[1819–24]. (Dar al-Salam 1890) Abu ʿĀmir al-Ashʿarī ʿAbdullāh ibn Barrād and Muhammad ibn al-ʿAlā' narrated:[i] both said: Abu Usāmah narrated; from Burayd; from Abu Burdah; from Abu Mūsā. He said: **'The sun was eclipsed during the Prophet's time. He stood up perturbed, fearing that it might be the Last Hour, and came to the mosque. He stood up doing the longest standing, bowing and prostrating. I never saw him doing this in any prayer. He then said: "These signs that God sends are not for the death or the life of anyone. God sends them to put fear into His servants' hearts. If you**

i. Related by al-Bukhari, 1059; al-Nasā'ī, 1502.

see any of them, resort to glorifying Him, supplication and seeking His forgiveness".'

In Ibn al-ʿAlā's narration there is a slight difference in a couple of words.

حَدَّثَنَا أَبُو عَامِرٍ الأَشْعَرِيُّ عَبْدُ اللهِ بْنُ بَرَّادٍ وَمُحَمَّدُ بْنُ الْعَلاَءِ، قَالا: حَدَّثَنَا أَبُو أُسَامَةَ عَنْ بُرَيْدٍ، عَنْ أَبِي بُرْدَةَ، عَنْ أَبِي مُوسَى قَالَ: خَسَفَتِ الشَّمْسُ فِي زَمَنِ النَّبِيِّ صَلَّى اللهُ عَلَيْهِ وَسَلَّمَ فَقَامَ فَزِعًا، يَخْشَى أَنْ تَكُونَ السَّاعَةُ. حَتَّى أَتَى الْمَسْجِدَ فَقَامَ يُصَلِّي بِأَطْوَلِ قِيَامٍ وَرُكُوعٍ وَسُجُودٍ. مَا رَأَيْتُهُ يَفْعَلُهُ فِي صَلاَةٍ قَطُّ. ثُمَّ قَالَ: «إِنَّ هَذِهِ الآيَاتِ الَّتِي يُرْسِلُ اللهُ لاَ تَكُونُ لِمَوْتِ أَحَدٍ وَلاَ لِحَيَاتِهِ، وَلَكِنَّ اللهَ يُرْسِلُهَا يُخَوِّفُ بِهَا عِبَادَهُ. فَإِذَا رَأَيْتُمْ مِنْهَا شَيْئًا فَافْزَعُوا إِلَى ذِكْرِهِ وَدُعَائِهِ وَاسْتِغْفَارِهِ».

وَفِي رِوَايَةِ ابْنِ الْعَلاَءِ كَسَفَتِ الشَّمْسُ وَقَالَ «يُخَوِّفُ عِبَادَهُ».

[1820–25]. (Dar al-Salam 1991) ʿUbaydullāh ibn ʿUmar al-Qawārīrī narrated to me:[i] Bishr ibn al-Mufaḍḍal narrated; al-Jurayrī narrated; from Abu al-ʿAlā' Ḥayyān ibn ʿUmayr; from ʿAbd al-Raḥmān ibn Samurah. He said: **'I was shooting with my arrows during God's Messenger's lifetime when the sun went into eclipse. I put them aside and said: "I shall see what God's Messenger (peace be upon him) will do today as the sun is eclipsed". When I reached him, I saw him supplicating with his arms raised, glorifying and praising God and asserting His Oneness until the sun was clear. He recited two surahs and prayed two *rakʿahs*'.**

وَحَدَّثَنِي عُبَيْدُ اللهِ بْنُ عُمَرَ الْقَوَارِيرِيُّ، حَدَّثَنَا بِشْرُ بْنُ الْمُفَضَّلِ، حَدَّثَنَا الْجُرَيْرِيُّ، عَنْ أَبِي الْعَلاَءِ حَيَّانَ بْنِ عُمَيْرٍ، عَنْ عَبْدِ الرَّحْمَنِ بْنِ سَمُرَةَ، قَالَ بَيْنَمَا أَنَا أَرْمِي بِأَسْهُمِي فِي

i. Related by Abu Dāwūd, 1195; al-Nasā'ī, 1459.

حَيَاةِ رَسُولِ اللهِ صَلَّى اللهُ عَلَيْهِ وَسَلَّمَ، إِذِ انْكَسَفَتِ الشَّمْسُ، فَنَبَذْتُهُنَّ وَقُلْتُ لأَنْظُرَنَّ إِلَى مَا يَحْدُثُ لِرَسُولِ اللهِ صَلَّى اللهُ عَلَيْهِ وَسَلَّمَ فِي انْكِسَافِ الشَّمْسِ الْيَوْمَ. فَانْتَهَيْتُ إِلَيْهِ وَهُوَ رَافِعٌ يَدَيْهِ يَدْعُو وَيُكَبِّرُ وَيَحْمَدُ وَيُهَلِّلُ، حَتَّى جُلِّيَ عَنِ الشَّمْسِ، فَقَرَأَ سُورَتَيْنِ وَرَكَعَ رَكْعَتَيْنِ.

[1821–26]. (Dar al-Salam 1992) Abu Bakr ibn Abi Shaybah narrated: ʿAbd al-Aʿlā ibn ʿAbd al-Aʿlā narrated; from al-Jurayrī; from Ḥayyān ibn ʿUmayr; from ʿAbd al-Raḥmān ibn Samurah who was one of the Prophet's Companions. He said: **'I was practising with my arrows in Madinah during God's Messenger's lifetime when the sun was eclipsed. I put them aside and said: "By God, I shall see what happens to God's Messenger when the sun is eclipsed". I went to him and he was standing in prayer, with his arms raised. He continued to glorify and praise God, declaring His Oneness and supplicating until it was clear. When it was clear, he recited two surahs and prayed two *rakʿahs*'.**

وَحَدَّثَنَا أَبُو بَكْرِ بْنُ أَبِي شَيْبَةَ، حَدَّثَنَا عَبْدُ الأَعْلَى بْنُ عَبْدِ الأَعْلَى، عَنِ الْجُرَيْرِيِّ، عَنْ حَيَّانَ بْنِ عُمَيْرٍ، عَنْ عَبْدِ الرَّحْمَنِ بْنِ سَمُرَةَ، - وَكَانَ مِنْ أَصْحَابِ رَسُولِ اللهِ صَلَّى اللهُ عَلَيْهِ وَسَلَّمَ-قَالَ: كُنْتُ أَرْتَمِي بِأَسْهُمٍ لِي بِالْمَدِينَةِ فِي حَيَاةِ رَسُولِ اللهِ صَلَّى اللهُ عَلَيْهِ وَسَلَّمَ إِذْ كَسَفَتِ الشَّمْسُ، فَنَبَذْتُهَا، فَقُلْتُ وَاللهِ لأَنْظُرَنَّ إِلَى مَا حَدَثَ لِرَسُولِ اللهِ صَلَّى اللهُ عَلَيْهِ وَسَلَّمَ فِي كُسُوفِ الشَّمْسِ. قَالَ: فَأَتَيْتُهُ وَهُوَ قَائِمٌ فِي الصَّلاَةِ رَافِعٌ يَدَيْهِ، فَجَعَلَ يُسَبِّحُ وَيَحْمَدُ وَيُهَلِّلُ وَيُكَبِّرُ وَيَدْعُو حَتَّى حُسِرَ عَنْهَا. قَالَ: فَلَمَّا حُسِرَ عَنْهَا قَرَأَ سُورَتَيْنِ وَصَلَّى رَكْعَتَيْنِ.

[1822–27]. (Dar al-Salam 1993) Muhammad ibn al-Muthannā narrated: Sālim ibn Nūḥ narrated; al-Jurayrī reported; from

Ḥayyān ibn ʿUmayr; from ʿAbd al-Raḥmān ibn Samurah. He said: **'While I was practising with my arrows during the Prophet's lifetime, the sun was eclipsed…'. He added a similar text.**

حَدَّثَنَا مُحَمَّدُ بْنُ الْـمُثَنَّى، حَدَّثَنَا سَالِمُ بْنُ نُوحٍ، أَخْبَرَنَا الْجُرَيْرِيُّ، عَنْ حَيَّانَ بْنِ عُمَيْرٍ، عَنْ عَبْدِ الرَّحْمَنِ بْنِ سَمُرَةَ قَالَ: بَيْنَمَا أَنَا أَتَرَمَّى بِأَسْهُمٍ لِي عَلَى عَهْدِ رَسُولِ اللهِ صَلَّى اللهُ عَلَيْهِ وَسَلَّمَ، إِذْ خَسَفَتِ الشَّمْسُ. ثُمَّ ذَكَرَ نَحْوَ حَدِيثِهِمَا.

[1823–28]. (Dar al-Salam 1994) Ḥarūn ibn Saʿīd al-Aylī narrated to me:[i] Ibn Wahb narrated; ʿAmr ibn al-Ḥārith reported to me; that ʿAbd al-Raḥmān ibn al-Qāsim narrated to him; from his father al-Qāsim ibn Muhammad ibn Abi Bakr al-Ṣiddīq; from ʿAbdullāh ibn ʿUmar; that he used to report from God's Messenger (peace be upon him) that he said: **'The sun and the moon are not eclipsed for the death or the life of anyone. They are signs of God's. When you see them [eclipsed], pray'.**

وَحَدَّثَنِي هَارُونُ بْنُ سَعِيدٍ الأَيْلِيُّ، حَدَّثَنَا ابْنُ وَهْبٍ، أَخْبَرَنِي عَمْرُو بْنُ الْحَارِثِ، أَنَّ عَبْدَ الرَّحْمَنِ بْنَ الْقَاسِمِ حَدَّثَهُ، عَنْ أَبِيهِ الْقَاسِمِ بْنِ مُحَمَّدِ بْنِ أَبِي بَكْرٍ الصِّدِّيقِ، عَنْ عَبْدِ اللهِ بْنِ عُمَرَ، أَنَّهُ كَانَ يُخْبِرُ عَنْ رَسُولِ اللهِ صَلَّى اللهُ عَلَيْهِ وَسَلَّمَ أَنَّهُ قَالَ: «إِنَّ الشَّمْسَ وَالْقَمَرَ لاَ يَخْسِفَانِ لِمَوْتِ أَحَدٍ وَلاَ لِحَيَاتِهِ، وَلَكِنَّهُمَا آيَةٌ مِنْ آيَاتِ اللهِ فَإِذَا رَأَيْتُمُوهُمَا فَصَلُّوا».

[1824–29]. (Dar al-Salam 1995) Abu Bakr ibn Abi Shaybah and Muhammad ibn ʿAbdullāh ibn Numayr narrated:[ii] both said: Muṣʿab (who is Ibn al-Miqdām) narrated; Zā'idah narrated; Ziyād ibn ʿIlāqah narrated (but in Abu Bakr's narration: Ziyād ibn ʿIlāqah said); I heard al-Mughīrah ibn Shuʿbah say: **'The**

i. Related by al-Bukhari, 1042 and 3201; al-Nasā'ī, 1460.
ii. Related by al-Bukhari, 1043, 1060 and in a shorter version, 6199.

sun was eclipsed during God's Messenger's lifetime, on the day Ibrāhīm died. God's Messenger (peace be upon him) said: "The sun and the moon are two of God's signs, and they are not eclipsed for the decease or the life of anyone. When you see them [eclipsed], supplicate to God and pray until it is clear".'

وَحَدَّثَنَا أَبُو بَكْرِ بْنُ أَبِي شَيْبَةَ وَمُحَمَّدُ بْنُ عَبْدِ اللهِ بْنِ نُمَيْرٍ، قَالاَ: حَدَّثَنَا مُصْعَبٌ، - وَهُوَ ابْنُ الْمِقْدَامِ، حَدَّثَنَا زَائِدَةُ، حَدَّثَنَا زِيَادُ بْنُ عِلاَقَةَ، (وَفِي رِوَايَةِ أَبِي بَكْرٍ قَالَ: قَالَ زِيَادُ بْنُ عِلاَقَة)، سَمِعْتُ الْمُغِيرَةَ بْنَ شُعْبَةَ يَقُولُ: انْكَسَفَتِ الشَّمْسُ عَلَى عَهْدِ رَسُولِ اللهِ صَلَّى اللهُ عَلَيْهِ وَسَلَّمَ يَوْمَ مَاتَ إِبْرَاهِيمُ. فَقَالَ رَسُولُ اللهِ صَلَّى اللهُ عَلَيْهِ وَسَلَّمَ: «إِنَّ الشَّمْسَ وَالْقَمَرَ آيَتَانِ مِنْ آيَاتِ اللهِ لاَ يَنْكَسِفَانِ لِمَوْتِ أَحَدٍ وَلاَ لِحَيَاتِهِ. فَإِذَا رَأَيْتُمُوهُمَا، فَادْعُوا اللهَ وَصَلُّوا حَتَّى يَنْكَشِفَ».

Text Explanation

In hadith No. 1815, ʻĀ'ishah says that she never bowed or prostrated longer than on this occasion, when she joined the congregational prayer at the time of a solar eclipse. Abu Mūsā al-Ashʻarī makes the same remark in hadith No. 1819. These two hadiths provide a basis for the preferred view that a long prostration in this prayer is desirable. The fact that most narrations do not mention long prostration does not detract from the validity of this view because it is based on an addition by reliable narrators, and such additions are accepted. Moreover, long prostration is confirmed by a number of the Prophet's Companions' reports. Muslim mentions it as reported by ʻĀ'ishah and Abu Mūsā, while al-Bukhari mentions it reported by other Companions of the Prophet, and Abu Dāwūd by others still. Thus, it is confirmed in hadiths with several chains of transmission. Hence, it should be upheld and implemented.

In hadith No. 1819, the Prophet is reported to have 'stood up perturbed, fearing that it might be the Last Hour'. This may sound problematic because the Last Hour is preceded by many signs that must occur and none of them had occurred at the time, such as the sun rising in the west, the appearance of the talking animal, the fire, the Impostor and fighting against some Turkic forces. It is also preceded by other events that must occur before the Last Hour, such as the liberation of Syria, Iraq, Egypt and other areas by the Muslim community, and also spending the treasures of the Persian emperor in support of God's cause, fighting against the Khawārij and other events mentioned in authentic hadiths.

Several answers may be given in response: 1) This eclipse might have occurred before the Prophet was informed of these matters; 2) He might have feared that the eclipse was a precursor of these events; 3) The narrator might have thought that the Prophet feared that this signalled the approach of the Last Hour but his thoughts need not be correct. The Prophet might simply have gone out quickly, focusing on the need to start the prayer and attend to other matters relating to the eclipse; 4) The Prophet might have thought that it was some sort of punishment, just as he looked worried when it was windy, fearing that it might bring punishment, as mentioned in the Book of Prayer for Rain. The narrator might have mistaken the Prophet's agitation and given it his own interpretation, which need not be considered.

In hadith No. 1820, the narrator says that when he reached the Prophet, he 'saw him supplicating with his arms raised, glorifying and praising God and asserting His Oneness until the sun was clear. He recited two surahs and prayed two *rakʿahs*'. In the next hadith, he said that the Prophet 'was standing in prayer, with his arms raised. He continued to glorify and praise God, declaring His Oneness and supplicating until it was clear. When it was clear, he recited two surahs and prayed two *rakʿahs*'. These reports may sound problematic, and it may be thought that the Prophet started the prayer after the sun was once again clear. It is not so, because this prayer cannot be started after the end of the eclipse. This hadith is understood as meaning that the Prophet was actually in prayer when his Companion arrived, as is clearly stated in the second report. The narrator then mentioned all that the prayer included of supplication, glorification, declaration of God's Oneness, praises of God and the recitation of two surahs in the last two standings of the second *rakʿah*. Recitation of the two surahs took place after the sun was clear, so as to complete the prayer. Thus, the total prayer was in two *rakʿahs;* it was started during the eclipse and was completed after it had ended. This understanding is necessary because it agrees with the second narration, in hadith No. 1821 and also with the rules of Fiqh and the narrations by other Companions of the Prophet. The first narration is understood in its light, so that the two narrations are consistent with each other. *Qadi* ʿIyāḍ quotes Imam al-Māzarī as suggesting that the Prophet added two separate voluntary *rakʿahs* after the end of the eclipse, but this understanding is not very solid and even contrary to the apparent meaning of the second narration, but God knows best.

In hadith No. 1821 the narrator says that the Prophet 'was standing in prayer, with his arms raised. He continued to glorify and praise God, declaring His Oneness and supplicating...'. This provides evidence in support of the view of our scholars that arms are raised when supplicating during prayer. This conflicts with the view of those who say that arms are not raised during such supplication in prayer.

In hadith No. 1823 and other hadiths in this book, the Prophet says: 'The sun and the moon are not eclipsed for the death or the life of anyone. They are signs of God's. When you see them [eclipsed], pray'. This provides evidence in support of the view of al-Shāfiʿī and Hadith scholars who are well versed in Fiqh, that the same form of prayer during a solar eclipse is also desirable when there is a lunar eclipse. This is reported from a number of the Prophet's Companions and others. However, Mālik and Abu Ḥanīfah argue that prayer during a lunar eclipse does not carry the same form. Rather, it is offered in two normal *rakʿahs,* like other prayers, and prayed individually, not in congregation, but God knows best.

BOOK OF FUNERAL PRAYER

CHAPTER 1

REMIND THE DYING TO DECLARE GOD'S ONENESS

[1825–1]. (Dar al-Salam 1996–1997) Abu Kāmil al-Jaḥdarī Fuḍayl ibn Ḥusayn and ʿUthmān ibn Abi Shaybah narrated:[i] both from Bishr. Abu Kāmil said: Bishr ibn al-Mufaḍḍal narrated; ʿUmārah ibn Ghaziyyah narrated; Yaḥyā ibn ʿUmārah narrated; he said: I heard Abu Saʿīd al-Khudrī say: **'God's Messenger (peace be upon him) said: "Get your dying people to say: 'There is no deity other than God'."'**

وَحَدَّثَنَا أَبُو كَامِلٍ الْجَحْدَرِيُّ فُضَيْلُ بْنُ حُسَيْنٍ وَعُثْمَانُ بْنُ أَبِي شَيْبَةَ، كِلاَهُمَا عَنْ بِشْرٍ، - قَالَ أَبُو كَامِلٍ حَدَّثَنَا بِشْرُ بْنُ الْمُفَضَّلِ، - حَدَّثَنَا عُمَارَةُ بْنُ غَزِيَّةَ، حَدَّثَنَا يَحْيَى بْنُ عُمَارَةَ قَالَ: سَمِعْتُ أَبَا سَعِيدٍ الْخُدْرِيَّ يَقُولُ: قَالَ رَسُولُ اللهِ صَلَّى اللهُ عَلَيْهِ وَسَلَّمَ: «لَقِّنُوا مَوْتَاكُمْ لاَ إِلَهَ إِلاَّ اللهُ».

Qutaybah ibn Saʿīd narrated: ʿAbd al-ʿAzīz (meaning al-Darāwardī) narrated [H]. Also, Abu Bakr ibn Abi Shaybah narrated; Khālid ibn Makhlad narrated; Sulaymān ibn Bilāl narrated; all with the same chain of transmission: **the same text.**

وَحَدَّثَنَاهُ قُتَيْبَةُ بْنُ سَعِيدٍ، حَدَّثَنَا عَبْدُ الْعَزِيزِ يَعْنِي الدَّرَاوَرْدِيَّ، ح. وَحَدَّثَنَا أَبُو بَكْرِ بْنُ أَبِي شَيْبَةَ، حَدَّثَنَا خَالِدُ بْنُ مَخْلَدٍ، حَدَّثَنَا سُلَيْمَانُ بْنُ بِلاَلٍ، جَمِيعًا بِهَذَا الإِسْنَادِ.

---

i. Related by Abu Dāwūd, 3117; al-Tirmidhī, 976; al-Nasāʾī, 1825; Ibn Mājah, 1445.

[1826–2]. (Dar al-Salam 1998) Abu Bakr and ʿUthmān, sons of Abi Shaybah narrated[i] [H]. Also, ʿAmr al-Nāqid narrated to me; all said; Abu Khālid al-Aḥmar narrated; from Yazīd ibn Kaysān; from Abu Ḥāzim; from Abu Hurayrah: **'God's Messenger (peace be upon him) said: "Get your dying people to say: 'There is no deity other than God'."'**

وَحَدَّثَنَا أَبُو بَكْرٍ وَعُثْمَانُ، ابْنَا أَبِي شَيْبَةَ ح. وَحَدَّثَنِي عَمْرٌو النَّاقِدُ، قَالُوا جَمِيعًا: حَدَّثَنَا أَبُو خَالِدٍ الأَحْمَرُ، عَنْ يَزِيدَ بْنِ كَيْسَانَ، عَنْ أَبِي حَازِمٍ، عَنْ أَبِي هُرَيْرَةَ قَالَ: قَالَ رَسُولُ اللهِ صَلَّى اللهُ عَلَيْهِ وَسَلَّمَ «لَقِّنُوا مَوْتَاكُمْ لاَ إِلَهَ إِلاَّ اللهُ».

Text Explanation

The Prophet (peace be upon him) urges us that when a person is about to die, that person should be reminded to say: 'There is no deity other than God' so that it will be the last word he or she utters. Another hadith quotes the Prophet as saying: 'A person whose final words are, "There is no deity other than God", enters Heaven'. The Prophet's order to remind the dying to say this is one of recommendation. Scholars are unanimous that this is what should be urged on a person approaching death. However, they discourage insistence and frequent repetition lest the dying person become irritated, particularly one who is suffering. The dying person might then feel unwilling to say it and might say what is unsuitable.

If the dying person says 'There is no deity other than God' once, they should not be urged to say it again, unless they say some other words. If they do, then they are encouraged to say it again so that these are the last words they say. The hadith implies staying near anyone who is approaching death so as to remind and comfort them, close their eyes and do what is due to them. This is unanimously agreed upon by all scholars.

---

i. Related by Ibn Mājah, 1444.

Transmission

After the first hadith in this chapter, Muslim mentions the following chain of transmission: 'Qutaybah ibn Saʿīd narrated: ʿAbd al-ʿAzīz (meaning al-Darāwardī) narrated [H]. Also, Abu Bakr ibn Abi Shaybah narrated; Khālid ibn Makhlad narrated; Sulaymān ibn Bilāl narrated; all with the same chain of transmission'. This is how it appears in all copies, and it is correct. Abu ʿAlī al-Ḥusayn ibn Muhammad al-Ghassānī and other scholars explain that it means 'from ʿUmārah ibn Ghaziyyah' who is mentioned in the chain of transmission of the first hadith, No. 1825. This means that both al-Darāwardī and Sulaymān ibn Bilāl reported from ʿUmārah. It is as Abu ʿAlī said. Had Muslim said: 'all from ʿUmārah ibn Ghaziyyah with the same chain of transmission', it would have been better and clearer. This is what he normally does in his book, but he omitted it in this instance because it is clear for anyone who is versed in this discipline.

CHAPTER 2

WHAT TO SAY WHEN SUFFERING A CALAMITY

[1827–3]. (Dar al-Salam 1999) Yaḥyā ibn Ayyūb, Qutaybah and Ibn Ḥujr narrated: all from Ismāʿīl ibn Jaʿfar; Ibn Ayyūb said: Ismāʿīl narrated; Saʿd ibn Saʿīd reported to me; from ʿUmar ibn Kathīr ibn Aflaḥ; from Ibn Safīnah; from Umm Salamah; that she said: I heard God's Messenger (peace be upon him) say: **'Any Muslim who suffers a calamity and says what God has ordered to be said: "We all belong to God and to Him we shall return. My Lord, reward me in this calamity of mine and compensate me with what is better". God will certainly compensate him [or her] with what is better'. She said: 'When Abu Salamah died, I said: "Who among the Muslims is better than Abu Salamah? His was the first family to migrate, joining God's Messenger (peace be upon him)". I then said it, and God compensated me [by marrying] God's Messenger'.**

She said: 'God's Messenger (peace be upon him) sent Ḥāṭib ibn Abi Baltaʿah with his proposal. I said: "I have a young girl and I am a jealous [woman]". He said: "As for her daughter, we shall pray that God will give her [i.e. the girl] what is sufficient for her, and I shall pray to God to do away with the jealousy".'

حَدَّثَنَا يَحْيَى بْنُ أَيُّوبَ وَقُتَيْبَةُ وَابْنُ حُجْرٍ، جَمِيعًا عَنْ إِسْمَاعِيلَ بْنِ جَعْفَرٍ، - قَالَ ابْنُ أَيُّوبَ حَدَّثَنَا إِسْمَاعِيلُ، - أَخْبَرَنِي سَعْدُ بْنُ سَعِيدٍ، عَنْ عُمَرَ بْنِ كَثِيرِ بْنِ أَفْلَحَ، عَنِ ابْنِ سَفِينَةَ، عَنْ أُمِّ سَلَمَةَ أَنَّهَا قَالَتْ: سَمِعْتُ رَسُولَ اللهِ صَلَّى اللهُ عَلَيْهِ وَسَلَّمَ يَقُولُ:

«مَا مِنْ مُسْلِمٍ تُصِيبُهُ مُصِيبَةٌ فَيَقُولُ مَا أَمَرَهُ اللهُ: إِنَّا لِلهِ وَإِنَّا إِلَيْهِ رَاجِعُونَ. اللَّهُمَّ أْجُرْنِي فِي مُصِيبَتِي، وَأَخْلِفْ لِي خَيْرًا مِنْهَا، إِلاَّ أَخْلَفَ اللهُ لَهُ خَيْرًا مِنْهَا». قَالَتْ: فَلَمَّا مَاتَ أَبُو سَلَمَةَ قُلْتُ أَيُّ الْـمُسْلِمِينَ خَيْرٌ مِنْ أَبِي سَلَمَةَ، أَوَّلُ بَيْتٍ هَاجَرَ إِلَى رَسُولِ اللهِ صَلَّى اللهُ عَلَيْهِ وَسَلَّمَ؟ ثُمَّ إِنِّي قُلْتُهَا، فَأَخْلَفَ اللهُ لِي رَسُولَ اللهِ صَلَّى اللهُ عَلَيْهِ وَسَلَّمَ. قَالَتْ: أَرْسَلَ إِلَيَّ رَسُولُ اللهِ صَلَّى اللهُ عَلَيْهِ وَسَلَّمَ حَاطِبَ بْنَ أَبِي بَلْتَعَةَ يَخْطُبُنِي لَهُ. فَقُلْتُ: إِنَّ لِي بِنْتًا وَأَنَا غَيُورٌ. فَقَالَ: «أَمَّا ابْنَتُهَا فَنَدْعُو اللهَ أَنْ يُغْنِيَهَا عَنْهَا، وَأَدْعُو اللهَ أَنْ يَذْهَبَ بِالْغَيْرَةِ».

[1828–4]. (Dar al-Salam 2000) Abu Bakr ibn Abi Shaybah narrated: Abu Usāmah narrated; from Saʿd ibn Saʿīd; he said: ʿUmar ibn Kathīr ibn Aflaḥ reported to me; he said: I heard Ibn Safīnah narrating; that he heard Umm Salamah, the Prophet's wife, say: I heard God's Messenger (peace be upon him) say: **'Anyone who suffers a calamity and says: "We all belong to God and to Him we shall return. My Lord, reward me in this calamity of mine and compensate me with what is better". God will certainly reward him for his calamity and compensate him with what is better.' She said: 'When Abu Salamah died, I said as God's Messenger ordered and God compensated me with one who is better than him: God's Messenger (peace be upon him) himself'.**

وَحَدَّثَنَا أَبُو بَكْرِ بْنُ أَبِي شَيْبَةَ، حَدَّثَنَا أَبُو أُسَامَةَ، عَنْ سَعْدِ بْنِ سَعِيدٍ قَالَ: أَخْبَرَنِي عُمَرُ بْنُ كَثِيرِ بْنِ أَفْلَحَ قَالَ: سَمِعْتُ ابْنَ سَفِينَةَ يُحَدِّثُ أَنَّهُ سَمِعَ أُمَّ سَلَمَةَ، زَوْجَ النَّبِيِّ صَلَّى اللهُ عَلَيْهِ وَسَلَّمَ تَقُولُ: سَمِعْتُ رَسُولَ اللهِ صَلَّى اللهُ عَلَيْهِ وَسَلَّمَ يَقُولُ: «مَا مِنْ عَبْدٍ تُصِيبُهُ مُصِيبَةٌ فَيَقُولُ: إِنَّا لِلهِ وَإِنَّا إِلَيْهِ رَاجِعُونَ. اللَّهُمَّ أْجُرْنِي فِي مُصِيبَتِي وَأَخْلِفْ لِي خَيْرًا مِنْهَا، إِلاَّ أَجَرَهُ اللهُ فِي مُصِيبَتِهِ، وَأَخْلَفَ لَهُ خَيْرًا مِنْهَا». قَالَتْ: فَلَمَّا تُوُفِّيَ أَبُو سَلَمَةَ قُلْتُ كَمَا أَمَرَنِي رَسُولُ اللهِ صَلَّى اللهُ عَلَيْهِ وَسَلَّمَ، فَأَخْلَفَ اللهُ لِي خَيْرًا مِنْهُ: رَسُولَ اللهِ صَلَّى اللهُ عَلَيْهِ وَسَلَّمَ.

[1829–5]. (Dar al-Salam 2001) Muhammad ibn ʿAbdullāh ibn Numayr narrated: my father narrated; Saʿd ibn Saʿīd narrated; ʿUmar (meaning ibn Kathīr) reported to me; from Ibn Safīnah, Umm Salamah's *mawlā*; from Umm Salamah, the Prophet's wife; she said: I heard God's Messenger say: **the same as narrated by Abu Usāmah. And he added: 'She said: "When Abu Salamah died, I thought who is better than Abu Salamah, God's Messenger's Companion? Then God gave me the will and I said it. I then married God's Messenger (peace be upon him)".'**

وَحَدَّثَنَا مُحَمَّدُ بْنُ عَبْدِ اللهِ بْنِ نُمَيْرٍ، حَدَّثَنَا أَبِي، حَدَّثَنَا سَعْدُ بْنُ سَعِيدٍ، أَخْبَرَنِي عُمَرُ، - يَعْنِي ابْنَ كَثِيرٍ - عَنِ ابْنِ سَفِينَةَ، مَوْلَى أُمِّ سَلَمَةَ، عَنْ أُمِّ سَلَمَةَ، زَوْجِ النَّبِيِّ صَلَّى اللهُ عَلَيْهِ وَسَلَّمَ قَالَتْ: سَمِعْتُ رَسُولَ اللهِ صَلَّى اللهُ عَلَيْهِ وَسَلَّمَ يَقُولُ: بِمِثْلِ حَدِيثِ أَبِي أُسَامَةَ. وَزَادَ قَالَتْ: فَلَمَّا تُوُفِّيَ أَبُو سَلَمَةَ قُلْتُ مَنْ خَيْرٌ مِنْ أَبِي سَلَمَةَ، صَاحِبِ رَسُولِ اللهِ صَلَّى اللهُ عَلَيْهِ وَسَلَّمَ؟ ثُمَّ عَزَمَ اللهُ لِي فَقُلْتُهَا. قَالَتْ: فَتَزَوَّجْتُ رَسُولَ اللهِ صَلَّى اللهُ عَلَيْهِ وَسَلَّمَ.

Text Explanation

In hadith No. 1827, the Prophet says: 'Any Muslim who suffers a calamity and says what God has ordered to be said: "We all belong to God and to Him we shall return".' This stresses the importance of saying this. It also serves as evidence in support of the agreed view that a recommended matter is given as an order because God's Messenger (peace be upon him) is commanded to say it, although the relevant Qur'anic verse implies a recommendation, and this is unanimously agreed upon by all Muslims.

The hadith adds that when suffering a calamity, a Muslim should also say: 'My Lord, reward me in this calamity of mine and compensate me with what is better'. The reward is for one's patience and grief when meeting such a calamity. As for the compensation, scholars of Arabic say that if the calamity is the loss of someone or something that may be replaced by similar, such as the loss of property, a child or a relative, then we say to the sufferer: 'May God compensate you with similar to what you have lost'. If what is lost cannot be replaced, such as the loss of a parent, an uncle or a brother while one's parents are dead, then we say to the sufferer: 'May God be your compensation for your loss'.

When the Prophet sent Umm Salamah his proposal, she replied saying: 'I am a jealous woman'.[i] She meant that she was very jealous, and the Prophet said that he would pray to God to free her of her jealousy.

Umm Salamah mentions her feelings when she lost her husband and her hesitation to pray for a better compensation: 'Then God gave me the will and I said it'. God answered her prayer and gave her for a husband the best of all men, God's Messenger (peace be upon him) himself.

i. Al-Nawawī does not mention her other reason, which is: 'I have a young daughter', because he considers that it is self-explanatory. What she meant was that she feared that she might not be able to do her duty by the Prophet as her husband because of attending to the needs of her daughter who was still a baby. The Prophet replied saying that he would pray that God would give the girl what would be sufficient for her. He meant that he would be looking after the young girl and Umm Salamah's three other children. It is repeatedly recorded that God answered every supplication by the Prophet in the best and most complete way.

CHAPTER 3

WHEN ATTENDING SOMEONE WHO IS ILL OR DECEASED

[1830–6]. (Dar al-Salam 2002) Abu Bakr ibn Abi Shaybah and Abu Kurayb narrated:[i] both said: Abu Muʿāwiyah narrated; from al-Aʿmash; from Shaqīq; from Umm Salamah. She said: **'God's Messenger (peace be upon him) said: "When you attend someone who is ill, or a deceased person, say something good. The angels will support what you say".' She said: 'When Abu Salamah passed away, I went to the Prophet and said: "Messenger of God, Abu Salamah has passed away". He said: "Say: 'My Lord, forgive me and him, and grant me good compensation for my loss'." I said that, and God compensated me by one who is better to me than him: Muhammad (peace be upon him) himself.'**

حَدَّثَنَا أَبُو بَكْرِ بْنُ أَبِي شَيْبَةَ وَأَبُو كُرَيْبٍ قَالا: حَدَّثَنَا أَبُو مُعَاوِيَةَ، عَنِ الأَعْمَشِ، عَنْ شَقِيقٍ، عَنْ أُمِّ سَلَمَةَ قَالَتْ: قَالَ رَسُولُ اللهِ صَلَّى اللهُ عَلَيْهِ وَسَلَّمَ: «إِذَا حَضَرْتُمُ الْمَرِيضَ أَوِ الْمَيِّتَ، فَقُولُوا خَيْرًا. فَإِنَّ الْمَلائِكَةَ يُؤَمِّنُونَ عَلَى مَا تَقُولُونَ». قَالَتْ: فَلَمَّا مَاتَ أَبُو سَلَمَةَ أَتَيْتُ النَّبِيَّ صَلَّى اللهُ عَلَيْهِ وَسَلَّمَ فَقُلْتُ: يَا رَسُولَ اللهِ إِنَّ أَبَا سَلَمَةَ قَدْ مَاتَ. قَالَ: «قُولِي اللَّهُمَّ اغْفِرْ لِي وَلَهُ، وَأَعْقِبْنِي مِنْهُ عُقْبَى حَسَنَةً». قَالَتْ: فَقُلْتُ فَأَعْقَبَنِي اللهُ مَنْ هُوَ خَيْرٌ لِي مِنْهُ، مُحَمَّدًا صَلَّى اللهُ عَلَيْهِ وَسَلَّمَ.

---

i. Related by Abu Dāwūd, 3115; al-Tirmidhī, 977; al-Nasāʾī, 1824; Ibn Mājah, 1447.

Text Explanation

This hadith recommends that we say only what is good in these situations. We supplicate and pray for the forgiveness of the person who is ill, and pray that God lessens his or her suffering, etc. The hadith also makes clear that angels are present in such situations and that they support and endorse our supplications.

CHAPTER 4

CLOSING THE DECEASED'S EYES AND PRAYING FOR THEM

[1831–7]. (Dar al-Salam 2003) Zuhayr ibn Ḥarb narrated to me:[i] Muʿāwiyah ibn ʿAmr narrated; Abu Isḥāq al-Fazārī narrated; from Khālid al-Ḥadhdhā'; from Abu Qilābah; from Qabīṣah ibn Dhu'ayb; from Umm Salamah. She said: **'God's Messenger (peace be upon him) entered where Abu Salamah [was laid]. His eyes were fixed open, and he closed them. He said: "When the soul is gathered, the eyes follow it". Some of his family lamented. The Prophet said: "Do not invoke on yourselves anything but what is good because the angels endorse what you say". He then said: "My Lord, forgive Abu Salamah and raise his rank among those who are rightly guided. Be his compensation for his offspring. Lord of all the worlds, forgive us and him, and grant him space in his grave and give him light therein".'**

حَدَّثَنِي زُهَيْرُ بْنُ حَرْبٍ، حَدَّثَنَا مُعَاوِيَةُ بْنُ عَمْرٍو، حَدَّثَنَا أَبُو إِسْحَاقَ الْفَزَارِيُّ، عَنْ خَالِدٍ الْحَذَّاءِ، عَنْ أَبِي قِلاَبَةَ، عَنْ قَبِيصَةَ بْنِ ذُؤَيْبٍ، عَنْ أُمِّ سَلَمَةَ قَالَتْ: دَخَلَ رَسُولُ اللهِ صَلَّى اللهُ عَلَيْهِ وَسَلَّمَ عَلَى أَبِي سَلَمَةَ وَقَدْ شَقَّ بَصَرُهُ، فَأَغْمَضَهُ ثُمَّ قَالَ: «إِنَّ الرُّوحَ إِذَا قُبِضَ تَبِعَهُ الْبَصَرُ». فَضَجَّ نَاسٌ مِنْ أَهْلِهِ فَقَالَ: «لاَ تَدْعُوا عَلَى أَنْفُسِكُمْ إِلاَّ بِخَيْرٍ، فَإِنَّ الْمَلاَئِكَةَ يُؤَمِّنُونَ عَلَى مَا تَقُولُونَ». ثُمَّ قَالَ: «اللَّهُمَّ اغْفِرْ لأَبِي سَلَمَةَ، وَارْفَعْ

---

i. Related by Abu Dāwūd, 3118; Ibn Mājah, 1454.

دَرَجَتَهُ فِي الْـمَهْدِيِّينَ، وَاخْلُفْهُ فِي عَقِبِهِ فِي الْغَابِرِينَ، وَاغْفِرْ لَنَا وَلَهُ يَا رَبَّ الْعَالَمِينَ، وَافْسَحْ لَهُ فِي قَبْرِهِ، وَنَوِّرْ لَهُ فِيهِ».

[1832–8]. (Dar al-Salam 2004) Muhammad ibn Mūsā al-Qaṭṭān al-Wāsiṭī narrated: al-Muthannā ibn Muʿādh ibn Muʿādh narrated; my father narrated; ʿUbaydullāh ibn al-Ḥasan narrated; Khālid al-Ḥadhdhā' narrated; with this same chain of transmission: **a similar text, except that he said: 'Be his compensation for those he has left behind', and 'make his grave spacious', not 'grant him space'. And added: 'Khālid al-Ḥadhdhā' said: "And a seventh supplication but I forgot it".'**

وَحَدَّثَنَا مُحَمَّدُ بْنُ مُوسَى الْقَطَّانُ الْوَاسِطِيُّ، حَدَّثَنَا الْـمُثَنَّى بْنُ مُعَاذِ بْنِ مُعَاذٍ، حَدَّثَنَا أَبِي، حَدَّثَنَا عُبَيْدُ اللهِ بْنُ الْحَسَنِ، حَدَّثَنَا خَالِدٌ الْحَذَّاءُ، بِهَذَا الإِسْنَادِ: نَحْوَهُ، غَيْرَ أَنَّهُ قَالَ: «وَاخْلُفْهُ فِي تَرِكَتِهِ». وَقَالَ: «اللَّهُمَّ أَوْسِعْ لَهُ فِي قَبْرِهِ». وَلَمْ يَقُلْ: «افْسَحْ لَهُ». وَزَادَ: قَالَ خَالِدٌ الْحَذَّاءُ وَدَعْوَةٌ أُخْرَى سَابِعَةٌ نَسِيتُهَا.

Text Explanation

In hadith No. 1831 'His eyes were fixed open'. This happens to a person as he is about to die. He looks at something and cannot divert his eyes. The Prophet closed Abu Salamah's eyes, and this shows that it is desirable to do so. All Muslims are unanimous on this. The Prophet said: 'When the soul is gathered, the eyes follow it'. This means that when the soul departs from the body, the eyes follow it looking where it is going. This statement is seen as evidence supporting the view of our theologians that souls are fine bodies residing in one's body. When they depart from the body, life departs from it. It is neither a state nor a blood as others say. Theologians have widely different opinions about the soul.

The Prophet prays for Abu Salamah starting with a supplication that God forgives him. This shows the desirability of praying for a person when he dies and praying for his family and offspring, that God may grant them of the good things of this life and the life to come.

CHAPTER 5

THE EYES FOLLOW THE DECEASED PERSON

[1833–9]. (Dar al-Salam 2005–2006) Muhammad ibn Rāfiʿ narrated: ʿAbd al-Razzāq narrated; Ibn Jurayj reported; from al-ʿAlāʾ ibn Yaʿqūb; he said: my father reported to me; that he heard Abu Hurayrah say: **'God's Messenger (peace be upon him) said: "Have you not seen that when a man dies, his eyes are fixed?" They said: "Yes". He said: "This is because his eyes follow his own self".'**

وَحَدَّثَنَا مُحَمَّدُ بْنُ رَافِعٍ، حَدَّثَنَا عَبْدُ الرَّزَّاقِ، أَخْبَرَنَا ابْنُ جُرَيْجٍ، عَنِ الْعَلاَءِ بْنِ يَعْقُوبَ قَالَ: أَخْبَرَنِي أَبِي أَنَّهُ سَمِعَ أَبَا هُرَيْرَةَ يَقُولُ: قَالَ رَسُولُ اللهِ صَلَّى اللهُ عَلَيْهِ وَسَلَّمَ: «أَلَمْ تَرَوُا الإِنْسَانَ إِذَا مَاتَ شَخَصَ بَصَرُهُ؟» قَالُوا بَلَى. قَالَ: «فَذَلِكَ حِينَ يَتْبَعُ بَصَرُهُ نَفْسَهُ».

Qutaybah ibn Saʿīd narrated: ʿAbd al-ʿAzīz (meaning al-Darāwardī) narrated; from al-ʿAlāʾ; with this same transmission: **the same text.**

وَحَدَّثَنَا قُتَيْبَةُ بْنُ سَعِيدٍ، حَدَّثَنَا عَبْدُ الْعَزِيزِ، يَعْنِي الدَّرَاوَرْدِيَّ، عَنِ الْعَلاَءِ، بهذا الإسناد.

Text Explanation

'Self' in this hadith means the spirit or the soul. *Qadi* ʿIyāḍ said: 'The hadith means that death is moving from one state to another, not an extinction and perishing. It involves the perishing of the body but not the soul, except for the imperishable tail part.[i] It also serves as evidence supporting the view that the soul and the spirit refer to the same thing'.

i. This is normally understood to refer to the coccyx.

CHAPTER 6

WEEPING FOR THE DECEASED

[1834–10]. (Dar al-Salam 2007) Abu Bakr ibn Abi Shaybah, Ibn Numayr and Isḥāq ibn Ibrāhīm narrated: all from Ibn ʿUyaynah; Ibn Numayr said: Sufyān narrated; from Ibn Abi Nujayḥ; from his father; from ʿUbayd ibn ʿUmayr; he said: Umm Salamah said: **'When Abu Salamah died, I said: "[He dies] a stranger in a foreign land! I shall weep for him in a way that will be famous". I was getting ready to weep for him when a woman came from the upper part [of Madinah] wanting to support me. God's Messenger (peace be upon him) met her and said: "Do you wish to bring Satan into a home from which God has thrown him out?" repeating this twice. I withheld myself and did not weep for him'.**

وَحَدَّثَنَا أَبُو بَكْرِ بْنُ أَبِي شَيْبَةَ وَابْنُ نُمَيْرٍ وَإِسْحَاقُ بْنُ إِبْرَاهِيمَ، كُلُّهُمْ عَنِ ابْنِ عُيَيْنَةَ - قَالَ ابْنُ نُمَيْرٍ حَدَّثَنَا سُفْيَانُ - عَنِ ابْنِ أَبِي نَجِيحٍ، عَنْ أَبِيهِ، عَنْ عُبَيْدِ بْنِ عُمَيْرٍ قَالَ: قَالَتْ أُمُّ سَلَمَةَ: لَمَّا مَاتَ أَبُو سَلَمَةَ قُلْتُ غَرِيبٌ وَفِي أَرْضِ غُرْبَةٍ. لأَبْكِيَنَّهُ بُكَاءً يُتَحَدَّثُ عَنْهُ. فَكُنْتُ قَدْ تَهَيَّأْتُ لِلْبُكَاءِ عَلَيْهِ، إِذْ أَقْبَلَتِ امْرَأَةٌ مِنَ الصَّعِيدِ تُرِيدُ أَنْ تُسْعِدَنِي، فَاسْتَقْبَلَهَا رَسُولُ اللهِ صَلَّى اللهُ عَلَيْهِ وَسَلَّمَ وَقَالَ: «أَتُرِيدِينَ أَنْ تُدْخِلِي الشَّيْطَانَ بَيْتًا أَخْرَجَهُ اللهُ مِنْهُ؟» مَرَّتَيْنِ، فَكَفَفْتُ عَنِ الْبُكَاءِ فَلَمْ أَبْكِ.

[1835–11]. (Dar al-Salam 2008–2009) Abu Kāmil al-Jaḥdarī narrated:[i] Ḥammād (meaning Ibn Zayd) narrated; from ʿĀṣim al-

i. Related by al-Bukhari, 1284, 5655, 6602, 6655, 7377 and 7448; Abu Dāwūd, 3215; al-Nasāʾī, 1867; Ibn Mājah, 1588.

Aḥwal; from Abu ʿUthmān al-Nahdī; from Usāmah ibn Zayd. He said: **'We were at the Prophet's when one of his daughters sent him a message requesting him to go to her and telling him that a son of hers was about to die. He said to the messenger: "Go back and tell her: 'To God belongs what He takes and what He gives. Everything has with Him a specified time. Accept with resignation and hope for God's reward'." The messenger came back saying that she appealed to him by God that he should go to her. The Prophet stood up and with him were Saʿd ibn ʿUbādah and Muʿadh ibn Jabal. I also went with them. The child was lifted to the Prophet and his life looked precarious; he was "like a worn out waterskin", and the Prophet was in tears. Saʿd said: "Messenger of God, what is this?" The Prophet said: "This is the compassion God has placed in His servants' hearts. God is specifically merciful to those of His servants who are compassionate".'**

حَدَّثَنَا أَبُو كَامِلٍ الْجَحْدَرِيُّ، حَدَّثَنَا حَمَّادٌ - يَعْنِي ابْنَ زَيْدٍ، عَنْ عَاصِمٍ الأَحْوَلِ، عَنْ أَبِي عُثْمَانَ النَّهْدِيِّ، عَنْ أُسَامَةَ بْنِ زَيْدٍ قَالَ: كُنَّا عِنْدَ النَّبِيِّ صَلَّى اللهُ عَلَيْهِ وَسَلَّمَ، فَأَرْسَلَتْ إِلَيْهِ إِحْدَى بَنَاتِهِ تَدْعُوهُ وَتُخْبِرُهُ أَنَّ صَبِيًّا لَهَا - أَوِ ابْنًا لَهَا - فِي الْمَوْتِ. فَقَالَ لِلرَّسُولِ: «ارْجِعْ إِلَيْهَا فَأَخْبِرْهَا إِنَّ للهِ مَا أَخَذَ وَلَهُ مَا أَعْطَى، وَكُلُّ شَيْءٍ عِنْدَهُ بِأَجَلٍ مُسَمًّى، فَمُرْهَا فَلْتَصْبِرْ وَلْتَحْتَسِبْ». فَعَادَ الرَّسُولُ فَقَالَ: إِنَّهَا قَدْ أَقْسَمَتْ لَتَأْتِيَنَّهَا. قَالَ: فَقَامَ النَّبِيُّ صَلَّى اللهُ عَلَيْهِ وَسَلَّمَ، وَقَامَ مَعَهُ سَعْدُ بْنُ عُبَادَةَ وَمُعَاذُ بْنُ جَبَلٍ، وَانْطَلَقْتُ مَعَهُمْ. فَرُفِعَ إِلَيْهِ الصَّبِيُّ وَنَفْسُهُ تَقَعْقَعُ كَأَنَّهَا فِي شَنَّةٍ، فَفَاضَتْ عَيْنَاهُ. فَقَالَ لَهُ سَعْدٌ: مَا هَذَا يَا رَسُولَ اللهِ؟ قَالَ: «هَذِهِ رَحْمَةٌ جَعَلَهَا اللهُ فِي قُلُوبِ عِبَادِهِ. وَإِنَّمَا يَرْحَمُ اللهُ مِنْ عِبَادِهِ الرُّحَمَاءَ».

Muhammad ibn ʿAbdullāh ibn Numayr narrated: Ibn Fuḍayl narrated [H]. Also, Abu Bakr ibn Abi Shaybah narrated: Abu

Muʿāwiyah narrated; all from ʿĀṣim al-Aḥwal; with this chain of transmission: **the same, but Ḥammād's narration is longer and more complete.**

وَحَدَّثَنَا مُحَمَّدُ بْنُ عَبْدِ اللهِ بْنِ نُمَيْرٍ، حَدَّثَنَا ابْنُ فُضَيْلٍ، ح. وَحَدَّثَنَا أَبُو بَكْرِ بْنُ أَبِي شَيْبَةَ، حَدَّثَنَا أَبُو مُعَاوِيَةَ، جَمِيعًا عَنْ عَاصِمٍ الأَحْوَلِ، بِهَذَا الإِسْنَاد. غَيْرَ أَنَّ حَدِيثَ حَمَّادٍ أَتَمُّ وَأَطْوَلُ.

[1836–12]. (Dar al-Salam 2010) Yūnus ibn ʿAbd al-Aʿlā al-Ṣadafī and ʿAmr ibn Sawwād al-ʿĀmirī narrated: both said: ʿAbdullāh ibn Wahb reported; ʿAmr ibn al-Ḥārith reported to me; from Saʿīd ibn al-Ḥārith al-Anṣārī; from ʿAbdullāh ibn ʿUmar. He said: **'Saʿd ibn ʿUbādah was ill, and the Prophet went to visit him, accompanied by ʿAbd al-Raḥmān ibn ʿAwf, Saʿd ibn Abi Waqqāṣ and ʿAbdullāh ibn Masʿūd. When he entered, he found him unconscious. He asked: "Has he passed away?" They said: "No, Messenger of God." The Prophet wept, and when the people saw him weeping, they wept. He said: "Will you listen? God does not punish people for weeping or being in grief. He punishes them for this – pointing to his tongue – or He may bestow mercy".'**

حَدَّثَنَا يُونُسُ بْنُ عَبْدِ الأَعْلَى الصَّدَفِيُّ وَعَمْرُو بْنُ سَوَّادٍ الْعَامِرِيُّ، قَالا: أَخْبَرَنَا عَبْدُ اللهِ بْنُ وَهْبٍ، أَخْبَرَنِي عَمْرُو بْنُ الْحَارِثِ، عَنْ سَعِيدِ بْنِ الْحَارِثِ الأَنْصَارِيِّ، عَنْ عَبْدِ اللهِ بْنِ عُمَرَ قَالَ: اشْتَكَى سَعْدُ بْنُ عُبَادَةَ شَكْوَى لَهُ، فَأَتَى رَسُولُ اللهِ صَلَّى اللهُ عَلَيْهِ وَسَلَّمَ يَعُودُهُ مَعَ عَبْدِ الرَّحْمَنِ بْنِ عَوْفٍ وَسَعْدِ بْنِ أَبِي وَقَّاصٍ وَعَبْدِ اللهِ بْنِ مَسْعُودٍ. فَلَمَّا دَخَلَ عَلَيْهِ وَجَدَهُ فِي غَشِيَّةٍ، فَقَالَ: «أَقَدْ قَضَى؟» قَالُوا: لا يَا رَسُولَ اللهِ. فَبَكَى رَسُولُ

i. Related by al-Bukhari, 1304.

اللهِ صَلَّى اللهُ عَلَيْهِ وَسَلَّمَ، فَلَمَّا رَأَى الْقَوْمُ بُكَاءَ رَسُولِ اللهِ صَلَّى اللهُ عَلَيْهِ وَسَلَّمَ بَكَوْا. فَقَالَ: «أَلا تَسْمَعُونَ: إِنَّ اللهَ لاَ يُعَذِّبُ بِدَمْعِ الْعَيْنِ وَلاَ بِحُزْنِ الْقَلْبِ، وَلَكِنْ يُعَذِّبُ بِهَذَا. وَأَشَارَ إِلَى لِسَانِهِ، أَوْ يَرْحَمُ.

Text Explanation

In hadith No. 1834, Umm Salamah describes her deceased husband as 'a stranger dying in a foreign land'. She meant that he was from Makkah and died in Madinah. The woman who came to her wanted to join her in weeping and lamenting for the loss of her husband. The rest of the hadith is self-explanatory.

In hadith No. 1835, the Prophet tells his daughter that to God belongs whatever He takes and whatever He gives, and that everything has its specific time. He said this to encourage her to show patience in this adversity and to submit to God's will. His words stress that what God has taken from you is His own, not yours. He only took what belonged to Him. Therefore, you should not be in terrible grief, just like a person who returns what he has borrowed. The Prophet also said that to God belongs what He gives. This means that when God gives something to anyone, what He gives remains within His dominion and He does with it whatever He will.

The Prophet says: 'Everything has with Him a specified time'. This urges people to remain patient in every adversity and they should not panic. When people die, their life span is over, and their specified time has arrived. It cannot be brought forward or set back. When people realise this, they are better able to show patience and resign themselves to God's will, but God knows best. This hadith sets one of the essential principles of Islam that includes several basic values and sets acceptable practices.

The Prophet's dying grandchild is described as making a sound 'like a worn out waterskin'. This means that his chest made a sound like water being poured into a very old waterskin.

The hadith concludes: 'The Prophet was in tears. Saʿd said: "Messenger of God, what is this?" The Prophet said: "This is the compassion God has placed in His servants' hearts. God is specifically merciful to those of His servants who are compassionate".' This means that Saʿd must have thought all weeping is forbidden, including tears. He also thought that the Prophet might have forgotten this, and he wished to remind him. The Prophet tells him that mere weeping and shedding tears is neither forbidden nor discouraged. On the contrary, it is a good sign of compassion. What is forbidden is weeping that is coupled with wailing and lamentation, or either of these, as made clear in other hadiths: 'God does not punish people for weeping or being in grief. He punishes them for this – pointing to his tongue – or He may bestow mercy' and 'The eye is tearful, the heart is sorrowful, but we do not say what incurs God's displeasure'.

Hadith No. 1836 mentions that the Prophet went to visit Saʿd ibn ʿUbādah when he was ill, and he was accompanied by ʿAbd al-Raḥmān ibn ʿAwf, Saʿd ibn Abi Waqqās and ʿAbdullāh ibn Masʿūd. This hadith makes it clear that visiting those who are ill is desirable and that a leader may visit his subordinates, and a ruler, a judge or a scholar may visit those who are under him.

CHAPTER 7

VISITING UNWELL PEOPLE

[1837–13]. (Dar al-Salam 2011) Muhammad ibn al-Muthannā al-ʿAnazī narrated: Muhammad ibn Jahḍam narrated; Ismāʿīl (who is Ibn Jaʿfar) narrated; from ʿUmārah (meaning Ibn Ghaziyyah); from Saʿīd ibn al-Ḥārith ibn al-Muʿallā; from ʿAbdullāh ibn ʿUmar. He said: **'We were sitting with God's Messenger (peace be upon him) when a man from the Anṣār came and greeted him. Then the Anṣārī man turned to leave. The Prophet said: "My Anṣārī brother, how is my brother Saʿd ibn ʿUbādh?" The man said: "Not bad". The Prophet said: "Who of you will come to visit him?" He stood up and we stood with him, and we were more than ten people. We had neither shoes nor socks, nor caps nor shirts. We walked on barren land until we reached his place. His own people stepped back from around him, so as to allow God's Messenger and his Companions who were with him to get nearer'.**

وَحَدَّثَنَا مُحَمَّدُ بْنُ الْـمُثَنَّى الْعَنَزِيُّ، حَدَّثَنَا مُحَمَّدُ بْنُ جَهْضَمٍ، حَدَّثَنَا إِسْمَاعِيلُ، وَهُوَ ابْنُ جَعْفَرٍ، عَنْ عُمَارَةَ، - يَعْنِي ابْنَ غَزِيَّةَ - عَنْ سَعِيدِ بْنِ الْحَارِثِ بْنِ الْـمُعَلَّى، عَنْ عَبْدِ اللهِ بْنِ عُمَرَ أَنَّهُ قَالَ: كُنَّا جُلُوسًا مَعَ رَسُولِ اللهِ صَلَّى اللهُ عَلَيْهِ وَسَلَّمَ، إِذْ جَاءَهُ رَجُلٌ مِنَ الأَنْصَارِ فَسَلَّمَ عَلَيْهِ، ثُمَّ أَدْبَرَ الأَنْصَارِيُّ. فَقَالَ رَسُولُ اللهِ صَلَّى اللهُ عَلَيْهِ وَسَلَّمَ: «يَا أَخَا الأَنْصَارِ، كَيْفَ أَخِي سَعْدُ بْنُ عُبَادَةَ؟». فَقَالَ: صَالِحٌ. فَقَالَ رَسُولُ اللهِ صَلَّى اللهُ عَلَيْهِ وَسَلَّمَ: «مَنْ يَعُودُهُ مِنْكُمْ؟». فَقَامَ وَقُمْنَا مَعَهُ، وَنَحْنُ بِضْعَةَ عَشَرَ مَا عَلَيْنَا نِعَالٌ وَلاَ خِفَافٌ وَلاَ قَلاَنِسُ وَلاَ قُمُصٌ، نَمْشِي فِي تِلْكَ السِّبَاخِ، حَتَّى جِئْنَاهُ. فَاسْتَأْخَرَ قَوْمُهُ مِنْ حَوْلِهِ حَتَّى دَنَا رَسُولُ اللهِ صَلَّى اللهُ عَلَيْهِ وَسَلَّمَ وَأَصْحَابُهُ الَّذِينَ مَعَهُ.

Text Explanation

The narrator mentions that they went to visit Saʿd, having neither shoes nor socks, nor caps nor shirts.[i] This indicates that the Prophet's Companions did not care much for the comforts of life and that they did not care for fine clothing and any luxuries. The hadith shows that it is permissible to walk barefoot. It also indicates that a leader or a scholar may take his friends to visit someone who is unwell.

i. According to scholars, this statement means that most of them did not have these, or some of these, articles.

CHAPTER 8

PATIENCE AT THE INITIAL SHOCK

[1838–14]. (Dar al-Salam 2012) Muhammad ibn Bashshār al-ʿAbdī narrated:[i] Muhammad (meaning Ibn Jaʿfar) narrated; Shuʿbah narrated; from Thābit; he said: I heard Anas ibn Mālik say: **'God's Messenger (peace be upon him) said: "True patience is that shown at the initial shock".'**

حَدَّثَنَا مُحَمَّدُ بْنُ بَشَّارٍ الْعَبْدِيُّ، حَدَّثَنَا مُحَمَّدٌ، يَعْنِي ابْنَ جَعْفَرٍ، حَدَّثَنَا شُعْبَةُ، عَنْ ثَابِتٍ قَالَ: سَمِعْتُ أَنَسَ بْنَ مَالِكٍ يَقُولُ: قَالَ رَسُولُ اللهِ صَلَّى اللهُ عَلَيْهِ وَسَلَّمَ: «الصَّبْرُ عِنْدَ الصَّدْمَةِ الأُولَى».

[1839–15]. (Dar al-Salam 2013) Muhammad ibn al-Muthannā narrated: ʿUthmān ibn ʿUmar narrated; Shuʿbah reported; from Thābit al-Bunānī; from Anas ibn Mālik: **'The Prophet passed a woman weeping, having lost her son. He said to her: "Fear God and be patient in your adversity". She did not recognise him but said: "What do you care about my tragedy". When he left, she was informed that he was God's Messenger. She had such a shock, almost like death. Later she went to him and found no doorkeeper at his home. She said: "Messenger of God, I did not recognise you". He said: "True patience is that shown at the initial shock".'**

---

i. Related by al-Bukhari, 1252, 1283, 1302 and 7154; Abu Dāwūd, 3124, al-Tirmidhī, 988; al-Nasāʾī, 1868.

وَحَدَّثَنَا مُحَمَّدُ بْنُ الْـمُثَنَّى، حَدَّثَنَا عُثْمَانُ بْنُ عُمَرَ، أَخْبَرَنَا شُعْبَةُ، عَنْ ثَابِتٍ الْبُنَانِيِّ، عَنْ أَنَسِ بْنِ مَالِكٍ أَنَّ رَسُولَ اللهِ صَلَّى اللهُ عَلَيْهِ وَسَلَّمَ أَتَى عَلَى امْرَأَةٍ تَبْكِي عَلَى صَبِيٍّ لَهَا، فَقَالَ لَهَا: «اتَّقِي اللهَ وَاصْبِرِي». فَقَالَتْ: وَمَا تُبَالِي بِمُصِيبَتِي؟ فَلَمَّا ذَهَبَ قِيلَ لَهَا إِنَّهُ رَسُولُ اللهِ صَلَّى اللهُ عَلَيْهِ وَسَلَّمَ. فَأَخَذَهَا مِثْلُ الْـمَوْتِ، فَأَتَتْ بَابَهُ فَلَمْ تَجِدْ عَلَى بَابِهِ بَوَّابِينَ. فَقَالَتْ يَا رَسُولَ اللهِ لَمْ أَعْرِفْكَ. فَقَالَ: «إِنَّمَا الصَّبْرُ عِنْدَ أَوَّلِ صَدْمَةٍ». أَوْ قَالَ: «عِنْدَ أَوَّلِ الصَّدْمَةِ».

[1840–000]. (Dar al-Salam 2014) Yaḥyā ibn Ḥabīb al-Ḥārithī narrated: Khālid (meaning Ibn al-Ḥārith) narrated [H]. Also, ʿUqbah ibn Mukram al-ʿAmmī narrated; ʿAbd al-Malik ibn ʿAmr narrated [H]. And, Ahmad ibn Ibrāhīm al-Dawraqī narrated to me; ʿAbd al-Ṣamad narrated; all said: Shuʿbah narrated; with this same chain of transmission: **the same story as narrated by ʿUthmān ibn ʿUmar.**

In ʿAbd al-Ṣamad's narration: **'The Prophet passed by a woman sitting by a grave'.**

وَحَدَّثَنَاهُ يَحْيَى بْنُ حَبِيبٍ الْحَارِثِيُّ، حَدَّثَنَا خَالِدٌ يَعْنِي ابْنَ الْحَارِثِ، ح. وَحَدَّثَنَا عُقْبَةُ بْنُ مُكْرَمٍ الْعَمِّيُّ، حَدَّثَنَا عَبْدُ الْـمَلِكِ بْنُ عَمْرٍو، ح. وَحَدَّثَنِي أَحْمَدُ بْنُ إِبْرَاهِيمَ الدَّوْرَقِيُّ، حَدَّثَنَا عَبْدُ الصَّمَدِ، قَالُوا جَمِيعًا: حَدَّثَنَا شُعْبَةُ، بِهَذَا الإِسْنَادِ نَحْوَ حَدِيثِ عُثْمَانَ بْنِ عُمَرَ بِقِصَّتِه. وَفِي حَدِيثِ عَبْدِ الصَّمَدِ مَرَّ النَّبِيُّ صَلَّى اللهُ عَلَيْهِ وَسَلَّمَ بِامْرَأَةٍ عِنْدَ قَبْرٍ.

Text Explanation

The Prophet stresses that true patience is that shown at the initial shock. This means that true and genuine patience that earns rich reward from God is the one shown at the outset because it requires great effort.

Hadith No. 1939 mentions that the Prophet passed a woman weeping for the loss of her son. He told her to fear God and show patience. This confirms that enjoining what is right and forbidding what is wrong should be with everyone. The woman first says to him that he cannot possibly care about her calamity but later tells him that she did not recognise him. This encourages apologising to people when one misbehaves towards them, even though one might not be aware of the other person's status.

The hadith mentions that when the woman went to see the Prophet, she found no doorkeeper at his place. This shows that the Prophet led a modest lifestyle. It also shows that a leader or a judge should not have a doorkeeper if he does not have real need for one. This is what our scholars say.

CHAPTER 9

THE DEAD ARE TORMENTED BY THEIR FAMILY'S LAMENTATIONS

[1841–16]. (Dar al-Salam 2015) Abu Bakr ibn Abi Shaybah and Muhammad ibn ʿAbdullāh ibn Numayr narrated:[i] both from Ibn Bishr. Abu Bakr said: Muhammad ibn Bishr al-ʿAbdī narrated; from ʿUbaydullāh ibn ʿUmar; he said: Nāfiʿ narrated; from ʿAbdullāh; that Ḥafṣah wept for ʿUmar. He said: **'Easy, girl! Do you not know that God's Messenger (peace be upon him) said: "A dead person is tormented by his family's lamentations".'**

حَدَّثَنَا أَبُو بَكْرِ بْنُ أَبِي شَيْبَةَ، وَمُحَمَّدُ بْنُ عَبْدِ اللهِ بْنِ نُمَيْرٍ، جَمِيعًا عَنِ ابْنِ بِشْرٍ، - قَالَ أَبُو بَكْرٍ حَدَّثَنَا مُحَمَّدُ بْنُ بِشْرٍ الْعَبْدِيُّ، - عَنْ عُبَيْدِ اللهِ بْنِ عُمَرَ، قَالَ حَدَّثَنَا نَافِعٌ، عَنْ عَبْدِ اللهِ، أَنَّ حَفْصَةَ بَكَتْ عَلَى عُمَرَ. فَقَالَ مَهْلاً يَا بُنَيَّةُ، أَلَمْ تَعْلَمِي أَنَّ رَسُولَ اللهِ صَلَّى اللهُ عَلَيْهِ وَسَلَّمَ قَالَ: «إِنَّ الْمَيِّتَ يُعَذَّبُ بِبُكَاءِ أَهْلِهِ عَلَيْهِ».

[1842–17]. (Dar al-Salam 2016) Muhammad ibn Bashshār narrated:[ii] Muhammad ibn Jaʿfar narrated; Shuʿbah narrated; he said: I heard Qatādah narrating from Saʿīd ibn al-Musayyib; from Ibn ʿUmar; from ʿUmar; from the Prophet (peace be upon him). He said: **'A dead person is tormented in his grave by others wailing for him'.**

i. Related by al-Nasāʾī, 1847.
ii. Related by al-Bukhari, 1292; al-Nasāʾī, 1852; Ibn Mājah, 1953.

حَدَّثَنَا مُحَمَّدُ بْنُ بَشَّارٍ، حَدَّثَنَا مُحَمَّدُ بْنُ جَعْفَرٍ، حَدَّثَنَا شُعْبَةُ قَالَ: سَمِعْتُ قَتَادَةَ يُحَدِّثُ عَنْ سَعِيدِ بْنِ الْـمُسَيَّبِ، عَنِ ابْنِ عُمَرَ، عَنْ عُمَرَ، عَنِ النَّبِيِّ صَلَّى اللهُ عَلَيْهِ وَسَلَّمَ قَالَ: «الْـمَيِّتُ يُعَذَّبُ فِي قَبْرِهِ بِمَا نِيحَ عَلَيْهِ».

[1843–000]. (Dar al-Salam 2017) Muhammad ibn al-Muthannā narrated: Ibn Abi ʿAdiy narrated; from Saʿīd; from Qatādah; from Saʿīd ibn al-Musayyib; from Ibn ʿUmar; from ʿUmar; from the Prophet (peace be upon him). He said: **'A dead person is tormented in his grave by others wailing for him'.**

وَحَدَّثَنَاهُ مُحَمَّدُ بْنُ الْـمُثَنَّى، حَدَّثَنَا ابْنُ أَبِي عَدِيٍّ، عَنْ سَعِيدٍ، عَنْ قَتَادَةَ، عَنْ سَعِيدِ بْنِ الْـمُسَيَّبِ، عَنِ ابْنِ عُمَرَ، عَنْ عُمَرَ، عَنِ النَّبِيِّ صَلَّى اللهُ عَلَيْهِ وَسَلَّمَ قَالَ: «الْـمَيِّتُ يُعَذَّبُ فِي قَبْرِهِ بِمَا نِيحَ عَلَيْهِ».

[1844–18]. (Dar al-Salam 2018) ʿAlī ibn Ḥujr al-Saʿdī narrated to me: ʿAlī ibn Mushir narrated; from al-Aʿmash; from Abu Ṣāliḥ; from Ibn ʿUmar. He said: **'When ʿUmar was stabbed, he lost consciousness. People lamented. When he came to, he said: 'Do you not know that God's Messenger (peace be upon him) said: "A dead person is tormented by the crying of those who are alive?".'**

وَحَدَّثَنِي عَلِيُّ بْنُ حُجْرٍ السَّعْدِيُّ، حَدَّثَنَا عَلِيُّ بْنُ مُسْهِرٍ، عَنِ الأَعْمَشِ، عَنْ أَبِي صَالِحٍ، عَنِ ابْنِ عُمَرَ قَالَ: لَمَّا طُعِنَ عُمَرُ أُغْمِيَ عَلَيْهِ، فَصِيحَ عَلَيْهِ. فَلَمَّا أَفَاقَ قَالَ: أَمَا عَلِمْتُمْ أَنَّ رَسُولَ اللهِ صَلَّى اللهُ عَلَيْهِ وَسَلَّمَ قَالَ: «إِنَّ الْـمَيِّتَ لَيُعَذَّبُ بِبُكَاءِ الْحَيِّ».

[1845–19]. (Dar al-Salam 2019) ʿAlī ibn Ḥujr narrated to me:[i] ʿAlī ibn Mushir narrated; from al-Shaybānī; from Abu Burdah;

---

i. Related by al-Bukhari, 1290.

from his father. He said: **'When ʿUmar was stabbed, Ṣuhayb cried: "O Brother!" ʿUmar said to him: "Ṣuhayb, do you not know that God's Messenger (peace be upon him) said: "A dead person is tormented by the crying of those who are alive?".'**

حَدَّثَنِي عَلِيُّ بْنُ حُجْرٍ، حَدَّثَنَا عَلِيُّ بْنُ مُسْهِرٍ، عَنِ الشَّيْبَانِيِّ، عَنْ أَبِي بُرْدَةَ، عَنْ أَبِيهِ قَالَ: لَمَّا أُصِيبَ عُمَرُ جَعَلَ صُهَيْبٌ يَقُولُ: وَاأَخَاهُ. فَقَالَ لَهُ عُمَرُ: يَا صُهَيْبُ أَمَا عَلِمْتَ أَنَّ رَسُولَ اللهِ صَلَّى اللهُ عَلَيْهِ وَسَلَّمَ قَالَ: «إِنَّ الْـمَيِّتَ لَيُعَذَّبُ بِبُكَاءِ الْحَيِّ».

[1846–20]. (Dar al-Salam 2020) ʿAlī ibn Ḥujr narrated to me: Shuʿayb ibn Ṣafwān Abu Yaḥyā reported; from ʿAbd al-Malik ibn ʿUmayr; from Abu Burdah ibn Abi Mūsā; from Abu Mūsā. He said: **'When ʿUmar was stabbed, Ṣuhayb came over from his home and entered ʿUmar's home. He stood up beside him weeping. ʿUmar said: "Why are you weeping? Are you weeping for me?" He said: "Yes, by God, I am weeping for you, *Amīr al-Mu'minīn*". ʿUmar said: "By God, you should know that God's Messenger (peace be upon him) said: 'The one who is cried for is tormented'."'**

He said: 'I mentioned this to Mūsā ibn Ṭalḥah and he said: "ʿĀ'ishah used to say: 'Those were the Jews'."'

وَحَدَّثَنِي عَلِيُّ بْنُ حُجْرٍ، أَخْبَرَنَا شُعَيْبُ بْنُ صَفْوَانَ أَبُو يَحْيَى، عَنْ عَبْدِ الْـمَلِكِ بْنِ عُمَيْرٍ، عَنْ أَبِي بُرْدَةَ بْنِ أَبِي مُوسَى، عَنْ أَبِي مُوسَى قَالَ: لَمَّا أُصِيبَ عُمَرُ أَقْبَلَ صُهَيْبٌ مِنْ مَنْزِلِهِ حَتَّى دَخَلَ عَلَى عُمَرَ، فَقَامَ بِحِيَالِهِ يَبْكِي. فَقَالَ عُمَرُ: عَلامَ تَبْكِي؟ أَعَلَيَّ تَبْكِي؟ قَالَ: إِي وَاللهِ، لَعَلَيْكَ أَبْكِي يَا أَمِيرَ الْـمُؤْمِنِينَ. قَالَ: وَاللهِ لَقَدْ عَلِمْتَ أَنَّ رَسُولَ اللهِ صَلَّى اللهُ عَلَيْهِ وَسَلَّمَ قَالَ: «مَنْ يُبْكَى عَلَيْهِ يُعَذَّبُ».

قَالَ: فَذَكَرْتُ ذَلِكَ لِمُوسَى بْنِ طَلْحَةَ فَقَالَ: كَانَتْ عَائِشَةُ تَقُولُ إِنَّمَا كَانَ أُولَئِكَ الْيَهُودَ.

[1847–21]. (Dar al-Salam 2021) ʿAmr al-Nāqid narrated to me: ʿAffān ibn Muslim narrated; Ḥammād ibn Salamah narrated; from Thābit; from Anas; that **'When ʿUmar ibn al-Khaṭṭāb was stabbed, Ḥafṣah lamented for him. He said: "Ḥafṣah, have you not heard God's Messenger's say: 'The one who is lamented for is tormented'? And Ṣuhayb lamented for him. ʿUmar said: 'Ṣuhayb, do you not know that the one who is lamented for is tormented?'".'**

وَحَدَّثَنِي عَمْرٌو النَّاقِدُ، حَدَّثَنَا عَفَّانُ بْنُ مُسْلِمٍ، حَدَّثَنَا حَمَّادُ بْنُ سَلَمَةَ، عَنْ ثَابِتٍ، عَنْ أَنَسٍ أَنَّ عُمَرَ بْنَ الْخَطَّابِ، لَمَّا طُعِنَ عَوَّلَتْ عَلَيْهِ حَفْصَةُ، فَقَالَ: يَا حَفْصَةُ أَمَا سَمِعْتِ رَسُولَ اللهِ صَلَّى اللهُ عَلَيْهِ وَسَلَّمَ يَقُولُ: «الْـمُعَوَّلُ عَلَيْهِ يُعَذَّبُ». وَعَوَّلَ عَلَيْهِ صُهَيْبٌ فَقَالَ عُمَرُ: «يَاصُهَيْبُ، أَمَا عَلِمْتَ أَنَّ الْـمُعَوَّلَ عَلَيْهِ يُعَذَّبُ».

[1848–22]. (Dar al-Salam 2022) Dāwūd ibn Rushayd narrated:[i] Ismāʿīl ibn ʿUlayyah narrated; Ayyūb narrated; from ʿAbdullāh ibn Abi Mulaykah. He said: **'I was sitting next to Ibn ʿUmar as we were awaiting the funeral of Umm Abān bint ʿUthmān. With him was ʿAmr ibn ʿUthmān. Ibn ʿAbbās came over led by someone, and I think that he told him where Ibn ʿUmar was seated. He came up and sat beside me so that I was between the two. A shout was heard from the house. Ibn ʿUmar said (as though suggesting to ʿAmr to go and speak to them): "I heard God's Messenger (peace be upon him) say: 'The deceased is tormented by his family's crying'." ʿAbdullāh left it general.**

Ibn ʿAbbās said: **'We were with the *Amīr al-Mu'minīn* ʿUmar ibn al-Khaṭṭāb, and when we were in the desert, we saw a man resting under a tree. He said to me: "Go and find out for me**

i. Related by al-Bukhari, 1286; al-Nasāʾī, 1857.

who that man is". I went and he was Ṣuhayb. I returned and said: "You ordered me to learn for you who that man was, and he is Ṣuhayb". He said: "Tell him to join us". I said: "He has his family with him". He said: "Even though his family is with him". (Ayyūb perhaps said: "Tell him to join us".) When we arrived, it was a short time before the *Amīr al-mu'minīn* was stabbed. Ṣuhayb came over, saying: "O my brother! O my friend!" ʿUmar said: "Do you not know or have you not heard that God's Messenger (peace be upon him) said: 'The deceased person is tormented by some of his family's crying'."' ʿAbdullāh left it general, while ʿUmar said "by some".

'I stood up and went to ʿĀ'ishah. I told her what Ibn ʿUmar said. She said: "No, by God. God's Messenger never said that the deceased is tormented by anyone's crying, but he said: 'God increases the torment of an unbeliever by his family's lamentations. It is indeed God who causes people to laugh and weep. Indeed, no soul shall bear the burden of another'."'

Ayyūb said: Ibn Abi Mulaykah said: al-Qāsim ibn Muhammad narrated to me, saying: **'When ʿĀ'ishah heard what ʿUmar and Ibn ʿUmar said, she said: "You are quoting to me two men who were neither liars nor disbelieved, but mistakes in what is heard may happen".'**

حَدَّثَنَا دَاوُدُ بْنُ رُشَيْدٍ، حَدَّثَنَا إِسْمَاعِيلُ ابْنُ عُلَيَّةَ، حَدَّثَنَا أَيُّوبُ، عَنْ عَبْدِ اللهِ بْنِ أَبِي مُلَيْكَةَ قَالَ: كُنْتُ جَالِسًا إِلَى جَنْبِ ابْنِ عُمَرَ وَنَحْنُ نَنْتَظِرُ جَنَازَةَ أُمِّ أَبَانٍ بِنْتِ عُثْمَانَ، وَعِنْدَهُ عَمْرُو بْنُ عُثْمَانَ. فَجَاءَ ابْنُ عَبَّاسٍ يَقُودُهُ قَائِدٌ فَأُرَاهُ أَخْبَرَهُ بِمَكَانِ ابْنِ عُمَرَ، فَجَاءَ حَتَّى جَلَسَ

إِلَى جَنْبِي فَكُنْتُ بَيْنَهُمَا فَإِذَا صَوْتٌ مِنَ الدَّارِ، فَقَالَ ابْنُ عمر: كَأَنَّهُ يَعْرِضُ عَلَى عَمْرٍو أَنْ يَقُومَ فَيَنْهَاهُمْ. سَمِعْتُ رَسُولَ اللهِ صَلَّى اللهُ عَلَيْهِ وَسَلَّمَ يَقُولُ: «إِنَّ الْمَيِّتَ لَيُعَذَّبُ بِبُكَاءِ أَهْلِه». قَالَ: فَأَرْسَلَهَا عَبْدُ اللهِ مُرْسَلَةً.

فَقَالَ ابْنُ عَبَّاسٍ: كُنَّا مَعَ أَمِيرِ الْـمُؤْمِنِينَ عُمَرَ بْنِ الْخَطَّابِ، حَتَّى إِذَا كُنَّا بِالْبَيْدَاءِ إِذَا هُوَ بِرَجُلٍ نَازِلٍ فِي شَجَرَةٍ. فَقَالَ لِيَ: اذْهَبْ فَاعْلَمْ لِي مَنْ ذَاكَ الرَّجُلُ. فَذَهَبْتُ فَإِذَا هُوَ صُهَيْبٌ. فَرَجَعْتُ إِلَيْهِ فَقُلْتُ إِنَّكَ أَمَرْتَنِي أَنْ أَعْلَمَ لَكَ مَنْ ذَاكَ وَإِنَّهُ صُهَيْبٌ. قَالَ: مُرْهُ فَلْيَلْحَقْ بِنَا. فَقُلْتُ: إِنَّ مَعَهُ أَهْلَهُ. قَالَ: وَإِنْ كَانَ مَعَهُ أَهْلُهُ - وَرُبَّمَا قَالَ أَيُّوبُ مُرْهُ فَلْيَلْحَقْ بِنَا. فَلَمَّا قَدِمْنَا لَمْ يَلْبَثْ أَمِيرُ الْـمُؤْمِنِينَ أَنْ أُصِيبَ، فَجَاءَ صُهَيْبٌ يَقُولُ وَاأَخَاهْ وَاصَاحِبَاهْ. فَقَالَ عُمَرُ: أَلَمْ تَعْلَمْ أَوْ لَمْ تسمع. قَالَ أَيُّوبُ: أَوْ قَالَ أَوَلَمْ تَعْلَمْ أَوَلَمْ تَسْمَعْ أَنَّ رَسُولَ اللهِ صَلَّى اللهُ عَلَيْهِ وَسَلَّمَ قَالَ: «إِنَّ الْـمَيِّتَ لَيُعَذَّبُ بِبَعْضِ بُكَاءِ أَهْلِهِ». قَالَ فَأَمَّا عَبْدُ اللهِ فَأَرْسَلَهَا مُرْسَلَةً، وَأَمَّا عُمَرُ فَقَالَ بِبَعْضٍ.

فَقُمْتُ فَدَخَلْتُ عَلَى عَائِشَةَ فَحَدَّثْتُهَا بِمَا قَالَ ابْنُ عُمَرَ فَقَالَتْ: لا وَاللهِ، مَا قَالَ رَسُولُ اللهِ صَلَّى اللهُ عَلَيْهِ وَسَلَّمَ قَطُّ «إِنَّ الْـمَيِّتَ يُعَذَّبُ بِبُكَاءِ أَحَدٍ». وَلَكِنَّهُ قَالَ: «إِنَّ الْكَافِرَ يَزِيدُهُ اللهُ بِبُكَاءِ أَهْلِهِ عَذَابًا. وَإِنَّ اللهَ لَهُوَ أَضْحَكَ وَأَبْكَى. وَلاَ تَزِرُ وَازِرَةٌ وِزْرَ أُخْرَى». قَالَ أَيُّوبُ، قَالَ ابْنُ أَبِي مُلَيْكَةَ، حَدَّثَنِي الْقَاسِمُ بْنُ مُحَمَّدٍ قَالَ: لَـمَّا بَلَغَ عَائِشَةَ قَوْلُ عُمَرَ وَابْنِ عُمَرَ قَالَتْ إِنَّكُمْ لَتُحَدِّثُونِّي عَنْ غَيْرِ كَاذِبَيْنِ وَلاَ مُكَذَّبَيْنِ، وَلَكِنَّ السَّمْعَ يُخْطِئُ.

[1849–23]. (Dar al-Salam 2023) Muhammad ibn Rāfiʿ and ʿAbd ibn Ḥumayd narrated: Ibn Rāfiʿ said: ʿAbd al-Razzāq narrated; Ibn Jurayj reported; ʿAbdullāh ibn Abi Mulaykah reported to me: **'A daughter of ʿUthmān ibn ʿAffān died in Makkah. We came to attend her funeral, and Ibn ʿUmar and Ibn ʿAbbās attended. I was seated between them; I first sat next to one of them, then the other came over and sat next to me. ʿAbdullāh ibn ʿUmar said to ʿAmr ibn ʿUthmān, who was facing him: "Will you not censure crying? God's Messenger (peace be upon him) said: 'The deceased person is tormented by his family's lamentations for him'."'**

Ibn ʿAbbās said: **'ʿUmar used to say something of this'. He then narrated: 'I travelled with ʿUmar from Makkah, and we**

were in the open desert, he saw a group stopping under a tree. He said [to me]: "Go and find out who these people are". I found that it was Ṣuhayb, and I told him. He said: "Tell him to join me". I went back to Ṣuhayb and said: "Move on and join the *Amīr al-Mu'minīn*". Then when ʿUmar was stabbed, Ṣuhayb came in crying and saying "O my brother! O my friend!" ʿUmar said: "Ṣuhayb, are you lamenting for me, yet God's Messenger (peace be upon him) said: 'A deceased person is tormented by some of his family's crying for him'."'

Ibn ʿAbbās said: **'When ʿUmar passed away, I mentioned this to ʿĀ'ishah and she said: "May God bestow mercy on ʿUmar. No, by God! God's Messenger never said: 'God punishes a believer by the lamentation of anyone', but he said: 'God increases an unbeliever's torment by his family's lamentations for him'."' He said: 'and ʿĀ'ishah said: "It is enough for you to read the Qur'an: 'No soul shall bear the burden of another'."' (35: 18) Ibn ʿAbbās said at this point: 'It is God who causes people to laugh and weep'.**

Ibn Abi Mulaykah said: **'By God, Ibn ʿUmar did not say anything'.**

حَدَّثَنَا مُحَمَّدُ بْنُ رَافِعٍ وَعَبْدُ بْنُ حُمَيْدٍ، قَالَ ابْنُ رَافِعٍ حَدَّثَنَا عَبْدُ الرَّزَّاقِ، أَخْبَرَنَا ابْنُ جُرَيْجٍ، أَخْبَرَنِي عَبْدُ اللهِ بْنُ أَبِي مُلَيْكَةَ قَالَ: تُوُفِّيَتِ ابْنَةٌ لِعُثْمَانَ بْنِ عَفَّانَ بِمَكَّةَ. قَالَ: فَجِئْنَا لِنَشْهَدَهَا - قَالَ - فَحَضَرَهَا ابْنُ عُمَرَ وَابْنُ عَبَّاسٍ. قَالَ: وَإِنِّي لَجَالِسٌ بَيْنَهُمَا. قَالَ: جَلَسْتُ إِلَى أَحَدِهِمَا ثُمَّ جَاءَ الآخَرُ فَجَلَسَ إِلَى جَنْبِي، فَقَالَ عَبْدُ اللهِ بْنُ عُمَرَ لِعَمْرِو بْنِ عُثْمَانَ وَهُوَ مُوَاجِهُهُ: أَلاَ تَنْهَى عَنِ الْبُكَاءِ فَإِنَّ رَسُولَ اللهِ صَلَّى اللهُ عَلَيْهِ وَسَلَّمَ قَالَ: «إِنَّ الْمَيِّتَ لَيُعَذَّبُ بِبُكَاءِ أَهْلِهِ عَلَيْهِ».

فَقَالَ ابْنُ عَبَّاسٍ: قَدْ كَانَ عُمَرُ يَقُولُ بَعْضَ ذَلِكَ، ثُمَّ حَدَّثَ فَقَالَ: صَدَرْتُ مَعَ عُمَرَ مِنْ مَكَّةَ، حَتَّى إِذَا كُنَّا بِالْبَيْدَاءِ إِذَا هُوَ بِرَكْبٍ تَحْتَ ظِلِّ شَجَرَةٍ. فَقَالَ اذْهَبْ فَانْظُرْ مَنْ

هَؤُلَاءِ الرَّكْبُ. فَنَظَرْتُ فَإِذَا هُوَ صُهَيْبٌ. قَالَ: فَأَخْبَرْتُهُ فَقَالَ ادْعُهُ لِي. قَالَ: فَرَجَعْتُ إِلَى صُهَيْبٍ فَقُلْتُ ارْتَحِلْ فَالْحَقْ أَمِيرَ الْمُؤْمِنِينَ. فَلَمَّا أَنْ أُصِيبَ عُمَرُ دَخَلَ صُهَيْبٌ يَبْكِي يَقُولُ: وَاأَخَاهْ! وَاصَاحِبَاهْ! فَقَالَ عُمَرُ: يَا صُهَيْبُ أَتَبْكِي عَلَيَّ وَقَدْ قَالَ رَسُولُ اللهِ صَلَّى اللهُ عَلَيْهِ وَسَلَّمَ: «إِنَّ الْمَيِّتَ يُعَذَّبُ بِبَعْضِ بُكَاءِ أَهْلِهِ عَلَيْهِ».

فَقَالَ ابْنُ عَبَّاسٍ: فَلَمَّا مَاتَ عُمَرُ ذَكَرْتُ ذَلِكَ لِعَائِشَةَ فَقَالَتْ: يَرْحَمُ اللهُ عُمَرَ. لَا وَاللهِ مَا حَدَّثَ رَسُولُ اللهِ صَلَّى اللهُ عَلَيْهِ وَسَلَّمَ «إِنَّ اللهَ يُعَذِّبُ الْمُؤْمِنَ بِبُكَاءِ أَحَدٍ»، وَلَكِنْ قَالَ: «إِنَّ اللهَ يَزِيدُ الْكَافِرَ عَذَابًا بِبُكَاءِ أَهْلِهِ عَلَيْهِ». قَالَ وَقَالَتْ عَائِشَةُ: حَسْبُكُمُ الْقُرْآنُ: «وَلَا تَزِرُ وَازِرَةٌ وِزْرَ أُخْرَى». قَالَ: وَقَالَ ابْنُ عَبَّاسٍ عِنْدَ ذَلِكَ: وَاللهُ أَضْحَكَ وَأَبْكَى.

قَالَ ابْنُ أَبِي مُلَيْكَةَ: فَوَاللهِ مَا قَالَ ابْنُ عُمَرَ مِنْ شَيْءٍ.

[1850–000]. (Dar al-Salam 2024) ʿAbd al-Raḥmān ibn Bishr narrated: Sufyān narrated; ʿAmr said; from Ibn Abi Mulaykah: **'We were attending the funeral of Umm Abān bint ʿUthmān…' he narrated the hadith but did not include ʿUmar's quotation of the hadith from the Prophet (peace be upon him) as it is quoted by Ayyūb and Ibn Jurayj. Their narrations are more complete than ʿAmr's.**

وَحَدَّثَنَا عَبْدُ الرَّحْمَنِ بْنُ بِشْرٍ، حَدَّثَنَا سُفْيَانُ، قَالَ عَمْرٌو، عَنِ ابْنِ أَبِي مُلَيْكَةَ: كُنَّا فِي جَنَازَةِ أُمِّ أَبَانٍ بِنْتِ عُثْمَانَ. وَسَاقَ الْحَدِيثَ وَلَمْ يَنُصَّ رَفْعَ الْحَدِيثِ عَنْ عُمَرَ عَنِ النَّبِيِّ صَلَّى اللهُ عَلَيْهِ وَسَلَّمَ كَمَا نَصَّهُ أَيُّوبُ وَابْنُ جُرَيْجٍ. وَحَدِيثُهُمَا أَتَمُّ مِنْ حَدِيثِ عَمْرٍو.

[1851–24]. (Dar al-Salam 2025) Ḥarmalah ibn Yaḥyā narrated to me: ʿAbdullāh ibn Wahb narrated; ʿUmar ibn Muhammad narrated to me; that Sālim narrated; from ʿAbdullāh ibn ʿUmar; that God's Messenger (peace be upon him) said: **'A deceased person is tormented by the crying of those who are alive'.**

وَحَدَّثَنِي حَرْمَلَةُ بْنُ يَحْيَى، حَدَّثَنَا عَبْدُ اللهِ بْنُ وَهْبٍ، حَدَّثَنِي عُمَرُ بْنُ مُحَمَّدٍ، أَنَّ سالـماً حَدَّثَهُ عَنْ عَبْدِ اللهِ بْنِ عُمَرَ، أَنَّ رَسُولَ اللهِ صَلَّى اللهُ عَلَيْهِ وَسَلَّمَ قَالَ: «إِنَّ الْـمَيِّتَ يُعَذَّبُ بِبُكَاءِ الْحَيِّ».

[1852–25]. (Dar al-Salam 2026) Khalaf ibn Hishām and Abu al-Rabīʿ al-Zahrānī narrated:[i] both from Ḥammād. Khalaf said: Ḥammād ibn Zayd narrated; from Hishām ibn ʿUrwah; from his father. He said: **'Ibn ʿUmar's statement that "A deceased person is tormented by his family's lamentations for him" was mentioned at ʿĀ'ishah's. She said: "May God bestow mercy on Abu ʿAbd al-Raḥmān. He heard something but he did not retain it in memory. What happened was that the funeral of a Jewish man passed by the Prophet, and his people were lamenting for him. He said: 'You are lamenting, and he is being tormented'."'**

وَحَدَّثَنَا خَلَفُ بْنُ هِشَامٍ وَأَبُو الرَّبِيعِ الزَّهْرَانِيُّ، جَمِيعًا عَنْ حَمَّادٍ. قَالَ خَلَفٌ: حَدَّثَنَا حَمَّادُ بْنُ زَيْدٍ، عَنْ هِشَامِ بْنِ عُرْوَةَ، عَنْ أَبِيهِ قَالَ: ذُكِرَ عِنْدَ عَائِشَةَ قَوْلُ ابْنِ عُمَرَ الْـمَيِّتُ يُعَذَّبُ بِبُكَاءِ أَهْلِهِ عَلَيْه. فَقَالَتْ: رَحِمَ اللهُ أَبَا عَبْدِ الرَّحْمَنِ، سَمِعَ شَيْئًا فَلَمْ يَحْفَظْهُ. إِنَّمَا مَرَّتْ عَلَى رَسُولِ اللهِ صَلَّى اللهُ عَلَيْهِ وَسَلَّمَ جَنَازَةُ يَهُودِيٍّ وَهُمْ يَبْكُونَ عَلَيْهِ، فَقَالَ: «أَنْتُمْ تَبْكُونَ وَإِنَّهُ لَيُعَذَّبُ».

[1853–26]. (Dar al-Salam 2027) Abu Kurayb narrated:[ii] Abu Usāmah narrated; from Hishām; from his father. He said: **'It was mentioned at ʿĀ'ishah's that Ibn ʿUmar attributed to the Prophet (peace be upon him) that he said: "A deceased**

i. Related by al-Bukhari, 3978; Abu Dāwūd, 3129; al-Nasā'ī, 1854.
ii. Related by al-Bukhari, 3979, 3980 and 3981; al-Nasā'ī, 2075.

person is tormented in his grave by his family's lamentations for him". She said: "He is mistaken. God's Messenger only said: 'He is being tormented for his sins, or sin, and his family are lamenting for him now'." This is the same as he said that, on the day of [the Battle of] Badr, God's Messenger (peace be upon him) stood by the well where the unbelievers who were killed were buried and addressed them. [He mentioned] that [the Prophet said:] 'they hear what I am saying'. He was wrong. The Prophet said: 'They now know that what I said is the truth'. She then recited: 'You cannot make the dead hear. (27: 80) You cannot make those who are in their graves hear you'. (35: 22)

He said: 'When they have seen their places in Hell'.

حَدَّثَنَا أَبُو كُرَيْبٍ، حَدَّثَنَا أَبُو أُسَامَةَ، عَنْ هِشَامٍ، عَنْ أَبِيهِ قَالَ: ذُكِرَ عِنْدَ عَائِشَةَ أَنَّ ابْنَ عُمَرَ يَرْفَعُ إِلَى النَّبِيِّ صَلَّى اللهُ عَلَيْهِ وَسَلَّمَ «إِنَّ الْمَيِّتَ يُعَذَّبُ فِي قَبْرِهِ بِبُكَاءِ أَهْلِهِ عَلَيْهِ». فَقَالَتْ: وَهَلَ! إِنَّمَا قَالَ رَسُولُ اللهِ صَلَّى اللهُ عَلَيْهِ وَسَلَّمَ: «إِنَّهُ لَيُعَذَّبُ بِخَطِيئَتِهِ أَوْ بِذَنْبِهِ، وَإِنَّ أَهْلَهُ لَيَبْكُونَ عَلَيْهِ الآنَ». وَذَاكَ مِثْلُ قَوْلِهِ إِنَّ رَسُولَ اللهِ صَلَّى اللهُ عَلَيْهِ وَسَلَّمَ قَامَ عَلَى الْقَلِيبِ يَوْمَ بَدْرٍ، وَفِيهِ قَتْلَى بَدْرٍ مِنَ الْمُشْرِكِينَ، فَقَالَ لَهُمْ مَا قَالَ «إِنَّهُمْ لَيَسْمَعُونَ مَا أَقُولُ». وَقَدْ وَهَلَ، إِنَّمَا قَالَ: «إِنَّهُمْ لَيَعْلَمُونَ أَنَّ مَا كُنْتُ أَقُولُ لَهُمْ حَقٌّ». ثُمَّ قَرَأَتْ: «إِنَّكَ لاَ تُسْمِعُ الْمَوْتَى»، «وَمَا أَنْتَ بِمُسْمِعٍ مَنْ فِي الْقُبُورِ».

يَقُولُ حِينَ تَبَوَّءُوا مَقَاعِدَهُمْ مِنَ النَّارِ.

[000–000]. (Dar al-Salam 2028) Abu Bakr ibn Abi Shaybah narrated: Wakīʿ narrated; Hishām ibn ʿUrwah narrated; with this chain of transmission: **the same meaning as Abu Usāmah's narration, but Abu Usāmah's narration is more complete.**

وَحَدَّثَنَاهُ أَبُو بَكْرِ بْنُ أَبِي شَيْبَةَ، حَدَّثَنَا وَكِيعٌ، حَدَّثَنَا هِشَامُ بْنُ عُرْوَةَ، بِهَذَا الإِسْنَادِ، بِمَعْنَى حَدِيثِ أَبِي أُسَامَةَ. وَحَدِيثُ أَبِي أُسَامَةَ أَتَمُّ.

[1854–27]. (Dar al-Salam 2029) Qutaybah ibn Saʿīd narrated:[i] from Mālik ibn Anas as part of what was read out to him; from ʿAbdullāh ibn Abi Bakr; from his father; from ʿAmrah bint ʿAbd al-Raḥmān; that she told him that she heard ʿĀ'ishah say: **'when she was informed that ʿAbdullāh ibn ʿUmar said that a deceased person is tormented because of the lamentations of those who are alive, she said: "May God forgive Abu ʿAbd al-Raḥmān. He certainly did not lie but forgot or was mistaken. It was only that God's Messenger (peace be upon him) passed by a [deceased] Jewish woman and people were lamenting for her. He said: 'They are lamenting for her and she is being tormented in her grave'."'**

وَحَدَّثَنَا قُتَيْبَةُ بْنُ سَعِيدٍ، عَنْ مَالِكِ بْنِ أَنَسٍ فِيمَا قُرِئَ عَلَيْهِ، عَنْ عَبْدِ اللهِ بْنِ أَبِي بَكْرٍ، عَنْ أَبِيهِ، عَنْ عَمْرَةَ بِنْتِ عَبْدِ الرَّحْمَنِ، أَنَّهَا أَخْبَرَتْهُ أَنَّهَا سَمِعَتْ عَائِشَةَ، وَذُكِرَ لَهَا أَنَّ عَبْدَ اللهِ بْنَ عُمَرَ يَقُولُ: إِنَّ الْمَيِّتَ لَيُعَذَّبُ بِبُكَاءِ الْحَيِّ. فَقَالَتْ عَائِشَةُ: يَغْفِرُ اللهُ لأَبِي عَبْدِ الرَّحْمَنِ. أَمَا إِنَّهُ لَمْ يَكْذِبْ، وَلَكِنَّهُ نَسِيَ أَوْ أَخْطَأَ. إِنَّمَا مَرَّ رَسُولُ اللهِ صَلَّى اللهُ عَلَيْهِ وَسَلَّمَ عَلَى يَهُودِيَّةٍ يُبْكَى عَلَيْهَا، فَقَالَ: «إِنَّهُمْ لَيَبْكُونَ عَلَيْهَا وَإِنَّهَا لَتُعَذَّبُ فِي قَبْرِهَا».

[1855–28]. (Dar al-Salam 2030–2032) Abu Bakr ibn Abi Shaybah narrated: Wakīʿ narrated; from Saʿīd ibn ʿUbayd al-Ṭā'ī and Muhammad ibn Qays; from ʿAlī ibn Rabīʿah. He said: **'The first one to be wailed for in Kufah was Quraẓah ibn Kaʿb. Al-Mughīrah ibn Shuʿbah said: "I heard God's Messenger (peace be upon him) say: 'Whoever is wailed for shall be suffering torment on the Day of Judgement, for that wailing'."'**

---

i. Related by al-Bukhari, 1289; al-Tirmidhī, 1006; al-Nasā'ī, 1853.

حَدَّثَنَا أَبُو بَكْرِ بْنُ أَبِي شَيْبَةَ، حَدَّثَنَا وَكِيعٌ، عَنْ سَعِيدِ بْنِ عُبَيْدٍ الطَّائِيِّ وَمُحَمَّدِ بْنِ قَيْسٍ، عَنْ عَلِيِّ بْنِ رَبِيعَةَ قَالَ: أَوَّلُ مَنْ نِيحَ عَلَيْهِ بِالْكُوفَةِ قَرَظَةُ بْنُ كَعْبٍ. فَقَالَ الْـمُغِيرَةُ بْنُ شُعْبَةَ: سَمِعْتُ رَسُولَ اللهِ صَلَّى اللهُ عَلَيْهِ وَسَلَّمَ يَقُولُ: «مَنْ نِيحَ عَلَيْهِ فَإِنَّهُ يُعَذَّبُ بِمَا نِيحَ عَلَيْهِ يَوْمَ الْقِيَامَةِ».

ʿAlī ibn Ḥujr al-Saʿdī narrated to me: ʿAlī ibn Mushir narrated; Muhammad ibn Qays al-Asdī reported; from ʿAlī ibn Rabīʿah al-Asdī; from al-Mughīrah ibn Shuʿbah; from the Prophet (peace be upon him): **the same text.**

وَحَدَّثَنِي عَلِيُّ بْنُ حُجْرٍ السَّعْدِيُّ، حَدَّثَنَا عَلِيُّ بْنُ مُسْهِرٍ، أَخْبَرَنَا مُحَمَّدُ بْنُ قَيْسٍ الأَسْدِيُّ، عَنْ عَلِيِّ بْنِ رَبِيعَةَ الأَسْدِيِّ، عَنِ الْـمُغِيرَةِ بْنِ شُعْبَةَ، عَنِ النَّبِيِّ صَلَّى اللهُ عَلَيْهِ وَسَلَّمَ: مِثْلَهُ.

Ibn Abi ʿUmar narrated: Marwān (meaning al-Fazārī) narrated; Saʿīd ibn ʿUbayd al-Ṭā'ī narrated; from ʿAlī ibn Rabīʿah; from al-Mughīrah ibn Shuʿbah; from the Prophet (peace be upon him): **the same text.**

وَحَدَّثَنَاهُ ابْنُ أَبِي عُمَرَ، حَدَّثَنَا مَرْوَانُ، - يَعْنِي الْفَزَارِيَّ، حَدَّثَنَا سَعِيدُ بْنُ عُبَيْدٍ الطَّائِيُّ، عَنْ عَلِيِّ بْنِ رَبِيعَةَ، عَنِ الْـمُغِيرَةِ بْنِ شُعْبَةَ، عَنِ النَّبِيِّ صَلَّى اللهُ عَلَيْهِ وَسَلَّمَ مِثْلَهُ.

Text Explanation

In these hadiths the Prophet is quoted as saying: 'A deceased person is tormented by his family's crying for him', 'A deceased person is tormented by some of his family's crying for him', '… by the crying of those who are alive' and 'A deceased person is tormented in his grave for his family's wailing'. All these narrations are by ʿUmar ibn al-Khaṭṭāb and his son, ʿAbdullāh (may God be pleased with them).

ʿĀ'ishah rejected these narrations and said that they must have forgotten or been mistaken. She denies that the Prophet might have said so, citing in support of her argument the verse that says: 'No soul shall bear the burden of another'. (35: 18) She added that the Prophet spoke about a Jewish woman that was suffering torment while her family were lamenting for her, but she was punished for her disbelief at the time of her family's lamentation, not because of their lamentations.

Scholars differ in their interpretation of these hadiths. Some understand them as referring to a person who requests his people to cry, lament or wail for him after he dies. If his request is fulfilled and acted upon, he is tormented for such lamentations and wailings because it occurs by his request. Their action is due to him and his will. They add that if the family do this, but the deceased person never asked or requested them to do so, he will not be tortured for their actions because of the rule stated by God Himself: 'No soul shall bear the burden of another'. Scholars further point out that it was a custom of the Arabs to make such requests, as we see in the poetry of Ṭarafah ibn al-ʿAbd who says: 'Maʿbad's daughter, when I am dead, lament for me as I deserve and tear the top of your dress'. They explain that the hadith is stated in general terms because it referred to what was customary among them.

Other scholars say that these hadiths apply to a person who urges his family to lament and wail for him or one who does not urge them to abandon such practices. If he urges lamentation or does not urge abandoning it, he will be tormented for his negligence. If he urges that no wailing or lamentation should be done, but his family do lament or wail for him, he is not tormented because he has fulfilled his obligation and he is not responsible for what happens later. The sum of this view is that it is one's duty to urge one's family not to cry, wail or lament for one. If one does not, then one is tormented for such practices because of negligence.

A third group of scholars say that these hadiths refer to a tradition whereby the relatives of the deceased person wail and lament shouting aloud the person's qualities, and these are extolled as fine, while they are forbidden by divine law. They say, for example, that as a fighter, he was the cause of women being widowed, children being orphaned, habitations being destroyed and mates being separated, etc. They consider these to demonstrate his bravery. All such actions, if true, are forbidden in Islam.

Some other scholars say that the deceased is tormented by being made to hear his family's laments and is distressed for them. This is the view supported by Muhammad ibn Jarīr al-Ṭabarī and others. *Qadi* 'Iyāḍ said: 'This is the best view'. They cite in support of this view a hadith which speaks of the Prophet rebuking a woman for lamenting for her father. He said: 'When you wail, your relative will weep. Servants of God, do not torment your brethren'.

'Ā'ishah (may God be pleased with her) said that the hadith means that an unbeliever or a sinner is being punished at the time of his family's lamenting, but his punishment is for his sins, not for their lamentations.

Of all these views, the correct one is that shared by the majority of scholars, making clear that whenever weeping or crying is mentioned, it refers to what is accompanied by loud cries, wailing and lamentation. It does not refer to weeping as the mere shedding of tears.

Hadith No. 1846 concludes: 'I mentioned this to Mūsā ibn Ṭalḥah and he said: "'Ā'ishah used to say: 'Those were the Jews'."' The one who said this is 'Abd al-Malik ibn 'Umayr.

In hadith No. 1848, 'Abdullāh ibn Abi Mulaykah says: 'I was sitting next to Ibn 'Umar as we were awaiting the funeral of Umm Abān bint 'Uthmān. With him was 'Amr ibn 'Uthmān. Ibn 'Abbās came over led by someone, and I think that he told him where Ibn 'Umar was seated. He came up and sat beside me, so that I was between the two'. This is considered as evidence that it is permissible, indeed desirable, to sit and meet waiting for a funeral. Ibn Abi Mulaykah sat in between 'Abdullāh ibn 'Umar and 'Abdullāh ibn 'Abbās, both of whom were superior to him as they were Companions of the Prophet and greater scholars, in addition to the fact that they were known for their piety and devotion, and further that they belonged to more honourable and older families than him. Good manners require that a junior person does not sit between two people who are his seniors and superiors, except for a valid reason. That he sat between them is understood to be for a good reason, such as perhaps the place where Ibn ʿAbbās sat was more comfortable for him, or some other reason.

In the same hadith, ʿAbdullāh ibn ʿUmar says: 'I heard God's Messenger (peace be upon him) say: "The deceased is tormented by his family's crying". ʿAbdullāh left it general'. This means that Ibn ʿUmar considered that the statement he quoted was of general application. He did not restrict it to the case of a Jew, as ʿĀ'ishah did, nor to one who urges his family to do so, as other scholars restrict it, nor did he refer it to some types of crying, as stated by his father.

And in the same hadith, ʿĀ'ishah says: 'No, by God. God's Messenger never said that the deceased is tormented by anyone's crying'. This shows that it is permissible to swear on the basis of implied evidence suggesting high probability, even though one cannot be absolutely certain. This is the view of our school. They said: 'A person may swear that a debt is owed to his deceased father if he sees a record of it in his father's handwriting and he thinks it correct'. It may be suggested that ʿĀ'ishah did not swear on the basis of what she thought, but on certain knowledge, as having heard it from the Prophet towards the end of his life. We say that this is improbable on two counts: the first is that ʿUmar and Ibn ʿUmar heard him say that a deceased person is tormented by the crying of his family. The second is that if ʿĀ'ishah heard such a statement by the Prophet towards the end of his life, she would have used this as her main argument, but she did not. She cited the verse that says, 'No soul shall bear the burden of another'. But God knows best. We shall discuss her denial of the dead being able to hear towards the end of this book where Muslim enters the relevant hadiths.

CHAPTER 10

STRICT PROHIBITION AGAINST WAILING

[1856–29]. (Dar al-Salam 2033) Abu Bakr ibn Abi Shaybah narrated: ʿAffān narrated; Abān ibn Yazīd narrated [H]. Also, Isḥāq ibn Manṣūr narrated to me (his text); Ḥabbān ibn Hilāl reported; Abān narrated; Yaḥyā narrated; that Zayd narrated to him; that Abu Sallām narrated to him; that Abu Mālik al-Ashʿarī narrated to him; that the Prophet (peace be upon him) said: **'Four pre-Islamic practices continue to be done by my community and they will not abandon these: boasting about ancestry, raising doubts about lineage, attributing rain to stars and wailing [for the dead]'. He also said: 'Unless a wailing woman repents before she dies, she shall be made to stand on the Day of Judgement wearing slacks made of black pitch and a shirt of scabies'.**

حَدَّثَنَا أَبُو بَكْرِ بْنُ أَبِي شَيْبَةَ، حَدَّثَنَا عَفَّانُ، حَدَّثَنَا أَبَانُ بْنُ يَزِيدَ، ح. وَحَدَّثَنِي إِسْحَاقُ، بْنُ مَنْصُورٍ - وَاللَّفْظُ لَهُ - أَخْبَرَنَا حَبَّانُ بْنُ هِلَالٍ، حَدَّثَنَا أَبَانٌ، حَدَّثَنَا يَحْيَى، أَنَّ زَيْدًا حَدَّثَهُ، أَنَّ أَبَا سَلَّامٍ حَدَّثَهُ، أَنَّ أَبَا مَالِكٍ الأَشْعَرِيَّ حَدَّثَهُ، أَنَّ النَّبِيَّ صَلَّى اللهُ عَلَيْهِ وَسَلَّمَ قَالَ: «أَرْبَعٌ فِي أُمَّتِي مِنْ أَمْرِ الْجَاهِلِيَّةِ لاَ يَتْرُكُونَهُنَّ: الْفَخْرُ فِي الأَحْسَابِ، وَالطَّعْنُ فِي الأَنْسَابِ، وَالاِسْتِسْقَاءُ بِالنُّجُومِ، وَالنِّيَاحَةُ». وَقَالَ: «النَّائِحَةُ إِذَا لَمْ تَتُبْ قَبْلَ مَوْتِهَا، تُقَامُ يَوْمَ الْقِيَامَةِ وَعَلَيْهَا سِرْبَالٌ مِنْ قَطِرَانٍ، وَدِرْعٌ مِنْ جَرَبٍ.

[1857–30]. (Dar al-Salam 2034) Ibn al-Muthannā and Ibn Abi ʿUmar narrated:[i] Ibn al-Muthannā said: ʿAbd al-Wahhāb narrated; he said: I heard Yaḥyā ibn Saʿīd say; ʿAmrah reported to me; that she heard ʿĀ'ishah say: **'When God's Messenger was informed of the deaths of Ibn Ḥārithah, Jaʿfar ibn Abi Ṭālib and ʿAbdullāh ibn Rawāḥah, he sat down with grief clearly apparent on his face. I was looking through a hole in the door when a man came in and said: "Messenger of God, Jaʿfar's women!" He mentioned their crying. The Prophet ordered him to go and tell them to stop. The man went away, then came back and said that they did not obey him. The Prophet ordered him again to go and tell them to stop. He went away, then came back and said: "By God, they will have their way, Messenger of God".' She said that the Prophet said to him: 'Go and put soil in their mouths'. ʿĀ'ishah said: 'I said [to the man]: "May God spite you. By God, you are not doing what God's Messenger has ordered you to do and you have not stopped troubling God's Messenger".'**

وَحَدَّثَنَا ابْنُ الْـمُثَنَّى وَابْنُ أَبِي عُمَرَ، قَالَ ابْنُ الْـمُثَنَّى حَدَّثَنَا عَبْدُ الْوَهَّابِ قَالَ: سَمِعْتُ يَحْيَى بْنَ سَعِيدٍ يَقُولُ: أَخْبَرَتْنِي عَمْرَةُ، أَنَّهَا سَمِعَتْ عَائِشَةَ تَقُولُ: لَـمَّا جَاءَ رَسُولَ اللهِ صَلَّى اللهُ عَلَيْهِ وَسَلَّمَ قَتْلُ ابْنِ حَارِثَةَ وَجَعْفَرِ بْنِ أَبِي طَالِبٍ وَعَبْدِ اللهِ بْنِ رَوَاحَةَ جَلَسَ رَسُولُ اللهِ صَلَّى اللهُ عَلَيْهِ وَسَلَّمَ يُعْرَفُ فِيهِ الْحُزْنُ. قَالَتْ: وَأَنَا أَنْظُرُ مِنْ صَائِرِ الْبَابِ – شَقِّ الْبَابِ – فَأَتَاهُ رَجُلٌ فَقَالَ: يَا رَسُولَ اللهِ إِنَّ نِسَاءَ جَعْفَرٍ، وَذَكَرَ بُكَاءَهُنَّ. فَأَمَرَهُ أَنْ يَذْهَبَ فَيَنْهَاهُنَّ. فَذَهَبَ، فَأَتَاهُ فَذَكَرَ أَنَّهُنَّ لَمْ يُطِعْنَهُ. فَأَمَرَهُ الثَّانِيَةَ أَنْ يَذْهَبَ فَيَنْهَاهُنَّ، فَذَهَبَ ثُمَّ أَتَاهُ فَقَالَ: وَاللهِ لَقَدْ غَلَبْنَنَا يَا رَسُولَ اللهِ. قَالَتْ فَزَعَمَتْ أَنَّ رَسُولَ اللهِ صَلَّى اللهُ عَلَيْهِ وَسَلَّمَ قَالَ: «اذْهَبْ فَاحْثُ فِي أَفْوَاهِهِنَّ مِنَ التُّرَابِ». قَالَتْ عَائِشَةُ فَقُلْتُ:

i. Related by al-Bukhari, 1305 and in similar wording 1299 and 4263; Abu Dāwūd, 3122; al-Nasā'ī, 1846.

أَرْغَمَ اللهُ أَنْفَكَ، وَاللهِ مَا تَفْعَلُ مَا أَمَرَكَ رَسُولُ اللهِ صَلَّى اللهُ عَلَيْهِ وَسَلَّمَ، وَمَا تَرَكْتَ رَسُولَ اللهِ صَلَّى اللهُ عَلَيْهِ وَسَلَّمَ مِنَ الْعَنَاءِ.

[1858–000]. (Dar al-Salam 2035) Abu Bakr ibn Abi Shaybah narrated: ʿAbdullāh ibn Numayr narrated [H]. Also, Abu al-Ṭāhir narrated to me; ʿAbdullāh ibn Wahb reported; from Muʿāwiyah ibn Ṣāliḥ [H]. And, Ahmad ibn Ibrāhīm al-Dawraqī narrated to me; ʿAbd al-Ṣamad narrated; ʿAbd al-ʿAzīz (meaning Ibn Muslim) narrated; all of them from Yaḥyā ibn Saʿīd; with this chain of transmission: **a similar text, but in ʿAbd al-ʿAzīz's narration: 'You have not stopped bothering God's Messenger'.**

وَحَدَّثَنَاهُ أَبُو بَكْرِ بْنُ أَبِي شَيْبَةَ، حَدَّثَنَا عَبْدُ اللهِ بْنُ نُمَيْرٍ، ح. وَحَدَّثَنِي أَبُو الطَّاهِرِ، أَخْبَرَنَا عَبْدُ اللهِ بْنُ وَهْبٍ، عَنْ مُعَاوِيَةَ بْنِ صَالِحٍ، ح. وَحَدَّثَنِي أَحْمَدُ بْنُ إِبْرَاهِيمَ الدَّوْرَقِيُّ، حَدَّثَنَا عَبْدُ الصَّمَدِ، حَدَّثَنَا عَبْدُ الْعَزِيزِ، - يَعْنِي ابْنَ مُسْلِمٍ. كُلُّهُمْ عَنْ يَحْيَى بْنِ سَعِيدٍ، بِهَذَا الإِسْنَادِ: نَحْوَهُ . وَفِي حَدِيثِ عَبْدِ الْعَزِيزِ: وَمَا تَرَكْتَ رَسُولَ اللهِ صَلَّى اللهُ عَلَيْهِ وَسَلَّمَ مِنَ الْعِيِّ.

[1859–31]. (Dar al-Salam 2036) Abu al-Rabīʿ al-Zahrānī narrated to me:[i] Ḥammād narrated; Ayyūb narrated; from Muhammad; from Umm ʿAṭiyyah. She said: **'When we gave God's Messenger (peace be upon him) our pledge of allegiance, he stipulated in addition that we shall not wail. No woman among us honoured that except five: Umm Sulaym, Umm al-ʿAlā', Abu Sabrah's daughter Muʿādh's wife; or Abu Sabrah's daughter and Muʿādh's wife'.**

---

i. Related by al-Bukhari, 1306; al-Nasāʾī in a shorter version, 4191.

حَدَّثَنِي أَبُو الرَّبِيعِ الزَّهْرَانِيُّ، حَدَّثَنَا حَمَّادٌ، حَدَّثَنَا أَيُّوبُ، عَنْ مُحَمَّدٍ، عَنْ أُمِّ عَطِيَّةَ قَالَتْ: أَخَذَ عَلَيْنَا رَسُولُ اللهِ صَلَّى اللهُ عَلَيْهِ وَسَلَّمَ مَعَ الْبَيْعَةِ أَلاَّ نَنُوحَ، فَمَا وَفَتْ مِنَّا امْرَأَةٌ إِلاَّ خَمْسٌ: أُمُّ سُلَيْمٍ وَأُمُّ الْعَلاَءِ وَابْنَةُ أَبِي سَبْرَةَ امْرَأَةُ مُعَاذٍ أَوِ ابْنَةُ أَبِي سَبْرَةَ وَامْرَأَةُ مُعَاذٍ.

[1860–32]. (Dar al-Salam 2037) Isḥāq ibn Ibrāhīm narrated: Asbāṭ reported; Hishām narrated; from Ḥafṣah; from Umm ʿAṭiyyah. She said: **'When we gave our pledge of allegiance, God's Messenger stipulated a condition that "you shall not wail". Only five of us honoured this condition, and one of them was Umm Sulaym'.**

حَدَّثَنَا إِسْحَاقُ بْنُ إِبْرَاهِيمَ، أَخْبَرَنَا أَسْبَاطٌ، حَدَّثَنَا هِشَامٌ، عَنْ حَفْصَةَ، عَنْ أُمِّ عَطِيَّةَ قَالَتْ: أَخَذَ عَلَيْنَا رَسُولُ اللهِ صَلَّى اللهُ عَلَيْهِ وَسَلَّمَ فِي الْبَيْعَةِ أَلاَّ تَنُحْنَ، فَمَا وَفَتْ مِنَّا غَيْرُ خَمْسٍ، مِنْهُنَّ أُمُّ سُلَيْمٍ.

[1861–33]. (Dar al-Salam 2038) Abu Bakr ibn Abi Shaybah, Zuhayr ibn Ḥarb and Isḥāq ibn Ibrāhīm narrated: all from Abu Muʿāwiyah; Zuhayr said: Muhammad ibn Khāzim narrated; ʿĀṣim narrated; from Ḥafṣah; from Umm ʿAṭiyyah. She said: **'When this verse was revealed: "[When believing women] pledge to you that they will not associate any partner with God… nor disobey you in anything reasonable",[i] a further stipulation was the prohibition of wailing. I said: "Messenger of God, except for this particular family: they did that for me before Islam and I must do likewise for them".**

i. The verse says: 'Prophet! When believing women come and pledge to you that they will not associate any partner with God, nor steal, nor commit adultery, nor kill their children, nor lie about who fathered their children, nor disobey you in anything reasonable, then accept their pledge of allegiance and pray to God to forgive them'. (60: 12)

God's Messenger (peace be upon him) said: "except for this particular family".'

وَحَدَّثَنَا أَبُو بَكْرِ بْنُ أَبِي شَيْبَةَ وَزُهَيْرُ بْنُ حَرْبٍ وَإِسْحَاقُ بْنُ إِبْرَاهِيمَ، جَمِيعًا عَنْ أَبِي مُعَاوِيَةَ، - قَالَ زُهَيْرٌ حَدَّثَنَا مُحَمَّدُ بْنُ خَازِمٍ، - حَدَّثَنَا عَاصِمٌ، عَنْ حَفْصَةَ، عَنْ أُمِّ عَطِيَّةَ قَالَتْ: لَمَّا نَزَلَتْ هَذِهِ الآيَةُ «يُبَايِعْنَكَ عَلَى أَنْ لاَ يُشْرِكْنَ بِاللهِ شَيْئًا... وَلاَ يَعْصِينَكَ فِي مَعْرُوفٍ» قَالَتْ: كَانَ مِنْهُ النِّيَاحَةُ. قَالَتْ: فَقُلْتُ يَا رَسُولَ اللهِ إِلاَّ آلَ فُلاَنٍ، فَإِنَّهُمْ كَانُوا أَسْعَدُونِي فِي الْجَاهِلِيَّةِ، فَلاَ بُدَّ لِي مِنْ أَنْ أُسْعِدَهُمْ. فَقَالَ رَسُولُ اللهِ صَلَّى اللهُ عَلَيْهِ وَسَلَّمَ «إِلاَّ آلَ فُلاَنٍ».

Text Explanation

In hadith No. 1856, the Prophet says that 'if a wailing woman does not repent before she dies' she will have such punishment. This is clear evidence that wailing is forbidden in Islam. This is unanimously agreed upon. It also shows that genuine repentance before death is accepted, provided that the person concerned is not in the last throes of death.

The Prophet ordered the man who reported to him that Jaʿfar's women were crying to put soil in their mouths. This is a more forceful ordering of them to stop. A number of scholars understand this as meaning that they cried and wailed. Hence, the prohibition was repeated. Had it been only weeping, the Prophet would not have prohibited it. He himself wept and said that it was not forbidden and described it as compassion. Some scholars understood the hadith as referring to weeping without laments or loud crying. They add that it is improbable that the female Companions of the Prophet would continue to do something forbidden, despite being ordered to stop. They were merely weeping, and the order sent to them was not one of prohibition, but rather one of discouragement. This is how they understood it and continued to weep.

In the same hadith, No. 1857, ʿĀ'ishah said to the man the Prophet sent to those women: 'May God spite you. By God, you are not doing what God's Messenger has ordered you to do and you have not stopped troubling God's Messenger'. She felt that he was not doing enough to ensure obedience of the Prophet's order. Nor did he tell the Prophet of his inability so that he might send someone else and stop being bothered.

In the last three hadiths, No. 1859–1861 Umm ʿAṭiyyah mentions that the Prophet added to the women's pledge of allegiance a condition that they would not wail and lament for the dead. This stresses the prohibition of wailing and lamentation, as well as the care taken by the Prophet to enforce its prohibition because it increases sorrow, reduces patience and is contrary to the general obligation of resigned submission to God's will.

Umm ʿAṭiyyah said that no woman among us honoured this except five. *Qadi* ʿIyāḍ said: 'This means that only five of the women who pledged allegiance with Umm ʿAṭiyyah, at the time she made her pledge, honoured this commitment. It does not mean that only five Muslim women stopped wailing for the dead'.

The last hadith mentions that Umm ʿAṭiyyah requested and was granted an exception in the case of a particular family. This meant that wailing and lamentation are not permitted for her or any other woman except for that particular family, as clearly stated in the hadith. The legislator may make any exception from any general ruling, and this is what applies in this hadith. *Qadi* ʿIyāḍ and others found this hadith problematic and said some strange things about it. I simply wish to warn against accepting these because some Mālikī scholars say that wailing is not forbidden, citing this hadith and hadith No. 1857, mentioning Jaʿfar's women as the basis for their view. They add that what is forbidden is only wailing accompanied by other practices of the days of ignorance, such as tearing one's clothes and scratching one's cheeks. The correct view is as we mentioned earlier, stating that all wailing and lamentation are forbidden. This is the view of all scholars. There is no evidence to support what this scholar mentioned about wailing accompanied by other ignorant practices, but God knows best.

CHAPTER 11

WOMEN SHOULD NOT MARCH WITH FUNERALS

[1862–34]. (Dar al-Salam 2039) Yaḥyā ibn Ayyūb narrated: Ibn ʿUlayyah narrated; Ayyūb reported; from Muhammad ibn Sīrīn; he said: Umm ʿAṭiyyah said: **'We used to be told not to follow funerals, but we were not given a strict order'.**

حَدَّثَنَا يَحْيَى بْنُ أَيُّوبَ، حَدَّثَنَا ابْنُ عُلَيَّةَ، أَخْبَرَنَا أَيُّوبُ، عَنْ مُحَمَّدِ بْنِ سِيرِينَ قَالَ: قَالَتْ أُمُّ عَطِيَّةَ: كُنَّا نُنْهَى عَنِ اتِّبَاعِ الْجَنَائِزِ، وَلَمْ يُعْزَمْ عَلَيْنَا.

[1863–35]. (Dar al-Salam 2040) Abu Bakr ibn Abi Shaybah narrated:[i] Abu Usāmah narrated [H]. Also, Iisḥāq ibn Ibrāhīm narrated; ʿĪsā ibn Yūnus reported; both from Hishām; from Ḥafṣah; from Umm ʿAṭiyyah. She said: **'We were told not to follow funerals, but we were not given a strict order'.**

وَحَدَّثَنَا أَبُو بَكْرِ بْنُ أَبِي شَيْبَةَ، حَدَّثَنَا أَبُو أُسَامَةَ، ح. وَحَدَّثَنَا إِسْحَاقُ بْنُ إِبْرَاهِيمَ، أَخْبَرَنَا عِيسَى بْنُ يُونُسَ، كِلَاهُمَا عَنْ هِشَامٍ، عَنْ حَفْصَةَ، عَنْ أُمِّ عَطِيَّةَ، قَالَتْ: نُهِينَا عَنِ اتِّبَاعِ الْجَنَائِزِ، وَلَمْ يُعْزَمْ عَلَيْنَا.

Text Explanation

This hadith means that God's Messenger did not issue a strict order of prohibition. He only implied this as discouragement. According to

---

i. Related by al-Bukhari in similar wording and a longer version, 313; Ibn Mājah, 1577.

our Shāfiʿī School, it is not forbidden for women to follow a funeral but discouraged. *Qadi* ʿIyāḍ said: 'The majority of scholars say that women should be prevented from following funerals, but scholars of Madinah permit it. Mālik permits it but discourages young women from doing it'.

CHAPTER 12

WASHING THE BODY OF THE DECEASED

[1864–36]. (Dar al-Salam 2041) Yaḥyā ibn Yaḥyā narrated:[i] Yazīd ibn Zurayʿ reported; from Ayyūb; from Muhammad ibn Sīrīn; from Umm ʿAṭiyyah. She said: **'The Prophet came to us when we were washing his [deceased] daughter. He said: "Wash her three times, or five, or more if you think it is needed, using water and *sidr*.[ii] Add camphor, or some camphor, to the last wash. Let me know when you have finished". When we finished, we told him, and he gave us a garment of his and said: "Wrap her with it".'**

وَحَدَّثَنَا يَحْيَى بْنُ يَحْيَى، أَخْبَرَنَا يَزِيدُ بْنُ زُرَيْعٍ، عَنْ أَيُّوبَ، عَنْ مُحَمَّدِ بْنِ سِيرِينَ، عَنْ أُمِّ عَطِيَّةَ قَالَتْ: دَخَلَ عَلَيْنَا النَّبِيُّ صَلَّى اللهُ عَلَيْهِ وَسَلَّمَ وَنَحْنُ نَغْسِلُ ابْنَتَهُ فَقَالَ: «اغْسِلْنَهَا ثَلَاثًا أَوْ خَمْسًا، أَوْ أَكْثَرَ مِنْ ذَلِكَ إِنْ رَأَيْتُنَّ ذَلِكَ، بِمَاءٍ وَسِدْرٍ. وَاجْعَلْنَ فِي الآخِرَةِ كَافُورًا أَوْ شَيْئًا مِنْ كَافُورٍ، فَإِذَا فَرَغْتُنَّ فَآذِنَّنِي». فَلَمَّا فَرَغْنَا آذَنَّاهُ، فَأَلْقَى إِلَيْنَا حِقْوَهُ فَقَالَ: «أَشْعِرْنَهَا إِيَّاهُ».

[1865–37]. (Dar al-Salam 2042) Yaḥyā ibn Yaḥyā narrated:[iii] Yazīd ibn Zurayʿ reported; from Ayyūb; from Muhammad ibn

---

i. Related by al-Bukhari, 1253, 1254, 1258 and 1260; Abu Dāwūd, 3142 and 3146; al-Nasāʾī, 1880, 1885, 1886, 1889 and 1892; Ibn Mājah, 1458 and 1459.

ii. *Sidr* is the Arabic name of a tree known as Ziziphus Spina-Christi. It is native to the regions of the Levant, East Africa and some tropical countries, as well as Southern and Western Asia. Its fruit has a fine smell and a sweet taste.

iii. Related by Abu Dāwūd, 3143; al-Nasāʾī, 1890.

Sīrīn; from Ḥafṣah bint Sīrīn; from Umm ʿAṭiyyah. She said: **'We plaited her hair in three plaits'.**

وَحَدَّثَنَا يَحْيَى بْنُ يَحْيَى، أَخْبَرَنَا يَزِيدُ بْنُ زُرَيْعٍ، عَنْ أَيُّوبَ، عَنْ مُحَمَّدِ بْنِ سِيرِينَ، عَنْ حَفْصَةَ بِنْتِ سِيرِينَ، عَنْ أُمِّ عَطِيَّةَ قَالَتْ: مَشَطْنَاهَا ثَلَاثَةَ قُرُونٍ.

[1866–38]. (Dar al-Salam 2043) Qutaybah ibn Saʿīd narrated; from Mālik ibn Anas [H]. Also, Abu al-Rabīʿ al-Zahrānī and Qutaybah ibn Saʿīd narrated; both said: Ḥammād narrated [H]. Yaḥyā ibn Ayyūb narrated; Ibn ʿUlayyah narrated; all of them from Ayyūb; from Muhammad; from Umm ʿAṭiyyah. She said: **'One of the Prophet's daughters passed away'.**

In Ibn ʿUlayyah's narration: **'God's Messenger (peace be upon him) came to us as we were washing his daughter's body'.**

In Mālik's narration: **'God's Messenger (peace be upon him) came in when his daughter passed away...' the same text as Yazīd ibn Zurayʿ's narration from Ayyūb, from Muhammad, from Umm ʿAṭiyyah.**

وَحَدَّثَنَا قُتَيْبَةُ بْنُ سَعِيدٍ، عَنْ مَالِكِ بْنِ أَنَسٍ، ح. وَحَدَّثَنَا أَبُو الرَّبِيعِ الزَّهْرَانِيُّ وَقُتَيْبَةُ بْنُ سَعِيدٍ قَالَا: حَدَّثَنَا حَمَّادٌ، ح. وَحَدَّثَنَا يَحْيَى بْنُ أَيُّوبَ، حَدَّثَنَا ابْنُ عُلَيَّةَ، كُلُّهُمْ عَنْ أَيُّوبَ، عَنْ مُحَمَّدٍ، عَنْ أُمِّ عَطِيَّةَ قَالَتْ: تُوُفِّيَتْ إِحْدَى بَنَاتِ النَّبِيِّ صَلَّى اللهُ عَلَيْهِ وَسَلَّمَ.

وَفِي حَدِيثِ ابْنِ عُلَيَّةَ قَالَتْ: أَتَانَا رَسُولُ اللهِ صَلَّى اللهُ عَلَيْهِ وَسَلَّمَ وَنَحْنُ نَغْسِلُ ابْنَتَهُ.

وَفِي حَدِيثِ مَالِكٍ قَالَتْ: دَخَلَ عَلَيْنَا رَسُولُ اللهِ صَلَّى اللهُ عَلَيْهِ وَسَلَّمَ حِينَ تُوُفِّيَتِ ابْنَتُهُ. بِمِثْلِ حَدِيثِ يَزِيدَ بْنِ زُرَيْعٍ عَنْ أَيُّوبَ عَنْ مُحَمَّدٍ عَنْ أُمِّ عَطِيَّةَ.

[1867–39]. (Dar al-Salam 2044) Qutaybah ibn Saʿīd narrated:[i] Ḥammād narrated; from Ayyūb; from Ḥafṣah; from Umm ʿAṭiyyah: **a similar text, except that he said: 'Three, or five, or seven times, or more if you think it is needed'.**

Ḥafṣah reported from Umm ʿAṭiyyah: **'We arranged her hair in three plaits'.**

وَحَدَّثَنَا قُتَيْبَةُ بْنُ سَعِيدٍ، حَدَّثَنَا حَمَّادٌ، عَنْ أَيُّوبَ، عَنْ حَفْصَةَ، عَنْ أُمِّ عَطِيَّةَ: بِنَحْوِهِ، غَيْرَ أَنَّهُ قَالَ: «ثَلاَثًا أَوْ خَمْسًا أَوْ سَبْعًا، أَوْ أَكْثَرَ مِنْ ذَلِكِ إِنْ رَأَيْتُنَّ ذَلِكِ».

فَقَالَتْ حَفْصَةُ عَنْ أُمِّ عَطِيَّةَ: وَجَعَلْنَا رَأْسَهَا ثَلاَثَةَ قُرُونٍ.

[1868–000]. (Dar al-Salam 2045) Yaḥyā ibn Ayyūb narrated:[ii] Ibn ʿUlayyah narrated and Ayyūb reported; he said: Ḥafṣah said, from Umm ʿAṭiyyah; she said [that the Prophet said]: **'Wash her an odd number of times: three or five or seven'. He [meaning Ayyūb] said: 'and Umm ʿAṭiyyah said: "We plaited her hair in three plaits".'**

وَحَدَّثَنَا يَحْيَى بْنُ أَيُّوبَ، حَدَّثَنَا ابْنُ عُلَيَّةَ، وَأَخْبَرَنَا أَيُّوبُ قَالَ: وَقَالَتْ حَفْصَةُ عَنْ أُمِّ عَطِيَّةَ، قَالَتِ: اغْسِلْنَهَا وِتْرًا ثَلاَثًا أَوْ خَمْسًا أَوْ سَبْعًا. قَالَ: وَقَالَتْ أُمُّ عَطِيَّةَ: مَشَطْنَاهَا ثَلاَثَةَ قُرُونٍ.

[1869–40]. (Dar al-Salam 2046) Abu Bakr ibn Abi Shaybah and ʿAmr al-Nāqid narrated: both from Abu Muʿāwiyah; ʿAmr said: Muhammad ibn Khāzim Abu Muʿāwiyah narrated; ʿĀṣim al-Aḥwal narrated; from Ḥafṣah bint Sīrīn; from Umm ʿAṭiyyah.

i. Related by al-Bukhari, 1254 and in similar wording, 1258; al-Nasāʾī, 1887.
ii. Related by al-Bukhari in varying versions, 1254, 1259 and 1260; al-Nasāʾī, 1882 and 1891.

She said: **'When Zaynab, God's Messenger's daughter, passed away, God's Messenger said to us: "Wash her three times, or five and add camphor, or some camphor, in the fifth. When you are done, let me know". We informed him, and he gave us his garment and said: "Wrap her with it".'**

حَدَّثَنَا أَبُو بَكْرِ بْنُ أَبِي شَيْبَةَ وَعَمْرٌو النَّاقِدُ، جَمِيعًا عَنْ أَبِي مُعَاوِيَةَ، - قَالَ عَمْرٌو حَدَّثَنَا مُحَمَّدُ بْنُ خَازِمٍ أَبُو مُعَاوِيَةَ، - حَدَّثَنَا عَاصِمٌ الأَحْوَلُ، عَنْ حَفْصَةَ بِنْتِ سِيرِينَ، عَنْ أُمِّ عَطِيَّةَ قَالَتْ: لَمَّا مَاتَتْ زَيْنَبُ بِنْتُ رَسُولِ اللهِ صَلَّى اللهُ عَلَيْهِ وَسَلَّمَ قَالَ لَنَا رَسُولُ اللهِ صَلَّى اللهُ عَلَيْهِ وَسَلَّمَ: «اغْسِلْنَهَا وِتْرًا ثَلاَثًا أَوْ خَمْسًا، وَاجْعَلْنَ فِي الْخَامِسَةِ كَافُورًا أَوْ شَيْئًا مِنْ كَافُورٍ، فَإِذَا غَسَلْتُنَّهَا فَأَعْلِمْنَنِي». قَالَتْ فَأَعْلَمْنَاهُ. فَأَعْطَانَا حِقْوَهُ وَقَالَ: «أَشْعِرْنَهَا إِيَّاهُ».

[1870–41]. (Dar al-Salam 2047) ʿAmr al-Nāqid narrated:[i] Yazīd ibn Ḥarūn narrated; Hishām ibn Ḥassān reported; from Ḥafṣah bint Sīrīn; from Umm ʿAṭiyyah. She said: **'God's Messenger (peace be upon him) came in as we were washing one of his daughters' body. He said: "Wash her an odd number of times: five or more..."' in a similar text to Ayyūb's and ʿĀṣim's narration. He said in the hadith: 'She said: "We plaited her hair in three parts: two on the sides and one in front".'**

وَحَدَّثَنَا عَمْرٌو النَّاقِدُ، حَدَّثَنَا يَزِيدُ بْنُ هَارُونَ، أَخْبَرَنَا هِشَامُ بْنُ حَسَّانَ، عَنْ حَفْصَةَ بِنْتِ سِيرِينَ، عَنْ أُمِّ عَطِيَّةَ قَالَتْ: أَتَانَا رَسُولُ اللهِ صَلَّى اللهُ عَلَيْهِ وَسَلَّمَ وَنَحْنُ نَغْسِلُ إِحْدَى بَنَاتِهِ، فَقَالَ: «اغْسِلْنَهَا وِتْرًا: خَمْسًا أَوْ أَكْثَرَ مِنْ ذَلِكِ»، بِنَحْوِ حَدِيثِ أَيُّوبَ وَعَاصِمٍ وَقَالَ فِي الْحَدِيثِ قَالَتْ: فَضَفَرْنَا شَعْرَهَا ثَلاثَةَ أَثْلاثٍ: قَرْنَيْهَا وَنَاصِيَتَهَا.

---

i. Related by al-Bukhari, 1263; al-Tirmidhī, 990; al-Nasāʾī, 1884.

[1871–42]. (Dar al-Salam 2048) Yaḥyā ibn Yaḥyā narrated:[i] Hushaym reported; from Khālid; from Ḥafṣah bint Sīrīn; from Umm ʿAṭiyyah; that **'When God's Messenger (peace be upon him) instructed her to wash his daughter's body, he said to her: "Start with the right parts of her body and with the places of ablution".'**

وَحَدَّثَنَا يَحْيَى بْنُ يَحْيَى، أَخْبَرَنَا هُشَيْمٌ، عَنْ خَالِدٍ، عَنْ حَفْصَةَ بِنْتِ سِيرِينَ، عَنْ أُمِّ عَطِيَّةَ، أَنَّ رَسُولَ اللهِ صَلَّى اللهُ عَلَيْهِ وَسَلَّمَ حَيْثُ أَمَرَهَا أَنْ تَغْسِلَ ابْنَتَهُ قَالَ لَهَا: «ابْدَأْنَ بِمَيَامِنِهَا وَمَوَاضِعِ الْوُضُوءِ مِنْهَا».

[1872–43]. (Dar al-Salam 2049) Yaḥyā ibn Ayyūb, Abu Bakr ibn Abi Shaybah and ʿAmr al-Nāqid narrated: all from Ibn ʿUlayyah. Abu Bakr said: Ismāʿīl ibn ʿUlayyah narrated; from Khālid; from Ḥafṣah; from Umm ʿAṭiyyah; that **'God's Messenger (peace be upon him) told them regarding washing his daughter's body: "Start with the right parts of her body and with the places of ablution".'**

حَدَّثَنَا يَحْيَى بْنُ أَيُّوبَ وَأَبُو بَكْرِ بْنُ أَبِي شَيْبَةَ وَعَمْرٌو النَّاقِدُ: كُلُّهُمْ عَنِ ابْنِ عُلَيَّةَ، - قَالَ أَبُو بَكْرٍ حَدَّثَنَا إِسْمَاعِيلُ ابْنُ عُلَيَّةَ، - عَنْ خَالِدٍ، عَنْ حَفْصَةَ، عَنْ أُمِّ عَطِيَّةَ أَنَّ رَسُولَ اللهِ صَلَّى اللهُ عَلَيْهِ وَسَلَّمَ قَالَ لَهُنَّ فِي غَسْلِ ابْنَتِهِ: «ابْدَأْنَ بِمَيَامِنِهَا وَمَوَاضِعِ الْوُضُوءِ مِنْهَا».

Text Explanation

The hadiths mention the Prophet's clear instructions to the women who were washing the body of his deceased daughter, telling them to wash her three or five or seven times or more. All these narrations

---

i. Related by al-Bukhari, 1167, 1255 and 1256; Abu Dāwūd, 3145; al-Tirmidhī, 990; al-Nasāʾī, 1883.

give the same meaning, even though they differ in wording. The Prophet's instructions mean that the washing should be an odd number of times, perhaps three. If more is needed to ensure complete cleanliness, then five, and if more is needed, then seven times, and so on. The sum of the instructions makes an odd number obligatory, and three times recommended. If complete cleanliness is achieved with three times, then a fourth is unnecessary. Otherwise, more times are added until complete cleanliness is achieved. In this case of addition, an odd number is recommended.

Washing the body of a deceased person is a collective duty[i] and so is wrapping the body, carrying the deceased to the graveyard, offering the special prayer and burying the deceased. All are collective duties. What is obligatory in washing the body is to wash it all once. This is the sum of the rulings applicable to the deceased.

In hadiths No. 1864 and 1867, the Prophet instructs Umm ʿAṭiyyah to wash the body more times 'if you think it is needed'. This stresses the point of need, which means that if more is needed, then more must be done. It is not a choice left to the women or men performing the washing. Umm ʿAṭiyyah, who washed the bodies of deceased women in preparation for burial, was one of the distinguished female Companions of the Prophet from the Anṣār. Her name was Nusaybah, or Nasībah. The Prophet's deceased daughter was Zaynab, according to the majority of scholars. *Qadi* ʿIyāḍ said: 'Some historians say that she was Umm Kulthūm, but the correct view is that she was Zaynab, as Muslim names her in the next hadith [No. 1869]'.

In hadith No. 1864, the Prophet tells Umm ʿAṭiyyah to use water and *sidr*, which makes it clear that the use of *sidr* is desirable, and this is the view of all scholars. It should be used in the obligatory wash, but some scholars say that it may be used in both the obligatory and recommended times. The Prophet's other instruction is to use camphor, or some camphor, in the last wash. This is desirable and

---

i. A collective duty means a duty binding on the Muslim community. If some or any of them performs this duty it is deemed to be discharged. If none does it, all of them incur a sin.

agreed upon by all our scholars. It is also agreed by Mālik, Ahmad and the majority of scholars. However, Abu Ḥanīfah said that it is not desirable. The view of the majority is based on this hadith and on the fact that it gives a good smell to the body and makes it stiffer and cooler, thereby slowing its decay. This is a gesture of respect to the deceased.

The Prophet gave his garment to Umm ʿAṭiyyah and told her to wrap his daughter in it. That her shroud was the Prophet's own garment, acted as a form of blessing. The hadith suggests that it is appropriate to seek a blessing through the use of articles and clothing belonging to devout people. It also shows that it is permissible to give a deceased woman a man's garment as a shroud in which she is to be buried.

Umm ʿAṭiyyah mentions that they combed her hair and made in it three plaits - two on the sides of her head and one in front. The hadith shows that it is desirable to comb the hair of the deceased person and to make it into plaits, if suitable. This is agreed by al-Shāfiʿī, Ahmad and Isḥāq. However, al-Awzāʿī and Kufi scholars say that it is not desirable to comb or plait the hair but that it should rather be left loose on her two sides. Our evidence is this hadith, and it appears that the Prophet was aware of this and his permission was granted, as the rest of the hadith shows.

In hadith No. 1871 and 1872, the Prophet tells the women to start with the deceased's right side and the places of ablution. This shows that it is desirable to start with the right side when washing the body of a deceased person and indeed in all types of cleansing. The same applies to all good actions. There are numerous hadiths confirming this and they are related in authentic anthologies. The hadiths also show that it is desirable to perform the ablution for the deceased. This is the view of our school, the Mālikī School and the majority of scholars. Abu Ḥanīfah says that it is not desirable. According to us, the ablution is performed at the beginning of the bath, in the same way as when taking a bath to remove a state of ceremonial impurity.

This hadith by Umm ʿAṭiyyah is evidence in support of the more correct view of our school, which is that it is more preferable for women to perform the washing of a deceased woman's body than her husband. However, its evidence may be set aside until it is ascertained that her husband was present at the time of her death, had no reason preventing him from washing her and that he did not assign the matter to the women. The view of our school and the majority of scholars is that a husband may wash the body of his deceased wife, but al-Shaʿbī, al-Thawrī and Abu Ḥanīfah said that it is not permissible. Scholars, however, unanimously agree that a woman may wash the body of her deceased husband.

Some scholars take this hadith as evidence that it is not obligatory for the one who washes a deceased person to take a bath. The evidence is in the fact that the Prophet was teaching them how to do the washing. Had taking a bath after it been obligatory, the Prophet would have taught them. The view of our school and the majority of scholars is that it is not obligatory, but it is desirable for whoever washes the body of a deceased person to take a bath. Imam Ḥamad ibn Muhammad al-Khaṭṭābī said: 'I do not know that anyone considers it obligatory'. Ahmad and Isḥāq consider performing the ablution after it to be obligatory, but the majority of scholars consider this as desirable, not obligatory. An odd view of our school suggests that it is obligatory, but this view need not be considered because the hadith cited in reference is not authentic according to the agreed view of Hadith scholars. This hadith says: 'Whoever washes a deceased person should take a bath, and whoever touches a deceased one should perform an ablution'.

CHAPTER 13

A DECEASED PERSON'S SHROUD

[1873–44]. (Dar al-Salam 2050–2051) Yaḥyā ibn Yaḥyā al-Tamīmī, Abu Bakr ibn Abi Shaybah, Muhammad ibn ʿAbdullāh ibn Numayr and Abu Kurayb narrated (Yaḥyā's text):[i] Abu Muʿāwiyah (Yaḥyā said: 'reported' while the others said: 'narrated'); from al-Aʿmash; from Shaqīq; from Khabbāb ibn al-Aratt. He said: **'We migrated with God's Messenger (peace be upon him) for God's sake, seeking God's pleasure, and our reward became due from God. Some of us have gone having received nothing of their reward, and one of these was Muṣʿab ibn ʿUmayr. He was killed in the Battle of Uḥud. There was nothing to use as a shroud for him except a striped garment. If we placed it on his head, his feet were uncovered, and if we covered his feet with it, his head was uncovered. The Prophet said: "Place it near his head and put some *idhkhir*[ii] on his feet". Some others have had their fruit ripe, and they are enjoying it'.**

وَحَدَّثَنَا يَحْيَى بْنُ يَحْيَى التَّمِيمِيُّ وَأَبُو بَكْرِ بْنُ أَبِي شَيْبَةَ وَمُحَمَّدُ بْنُ عَبْدِ اللهِ بْنِ نُمَيْرٍ وَأَبُو كُرَيْبٍ (وَاللَّفْظُ لِيَحْيَى). قَالَ يَحْيَى أَخْبَرَنَا وَقَالَ الآخَرُونَ حَدَّثَنَا أَبُو مُعَاوِيَةَ، عَنِ الأَعْمَشِ، عَنْ شَقِيقٍ، عَنْ خَبَّابِ بْنِ الأَرَتِّ قَالَ: هَاجَرْنَا مَعَ رَسُولِ اللهِ صَلَّى اللهُ عَلَيْهِ

---

i. Related by al-Bukhari, 1276, 3897, 3914, 4047, 4082, 6432 and 6448; Abu Dāwūd, 2876; al-Tirmidhī, 3852; al-Nasā'ī, 1902.

ii. *Idhkhir* is a type of thin and narrow grass, which looks white when dry. It is soft and has a pleasant smell.

وَسَلَّمَ فِي سَبِيلِ اللهِ، نَبْتَغِي وَجْهَ اللهِ، فَوَجَبَ أَجْرُنَا عَلَى اللهِ. فَمِنَّا مَنْ مَضَى لَمْ يَأْكُلْ مِنْ أَجْرِهِ شَيْئًا، مِنْهُمْ مُصْعَبُ بْنُ عُمَيْرٍ: قُتِلَ يَوْمَ أُحُدٍ، فَلَمْ يُوجَدْ لَهُ شَيْءٌ يُكَفَّنُ فِيهِ إِلاَّ نَمِرَةٌ. فَكُنَّا إِذَا وَضَعْنَاهَا عَلَى رَأْسِهِ خَرَجَتْ رِجْلاهُ، وَإِذَا وَضَعْنَاهَا عَلَى رِجْلَيْهِ خَرَجَ رَأْسُهُ. فَقَالَ رَسُولُ اللهِ صَلَّى اللهُ عَلَيْهِ وَسَلَّمَ: «ضَعُوهَا مِمَّا يَلِي رَأْسَهُ وَاجْعَلُوا عَلَى رِجْلَيْهِ الإِذْخِرَ». وَمِنَّا مَنْ أَيْنَعَتْ لَهُ ثَمَرَتُهُ فَهُوَ يَهْدِبُهَا.

ʿUthmān ibn Abi Shaybah narrated: Jarīr narrated [H]. Also, Isḥāq ibn Ibrāhīm narrated; ʿĪsā ibn Yūnus reported [H]. And, Minjāb ibn al-Ḥārith al-Tamīmī narrated; ʿAlī ibn Mushir reported [H]. Also, Isḥāq ibn Ibrāhīm and Ibn Abi ʿUmar narrated; all from Ibn ʿUyaynah; from al-Aʿmash; with this chain of transmission: **a similar text.**

وَحَدَّثَنَا عُثْمَانُ بْنُ أَبِي شَيْبَةَ، حَدَّثَنَا جَرِيرٌ، ح. وَحَدَّثَنَا إِسْحَاقُ بْنُ إِبْرَاهِيمَ، أَخْبَرَنَا عِيسَى بْنُ يُونُسَ، ح. وَحَدَّثَنَا مِنْجَابُ بْنُ الْحَارِثِ التَّمِيمِيُّ، أَخْبَرَنَا عَلِيُّ بْنُ مُسْهِرٍ، ح. وَحَدَّثَنَا إِسْحَاقُ بْنُ إِبْرَاهِيمَ وَابْنُ أَبِي عُمَرَ، جَمِيعًا عَنِ ابْنِ عُيَيْنَةَ، عَنِ الأَعْمَشِ، بِهَذَا الإِسْنَادِ: نَحْوَهُ.

[1874–45]. (Dar al-Salam 2052) Yaḥyā ibn Yaḥyā, Abu Bakr ibn Abi Shaybah and Abu Kurayb narrated (Yaḥyā's text): Abu Muʿāwiyah (Yaḥyā said: 'reported' and the other two said: 'narrated'); from Hishām ibn ʿUrwah; from his father; from ʿĀ'ishah. She said: **'The Prophet's shroud was three white Saḥūlī garments made of cotton. They included neither a shirt nor a turban. As for the suit, people were confused regarding it. It was bought for him to be his shroud, but it was abandoned and three white Saḥūlī garments were made his shroud. The suit was taken by ʿAbdullāh ibn Abi Bakr who said: "I will keep it so that it will be my shroud". He**

subsequently said: "Had God accepted it for His Prophet, it would have been used as his shroud". He sold it and donated its price to charity'.

حَدَّثَنَا يَحْيَى بْنُ يَحْيَى وَأَبُو بَكْرِ بْنُ أَبِي شَيْبَةَ وَأَبُو كُرَيْبٍ - وَاللَّفْظُ لِيَحْيَى. قَالَ يَحْيَى أَخْبَرَنَا وَقَالَ الآخَرَانِ حَدَّثَنَا أَبُو مُعَاوِيَةَ، عَنْ هِشَامِ بْنِ عُرْوَةَ، عَنْ أَبِيهِ، عَنْ عَائِشَةَ قَالَتْ: كُفِّنَ رَسُولُ اللهِ صَلَّى اللهُ عَلَيْهِ وَسَلَّمَ فِي ثَلاَثَةِ أَثْوَابٍ بِيضٍ سَحُولِيَّةٍ مِنْ كُرْسُفٍ، لَيْسَ فِيهَا قَمِيصٌ وَلاَ عِمَامَةٌ. أَمَّا الْحُلَّةُ فَإِنَّمَا شُبِّهَ عَلَى النَّاسِ فِيهَا أَنَّهَا اشْتُرِيَتْ لَهُ لِيُكَفَّنَ فِيهَا، فَتُرِكَتِ الْحُلَّةُ، وَكُفِّنَ فِي ثَلاَثَةِ أَثْوَابٍ بِيضٍ سَحُولِيَّةٍ. فَأَخَذَهَا عَبْدُ اللهِ بْنُ أَبِي بَكْرٍ فَقَالَ: لأَحْبِسَنَّهَا حَتَّى أُكَفِّنَ فِيهَا نَفْسِي. ثُمَّ قَالَ: لَوْ رَضِيَهَا اللهُ عَزَّ وَجَلَّ لِنَبِيِّهِ لَكَفَّنَهُ فِيهَا. فَبَاعَهَا وَتَصَدَّقَ بِثَمَنِهَا.

[1875–46]. (Dar al-Salam 2053–2054) ʿAlī ibn Ḥujr al-Saʿdī narrated to me: ʿAlī ibn Mushir reported; Hishām ibn ʿUrwah narrated; from his father; from ʿĀ'ishah. She said: **'God's Messenger (peace be upon him) was wrapped in a Yemeni suit that belonged to ʿAbdullāh ibn Abi Bakr, but then it was removed. He was then given a shroud made of three Saḥūlī garments made in Yemen, and they included neither a turban nor a shirt. ʿAbdullāh took the suit and said: "It will be my shroud". He subsequently said: "God's Messenger (peace be upon him) was not given it as a shroud and will it be my shroud!" He gave it to charity'.**

وَحَدَّثَنِي عَلِيُّ بْنُ حُجْرٍ السَّعْدِيُّ، أَخْبَرَنَا عَلِيُّ بْنُ مُسْهِرٍ، حَدَّثَنَا هِشَامُ بْنُ عُرْوَةَ، عَنْ أَبِيهِ، عَنْ عَائِشَةَ قَالَتْ: أُدْرِجَ رَسُولُ اللهِ صَلَّى اللهُ عَلَيْهِ وَسَلَّمَ فِي حُلَّةٍ يَمَنِيَّةٍ، كَانَتْ لِعَبْدِ اللهِ بْنِ أَبِي بَكْرٍ، ثُمَّ نُزِعَتْ عَنْهُ، وَكُفِّنَ فِي ثَلاَثَةِ أَثْوَابٍ سُحُولٍ يَمَانِيَةٍ، لَيْسَ فِيهَا عِمَامَةٌ وَلاَ قَمِيصٌ. فَرَفَعَ عَبْدُ اللهِ الْحُلَّةَ فَقَالَ أُكَفَّنُ فِيهَا. ثُمَّ قَالَ: لَمْ يُكَفَّنْ فِيهَا رَسُولُ اللهِ صَلَّى اللهُ عَلَيْهِ وَسَلَّمَ وَأُكَفَّنُ فِيهَا! فَتَصَدَّقَ بِهَا.

Abu Bakr ibn Abi Shaybah narrated:[i] Ḥafṣ ibn Ghiyāth, Ibn ʿUyaynah, Ibn Idrīs, ʿAbdah and Wakīʿ narrated [H]. Also, Yaḥyā ibn Yaḥyā narrated: ʿAbd al-ʿAzīz ibn Muhammad reported; all from Hishām; with the same chain of transmission: **but they do not include the part concerning ʿAbdullāh ibn Abi Bakr.**

وَحَدَّثَنَاهُ أَبُو بَكْرِ بْنُ أَبِي شَيْبَةَ، حَدَّثَنَا حَفْصُ بْنُ غِيَاثٍ وَابْنُ عُيَيْنَةَ وَابْنُ إِدْرِيسَ وَعَبْدَةُ وَوَكِيعٌ ح. وَحَدَّثَنَاهُ يَحْيَى بْنُ يَحْيَى، أَخْبَرَنَا عَبْدُ الْعَزِيزِ بْنُ مُحَمَّدٍ، كُلُّهُمْ عَنْ هِشَامٍ، بِهَذَا الإِسْنَادِ. وَلَيْسَ فِي حَدِيثِهِمْ قِصَّةُ عَبْدِ اللهِ بْنِ أَبِي بَكْرٍ.

[1876–47]. (Dar al-Salam 2055) Ibn Abi ʿUmar narrated to me: ʿAbd al-ʿAzīz narrated; from Yazīd; from Muhammad ibn Ibrāhīm; from Abu Salamah. He said: **'I asked ʿĀ'ishah, the Prophet's wife, saying: "How many garments made God's Messenger's shroud?" She said: "Three Saḥūlī garments".'**

وَحَدَّثَنِي ابْنُ أَبِي عُمَرَ، حَدَّثَنَا عَبْدُ الْعَزِيزِ، عَنْ يَزِيدَ، عَنْ مُحَمَّدِ بْنِ إِبْرَاهِيمَ، عَنْ أَبِي سَلَمَةَ أَنَّهُ قَالَ: سَأَلْتُ عَائِشَةَ زَوْجَ النَّبِيِّ صَلَّى اللهُ عَلَيْهِ وَسَلَّمَ فَقُلْتُ لَهَا: فِي كَمْ كُفِّنَ رَسُولُ اللهِ صَلَّى اللهُ عَلَيْهِ وَسَلَّمَ؟ فَقَالَتْ: فِي ثَلَاثَةِ أَثْوَابٍ سَحُولِيَّةٍ.

Text Explanation

In hadith No. 1873, Khabbāb ibn al-Aratt, one of the earliest people to accept Islam, says: 'Our reward became due from God'. This means that the fulfilment of God's promise became due according to Islamic law. It is not a rationally necessitated obligation, as claimed by the Muʿtazilah. Indeed, it is similar to the hadith that mentions people's right from God, which we explained in the Book of Faith. Khabbāb

---

i. Related by Abu Dāwūd as narrated by Ḥafṣ ibn Ghiyāth, 996; al-Nasā'ī, 1898; Ibn Mājah, 1469.

says: 'Some of us have gone having received nothing of their reward'. This means that they had nothing of the comforts of this present life, and no part of their reward was granted to them in this life. Khabbāb describes the condition of Muṣʿab ibn ʿUmayr when he fell a martyr in the Battle of Uḥud: 'There was nothing to use as a shroud for him except a striped garment'. The hadith implies that the shroud in which a person is wrapped for burial is taken from his estate and it is of higher priority even than the deceased's debts. The Prophet ordered that Muṣʿab be wrapped in his striped garment, without asking whether he had enough to repay his debts. A person who had nothing but an outer garment to be used as his shroud was certainly likely to be in debt. Our scholars make an exception that applies to a debt related to money itself, such as a pledged property, money that is liable to zakat which must be paid and similar matters.

The Prophet instructed his Companions who were preparing Muṣʿab for burial: 'Place it near his head and put some *idhkhir* on his feet'. This is evidence that if the available material is too small to cover the whole body of a deceased person, it should be placed towards the person's head and the shortfall towards the feet. The head should be covered. If the material available is too small, the private area [i.e. from the waistline to the knees] should be covered. If the material covers more than this, the part of the body above the waistline should be covered. If the material is too small to cover the private area, then the deceased's genitals should be covered, because they are the most important part to cover.

This hadith may be cited as evidence that what must be covered by the shroud is the private area, but it is not necessary to cover the rest of the deceased's body, even when this is available. It may be said that the people were not able to cover the whole of Muṣʿab's body because the hadith mentions that he had nothing other than his striped garment. The answer is that what the deceased owned was that garment. Had covering the whole body been obligatory, it would have been the duty of all Muslims who were present to complete the shortage, unless there was among them a relative of Muṣʿab to bear his expenses. If such a relative was present, he had to fulfil that duty. Again, it may be said that they were unable to address this need because this happened at the end of the Battle of Uḥud, a battle in which many Muslims were killed. People were very busy burying them and at the same time they were worried lest the enemy should attack again. The answer is that it was unlikely that none of those who were undertaking the task of burying Muṣʿab did not have a piece of material or garment that could be used for the purpose, but God knows best.

The narrator adds the other condition: 'Some others have had their fruit ripe, and they are enjoying it'. This is a metaphor describing the wealth that they were given.

In hadith No. 1874, ʿĀ'ishah mentions: 'The Prophet's shroud was three white Saḥūlī garments made of cotton. They included neither a shirt nor a turban'. These garments are described as Saḥūlī. Some scholars say that it means that they are clean white cotton garments, but others say they are not necessarily cotton. Other scholars say that they are named after a town in Yemen where they are normally made.

This hadith and the previous one mentioning the case of Muṣʿab ibn ʿUmayr and others, make clear that it is obligatory that a deceased person should be wrapped in a shroud. This is unanimously agreed upon by scholars. It is a duty that is paid for from the estate of the deceased. If the deceased leaves nothing, then the person who looked after him or her during their lifetime is responsible for it. If not, then the state pays for it. If the state does not have the money, it is a duty on Muslims, and the ruler may assign this duty to any rich person(s). The hadith also indicates that the sunnah is to shroud a man with three garments. This is the view of our school and the great majority of scholars, but the duty is to use one garment, as we explained earlier. In the case of deceased women, it is desirable to use five garments. It is permissible to use five for a man, but it is more desirable not to exceed three. To exceed five for either man or woman is extravagant.

According to the hadith, it is desirable to choose white for a shroud. This is unanimously agreed upon. In an authentic hadith, the Prophet says in reference to white garments: 'Use them for shrouds for your dead'. Dyed and flashy material are discouraged. As for silk material, our scholars say that it is forbidden to use as a shroud for a man, but it is permissible for a woman, yet it is discouraged. Mālik and most scholars say that using silk for shrouds is discouraged in all cases. Ibn al-Mundhir said: 'I do not know of any other view'.

'Ā'ishah further mentions that there was neither a shirt nor a turban. This means that the Prophet was given a shroud consisting of three garments with no shirt or turban. There was nothing other than the three garments. This is how the hadith is interpreted by al-Shāfiʿī and the majority of scholars, and this is the right thing to say, according to the apparent meaning of the hadith. They say that it is desirable that the shroud should not include a shirt or a turban. Mālik and Abu Ḥanīfah say that including them is desirable, understanding the hadith as meaning that the shirt and turban were not part of the three garments but added to them. This understanding is not solid, as there is no confirmation that the Prophet had a shirt and a turban as part of his shroud. In fact, the hadith implies that the shirt that was on the Prophet at the time of washing his body was taken off when he was wrapped in his shroud. This is the correct meaning and nothing else can be valid. Had his shirt been left on him, wet as it was, it would have affected the shroud.

A hadith related by Abu Dāwūd and narrated by Ibn 'Abbās mentions that the Prophet was wrapped in a shroud consisting of three garments: the suit consisted of two garments and his shirt which was on him when he died. This hadith is poor in authenticity. One of its narrators is Yazīd ibn Abi Ziyād, and he is graded by Hadith scholars as unreliable. Moreover, it is contrary to what reliable narrators state.

'Ā'ishah added: 'As for the suit, people were confused regarding it'. A suit consists of two garments: a lower one covering from the waistline to well below the knees and an upper garment covering the upper part of the body down to one's hips and even lower. Hadith No. 1875 mentions that the suit belonged to 'Abdullāh ibn Abi Bakr. The Prophet, however, was given a shroud of three white cotton garments.

Ṣaḥīḥ Muslim